*Teaching Mathematics to Students
with Learning Disabilities*

Teaching Mathematics

to Students with Learning Disabilities

◆ ◆ ◆

THIRD EDITION

Nancy S. Bley

Carol A. Thornton

pro·ed
An International Publisher

8700 Shoal Creek Boulevard
Austin, Texas 78757-6897

© 1995, 1989 by PRO-ED, Inc.
8700 Shoal Creek Boulevard
Austin, Texas 78757-6897

Library of Congress Cataloging-in-Publication Data

Bley, Nancy S.
   Teaching mathematics to students with learning disabilities /
Nancy S. Bley and Carol A. Thornton.—3rd ed.
     p.   cm.
   Rev. ed. of: Teaching mathematics to the learning disabled.
   Includes bibliographical references and index.
   ISBN 0-89079-603-3
   1. Mathematics—Study and teaching (Elementary) 2. Learning
disabled children—Education—Mathematics. I. Thornton, Carol A.
II. Bley, Nancy S. Teaching mathematics to the learning disabled.
III. Title.
QA135.5.B56 1994
371.9′0447—dc20   94-6988
                                            CIP

Production Manager: Alan Grimes
Production Coordinator: Adrienne Booth
Art Director: Lori Kopp
Reprints Buyer: Alicia Woods
Editor: Tracy Sergo
Editorial Assistant: Claudette Landry

Printed in the United States of America

5 6 7 8 9 10   98

To our husbands, Michael and Denis,
our children,
Chris, Stephanie, and Jennifer,
and to
Gail and Genny,
for their patient understanding and support
throughout this project.

Contents

CHAPTER 8

Rational Numbers: Early Concept Work with Fractions and Decimals *349*

CHAPTER 9

Extending Understanding and Application of Fractions and Decimals *391*

CHAPTER 10

Hard-to-Learn, Upper-Grade Topics *443*

Preface

LIKE THE PREVIOUS editions of *Teaching Mathematics to the Learning Disabled*, this third edition is written in the belief that, though they learn differently, most students with learning disabilities can master important mathematical concepts so that these concepts can be applied in their daily lives. This belief has evolved out of our own personal experiences working with students with learning disabilities. Approaches and techniques that we have found most successful are interwoven in the suggestions given throughout the text.

Major changes in this edition include a reorganization of chapters; a stronger emphasis on encouraging problem solving, decision making, and reasoning; and a section devoted to nonverbal learning disabilities and their impact on understanding and using mathematics effectively. Additionally, ways of incorporating the increased availability of calculators have been added in the hope of encouraging teachers to think more about the most efficient method of determining answers than about actual details of long computations. Similarly there is added emphasis on mental calculation where appropriate. The authors also have tried to highlight the importance of reconsidering the concept of a "right answer." In today's world it is usually much more important to be able to determine and use efficient methods of arriving at a solution that will help solve a problem. There may be a variety of useful solutions, and sometimes the right answer to a computation problem is the wrong answer to the related problem.

Rather than treat comprehensively all topics in the school mathematics curriculum, from the perspective of the *Curriculum and Evaluation Standards for School Mathematics* (National Council of Teachers of Mathematics, 1989), emphasis again has been placed on topics that potentially can or commonly do cause the most difficulty for students with learning disabilities. Background information at the beginning of each section summarizes standard approaches to topics and points out particular problems that students with learning disabilities may encounter with a given concept or application. Then, in follow-up, a sequence of suggested activities is presented to highlight the fact that instructional alternatives are sometimes necessary to meet the needs of these students. The assumption is that teachers are familiar with standard approaches to handling the topics.

A variety of adaptations are provided, including such methods as color coding, organizing file pages spatially, and previewing. (A note of caution: when using color coding as an approach, it is suggested that students be checked for intact color vision. If they show any difficulty, similar techniques like bold print or underscoring might be used instead.) Many of the "file pages" now can be done on a computer, saved to a disk, retrieved as needed, and adjusted to meet individual needs easier than when only paper-and-pencil file pages were available. Adaptations used during early instruction gradually are withdrawn as students become more confident and able to work independently. Indeed, that is the goal: to help students learn to compensate for their learning disabilities and to deal effectively with mathematics both in academic and everyday situations. Any inspiration we can provide toward accomplishing this goal comes primarily from the students with whom we have worked and from whom we ourselves have learned.

Nancy S. Bley
Carol A. Thornton

REFERENCE

National Council of Teachers of Mathematics. (1989). *Curriculum and evaluation standards for school mathematics*. Reston, VA: Author.

CHAPTER I

Planning Instruction for Special Needs

STUDENTS WITH LEARNING DISABILITIES are unable to learn the way most students do. For this reason, there characteristically is a discrepancy between their learning potential and performance in mathematics. Probably, the single biggest obstacle to learning for these students is their inability to perform well independently. This may be for a variety of reasons, including:

- an inability to use critical thinking without specific training;

- visual perception difficulties that preclude accurately perceiving what is written on a page;

- poor retention; or

- an auditory misperception of words or parts of words.

Some students with learning disabilities have good study skills and are highly motivated. They are willing to learn and try to stay on task. Typically, this willingness decreases with age as problems, like those just mentioned, continually frustrate learning attempts. Students then often begin to misbehave, withdraw, or simply not attend.

The problem may be compounded when these students are mainstreamed or taught in resource rooms along with children who have uniquely different learning styles, abilities, and interests. The mathematics teacher somehow must deal with each student's diverse learning needs. In some instances, the curricular goals set by the school district seem unrealistic for certain individuals. How does one adequately teach the expected content and still help those students who have legitimate learning difficulties?

In regular mathematics classes, even the best attempts to handle the different learning needs of students with learning disabilities through individual assignments or cooperative learning schemes are sometimes thwarted. Although the teacher may be able to spend some time working individually with a child or a small group, overall, the setting still demands considerable independent work skills. It cannot be assumed that students with learning disabilities possess these skills. Instead, they must be taught these skills specifically and then monitored regularly, not just in the resource room but in the larger classroom setting as well.

The teacher encounters additional problems when attempting to use textual materials typically written for regular class students. Most commercial texts are visually confusing, with the result being that students with learning disabilities lose their place, have difficulty focusing on or copying problems, and also may have trouble spacing their work in workbooks. Lessons frequently are not sequenced to provide transition between topics, and there is often not enough review of important concepts. For students who cannot readily transfer concepts from the concrete to the abstract without teacher assistance, the use of manipulatives may be confusing at best and perhaps even meaningless.

All these issues are being addressed in the context of new thrusts in school mathematics. Students who entered kindergarten in 1988 can expect to graduate from high school in the year 2001. By then, there will be far less need for computation skills as we know them today. Rather, students graduating in the 21st century will have to be able to evaluate the most efficient and relevant way to compute an answer. They will have to be able to choose from and effectively use a variety of formats—a calculator, mental calculation, estimation, a computer, or paper and pencil. They will also have to be able to adjust to subtle differences between the available tools, such as between different types of calculators or different models of computers. Yet these students who will graduate in the 21st century still frequently face the computation-dominated curriculum that is more suitable for the 19th century. To address this inconsistency, the National Council of Teachers of Mathematics (NCTM) issued its *Curriculum and Evaluation Standards for School Mathematics* (1989).

The position taken by leaders in mathematics education is that, while computation is still vital in the current information age, it is obvious that obtaining answers by standard paper-and-pencil methods is not sufficient nor is it always preferable. There is now a need to be flexible in choosing the most efficient method from the available resources. There is also an important need to be able to judge whether answers are "reasonable" and even whether an exact answer is required.

Wise decision making and the ability to think critically are the keys. This sometimes involves the ability to judge which operation should be carried out in a specific setting. Practical problem solving rooted in a good sense of number and relationships between numbers, as well as adequate understanding of each of the operations, is necessary.

The National Council of Supervisors of Mathematics (NCSM) has endorsed the position taken by NCTM. Thus, their official statement, the *Twelve Components of Essential Mathematics* (see Table 1.1), also summarized the thinking NCTM expresses in its *Standards* document (1989). The full text of their position (NCSM, 1988) contained additional statements concerning (a) the need to promote a positive climate for mathematics learning, (b) the use of technology in school mathematics, and (c) implications for evaluation.

A word of caution is also in order concerning the use of standardized tests that emphasize only computation. Recommendations, which already are impacting new versions of standardized tests, include:

- more analysis of applied problem solving and critical thinking/reasoning in mathematics;

Table 1.1 Twelve Components of Essential Mathematics

Problem Solving

Learning to solve problems is the principal reason for studying mathematics. Problem solving is the process of applying previously acquired knowledge to new and unfamiliar situations. Solving word problems in texts is one form of problem solving, but students also should be faced with non-text problems. Problem-solving strategies involve posing questions, analyzing situations, translating results, illustrating results, drawing diagrams, and using trial and error. Students should see alternate solutions to problems; they should experience problems with more than a single solution.

Communicating Mathematical Ideas

Students should learn the language and notation of mathematics. For example, they should understand place value and scientific notation. They should learn to receive mathematical ideas through listening, reading, and visualizing. They should be able to present mathematical ideas by speaking, writing, drawing pictures and graphs, and demonstrating with concrete models. They should be able to discuss mathematics and ask questions about mathematics.

Mathematical Reasoning

Students should learn to make independent investigations of mathematical ideas. They should be able to identify and extend patterns and use experiences and observations to make conjectures (tentative conclusions). They should learn to use a counter-example to disprove a conjecture and they should learn to use models, known facts, and logical arguments to validate a conjecture. They should be able to distinguish between valid and invalid arguments.

Applying Mathematics to Everyday Situations

Students should be encouraged to take everyday situations, translate them into mathematical representations (graphs, tables, diagrams, or mathematical expressions), process the mathematics, and interpret the results in light of the initial situation. They should be able to solve ratio, proportion, percent, and direct variation and inverse variation problems. Not only should students see how mathematics is applied in the real world, but also they should observe how mathematics grows from the world around them.

Alertness to the Reasonableness of Results

In solving problems, students should question the reasonableness of a solution or conjecture in relation to the original problem. Students must develop the number sense to determine if results of calculations are reasonable in relation to the original numbers and the operations used. With the increase in the use of calculating devices in society, this capability is more important than ever.

Estimation

Students should be able to carry out rapid approximate calculations through the use of mental arithmetic and a variety of computational estimation techniques. When computation is needed in a problem or consumer setting, an estimate can be used to check reasonableness, examine a conjecture, or make a decision. Students should acquire simple techniques for estimating measurements such as length, area, volume, and mass (weight). They should be able to decide when a particular result is precise enough for the purpose at hand.

Appropriate Computational Skills

Students should gain facility in using addition, subtraction, multiplication, and division with whole numbers and decimals. Today, long, complicated computations should be done with a calculator or computer. Knowledge of single-digit number facts is essential, and using mental arithmetic is a valuable skill. In learning to apply computation, students should have

(continues)

Table 1.1 *Continued*

practice in choosing the appropriate computational method: mental arithmetic, paper-pencil algorithm, or calculating device. Moreover, there are everyday situations that demand recognition of, and simple computation with, common fractions. In addition, the ability to recognize, use, and estimate with percents must also be developed and maintained.

Algebraic Thinking

Students should learn to use variables (letters) to represent mathematical quantities and expressions; they should be able to represent mathematical functions and relationships using tables, graphs, and equations. They should understand and correctly use positive and negative numbers, order of operations, formulas, equations, and inequalities. They should recognize the ways in which one quantity changes in relation to another.

Measurement

Students should learn the fundamental concepts of measurement through concrete experiences. They should be able to measure distance, mass (weight), time, capacity, temperature, and angles. They should learn to calculate simple perimeters, areas, and volumes. They should be able to perform measurement in both metric and customary systems using the appropriate tools and levels of precision.

Geometry

Students should understand the geometric concepts necessary to function effectively in the three-dimensional world. They should have knowledge of concepts such as parallelism, perpendicularity, congruence, similarity, and symmetry. Students should know properties of simple plane and solid geometric figures. Students should visualize and verbalize how objects move in the world around them using terms such as slides, flips, and turns. Geometric concepts should be explored in settings that involve problem solving and measurement.

Statistics

Students should plan and carry out the collection and organization of data to answer questions in their everyday lives. Students should know how to construct, read, and draw conclusions from simple tables, maps, charts, and graphs. They should be able to present information about numerical data such as measures of central tendency (mean, median, mode) and measures of dispersion (range, deviation). Students should recognize the basic uses and misuses of statistical representation and inference.

Probability

Students should understand elementary notions of probability to determine the likelihood of future events. They should identify situations where immediate past experience does not affect the likelihood of future events. They should become familiar with how mathematics is used to help make predictions such as election results, business forecasts, and outcomes of sporting events. They should learn how probability applies to research results and to the decision-making process.

Note. From *Twelve Components of Essential Mathematics* by National Council of Supervisors of Mathematics, 1988, Minneapolis: Author. Reprinted by permission.

- allowing the use of calculators on the tests; and

- using a "portfolio" method of evaluating students' progress.

Clearly, the emergence of a mathematics curriculum that emphasizes the essentials summarized in Table 1.1 has implications for writing individual educational programs in mathematics for students with learning disabilities. These plans also should capture the spirit of NCSM (1988) and NCTM (1989), which emphasize ideas like the following:

- Problem solving should be integrated at all levels and into all facets of a child's mathematics program.

- Students typically learn mathematics best through interacting with their environment and/or concrete materials. That environment should be planned carefully to nurture the development of mathematical concepts at all levels.

- Written symbols/computational procedures should be introduced in conjunction with or after exploratory work that focuses on providing meaning to what is written.

- Internalization of mathematical concepts and development of language skills are two aspects of learning that can and should reinforce each other. Instructional activities should offer students opportunities to discuss their thinking, ask questions, and present their interpretation of a mathematical idea or procedure. As with independent study skills, many students with learning disabilities do not automatically develop the appropriate mathematical language; consequently, they must be taught the specifics involved.

- Students' feelings about themselves as learners and about their experiences with mathematics can greatly influence the level of their efforts and eventual success. By providing an environment that is accepting, encouraging, stimulating, and enjoyable, a program can foster a strong self-image and a positive attitude toward mathematics.

The following chapters will share techniques and ideas for incorporating these new theories into mathematics programs for students with learning disabilities in primary, intermediate, and middle/junior high schools. These chapters also will illustrate, for selected topics and for new thrusts related to these topics, how specialized techniques can be used within traditional sequences of instruction.

The overriding goal of this text is to provide ideas for arranging instruction so that teachers can provide an environment in which children will learn. Sometimes it is necessary to alter the standard mathematics sequence to meet the individual needs of students with learning disabilities. At other times, it is better to circumvent difficulties, using specialized methods, so these students

- can learn in a way that is appropriate for them and

- will learn more general compensatory techniques that will enable them to continue to learn and use mathematics in ways that are best for them.

We hope the ideas suggested will act as a springboard for teachers to develop their own ideas for teaching children with learning disabilities. Based on this perspective, the remainder of this chapter is devoted to

- providing the reader with an overview of learning disabilities as they relate to school mathematics through grade 8 and

- suggesting general techniques that can aid classroom instruction and planning for students with learning disabilities.

LEARNING DISABILITIES AND THEIR EFFECT ON MATHEMATICS PERFORMANCE

Most mathematics teachers are familiar with at least some of the following situations:

- an assignment that is "wrong" because sloppy writing led to misreading or nonalignment of digits

- the child who consistently receives high scores on quizzes of isolated basic facts yet has difficulty when required to retrieve these same facts to solve word problems or longer computations

- the child who never seems to pay attention during oral quizzes or explanations and cannot answer questions in class

- the older elementary student who "refuses" to learn the basic facts

- children who add when they should multiply or skip steps in division problems

- the child who cannot differentiate between when to use the four operations in an application

The list is endless, and every teacher probably can pinpoint at least one child who matches each of these descriptions.

Such situations can be very frustrating for both teacher and student. While these students may represent only a small percentage of the students in a class, the nature and magnitude of the problems may be large enough to affect presentation of material and overall instruction.

Each case could involve a child with learning disabilities. Since these students typically have average or above average intelligence, teachers mistakenly may think that the students are not trying, that they are lazy, or that they are not paying attention. Because they frequently, and often rightly, feel like they understood something but were unable to show their understanding in a meaningful or perhaps acceptable way to the teacher or their peers, many students with learning disabilities have mixed feelings about themselves. They do not look different but they feel different. They often see themselves participating successfully in certain areas, such as sports, conversations, or even some academic areas. They work at least as hard if not harder than their classmates and make an effort to take notes and to complete homework but still are not able to achieve in mathematics. They fail written tests. Even though there is evidence that cooperative learning can be effective, often students with learning disabilities do not study with peers for fear they will appear dumb. Outwardly they may profess to study better alone, but inwardly they feel they are missing out on a lot of fun and help. These students come in many variations. Enrolled in a resource room, they feel labeled. Even in mainstreamed situations they often feel left out.

Understanding a child's disability and the interaction between learning theories and learning disabilities sometimes helps teachers plan instruction to minimize the frustrations and social pressure. Toward this end, the following paragraphs review common learning disabilities that influence success in mathematics. The major disabilities have been divided into several areas based on the related visual and/or auditory deficit. These areas include perceptual, memory, and integrative processing deficits (see Table 1.2). Additionally, the area of nonverbal learning disabilities is also included (see Table 1.3 on p. 10 and related text on pp. 18–19). Comments on the implications of constructivism and Piaget's developmental theory for teaching students with learning disabilities conclude the section.

Visual and Auditory Perception Problems

Figure-ground difficulties

Children with visual figure-ground difficulties may exhibit a variety of symptoms. These are the children who frequently lose their place on the page, do not finish all their work, or appear not to concentrate when copying problems from the book. Also, they tend to mix up parts of problems and often copy symbols incorrectly. Because most mathematics books present many problems on a page, students with learning disabilities may not differentiate between the problem number and the problem itself and may include neighboring digits in the computation. As a result, their work appears carelessly done.

The worksheet shown in Figure 1.1 illustrates some of these difficulties. The computation in the first problem is almost accurate but includes the problem number in the final step. Problem 2 is started correctly. The answer to 12 subtract 6 is 6, but the answer is placed under problem 3. Since 7 subtract 1 is also 6, the student proceeded with this computation, not realizing that an entire problem had been skipped. In problem 5, the child is still adding, possibly because of the similarity of numbers in problems 4 and 5. Problem 6 was begun but not finished, without the student being aware of it.

Figure-ground deficits also may interfere with the ability to accurately use a calculator or to read multidigit numbers. The proximity of the calculator keys and the size of the keys may make it hard for a student to locate the desired button. The calculator in Figure 1.2 is fairly typical and one that most students can use but that is often difficult for students with learning disabilities to use, especially since the operation keys are clustered together. Reading multidigit numbers also is often confusing since students with figure-ground difficulties tend to focus on the individual digits and do not spontaneously group them. In the example of Figure 1.3, despite a firm understanding of place value for three-digit numbers, a child may be unsure whether to say "sixty-one two" or "six hundred twelve."

Table 1.2 Examples of Learning Disabilities Affecting Performance in Mathematics

	VISUAL DEFICIT	AUDITORY DEFICIT
Perceptual		
Figure-Ground	• may not finish all problems on page • frequently loses place • difficulty seeing subtraction within a division problem • difficulty reading multidigit number (see *Closure*)	• trouble hearing pattern in counting • difficulty attending in the classroom
Discrimination	• difficulty differentiating coins • difficulty differentiating between or writing numbers (3 for 8; 2 for 5) • cannot discriminate between operation symbols • cannot discriminate between size of hands on clock • difficulty associating operation sign with problem (see *Abstract Reasoning*)	• cannot distinguish between 30 and 13 (see *Receptive Language*) • difficulty with decimal numbers
Reversal	• reverses digits in a number (may also be a sequential memory problem) • difficulty with regrouping	
Spatial	• trouble writing on lined paper • difficulty with concept of *before/after*, so trouble telling time • trouble noticing size differences in shapes • trouble with fraction concept due to inability to note equal-sized parts • difficulty writing decimals • difficulty aligning numbers • difficulty with ordinal numbers • difficulty writing fractional numbers (may also be reversal)	• difficulty following directions using ordinal numbers
Memory		
Short-Term	• trouble retaining newly presented material • difficulty copying problems from the board (may be spatial)	• difficulty with oral drills • difficulty with dictated assignments
Long-Term	• inability to retain basic facts or processes over a long period • difficulty solving multi-operation computation	

(continues)

Table 1.2 *Continued*

	VISUAL DEFICIT	**AUDITORY DEFICIT**
Sequential	• difficulty telling time • difficulty following through a multiplication problem • difficulty following through long division problems • difficulty solving column addition problems • difficulty solving multistep word problems	• cannot retain story problem that is dictated
Integrative		
Closure	• difficulty visualizing groups • difficulty reading multidigit number (see *Figure-Ground*) • difficulty with missing addends and missing factors • inability to draw conclusions, therefore, trouble noticing and continuing patterns • difficulty with word problems • trouble continuing counting pattern from within a sequence	• difficulty counting on from within a sequence
Expressive Language	• rapid oral drills very difficult	• difficulty counting on • difficulty explaining why a problem is solved as it is
Receptive Language	• difficulty relating words to meaning (may be spatial) • difficulty with words that have multiple meanings	• difficulty relating words to meaning • difficulty writing numbers from dictation
Abstract Reasoning	• inability to solve word problems • inability to compare size of numbers, using symbols • cannot understand patterning in counting • difficulty with decimal concept	

In such cases, if the teacher verbalizes alternatives for the number, the child often can associate correctly.

Children with auditory figure-ground deficits may have trouble attending in class. For example, they cannot sort out extraneous stimuli, such as the sound of chalk, from the teacher's explanation. Or they may seem to be daydreaming or disruptive when, in fact, they are trying to attend but simply cannot listen and learn simultaneously.

Table 1.3 Nonverbal Learning Disabilities and Their Effects on Mathematics

CHARACTERISTICS OF STUDENTS WITH NONVERBAL LEARNING DISABILITIES	RELATIONSHIP TO THE STANDARDS
Good at computation and use of formulas	Decreased use of formulas and algorithms
Poor visual imagery	Increased use of concrete aids
Poor abstract reasoning	Increased use of concrete aids; decreased attention to rote procedures
Need for labels and vocabulary	Decreased use of key words and geometric names
Difficulty writing	Decreased use of paper-and-pencil tasks
Describes ''around'' a word or situation	Increased mathematical discussions
Benefits from scanning for signal words	Decreased attention to key words

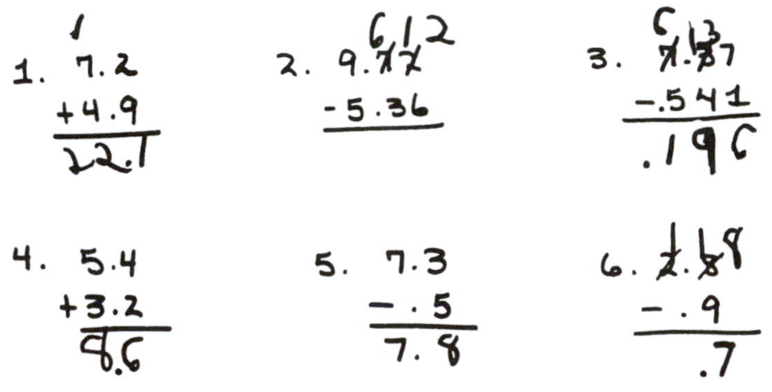

FIGURE 1.1

FIGURE 1.2

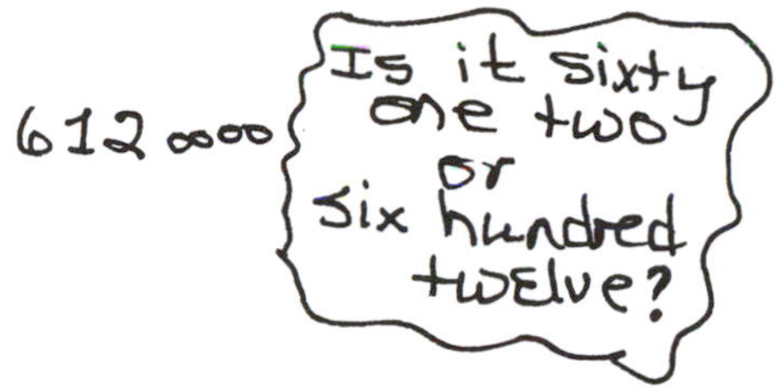

FIGURE 1.3

Auditory figure-ground difficulties also can interfere with a student's ability to hear counting patterns. Although place-value ideas form the basis of our number system, most young children learn to count by tuning in to repetitive patterns they hear. Even 5- and 6-year-olds learn to count by 5s and 10s, although they have no idea of place value. Learning to skip count often does not come easily to children with learning disabilities. Thus, they often are unable to discover the pattern (i.e., localize the repetitive part and repeat it) without a much stronger oral emphasis than is generally used.

Discrimination problems

Visual discrimination errors may cause students to misread or incorrectly write numbers. Very young children often are not developmentally ready to discriminate one number from another. As a result, they tend to write numbers backwards, especially 2, 3, or 5, often without even noticing the reversal. This difficulty is generally outgrown by the age of 7. Children with learning disabilities, however, may exhibit the problem more frequently or beyond the normal developmental stage. Because they do not perceive the numbers correctly, the task of writing numbers, copying problems from the board, spontaneously writing them from dictation, or using a calculator can be extremely difficult. By the time they have written a number or keyed it into the calculator, they may have lost their place or be so far behind that the teacher is ready to erase the board or change subjects.

Telling time or recognizing coins also can be very hard for children who are unable to discriminate size differences. The ability to recognize and differentiate between coins requires that a child notice discrete differences in size. Some children may recognize size differences in general but are unable to apply this skill to a practical situation. They may perform slower than classmates because of the perceptual deficit. Telling time, for example, takes these students longer because they must consciously locate the smaller hand on the clock while their peers locate it automatically.

As children encounter more and more symbols, perceptual problems become more prominent. Figure 1.4 illustrates several perceptually related errors made by children who, in fact, knew how to handle the computation involved.

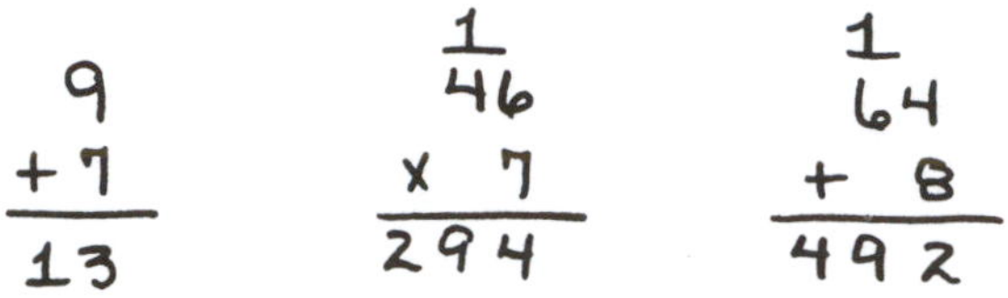

$$
\begin{array}{r}
9 \\
+\,7 \\
\hline
13
\end{array}
\qquad
\begin{array}{r}
\overset{1}{4}6 \\
\times\;\;7 \\
\hline
294
\end{array}
\qquad
\begin{array}{r}
\overset{1}{6}4 \\
+\;\;8 \\
\hline
492
\end{array}
$$

FIGURE 1.4

In the first example, the child read 9 as 6. The computation for what was seen, however, is correct. In the next example, the computational process is right. The errors are due to interpreting the 6 as a 2. The third example shows what can happen when a child has trouble discriminating operation signs. At first the sign was correctly seen as a "plus" sign and addition was consequently performed. At the second step of the problem, however, the child perceived the sign as a multiplication sign and proceeded to use that operation.

Auditory discrimination problems are exemplified in the inability to perceive numbers correctly. This, in turn, can affect a child's ability to count. Often children misperceive endings of words, leading to a counting pattern such as the following: "... 9, 10, 11, 12, 30, 40, 50, 60, 70, 80, 90, 20." The subtlety of this situation is that children, if asked to count aloud, may in fact *say the numbers correctly*. Internally, however, they misperceive what they hear themselves say. Depending on the severity of the problem, these children may or may not be able to correct the pattern if the symbols for 13 through 20 are placed before them.

Reversals

Another common perceptual difficulty results in reversals. Children who tend to make reversals not only make mirror images of individual digits as noted in the section on discrimination; they may also reverse the digits of a two-digit number when reading or writing. This problem naturally leads to errors in computation. For example, children may carry the wrong number when regrouping. The most common reversals occur in the teens: 21 for 12, 31 for 13, 41 for 14, and so on. An example of how reversals can affect multiplication computation is illustrated in Figure 1.5.

The child read 31 for 13 in the first problem and, consequently, multiplied 1 by 9. In the subsequent step, the 1 was correctly located in the 10s place and was multiplied next. Again, 9 was recorded in the product.

In the second problem, the digits were reversed when written down, thus accounting for the 7 in the 1s place. The rest of the problem was computed accurately.

This last example illustrates the importance of teaching children, especially those with learning disabilities, first to write the number that is to be regrouped. When using a calculator students should be encouraged either (1) to write the problem down first and to check that what they wrote is what they meant to write

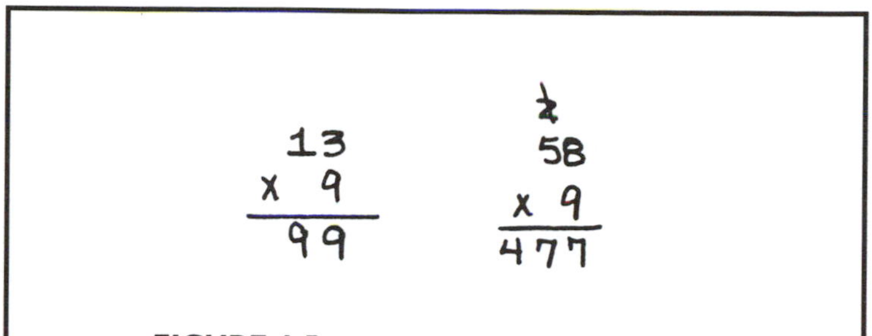

FIGURE 1.5

or (2) to keep a clearly spaced 100s chart in front of them so they can look at the number they mean to key into the calculator. More severe reversal and discrimination problems may require color coding or alternate methods of computing. Some of these approaches are discussed in Chapters 5 and 7.

Spatial and Temporal Deficits

Spatial and temporal organization can greatly affect a child's mathematics performance and the ability to apply practical applications outside the classroom. Although children with temporal disabilities may be able to tell time by rote, their concept of time and, therefore, their general planning ability are often considerably impaired.

Other problems characterize the child with spatial disabilities. For example, difficulty locating position in space—knowing right from left or up from down—can make the task of number alignment almost insurmountable. Renaming in computation becomes even more difficult. Children with this disability (a) need to understand *why* the regrouped number is placed above the 10s digit and (b) need visual and kinesthetic clues to help them locate and feel what *above* means.

Difficulties with spatial organization can prevent children from properly forming a number that they actually see accurately. They may reverse the position or invert it. Verbal cues such as "right" and "left" or "top" and "bottom" carry little meaning and are, therefore, no help in starting the number. Specific training involving motor activities, color coding, verbalization, and continual integration in daily relevant experiences is essential.

At the upper grade levels, spatial difficulties can interfere with the study of decimals, fractions, and word problems. Even when conceptual understanding is strong, difficulties still may arise. Locating where the decimal point belongs, determining the correct sequence of steps in a word problem, or properly placing the numbers in a fraction or a mixed number can be extremely difficult for a child with these deficits.

Motor Deficits

For many children, the process of writing numbers may be so difficult that it greatly affects their ability to succeed in mathematics. Children with perceptual motor difficulties have trouble relating what they see to what they write. They cannot coordinate their eyes with the proper hand movements. As mathematical problems become longer and more involved, these children find it extremely difficult to complete written assignments because they expend so much time and energy retrieving and applying the necessary finger movements for number formation that they forget what they are doing. For these students the increased availability of calculators and computers is invaluable and is strongly encouraged.

Memory Deficits

Although memory difficulties can be classified under perceptual deficits, we have chosen to separate them for the purposes of remediation and planning. Many children seem to understand what is presented in class and may even accurately complete classroom assignments. But these same students may not carry through on homework, or they may appear lost when the teacher continues a topic the next class day after only a short review. Initially they may do quite well when a topic is presented, but because there is only a limited review in the text, they quickly forget and appear never to have learned the material. These are the children who are often accused of not listening, of copying a friend's work, or of doing careless work.

In other cases, teachers may be baffled because, while students' classwork and homework are good, later they are unable to use the material as a basis for learning a new concept or skill, and when it comes time for a unit test on the material, they do poorly.

The difficulty in each of these examples may be due to specific short- or long-term memory problems that preclude retention of material over time. These children require training to acquire ways of remembering. They also need a considerable amount of overlearning before they are capable of retaining a concept. Additionally, they benefit greatly from "experiencing" what they are learning.

Short-term visual memory deficits manifest themselves in several ways. For some, the process of copying numbers from the board or from a textbook is extremely difficult. The inability to retain visual images long enough to write them on paper causes slowness and errors. Even using a calculator is difficult, especially if the entire problem is not displayed, as is usually the case. Unlike their peers who can hold an entire problem in their minds (e.g., $48 + 63$), these children must keep checking to see what they are to write or to key into the calculator. The time involved in this process greatly impedes the amount of work that can be done. Even when worksheets are provided, making it unnecessary for them to copy the problems, students still may be unable to retain enough information to perform accurate and quick computations.

Auditory short-term memory deficits often result in an inability to learn basic facts. For example, when presented with oral drills children may not be able to retain the isolated numbers long enough to give an answer. In addition, visual memory deficits may prevent retrieval of the correct answer, even if the problem is written down for the child.

Visual and auditory short-term memory problems also can hamper the ability to solve word problems. Although children may have no difficulty reading or comprehending the material, they may be unable to retain information long enough to solve a problem. This may be especially true of problems involving two or more steps.

For some children who are able to learn visually from textbooks, the pace may be too fast. Often there is not enough review and skill incorporation for the necessary overlearning to occur. As a result, these students, although understanding the material when presented, might be unable to retain it or use it as a building block for future learning.

Many areas of mathematics require considerable sequencing ability. Obviously, students with sequential-memory deficits encounter special problems here. Most children, for example, learn to tell time by the age of 7 or 8. But if they have trouble retaining a sequence, an otherwise simple task suddenly causes more trouble. Think for a moment of the basic steps involved in telling time:

- Which hand do I look at first?
- What number does that hand refer to?
- What number should I say first?
- What number does the other hand refer to?
- How do I count by 5s?

Assuming there is no spatial or temporal difficulty, the task of telling time requires that a considerable number of steps be sequenced properly. In order to use each step as a transition to the next, children with sequential-memory problems must be taught each step to the point of overlearning.

Sequential memory also affects the ability to count money, to compute using the four basic operations, and to solve word problems. In addition, it affects a student's overall ability to process and understand what is taught to the class as a whole. As a result, some children only retain isolated segments of what is said.

Figure 1.6 shows the work of a student whose primary disabilities are long-term and sequential memory. A close look will show that the child probably understands basic computation at the middle grade level. Since the processes at this level are long and involved, they place great demands on the child's retention and sequencing abilities. This child is probably unaware that the problems are incomplete. Only so much could be held in the memory at one time.

Integrative Deficits

Children with learning disabilities often have trouble integrating and applying what they learn. Some type of interference prevents them from pulling information together to draw conclusions, to make associations, or simply to use building blocks of information to learn material adequately. Following are some examples of common integrative problems.

Closure difficulties

Children with closure problems may find it especially difficult to read multi-digit numbers. They fail to group digits logically as they read the numbers. They may

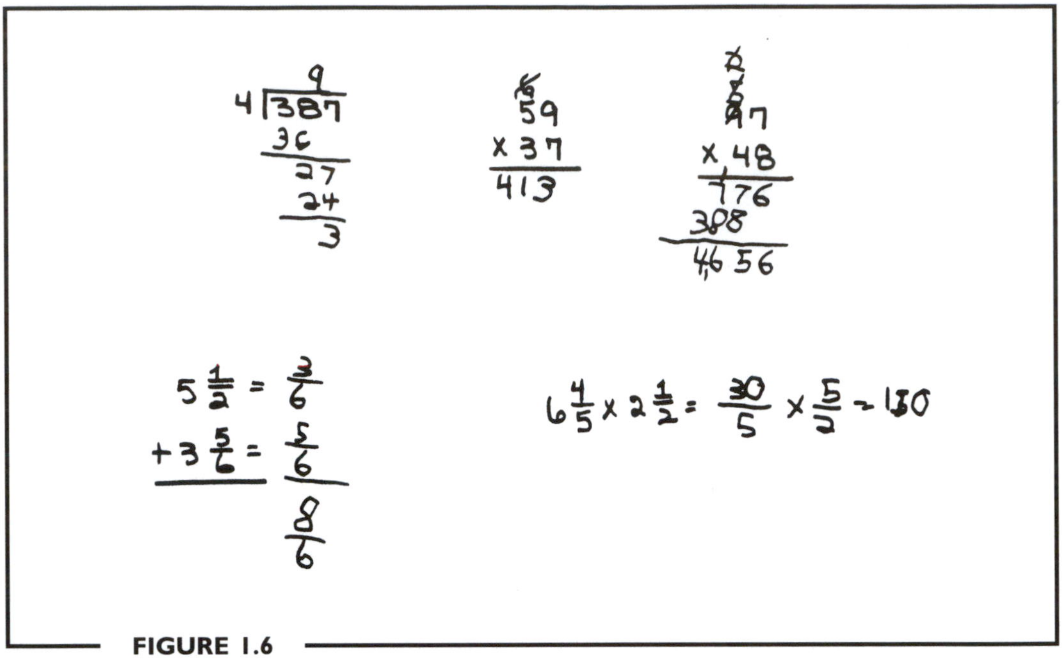

$$4\overline{)387} \quad \begin{array}{r} 9 \\ \underline{36} \\ 27 \\ \underline{24} \\ 3 \end{array}$$

$$\begin{array}{r} 59 \\ \times\ 37 \\ \hline 413 \end{array} \qquad \begin{array}{r} 97 \\ \times\ 48 \\ \hline 776 \\ 368 \\ \hline 46\ 56 \end{array}$$

$$\begin{array}{r} 5\frac{1}{2} = \frac{3}{6} \\ +3\frac{5}{6} = \frac{5}{6} \\ \hline \frac{8}{6} \end{array} \qquad\qquad 6\frac{4}{5} \times 2\frac{1}{2} = \frac{30}{5} \times \frac{5}{2} = 130$$

FIGURE 1.6

be able to count by rote or continue a sequence of four or five numbers, and yet given a single number and asked what comes next, they may not be able to respond independently.

These same children have trouble with classification tasks. At a primary level, they have difficulty sorting shapes by one characteristic. Further, as they begin to use symbols, they may be unable to determine the similarity between a group of numbers (e.g., all even numbers). (Regardless of the specific disability, it is generally much harder for children with learning disabilities to find similarities than to find differences.)

Word problems, and applications in general, also involve closure. With the ever-increasing emphasis on this area and a decreasing emphasis on isolated computation skills, students with learning disabilities may have increased reasons for being concerned about their ability to be successful in math. The ability to solve word problems greatly depends on developing an intuitive understanding of the different patterns that cause one to add, subtract, multiply, or divide. These students find it much more difficult to build up this background of problem-solving patterns. Thus, they often need a "supply box" of examples as well as practice comparing words to symbols.

Counting on, a technique often taught early in the primary grades, can be very difficult for these students. Although they may have little trouble locating the starting point, eliciting the next number may be impossible. Counting on from within a sequence, especially when skip counting is involved (e.g., counting coins), is extremely difficult and considerable drill and training usually is required to internalize the technique.

Expressive language problems

Children with expressive language difficulties cannot verbalize clearly, if at all, what they may really understand. These are the children who have trouble with rapid oral drills. As a result, they may not participate in class because they cannot express in words what they are thinking. They tend to do better on written homework or in situations where they receive visual cues and have enough time to respond. They cannot produce on demand; therefore, timed tests, whether oral or written, only make this disability more apparent.

Teachers commonly ask children to show that they understand a given concept by having them explain or apply it, either verbally or manually. Children with expressive language problems may need visual cues to help them retrieve the words and sequence the steps once recalled. Often these students can more easily distinguish between right and wrong processes than they can explain them. As a result, when a mistake occurs, they may recognize that something is not right but are unable to correct it spontaneously unless given alternatives.

Reading and writing decimals can be hard for children with expressive language difficulties. By comparison, fractions are easier. When one writes "$\frac{2}{100}$" or says "two one hundredths," it is clear that a 2 and a 100 are included among the digits for the fractions. Decimals lack this cuing. Hearing "two one hundredths" does not readily reveal the number of decimal digits in the number. Similarly, reading ".02" on a calculator does not automatically cue the response "two one hundredths."

Receptive language difficulties

"What do you mean?" "Please repeat that." "Can I have a clue?" These questions, and many others, are frequently asked by children with receptive language deficits because they have difficulty associating meaning with words. On occasion, all of us hear common words, perhaps in context, and temporarily "blank out" on the meaning. Usually the lapse is only temporary, a second or two. This is similar to what regularly happens to children with learning disabilities: they hear a word, recognize it as a unit, but fail to grasp the intended meaning.

In mathematics, this disability manifests itself in some or all of the following ways:

- difficulty following directions;
- difficulty understanding mathematical terms, especially those with multiple meanings such as *sum, times, difference,* and so on;
- difficulty solving a problem set up differently than originally presented;
- difficulty solving word problems.

Children with receptive language deficits often appear very literal. They may not understand simple jokes and generally find it hard to make sense of much of what they hear or read. Although they can repeat the exact words and may go through rote processes that are similar, they often are unable to repeat the same process if presented with the slightest variation.

Abstract-reasoning problems

One of the most difficult areas for children with learning problems, and for their mathematics teachers, involves abstract reasoning. As a general rule, new mathematical topics can and should be presented concretely. Many learning aids assist children in seeing, feeling, and dramatizing new concepts. Presented in this hands-on manner and subsequently discussed, the concepts become a natural basis for the transfer of meaning to written symbols. Indeed, written symbols should be associated with the models that illustrate the idea or process before being used alone.

Generally, when concrete aids are used, at least one of the following abilities is required:

- verbalizing what has been learned or observed;

- associating what is happening with symbolic representation; or

- understanding, auditorially or receptively, what is being explained or shown.

Children who have trouble making associations because of poor abstract reasoning often find it impossible to perform any of the above tasks. These children need the immediate and repeated association of numbers, operation signs, and other mathematical symbols that we substitute for words to understand the concept.

For children with learning disabilities of this type, repetition and practice may help them feel comfortable with a given process or idea. The confidence they develop from mastering the steps tends to allow them to focus their energy on understanding and applying the information. They can then more easily begin to make associations that eventually will lend meaning to what they do. As a result of this repeated practice and reassociation, the child develops:

- an understanding of the specific concepts;

- the ability to reason and associate in general; and

- a stepping stone for later reasoning.

As noted earlier, children with learning disabilities require a considerable amount of overlearning to succeed. Most textbooks provide drill for both computation and word problems. However, for students with reasoning deficits, such pages may act as a hindrance. The repetition of a process relieves the need to make decisions. An entire page of word problems that require multiplication does not help the child learn *when* to multiply and when not to multiply. Instead, if the goal is, in fact, learning when to multiply, it may be sufficient for the child to cross out all the problems that do not require multiplication.

Nonverbal Learning Disabilities

The child who has nonverbal learning disabilities typically has a significantly higher Verbal than Performance IQ on the *Wechsler Intelligence Scale for Children–Revised* or the *Wechsler Intelligence Scale for Children–Third Edition,* though not all students with this discrepancy have nonverbal learning disabilities (Denckla, 1991). The child with nonverbal learning disabilities "is usually good at word recognition and spelling, but tends to be poor in arithmetic" (Badian, 1992, p. 160). These students misperceive social cues such as tone of voice and facial expression and have considerable difficulty with visual-spatial organization. They have trouble with abstract reasoning, "lack understanding of mathematics concepts and do not readily solve problems in mathematics" (Foss, 1991, p. 129). They are, however, good rote learners. They also may have visual motor difficulties that make writing laborious and their work sloppy. Organizational skills may be weak, and they also tend to have poor visual imagery. These students can learn to relate ideas and to apply their knowledge but they generally require a highly structured, carefully sequenced program that provides them with a considerable amount of verbal mediation and small learning increments.

Attention Deficit Disorder With and Without Hyperactivity

Many, but not all, children with learning disabilities also have attention deficit disorder with or without hyperactivity (ADHD, ADD). These children may be easily distracted either by external stimuli that most of us ignore or by internal stimuli of which we often are unaware. Consequently they may only be able to process very slowly. In general, they find it difficult to stay on task—they may seem to be in constant motion and to never pay attention; the slightest sound or sight distracts them; they lose their place but may not even know that they have lost it. They may appear to be purposely thinking about other things in order to avoid work. These are the children who are inordinately attentive to marks on a page or to specks of dust. The mere sound of the chalk on the board may prevent them from listening to the teacher. In fact, they cannot sustain attention for a long period of time. When they appear to short-circuit, it often is necessary to let them change activities to allow them to regain their attention. According to Zentall and Ferkis (1993):

> The . . . mathematical instruction of youth with LD, ADD, and ADHD call for: (a) mastery learning, which builds on prerequisite skills and understandings, rather than spiral learning; (b) learning that involves active construction of meanings; (c) verbal teacher interactions with the child to assess and stimulate problem-solution strategies; (d) increased emphasis on assessment and teaching of mathematical concepts; (e) use of strategies, where appropriate, related to the requirements for reading comprehension and for memory in problem solving (e.g., for multiple step problems); (f) attentional cues to help students prepare for changes in problem action, operation, and order of operation; and (g) novel instructional activities to facilitate overlearning basic calculations (i.e., to increase automatization). (p. 16)

Behavioral Difficulties

Before we conclude this overview of learning disabilities, it is important to note those behavioral disabilities that can affect classroom performance and mathematics achievement. Following are the more common problems of this type.

Perseveration

Perseveration (the repetition of an activity even though a change is required) shows up in many ways. Children may perform the same operation throughout a page because they do not notice the signs have changed. Or they may continue doing whatever was required in the first problem. Such behavior patterns may be compulsive, not merely careless.

Figure 1.7 illustrates other ways in which perseveration can affect a child's computational work. In the first step, $17 - 9$, the child continued counting backwards, unable to stop at 8. Similarly, in the second problem the count was extended further than necessary for $6 + 5$. In other words, this child has no internalized means of stopping.

Once children have begun to attend, it may be extremely difficult for them to change activities unless they are reminded or physically drawn into doing so. In extreme cases, techniques such as handing children a clean sheet of paper on which to write or asking them to move from their seats to the board may help. Perseverations should be stopped whenever they are noted. Change from one academic subject to another may be necessary to prevent perseverating.

Disinhibition and impulsivity

Children who exhibit disinhibition or impulsivity often have trouble making transitions from one topic to another. For example, turning the page of a book to begin a new topic may divert their attention from the introduction given by the teacher. These children are usually quick to answer questions but often give irrelevant responses. Similarly, estimating answers is extremely difficult for them since they tend to guess wildly. Their thoughts often are triggered by some word they read or hear without their realizing that they made the association. As with perseveration, it often is necessary to change activities in order to refocus attention.

Reading problems

Although not ordinarily classified as behavior disorders, reading difficulties are included in this section because, when they interfere with mathematics performance, they can affect behavior. Although there are major changes taking place in the textbook market, most mathematics textbooks involve a lot of reading, which often puts children with learning disabilities at a severe disadvantage. In addition,

FIGURE 1.7

most texts require a high degree of abstract reasoning and the ability to transfer and retain skills over time. They also require that the child demonstrates at least on–grade level reading. Many children with learning disabilities do not read at grade level. Yet they are capable of performing on grade level or above in math if little reading is required. In the higher grades, mathematics may become increasingly difficult for these learners due to its dependence on reading.

LEARNING THEORY AND LEARNING DISABILITIES

As the nature and emphasis in mathematics education is changing, there has been an increased awareness of the importance of the constructivist approach to teaching and of the influence of metacognition in helping all students learn. Constructivist education emphasizes the child as an active learner who creates his or her own learning environment. Metacognition emphasizes self-awareness of how one approaches a task in order to plan, evaluate, and monitor progress. These two approaches form an integral part of the current trend in mathematics education, in which students are encouraged to participate actively in their learning by "inventing" (accurate) reasons for what they are doing. In this way, they will be better able to understand and apply what they are learning.

At the same time, however, that children should be encouraged to explore in order to understand and apply their knowledge, it is still necessary to remember the developmental issues of childhood. Most mathematics teachers, and primary-school teachers in particular, are aware of the implications of Piaget's developmental theory of mathematics learning. Children progress through certain developmental stages as they master mathematics concepts. Children with learning disabilities, however, who have difficulty making associations may need to have their programs (even at the middle- and upper-elementary levels) geared toward these stages as new and more abstract ideas are attempted and learned. The purpose of the following paragraphs is to give the teacher an idea of how this type of instruction might be carried out with children with learning disabilities.

One-to-One and One-to-Many Correspondence

Most children begin developing the idea of one-to-one matching at the concrete level by the time they are 5 or 6 years old. Gradually, this skill develops to the point where the child can count and perform simple computational problems. This last step, though at a higher level cognitively, represents a one-to-many correspondence. As children begin to internalize their thinking, specific instruction usually ceases, and they generally are able to extend the simpler one-to-one matching skill to computational situations requiring one-to-many matchings.

In terms of one-to-many matchings, application to multiplication involving single-digit or multidigit multipliers is apparent. Regardless of the presentation method, children ultimately must use one-to-many matching to be sure they have finished a given problem. For example, in Figure 1.8, it would not be unusual for a teacher to remind students to multiply all parts of the number 58 by 9. Even when students are encouraged to use a calculator for this type of calculation, a review of one-to-one and one-to-many matchings before teaching multiplication will make the process much simpler.

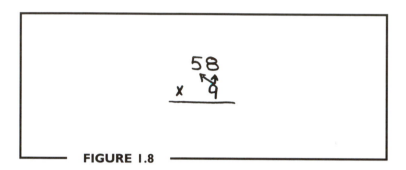

FIGURE I.8

Classification

Classification involves the ability to group objects or ideas by a common characteristic. This skill can involve any of the following abilities:

- spatial organization;
- reasoning;
- discrimination (visual or auditory); and/or
- expressive language (verbal or manual).

As mathematics becomes more symbolic, concrete presentation of classification generally is de-emphasized. However, children learning about equivalent fractions and decimals need a high degree of internalized classification. Suppose, for example, these children are presented with different sizes and shapes, each having one of four equal parts shaded. On the basis of this common characteristic, the children must be able to classify each shaded part as the equivalent of one fourth.

Children with learning disabilities may find this concept extremely difficult even though they are otherwise developmentally ready for it. For example, students with a reasoning deficit may not be able to determine the similarity without the help of specific aids, such as a flip chart (see Figure 1.9). Each page shows a different fractional relationship, and the child can match the concrete shapes to the pictorial representation and accompanying word. Children with figure-ground problems, in turn, may not see the four equal parts because they cannot properly focus their attention. These children would be aided by writing a number in each section, beginning with the shaded one. This would allow them to circle the number 1 in the shaded section, thereby seeing more readily the 1-out-of-4 idea.

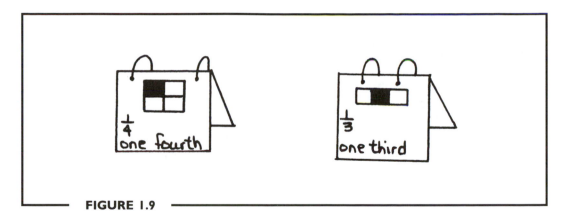

FIGURE 1.9

Flexibility

Children exhibit flexibility of thought when they show they can deal with:

- multiple meanings;
- different ways to express given sums or products; and
- horizontal and vertical formats for basic facts.

In general, flexibility is the ability to classify by more than one characteristic. It also involves being capable of using those characteristics to solve more advanced problems.

How does flexibility apply to mathematics beyond the developmentally concrete stages? Figure 1.10 shows the work of an 11-year-old boy who failed to exhibit true flexibility of thought. When questioned whether he noticed the signs, he replied, "Sure, but you always change the bottom number when they're written this way." This child had learned to multiply mixed numbers horizontally and to add them vertically. Although he readily recognized that the second problem involved multiplication, its vertical position confused him. In this case, it might be necessary to review, briefly, the horizontal and vertical multiplication of whole numbers before relating this idea to fractions. (Chapter 9 will offer further suggestions for how to handle problems of this nature.)

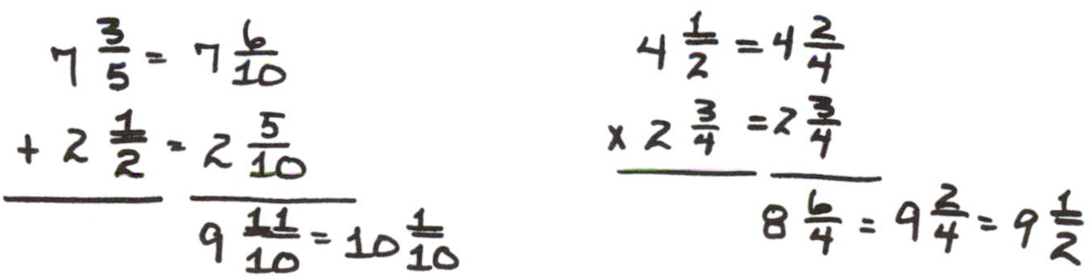

$$7\frac{3}{5} = 7\frac{6}{10}$$
$$+\ 2\frac{1}{2} = 2\frac{5}{10}$$
$$\overline{\qquad 9\frac{11}{10} = 10\frac{1}{10}}$$

$$4\frac{1}{2} = 4\frac{2}{4}$$
$$\times\ 2\frac{3}{4} = 2\frac{3}{4}$$
$$\overline{\qquad 8\frac{6}{4} = 9\frac{2}{4} = 9\frac{1}{2}}$$

FIGURE 1.10

Seriation

Seriation involves discrimination as well as spatial or temporal organizational abilities—areas in which many children with learning difficulties in mathematics have disabilities. To be able to organize numbers in some specific order requires that one understand the concepts of *more* and *less, before* and *after,* as well as ordinal counting. Some children may understand these concepts and how to order numbers yet find it difficult to apply the seriation skill to more advanced mathematical ideas, such as solving multistep problems or ordering decimals and fractions. For example, when presented with the specific steps of a word problem (not necessarily in the right order) and some concrete aids if needed, children may be able to explain what to do first, second, third, and so on. Yet when asked to organize these steps spontaneously and without concrete aids or written (verbal) choices, these same children may be unable to do so. In other words, their learning deficits require that they be provided clues that other students might not need. Eventually, and with enough repetition, many students with learning disabilities internalize these clues so they can begin to solve problems independently. Another way of helping with multistep problems involves highlighting each step using a different color. The first step would be green and the last red, reminding students of traffic lights where you "go on green and stop on red." An accompanying worksheet would list the step numbers in matching colors.

Conservation

The ability to conserve implies the understanding that the basic value or amount of something does not change even though its shape or arrangement does. Some children are slow to understand this concept. Children with learning disabilities, in particular, tend to have difficulty applying the notion of conservation to advanced mathematical ideas.

The early stages of conservation require that children recognize the invariance of quantity in spite of changes in shape. Similarly, the older child who is studying basic facts, using symbols only, needs to realize that 6×4 equals 4×6. When children use a calculator they need a solid understanding of the equivalence of fractions and decimals. Conservation emerges as the basis for understanding equivalence.

The preceding discussion illustrates the importance of allowing children to learn in the way that is best for them while keeping in mind developmental stages of learning. From the Piagetian perspective, the examples serve to emphasize the developmental readiness required to master particular concepts and topics. The constructivist and metacognitive approaches also account for this since children can actively learn what they are developmentally ready to learn. Children with learning disabilities may need more review and reminders, however, in order to move through mathematical concepts both horizontally and vertically.

GENERAL TECHNIQUES FOR DEALING WITH LEARNING DISABILITIES IN THE MATHEMATICS CLASSROOM

J. is very attentive in class, seems to follow most presentations, and usually is able to answer the teacher's questions. However, his work is always sloppily done, answers to problems run into each other, and the teacher generally is unable to match his work with either the assignment or his solutions.

A. regularly gets 100% on weekly basic fact tests but can never seem to give the correct answers to facts when called upon to do so in class. She consistently makes errors when solving application problems although she obviously understands the concepts involved.

Then there is P., who never seems to complete his work—especially classroom assignments. When given time during class to copy problems, he asks to get a drink, breaks a pencil, or otherwise wastes time. When he does manage to copy and finish an assignment, he makes many errors—his method of solving may be correct but his solutions are wrong.

These situations represent some of the problems a mathematics teacher might encounter and illustrate the demands placed on teachers to meet the needs of all students within the class. The children described, though seemingly covered by an umbrella of carelessness, may all be exhibiting learning disabilities with which they are inefficiently trying to cope. An overriding goal of the mathematics teacher is to plan and implement instruction so that all students in the class will benefit. What can be done to avoid spending an inordinate amount of time with one child to the exclusion of others, or vice versa? The techniques described in the remainder of this section are intended to help teachers in this regard.

Use Visuals and Manipulatives To Illustrate Important Ideas

Children with learning disabilities, like their peers in regular class mathematics, often are concrete in their thinking. As a general rule, the use of simple or familiar objects to illustrate facts, ideas, and written symbols or processes promotes both understanding and retention.

Use Visual Cuing: Boxes, Circles, and Lines

In an earlier section we showed how children with figure-ground difficulties may find it hard to locate the assigned problems in standard textbooks; that is, they cannot visually separate the problems from each other. A useful, inexpensive tool for handling this difficulty is a geometric shape template. The template can be used to box the problems in the book so that they can be found readily. Separating problems from each other prevents a child from seeing all of them as one.

Another common difficulty involves separating the problem number from the problem itself. In more and more textbooks, numbers are colored to differentiate them from the problems.

Homework, especially from the text, can be a mammoth undertaking for a child with either fine motor or figure-ground difficulties. Particularly at the intermediate and upper grade levels, it is not unusual for students to be assigned a page of 25 or 30 computational problems. Often these problems must be copied out of the book before they are solved. Many children with learning disabilities are so overwhelmed by the magnitude of the task that they do not do it at all. As a result, they are accused of being lazy or irresponsible.

Consider for a moment what is involved in a seemingly easy task of copying problems from a book. Children must be able to:

- sort the problem number from the problem itself;

- remember what they are copying and what the numbers look like;

- space the problems on the page so they can read the numbers and later solve the problems without mixing one problem with another; and

- align the numbers properly while copying to avoid errors in subsequent computation.

Due to this complexity, it may be necessary to shorten the task or split it into a two-night assignment. One night the student copies the problems, circles the problem numbers, boxes the problems, and sets up the worksheet. The second night the actual computation is done, hopefully with a calculator for at least part of the assignment. Also, it may be necessary to help children use the shape template or a ruler to organize their papers spatially before beginning an assignment. Rather than lined paper, provide centimeter-square graph paper that can be boxed, as shown in Figure 1.11.

NOTE: *With the increased emphasis on the use of mental calculation, estimation, and calculators, it is hoped that teachers are assigning fewer computation problems, both in class and for homework.*

For some children with learning disabilities, the use of lined paper, even as an aid for number alignment, only adds further confusion. The added visual stimulus of the lines makes it hard for them to organize their work, especially if fine motor deficits are involved. These students may have so much trouble staying on or within the lines and figuring out how to use them that their work becomes even more illegible than ever. In these cases, insist that the children use unlined paper. (Figures 1.12 through 1.15 show sample sheets teachers can keep in a file and draw upon as needed. Chapter 7 suggests more specific uses for pages of this type as an aid to computation.)

Before school starts each year, solicit the help of a parent, aide, or other volunteer to prepare textbook pages and different kinds of spatially formatted papers. The

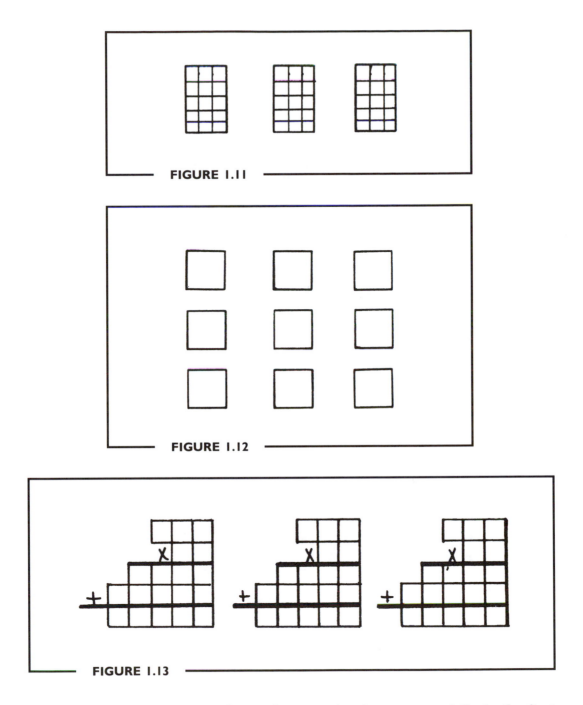

FIGURE 1.11

FIGURE 1.12

FIGURE 1.13

geometric shape template can be used to organize the pages spatially in the first chapters of the textbook. Problem numbers also could be circled. Important directions or examples may be underlined with bright colors or heavy lines. A file drawer containing special worksheet formats for children with spatial or perceptual difficulties also could be stocked at this time.

Eventually, children should learn to perform some of these self-help skills themselves. Early in the school year, therefore, it may be a good idea to set aside 5 to

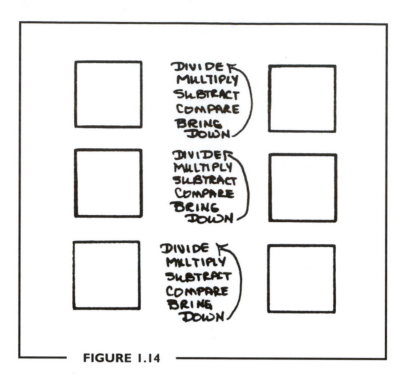

FIGURE 1.14

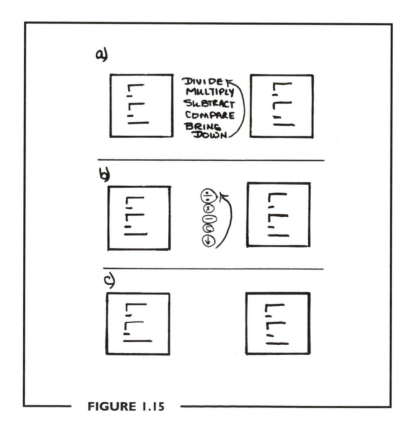

FIGURE 1.15

10 minutes each day for children with learning problems to learn how to box, circle, or underline as needed. This exercise may be equally important as a part of a specific assignment as the computation itself. Activities such as these are important, since they teach the children ways of dealing with their disabilities. Compensatory techniques, such as boxing or otherwise delineating the material, allow the children to keep up and be more a part of the mathematics class. These techniques also have carryover to other subjects.

Assign Fewer Problems and Minimize or Eliminate Copying from the Textbook or Board

It is important to remember the goal of a mathematics lesson. Suppose the purpose is to review a computational procedure. For students with severe spatial, motor, or perceptual deficits, teachers can better evaluate performance if other difficulties are minimized. This may mean employing techniques like those described previously, or it might mean:

- assigning only every fourth or fifth problem, rather than all the problems on a page;
- providing worksheets so children do not have to copy problems; or
- pairing students so that one acts as the "secretary" while they figure out the answers together.

If students are highly distractible, it may be helpful to:

- have them place an X, a chip, or their fingers on the problem while computing so they do not lose their place;
- create several standard formats for worksheets and provide construction paper masks that blot out all but one fourth or one third of the page; or
- cut a worksheet into fourths or thirds and assign only one small section at a time.

Use Visual Cuing: Color Code

Color coding, although it can appear confusing to those of us without memory or perceptual difficulties, can be an effective way to teach many children with learning disabilities. It provides them with any or all of the following:

- ways of focusing attention;
- ways of properly sequencing steps;
- increased ability to recall information;
- ways of identifying starting and stopping points;

- cues to the appropriate response; or

- increased ability to be independent.

As previously mentioned, it generally is advisable to code the first step in green and the last step in red. When using more than two colors, choose ones that are easily distinguished from each other. Do not make Step 2 orange and Step 3 red. For those few students who are color blind, use heavy lines instead of colors.

If students have auditory memory or perceptual difficulties, try to keep verbal directions and explanations short and to the point. Reinforce them with visual cues. In the case of children with reading or language interference, present concrete examples or illustrations that they can look at while explanations are being given. The use of color to focus, delineate, or cue in illustrations and other visuals also is useful for students with visual perception or memory problems. Teachers can use colored chalk or marking pens during teaching sessions for this purpose. Later, using the same colors, they can make special follow-up worksheets for individual students. (Figures 1.16 and 1.17 present ideas for color-coded pages that can be kept on file and distributed as needed. Other ideas are included in subsequent chapters.)

Colors also can be used when boxing, circling, or underlining sections of a textbook. For example, directions might be underlined in green to remind students to "read these first." This simple technique will prevent children from spending an inordinate amount of time searching for the directions or trying to separate them from the problems.

Alter, Adjust, or Reinforce the Standard Text Presentation When This Meets a Special Need

Most textbooks provide a standard sequence to be followed, but with some children it may not be appropriate. For example, more and more texts introduce decimals and decimal computation before fractional computation. For children with auditory discrimination, spatial organization, or abstract-reasoning problems, a more careful review of basic fraction concepts and symbolism along with simultaneous presentation of fractions and decimals may be necessary. Even in written form, fractions are more concrete than decimals—they more graphically trigger the visual image of what is represented. The suggested review in Chapter 8 provides a basis for helping children learn decimal notation by associating it with fractions.

If students have memory difficulties and are familiar only with certain basic facts, use these facts when presenting a new procedure or concept. Make it a game. Let the class know that all the experimenting and work today will be with only a couple of facts. Controlling the lesson with known facts will allow the children with learning disabilities to learn along with their classmates more readily. Additionally, this approach provides the overlearning that is so essential and eliminates the need for children (even those who do not have learning disabilities) to draw on weaknesses while trying to learn something new.

A final technique deals with homework assignments. Instead of assigning all problems on a given page, draw from several pages. Selectively list the problems

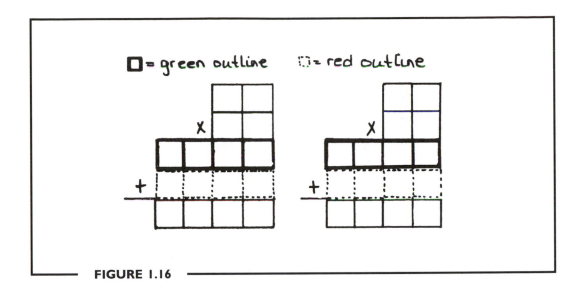

FIGURE 1.16

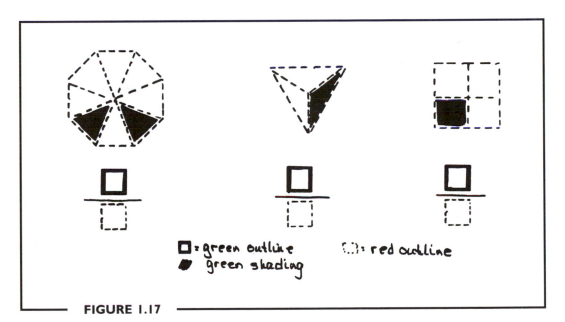

FIGURE 1.17

and the order in which they should be completed. An assignment might look like this:

- page 235: problems 3, 7, 8, 5 (These problems may be three of one kind and a fourth that is slightly different.)
- page 182: problems 2 and 14
- page 203: problems 1 through 4, and 7
- page 182: problems 7 and 1

Insist that the children solve the problems in the order presented as a means of avoiding perseveration, developing sequencing skills, and improving reasoning. This approach can be used with an entire class.

Allow Children To Finger Trace or Use Other Tactile Cues

In some cases, seeing or hearing is not enough. More involvement is required. Standard procedures parallel those often used in reading: finger trace, say, then write. Sometimes children may be instructed to close their eyes while finger tracing a textured example. For reversals, it is recommended that students finger trace a textured numeral then retrace the shape in midair or on paper before writing it.

Another technique can be used to reinforce retention of basic facts. Using the answer side of a flash card, children with visual memory problems might finger trace both the problem and the answer. Upon turning the card over, they should try to give the answer immediately. If they forget, finger tracing the problem again often triggers the correct response. Similarly, pair students and have one "write" on the other's back while that student says and writes the number on a piece of paper or on the blackboard.

Capitalize on Patterns and Other Associations To Promote Understanding or Retention

Many children with learning disabilities are helped by instruction that is based on using patterns or relevant associations. One technique is drawn from the area of basic facts. Often children can learn difficult facts by associating them with easier, known ones. The one-more-than idea is powerful in this regard (e.g., $5 + 5 = 10$, so $5 + 6$ is one more [11]). Three additional examples that employ associations are illustrated in Figure 1.18. Other suggestions are detailed throughout the following chapters.

Use Auditory Cuing

Children with visual, perceptual, or memory disabilities generally require a high degree of auditory reinforcement. At times, for example, it may be helpful for children to close their eyes to block out distracting visual stimuli and just listen. They might read a basic problem and its answer into a tape recorder then listen to the playback for reinforcement. Examples of this basic approach are presented throughout the following chapters.

Make Samples for Students Who Need Them

Number charts

In many classrooms wall charts stretch all the way around the room, often showing manuscript or cursive letters. Be sure to include a number chart as well,

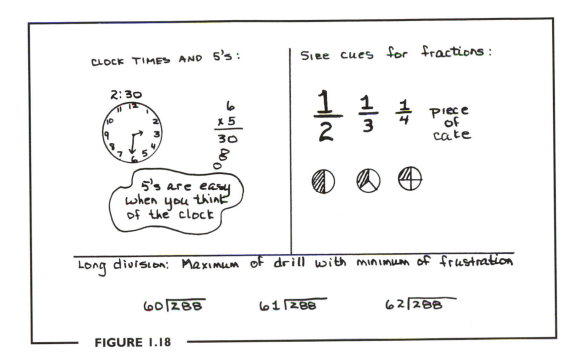

FIGURE 1.18

even at the upper grade levels. It will help students who are capable of proceeding mathematically but lack visual memory or other capabilities to put the skills into practice. The chart will serve as an unobtrusive aid and will minimize the chance that students with learning difficulties will be teased.

Charts for special ideas

Figure 1.19 presents a useful chart for children with receptive language deficits. Similarly, the technique pictured in Figure 1.20 has proven helpful to many students with learning difficulties in mathematics. Charts like these are necessary references for many children with special problems while also being helpful to the rest of the class.

Other techniques

To help children with nonverbal learning disabilities or those who confuse or forget the sequence of computation, techniques like those illustrated in Figure 1.21 might be employed, including:

- visual directional clues in a sample problem;

- flip charts for a sample problem, with a separate page for each step; and

- a sample problem, completed step by step, at the top of a worksheet.

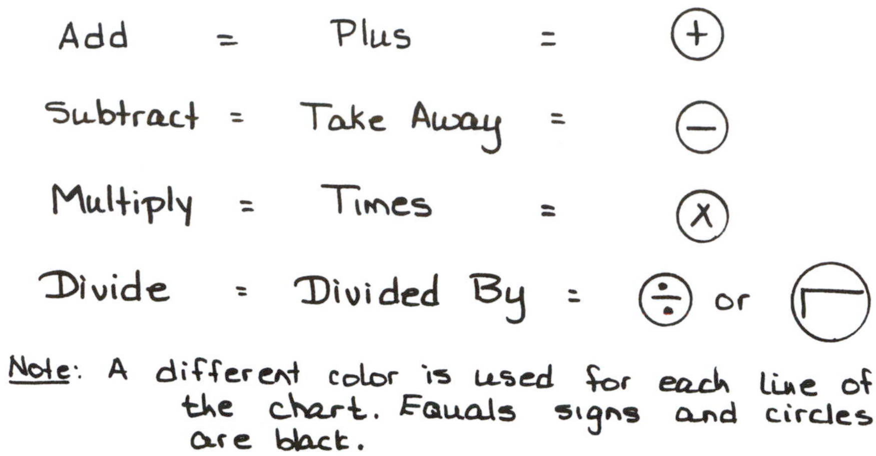

Add   =   Plus   =   ⊕

Subtract =   Take Away =   ⊖

Multiply =   Times   =   ⊗

Divide   = Divided By = ⊙ or ⌐⃝

<u>Note</u>: A different color is used for each line of the chart. Equals signs and circles are black.

FIGURE 1.19

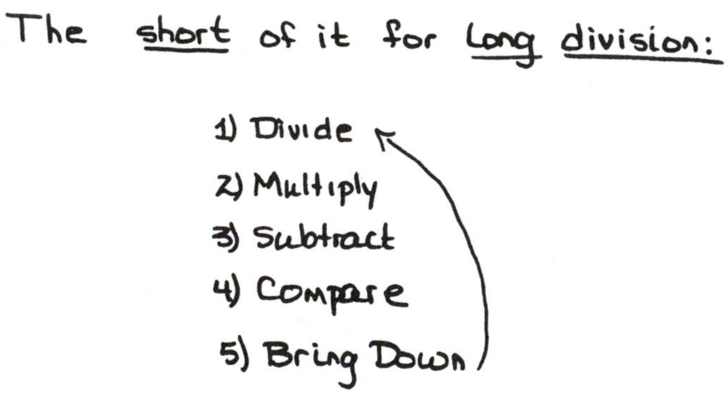

The <u>short</u> of it for <u>long</u> <u>division</u>:

1) Divide
2) Multiply
3) Subtract
4) Compare
5) Bring Down

FIGURE 1.20

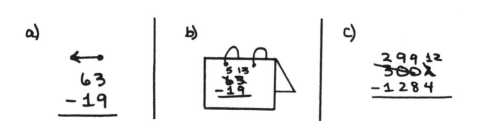

a)

63
−19

b)

c)

29 9 12
300 1
−1284

FIGURE 1.21

Carefully Sequence Instruction in Small Steps, with Adequate Provision for Practice and Review

Proper sequencing of instruction is critical for students with learning disabilities, as is extra developmental and practice time for both understanding and retention of concepts and processes. In addition, breaking the learning process into small, meaningful segments makes understanding possible rather than overwhelming for these students. Specific suggestions for how to apply this technique are outlined for selected topics in each of the chapters that follow.

Sometimes teachers find it helpful to think of each of the following elements when planning a mathematics lesson:

- daily review;

- "Look Ahead" activity (to teach/review a concept or skills embedded in an upcoming lesson);

- major thrust for the day; or

- minimath activities (connected with or separate from the lesson itself, and focusing on concepts or skills that are best developed over time rather than in 2-week units. Examples include problem solving, estimation, mental math, counting skills, calendar math, and time.)

Sometimes, in conjunction with one or more of these aspects of a lesson, learning packets with special practice pages can be prepared in advance to satisfy the need for smaller increments and more review. A tape recorder also can be used to provide extra practice for those requiring auditory learning. In addition, a tape recorder often is helpful for students with visually based difficulties who are strong auditorially.

Many motivating games can be used to reinforce the learning of each small step. However, students must transfer from games to more applicable methods of showing understanding. Many students with learning disabilities cannot make this transfer independently. For example, some children can play basic-fact dice games very easily. They can recognize the groupings and may be able to give answers without counting. However, they may not be able to perform the same computations on paper or mentally. They simply do not make the associations independently. For these children, it may be necessary to keep visuals such as those illustrated in Figure 1.22 to aid in the transition from games to other assignments.

It often is possible to make assignments or plan activities that build perception, auditory association, visual memory, or other processing skills. For example, allow students to use a computer to type in number sentences that are either dictated by the teacher or prerecorded on the microphone. Other children may be assigned numbers or number sentences to copy, just as other children practice handwriting.

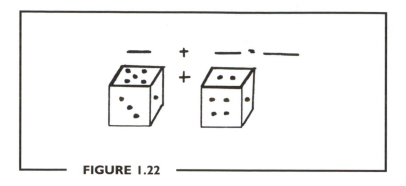

FIGURE 1.22

DISCUSSION

This chapter has focused on several important aspects of planning effective mathematics instruction for students with specific learning disabilities. It first presented an overview of the major disabilities from the perspective of their effect on mathematics performance. Knowing and understanding a disability is a prerequisite for dealing effectively with it during instruction. Ten general techniques for meeting the needs in the mathematics classroom of students with learning disabilities were then discussed. More detailed applications of these techniques to selected mathematical topics appear in the chapters that follow.

No attempt will be made to deal here with the content of the entire elementary school mathematics curriculum. It is assumed that teachers are familiar with standard sequences and approaches to presenting topics basic to that curriculum. Instead, the emphasis is on selected areas that commonly cause difficulties for students with learning disabilities. Instructional sequences that incorporate special techniques and adaptations for meeting special needs will be outlined. Most of these suggestions can be carried out in regular classrooms as well as in resource, clinical, or self-contained settings. We hope the sample sequences and accompanying teaching ideas will encourage teachers to apply similar approaches to other areas of mathematics.

REFERENCES

Badian, N. A. (1992). Nonverbal learning disability, school behavior, and dyslexia. *Annals of Dyslexia, 42,* 160.

Denckla, M. B. (1991). Academic and extracurricular aspects of nonverbal learning disabilities. *Psychiatric Annals, 1*(21), 717–724.

Foss, J. M. (1991). Nonverbal learning disabilities and remedial interventions. *Annals of Dyslexia, 41,* 129.

National Council of Supervisors of Mathematics. (1988). *Twelve components of essential mathematics.* Minneapolis: Author.

National Council of Teachers of Mathematics. (1989). *Curriculum and evaluation standards for school mathematics.* Reston, VA: Author.

Zentall, S. S., & Ferkis, M. A. (1993). Mathematical problem solving for youth with ADHD, with and without learning disabilities. *Learning Disability Quarterly, 1,* 16.

CHAPTER 2

Problem Solving

THE NATIONAL COUNCIL of Teachers of Mathematics (NCTM), in *An Agenda for Action: Recommendations for School Mathematics of the 1980s,* set goals that called for greater emphasis on problem solving at all levels (NCTM, 1980, p. 1). Since then, NCTM has gone on to address these goals by developing the *Curriculum and Evaluation Standards for School Mathematics* (1989). This document not only stresses the importance of emphasizing problem solving throughout the mathematics curriculum but also addresses these needs in relation to a changing society—one in which more calculators and computers are available. Suggestions also are made for changing the focus of instruction and for revising textbook material. (See Table 2.1 for a summary of these changes.)

Problem solving is a difficult area to teach and one that is often avoided, especially when teaching students with learning disabilities. Yet it is one of the most important areas in mathematics instruction as it affects all aspects of a person's life. Students must feel confident that, when they approach new or difficult situations, they possess the skills necessary to make a reasonable attempt to solve the problem, whether it involves determining if there is enough money to buy something or if they have enough time to go to a movie with a friend before going to work. Academic and socialization skills often depend on our ability to feel confident about our reasoning skills.

In the past, too often problem solving in the mathematics curriculum placed heavy emphasis on reaching a final answer, rather than on the process of reasoning. The thrust is changing and the mathematics curriculum now includes more problems that stress the process of arriving at an acceptable solution rather than the "right answer." At the lower grade levels, teachers should encourage students to feel comfortable with situations that involve words such as *some* or *a few.* In daily life, we talk about going places with "some friends" or "losing a few things." As children progress in math they must become more aware that there are a variety of ways to solve a problem. Strategies such as the following constitute an important component of any mathematics curriculum and rely less on the exact answer than on the procedure:

- making an organized list;
- noticing a pattern;

Table 2.1 Summary of Changes in Content and Emphasis

	INCREASED ATTENTION	DECREASED ATTENTION
Grades K–4		
Number	• Number sense • Place value concepts • Meaning of fractions and decimals • Estimation	• Symbolic representation
Operations and Computation	• Meaning of operations • Mental computation • Estimation/reasonableness • Computation method • Use of calculators • Basic fact thinking strategies	• Complex and isolated paper/pencil work • Addition/subtraction without regrouping • Isolated division facts • Long division with and without remainders • Paper/pencil fraction computation • Use of rounding to estimate
Geometry/ Measurement	• Properties of figures • Relationships • Spatial sense • Process of measuring • Concepts • Actual measuring • Estimation • Curriculum generalization	• Naming figures • Memorizing measurement equivalents
Probability/ Statistics	• Data collection and organization • Exploration of chance	
Patterns and Relationships	• Pattern recognition and description • Variables to express relationships	
Problem Solving	• Word problems with a variety of structures • Everyday problems • Applications • Study of patterns and relationships • Strategies	• Clue words
Instructional Practices	• Use of manipulatives • Cooperative work • Discussion • Questioning • Justification of thinking • Writing about math • Problem-solving instruction approach • Content integration • Use of calculators and computers	• Rote practices • Rote memorization of rules • One answer/one method • Use of worksheets • Written practice • Teaching by telling

(continues)

Table 2.1　*Continued*

	INCREASED ATTENTION	DECREASED ATTENTION
Grades 5–8		
Problem Solving	• Open-ended problems • Extended projects • Investigation/formulation • Variety of representation	• Practice in routine, one-step problems • Categorized problems
Communication	• Discussing, writing, reading, and listening to ideas	• Fill-in-the-blank worksheets • Answering yes/no questions
Reasoning	• In spatial contexts • With proportions • From graphs • Inductive/deductive	• Relying on teacher/answer key
Connections	• Generalization to outside • Connecting math topics • Application	• Learning isolated topics • Developing skills out of context
Number/ Operation/ Computation	• Developing number sense • Developing operation sense • Creating algorithms and procedures • Use of estimation • Exploring relationships • Understanding ratio, proportions, and percents	• Memorizing rules and algorithms • Paper/pencil work • Exact answers • Memorizing procedures • Rounding out of context
Patterns/ Functions	• Identifying/using functional relationships • Developing/using tables, graphs, rules for situations • Interpreting mathematical relationships	• Seldom in curriculum
Algebra	• Understanding variables, expressions, equations • Various approaches to solving equations • Informal study of inequal and nonlinear equations	• Manipulating symbols • Memorizing procedures • Drill on solving equations
Statistics	• Analyze, evaluate, decide	• Memorizing formulas
Probability	• Create situations	• Memorizing formulas
Geometry	• Understand relationships • Use in solving problems	• Memorizing vocabulary • Memorizing facts and relationships
Measurement	• Estimating	• Manipulating formulas • Converting measures
Instructional Practices	• Active student involvement • Use of appropriate technology • Use of concrete materials • Teacher/facilitator	• Computation out of context • Paper-and-pencil work • Isolated topics • Memorization

- analyzing a survey;

- working a problem backwards;

- using reasonable guess-and-check tests; or

- simulating a procedure.

When methods such as these are used, students begin to feel comfortable about taking risks, viewing mistakes as part of learning, and with different ways of thinking and approaching problems. They learn that sometimes there is more than one way to solve a problem and that there may be no "right" answer.

Other important aspects of problem solving include the ability to:

- recognize whether a problem contains enough information or extraneous information;

- use a chart or table to obtain needed data;

- comfortably estimate and use such an estimate rather than an exact answer; and

- retell a problem in one's own words.

    NOTE: *Children with expressive language problems may need help with this. For example, rather than being asked to restate a problem, they might be allowed to read/hear a variety of restatements and be asked to choose the correct one.*

Teachers must continually use and encourage a variety of ways to approach problem solving. Even young children can begin to learn to use reasoning skills, especially if the mathematics curriculum is approached developmentally. Some effective approaches, which can be used at various levels, are summarized as follows.

- Use interesting problems that are within a child's experience. Young children and children with learning disabilities respond best when problem situations are meaningful. "About how long until recess?" Even if the answer is "About two big dots" (as described by one child who looked at an analog clock), students are still learning to "feel" time.

- Encourage and reinforce children's estimates, even if the answers are way off or the approach is not efficient. Help them learn other approaches but remember that, either because of their developmental level or their own learning style, *what is efficient for one person may not be efficient for another.*

- Pose problem situations orally. This is especially appropriate for younger students and children who have trouble reading.

    NOTE: *Providing concrete, visual reinforcement, which includes the use of symbols, for each orally presented problem, regardless of the student's age, helps students who have auditory-processing or abstract-reasoning difficulties.*

- Calculators and computers serve important functions in our society. When introduced properly at an early age, these tools need not be considered a crutch. Help students learn to use them and to recognize when they offer a more efficient procedure than the use of pencil-and-paper calculation.

- Begin early to encourage children to develop their mental calculation skills. For students with learning disabilities mental calculation can be difficult, but it does not have to be impossible. Rapidly flash pictures, numbers, objects, and the like to young children or students with memory problems. Help them concentrate on remembering what they saw *first, second, third.* Encourage older students to use place value to find answers to larger computation problems mentally.

- Use concrete objects, drawings, and diagrams at all levels of instruction to clarify a problem, find a solution, and verify the answer. Have children act out problems.

- Encourage students to feel comfortable with incorrect answers and teach them to understand that they can learn from errors. Start with a page of solved word problems that include incorrect answers. Work with students to locate the wrong answers by talking about unreasonable answers. Especially if introduced at a young age, this approach takes the fear out of making mistakes, teaches students to view mistakes as a learning process, and helps them develop self-confidence.

  NOTE: *Do not use problems that students in class have solved. The teacher should solve the problems, purposely making mistakes.*

- Help students understand that something which is difficult for one student may be easier for another. Encourage them to help each other so that everyone feels comfortable with their strengths and weaknesses.

- Have children, even very young ones, write (match) mathematical sentences for problems without computing the answers. This emphasizes the importance of a procedure, rather than the correct answer.

  NOTE: *Allow children with expressive language difficulties to choose an appropriate sentence from several that are provided. Encourage the use of concrete aids, as needed.*

- Use open-ended problems (those with more than one solution) to foster creative thinking and to develop a confidence that people think in different ways.

- Use problems containing too much or too little information and ask students to identify what is still needed or what information is extra.

- Help students understand that we use math all the time and that most of the time the math we use does not require exact answers. For example, we only need to estimate how long it will take to go to the airport or how many CDs can be bought for $15.00.

- Have students make up problems to be solved in class. To offset the tendency to make problems too difficult, require that they be able to solve their own problems or explain why the problems cannot be solved.

  NOTE: *By pairing students with different strengths and weaknesses, cooperative learning works well for this approach. One student dictates, one writes, others try to solve in a variety of ways.*

- Help students develop the language and thought process necessary for solving problems.

  1. Read the problem.

  2. Picture what is happening.

  3. Think: What is the question? Is there enough (too much) information to arrive at a solution?

  4. Is an exact answer required?

  5. What operation(s) are needed?

  6. What is the best method for determining the answer—calculator, mental calculation, paper and pencil?

  7. Check. Is it reasonable?

  Break down this sequence in steps and help students overlearn each step.

- Encourage children to devise word problems or use manipulatives to describe computation problems. Problems should relate to situations that are part of their experiences.

- Use problems with words such as *some* or *many* instead of numbers to check that students know when to use each operation. Encourage students to insert low numbers to help determine the operation.

- Use problems without a stated question and have students ask a question about the information. Do this in a small group and require each student to ask a different question.

- Make sure you understand children's thinking before commenting on the work or marking an answer as wrong. Remember, given their thinking or what they saw, their answer may be correct.

- Post a "problem of the week" on the bulletin board.

- In class discussions, ask for alternative suggestions or methods for solving a problem.

- Be sure the children know the mathematics needed to solve assigned problems. For example, if they understand which operation to use but have not memorized the facts involved, allow them to use a cross-out list, as suggested in Chapter 7. Work on learning the facts another time.

Given the continually expanding scope of problem solving in school mathematics, this chapter will focus on the related subskills needed to develop problem-solving ability. The techniques suggested apply not only to helping students determine correct answers but also to helping them develop the confidence and ability to solve nonroutine or process problems. Throughout, recommendations also are made to assist teachers in relating isolated components of problem solving to real-world situations.

PROBLEM SOLVING AND THE STUDENT WITH LEARNING DISABILITIES

The suggestions in the previous section are important for *all* students. The approach to teaching students with learning disabilities, however, may need to be different and involve more review or topic breakdown. Nonetheless, the ideas are essential for developing a sense of confidence and the "belief that they [all students] have the power to do mathematics and that they have control over their own success or failure" (NCTM, 1989, p. 26).

Problem-solving situations call upon children to retrieve previously learned information and apply it in new or varying situations. Knowing basic arithmetic skills and knowing when and how to incorporate these skills in new contexts are two completely different tasks. All too often we assume that students understand how to solve a problem if they understand and can carry out the operations involved.

As difficult as it may be for students with learning disabilities to master a particular skill, it generally is considerably more difficult for them to decide when and how to use that skill in new contexts. This appears to be especially hard for students with nonverbal learning disabilities. "When academic demands shifted from rote learning of skills, facts, and procedures to more complex integrated learnings and applications, these individuals began to fail and to cease to try. . . . To be effective, interventions must address the problem areas directly and explicitly. They must also involve the student in planning to apply newly learned behaviors to similar tasks and situations beyond the training exercises" (Foss, 1991). In general, students with learning disabilities will develop confidence in their ability to use the problem-solving process if they are provided specific help with:

- decision making,
- information use,
- vocabulary,
- sequencing, and
- patterning.

Because of their importance in the problem-solving process, each of these areas deserves special consideration in a mathematics program for students with learning disabilities.

Decision Making

All problem solving involves making decisions. Very young children make a decision when they indicate whether the symbol in front of them is a 2 or a 3. They also make decisions when playing a game, such as Bingo, where they must use an understanding of *more* and *less* to decide where to put their chips. As children progress and learn more skills, decision making continues to enter their daily life. Thus, they are confronted not only with deciding what a sign means or whether to regroup but also with answering such questions as what operation to use, which problem to solve first, or whether they have enough money to buy something.

The decision-making process is complex. It requires the ability (a) to use strong abstract-reasoning, (b) to both understand and express words in a meaningful way, (c) to draw on previously learned concepts and skills, (d) to distinguish among them, and (e) to choose the concept or skill that is most appropriate in a given situation.

Information Use

In order to solve problems, students must be able to interpret information accurately and to formulate and express the key ideas involved. They must understand what question/questions are being asked. In addition, they must be able to isolate given information within a problem. In some problems, sorting out irrelevant information is essential. In real-life situations, we are not always told in advance that some of the information is not important. Similarly, on a day-to-day basis, we are not always given the information we need to know in order to solve a problem. We must determine what information is missing. All these requirements demand strong language ability—both receptive and expressive. For many children, problem solving is difficult, not because of the computation involved or even because of the difficulty with abstract reasoning. These students may find problem solving hard because they are unable to understand and use language efficiently. They are unable to express their ideas or associate the words with the appropriate meanings involved.

Vocabulary

Due to the many special problems involved, vocabulary is considered apart from the more general use of language in relation to problem solving. Like reading, mathematics has a vocabulary. Although the vocabulary varies depending on the level of the material, it is still an integral part of the mathematics problem. For younger children, the relevant vocabulary involves associating one or more words with a symbol, as in Figure 2.1, and understanding those words when they are spoken or read. Older students, generally fourth grade and above, must acquire a rapidly expanding vocabulary, including many words with multiple meanings (e.g., *and, factor, times*). When new vocabulary is used, many students with learning disabilities may not automatically know the meaning just from the context. At best, they may know that a familiar word does not make sense in its current context.

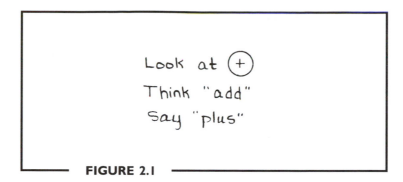

FIGURE 2.1

Sequencing

Problem solving requires not only using information that has been learned previously but also choosing which previously learned information is needed and using it in a properly organized way. In other words, sequencing is important to success in problem solving. Unlike computation where the sequence does not vary, the sequences needed to handle real-life problems can vary from situation to situation. In one instance, it may be necessary to add first and then multiply, whereas in another, the reverse procedure might be required.

Patterning

Generally, when we think of patterning in mathematics, we think of numbers or shapes that follow a specific order, as in Figure 2.2. Patterning, however, is also an important part of solving common daily problems. In Chapter 4 the complex patterning needed to count money will be addressed. An extension of this type of patterning underlies the ability to decide which of the four basic operations to apply in a given situation. Can students notice and retrieve the similarities and differences between a given problem and those previously worked using a particular operation? (See Figure 2.3.) Some students with learning disabilities cannot

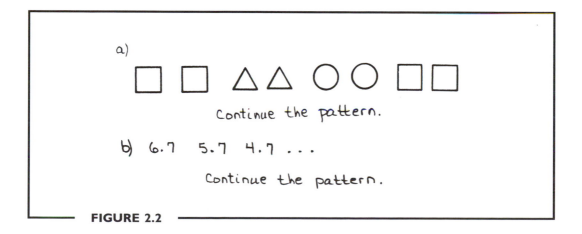

FIGURE 2.2

visualize what is laid out from just the words of a problem—that the situation really fits the pattern of addition or division, for example. They do not see the similarity between this and previous work with addition, division, or some other operation. Unfortunately, it often is easier for students with learning disabilities to express the differences than to express the similarities between things. In order for them to expand their problem-solving skills, it is helpful and often necessary for similarities to be isolated and for repeated practice to focus on recognizing those similarities.

Decision making, information use, vocabulary, sequencing, and patterning are all key aspects of the problem-solving process. When certain prerequisite skills, those discussed in the next section, are intact, teachers of students with learning disabilities can give these aspects of problem solving the attention they deserve.

FIGURE 2.3

PREREQUISITES FOR EFFICIENT PROBLEM SOLVING

Good problem solvers can estimate, predict, draw conclusions, and use information effectively. Too often these skills are only taught in the reading curriculum. It is important for mathematics teachers to realize that children's abilities to handle these tasks greatly affect their confidence and success in many areas of mathematics, including problem solving. The following are suggestions for how to develop these areas.

1. **Rounding.** Repeated work on understanding the relationship between rounding isolated numbers and problem solving is essential. Too often students view rounding as a computational skill and are unable to apply it when needed. Help them understand that rounding a computation, such

as that shown in Figure 2.4, is similar to what you might do if you want to make sure you have enough money with you to go to a movie ($6.50), buy a book ($7.45, without tax), and have dinner ($11.00).

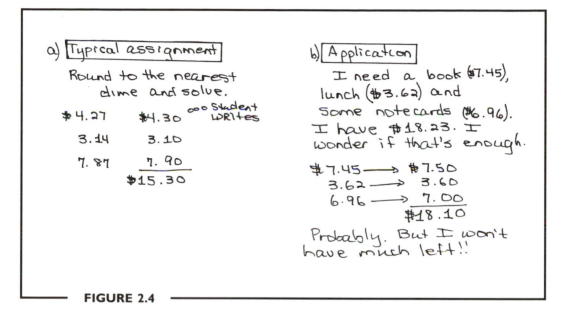

FIGURE 2.4

2. **Choosing efficient methods.** Starting with very young children, develop the ability to choose the best method for calculating. Sometimes the use of a calculator is the best, sometimes mental calculation is preferable, and sometimes paper and pencil is more efficient. Using an analog clock, ask students to time how long it takes to solve a problem mentally. Compare the results to the time it takes to solve the same problem using a calculator or paper and pencil. "Which is more efficient?"

NOTE 1: *For young children or those with visual perceptual problems, use a calculator with large keys, a large display, and large print on the keys.*

NOTE 2: *Think developmentally! An approach that is not efficient for an adult or an older child may be efficient for younger students or those with different types of learning disabilities. Children with abstract-reasoning difficulties, for example, may be able to punch the keys on a calculator quickly without understanding what is happening unless they have access to manipulatives or unless they imagine a picture.*

3. **Predicting.** Extensive work with blocks, coins, and other real-life objects often helps children think about "What might happen if we did this?" Spread some centimeter cubes out on the table and ask children what might happen if the cubes were all pushed together. Encourage different answers: "They'd be closer together." "I'd be able to carry them easier." "I'd be able to count them easier." All these answers (a) are acceptable, (b) involve

predicting, (c) help children recognize different ways of thinking, and (d) develop self-confidence.

4. **Introducing the language of estimation.** Make sure children understand the difference in meaning between such expressions as "I *have* 7 crayons" and "I *have about* 7 crayons." Practice different situations where students describe a picture or event, first using factual words such as *is* and *have* and then using estimation words like *about, nearly, almost,* and so on.

5. **Estimating.** Provide ample practice estimating an answer ahead of time. Do this in small groups and have students explain how they arrived at their answer. Plot the answers on a number line and talk about situations in which the different estimates would be acceptable. Check estimates using the calculator. The goal of this task is to develop comfort with estimates, as opposed to "correct" estimates and computation.

Rather than presenting an all-encompassing approach, the following pages are intended to stimulate teachers to recognize how often math is used to solve a problem. Numerous topics need to be considered, and it is far beyond the scope of this book to address them all. What is needed, however, is more flexibility in approaching different situations and more focus on making children feel comfortable with math as it relates to their own everyday lives.

DETERMINING THE CORRECT OPERATION

Typical Disabilities Affecting Progress: Difficulty with abstract reasoning, visual memory, receptive or expressive language, and nonverbal learning disabilities.

Background: The need to decide whether to add, subtract, multiply, or divide enters many facets of daily life. At the store we must decide whether the correct change has been given or how much money to give the clerk. Purchasing school supplies requires that we decide when to multiply and when to add. The following activities describe some specific decision-making skills at the computation level. Teachers are encouraged to relate these ideas to more meaningful situations to help students understand the relationship between computation and problem solving and apply their mathematical knowledge accordingly.

SUGGESTED SEQUENCE OF ACTIVITIES

1. **Prerequisites.** Be sure children have a strong mental picture of each operation. For young children who are still working at the concrete level, use objects and color-coded pages, as in Figure 2.5, to help them associate the idea of subtraction with the number sentence and the subtraction symbol. Review other operations in a similar manner.

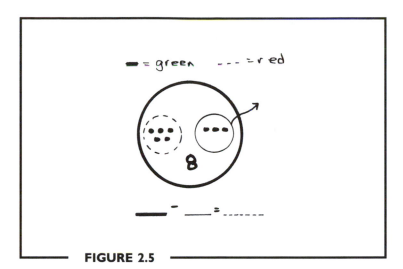

FIGURE 2.5

- *Variation:* Relate this activity to their daily lives by having students describe (show) what they do when called upon to share their toys or take playing chips from a box so their friends each has the same amount.

2. **You tell.** In early work with simple number combinations, help students develop reasoning skills by presenting problems with answers but without signs, as in Figure 2.6. Have students supply the correct sign. As a preliminary exercise, discuss what the possibilities are. For a page like the one illustrated, help children verbalize that the answers to addition problems have to be larger than the addends involved. Similarly, the answers to subtraction problems must be smaller than what you start with (the subtrahend).

NOTE: *Similar work would be carried out in early work with multiplication and division. Once facts are learned, answers are given spontaneously, and students tend to ignore the real reason for the sign. Given 5, 6, and 30, for example, they will choose the multiplication problem because "I know that 5 × 6 = 30." Hence, it is essential to incorporate these exercises early, before children commit facts to memory.*

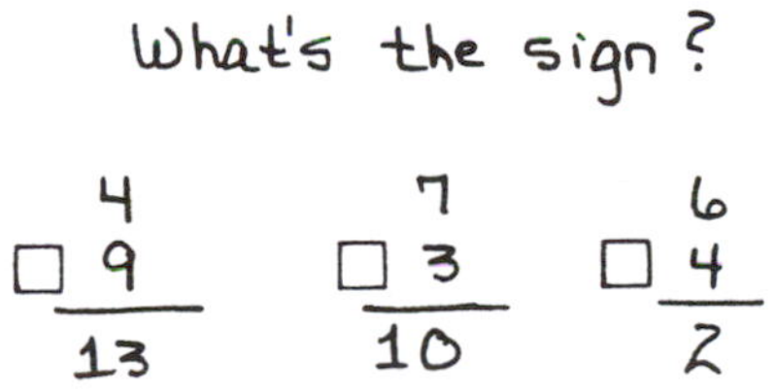

What's the sign?

	4		7		6
□	9	□	3	□	4
	13		10		2

FIGURE 2.6

3. **Do it with big numbers.** As students begin to work with larger numbers, a similar exercise can be used (see Figure 2.7). When using larger numbers, keep the pace fairly quick so the children do not have time to compute the answer. Discuss the numbers involved. Make sure students can tell whether (and why) the answer will be larger or smaller than what you start with.

4. **Special help.** Students with visual memory or visual discrimination deficits may have trouble retrieving the correct sign without having the symbols nearby. For them, keep strips as in Figure 2.8 to be used by students at their desks. The strip will serve as a visual reminder of the association.

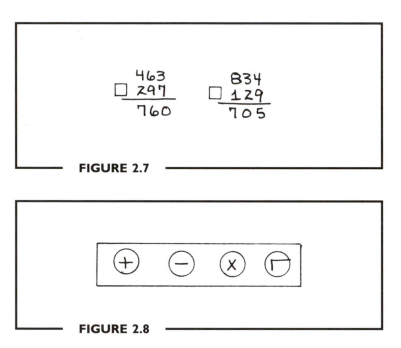

FIGURE 2.7

FIGURE 2.8

5. **Do the easy one first.** Older students who have learned when to use each of the four operations in situations involving whole numbers often have trouble with fractions and decimals when trying to:

   • recognize which operation to use; and

   • carry out the appropriate operation.

For these students, it is helpful to parallel two problems that are solved similarly but involve different types of numbers. Figure 2.9b shows an equation that gives many middle school and junior high students trouble. It is made much simpler when paralleled with that in Figure 2.9a.

NOTE: *The goal of this assignment is for students to understand how to solve equations with a variety of numbers. Rather than requiring paper and pencil, teachers should encourage use of the calculator, estimation,*

a) $9A = 73$

$A = 72 \div 9$

$A = 9\overline{)73} = 8\frac{1}{9}$
$\underline{-72}$
1

$A = 8\frac{1}{9}$

b) $4\frac{1}{2}A = 64$

$A = 64 \div 4\frac{1}{2}$

$A = 64 \div \frac{9}{2}$

$64 \times \frac{2}{9} = \frac{128}{9} = 14\frac{2}{9}$

$A = 14\frac{2}{9}$

FIGURE 2.9

or mental calculation. If the ability to solve these computations accurately is in question, it may be wise to make this a two-part assignment.

6. **Tell what to do, then stop.** Follow through on these ideas in verbal problems by having students:

- read the problem;
- picture what is happening;
- use objects or draw to picture the problem if this helps;
- think about what is being asked; and
- tell what to do (add, subtract, multiply, divide).

At first, do not require that the children actually compute. After their papers are checked, the computation can be carried out and the result checked.

DETERMINING WHETHER AN ANSWER IS REASONABLE

Typical Disabilities Affecting Progress: Difficulty with abstract reasoning and closure.

SUGGESTED SEQUENCE OF ACTIVITIES

1. **Choose.** Present questions and multiple-choice answers as in Figure 2.10. Students select the most reasonable answer. Discuss why the other choices won't work.

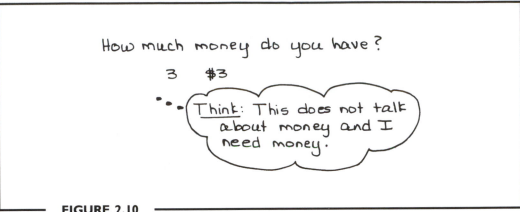

FIGURE 2.10

2. **Estimate.** Before they compute, help children estimate answers by getting a "ballpark" answer, as in Figure 2.11.

   - *Follow-up:* Have students tell/show how they arrived at the ballpark answer. Hearing/seeing how others derive estimates gives them ideas on how to proceed and makes them more confident about trying themselves.

3. **The whole thing.** When students arrive at an answer to a written word problem, they must fill in the word the answer describes, as in Figure 2.12. Have them read or say the entire sentence as illustrated to determine whether, in context, the answer makes sense.

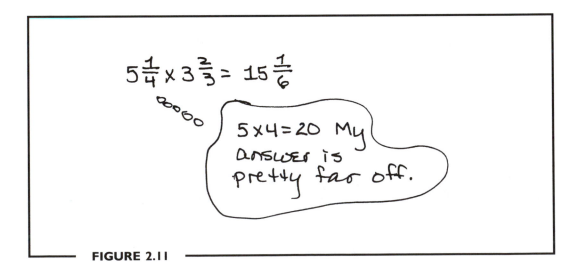

FIGURE 2.11

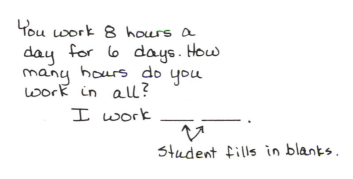

You work 8 hours a day for 6 days. How many hours do you work in all?

I work ___ ___ .

Student fills in blanks.

FIGURE 2.12

COMPUTATION: CHOOSING THE CALCULATION METHOD

Computation must be taught meaningfully. This means careful attention to underlying concepts and relationships. A conceptual approach to computation often prevents many of the problems children otherwise would experience in learning to compute.

One also must be mindful that technology has drastically changed the methods by which we compute and that a meaningful approach also includes making good choices. To function in today's world, therefore, it is necessary to be able to compute and estimate in a variety of settings. Inexpensive calculators are readily available to perform routine computations accurately and quickly. The National Council of Teachers of Mathematics (1989) recommends that students be encouraged to choose and use the method that is most appropriate in a given situation: estimation, a quick mental calculation, computing with paper and pencil, or using a calculator.

Students with learning disabilities often encounter difficulty using a calculator for perceptual reasons, but by choosing a calculator with a large display window and large numbers on the keys students can overcome this problem. Students with abstract-reasoning or short-term memory problems may encounter difficulty keying in numbers and operations. Additionally, ongoing decision making related to the choice of calculation often is hampered by a lack of flexibility in thinking that is required to make good judgments. Some ideas that might help students follow.

- *Provide good role modeling.* For example, given a multiplication problem in problem-solving situations beyond two digits: "Let's use a calculator. It's not worth the time to crank that one out." Do a quick estimate to check whether the answer obtained makes sense.

- *First do the "good" mental-calculation problems;* do the rest using paper and pencil. Provide specific exercises using a mix of problems—some that lend themselves to quick mental calculation. Challenge students to find and do the "quick math" problems in their heads. For example: 30.15 + 26.14. Children can think 30 + 26, about 56 plus some.

- *Build estimation skills.* Modify the ideas presented in Chapter 7 for whole numbers. Frequently ask students to take a minute before doing an exercise and identify sums (differences, products, or quotients) that are close to $10.00 (or to some other target number). To carry out this direction, students will need to estimate. Afterwards, allow them to use a calculator to check their thinking.

- *Emphasize situations where an estimate is good enough.* Many daily situations require only an estimate. Newspaper headlines and daily articles carry examples of estimates. As situations present themselves, help students sort out when an estimate is good enough and when it is not. For example, if there are 11 of us at a party, is it good enough to say, "That's close to 10, so I'll ask for 10 party treats?" (Of course not!) On the other hand, when figuring whether $5.00 is enough to pay for two gallons of milk and a loaf of bread, an estimate will do. Use real-world applications like these extensively in mathematics to communicate the message that estimation is useful and important.

- *Foster a positive attitude.* Children take a risk when they follow your direction to choose a calculation method or to estimate. Decision making is required, and more than one response may be correct. (This situation parallels real-world use of numbers in daily problem settings.) Students are stimulated and encouraged in a nonthreatening, supportive environment. Hold back from labeling a response as *right* or *wrong*. Accept a broad range of answers and alternative solutions. When comparing calculator answers to estimates, explore with students ways to get closer when estimating.

CHECKING: IS THE ANSWER REASONABLE?

Asking students to check their work is not a new requirement in classroom teaching. What is new is the introduction of a sequence, similar to the following, that allows students to recognize errors and, consequently, become more accurate in their work. Prior to introducing any new computational procedure,

1. develop mental estimation skills that allow children to check completed problems quickly;

2. present calculations that already are complete: some that are correct, others with answers that are way off target; and

3. ask students to find and circle answers that do not make sense.

Experience has shown that this simple sequence helps sensitize students so that they become more willing and able to recognize their own computational errors.

As suggested in Chapter 1, many teachers find that children are more successful if they can carry out some mental math daily (or at least frequently). Toward this end, regular 5- to 10-minute mini-math sessions that focus on topics like estimation, quick (mental) math, and checking whether given answers make sense, carried out throughout the school year, reap big rewards.

Students with learning disabilities also can extend their mental computation ability, but they need a more directed approach. For example, expressive language deficits may make it difficult, initially, for students to elicit the numbers, especially if they are calculating silently. Teachers may need to assist them in their practice by providing frequent, structured, oral mental calculation where the students' thoughts and words are guided. In this way, a language base is being established for future use. In general, be aware of (or better yet, try to anticipate) what may be interfering with these skills.

Without calculator assistance, students must be able to estimate and do simple calculations in their heads. The ability to do so helps them outside the classroom in many daily situations. Both within and apart from problem-solving settings, this ability also helps in day-to-day checking of written, mental, and calculator-derived computations.

MAKING GOOD USE OF INFORMATION

Typical Disabilities Affecting Progress: Difficulty with long-term memory, abstract reasoning, and receptive and expressive language.

SUGGESTED SEQUENCE OF ACTIVITIES

1. **X what is not needed.** Present problems as in Figure 2.13 and have the students cross out any information that is not needed (in this case, the number of pages). Generally, the assignment is best spread over 2 days so responses can be checked and discussed before the students actually carry out the computation. For younger students or for initial presentation, highlight the needed items, as in Figure 2.14. As they become more proficient, have the children themselves highlight the items in the question and then in the statement part of the problem.

2. **Just give the data.** Present short problems that do not ask a question but merely supply information. Have students determine what they know from this small amount of information. Figure 2.15 illustrates the format for an

18 📘s on the first shelf.

6 pages in each book.

7 📘s on the second shelf.

How many books? ___

FIGURE 2.13

18 📘s on the first shelf.

6 pages in each book.

7 📘s on the second shelf.

How many **books**? ___

FIGURE 2.14

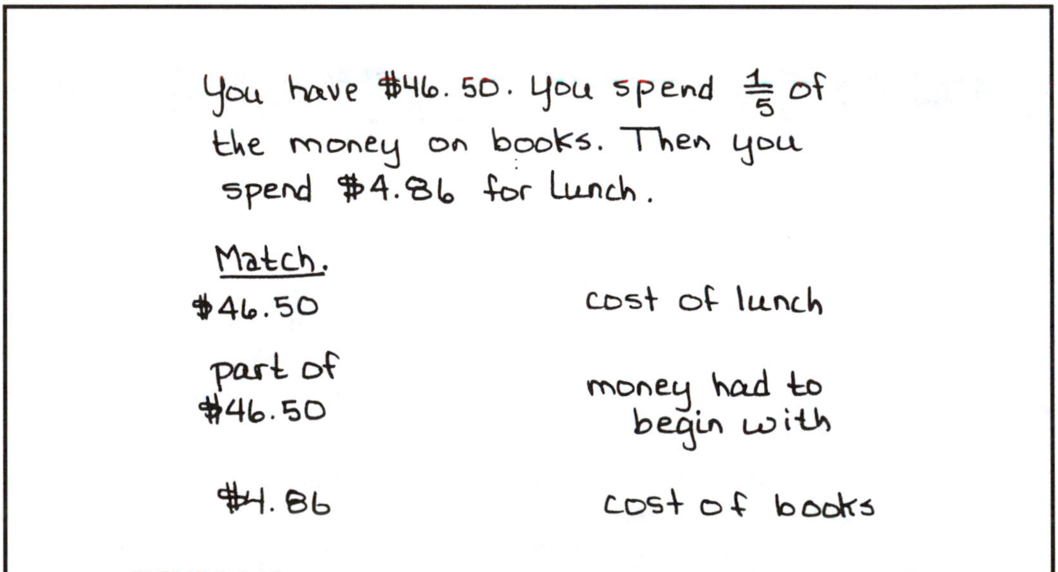

You have $46.50. You spend $\frac{1}{5}$ of the money on books. Then you spend $4.86 for lunch.

Match.

$46.50   cost of lunch

part of
$46.50   money had to
                                    begin with

$4.86   cost of books

FIGURE 2.15

initial presentation that has proven effective, even with students who have retrieval or expressive language deficits. The goal, at this point, is to identify what information is supplied and what information will be useful in solving the problem.

3. **Tell what's missing.** A similar procedure can be used to help students determine missing information, Initially, present problems in which the question asks for something that cannot be learned from the information given. Highlight the word in the question that calls for the missing information.

   NOTE: *At the verbal level, when manipulatives are not used, this type of problem can be very difficult, especially for students with learning disabilities. Check the child's developmental level (see the Prerequisites for Efficient Problem Solving section, p. 46) and provide a lot of practice using concrete aids. Make the transition to written and oral word problems very gradually.*

4. **Number word to numeral.** Many children are unable to attach meaning to verbal number names used in some problems. Practice pages like that in Figure 2.16 often are helpful. Initially, the student fills in the numeral names. Later, the appropriate operation can be determined and the computation carried out.

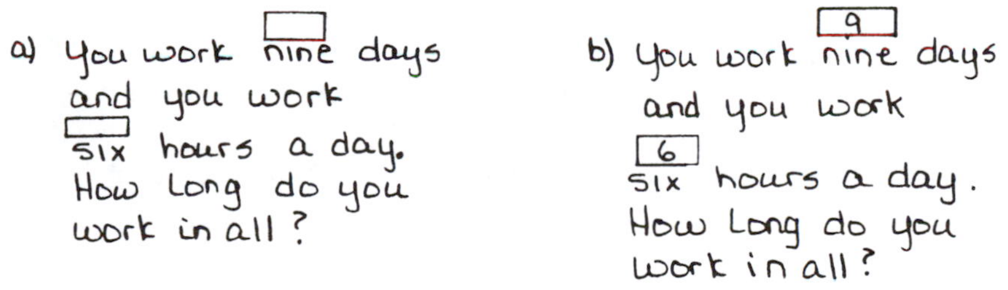

FIGURE 2.16

5. **Two steps.** Problems involving two steps can be color coded as shown in Figure 2.17 to help associate the necessary information with the correct step. As before, do not require that students compute answers to the problems until they have been checked to be sure the proper information for each step is available.

   NOTE: *To help develop their independence, encourage students to do their own highlighting prior to solving the problem. This will make them more aware of the thought process involved and the task sequence.*

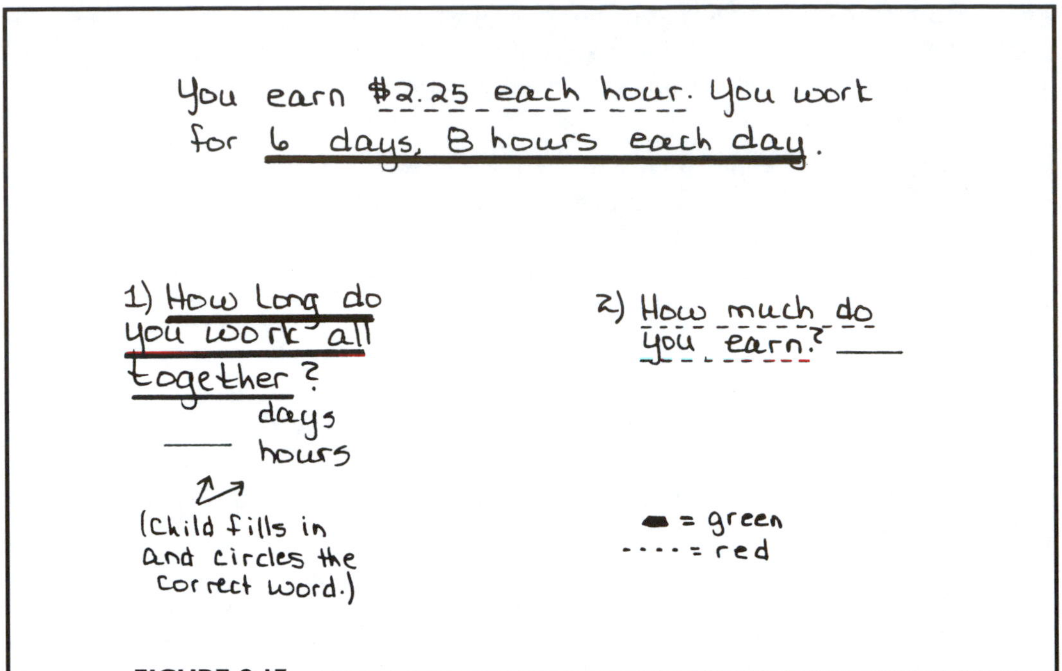

You earn $2.25 each hour. You work
for 6 days, 8 hours each day.

1) How long do
you work all
together?

_____ days
_____ hours

↱
(Child fills in
and circles the
correct word.)

2) How much do
you earn? _____

▬ = green
----- = red

FIGURE 2.17

6. **Special help.** Even when the children are better able to identify, in context, numerals in written form, they still may have trouble verbalizing, either aloud or to themselves, what they need to do to solve the problem. To help in such situations, present problems like that of Figure 2.18. Steps for solving the problem are shown in random order at the right. Seeing the information usually helps children verbalize what needs to be done. Then, step by step, in the spaces provided, they write the computation in the correct order to solve the problem. As the children become more proficient with practice, eliminate showing one or more of the completed steps.

7. **Picture choice.** For younger children a variation of the preceding procedure consists of presenting a choice of pictures as in Figure 2.19. Children choose the picture that best describes the problem. Encourage them to state the completed number sentence orally.

MATHEMATICAL MEANING OF WORDS AND SYMBOLS

Typical Disabilities Affecting Progress: Nonverbal learning disabilities and difficulties with closure, abstract reasoning, memory, and receptive language.

Copy the correct solution for each step in the right spaces and then solve.

You buy 14 pads of paper for 3¢ a pad. You sell them for 5¢ a pad. What is your profit?

$$14 \times 5¢$$
$$(14 \times 5¢) - (14 \times 3¢)$$
$$14 \times 3¢$$

Step 1   Step 2

Step 3

FIGURE 2.18

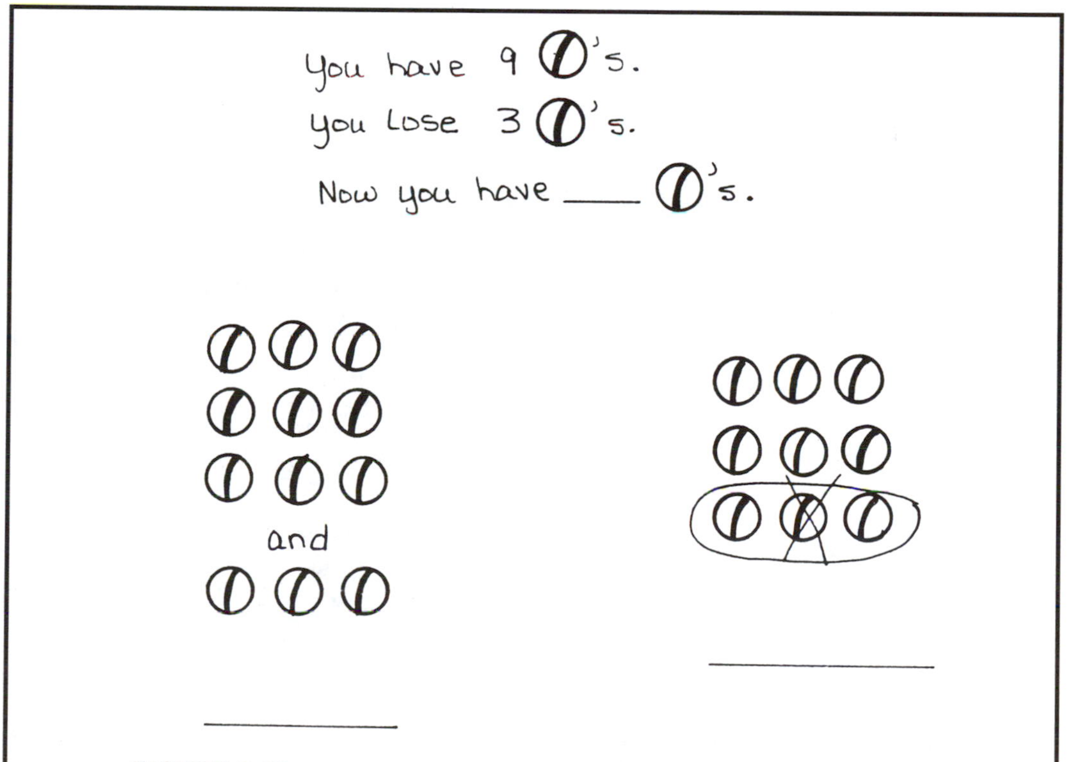

You have 9 ⓘ's.
You lose 3 ⓘ's.
Now you have ___ ⓘ's.

ⓘ ⓘ ⓘ
ⓘ ⓘ ⓘ
ⓘ ⓘ ⓘ
and
ⓘ ⓘ ⓘ

ⓘ ⓘ ⓘ
ⓘ ⓘ ⓘ
ⓘ ⓘ ⓘ

___

___

FIGURE 2.19

SUGGESTED SEQUENCE OF ACTIVITIES

1. **Focus.** Help students associate words with numbers and symbols by presenting exercises like those shown in Figure 2.20. Figure 2.20a is used in conjunction with word problems that contain the troublesome terms *each* and *many*. The exercise helps students internalize the numerical meaning of the terms. In the first problem, *each* means 1, not 9, 3, or 7. *Many* may mean 8 or 43 but never 0 or 1. The exercise in Figure 2.20b focuses on developing meaning for the term *earn*. Similar exercises should be developed for other vocabulary terms that cause students difficulty.

2. **Key words.** Exercises like that in Figure 2.21 help children begin to associate mathematical meaning with words. Key words and their meaning are placed just before each problem and are highlighted within the problem.

DETERMINING THE CORRECT SEQUENCE

Typical Disabilities Affecting Progress: Difficulty with expressive language, abstract reasoning, short-term memory, spatial and temporal organization, and closure.

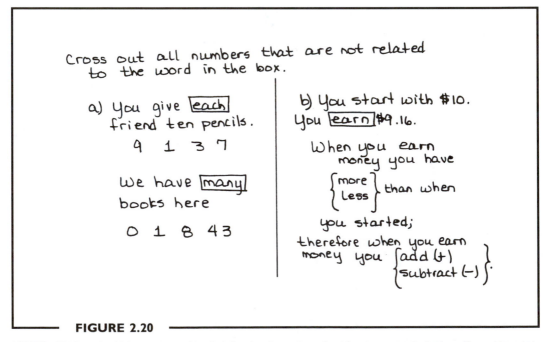

FIGURE 2.20

NOTE: Children should be encouraged to describe situations where 8 might mean *many* (a few) so 43 would mean a *whole lot* (many).

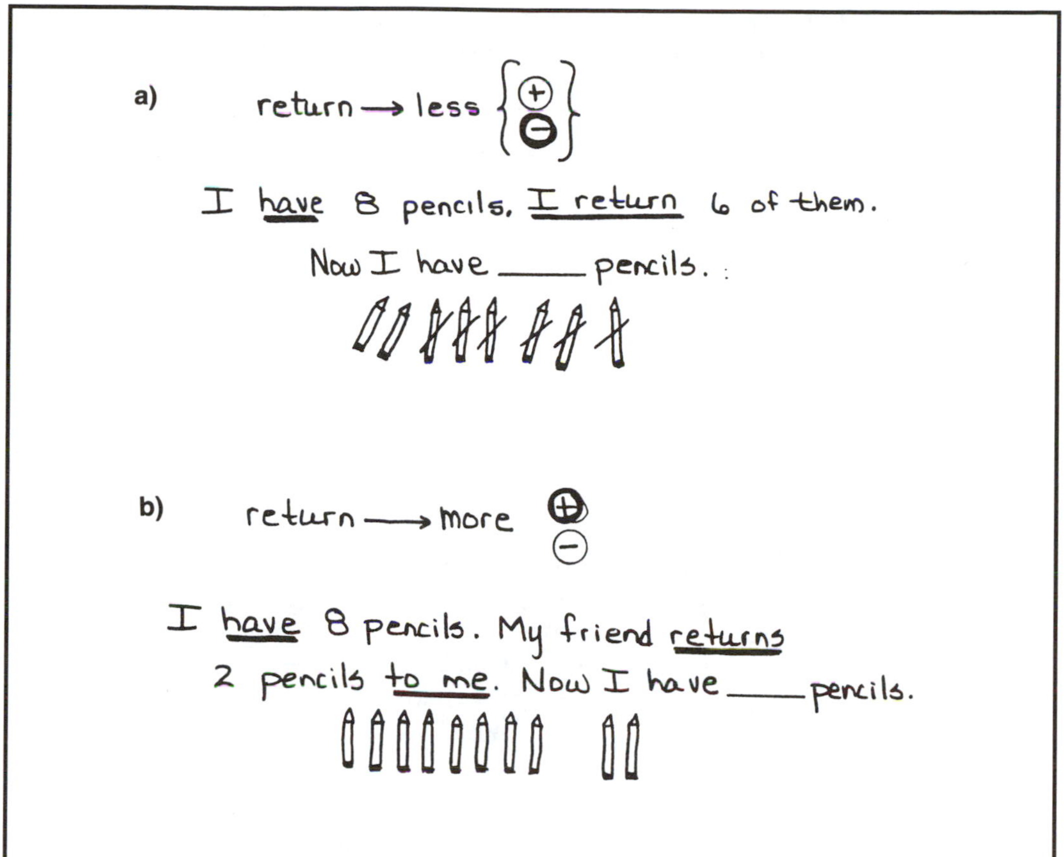

a) return → less $\left\{\begin{array}{c}\oplus\\\ominus\end{array}\right\}$

I have 8 pencils. I return 6 of them.

Now I have _____ pencils.

b) return → more $\begin{array}{c}\oplus\\\ominus\end{array}$

I have 8 pencils. My friend returns 2 pencils to me. Now I have _____ pencils.

FIGURE 2.21

Background: In order for students to determine the correct sequence for a problem, they must possess a good understanding of the concepts *before* and *after*, regardless of whether the expected outcome is an exact numerical answer. Sometimes the best answer does not involve a number. Rather, a decision must be made as to what sequence to follow. The correct sequence can vary, however, depending on the situation, and children must feel comfortable with the ideas of *before* and *after* to make these decisions.

Many students with learning disabilities need specific help with these concepts, even as they get older. Often this means reviewing the ideas prior to problem-solving situations. For example, asking a student with learning disabilities whether he or she wants to see a movie before lunch or after lunch may involve briefly reviewing temporal concepts first. The following activities propose some ways of helping students of all ages in this area. The suggestions are presented in the format of word problems so they can be more easily transferred to daily situations as they arise.

SUGGESTED SEQUENCE OF ACTIVITIES

1. **Before/after.** While most children learn to sequence steps as they mature, many students with learning disabilities must be taught a thought pro-

cess to help them determine a given sequence of steps. To this end, it often helps to set up problems with the *before/after* concept clearly presented. This is especially true for situations involving two steps, one of which is not clearly stated (see Figure 2.22a). Provide worksheets, as shown in Figure 2.22b. Ask students to cross out the wrong choice and then to solve the problem.

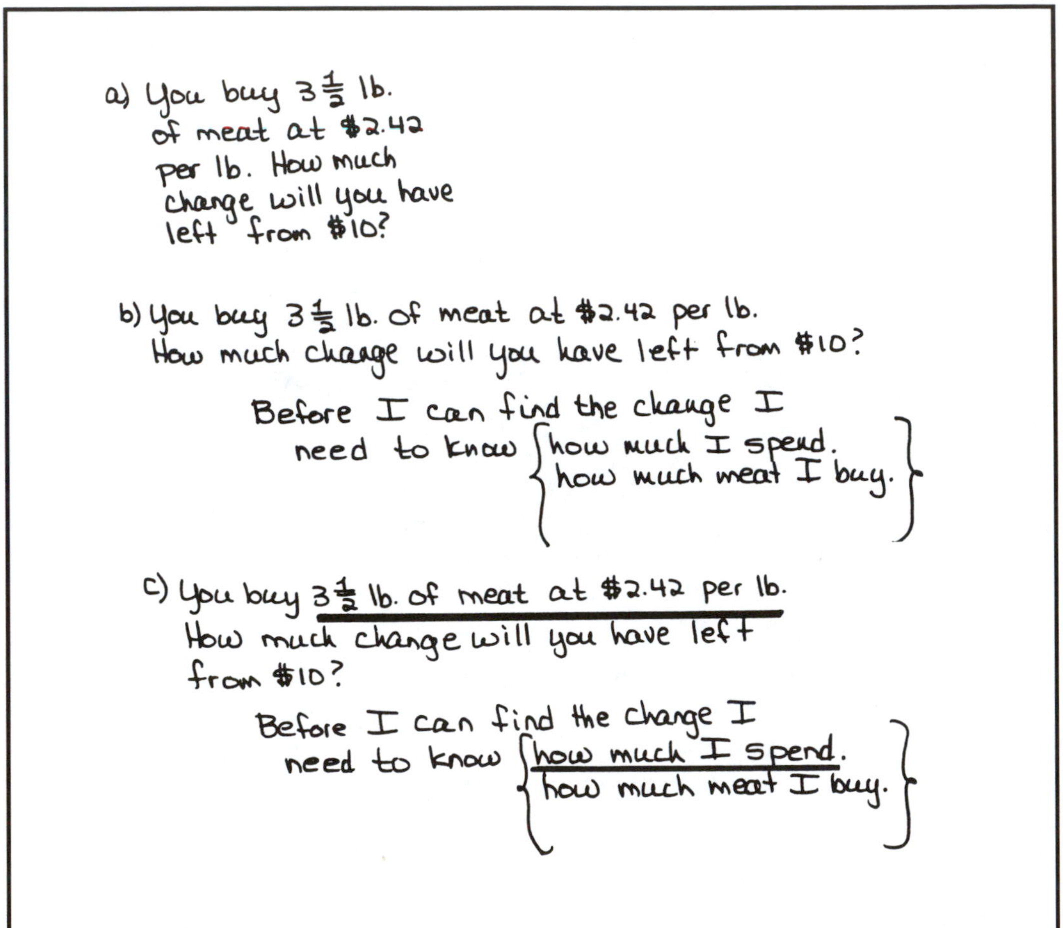

FIGURE 2.22

NOTE: Prior to the start of the school year, have an aide or adult volunteer preview the textbook and make up pages, as shown, to go along with the problems in the book. If necessary, color code as illustrated in Figure 2.22c.

- *Variation 1:* Encourage children to predict what they would have to do in similar situations. Use coins or other manipulatives to assist.

- *Variation 2:* Present two- and three-step problems along with the needed steps on individual strips or on the computer in a word-processing program. Talk with children, use manipulatives, and help them determine the correct sequence. Have them arrange the strips or use "cut" and "paste" functions on the computer to solve the problem. For some students, especially those with memory problems, this task may be a two- or three-part assignment. Use the manipulatives one day; the next day, sequence the written words and encourage students to "picture what you did with the coins yesterday." Check the sequencing before they continue. Finally, have them solve the problem.

2. **Color cue.** Various activities in the previous pages have highlighted the effectiveness of color coding as an aid to sequencing. Figure 2.23 shows another way to color code a word problem so students begin to internalize the thought process and procedure for sequencing problems.

3. **Phase out.** As children develop sequencing skills, randomly list the necessary steps and have them number them in the correct order. If necessary, color code either the word problem or the steps, but not both (as in Figure 2.24). When checking the numbering, have the students note alternative sequences that their friends might have chosen. After the sequences have been checked, students can solve the problems.

NOTE: *The computer program,* Math Blaster Mystery *(Davidson Software), is a good program to use in this area. There are word problems included, requiring students to think about how to sequence problems. The teacher also can enter problems and save them to a data disk so that the program can easily be individualized to meet the needs of most students. (See the appendix in Chapter 3 for addresses of software publishers.)*

RECOGNIZING THE PATTERN OF A PROBLEM

Typical Disabilities Affecting Progress: Difficulty with abstract reasoning and auditory processing, nonverbal learning disabilities.

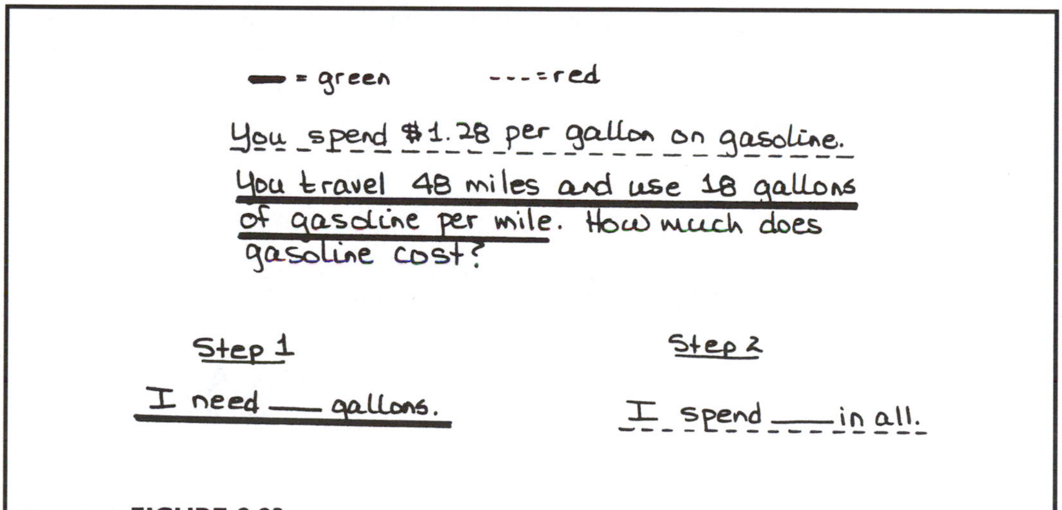

FIGURE 2.23

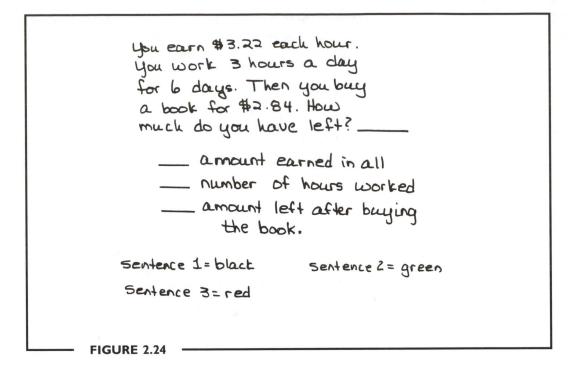

You earn $3.22 each hour.
You work 3 hours a day
for 6 days. Then you buy
a book for $2.84. How
much do you have left? ____

____ amount earned in all
____ number of hours worked
____ amount left after buying
the book.

Sentence 1 = black   Sentence 2 = green

Sentence 3 = red

FIGURE 2.24

SUGGESTED SEQUENCE OF ACTIVITIES

1. **See the pattern.** Present simple visual problems, as in Figure 2.25, and have students circle the best solution.

2. **Word problems now.** As children become better at recognizing patterns for the operations, gradually introduce word problems. At first, present assignments in which students use only one operation. Choose different numbers in the problems and help students manipulate concrete aids or draw a picture of the problem, as in Figure 2.25. Rather quickly move to pages with mixed types of problems. Throughout, encourage students to

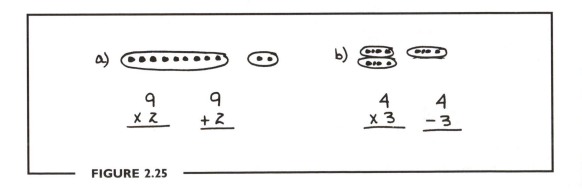

FIGURE 2.25

look for a pattern: separating groups, finding the total of groups equal in size, and so on. Allow the children to use the concrete aids or to draw a picture of the problem as long as this seems helpful.

3. **Easy one first.** Sometimes working a parallel problem with whole numbers can help students solve a problem that contains fractions or decimals. A similar technique helps students solve problems in general. Some students go blank when they notice that a word problem contains a fraction or a decimal. Giving these students a parallel problem with whole numbers often helps them recognize the general pattern to the solution, such as the sequence of operations, which they then can apply to the original problem with fractions or decimals.

PROBLEM SOLVING IN THE REAL WORLD

Although essential, the activities in the preceding sections are only of value if students can apply and use the basic problem-solving skills in their daily lives. It is hoped that by considering a nonstandard topic (e.g., vocabulary or decision making) as a specific skill and helping students learn ways to use the skill to approach problem-solving situations, teachers will make students more aware of how to use these skills in a variety of instances.

SUGGESTED SEQUENCE OF ACTIVITIES

1. **What works.** Give students opportunities to choose whatever method they want for solving a problem, even if their choice might not be the most efficient. Later, as a separate activity, help them identify more efficient methods.

2. **Each one different.** Present a problem to a small group of students and require that each student solve the problem in a different way. (If there are too many students, group them and require each group to come up with a different solution.) In order to follow these directions, students will have to find several different methods themselves in case someone else presents their solution first. Help students see why the various approaches resulted in the same, or different, solutions. Analyze why some approaches worked and some did not.

3. **Plan ahead.** Before going on a field trip, discuss with students the possible price of things they may want to do or buy. Include the actual cost of such things as entrance fees. Write the prices on the board and help students estimate a reasonable amount of money to bring on the trip.

4. **What's first?** Have students plan a segment of the morning schedule. Present alternatives that include required subjects as well as free-time activities. List the activities on the board along with the approximate times needed for each. Let the children decide on a sequence they think will work.

NOTE: *To help students see that not all sequences work out, let them choose whatever sequence the group selects. This may mean that not all work will be completed or that students will miss an activity. That's okay! Students will have learned a valuable lesson about planning ahead while they also learn about sequencing.*

- *Variation:* Some students, especially those with expressive language, short-term memory, or temporal difficulties, may be helped by having the activities written out on strips and the times noted on pie segments of an analog clock. They then can fill in the clock with the activities as shown in Figure 2.26.

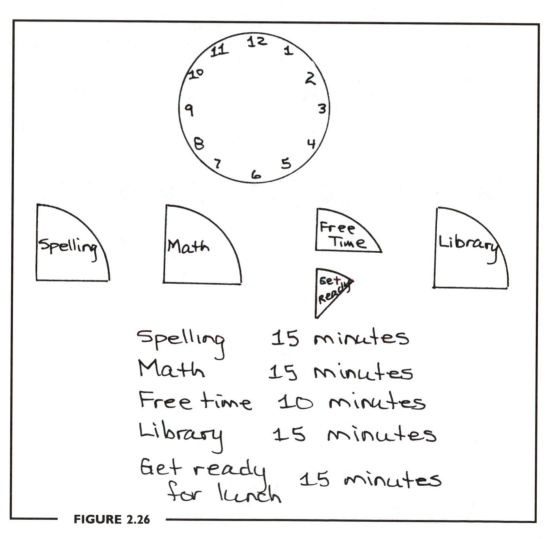

FIGURE 2.26

REFERENCES

Foss, J. M. (1991). Nonverbal learning disabilities and remedial interventions. *Annals of Dyslexia, 41,* 133.

National Council of Teachers of Mathematics. (1980). *An agenda for action: Recommendations for school mathematics of the 1980s.* Reston, VA: Author.

National Council of Teachers of Mathematics. (1989). *Curriculum and evaluation standards for school mathematics.* Reston, VA: Author.

CHAPTER 3

Mathematics, Microcomputers, and Students with Learning Disabilities

CURRENT TRENDS

In recent years, due to legislation such as the Individuals with Disabilities Education Act (IDEA), the Regular Education Initiative (REI), and a great deal of emphasis placed on improving professional education, teachers are beginning to be better equipped to handle a variety of learning styles in the classroom. More and more students are being mainstreamed, and teachers are striving to provide material that is individualized enough to help these children learn and retain what is presented while actively and successfully participating within the regular classroom setting. The increased availability of and knowledge about computers has opened the door to the ability to individualize where needed more easily. In addition, a greater awareness of the need to ensure as much independence as possible for students with learning disabilities has resulted in teachers beginning to feel more comfortable about helping these children learn in spite of their differing needs.

Even with these improvements, planning and implementation of instruction still can be overwhelming. However, teachers have a potential helpmate as a result of both the changes occurring in mathematics education based on the *Curriculum and Evaluation Standards for School Mathematics* (National Council of Teachers of Mathematics, 1989) and the improvements in both ease of using microcomputers and the quality of available software.[1] If used properly by a teacher who feels comfortable with it, the computer can provide simulated real-life experiences, practice at a pace that is slow and individualized enough for students to process material and overlearn where necessary, and the ability to learn in a cooperative manner. For most students, the computer is highly motivating. Those who are reluctant to join in social situations involving a lot of conversation (e.g., students with expres-

---

1. Although the authors recognize the increased value, availability, and variety of multimedia, there is not enough space in this book to address these topics in full. The emphasis, instead, is on computer software, since it is more readily available in a variety of settings.

sive and receptive language difficulties or those with nonverbal learning disabilities) often can develop improved socialization skills by interacting with a peer at the computer. Additionally, a computer's response to mistakes can be less threatening than the personal response of a teacher, peer, or parent.

Mathematics teachers can effectively use computers in a variety of ways, such as:

- to increase students' logic, reasoning, and problem-solving skills through simulation and nonverbal understanding of relationships;

- to improve retention of basic facts, computation procedures, and vocabulary relationships;

- to help students develop self-confidence through overlearning;

- to foster cooperative learning and application of mathematics;

- to improve understanding of relationship of mathematical ideas to life skills through simulation and interactive tutorial presentations; and

- to develop understanding of data bases and spreadsheets.

Although the computer can be of tremendous assistance, especially in a mainstreamed classroom, teachers must recognize some of the difficulties students with learning disabilities may encounter while using the computer. Specifically, consideration of how students' learning disabilities can interfere with successful computer use will help the teacher plan more effectively. The following section addresses learning disabilities that have been mentioned throughout this book but, this time, in terms of their interaction with the computer. At the end of each section suggestions for general remediation techniques are provided. The major disabilities have been subdivided similarly to the overview in Table 1.1 (see Chapter 1). Table 3.1 summarizes the discussion as it is presented in this chapter.

LEARNING DISABILITIES AND THE COMPUTER

Most teachers have encountered one or more of the following situations while students are using a computer.

- A student continues to hit a key/keys, randomly, until the screen changes.

- A student is unable to locate the correct response key even though the program only requires the use of, for example, numbers and the *return* key, or the *return* key and the *space bar*.

- A student forgets why and how a particular screen was accessed and what the relevance of that screen is to what is being done.

- A student is able to play any available computer game successfully, even if use of the basic facts is involved. However, the same student is unable to memorize the facts and accurately integrate their use into everyday experiences.

Table 3.1　Learning Disabilities and the Computer

DISABILITY	PROBLEM AREA	WAYS OF HELPING
Figure-Ground	Visual — size of type — amount on screen — tracking from 　• screen to keyboard 　• screen to paper — locating keys on keyboard	— use large type — skip lines — allow enough time — bold type — heavy cursor
	Auditory — use of sound — number of computers in room	— choose programs that reinforce without sound
Discrimination	Visual — noticing punctuation — too much on screen — line spacing — type of screen reinforcement	— tilt screen or place to side of keyboard — use paper to track — underlining capability — ability to control speed of presentation
	Auditory — misperception of endings	— highlight word/number as said — make tape to match lesson
Spatial Perception	— use of arrow keys — solving multistep problems	— programs with arrow pointing to steps — encourage use of I-J-K-M
Memory	Short/Long Term — screen-to-screen retention — too much skill/subject isolation — keyboard/screen retention	— ease of returning to 　• menu 　• previous frame — paper/pencil use
	Visual Memory — lack of realistic pictures — low vocabulary	— preview vocabulary — off-computer activities for keyboard recognition
Language	Receptive Language — difficulty relating word to meaning	— provide visual cues — preview vocabulary
	Expressive Language — difficulty with timed programs	— allow student to determine timing
Abstract Reasoning	— lack of concrete representation	— interactive program — concrete aids — branching capability

• A student is confused over the way symbols are represented on the keyboard versus the screen. (See Figure 3.1.)

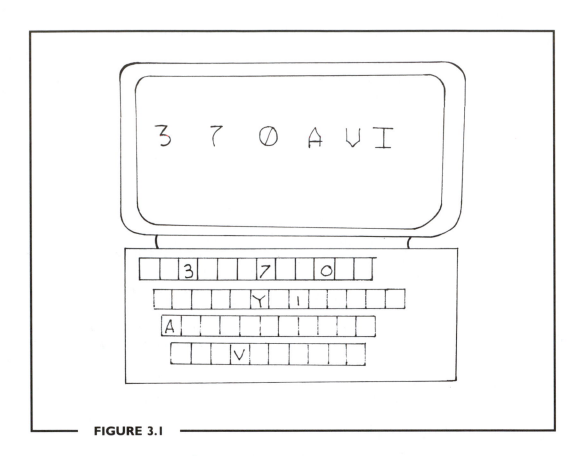

FIGURE 3.1

Visual and Auditory Perceptual Problems

Figure-ground difficulties

Background: Students with visual figure-ground deficits tend to have trouble keeping their place on the keyboard, especially if they need to look back and forth from the screen to the keyboard. Even those students who seem to know their way around a keyboard may have trouble because the keys are close together. These students especially have trouble with the number keys and other keys that carry two symbols. Additionally, many programs use small print on the screen, making it still more difficult for students to sort out the information being presented.

Auditory figure-ground difficulties are compounded by the sound from other computers and computer users in the room. Even if no game is being played and the sound is turned off, the mere sound of typing can interfere with students' thought processes. If a sound factor is added, either to the individual student's program or to that of another child, even more confusion results.

SUGGESTED SEQUENCE OF ACTIVITIES

1. **Cover it.** For those programs that require that only a few keys be used for responses, it often is helpful to cover up the remaining keys. For example, if only the number keys and perhaps the *space bar* or *return* key[2] are required, cover up the remaining keys, as in Figure 3.2.

   NOTE: *See Activity 4 on page 78 in the Visual Discrimination Difficulties section for a variation of this activity.*

2. **Practice it.** At the beginning of the year have an assistant or a talented student make up a picture of the computer's keyboard as in Figure 3.3 and

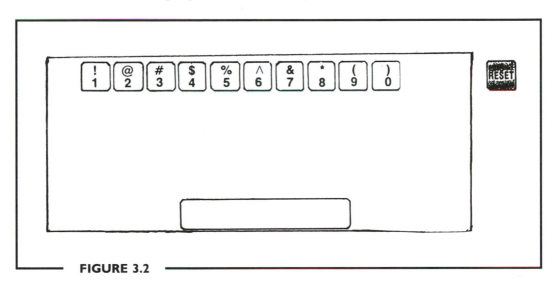

FIGURE 3.2

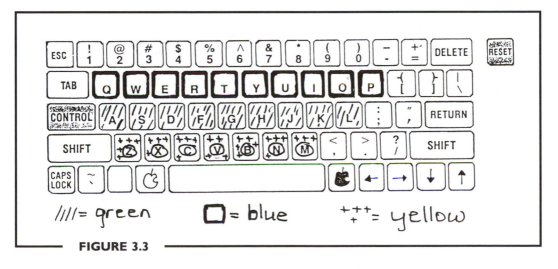

//// = green   ☐ = blue   ⁺⁺⁺ = yellow

FIGURE 3.3

---

2. The key names used throughout this chapter refer to the Apple family of microcomputers. If your system uses different terms, adjust accordingly.

some tape-recorded or paper instructions for typing. Enlarge the picture so that fingers can fit easily on the keys. Have students practice locating the keys. Initially highlight as shown, but gradually reduce the highlighting.

NOTE: *Paper keyboards are available commercially. Be sure to use one that matches your computer so students do not have to unlearn*

- *Variation:* Highlight the keyboard by placing removable colored dots on the keys that the child will be using (see Figure 3.4). Leave the other keys alone. In this way, familiarity with the keyboard continues to grow, but progress and use of the computer is not greatly affected by any deficit area.

3. **Time out.** When choosing commercially prepared programs or developing your own, consider ones that allow for teacher or student decision making on timing. Students with figure-ground deficits (as well as other deficits) will be relieved if they do not need to work within a time frame as they search the keyboard.

4. **Hold still.** Select programs in which the location of the problem remains reasonably consistent from screen to screen. In this way, students can practice finding information in a specific location and off-computer work becomes easier to arrange (see Activity 5).

NOTE: *Consistency of problem location is even more important when students begin to use timed programs. There is less chance for them to lose their place if they know to look in the same place each time.*

5. **There it is.** Preview programs by providing worksheets like those shown in Figure 3.5. Discuss the sheet and use it with the actual program so students become aware of their eye movement. Help them realize how they locate the problem on the worksheet and what it "feels" like to find it on both the worksheet and the monitor.

6. **Block it.** Allow students to use earphones, even for games that depend on a bell or another type of sound. The sound of the other computers will not interfere as much, allowing students to attend more easily to what is required.

7. **Mouse it.** Choose programs that allow the use of a mouse. Even students with fine motor problems generally are able to use a mouse, and the decreased need to look back and forth from keyboard to screen helps those with visual perceptual problems.

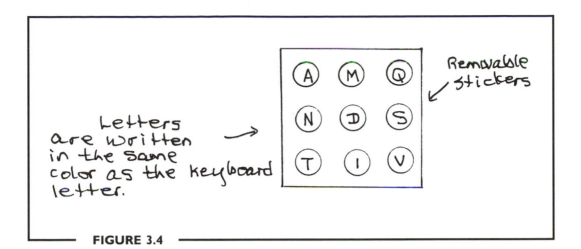

Letters are written in the same color as the keyboard letter.

Removable stickers

FIGURE 3.4

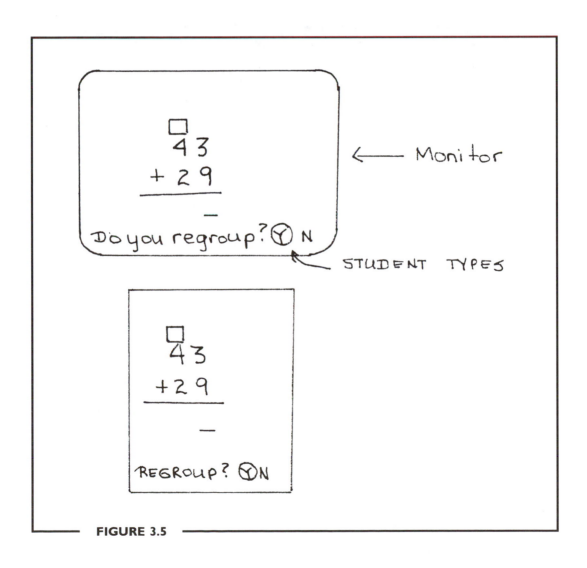

Monitor

Do you regroup? Y N

STUDENT TYPES

REGROUP? Y N

FIGURE 3.5

Visual discrimination difficulties

Background: Students with visual discrimination difficulties who often misread numbers on a written or typed page tend to have similar problems when using a computer. The clarity of the print on the screen, the color of the monitor, and the size of the print all play a part in how well a child can discern the information on the screen. These children may have an especially difficult time reading decimal numbers, as it is often hard for them to see the decimal point. Even using the arrow keys can be confusing as these students try to figure out which way the arrows go. Frequently, there is too much on the screen, the text is too close together, the type is too small, and the clarity of the color or monochrome background interferes with a child's perception of the material. Additionally, often the graphics that accompany the text are unclear in spite of continued improvements in this area.

SUGGESTED SEQUENCE OF ACTIVITIES

1. **Look closely.** Preview the programs students will be using to locate any oddly shaped words or letters. For example, sometimes an *m* may look something like that in Figure 3.6, or a "+" sign may be hard to read. Check the documentation for examples of the pictures used on the screen. Make copies so students can become familiar with them before using the program. Play matching games, make flash cards, or devise other means of acquainting students with hard-to-read visuals.

2. **Go for big.** Use programs with large numbers. The examples in Figure 3.7 represent two math programs that both offer good presentations. However, the first one is far easier for most students to use simply because the numbers are larger and clearer.

FIGURE 3.6

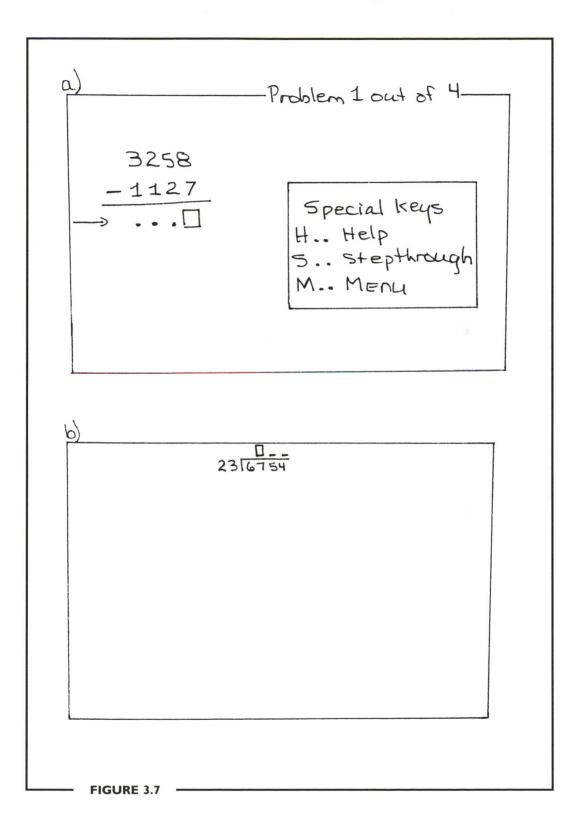

a)

———— Problem 1 out of 4 ————

3258
− 1127
———————
→ . . . ☐

Special keys
H.. Help
S.. Stepthrough
M.. Menu

b)

```
      ☐ _ _
23|6754
```

FIGURE 3.7

3. **Highlight it.** If a program with smaller print must be used, assist students by providing a tachistoscopic card. It is easiest to use the card with a program that always places the numbers in the same location. This allows the card to be attached to the monitor, as in Figure 3.8.

4. **Hide it.** Some students have trouble using the number keys because there are two symbols on each. (See Activity 1, page 73, in the Figure-Ground Difficulties section.) Because of the size of the symbols, students may spend unnecessary time (a) trying to separate the symbols and (b) trying to figure

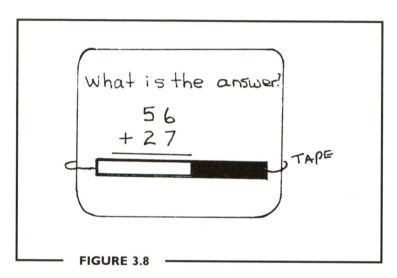

FIGURE 3.8

out which number they want. Since generally the goal is to locate the correct number, it often is helpful to use removable stickers with numbers on them to cover the keys.

NOTE: *Be sure the numbers on the stickers closely resemble the keyboard numbers, as in Figure 3.9.*

5. **Consistency, please.** Use programs in which the screen format does not vary greatly from screen to screen. This enables students to focus their eyes more easily. In addition, off-computer activities can help students know what to expect when they go to the computer.

6. **Find it.** Make flash cards of important computer words students need in order to load and/or run a program. If possible, make worksheets of some screens that involve these words and have students practice locating the words on the worksheet. Then have them locate the words on the keyboard and the monitor several times prior to running the program. Provide an acetate overlay that has a heavy line on it so students can place the card on the screen with the heavy line under the word.

Auditory discrimination

Background: Students with auditory discrimination problems encounter difficulties using computers even when no voice synthesizer is involved. For exam-

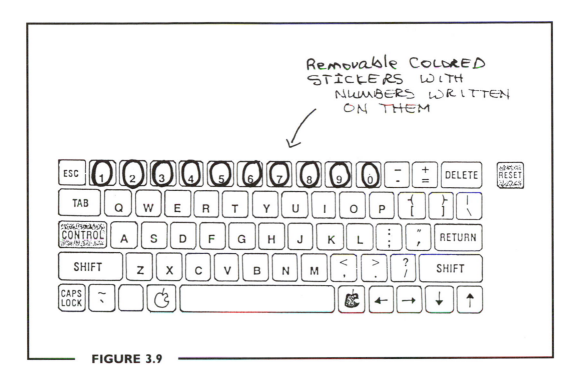

FIGURE 3.9

ple, those who misperceive endings on words or have trouble discriminating between the difference in ending sounds for numbers, such as between "nineteen" and "ninety," may encounter those same problems when using the computer. Unfortunately, it may not be noticed if there is no teacher–student interaction at the time. For example, a student attempting to solve a computation problem as shown in Figure 3.10 might run into problems. Depending on how friendly the computer feedback is when a mistake is made, frustration may occur.

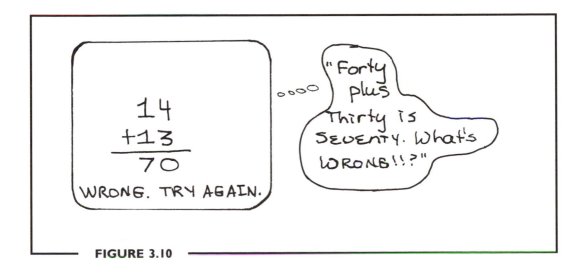

FIGURE 3.10

SUGGESTED SEQUENCE OF ACTIVITIES

1. **Preview it.** Particularly when students are solving problems involving teen numbers, it may be helpful to preview the work. Choose programs in which the presentation order of problems can be previewed, either on screen or in the documentation, and provide the student with practice ahead of time. Have students read the problems aloud and match or otherwise associate the individual numbers with the words. In this way, students are learning a method of checking themselves that can be helpful when they use the program independently.

2. **Tape it.** Choose programs in which the sequence can be predetermined. At the beginning of the school year, have an aide or volunteer tape problems from the program. Students can use the tape when working with the program and when a teacher or peer is unavailable to monitor the work.

   - *Variation:* Break computer use into two or three sessions. Initially, have students call up each problem and read the computation into a tape recorder. Next, have the students listen to the tape and write the numbers on paper at their desks. After having the work checked, the student should use the program.

3. **Sequence it.** Ideally, choose computational programs that allow students to key in the regrouped number first, as in Figure 3.11a. (Unfortunately, such programs are not widely available.) If it is necessary to use a program in which the regrouped number is typed in second, choose one that at least asks the student to think about whether or not regrouping is needed.

   NOTE: *Students with visual discrimination problems should not use programs if they are required to type in the solution from right to left. (See Figure 3.11b.)*

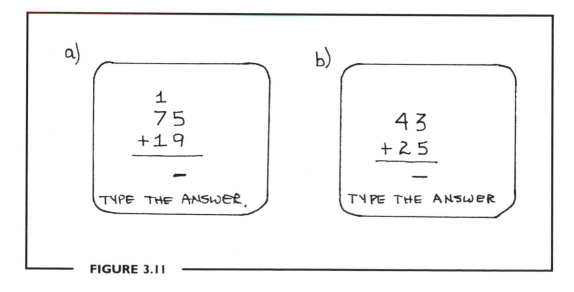

FIGURE 3.11

Spatial and temporal difficulties

Background: The arrow keys often are used to move the cursor around the screen. The idea behind this is sound; however, the purpose often is defeated by the location of the keys on the keyboard. Frequently, the keys have no actual relationship to space unless the student is looking at the arrow. (See Figure 3.12.)

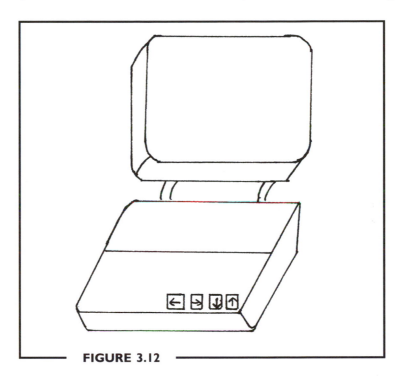

FIGURE 3.12

Concepts such as *up, down,* or *behind,* which already are difficult for some students to comprehend, become especially confusing on a computer monitor, where their meaning has a different orientation than on a piece of paper (Figure 3.13) or on any object that is parallel to the ground. Moreover, the ability to involve children motorically is limited because their hands and the keyboard are on a different plane than the monitor, making it hard to help them feel the direction. This confusion is compounded by the fact that accessing the next screen or the one before usually involves using the *control* key and some letter instead of a related letter such as *N* for *next* or *B* for *before.*

As discussed in other parts of this book, a sense of time is difficult for many children and especially for students with learning disabilities. Therefore, even if other areas are strong, these students' poor sense of time makes it hard for them to react effectively under a time pressure without specific assistance.

SUGGESTED SEQUENCE OF ACTIVITIES

1. **Stretch yourself.** In addition to the arrow keys, many programs also provide for cursor movement through use of the *I, J, K, M* keys or some other

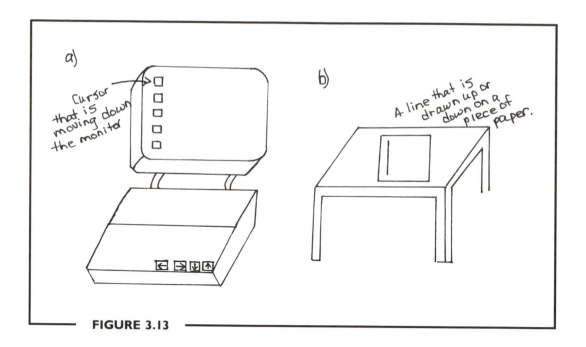

a)

Cursor
that is
moving down
the monitor

b)

A line that is
drawn up or
down on a
piece of
paper.

FIGURE 3.13

combination. These keys may be more helpful because they more closely replicate movement in space. However, practice in off-computer activities is probably still necessary. Start by placing direction arrows on removable stickers. Put the stickers on a large paper keyboard—one that is larger than the actual keyboard. (See Figure 3.14a.) Practice with students by saying, "Move the cursor up" or "Move the cursor left." Students also can be paired with a peer for this exercise.

- *Variation:* For younger children, make a large, blackboard-size keyboard, similar to the one in Figure 3.14b, where the movement keys are farther apart. Involving the gross motor movements will help students transfer to the fine motor movement required for the keyboard.

2. **See it.** Place removable stickers on the monitor. The color of the stickers on the monitor should match the color of the stickers on the keys. (See Figure 3.15.)

3. **Compare it.** Use a program in which the cursor movement is directed by one of the keys previously described. Pair students and have one of them place a finger on the up arrow or the *I* key. The other stands behind and runs a finger up the seated student's back while saying, "Feel the up direction; now feel 'up' on the computer." The student does this again while the seated student simultaneously depresses the up key and looks at the screen.

4. **aMAZING.** Some commercial programs involve mazes that are not too complex. Initially, students may be reluctant to use them, but with teacher

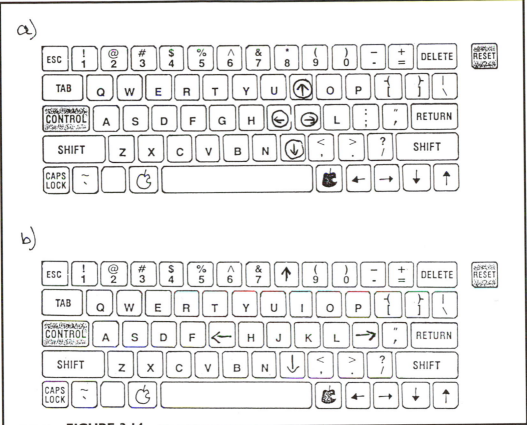

FIGURE 3.14

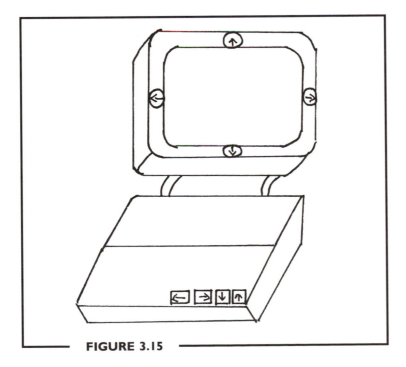

FIGURE 3.15

assistance, reduced timing, and clearly defined lines on the screen they usually begin to enjoy these games.

5. **See the time.** Some programs have on-screen clocks or timing bars at the bottom of the screen. Have students start by using programs like this and help them notice the movement of the clock or the bar. In this way, they can begin to "feel" the time and use it to help pace themselves.

NOTE: *Children with visual perceptual problems may find these on-screen aids too confusing.*

Memory Problems

Short- and long-term memory problems

Background: The computer is patient and can provide the overlearning that is essential to students with memory problems. At the same time, however, some students encounter unexpected problems because they are able to access only a certain amount of information at any one time. The screen holds relatively little information and, even though previous screens may be accessed easily, students must flip continually between screens. If access is not possible, the problem is compounded further.

The continual need to look back and forth between the screen and the keyboard often is problematic for students with memory deficits, especially if they are unfamiliar with the keyboard or lose their place easily. They may forget what they are looking for while their eyes move from screen to keyboard and back to the screen again. Worse, while they are searching the keyboard for the correct key, action may take place on the screen. Having missed it, by the time they look at the screen they no longer know what they are supposed to be looking for. The use of a mouse can greatly alleviate these difficulties.

Commercial programs that do not allow for teacher or student entry of curriculum-related information may cause *skill–subject isolation.* Specifically, students learn certain material in class, following a planned sequence that meets their needs. When these students then use a computer to reinforce what they have been learning, they may be faced with a variety of materials, only some of which are related to what they have been studying.

SUGGESTED SEQUENCE OF ACTIVITIES

1. **Help.** Increasingly, programs are providing help screens, rather than requiring students to access previous screens or start all over if they forget. If placed properly, these screens can be important aids.

2. **I've seen that.** Choose simulation programs and programs that allow for entry of curriculum-related material. In that way, overlearning can be achieved, and ideas and sequences that have been addressed in class can be reinforced.

3. **Picture it.** When the screen format remains fairly constant throughout a program, preview the screens and draw pictures of the format for students to use at their desks.

4. **New words.** As part of students' ongoing vocabulary development, include key computer words such as *return, control, delete,* and so on. Make flash cards or play concentration or matching games, making sure that the words are written as they are on the computer. For example, on Apple computers the major words are written in lowercase. Although instructions often refer to the control key as "ctrl," students must learn to refer to the correct key whenever they hear or see "control."

   NOTE: *If students use different models of computers, choose a separate color for each and write key word names in the color that matches the computer. Some students find it easier to recall the variation in words by associating the words with a color.*

Visual memory

Background: The need for visual aids to reinforce learning or to assist with recall is as important when students are using a computer as when they work out of a workbook or read a book. Realistic, clear pictures and graphics are essential. For example, a program designed to develop money skills should involve clear, simulated coins and bills, as well as the opportunity to use real coins while solving problems.

Students with visual memory deficits may find it especially hard to become familiar with the keyboard when there is no pattern (alphabetic) to the key location and nothing concrete for them to use to help recall the key placement.

SUGGESTED SEQUENCE OF ACTIVITIES

1. **That's it.** Off-computer keyboard activities are helpful when students are trying to remember the key location for a specific program. Highlight worksheets as shown in Figure 3.16 to assist recalling which keys are associated with which program. Make flash cards or concentration games for students to play with each other.

2. **Preview it.** (See Activity 1 in the Auditory Discrimination section on page 80.) The goal of this activity is to allow a student to use the computer independently, at least to start up a program. Therefore, although it is preferable that students read certain key computer words in varying contexts, students with visual memory problems may need to repeatedly practice these words in isolation.

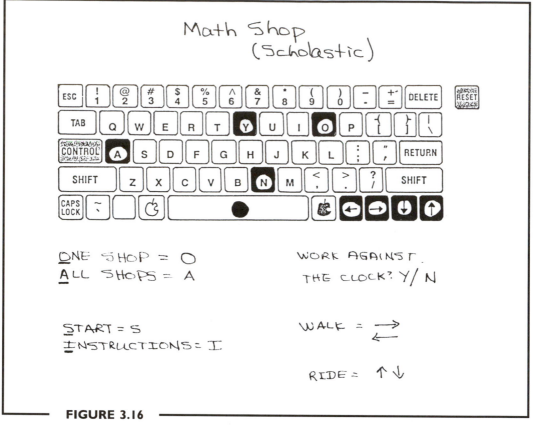

FIGURE 3.16

NOTE: Words and corresponding keys should be highlighted in the same color.

Expressive and Receptive Language Difficulties

Background: Much of the time spent using the computer involves responses that are elicited by the on-screen presentation. Often, to score a correct response, an answer must be supplied with a minimum amount of cuing. If the information being presented is related to the student's experience, responding is easier. However, for students with language difficulties the task can be confusing, especially if a time limit is involved. Timed situations for these students make eliciting or comprehending information more difficult.

SUGGESTED SEQUENCE OF ACTIVITIES

1. **Study it.** Most programs require at least a minimal amount of reading, even if only to be able to access a particular section. Before having a child use the program, preview it and make a list of the essential words the student should be able to recognize to run the program independently. Put each word on an individually numbered 3″ × 5″ card *in the same order* as

the words will appear when the program is running. Make sure the child can read the words before using the program. This way, children need not worry about all the other words but can search for the key word to tell them what to do.

2. **Crossword puzzle.** At the beginning of the school year, have an aide, parent, or student make keyboard crossword puzzles as in Figure 3.17. Use crayons to lightly color certain keys (on paper keyboards) and write the crossword number on the key. When using the puzzles, students fill in the word in the correct crossword puzzle box. Make different crossword puzzles to match different computer games.

3. **Let's play a game.** A variation of "Old Maid" can be played by two or three children. Make cards like those in Figure 3.18. Each student starts with seven cards; the rest of the cards are placed face down in the middle of the table. Students take turns requesting cards based on the cards they are holding. In Figure 3.18a the child holding the keyboard with the *return*

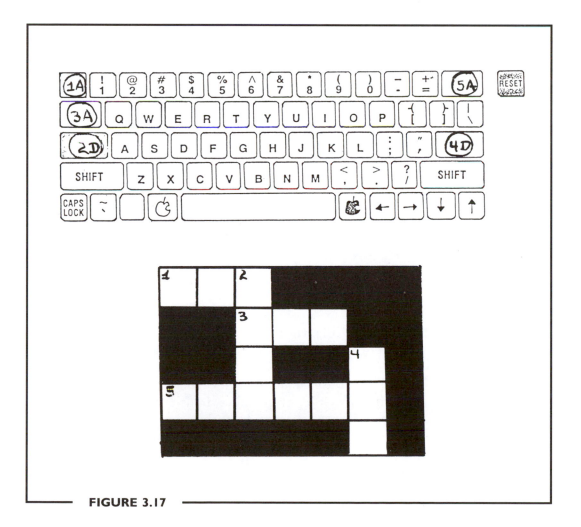

FIGURE 3.17

key highlighted would ask for a card that has the corresponding word on it. In Figure 3.18b the child would request a keyboard on which the *control* key is highlighted.

NOTE: *Allow students to keep paper keyboards in front of them to assist with language requirements as needed.*

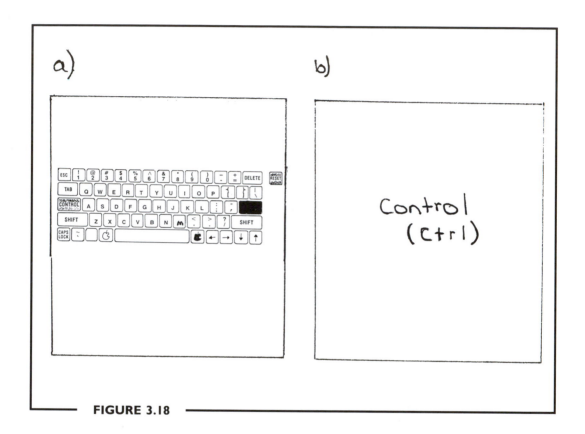

FIGURE 3.18

Abstract-Reasoning Skills

Background: The computer can serve as an effective tool for developing reasoning, logic, and problem-solving skills, yet many students find computers mystical because they are not concrete enough for children who have trouble drawing conclusions. "How does it remember so much?" "How does the disk know what to do?" "Why does *return* mean that it is the computer's turn?" These and many other questions are very reasonable for any child, even adults, to ask. Much can be done to help gain an understanding of these concepts. In reality, however, most teachers working with elementary school students have neither the expertise nor the time to explain what happens.

At the very basic level of mathematics, where we teach one-to-one correspondence or use very simple shapes and matching exercises, much of the computer's pictorial representation is good. Still, many students at this level and higher need concrete aids, and often computer timing factors or the nature of a given program do not allow for the use of concrete aids. As the material becomes more complex, pictorial representations often decrease and students must rely more and more on processes containing symbols. More and more programs, however, are incorporating good visual aids and encouraging interactive work. It is important to look for these carefully.

SUGGESTED SEQUENCE OF ACTIVITIES

1. **Is it gone?** Help students sort out the mystery of a computer by comparing it to a book. Have them find a problem on a page in their book and circle it. Close the book. "Did the problem go away or is it waiting for us to look at it again?" Compare this procedure to the way a computer works by showing a program that provides easy access to previous screens. Help students see that out of sight is *not* out of mind.

2. **Real things, please.** As much as possible, encourage (require) the use of concrete aids and manipulatives with programs students use. In many instances, this means that the time limits must be eliminated.

PROGRAM CONSIDERATIONS WITH REGARD TO LEARNING DISABILITIES

General Considerations

Although computers are more available, teachers, students, and administrators are only slightly more able to effectively incorporate them into the daily classroom environment. Part of good incorporation involves an awareness of what type of software will work in different situations. As with the more traditional type of learning tools, such as textbooks and workbooks, a wide variety of needs must be considered when choosing/using software with students. No one piece of software can meet all needs. Before discussing the relationships of specific software to specific learning disabilities, some general areas must be considered.

Choose programs that allow for the use of curriculum-related material.[3] Computers can be of tremendous help in developing problem-solving skills, building reten-

---

3. Authoring systems, such as *Hypercard* (available from Apple Computer, Cupertino, CA), which allow for complete curriculum integration, are not considered in this edition. Although they are ideal, if good, the authors recognize that most teachers do not have the time to implement them effectively. Instead, we have tried to emphasize ways in which teachers can use programs that are available on the market.

tion, and extending abstract reasoning, but only if the material presented is relevant and sequenced according to the students' needs. Therefore, programs should have the following characteristics:

- Teacher-made word problems can be entered that follow the desired sequence and allow for proper reading level. Provide the option of either an on-screen calculator or use of a real calculator for students who need to work on problem solving and fact retention separately.

- Basic facts can be entered according to the sequence described in Chapter 6. (Too many programs use the traditional, less appropriate method of "tables of.")

- The time needed to respond can vary and is under the control of the teacher and/or the student. In this way, if help screens, on-screen calculators, or other aids are not available, such tools still can be used.

- The presentation of basic facts and computation can be either horizontal or vertical.

- Students can easily access help screens or previous screens.

- Spelling errors are accepted, or the computer can at least be programmed so that it recognizes spelling variations. (Remember, language is an important and often neglected component in mathematics instruction.) A tic-tac-toe game where a student is required to type in a correct word (seventeen) in response to a question (How much is one ten and seven ones?) should not penalize the student for misspelling 17 (sevintene).

- Student input is recorded automatically so that, if direct observation is not possible, the teacher can check the work at a later date. Ideally, a printout (paper or screen) should be available, similar to Figure 3.19. Too often students work independently at the computer while the teacher is occupied with other students. As a result, there is no way for the teacher to evaluate their work later.

You have learned:
how to subtract with borrowing
how to multiply with carrying

You need to work on:
basic facts
making change
using decimal points
combining coins

FIGURE 3.19

- Computer response is helpful and can be under the teacher's control. For example, a program involving basic facts might present the correct answer immediately following an error; one teaching fraction concepts might offer various types of help. ("Do you want to see a picture?" "Shall I [the computer] help you?" "Did you mean to type that key?") In the former case, correct rather than wrong answers are being reinforced. In the latter instance, problem solving is being reinforced.

- Letters and numbers are clear and large enough for students to read easily.

- Students have the opportunity to review incorrect or difficult problems.

- Fractions are presented in vertical format with a horizontal fraction bar rather than a slash.

- Branching is possible, depending on the student's level. The option to branch (go) to another level—either to a more advanced one or to review—should be part of the program. It should, however, be under the control of the teacher and/or student, rather than automatically determined by the computer.

Specific Suggestions

The following is a description of various programs based on their applicability to various types of learning disabilities. In no way is it meant to be an endorsement for any one program or publisher, nor is the listing meant to be complete. The software market is changing constantly and teacher input is being incorporated into the design and development of software. The purpose of this section, rather, is to help teachers learn to evaluate the needs of the student in light of both learning disabilities and specific programs.

No one software program can meet all needs, and some are better suited than others to particular curriculum goals and specific learning disabilities. Even the most highly rated program, in terms of ease of use, teacher utility, and content, may not be equally useful to all students. Proper integration of computers in the ongoing instructional schedule requires an understanding of the relationship between curriculum goals and the effect of learning disabilities on successful use of computers. Additionally, teachers must evaluate the strengths and weaknesses of individual programs in light of student needs. (See the Appendix at the end of this chapter for a list of addresses of software publishers.)

NOTE: *Note: A dash (–) in front of a listing means that the user can customize it to some extent in order to meet specific curriculum needs.*

Type of learning disability: *figure-ground*

Considerations for determining the effectiveness of programs for students' figure-ground difficulties include:

- amount and size of the print on the screen;

- ability to track material on the screen by using a cursor within the program, teacher-made tachistoscopic materials, or a mouse;

• amount of key searching needed in order to work the program. The goal is to allow the student to focus more on the screen and less on going back and forth between the keyboard and the screen;

• whether teacher/student can adjust time factors;

• consistency of screen format; and

• whether sound is available but optional.

Program	Publisher
–*Tic Tac Show*	Scholastic
–*Grammar Examiner*	Designware
–*FasTrack Quizzer*	Creative Publications
–*Wiz Works*	DLM
–*MathBlaster Plus*	Davidson
–*Kids Time*	GreatWave

NOTE: *Provided the users make up their own game boards,* Grammar Examiner *is a good program for students with figure-ground deficits, especially if a color monitor is available. However, using the game boards provided with the program can be horribly confusing, difficult to follow, and long. Although written with the intent of teaching grammar, this program can be adapted to language-related math work; it will accept the use of numbers.*

Type of learning disability: *discrimination*

Considerations for determining the effectiveness of programs for students with discrimination difficulties include:

• size and spacing of numbers and words on the screen;

• method used to focus student's attention on the task;

• type of reinforcement used; and

• clarity of monitor, especially color monitors.

Program	Publisher
–*Match Wits*	CBS
–*Square Pairs*	Scholastic
–*MathBlaster Plus*	Davidson
–*Arcademic Drill Builders*	DLM
–*Clock*	Hartley
–*Addition Magician*	Learning Company
–*Hands on Math*	Ventura

Type of learning disability: *spatial*

Considerations for determining the effectiveness of programs for students with spatial difficulties include:

• how material on the screen deals with directionality;

- whether a minimal number of keys can be used to work the program and whether the keys are kinesthetically/visually related to the intended direction;

- how the program deals with movement in space—visual or temporal; and

- whether off-computer activities can be used to help the student understand the difference in directions between using a screen (vertical) and paper and pencil (different orientation).

Program	Publisher
–*Clock*	Hartley
Peanuts Mazes	Random House
Fences (Part of *Microzine #5*)	Scholastic
Bumble Plot	Learning Company
–*Turtle Tracks*	Scholastic
Addition Magician	Learning Company
Fraction Factory	Springboard

Type of learning disability: *memory difficulties*

Considerations for determining the effectiveness of programs for students with memory difficulties include:

- teacher/student ability to control the time limits within the program;

- whether repetition of material, if needed, is possible, especially after an error or at the end of the program for review;

- whether the presentation method of the material (i.e., random or sequential) can be controlled by the teacher;

- whether curriculum-related material can be entered into the program; and

- whether the teacher can preview some of the material so off-computer material can be used prior to or while students use the computer.

Program	Publisher
–*Match Wits*	CBS
–*Square Pairs*	Scholastic
–*Mystery Match* (part of *Math Rabbit*)	Learning Company
Success with Math	Mindscape
–*MathBlaster Plus*	Davidson
–*AlgeBlaster Plus*	Davidson
–*Magic Cash Register*	Metacomet
–*Kids Time*	GreatWave

Type of learning disability: *receptive and expressive language*

Considerations for determining the effectiveness of programs for students with receptive and expressive language difficulties include:

- ability to use a multiple-choice format;
- interactive ability with curriculum-related material;
- ability to control (remove) the time limits with the program;
- ability to access previous screens;
- provisions for previewing vocabulary; and
- consistency of format.

Program	Publisher
–*Word Attack*	Davidson
–*Tic Tac Show*	Scholastic
–*Arcademic Drill Builders*	DLM
–*FasTrack Quizzer*	DesignWare
–*Crossword Magic*	Mindscape
Number Connections	Sunburst/Wings for Learning
Clock	Hartley
Addition Magician	Learning Company
–*Clown Counting Program* and *Mystery Match* (part of *Math Rabbit*)	Learning Company
–*Magic Cash Register*	Metacomet

Type of learning disability: *abstract reasoning*

Considerations for determining the effectiveness of programs for students with abstract-reasoning difficulties include:

- ability to interact with the program using concrete aids;
- use of representative visual cues on the screen;
- ease of accessibility between screens;
- provisions for teacher preview of vocabulary; and
- ability to add help screens for curriculum-related material.

Program	Publisher
–*Magic Cash Register*	Metacomet
–*Math Word Problems*	Optimum Resources
–*Tightrope* (part of *Math Rabbit*)	Learning Company
The Factory	Sunburst
Sim City	Earthquest
–*Math Blaster Mystery*	Davidson
–*How the West Was One + Two × Four*	Sunburst
–*What Do You Do With a Broken Calculator*	Sunburst

RECOMMENDATIONS FOR SOFTWARE DEVELOPMENT

This section presents ideas for both publishers and teachers to consider with regard to developing software for students with learning disabilities. Even if teachers have the ability to develop software, they may have neither the time nor the interest in doing so. However, since much software is part of the public domain and can, therefore, be adjusted relatively easily to meet individual needs, we felt that a discussion of certain programming and software development issues were in order. Additionally, teaching assistants, parents, or students who are computer whizzes may be able to implement many of the following ideas into both commercial and public domain software or authoring systems.

Sequence

When selecting or developing programs it is important to consider not only the relevance of the content to the ongoing curriculum but also the sequence of the content presentation. Students with learning disabilities often need the presentation of instructional sequences altered from the traditional method in order to learn and retain information. For example, a child who requires a great deal of overlearning but who tends to perseverate would not benefit from a computation program that only presented one type of problem at a time, such as adding without regrouping. Yet, this same child might not be ready to solve problems with regrouping. Instead, an intermediate step might be helpful where the child learns to differentiate between problems that require regrouping and those that do not. If the teacher can insert a decision-making section/option into a computation program, the student has an opportunity to acquire the necessary skills without being impeded by a learning disability. (An example of one such idea is shown in Figure 3.20.)

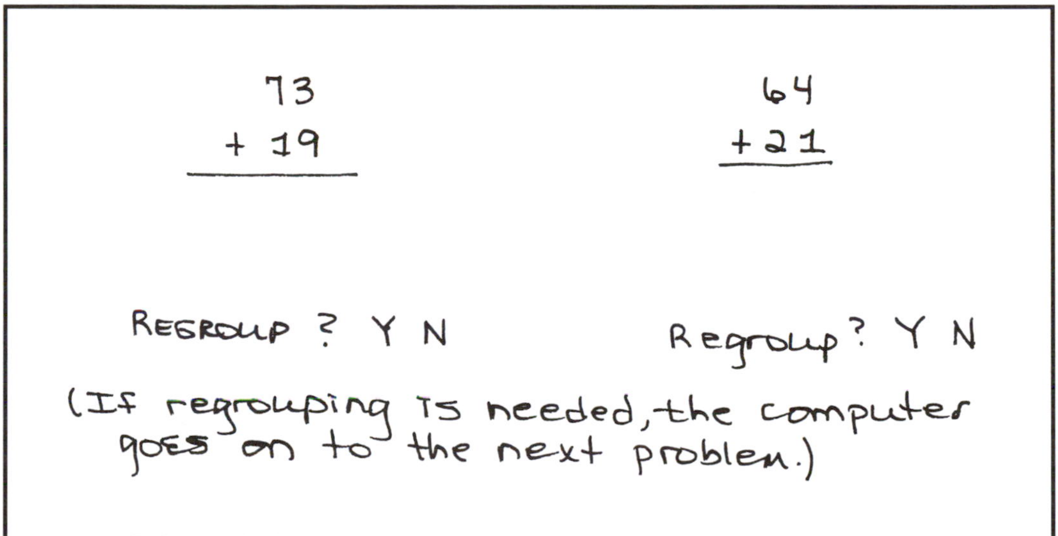

```
      73                        64
    + 19                      + 21
    _____                    _____


  REGROUP ? Y N            Regroup ? Y N

(If regrouping is needed, the computer
   goes on to the next problem.)
```

FIGURE 3.20

Other content-related suggestions include:

1. allowing for teacher input at various points within the program so that a student can review as needed;

2. changing the format of programs so that the teacher is able to:

   a. determine the sequence of presentation and

   b. substitute numbers within the problems without changing the basic structure (i.e., the basic structure of not regrouping would remain, but the basic facts could be changed as a child learned various clusters according to the sequence suggested in Chapter 6);

3. allowing for curriculum-related information to be entered at selected points, depending on student needs;

4. providing help screens that can be used by the teacher (such as one that is based on the teacher's assessment of a student's work); and

5. using programs in which work can be saved on a separate disk. Then, if students need to stop before completing a program they need not begin all over again unless that is preferable.

Response Format

Students with learning disabilities respond to information in various ways, depending on their specific disabilities. In order to instruct these students effectively, special education teachers must be able to clearly determine the goal of a particular assignment and then control the environment to the extent necessary. Only in this way will students learn the information without being held back due to learning deficits. For example, a student with expressive language difficulties may enjoy and benefit from using a computer if a multiple-choice format is available, while another student would do fine if required to provide an answer without language cues. Programs with a format choice have the potential of not only being more individualized but also allowing two students with different learning disabilities to work together. Some further suggestions along these lines include the following:

1. Games that allow the teacher to choose whether a student must type in an entire answer (see Figure 3.21a) or select from choices by typing in a number only (see Figure 3.21b) allow for broader use. Students with figure-ground, visual discrimination, or expressive language deficits might benefit from the second format, whereas students strong in these areas but who need to build up their memory might do better with the former.

   NOTE: *Figure 3.21b calls for the use of a number rather than a letter because less of the keyboard is involved. This feature enables students* *with figure-ground or discrimination problems to use the program successfully.*

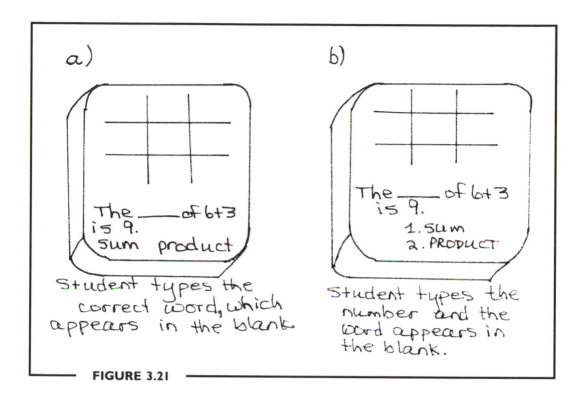

FIGURE 3.21

2. Computer response to student input should involve some evaluation on the student's part. A student with figure-ground difficulties or perceptual deficits may type in the wrong answer unknowingly. Before the computer immediately responds to the input, a question might be asked such as, "Are you sure that is the answer you want?" At the very least, some time should elapse before the computer responds to the answer.

Time Factors

For many students, time restrictions greatly inhibit progress. For example, students with language difficulties need time to process information. Figure-ground deficits may mean a student needs more time to locate the keys on the keyboard. Memory problems affect the student's speed. If there is no way to alter the built-in timing, many otherwise good programs lose their effectiveness. The following are additional considerations.

1. The teacher should easily be able to control the time factor of any program. This means being able to set the allotted time prior to when a student uses the program. In some cases, it also means allowing the student to control

the timing, within certain parameters, as the material is mastered. For example, prior to a student's beginning a program, the teacher could set the time to a certain speed and then establish parameters within which the student can increase or decrease the time. While working on the program at different levels that have been predetermined by the teacher, the student can choose how to handle the timing factor.

2. As they develop the confidence to work within a timed setting, some students benefit from seeing the elapsed time. In this way, they develop a sense of different lengths of time and learn to adjust them to different activities. An example of a type of screen is shown in Figure 3.22.

3. It should be possible to save timing changes for individual students so the same time structure can be used during a subsequent session. This feature also would allow another student to begin/continue at a different level without interfering with the work of other students.

Computation

When developing programs that are meant to teach either basic facts or computation skills, the following factors must be considered. The presentation order of the facts is essential, to avoid having students feel as if they have to learn 100 (or 90) isolated facts for each of the four operations. The method by which the problem

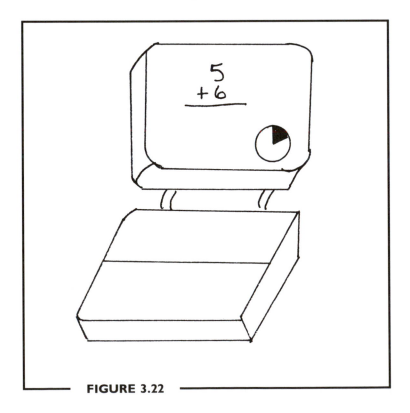

FIGURE 3.22

is presented (horizontal or vertical) and by which the student enters the digits in a computation problem also is important both in terms of specific learning disabilities and in terms of understanding a concept. In addition, the location and size of the material on the screen are critical.

1. When a student is required to solve computational problems on the monitor, the presentation should appear in a vertical position with input from right to left, except where regrouping is involved.

   NOTE: *In Chapter 6 a left-to-right sequence is described, which often is needed for students with severe reversal problems. Maybe someday the left-to-right option for computation problems also will be available on computers.*

2. Those programs that do not allow for vertical presentation of problems should offer one of the following characteristics.

   a. The teacher should be able to preview the problems and the order in which they are presented so that the student has paper and pencil available to solve the problem, if needed.

   b. An on-screen calculator should be presented or at least available. The student uses it by using a mouse or typing in the numbers from the keyboard. Perhaps keying numbers into the on-screen calculator could cause the numbers to be placed correctly on the screen, as in Figure 3.23.

   c. Ideally, the program will allow for a well-spaced printout of the problems so that the student has a worksheet.

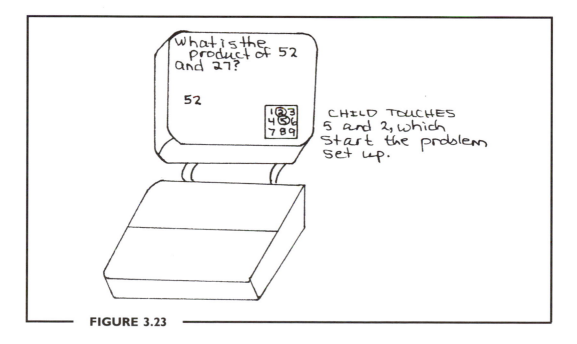

FIGURE 3.23

3. If regrouping is involved, the student should:

    a. be required to decide whether or not to regroup. If no regrouping is involved, a certain key can be designated to push so the problem can move along.

    b. be required to enter the answer so that the regrouped digit is entered first.

4. Numbers should be sufficiently large and centered well enough on the screen that they are read easily. Not only will this reduce the problems encountered by students with perceptual problems, it also will keep the numbers from appearing to jump out at the student.

5. When solving division problems, even short division, the option of using either division sign ($\sqrt{}$ or $\div$) should be available so that the teacher can determine ahead of time which one the student will use.

6. It is not always advisable to have students solve a page with mixed operations. However, the option should be available to the teacher ahead of time.

7. Fraction problems should use the horizontal bar instead of the slanted line, and computation should be presented vertically.

Branching Capabilities

Ideally, the computer should be an integral, related tool of the overall curriculum. As such, computers must enable users to retain the material presented without becoming bored or stagnating at a certain level. These are the same requirements that apply to any classroom instruction. To ensure that the computer meets these criteria, the following branching options must be available.

1. The computer must perform ongoing evaluation so that, as a student reaches mastery or continues to make errors, appropriate branching can occur.

2. The teacher should be able to exert some control over this branching by:

    a. accessing the student's input and noting the sequence in which the information was answered as well as the number of times it took for the student to obtain the correct answer and

    b. predetermining at what points the computer should decide when and where to branch.

3. The scope and sequence of the material presented in the software should be available, preferably in the printed documentation or via a help screen, while running the program. This allows the teacher to:

    a. decide whether a particular program serves the purposes of the curriculum;

  b. decide how and when to have the computer branch to another part and when review is needed;

  c. develop off-computer activities that are related to the material used in the program; and

  d. develop materials that the student can use while working on the computer.

Reading Level

Recognizing that it is not possible to eliminate all reading demands from programs, the level and amount should be controlled to the extent possible. At a minimum, language typically is needed to give instructions. However, software publishers are encouraged to consider the following recommendations.

1. In addition to the intended age and/or grade level, it also would help to delineate the reading level of the software program on the outside of the box. The age descriptions on the box frequently refer more to interest level than to the actual reading level.

2. Make directions as simple as possible, written in clear, large print, with generous space between the lines. An ongoing help line at the bottom of each screen would benefit students by reminding them of what to do in order to (a) return to the menu, (b) correct an error, or (c) receive help. If this feature is not possible, a simplified card containing the most basic user information should be included in the documentation. Such a card easily can be kept at the student's side while working.

3. To the extent possible, representative icons should be used to assist in understanding the directions.

4. Include a glossary of words that the student needs to understand to use a program successfully. This also would allow some off-computer activities to be developed prior to actual use of the program.

5. Programs aimed at developing problem-solving skills should specify both the interest and the reading level on the outside of the box and in the documentation.

6. On-screen help boxes with vocabulary and definitions or representative examples would assist students as they read the problems and possibly encounter words with which they are unfamiliar.

7. Software that is programmed to accept teacher-developed word problems is most helpful. The shell program could be written and published in such a way that the teacher could determine:

  a. reading level and material;

  b. number of steps in the problem;

  c. types of problems presented;

  d. help given in solving the problems, including:

    • steps listed in order,

    • steps listed out of order, or

    • things to consider prior to solving; and

  e. order in which the problems are presented (sequential or random).

Teacher Utility

One of the important advantages of having computers in the classroom is their potential for individualizing instruction. It is especially important, therefore, that the classroom teacher has some control over the software and is aware of how the student uses the software without having to be present at all times.

> **NOTE:** *Even though it is not realistic to expect teachers to watch students at the computer continuously, too often no monitoring takes place. In order to evaluate the usefulness of a given activity, teachers must take time to see how students are interacting with and responding to the computer. Otherwise, the computer simply becomes busywork.*

To enhance computer utility for teachers, the following suggestions should be considered.

1. The utility section must be easily accessible to the teacher but not to the student. In some instances, it is helpful for students to be able to access part of the utility section, but the record keeping and error analysis should be open only to the student with the assistance of the teacher.

2. Automatic record keeping should start as soon as a student signs on the computer by entering a name.

3. A paper printout showing the following information would help in assessing student progress:

  a. number of problems attempted;

  b. a copy of the problems, the numbers keyed in to derive the answers, and the final answers; and

  c. percent correct.

4. If correct answers involve words rather than numbers, the program should allow the teacher to include a spell checker—one that permits inclusion of odd spellings. Often, students with learning disabilities have trouble with spelling. If the answer to a math problem depends on correctly spelled words,

there is no way to measure math ability. At the very least, the program should accept spelling errors. Most teachers, however, are more familiar with the types of errors their students make than are software developers, hence the advantage of flexibility in this area.

General Recommendations

As we become more and more sophisticated in our approach to teaching and to integrating computers into instruction, our knowledge of what comprises useful software also has improved. The ideas in the preceding discussion apply to particular areas of learning and software. The following points are more general.

1. It is important for the student to be able to read what is on the screen. To that end, the type must be large. Just as some word processors offer a variation in the number of columns, math software should allow for varying the size of the type and perhaps even boldness of the type.

2. When solving word problems, the student should be required to include a word answer along with the correct computation. If spelling is a problem, the student should be presented with choices from which one answer must be selected. Figure 3.24 presents one suggestion for younger students or those who have difficulty with the keyboard.

3. The spacing between numbers and between words should be clear. At the very least, double spacing should be available to make it easier to read the material on the screen.

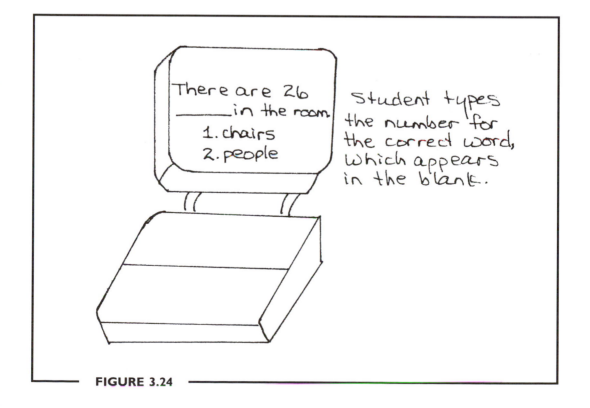

FIGURE 3.24

4. The use of underlining, arrows, and cursors to help focus attention is essential for many students. Screens change quickly, and many students with learning disabilities need help to refocus their attention to the correct place on the screen.

5. When graphics are included, many children, though enjoying and benefiting from them, nevertheless have trouble keeping their orientation. Therefore, these students need assistance, in terms of cursors and appropriate time limits, to locate the problem or the answer amidst the graphics.

6. Much software benefits from and/or requires color monitors. If this is the case, it is important that the colors are very clear and the type size of the numbers and letters is large enough so that the images are not blurred.

7. The area in which students solve the problems should be located centrally on the screen. If more than one problem is present or if an area is reserved for computation, the program should allow the teacher or student to organize the work space spatially.

8. Many programs provide off-computer activities. These should include activities focusing on the directions needed to work through material. This would enable the student to become familiar with the keyboard as it relates to a particular piece of software.

REFERENCES

Individuals with Disabilities Education Act. (1990). Public Law 101-476.

National Council of Teachers of Mathematics. (1989). *Curriculum and evaluation standards for school mathematics*. Reston, VA: Author.

APPENDIX

Software Publishers

Apple Computer
20525 Mariani Avenue
Cupertino, CA 95014
800-800-2775

CBS
(software distributed by)
Cambridge Development Lab
86 West St.
Waltham, MA 02154
800-637-0047

Creative Publications
5040 West 111th Street
Oak Lawn, IL 60453
800-624-0822

Davidson Software
P.O. Box 2961
Torrance, CA 90509
800-545-7677

DesignWare
185 Berry Street
San Francisco, CA 94107
800-572-7767

DLM
P.O. Box 4000
One DLM Park
Allen, TX 75002
800-527-4747

Earthquest Educational Division
125 University Avenue
Palo Alto, CA 94301
800-321-8925

GreatWave Software
5353 Scotts Valley Drive
Scotts Valley, CA 95066
408-438-1990

Hartley Courseware
3001 Coolidge Suite 400
East Lansing, MI 48823
800-247-1380

Learning Company
6493 Kaiser Drive
Freemont, CA 94555
510-792-9628

Metacomet
Cambridge Development Laboratories
86 West Street
Waltham, MA 02154
800-637-0047

Mindscape Educational Software
1345 Diversey Parkway
Chicago, IL 60614
800-829-1900

Optimum Resources
10 Stantinn Place
Norfolk, CT 06058
800-327-1473

Random House
American School Publishers
155 N. Wacker Dr.
P.O. Box 4520
Chicago, IL 60680-4520
800-843-8855

Scholastic Software
740 Broadway
New York, NY 10003
800-541-5513

Springboard Software
7808 Creekridge Circle
Minneapolis, MN 55435
612-944-3912

Sunburst/Wings for Learning
1600 Green Hills Road
Scotts Valley, CA 95067
800-321-7511

Ventura Educational Systems
3440 Brokenhill Street
Newbury Park, CA 91320
800-336-1022

Sunburst/Wings for Learning
1600 Green Hills Road
Scotts Valley, CA 95067
800-321-7511

Ventura Educational Systems
3440 Brokenhill Street
Newbury Park, CA 91320
800-336-1022

CHAPTER 4

Money and Time

EVEN BEFORE THEY enter school, many children can discriminate among a penny, a nickel, and a dime. They may not always associate the correct coin with the correct name, but they usually use one of the three names when referring to a coin. Most preschoolers also develop some sense of time, and many even learn to tell time by the hour. For example, they know dinner is at 6:00, when the "little hand is on the six." "If it's on the five, it's not dinner time."

Basic concepts and skills related to money and time are formally introduced, reinforced, and expanded during the primary school years. Thus, most mathematics programs gear early number work to the development of money and time skills. Usually by the end of first grade, children can tell time to the half hour, and most can recognize the difference between the five coins by name and value. Many can even find the value of coin groups to 25 cents and make change for amounts up to 10 cents.

As children's experience and training base broadens, most develop a feel for time that helps them know how long they have to complete an activity or wait for another to begin. Most youngsters also develop a general sense of how much money they need for particular items ("lots" or "a little"), what change is, and how long it will take to save enough money for something they want or need.

As children learn to handle larger amounts of money and to tell time more accurately, the vocabulary involved places greater demands on both receptive and expressive language skills. Children must now begin to deal with familiar words in new contexts. Expressions like "ten minutes *ago*," "*in* a half hour," "*later*," and "making *change*" all include words that may be part of their vocabularies, but are now presented in a different way. If children use these expressions, it should entail more than merely parroting what others say. For example, when a child says, "I'll be there in 10 minutes," it should be based on a real understanding of the underlying concepts.

As students progress through school, the demands on using time and money efficiently increase. By the time children reach the middle grades, they are expected to read time to the nearest minute and deal with large money amounts. Older students in middle school or junior high are expected to count out money amounts and make change without relying on paper-and-pencil calculations. They also must learn to write checks and handle bank accounts—daily living skills of practical importance.

Children's success in mastering concepts and skills for money and time can be greatly hindered by learning disabilities. Many of the tasks outlined in the preceding paragraphs require good visual and auditory memory, discrimination, and sequencing skills. To count money, for example, students must be able to discriminate between size differences and accurately retrieve, from memory, the correct name and/or value to match a given size. To tell time from a standard clock, they must discriminate the size of the hands as well as the correct digit and its meaning. Using money and time on a daily basis involves a high degree of visual and auditory memory, as well as visual and spatial discrimination.

This chapter addresses some of the common problems students with learning disabilities face in trying to master money and time skills. The first part of the chapter focuses on money. An introductory section suggests materials to keep in the classroom for use in teaching money. The remaining sections present ways to approach the following topics with students with learning disabilities:

1. Coin discrimination;

2. Counting money amounts to $1.00 (using a quarter, rather than coin substitutes for the quarter, for amounts over $.25);

3. Counting money amounts to $1.00 (using coin substitutes for the quarter for amounts over $.25);

4. Paying for items and making change greater than $1.00.

The last part of the chapter deals with teaching time to students with learning disabilities. After an introductory section on classroom materials helpful for this purpose, ways of handling the following topics are explored:

5. Reading clock times;

6. Reading and writing clock times;

7. Naming the correct hour;

8. Understanding the many ways to tell time; and

9. Understanding and using temporal expressions.

As in previous chapters, for each topic section, a basic sequence of activities and exercises is presented. When necessary, alternate approaches for meeting the needs of particular disabilities are also noted.

CLASSROOM MATERIALS FOR TEACHING MONEY

Concrete teaching aids and real-life applications help children build and develop confidence with new concepts and skills. This principle is particularly important when teaching children how to handle money. The following materials are useful for this purpose.

- Real money
- Coin and paper money stamps
- Ink pads and bottles of colored ink
- Laminated coin lines
- Play money, including color-coded coins
- Dice games and other money activities
- Practice pages (kept in a file, ready for use)
- Empty food cans (labels on, lids cut from the bottom) or other items for a play store

Real money should be used whenever possible, particularly in early activities (keep a bag of change—locked up when not in use). Experience has shown that even very young children can learn to handle money with care and not lose it. After all: "Money has *value*. We use it to buy what we need and want. People work hard to *earn* money. The coins in the bag belong to the teacher who has worked hard to get them, but who is loaning them out so you can learn about money." These are very basic concepts that are part of "money sense" for young learners.

As work progresses, continue to use real money whenever possible. At times, however, this is not practical, and money substitutes must be introduced. In such instances, it is essential that any play money and pictures used resemble real money as closely as possible. Like many of their peers, students with learning disabilities find it difficult enough to relate money substitutes to real money without the added frustration of poor resemblance.

Coin stamps, both heads and tails, and paper money stamps are useful items, which can be purchased from many school supply companies. Ink pads are needed for money stamps; keep several on hand for use with different colors of ink. Color-coded coins can be useful when teaching and reinforcing coin discrimination and when dealing with children with figure-ground problems. Use of these coins eliminates the interference of any learning deficit while strengthening retention and overlearning. Figure 4.1 is an example of a color-coded coin line that is easy to make, using either stamps and colored inks or colored paper. The sample can be laminated, covered with contact paper, or kept in a plastic holder for durability.

Although it takes time, realistic simulated money can be made using coin stamps and either colored paper or crayons. (Again, make sure the pennies are brown and the silver coins grey so they resemble real coins as much as possible.) Laminate the coins or cover them with clear contact paper to extend their lifetime. Students with severe visual discrimination problems may benefit initially from coins which match the colors used on the coin number line described in the previous paragraph.

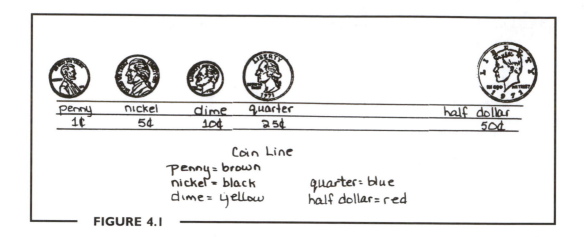

FIGURE 4.1

Once they have a stronger visual image, students can gradually proceed to using more closely color-related paper coins.

The following sections suggest how to use the color-coded coins and coin line. Additionally, other money and many dice games can be played to reinforce money skills. A master copy of several types of coin dice is provided in Figure 4.2. Ideas for using the dice are also included in the sections that follow.

Throughout the chapter, various worksheet ideas will be illustrated. These can be kept on file and be readily available for homework, learning centers, and extra reinforcement of specific skills.

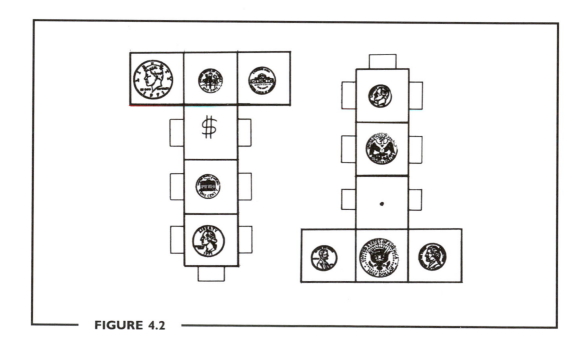

FIGURE 4.2

COIN DISCRIMINATION

Problem Area: Inability to discriminate coins by name and value.

Typical Disabilities Affecting Progress: Difficulty with visual discrimination, receptive and expressive language, figure-ground, and auditory memory.

Background: Very young children, preschool to about age 6, often have difficulty discriminating fine differences in size while readily seeing gross differences such as that between the size of a dinner plate and a quarter. Developmentally, they may not be ready to do much more than order coins by size with the aid of finger tracing or matching one on top of the other.

With continual exposure, most primary-grade children gradually learn to distinguish coins. They begin to look more closely at them, study them, and feel them. Their understanding of "bigger" and "smaller" may be weak and, thus, it often is meaningless or even confusing to say, "The bigger one is a nickel." What does "bigger" mean? How can it be bigger if the dime is worth 10 cents and the nickel is worth 5 cents? Does "bigger" mean size or value? Through repeated experience, careful instruction, and developmental growth, children learn to associate the correct name with a given coin. By the time they are 6 or 7, most children can accurately match the coin with its name, and often with its value.

For children with disabilities like those listed above, the discrete differences and sequencing required in discriminating coins preclude much chance of their automatically making these associations. A detailed analysis highlights the requirements and sequences involved in responding to the following request: "Give me the nickel, Peter."

- Receptively, the child must understand the meaning of the word "nickel."

- The child must be able to see that coins are, in fact, different sizes.

- The child must be able to (a) revisualize a nickel or (b) tactually feel the difference between the nickel and other coins.

- Once the image has been recalled, the child must be able to retain it long enough to associate it with the correct coin.

For most children, these steps probably take about 1 or 2 seconds to complete once the process has been mastered. However, for the child with learning disabilities, the effort to comply with the request may end in total frustration, wild guesses, or a refusal to answer. Therefore, more specialized instruction, such as that outlined below, is needed. The general approach presented can be adapted to the child's current level. When dealing remedially with an older student, for example, all five coins are introduced, one at a time, in the manner suggested. In introducing the coins to younger children, on the other hand, greater care is taken to correlate the work with the early number program. The quarter, for example, would be introduced only after children can meaningfully read and write 2-digit numbers.

SUGGESTED SEQUENCE OF ACTIVITIES

1. **Penny first.** The penny should be introduced first because it is more readily distinguished by its color. Show the children all five coins, but focus only on the penny. Let them pick it up and feel it. If they do not already know it, tell them its name (penny). Discuss similarities and differences between the penny and other coins in the pile. Emphasize color, size, images on the coin, and whether its edge is rough or smooth.

2. **Coin line.** Have the children place the penny on top of the penny pictured on a coin line. Show them how the size and color of the two coins are the same. Some children have difficulty relating a real coin to its picture, thus the need in early lessons to carefully relate the two. If possible, allow the children to use a penny coin stamp on brown construction paper to make their own penny pictures.

3. **Penny line-up.** Give each child an envelope of coins (pennies and silver coins). Have them sort out all the pennies and place them under the penny of the coin line. Personal coin lines may be given to each child for this purpose.

4. **Penny match.** Give each child about 15 pennies, using real coins if possible. If the number of students makes this impractical, use a penny stamp on brown construction paper to make play coins. Provide an activity sheet like the one in Figure 4.3 and instruct the children to cover each penny on the page with the ones given to them. "The penny pictures on the activity sheet are not colored, but they have the same picture and are the same size as the pennies you have. Can you find all of them?" If the page is covered correctly, the pennies should form the letter "P." When naming the penny, discuss how one makes the "P" sound.

   - *Variation:* For those children who learn best kinesthetically, give tracing paper along with the activity sheet of Figure 4.3. Ask them to place (or tape) the tracing paper over the sheet. Then, using a penny or a stencil the shape and size of a penny, show them how to trace over each penny on the sheet. When finished, the shape formed by the tracing should be the letter "P."

5. **One penny is worth 1¢.** Discuss how money has value, since we use it to buy what we need and want. Introduce the cent sign. Explain that a number with a cent sign (¢) next to it means that the number stands for an amount of money. The value of a penny is 1¢. Write on the board: 1 penny = 1¢. (Use "1 penny→1¢" if children do not understand the equal sign.) Give each student about 10 pennies. Ask questions and carry out activities like the following:

   - Have students put four pennies in a pile in front of them. "How many cents do you have there?" . . . "Put 2¢ in a pile in front of you. How many pennies do you have?"

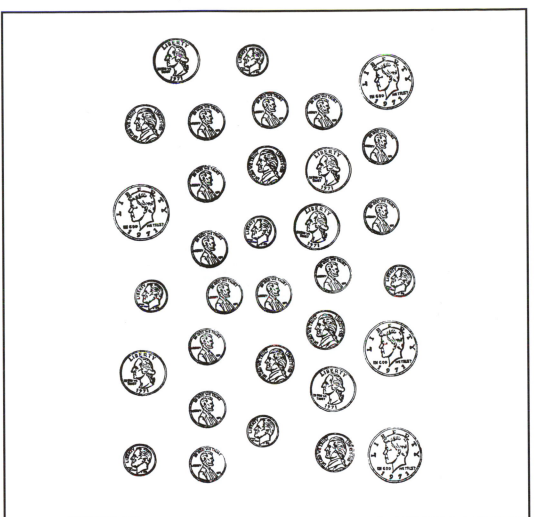

FIGURE 4.3

- "Suppose I wanted to trade with you. If I gave you three pennies, how many cents would you give me so we'd have a fair trade?"

- "If you give me 5¢ and I give you four pennies back, is that a fair trade?"

- "Suppose you are at a store and want to buy some gum. Look at the price tag (5¢). How many pennies do you need to pay the cashier?"

Continue until students recognize and understand the meaning of cent in relation to pennies.

6. **What coin next?** Use activities similar to those above to introduce other coins. The normal presentation of coins, in order, is: penny, nickel, dime, quarter, and half dollar. If a child has difficulty with visual discrimination or size perception, use the sequence penny, *quarter*, nickel, dime, and half dollar. In our experience, this sequence is easier because of the greater differ-

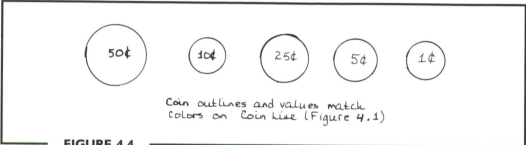

Coin outlines and values match
colors on Coin Line (Figure 4.1)

FIGURE 4.4

ence in size between the penny and the quarter. Even when size perception is no problem for students, deviation from the standard sequence is often recommended. After the penny and nickel, introduce the quarter. Both its value and its size are big.

7. **Size it up.** As the coins are introduced, provide reinforcement pages, like that of Figure 4.4, which are color coded to match the coin line. The purpose of these pages is to help the children respond to differences in coin size and emphasize the value of each coin. Initially children match the colored paper coins with the circles. Then these coins are replaced with real coins and gradually the color cues are eliminated. Children can be asked to name the coins they have placed on the sheet.

8. **Bingo.** For children with language deficits, a bingo game is a fun way to build up a weakness while using a possible strength—visual perception. The calling cards, the markers, the pictures on the bingo cards, or the space beneath each picture on the cards can be color coded to match the coin line colors. In the space below each coin picture in Figure 4.5, a child would place the correct word or value when it is called. The calling cards (Figure 4.6) list the name of the coin on one side and both the coin and the name on the other. The coin picture clue helps the student know what to call the coin. The winner is the child who covers a row in any direction—down, across, or diagonally.

   • *Variation:* Instead of writing the names of coins on the calling cards, write coin values. Children then cover the coin that matches the value called. For example, if 10¢ is called, they place a 10¢ marker beneath a picture of a dime.

COUNTING MONEY AMOUNTS TO ONE DOLLAR USING QUARTERS

Problem Area: Inability to determine the value of a group of coins in which quarters rather than quarter coin substitutes are used.

Typical Disabilities Affecting Progress: Difficulty with expressive language; sequential memory; visual perception, particularly figure-ground; and closure.

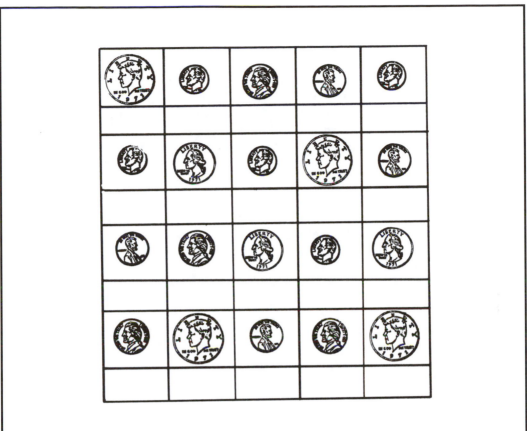

FIGURE 4.5

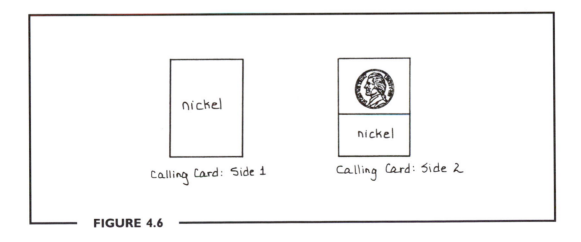

FIGURE 4.6

Background: Once coin recognition and basic values of coins have been established, most children learn to find the value of groups of coins. Early work starts with values up to 10 cents and gradually extends to counting money amounts to one dollar. At this point, it is helpful for children to begin to learn automatically to relate two nickels to 10¢. The ability to do so makes handling money and coin group values much easier.

Two prerequisites to successfully finding the value of coin groups are: (a) the ability to count on from midpoint, and (b) a strong understanding that quantity (size) and value do not always match. There may be fewer coins than the actual cent value, and it is generally easier to recognize small, known groups within a larger group and to count on from that value. A child's ability to perform these tasks often depends upon being able to apply skip counting by 2s, 5s, or 10s to a money situation and to *count on* by 2s, 5s, or 10s from various starting points.

Children having the difficulties identified at the beginning of this section may be unable to use their skip counting skills in this way. They may not recognize what pattern to use or when to switch from one pattern to another. The activities below are intended to help children cope with these problems. The following prerequisites are assumed:

- Students can recognize a number pattern as one that involves skip counting by 2s, 5s, or 10s.

- When dealing with numbers alone, apart from money, students can *continue* a skip counting pattern that has been started.

- Students have been introduced to "switch" skip counting (e.g., they start counting by 5s, then continue counting by 10s, or vice versa). An example of a written exercise that reinforces this skill is illustrated in Figure 4.7.

- Students can recognize the following substitutions: two nickels for a dime, five pennies for a nickel, two quarters for a half dollar, three quarters for 75 cents, and four quarters for one dollar. Automatic recognition of these coin equivalents is desirable. An example showing how to use tailed coins on a money line to reinforce coin equivalents is shown in Figure 4.8. Placed end to end, it takes *two* nickels to equal (the length of) the dime. Coin "tails" are made from masking tape, attached to the coin, then folded lengthwise in half. Tails can be colored to match the colors of the coins on the coin line.

25   30   35   __   __   __   60   70   __   __

20   30   40   __   __   __   75   80   85   __   __

Sample number sequence to reinforce switch skip counting

FIGURE 4.7

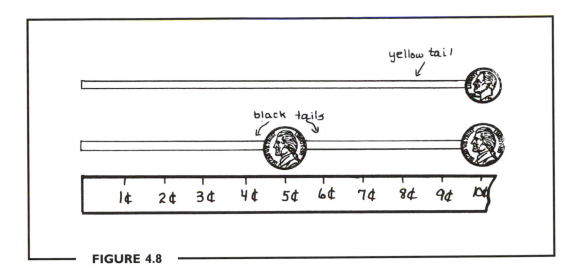

FIGURE 4.8

SUGGESTED SEQUENCE OF ACTIVITIES

1. **Count it out.** Keep dittos on hand, such as that illustrated in Figure 4.9. Each line should be a different color. Use colored dittos or give the child four crayons, each clearly different in color from the others but including a green and a red. The child underlines each row of words with a different color, beginning with the green and ending with the red. Next, give the children a shape stencil like that shown in Figure 4.10. The four shapes should be outlined to match, respectively, the colors of the four rows in Figure 4.9. Given a group of coins, the children place them inside the shapes in the appropriate sequence—greatest valued coins first, pennies last. This step will initially require teacher assistance. After grouping the coins, the child fills in the blanks on the worksheet. As each blank is filled, the child should be instructed to read the entire sentence aloud before going on to the next blank. For children with closure difficulties who have trouble finding starting points and continuing patterns, the colors provide the needed

I have _____.
Now I have _____.
Now I have _____.
Now I have _____.

I have _____.
Now I have _____.
Now I have _____.
Now I have _____.

FIGURE 4.9

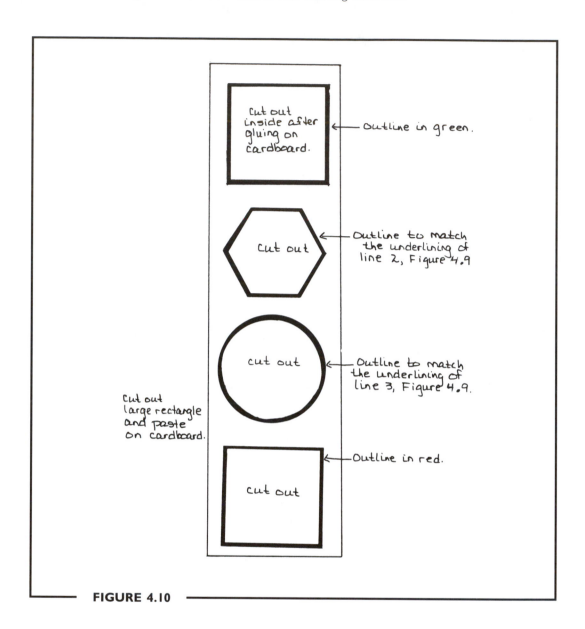

FIGURE 4.10

cues. For those who have trouble expressing thoughts or retaining a sequence, verbalizing the words "I have . . ." helps focus attention and initiate the thought process. The colors will help maintain the sequence.

2. **"Switch" skip counting.** Finding the value of coin groups can be difficult because it requires "switch" skip counting. Due to integrative processing deficits or perseveration, a student may be unable to switch from one counting pattern to another as is often required when using money. Consider the coin group of Figure 4.11. One way to organize the counting is shown in Figure 4.12. In this grouping, three counting patterns are involved: fives, tens, and ones. To help develop the needed counting skills, keep charts such as that presented in Figure 4.13. Insert the charts into plastic holders and

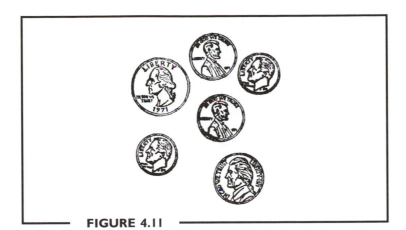

FIGURE 4.11

FIGURE 4.12

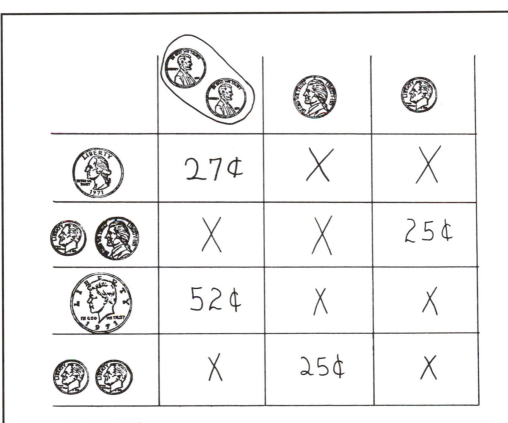

FIGURE 4.13

have the children write on the holders with grease pencils. Have them put a large X in any two squares in each row. In the empty box, instruct them to write the money value obtained after they count the coins to the left and above the empty space. If fine motor coordination is a problem, eliminate the writing (the goal is to develop switch counting, not writing). Have the children place chips, with the correct value written on them, in the empty spaces. When the card is filled in, the children can use an answer key to grade it, or the teacher or another student can check it. Children then can read the entire sequence aloud.

- *Examples* (refer to Figure 4.13):

    "Row 1: 25-27¢"
    "Row 2: 10-15-25¢"

- *Follow-Up:* Counting money requires good auditory processing and visual, auditory, and sequential memory. Writing values down while counting aids learning, but eventually one has to be able to add coin values mentally. Consequently, the next step in the preceding activity involves having children cover two squares in each row as before. Instead of writing the total value obtained, however, they are to count the entire sequence aloud to the teacher or a friend, or into a tape recorder.

3. **Money line** (alternate approach). Another approach to helping students count to determine the value of a group of coins consists of using tailed coins on a money line. In Figure 4.14a, for example, the child is given one quarter, one nickel, two dimes, and one penny to count. Tailed coins for each of these coins are chosen and placed end to end on the money line, greatest valued coins first (Figure 4.14b). Figure 4.15 illustrates the use of the money line to build or reinforce skills for "switch" skip counting. The children can practice using the tailed coins or refer to them, as necessary, until they master the technique using real coins.

COUNTING MONEY AMOUNTS TO ONE DOLLAR USING QUARTER COIN SUBSTITUTES

Problem Area: Difficulty determining the value of a group of coins which includes a cluster of coins equivalent to the quarter rather than a quarter itself.

Typical Disabilities Affecting Progress: Difficulty with integrative processing and closure.

Background: There are many ways to make amounts like 76¢ or 63¢ using different combinations of coins. Children must learn to recognize various equivalent coin combinations. This is usually most difficult for larger amounts—50¢ to

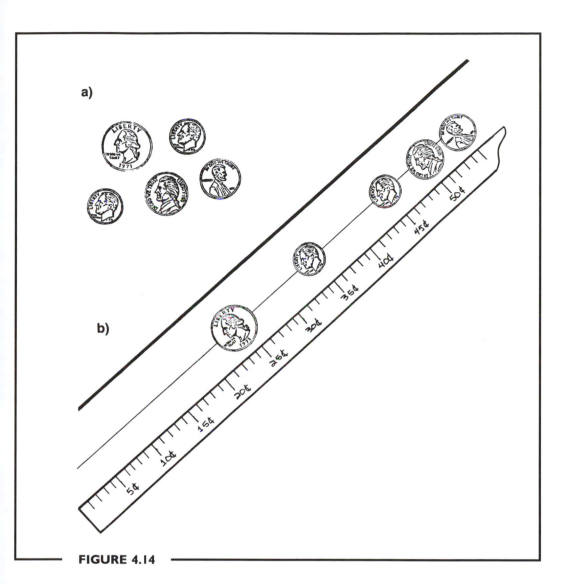

FIGURE 4.14

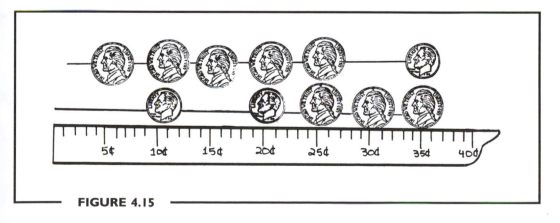

FIGURE 4.15

one dollar. The group of coins in Figure 4.16 is representative of a frequently used coin substitution. After a fair amount of experience counting coins, most children automatically recognize two dimes and one nickel as being worth 25 cents. The child with learning disabilities may recognize this, too. Unfortunately, however, there may not be an automatic transfer in thought to the conclusion "a quarter—therefore, the value of this group is 50 cents, because two quarters make 50 cents."

One approach to this problem would be to teach children to group the coins differently and to find another counting pattern. They could, for example, begin with the single coin that is worth the most money. However, for most older children, it is more expedient to recognize the substitution and learn to use it. The following activities help develop this skill.

FIGURE 4.16

SUGGESTED SEQUENCE OF ACTIVITIES

1. **The odd pieces.** Younger children enjoy puzzles. Those shown in Figure 4.17 can be cut out, pasted on 3″ × 5″ index cards, and used for individual activities in a learning center. Note the circling to cue recognition of the three coins as one unit, equivalent in value to a quarter. To encourage thinking, include one or two distractors in the puzzle set, like that shown in Figure 4.18. Children could be challenged to find the odd pieces (the distractors).

2. **Bingo.** Make bingo cards, similar to those in Figure 4.5. The calling cards should have coins pictured on them like those on the right of the Figure 4.17 puzzle pieces. The game is played like regular bingo.

3. **Fill in.** For older children, keep dittos such as those in Figure 4.19. Figure 4.19a is especially helpful for students with expressive language deficits. Gradually the transition can be made to pages like that of Figure 4.19b.

PAYING FOR ITEMS AND MAKING CHANGE FOR AMOUNTS TO ONE DOLLAR

Problem Areas: Difficulty selecting, from a larger collection of coins, money needed to pay for an item; difficulty making change for values to one dollar.

Typical Disabilities Affecting Progress: Difficulty with auditory sequencing, integrative processing, closure, sequential memory, visual figure-ground.

Background: Being able to count and tell the value of a group of coins is a prerequisite to a more challenging skill: being able to select, from a larger collection, those coins needed to make a given amount. This latter skill is needed in day-to-day situations as one examines the coins in a purse or pocket to see if there is enough to pay for an item. Some students with learning disabilities cannot apply the first skill to real-life situations. Children with figure-ground difficulties often

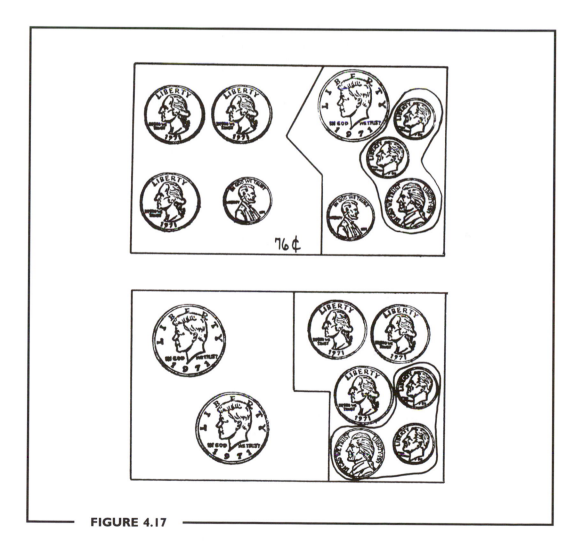

FIGURE 4.17

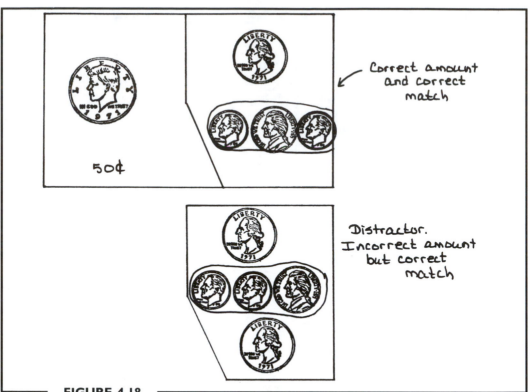

Correct amount and correct match

50¢

Distractor. Incorrect amount but correct match

FIGURE 4.18

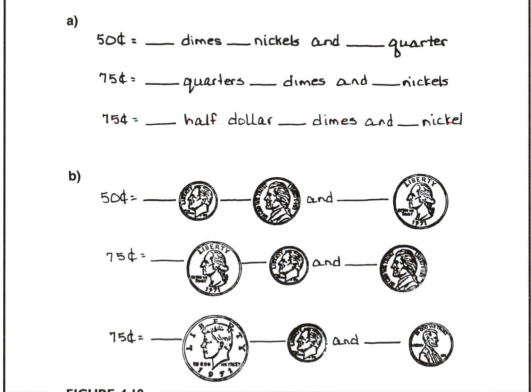

a)

50¢ = ___ dimes ___ nickels and ___ quarter

75¢ = ___ quarters ___ dimes and ___ nickels

75¢ = ___ half dollar ___ dimes and ___ nickel

b)

50¢ = ___ ⬤ ___ ⬤ and ___ ⬤

75¢ = ___ ⬤ ___ ⬤ and ___ ⬤

75¢ = ___ ⬤ ___ ⬤ and ___ ⬤

FIGURE 4.19

have problems finding the coins they want because they cannot sort them out from the group. Other children may become frustrated because the simplest (most familiar) way of making up a given amount is not possible with the coins they have. The first set of activities below suggests ways of handling these problems. The other activities in this section focus on another important skill—checking change received. Modern cash registers subtract the cost from the amount given to a clerk, telling how much change should be given in return. The most efficient way to check in this situation is to *count up* from the cost until the amount paid is reached. This, of course, is the common procedure used by cashiers for giving change if their registers do not internally subtract and display the amount to be given back.

Learning to count out one's change in this way is perhaps the most difficult money skill to master. Children must realize that the exact amount of money needed to pay for an item is not always available. Sometimes one has to pay more than an item is worth, and then receive change in return. To determine the amount of money to be given (or received) as change, a new counting process is required. When counting to find the value of a group of coins, children often start with the single coin of greatest value. It is now necessary to retain the purchase price in memory and count on from this cost using smaller valued coins first. Other coins are added until the amount paid is reached. Children with sequential-memory problems usually find this very difficult. Other children having the disabilities identified above may fail to recognize the different skip counting patterns involved or be unable to produce them automatically. The second set of activities that follows has proven helpful in dealing with these problems.

SUGGESTED SEQUENCE OF ACTIVITIES

Paying for an Item

1. **You find.** Some students with figure-ground difficulties find it hard to locate, from a larger collection, the coins they need to pay for an item. For them, laminated cards and priced items such as those of Figure 4.20 are helpful. The cards show the coins available to pay for an item. The child draws a card and takes (from a bank of extra coins) all the coins pictured on the card. If necessary, allow the student to place coins on top of those pictured until the card is full. These coins are then placed in a separate pile. Next show the child a picture of an item to be purchased, such as the bat in the first example of Figure 4.20. With a grease pencil draw a circle around the coins on the child's card that are needed to pay for that item. "You need a dime and a nickel" (Figure 4.20a). Instruct the child to select coins from the pile to cover those circled on the card. Repeat, using different cards or different items to be purchased. Children gradually learn to circle and tell the needed coins independently. As they become more proficient, the cir-

cling can be eliminated and they can merely cover the correct cards. In our experience, this approach leads to independent recognition of needed coins.

2. **Pay.** Set up a "store" in the classroom and give each child a purse or envelope of coins. (Alternatively, a container of coins could be placed on the cashier's counter for all the children to use.) At first, as students pay for items, accept any coins they give to pay for an item (as long as the amount given is correct). For example, a child may choose to use two nickels rather than a dime. By observing a child's pattern of coin selection, the teacher can gradually suggest better choices, in a manner that is logical to that student. One might provide enough coins so that a child can pay for a given item in at least two different ways. If the child uses the fewest possible coins to pay for an item, a compliment is in order. If, on the other hand, the child gives a combination that involves more coins than required, point out that there is a better way. "Yes, a dime and five pennies equals 15¢. That is good, but did you notice that you can use one nickel in place of these five pennies?" Or, "You used six coins. Can you pay using only two coins?"

- *Follow-Up:* Use worksheets such as that illustrated in Figure 4.21. If necessary, use the coin line color to outline the circles on the page. Gradually, eliminate this prompt.

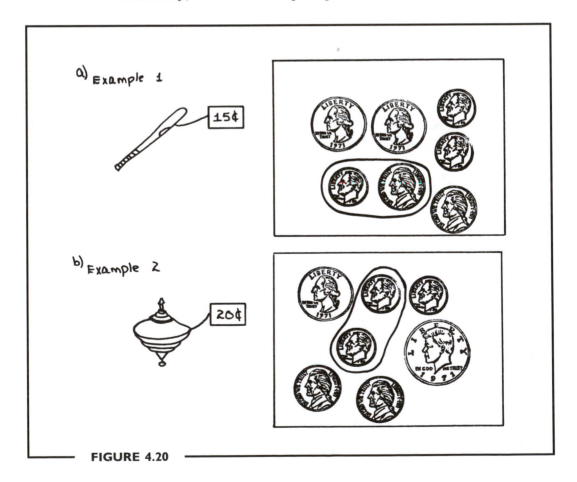

FIGURE 4.20

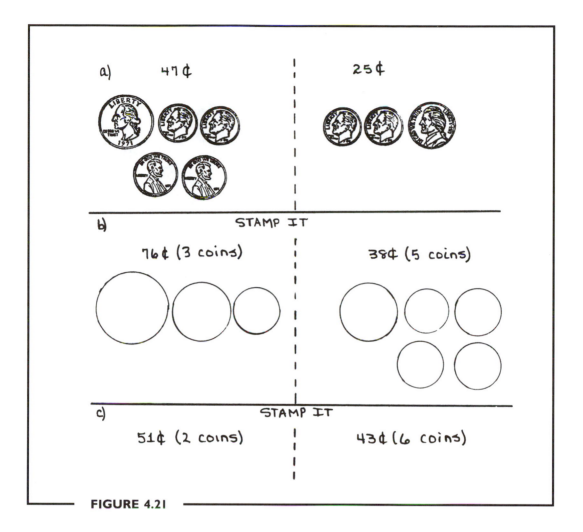

FIGURE 4.21

3. **Use what you have.** Point out that sometimes we do not have the proper coins to pay the way we would like. For example, we might want to buy ice cream that costs 25¢. If we do not have a quarter, then two dimes and a nickel, or five nickels, or even 25 pennies will do. Give the student several coins and ask for an amount of money that cannot be made in the "usual way" with the available coins. For example, give five nickels and ask for 20¢. As children become more proficient, give a quarter, five nickels, and four pennies for this task to force selection from a larger group of coins.

- *Follow-Up:* Use worksheets like that of Figure 4.22. For the example shown, the children can circle or place real coins on those pictured to show 20¢. If necessary, use coin line colors to outline the coins needed in the first few exercises.

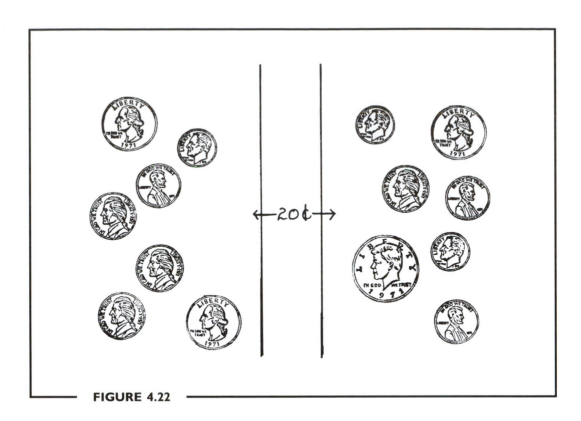

FIGURE 4.22

Making Change for Amounts Paid up to One Dollar

1. **Count up.** Use tailed coins on a money line, as in Figure 4.23, to introduce the idea of counting up to get from one number (the cost) to another (the amount paid). This approach concretizes the process of counting up and aids visual memory. A set of price tag cards, like that shown, is also needed. Children draw a card and place it on the line as illustrated to indicate where one starts the count. Tailed coins are then used to dramatize the counting on to 25¢. Children should be encouraged to use *as few coins as possible*—four pennies and one nickel rather than nine pennies in this example (Figure 4.23).

2. **Go and stop.** At this point, students with auditory-sequencing or memory deficits usually find it easier to turn to worksheets such as that illustrated in Figure 4.24. The first example is for younger children with low reading vocabulary, the second its parallel for older students. Students fill in the first four blanks. Then, as they count up from the cost, they check each coin as if they were actually picking it up. Next they count and record the change—in this example, 9¢.

   To cue meaning, the words "go on" ("begin at") could be written in green and "stop at" in red. For those in need of extra cueing, the word "cost" ("price") could also be coded in green and the words "you give" ("amount

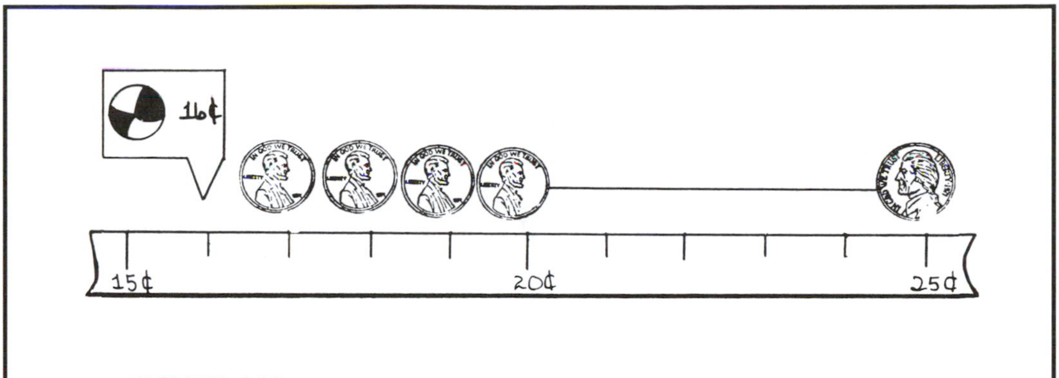

 16¢

15¢   20¢   25¢

FIGURE 4.23

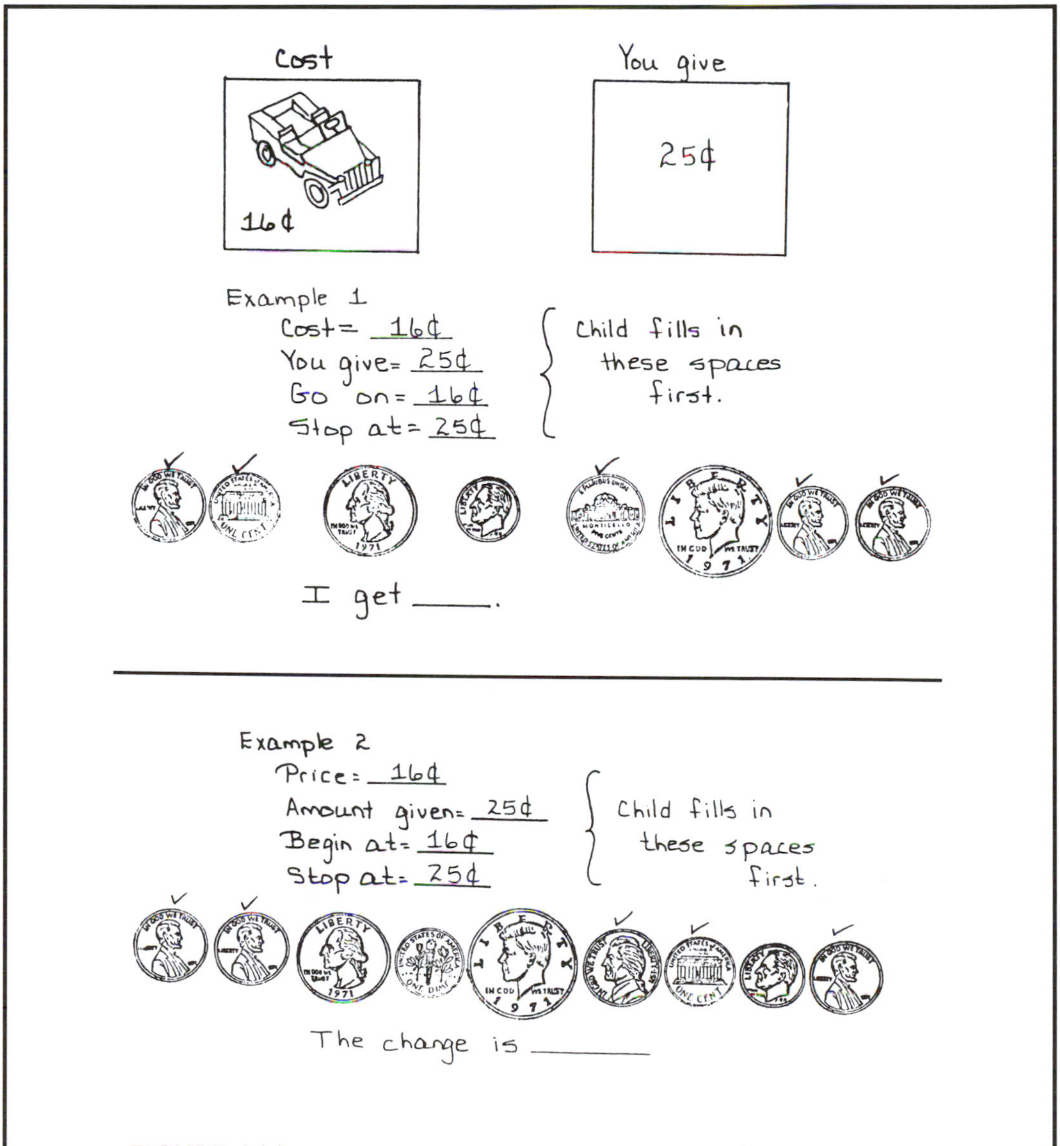

Cost 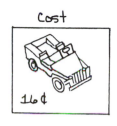 16¢

You give

25¢

Example 1
Cost = _16¢_
You give = _25¢_   } Child fills in
Go on = _16¢_   these spaces
Stop at = _25¢_   first.

I get _____.

Example 2
Price = _16¢_
Amount given = _25¢_   } Child fills in
Begin at = _16¢_   these spaces
Stop at = _25¢_   first.

The change is _____

FIGURE 4.24

given") in red. Answer lines would be colored to match the words. Gradually, all colors would be eliminated as the vocabulary meanings and the counting process itself become internalized. The amount of information to be personally recorded by students is also gradually reduced as they become more proficient at counting. Recording the numbers to "go on" and "stop at" is dropped first. As short-term memory or counting skills improve, the price and the amount given may be eliminated (Figure 4.24).

3. **Real coins now.** As before, but provide real coins rather than stamped pictures of coins. At first, it may be helpful to keep a worksheet showing the coin stamp as reference. If children tend to perseverate, do not be too quick to eliminate the writing while using real coins. It serves to break the counting and hence decreases perseveration.

NOTE: *Children with integrative processing deficits may have difficulty recognizing whether or not they have the correct coins to pay exactly or to make the needed change. They may try to ignore the problem, as in Figure 4.25. In this example, the value of the dimes became meaningless and they were treated as pennies. To help, have the children first fill in the charts of Activity 2 above. Then have them compare the coins they checked with the coins they have. In the example of Figure 4.25, the first coin needed is a penny so the child cannot give the needed change.*

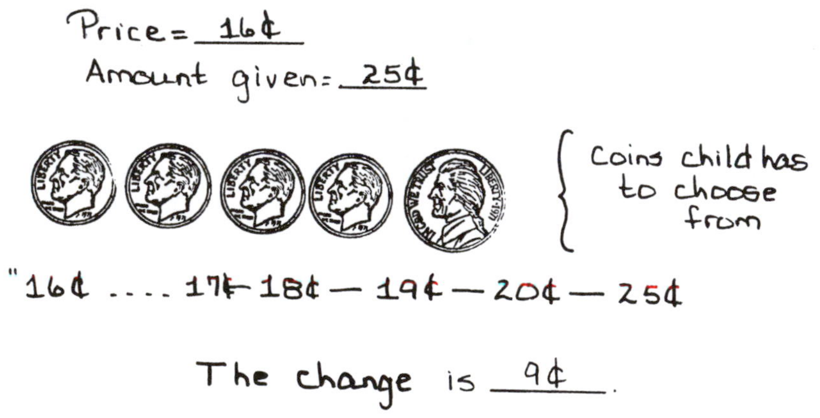

FIGURE 4.25

WRITING MONEY AMOUNTS GREATER THAN ONE DOLLAR

Problem Area: Reversal tendencies or other difficulties in writing money amounts using the dollar sign and decimal point.

Typical Disabilities Affecting Progress: Difficulty with spatial organization; visual perception.

Background: Children who are unable to organize their space due to visual or perceptual deficits or spatial disorganization may have considerable difficulty writing down money values. For example, since we say, "Three dollars and 16 cents," children often reverse the position of the dollar value and the dollar sign (see Figure 4.26). Or they may not associate all the words with symbols. Specifically, they may not "see" the dollar sign and decimal point when reading or writing the numbers. The activities outlined below are directed toward helping students with these problems.

Three dollars and sixteen cents = 3$.16

FIGURE 4.26

SUGGESTED SEQUENCE OF ACTIVITIES

1. **Dollar sign.** For those who have reversal tendencies, it often helps to approach the problem in small steps. If children learn well through kinesthetic involvement, have them finger trace felt numerals and symbols, *dollar value first, then the sign.* Then have them rewrite the pattern traced—*dollar value first, then the sign.* Although this is an unusual order, it provides a more immediate association between words and symbols. Each time a word is said, something is written. The more traditional way requires the student to write one symbol ($) while saying or thinking an unrelated symbol (e.g., 4). Figure 4.27 shows a sample page that might be used as

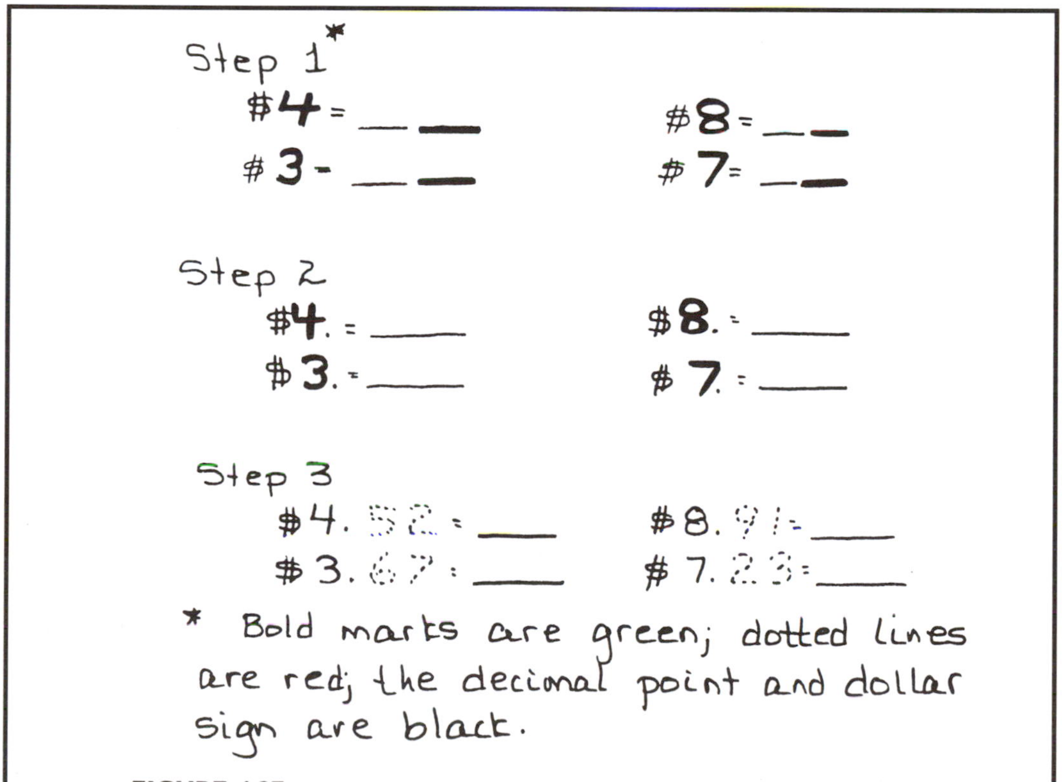

Step 1 *
  $4 = __ __ $8 = __ __
  $3 - __ __ $7 = __ __

Step 2
  $4. = ___ $8. = ___
  $3. = ___ $7. = ___

Step 3
  $4.52 = ___ $8.91 = ___
  $3.67 = ___ $7.23 = ___

* Bold marks are green; dotted lines are red; the decimal point and dollar sign are black.

FIGURE 4.27

a follow-up to this exercise. First, in Step 1, the children finger trace examples and write four dollars ($4) as just described. In Step 2 the decimal point is introduced and associated with the word "and." In the last step the number of cents is included. All three steps provide space (after the "equals" sign on the worksheet) for children to write the money amount independently.

2. **Greatest value.** This is a practice activity for two or three players. Provide the following five dice:

   - Die 1: "$" written on each of the six sides
   - Die 2: "." written on each of the six sides
   - Die 3: 0,1,2,3,4,5
   - Die 4: 0,5,6,7,8,9
   - Die 5: 3,4,5,6,7,8

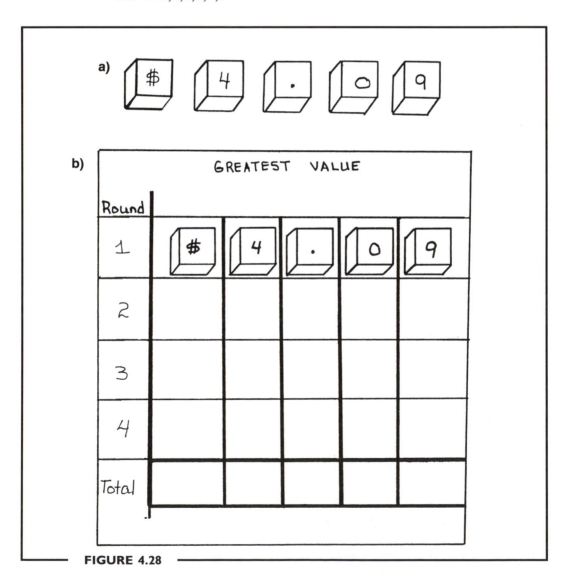

FIGURE 4.28

Also provide a five-space chart for the dice (Figure 4.28a) and a "greatest-value" record sheet for each player (Figure 4.28b). Children take turns throwing the dice and arranging them in the five spaces on the chart to show the greatest dollar value possible. If the amount is written and read (aloud) correctly, it is entered on the player's record sheet for that round. The player with the greatest total after four rounds wins.

NOTE 1: *Using grease pencils or washable markers on the laminated record sheet makes for easy reuse.*

NOTE 2: *If the column addition is too difficult for the students, use a tally system: one tally for dollar values $3.00 or less; two tallies for dollar values between $3.00 and $6.00; and three tallies for dollar values of $6.00 or greater.*

3. **Follow-up.** For additional drill, keep pages on file like that of Figure 4.29. Children read, then write the given dollar value. If reading is a problem, a cassette tape for the left part of the page can be prepared for the children to use while completing the page. The color coding, important in early work, can gradually be eliminated.

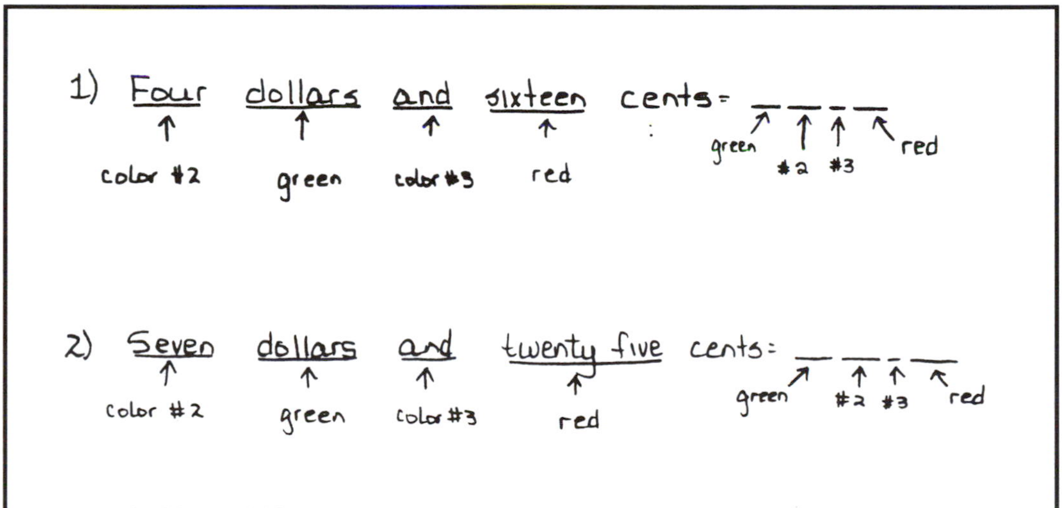

FIGURE 4.29

NOTE 1: It may be preferable to have some students write the dollar value first, then the sign, as explained in Activity 1.

NOTE 2: Being able to read and write number words is important for checkwriting, thus worth the practice focused on in this exercise.

CLASSROOM MATERIALS FOR TEACHING TIME

Most classrooms have a wall clock and perhaps a toy clock for students to use. However, except for workbook pages, there may be little else in the room that is realistically related to teaching time. Several items can greatly aid students in acquiring time concepts and skills:

- Small clock, about four inches in diameter

- Geared clock with a knob on the back to move the hands (the hands should be clearly different in size)

- Clock stamps and ink pads (one red, one green)

The small clock is useful for children with visual discrimination or other perceptual problems. These students may have difficulty with the wall clock because it is too far away for them to make any clear discriminations. Figure 4.30 gives an example of the size and face of the smaller clock. The size of the hands is clearly different, and the minute intervals are spaced far enough apart for the child to point with a finger or a pencil. This type of clock can be used to "feel" the time. This kinesthetic approach is often necessary for children with visual-perceptual or spatial difficulties.

Since it is impractical to teach time only on a real clock, a geared clock provides the next best aid. Children can see how the hands move at different rates. They can actually "feel" the slowness of the hour hand movement in contrast to that of the minute hand.

As digital clocks are so common, children must learn to read them. Most mathematics curricula now include a discussion of them within their chapters on time. Once children can read the numbers on a digital clock, they can be helped to make associations with the standard clock as an aid for "reading" its time.

At this point, it may be appropriate to give a word of caution regarding digital clocks. As convenient and useful as they are for teaching children to tell time, *they do not help develop a sense of time.* It is questionable, at best, whether this

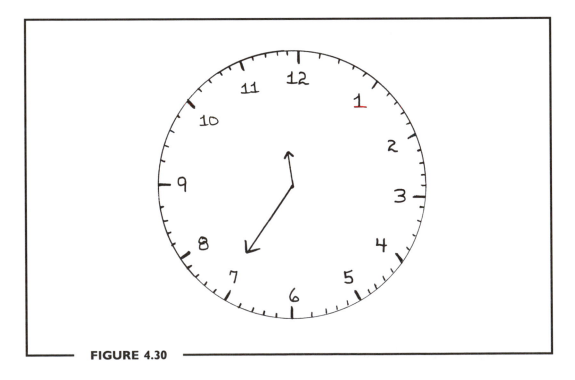

FIGURE 4.30

sense can be taught at all. The movement of time is mysterious enough, and digital clocks only reinforce the magic. A standard clock, however, at least allows some concrete way for children to develop a feel for how long an activity will last. One can, for example, use the overlay and shading technique of Figure 4.31 to illustrate the time allotted to an activity. On a digital clock this is impossible.

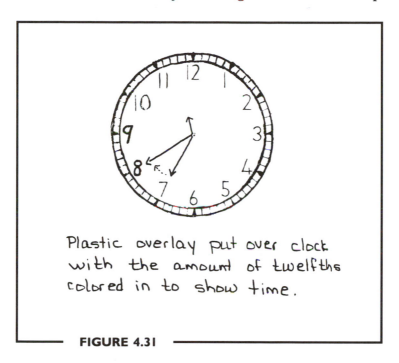

Plastic overlay put over clock with the amount of twelfths colored in to show time.

FIGURE 4.31

Clock stamps are available commercially, and they should be standard materials for every classroom. They can easily be used by both teacher and student. When drawing in the hands, be careful to distinguish clearly between the lengths of the minute and the hour hands. Figure 4.32 illustrates the type of clock stamp we have found most useful.

The sections that follow suggest ways of using these materials to help students with learning disabilities develop important time concepts and skills. In addition, several workpages are illustrated that can be kept on file and used for reinforcement, homework, and other independent work.

READING CLOCK TIMES

Problem Area: Difficulty associating the correct hand on a standard clock with the spoken or written word.

Typical Disabilities Affecting Progress: Difficulty with visual discrimination, visual-sequential memory, short-term memory, visual memory, expressive language.

Background: As mentioned earlier, many children develop some comprehension of time before they enter school. It is not uncommon for young children to be up earlier on school days than on weekends. Once the routine of going to school

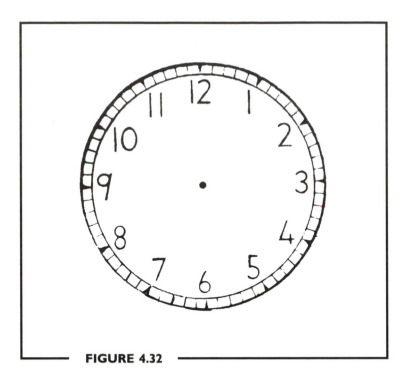

FIGURE 4.32

has been established, their internal clock begins to plan accordingly. They do not automatically begin dressing for school on Saturday. They may not know why they do not have to, but they have a sense that something is different.

Gradually parents' words begin to have meaning, and on school days children understand that at 8:00 it is time to leave. They may not actually tell time, but if a parent says, "In five minutes it will be eight o'clock," the child understands. Later the clock becomes more meaningful and the child thinks, "The little hand is on the 8. It must be time to go to school."

In the primary grades, intuitive understandings such as these are formally developed. While several sequences can be used to teach a child to read time from a standard clock, one of the more common is the following:

- time by the hour (e.g., 2:00);

- time by the half hour (e.g., 2:30);

- time by the quarter hour (e.g., 2:15 or 2:45);

- time by 5-minute intervals (e.g., 2:25 or 2:40); and finally

- time by minute intervals (e.g., 2:26 or 2:41).

For most children this sequence works well. When teaching time on the hour, many teachers simplify the clock as in Figure 4.33a. Using a clock with only an hour hand makes it possible for most children to "tell time" as soon as they can read the numerals 1 to 12. Then the child can relate this one-handed clock to a spinner and "read time" by telling the number the hand is closest to. When children can tell time to the nearest hour in this way, the teacher can point out the hour hand on a *two-handed clock*. The next step is to practice telling time on this type of clock by focusing on the hour hand as in Figure 4.33b. If necessary in early work with the two-handed clock, children may be instructed to cover the minute hand.

When children can read and write 2-digit numbers, the spinner idea can be introduced for reading minutes (Figure 4.33c). Now the child tells time more precisely by reading the "hour" then the "minute" spinner. Gradually, the association can be made between the minutes and the 12 clock digits. Additional experiences with a geared clock can help children see that as the hour hand moves from one hour to the next, the minute hand travels all the way around the clock. Children with good visual perception and long-term memory quickly learn to associate what

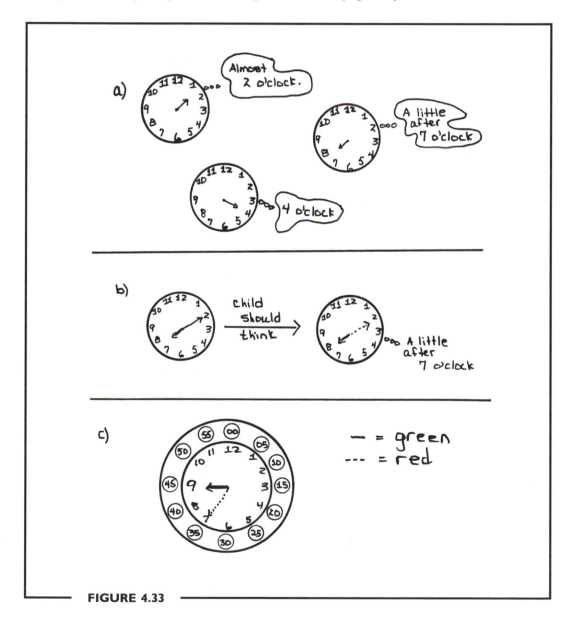

FIGURE 4.33

one says for given configurations of the hands. For example, "The little hand moves from one hour to the next, the minute hand travels all the way around the clock."

> **NOTE:** *The above approach often does not work with students who have memory difficulties as there is too much to recall and the sequence is not consistent. Instead, these students often benefit more from learning first to tell time by the hour and then by 5-minute increments. Emphasis is still on the meaning of the clock hands, but visual memory and sequencing are reinforced because the student gradually moves around the clock in a consistent manner. Additionally, students with memory problems, who may not automatically remember to say 6:45, for example, have a way of helping themselves by counting by fives. Later, after the student has learned to tell time in this manner, emphasis can be put on recognizing fractional segments of half hour and quarter hour.*

Students using the "5-minute" approach especially benefit from using the spinner depicted in Figure 4.33. The spinner provides a visual, logical framework for reading minutes and aids in recall when memory fails. In addition, as fractional segments are emphasized, most children can more easily learn to count on from these points.

Children with learning disabilities, particularly those with the disabilities described at the beginning of this section, may find even these simple approaches to telling time difficult. One common problem relates to correctly locating where the hands are pointing. Another involves being able correctly to associate each hand with what one should say in order to read the time indicated by the hand. For example, some students with learning disabilities who can skip count by fives, fail, even after repeated use of the skip counting technique, to make the necessary association. The following activities have proven successful in handling these difficulties. Since the goal is for children to read the hour first, followed by minutes, green color coding is used for hour times, red for minutes.

SUGGESTED SEQUENCE OF ACTIVITIES

1. **Hour hand first.** On a large tagboard circle, glue or draw small circles at each of the 12 clock positions, as in Figure 4.34a. Make a deck of 52 cards, all circles, similar to those shown in Figure 4.34b. The circles should be the same size as those drawn in the clock positions of the larger circle. Place the numerals 1 through 12 (four of each numeral) in the same relative position on the smaller circles as they would appear on a standard clock. Write the numeral 13 on the remaining four circles. The numerals and the small arrow that simulates the hour hand should be green. The child "deals," placing one card from the deck face down on each of the 12 clock positions of the large circle. A 13th card is placed in the center. This procedure continues until all 52 cards have been placed on the board (Figure 4.35).

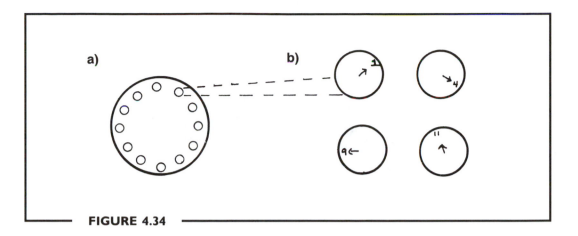

FIGURE 4.34

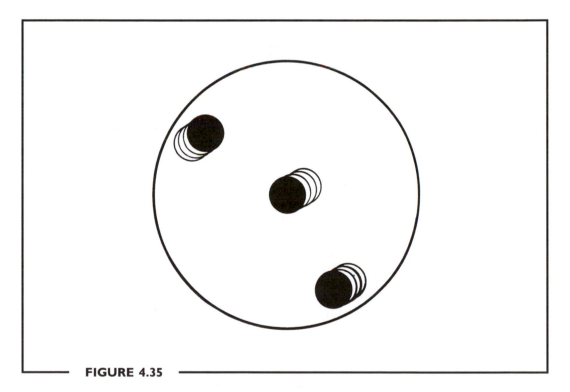

FIGURE 4.35

The child turns over the first card of the center pile and places it, face up, under the pile on the board that corresponds to the clock position shown (see Figure 4.36). The top card of that pile is then turned over and play continues as before. Every time "13" is turned over, it is placed face up under the four cards in the center. The child wins the game if all the cards are placed face up in the proper position on the board before the four cards with "13" are uncovered.

- *Variation:* As before, but the child says the hour time whenever a card is properly placed.

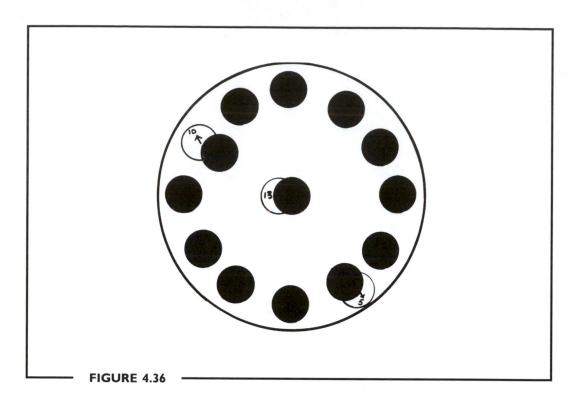

FIGURE 4.36

2. **Now minutes.** A game similar to that of Activity 1 can be played to reinforce the skip counting pattern of the minute hand. This time, make 52 cards beginning with 00 and stopping at 60 (the 60 is for the center pile). The hand pointing to the minutes numeral must be noticeably longer than the hour hand in Activity 1, and red, as shown in Figure 4.37. Use the large circle of Activity 1, but place a rim around the outside containing 12 circles for the 5-minute times (see Figure 4.38).

3. **Both hands.** Play the following bingo-type game. Make a set of calling cards picturing times on standard clocks. Use green for the hour hand and red for the minute hand. Provide 4″ × 4″ gameboards for students with times written at the bottom of each square, as shown in Figure 4.39. Give each child 16 "clock" chips that fit into the space above each time written on the gameboard (see Figure 4.40). These can be made by placing gummed

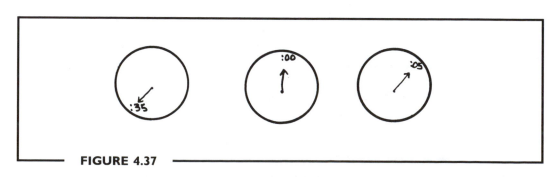

FIGURE 4.37

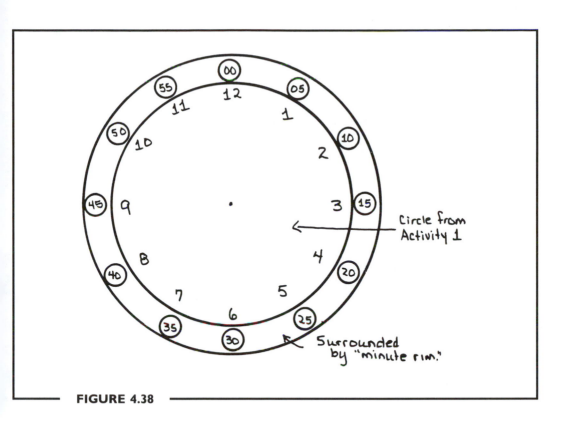

00
05
10
15
20
25
30
35
40
45
50
55
12
1
2
3
4
5
6
7
8
9
10
11
Circle from Activity 1
Surrounded by "minute rim."

FIGURE 4.38

4:30	3:10	6:55	8:40
9:20	2:15	7:30	10:50
5:40	6:05	12:45	9:10
8:00	2:30	1:25	4:35

FIGURE 4.39

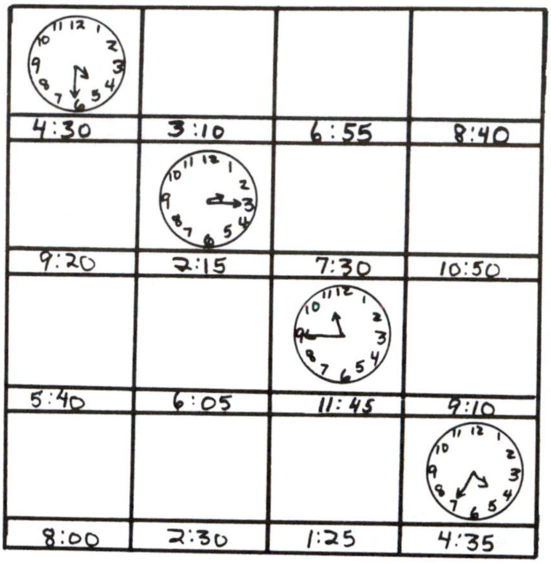

4:30	3:10	6:55	8:40
9:20	2:15	7:30	10:50
5:40	6:05	11:45	9:10
8:00	2:30	1:25	4:35

FIGURE 4.40

labels on ordinary gameboard chips and drawing a clock face on the label. Do not color code the hands on the clock chips. To play, a caller (child or teacher) holds up a color-coded clock. Players decide whether the time shown by that clock is on their gameboard. If so, they place a clock chip showing the same time on the gameboard just above the written time. The winner is the first person to complete a row in any direction.

NOTE: *If the gameboards are covered with acetate or clear contact paper, color coding can be used, when needed, and wiped off. Hour digit(s) would be green, minute digits red.*

- *Variation 1:* Alter the activity by placing clock faces on the gameboard and color-coded numbers on the calling cards. Game chips would also contain the written clock times. If necessary, these can also be color coded.

- *Variation 2:* Place clock chips upside down on the board to match the clock times shown. As a card is held up, the players decide whether they have that time on their individual board. If so, the chip is turned over. The first player to complete correctly a row in any direction wins.

READING AND WRITING CLOCK TIMES

Problem Area: Difficulty telling time on a real clock.

Typical Disabilities Affecting Progress: Difficulty with spatial organization, visual perception, visual-sequential memory, short-term memory, and expressive language.

Background: Many children with learning disabilities need a considerable amount of paper-and-pencil practice before they can use a real clock to tell time. The paper-and-pencil activities provide:

- Overlearning;

- Less interference from visual-perception deficits because of the proximity of the paper;

- Kinesthetic involvement for children who need it (they can run their fingers or pencils along the paper and feel where the hand is); and

- Sequencing cues.

The following ideas can be used to accomplish these goals.

SUGGESTED SEQUENCE OF ACTIVITIES

1. **Color-coded dittos.** Several types of dittos can be filed for ready use. In Figure 4.41 the numerals 1 through 12 are green while 00 through 55 are red. The boxes below the clock are also coded, the first green, the second red. The use of boxes rather than lines during early practice strengthens the relationship between digital and standard clocks, a relationship that must be directly reinforced for some children. One approach consists of hav-

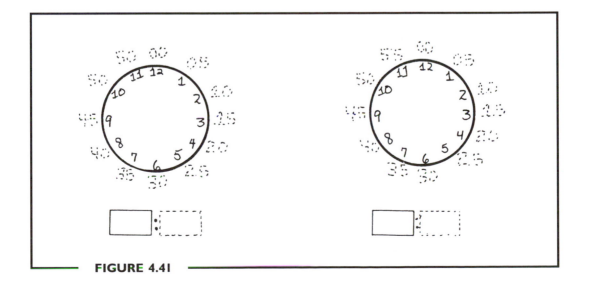

FIGURE 4.41

ing the students themselves draw a simple version of a digital clock and then use that picture as a model for the worksheet boxes.

2. **Fade the cue.** Figure 4.42 illustrates one way of gradually fading the color cue. First the red numbers are replaced with red dots. The next step eliminates the colors on the clock hands. For some children, especially those with severe visual perception difficulties, the colors in the boxes may be eliminated first, followed by the colors on the hands. An alternative would be to keep pages on file, such as those shown in Figure 4.43, with a color-coded example at the top. In Figure 4.43a, the remainder of the clocks have only green and red lines for answers. Make the green line noticeably shorter than the red line. Provide auditory cueing by asking the child which hand on the clock looks most like the short green line. "Which hand do you 'go' on?"

3. **Card to help.** For students needing color reinforcement, especially as they make the transition to the real clock, keep a tagboard clock in the room. Cover it with acetate or contact paper so it can be color coded when needed. If color cueing is necessary, the child can use a green and red marker or grease pencil to write over the numbers. (If this proves too difficult, motorically, the teacher should do it.) The child can use this card to help associate the clock hands and the sequence for reading clock times.

4. **Strips.** As children make the transition to a real clock, they may still need to write down what they see before they are able to express it. This is especially true for:

   • Students with memory problems that prevent them from retaining an entire sequence; and

   • Students with expressive language difficulties who have trouble learning if their flow of thought is interrupted.

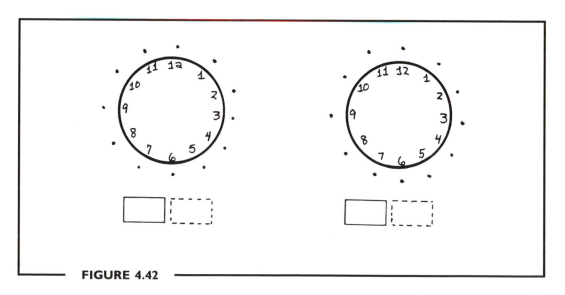

FIGURE 4.42

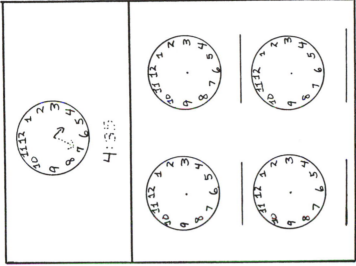

b)

Sample page for child who just needs a reminder, but is strong in skip counting by 5's. Nothing is color coded except example at the top. (Hour hand and "4" are green; dotted figures are red.)

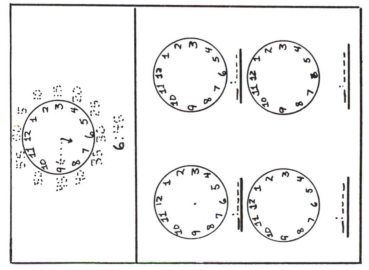

a)

Sample page for child who still needs colors but is beginning to make a transition. Bold hands and hour digits are green; dotted figures are red.

FIGURE 4.43

The writing process is an intermediate step that allows students to focus on one part of the sequence at a time until overlearning has occurred. Keep strips available such as those shown in Figure 4.44. The children can work in pairs to complete the strips. Using the geared clock, one child sets the time shown on one of the clocks in Figure 4.44a. The other writes the time down on paper, as in Figure 4.44b. If necessary, clocks on the strips can be color coded to aid students in expressing times correctly—hour first, then minutes. Make the hour hand green and the minute hand red, as suggested earlier.

NAMING THE CORRECT HOUR

Problem Area: Difficulty knowing which direction to look when the hour hand is between two numbers.

Typical Disabilities Affecting Progress: Difficulty with spatial orientation, visual perception, and memory.

Background: Some children may know what words and numbers to associate with each hand. They may have learned which hand to look at first. Yet, they may

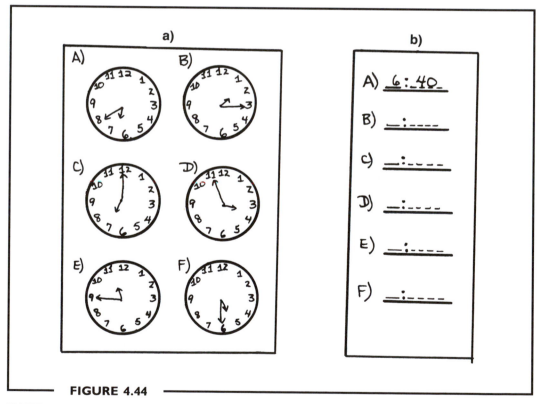

FIGURE 4.44

NOTE: The worksheets illustrated in this section, especially those with color coding and numbers around the outside rim, make it possible to teach time even to children who are weak on skip counting by fives. For many, this approach provides the way to overlearning.

still be uncertain about which number to use when the hour hand is between two numbers. If their spatial abilities are weak, telling them to look at the number "in front of" or "before" may be meaningless. Likewise, asking them to look at the lower number is also confusing. What is the "lower number"? There is no numeral underneath the 1. What happens when the hour hand is between the 12 and the 1? The following ideas should prove helpful in handling this problem.

SUGGESTED SEQUENCE OF ACTIVITIES

1. **Point the way.** Make a small green arrow, as in Figure 4.45 , which fits around the small desk clock. When the children are working with the clock, have them place the arrow at the top of the hour hand so it curves around and points to the correct number. A small hook could also be used on the clock pages.

   - *Variation:* If children have trouble manipulating the arrow, keep a clear plastic overlay that covers the clock face. Using a marker or grease pencil, draw an arrow on the face. The child can then place the plastic face over the real clock and rotate it until the arrow is in place.

2. **Reinforce.** When providing children with clock pages for practice, include the arrows on the page. Have the children run a pencil, or preferably a finger, over the line and say the number pointed to. In our experience, with continued kinesthetic reinforcement of this type, even young children are soon able to draw their own lines well enough to determine which number to look to for the hour.

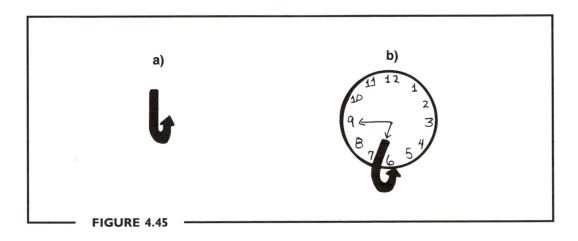

FIGURE 4.45

UNDERSTANDING THE MANY WAYS TO TELL TIME

Problem Area: Understanding temporal expressions including "past," "after," "before," and "until."

Typical Disabilities Affecting Progress: Difficulty with spatial organization, receptive language, and abstract reasoning.

Background: Time can be expressed in many different ways. For the child with abstract reasoning or receptive language deficits, this can prove very frustrating. When looking at the clock in Figure 4.46, for example, this child is likely to hear it described in any of the following ways:

- six forty;

- twenty minutes until seven;

- forty minutes after six;

- twenty minutes before seven; or

- forty minutes past six.

The child is expected to associate the correct time with all the possible descriptions. For the very young child or for the student with learning disabilities, it is often impossible to make these transfers. Even though the various ways of naming a certain time may not be formally taught, most young children gradually catch on to these expressions as they mature and repeatedly hear them in daily situations. However, because of the deficits just identified, many students with learning disabilities may be unable to relate to all these expressions without special help.

Children who have trouble with multiple meanings or synonyms need to learn the different expressions one at a time. Initially, tell the time by using only the numbers themselves: "It is now 1:20 and it's time for math." Do not confuse the

FIGURE 4.46

child by saying, "It's twenty past one," until you are sure the child understands the meaning of "past." It may be difficult to use only one format consistently, but it is essential for these children to have a carefully structured program. The various terms can be incorporated into the time unit by using the circular number line described in the following paragraph. After children clearly understand the similarity between 5:20 and 20 minutes after 5, the term "past" can be introduced. Similarly, when children can relate time expressions like 5:40 and 20 minutes before 6, then "until" may be introduced. The sequence outlined here can be adapted for this purpose.

SUGGESTED SEQUENCE OF ACTIVITIES

Minutes "After" and Minutes "Before"

1. **Circular number line.** Once children are able to tell time using numbers only, review the concepts "before" and "after" using a circular number line (spinner, with the numbers written in sequence rather than in random order). Establish the idea that, on the circle (spinner), "after" still means that the numbers get larger, only now the direction changes. Instead of going forwards and backwards, we are going around. To help establish eye movement on the clock, present pages such as those shown in Figure 4.47.

2. **Geared clock.** Once the ideas of "before" and "after" are clear to students, begin relating these concepts to a clock. Use the geared clock and ask the children to turn the hands according to your instructions (see Figure 4.48). At this point, the single goal is to get the children to "feel" how clock hands move in different directions.

3. **Worksheets.** Practice pages of color-coded clocks, such as that in Figure 4.49, are often helpful. On these clocks, the numerals 1 through 5 are green and 7 through 11 are red. The child writes the time shown and then fills in the second blank below the clock.

   NOTE: *A prerequisite at this point is knowing which hand represents minutes and which represents hours. The children will then know what hand to look to when deciding the number of minutes "before" or "after" an hour. Children should also know, for any given hour, what the* next *hour will be. This skill is necessary to help them determine the time before and after an hour. For example, 6:40 means 20 minutes before (the next hour) 7.*

4. **Toward "overlearning."** For students requiring overlearning, provide several practice pages using only one concept ("after" *or* "before"). Very shortly, however, the pages should be mixed, using both before and after. Mixing

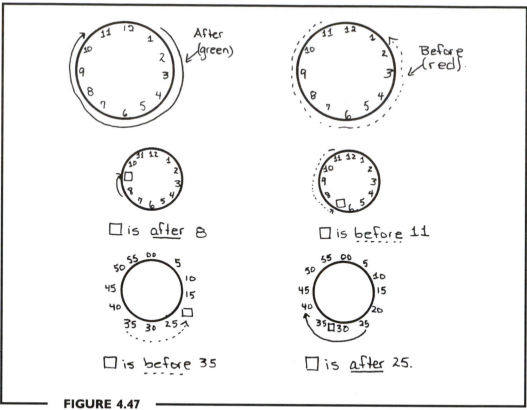

□ is <u>after</u> 8

□ is <u>before</u> 11

□ is <u>before</u> 35

□ is <u>after</u> 25.

FIGURE 4.47

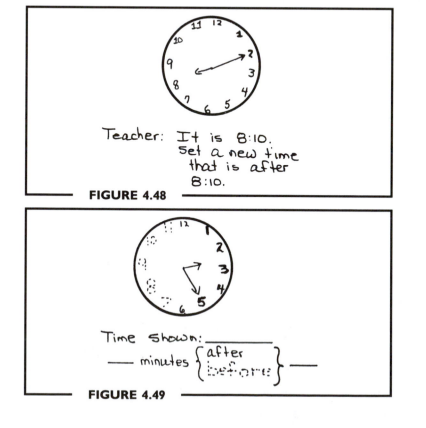

Teacher: It is 8:10.
Set a new time
that is after
8:10.

FIGURE 4.48

Time shown: _____
___ minutes { after / before } ___

FIGURE 4.49

the concepts will avoid perseveration while providing opportunities for reasoning and problem solving.

5. **One step only.** Figure 4.50 shows a useful sequence for students who need help developing a one-step procedure for telling time. As shown in Figure 4.50a, students first write the time and then the equivalent expression using "minutes before" or "minutes after." Initially, decision making is aided by color coding the words "before" and "after." Students who do not have fine motor problems should be encouraged to write over the phrase as they say it. As students become more secure with this two-step process, begin to eliminate the first step, that of writing down the digital time, and extend the decision-making process as in Figure 4.50b.

6. **Puzzle match.** For an independent activity, make puzzle cards like those shown in Figure 4.51. Whenever the word "before" is used, the clock is on the right. For the word "after," the clock is on the left.

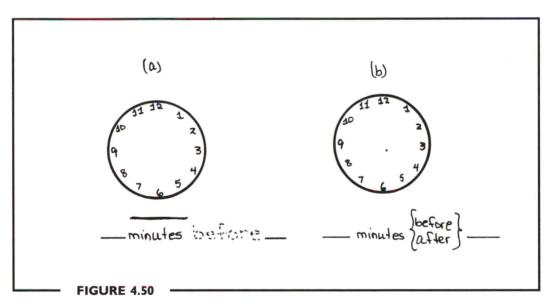

FIGURE 4.50

NOTE: An intermediate step might include highlighting each side of the clock in Figure 4.50b as in Figure 4.49.

7. **Special help.** For children with receptive language deficits, pages like that in Figure 4.52 present a helpful way to build up comprehension. Initially, allow the children to keep a standard clock in front of them. Gradually eliminate the clock, since the use of the words "before" and "after" in time expressions requires comprehension even though no clock may be visible. If the student has reading problems, provide a tape for use in conjunction with the page.

FIGURE 4.51

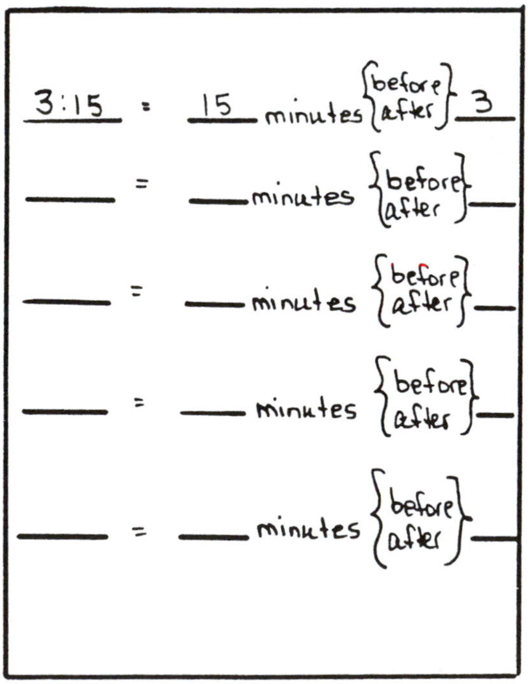

$$3:15 \; = \; \underline{\;15\;}\text{ minutes} \begin{Bmatrix} \text{before} \\ \text{after} \end{Bmatrix} \underline{\;3\;}$$

$$\underline{\qquad} \; = \; \underline{\qquad}\text{minutes} \begin{Bmatrix} \text{before} \\ \text{after} \end{Bmatrix} \underline{\qquad}$$

$$\underline{\qquad} \; = \; \underline{\qquad}\text{minutes} \begin{Bmatrix} \text{before} \\ \text{after} \end{Bmatrix} \underline{\qquad}$$

$$\underline{\qquad} \; = \; \underline{\qquad}\text{minutes} \begin{Bmatrix} \text{before} \\ \text{after} \end{Bmatrix} \underline{\qquad}$$

$$\underline{\qquad} \; = \; \underline{\qquad}\text{minutes} \begin{Bmatrix} \text{before} \\ \text{after} \end{Bmatrix} \underline{\qquad}$$

FIGURE 4.52

UNDERSTANDING AND USING TEMPORAL EXPRESSIONS

Problem Area: Difficulty understanding and correctly using temporal expressions like "in ____ minutes," "____ minutes ago," "earlier" and "later," and so on.

Typical Disabilities Affecting Progress: Difficulty with spatial organization, receptive or expressive language, and closure.

Background: For some children with learning disabilities, the process of telling time signifies nothing more than looking at the clock and saying some numbers. While this helps them get where they have to be on time and know what time an activity is to begin, this skill alone does not enable them to predict or plan their time. Some children, particularly those with language or spatial deficits, do not understand temporal expressions like "in 10 minutes" or "15 minutes ago," "earlier" or "later." They hear a familiar word, such as "in," but because it is used in an unfamiliar context they cannot meaningfully relate to it. Being able to read time from a clock and being able to interpret, predict, and plan, based on one's ability to tell time, are two distinct abilities. It is important that children develop both these skills. The activities that follow address one aspect of developing *a sense of time* or an *awareness of time* beyond merely reading clock numbers. The goal is to help students learn and meaningfully use expressions such as "in ____ minutes," "____ minutes ago"; "earlier," and "later." The basic ideas presented can be adapted for helping children with learning disabilities understand and use other temporal expressions as well.

SUGGESTED SEQUENCE OF ACTIVITIES

Prerequisite Skills: Children should be able to handle the following successfully:

- Skip counting by 5s to 55;

- Counting on from within this counting sequence, with visual reinforcement;

- Understanding the meanings of "before" and "after" for clock times;

- Understanding which hand moves most rapidly and, ideally, associate it with minutes; and

- Identifying the minute hand on the clock and realizing that one counts on from this hand (the minute hand, not the hour hand) to determine "in ____ minutes" or "____ ago."

Basic Sequence

1. **Move forward to see.** Set a time on a geared or a real clock. At first, use only "5-minute" times like 2:15, 2:25, or 2:40. Have the children tell or write

the time. Then, while moving the hands of the clock, ask the question, "What time will it be in 5 minutes?" As you say ". . . *in* 5 minutes," emphasize the word "in" and move the hands of the clock. The children then say or write the new time. Continue this procedure until the concept of "in" is firmly established. Do not change the hour during the activity.

2. **Move back.** Use the same procedure to answer the question, "What time was it 5 minutes ago?" Initially, it is important to keep the two questions separate. Once the child readily recognizes the difference between the two words, mix the questions. Children should practice moving the clock hands according to the teacher's instructions. At this point, the teacher may not even require children to tell the time—the major goal is for students to develop, kinesthetically, the feeling of the two expressions. Later, when they cannot move the hands of a clock, the feeling will still be there. Many children actually move their fingers as if turning the clock. This helps them determine, visually, in which direction to go on the clock when counting.

3. **Minute-hand card.** Give the child a clear plastic minute-hand card with a hole in the center and a long minute hand line (Figure 4.53a). Also provide a page of clocks showing various times. The hole in the card should match the dot where the two clock hands meet in the center. First, the child writes the time shown on a clock. Then the card is placed over the clock face so the minute hand points to the next number, as in Figure 4.53b. The child says, "In 5 minutes it will be 6:45." As the child gains proficiency, use intervals other than 5 minutes. Use the minute-hand card as long as it is needed. Direct the child to point it to the next numeral—that which indicates the next time for minutes. This will ensure counting on from the proper place.

   • *Variation:* For those with good visual imagery, an alternative is to have the child use a finger and point to the next number.

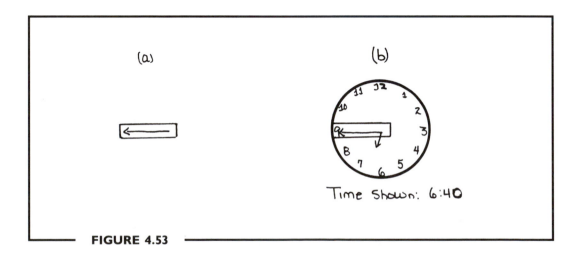

FIGURE 4.53

4. **Follow-up.** Sample pages to reinforce this skill are shown in Figure 4.54a. As noted in the previous section, it is often necessary for the children to go through the two-step process at first. Initially, the pages deal with only one concept. As students are ready, move to pages that mix the ideas, as in Figure 4.54b.

5. **One step only.** When the child no longer needs to write down the time, eliminate this step. Show the child how to use a finger or the minute card to determine the stated time. For auditory cuing, remind the student to "Think: It is now ____, so in 10 minutes it will be ____."

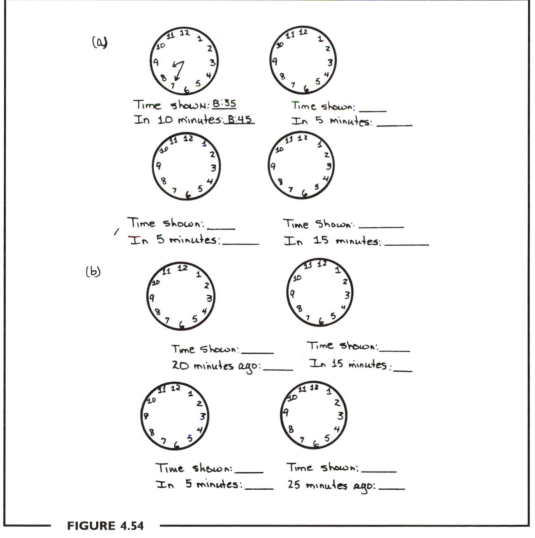

FIGURE 4.54

NOTE: Some children may need help associating "in" and "ago" with "after" and "before." If so, write "in" using green and "ago" using red (refer back to Figure 4.47).

6. **Card game** (for two or three players). A variation of the card game "Go Fish" can now be played. Make a deck of 20 cards with a clock face on each card (Deck A) (see Figure 4.55a). Make a second set of 20 cards with a temporal expression on each (Deck B), as in Figure 4.55b. Each child is dealt five cards from Deck A. The remainder of the cards are placed face down in the center. Deck B is placed face down next to it. Children take turns drawing a card from Deck B and thinking of a card in their hand. Suppose the child has the clock 6:20 from Deck A and draws the expression "in 15 minutes" from Deck B. The person on the left is asked for a clock showing the time 6:35. If that student has the card, it is given to the caller, who lays down the pair. The child places the expression card in a discard pile and the game moves on. If the child makes a mistake or if the child to the left does not have the requested clock, the caller draws from the fish pile until the correct clock is drawn or until five cards have been drawn, whichever occurs first. The winner is the one with the most pairs at the end. If necessary, the discard pile is shuffled and reused.

7. **Compare.** For those children who need concrete associations for particular temporal expressions, keep a gameboard such as that shown in Figure 4.56. Also provide a deck of cards with clock faces. Each space on the board counts for 5 minutes. In turn, children draw two cards and place them, in the order drawn, at the bottom of the gameboard. Children verbally fill in the blank and choose the correct word (e.g., "earlier" or "later"). They move by fives to dramatize the difference between the two clock times. Since the cards drawn in Figure 4.56 have a difference of 15 minutes, the child moves backwards three spaces, counting by fives. The move is backwards because the second clock shows an earlier time.

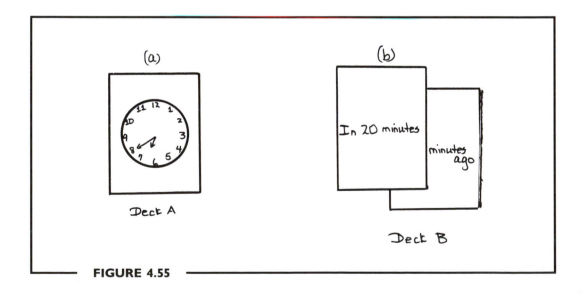

FIGURE 4.55

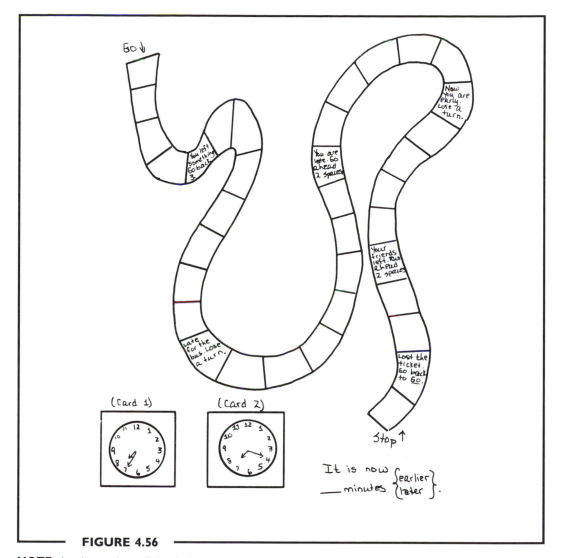

FIGURE 4.56

NOTE: It is best to keep all the clocks within a two-hour time span.

CHAPTER 5

Number and Place Value: Developing "Number Sense"

NUMBER AND PLACE VALUE topics play an important role in primary-school mathematics instruction. In the beginning, children deal only with the numbers 1 to 10 or 12. They count groups of objects and record the number counted; they see and record clock times; they measure and record inch or centimeter measures; they use these numbers in early addition and subtraction work. Once mastered, these topics can be used to help students extend their understanding and ability to deal successfully with 2-, 3-, and higher digit whole numbers.

Each step should begin by modeling the numbers and building accurate and efficient counting techniques. Then, when children can both read and write the associated numerals, number comparisons and sequencing tasks are introduced. Since number words are used in writing checks, these normally are dealt with as soon as a child's reading skills are developed well enough to handle them. Throughout, the overriding goal of developing "number sense" is achieved by providing problem-solving and practical experiences that nurture a "good feel" for the size of number, for operations on numbers, and for relationships between numbers.

It is assumed that teachers and educators using this book are familiar with standard sequences and techniques for developing these topics, as well as with the renewed curricular emphasis on developing "number sense." From the perspective of the child with learning disabilities, however, standard approaches often fall short of meeting specific learning needs. This chapter focuses on seven areas within the early number and place value program that typically are troublesome to students with learning disabilities:

1. Counting in early number work
2. Reversals
3. Extending counting skills: Skip counting by 10s and 5s
4. Comparing numbers
5. Rounding and estimation
6. Reading and interpreting quantitative data from the printed word
7. Writing mathematics

For each of the seven sections, typical disabilities contributing to the problem are identified, and a carefully structured sequence of learning activities and exercises is suggested. Special techniques, such as finger tracing and visual or auditory cueing, are also illustrated.

In an eighth section, Developing Number Sense, more general suggestions for developing number sense over time are presented. Most ideas can be carried out in regular education classrooms as well as in resource or clinical settings. A concluding section, "Using a Hand Calculator," outlines ideas to help students with learning disabilities with number and place-value topics.

COUNTING IN EARLY NUMBER WORK

Problem Area: Inability to count on or back two or three numbers; inability to visually recognize the number of objects in a 10-frame; inability to recognize whether two or three numbers have been said in a vocal count.

Typical Disabilities Affecting Progress: Difficulties with visual or auditory association, closure, figure-ground, expressive language.

Background: The early number program has its roots in counting. Children refine and rely heavily on this skill as they begin addition and subtraction. When the instructional goal shifts to memorizing basic facts, four extensions of counting contribute significantly to a child's success at quickly and accurately deriving answers to *unknown* facts:

- Counting on (2 + 7: "That's 7—8, 9." The child starts with the greater addend and counts on two. The answer or sum is 9.)

- Counting back (9 − 2: "That's 9—8, 7." The child starts with the total and counts back two numbers to 7.)

- Visual recognition of the 10-frame (6 and 4 fill the frame [see Figure 5.1]; 6 + 4 = 10. The 10-frame reference is useful for sums of 10 and related differences.)

- Auditorally recognizing when two or three numbers have been said. (11 − 9: "That's 9—10, 11." The child counted up *two* numbers. The answer is 2.)

Each of these skills involves an extension of counting that can and should be developed in the early number program prior to any work with number facts. Otherwise, we ask children to learn two things at once: (a) the number facts and (b) the counting skills for answering many of the easy number facts quickly. Rather, the goal is to assure that the extended counting skills are intact before we ask children to apply them in early addition-subtraction. After children learn to count linearly in sequence from one, we turn to developing these four useful extensions of counting.

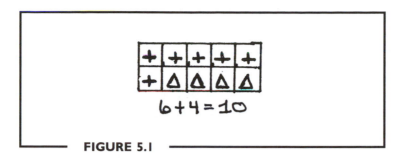

FIGURE 5.1

Auditory Patterning

Is it necessary for children to finger count as they count on to add or count back to subtract 1, 2, or 3? Experience has shown that the following auditory patterning activities, started early, help students internalize these short counts, eliminate the need to finger count, and assist in the counting on and counting backwards skills. The activities sensitize children to the differences between the auditory patterns which accompany the beats of two claps and three claps; the processing of two versus three numbers.

NOTE: *For children with auditory deficits, tap on the child's shoulder or back instead of clapping (Activity 1) or while saying the numbers (Activity 2).*

SUGGESTED SEQUENCE OF ACTIVITIES

1. **How many claps do you hear?** Clap 1, 2, or 3 times and ask students to tell how many claps they heard. When children become comfortable with this activity, proceed to the following activity.

2. **How many numbers do you hear?** Say two or three numbers in sequence (forwards or backwards), and ask students to tell how many numbers they heard.

   • *Examples:*

   > "6, 7, 8." ("Three numbers.")
   > "11, 10." ("Two numbers.")

Repeat this activity frequently. The pay-off comes later in the addition-subtraction program. Given 5 + 3, for example, students tend to begin to recognize (without finger counting) when they have counted on 3 more: "5—6, 7, 8." Or, for problems like 11 − 2, they tend to recognize (without finger counting) when they have counted back 2: "11—10, 9." The following activities involve body movement and further reinforce the auditory patterning for two or three.

3. **Say and stand.** Sit, hands on knees. Say a number (e.g., 9). *Count on two* before you stand. Say the number. Children repeat. Continue, using other numbers. When children are comfortable with the "two more" pattern, carry out the same activity but with the challenge to *count back* two before standing: "8—7, 6."

4. **Toe touch.** Have children stand, both hands above their head. Say a number (e.g., 8). *Count on three* before you touch your toes. Children repeat. Continue, using other numbers. When children are comfortable with the "three more" pattern, carry out a similar activity in which the challenge is to *count back* three before touching toes.

Counting On

Counting on involves two skills which are potentially especially difficult for students with learning disabilities: (a) visualizing groups of objects as a whole and (b) eliciting a number from midpoint. To assist students, ensure that first activities include countable objects or dot cards to reinforce sight groups less than five. Practice eliciting the number after using visual cues as needed. Later, the transition to numbers greater than five is made. Generally, the teacher's immediate goal should be to provide many opportunities in which the first vocal number in a count is *not* "1." These ideas are central to the following sample instructional sequence for children with learning deficits.

SUGGESTED SEQUENCE OF ACTIVITIES

Recognizing Sight Groups

1. **Is this two?** (For individuals or small groups; adapt to large-group instruction by using an overhead projector.) Place two small objects under each of five boxes on a table. Give each child a numeral "2" card showing two spots. One by one, lift each box so that children can have a quick peek before it is put back. Ask: "Is this two?" Start as a group activity, then call on individuals to respond. Check by allowing the children, in turn, to place each object over a spot on their "2" card. Repeat, but vary the arrangement of objects under the boxes. Sometimes place only one object under a box. In some cases, it may be necessary, at first, to use one color for all "2" clusters. Gradually, however, this cue is eliminated.

- *Example:* Let green be the cueing color. At first use only green objects for the "two" clusters: two green sticks under one box; two green beads under another; and so on. As a next step, use objects of different colors for the "two" clusters, but place them inside a green loop, such as that drawn with crayon on paper. Gradually fade the loop out of the picture.

- *Follow-Up Activity:* Have children paste cloth scraps or construction paper pieces, by twos, on cards. "See how many different ways you can make two." Later use the cards, along with others, showing one item or three items in an "Is This Two?" flash card activity.

NOTE: *With some children, especially those having expressive language deficits, it helps to associate the numeral 2 with the "two" clusters during early phases of the activity. The additional visual cueing provides a handle which helps students elicit the appropriate response and promotes overlearning as well.*

- *Example:* After students have pasted the cloth scraps on cards, by twos, have them match each card with a green numeral 2. As the cards showing one item are added as distractors, the green "2" cards may still be used (see Figure 5.2). The color cue, then the numeral itself, would gradually be eliminated.

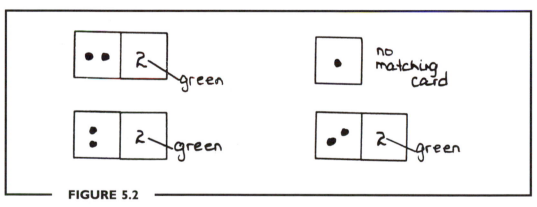

FIGURE 5.2

NOTE: If possible, cover the cards with contact paper or acetate. Then, if underscoring is necessary for only some students, the cards can more easily be wiped clean and reused with others.

2. **Say what you see.** Use flash cards from the previous activity (cards showing two or three objects). Include others showing only one item. Flash the cards, asking students to tell how many they see. Use a thin underscore (e.g., green for two, black for three) *only* if necessary, and plan systematically to fade the prompt.

3. **Circle what you see.** Pass out worksheets like that shown in Figure 5.3, containing one, two, or three items in each box. Flash a "2" or "3" numeral

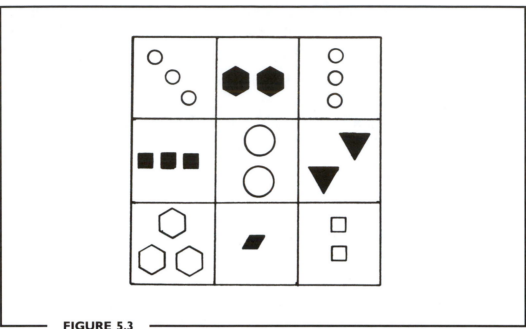

FIGURE 5.3

card and, each time, have the children circle a group to match. Initially, use colored numeral cards (e.g., a green "2," a black "3"). Gradually eliminate the color cue.

4. **Adapt these activities to nurture sight group recognition for four.**

SUGGESTED SEQUENCE OF ACTIVITIES

Counting On

1. **Small handful.** (Materials: 12 small counters in a box with lid.) Have a child take a small handful of counters (e.g., 5) from the box, count how many are taken, and place them into the lid of the box. Hold the box lid high, so no one can peek. "Let's put more counters into the lid. Count with me." "How many in the lid?" (5) "Now . . . (as, one by one, three additional counters are dropped into the lid) . . . there's 6, 7, 8." If it seems to help, allow children to recount from 1 to check. Then return all counters to the box and repeat for other "wee handfuls." Each time, have children count on aloud from the number of counters in the lid as, one by one, 1, 2 or 3 additional counters are dropped into the lid.

2. **Say, unfold, and count on!** (Materials: folded number/dot cards as shown in Figure 5.4. Use numbers 4–9 and one, two, or three dots on the cards.) Children say the number, unfold, and count on.

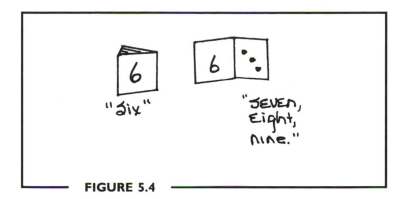

FIGURE 5.4

- As children become comfortable with the auditory patterning activities, the dot card can be replaced with a numeral card for 1, 2, and 3.

3. **Turn over.** Line up large numeral cards along the chalk tray (Figure 5.5). Let children see you turn one card over (e.g., the "7" card in Figure 5.5). Point to the card in front of the "7" and say, "Read this card, (name of child)." (6) "What comes after 6?" (7) Turn the card over to check.

FIGURE 5.5

NOTE: *It might help some children to say a number, finger trace and say the next few numbers after, then close their eyes while they repeat the sequence. If it seems helpful, allow children to recount from 1, emphasizing the last few numbers of the sequence.*

- *Follow-Up Activity 1:* As in Activity 3, but use a large-scale ruler or number line, decide on a number and cover all numbers to the right of it with an arrow card (Figure 5.6). "What's the arrow pointing to?" (6) Have children count on from the last number shown until you give a signal to stop.

- *Follow-Up Activity 2:* As before, but encourage the children to study the ruler or card sequence so they remember "in their heads" where the numbers are. Then have them close their eyes while you turn over a numeral card.

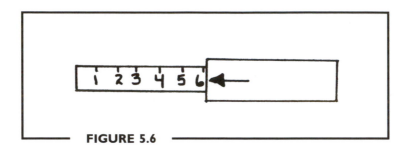

FIGURE 5.6

4. **Walk on!** Use a large walk-on number line. Have children close their eyes and walk on the number line until told to stop, silently counting their steps. Use shelf paper to cover up extra numbers. When the children stop and open their eyes, call on someone to tell you quickly the number after the one showing. As a follow-through, have the child stand on one number (e.g., 6) and show that just one more step takes you to the number after (7).

5. **Two more.** This activity prepares children to count on in addition problems with 2 as an addend (e.g., 6 + 2, 2 + 5, 7 + 2). Emphasis is on the auditory patterning involved. Use the ruler and arrow card from Follow-Up Activity 1 for *Turn Over*. Point the arrow to a numeral (4 to 9) and have the children tell you the number 2 more. Orally emphasize the auditory pattern that makes this activity easy.

   • *Example:*

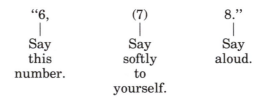

   "6,   (7)   8."
    | | |
   Say   Say   Say
   this   softly   aloud.
   number.   to
               yourself.

   Repeat with other numbers, and later extend to addition problems having 3 as an addend. Some children with auditory deficits or perseveration tendencies may have difficulty saying the middle number(s) softly. These children might be taught to tap the table while speaking softly.

6. **Come again.** Prepare two card decks:

   • Deck 1: 24 cards, four of each numeral, 4 through 9.

   • Deck 2: 24 cards, twelve "2" cards, twelve "3" cards. In turn, the children draw a card from each deck. A "2" draw from Deck 2 means "quickly tell the number 2 more than" that drawn from Deck 1. A "3" draw means "quickly tell the number 3 more than" that drawn from Deck 1. Students keep both cards if they answer quickly and correctly. (It should be obvious when children are counting on rather than counting from 1.)

Counting Back

Many special children find it difficult to count backwards, even for short counts. Because about one fourth of the subtraction basic facts can be quickly answered by counting backwards, this skill deserves greater and earlier emphasis in work with numbers through 10 or 12. Too many school programs fail to develop this skill specifically, leaving children to learn the skill while trying to apply it when answering unknown subtraction facts like 9 − 2, 8 − 3, 11 − 2, and others. Children with learning deficits are among the first to be frustrated and fail in these situations. To acquire the skill level necessary to be able to count back two or three numbers in subtraction, ideas like the following have proven helpful.

SUGGESTED SEQUENCE OF ACTIVITIES

1. **Up and back.** Have children use two body motions: clap hands while counting up to a number; clap knees while counting back from that number. Later, count up (teacher only) and let children count back.

   • *Example:*

       Teacher says: "1, 2, 3, 4" (while all clap hands).
       Children respond (while all clap knees): "4, 3, 2, 1."

   In a final phase, count forwards silently and say just the last number (e.g., "4"). Children count backwards, starting with this number ("4, 3, 2, 1"). Be sure children can count back from four before extending the backward count pattern to five. Then master that count pattern before extending further, and so on.

2. **Break away!** (Materials: 16 interlocking cubes.) Taking turns, children make an interlocking cube train (e.g., a "9" train) and count backwards as, one by one, they break a cube away from the train (Figure 5.7). For stu-

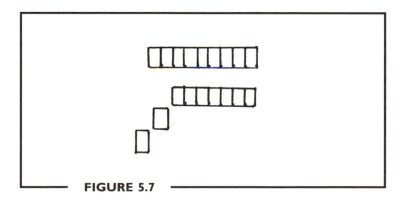

FIGURE 5.7

dents with expressive language difficulties, initially it may help to have numbers on each cube. Once they feel confident with the auditory pattern and have developed a visual image to assist them, the numbers can be removed.

Visual Patterning Based on the 10-Frame

Good visual imagery for the 10-frame is an important skill. One example of 10 things, or six or seven is that number of objects "in the frame" (see Figure 5.8). The following two basic activities help build visual imagery for the 10-frame.

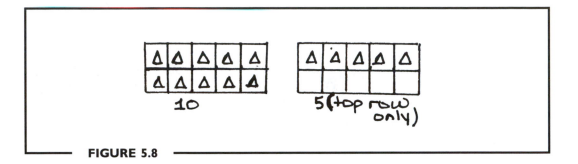

FIGURE 5.8

SUGGESTED SEQUENCE OF ACTIVITIES

Prerequisite Skills:

a. Sight recognition for groups less than 5

b. Sight recognition for group needed to make 5

c. Understanding of "top" and "bottom"

1. **10-frame flash.** (Materials: A set of 10-frame cards similar to those shown in Figure 5.9.) Flash each card briefly, then remove it from sight. "How many stars did you see?" Repeat, emphasizing 6–9 stars in the frame. It

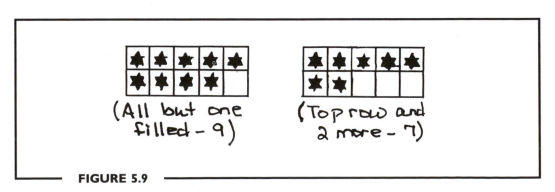

FIGURE 5.9

often is helpful to make comments like: "Nine stars—that must be *all but one* filled. Let's check." "Seven stars—that must be the top row and two more: 5—6, 7. Let's check."

2. **Frame fill.** (Materials: 10-frame cards, as in Activity 1.) Flash as before, then ask children to close their eyes. "Can you see the stars in the frame? How many would it take to fill the frame? . . . Let's check."

NOTE: *Good mental imagery for the 10-frame paves the way for success later with 10 sums and for subtracting any number from 10. It also is basic to using 10 as a bridge for adding facts like 6 + 8 and 7 + 5; for subtracting 13 − 8, 12 − 4 and other "harder" facts.*

Once children have been introduced to each of these types of activities, it is possible to provide a sample of each activity type (counting on, counting back, how many numbers heard [two or three] and 10-frame work) during a 5-minute "Quick Math" period some time during the day. Until children have mastered the number facts which rely on these skills, they should be treated in daily or at least biweekly mini-math sessions.

REVERSALS

Problem Area: Number reversals (Ɛ for 3, 6 for 9, 23 for 32), disorientations (J), mirror images, and other misperceptions.

Typical Disabilities Affecting Progress: Difficulties with visual/auditory memory or visual discrimination, spatial organization, and visual motor integration.

Background: Before children begin writing numerals, they should be able to count out the correct number of objects for each numeral being written. Further, those with severe visual-motor coordination difficulties should be provided preliminary work at the gross motor level. In extreme cases this may include movement exercises such as hopping, crawling, jumping, and ball catching. Gross motor writing activities may also be necessary.

For example, children might form (or trace over) numerals in damp sand, or use a finger or wet sponge to trace over large numerals drawn on the chalkboard. Guide the child's hand and give verbal cues to prompt correct formation if necessary. For example, "Down, around, the 6 curls up; the 6 sleeps sound." It sometimes helps to have children close their eyes as you guide their formation of a numeral. "Feel the 6 go down, around. Now you make it" first with eyes closed, then with eyes open. On a regular basis, have children draw or display the appropriate number of objects for a numeral that is formed.

Whenever possible, early number and place value work should be embedded in game, problem, or application settings to which children can relate. As larger numbers of objects are counted, children who can count by 10s may independently note that "grouping by 10s makes it quick and easy for others to check my count." Developing efficient ways to count, record, and communicate to others about larger numbers of objects is the stepping stone to place value understandings for multidigit numbers, which include grouping (by 10s), partitioning numbers in different ways (e.g., 23 can be 2 tens 3 ones or 1 ten 13 ones), and comparing numbers.

Recent research is emphasizing how place value concepts are *really learned* when children are routinely challenged to solve and justify their solutions to numeric problems. In other words, what appears to be a problem-solving or computational setting may indeed be an important forum for place value learning. All children, including those with learning disabilities, benefit and can grow in place value understandings by repeatedly engaging in extended problem-solving experiences like the following:

> Sami's sticker book holds 100 stickers. He has 17
> dog stickers and 56 horse stickers in his book.
> Does he have room for 47 bird stickers?

In the past it was thought that such problems were "too complicated" for many students with learning disabilities. Teachers are now finding that past expectations and, hence, results were not high enough. Calculators can do the computing. The challenge is to nurture children's abilities to *think mathematically*. Experience has shown that children become better thinkers and better problem solvers when they are systematically involved in solving problems. Children also gain richer insights into number when they are allowed, even encouraged to solve problems in personally meaningful ways, and when they can listen to and see different solution approaches used by other students.

In the sticker problem above, for example, one child focusing on the 10s digits might think: "10 and 50—that's 60, and 40 more is already 100. So the book is full before I add in the extra ones." Another child might do a paper-and-pencil computation and get 73 for the total number of stickers in the book, then count on by 10s while finger tabbing: 77—83, 93 (that's 20)—and 7 more to 100 makes 27. "There's only room for 27 more stickers, not 47."

A different student might use trains of 10 interlocking cubes and loose ones to represent the 17, 56, and 47 stamps, push all the 10-trains together (to obtain ten such trains) and count by 10s to 100. This child might even combine loose cubes into as many 10-trains as possible and finally note that the total number of cubes is more than 100, so the stickers won't all fit. "In fact, 14 won't fit." Other solution approaches are possible, some using only paper-and-pencil computations, some using a 100s chart, base 10 blocks, or other math aid. As the students work, they are likely to partition and regroup numbers in different ways, and hence reinforce or learn important place value concepts. They may:

- Group objects such as popsicle sticks or cubes by tens and then tell or write the number of tens and number of extra ones.

- Children count orally by tens and use objects to show the count: "2 tens, twenty; 6 tens, sixty," and so on.

- Use the objects (tens and ones) to help compare the number of stickers to 100.

If, as children work, consistent reversal tendencies are noted beyond the early primary level, then structured assistance, as suggested below, may be necessary. If the reversals mostly involve teen numbers, the reminder that "Teens are different. They are back-to-front numbers—what you hear first you write last," often helps to correct the problem. Sometimes recounting from one, following the page numbers of a book and comparing with what has been written, is helpful in highlighting and correcting the difficulty.

If a child has severe spatial organization problems, it is helpful to confine all writing activities to a horizontal plane. The down stroke on the "4" made by a child sitting at a desk, for example, has a different orientation to the body than that made while standing. It may be necessary in cases such as this to teach an alternate pattern for writing a 4 and a 5—one which involves only one stroke (see Figure 5.10). These patterns have also helped children with severe reversal tendencies. If children still have difficulty with reversals, the following basic sequence may help.

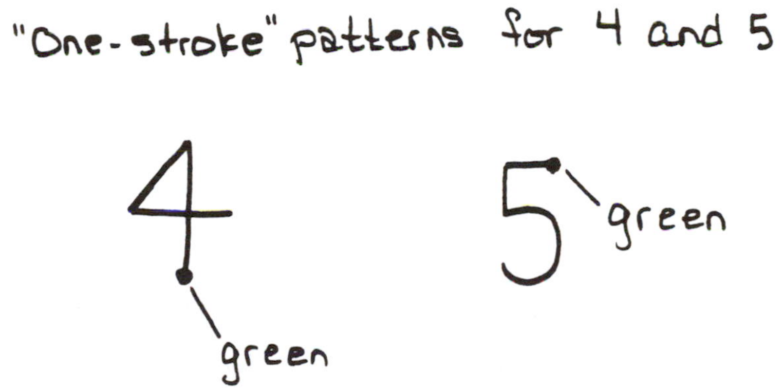

"One-stroke" patterns for 4 and 5

4 green

5 green

FIGURE 5.10

SUGGESTED SEQUENCE OF ACTIVITIES

1-Digit Reversals

1. **Stencil in.** Provide stencils children can use to write given numerals. Place a green dot on the stencil to indicate the starting place. In Figure 5.11 the loop is outlined in red. This helps distinguish the 6 from a 9. When necessary, have children finger trace before starting, and use verbal cues.

2. **Get the feel.**

   - *Variation 1:* (For children who confuse two numerals, such as 6 and 9.) Have children use stencils to form both numerals. Use green

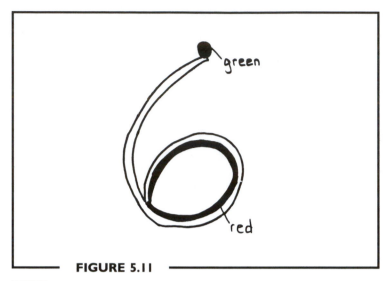

FIGURE 5.11

NOTE: If a child is confusing two numerals, such as 6 and 9, give verbal cues for only *one* of the digits. If the "curl around, sleep sound" cue is given for 6, then 9 is just the "other one." When cues are given for both numerals, children start confusing cues.

dots for both numerals to show the starting place. Orally name both numerals, but for one use additional color and verbal cueing, as above, to emphasize its shape. Then tell the child, "Close your eyes. I'll move your hand. Am I making a 6?" (If no, ask "Am I making a 9?") If the child is not ticklish, write one of the numerals on the child's back. "Tell me what I'm writing . . . Yes, 6. Go to the chalk tray and pick out a picture card showing six things."

NOTE: *It often helps to have textured numerals in front of the children while you finger trace on their backs. Felt numbers are better than sandpaper because they are less abrasive. While you trace, have the children look at the numerals to help fix the association. When finished, have them trace over the numeral they think you made. If correct, and if they are able to write numerals, they can be requested immediately to do so on the chalkboard, on paper, or in sand.*

- *Variation 2:* For children who make mirror images of given numerals (see Figure 5.12). Move the hand or write on the back so the child can "feel" the numeral being written. Then have the child form the numeral in the air (on the desk). This can be done as you write the numeral on the child's back.

3. **Count and trace.**

- *Variation 1:* (For children who confuse two numerals, such as 6 and 9.) Have children count and complete the numeral to show how many,

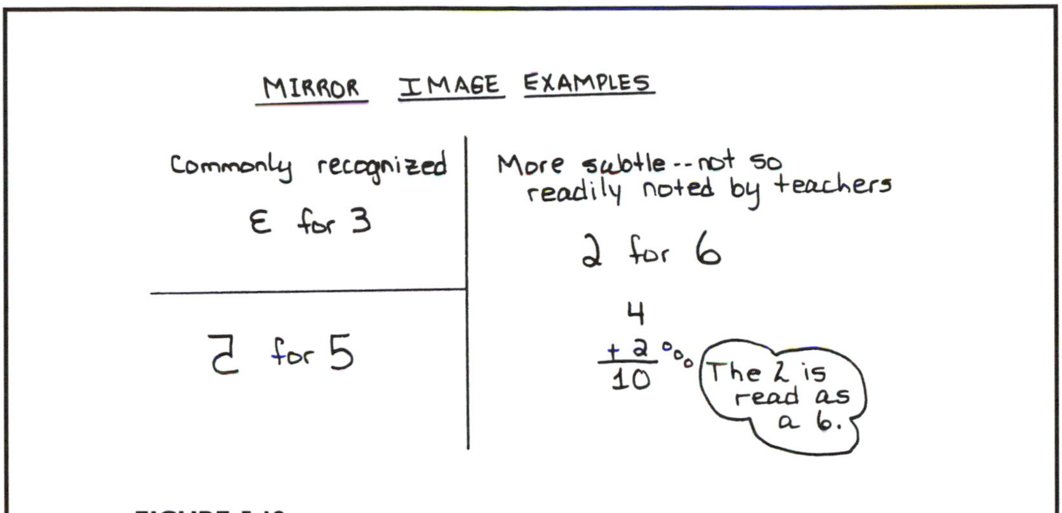

MIRROR IMAGE EXAMPLES

Commonly recognized

ƎＥ for 3

Ƨ for 5

More subtle--not so
readily noted by teachers

ᗱ for 6

$$\begin{array}{r} 4 \\ + 2 \\ \hline 10 \end{array}$$ °°°

The 2 is read as a 6.

FIGURE 5.12

as in Figure 5.13. If necessary, use a green dot to show the starting place, and have children trace the numeral before writing it. "Does it feel like the 6? Does it circle round 'to sleep sound'?" Use red outlining on the loop, as in the following variation, if this helps.

- *Variation 2:* For children who make mirror images of given numerals. Children count and write a row of the numeral showing "how many." Use color coding to start the numeral. In Figure 5.14, the top curve is green. First solid lines are used, then dotted. Children may need to finger trace a few numerals before using pencil.

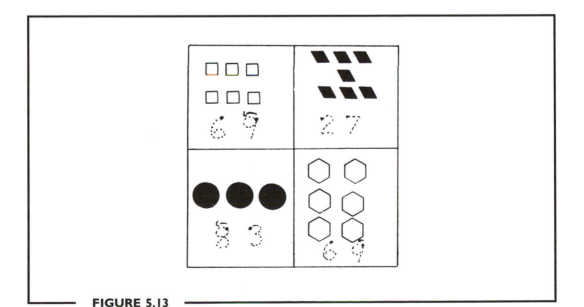

FIGURE 5.13

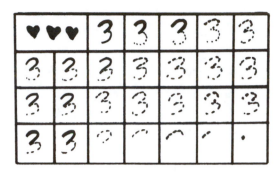

FIGURE 5.14

Prompt with verbal cues when necessary. We prefer not to include incorrect mirror images. In our experience, emphasizing correct models has more quickly remedied the problem.

- *Follow-Up Worksheet* (Figure 5.15): Children tend to revert to former reversal patterns. Though correctable, it does take time to resolve this problem. Worksheets like this, requiring only occasional independent writing of a numeral, provide self-correction when children forget the proper writing movement. As children trace over given samples, teachers might ask: "Do you feel you do it the same way when you write it?"

- *Optional Follow-Up:* For children who have been introduced to addition (or other operations and related basic facts), it may be necessary to help transfer the numeral recognition skill to problem situations. Figure 5.16 suggests a way of doing this. Children are asked to state the correct answer, complete the correct numeral, and cross out the wrong one. Children can also be helped to transfer number recognition to printed numerals. Have them find and circle given numerals appearing in newspaper ads, for example.

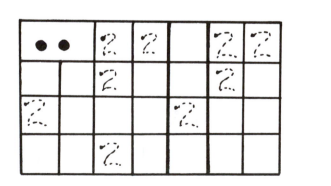

FIGURE 5.15

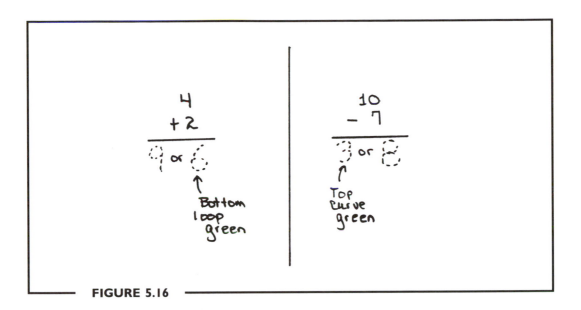

FIGURE 5.16

4. **You do.** As children need less structured cues to write "problem" numbers on paper, use a green dot to show where to start (Figure 5.17a). Children count the objects, trace the solid numeral, and use it as a pattern for writing other numerals in that row. If necessary, a yellow highlighter can be used when dotted lines no longer appear to guide correct formation.

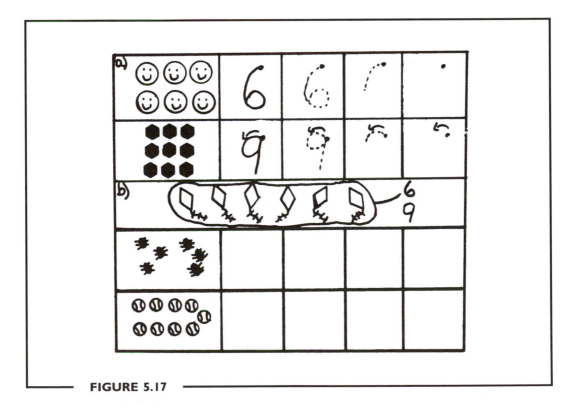

FIGURE 5.17

Eventually, numeral patterns are given only at the top of the worksheet (Figure 5.17b). In these examples, color outlining of the 6 loop is used if needed, but it would be eliminated gradually.

- *Optional Follow-Up:* Simple number combinations involving the numerals being worked on are again given. This time, however, the dotted numerals used in Figure 5.16 are not shown. Instead, Figure 5.18 illustrates a way of making the activity self-checking. Write problems on the bottom part of a sheet of construction paper, as shown. Cover this part with contact paper to allow use of a washable marker when answering. Children can fold the top part down over the problems and compare their answers with those given.

5. **Hand numbers.** Children can be taught to use their right hand to check the shape of many numerals. The curve of the 2, 3, and 5 all coincide with the shape formed by cupping the right hand. The numerals 7 and 9 can be "made" with the right hand and forearm, as in Figure 5.19. Left-handed children are at an advantage in this hand check—they do not even have to put their pencils down!

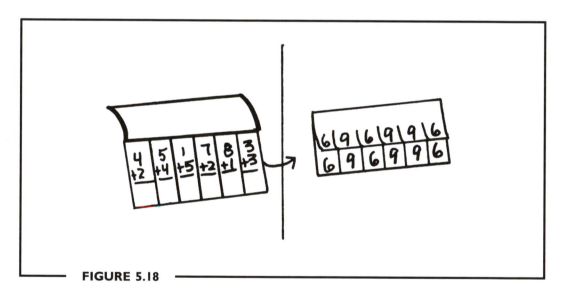

FIGURE 5.18

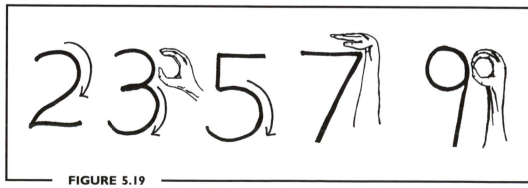

FIGURE 5.19

NOTE: *Activities and exercises similar to those in the preceding sequence can be used to help children who demonstrate other writing problems, including disorientation and misperception of numerals. Have model numbers available to which children can refer.*

SUGGESTED SEQUENCE OF ACTIVITIES

2-Digit Reversals

1. **Tens and ones.** Use colored chips or graph paper pieces (see Figure 5.20a). Give the child 2 tens and 4 ones. "How many stacks of 10?" (2) Have the child place a green textured numeral beneath the 2 ten-stacks. "How many ones?" (4) Position these to the right of the ten-stacks, and have the child place a red numeral beneath the 4 ones (Figure 5.20b). "Two tens and 4, that's twenty-four. Finger trace the 24 so you get the feel of it. Start with tens." The child should say the number aloud as it is traced.

   - *Follow-Up Discussion:* "Think of a traffic light. Suppose you want to walk across the street. When can you start walking?" (When the light is green.) "Yes, green means start. Red means stop. Look at the numerals we used. When you read or write numbers like this (point), you *start* with tens, the green one, and *stop* with ones."

   If the child has any difficulty relating 2 tens to twenty, 4 tens to forty, and so on, take time to reinforce this relationship. Use ten-stacks to dramatize the counting by tens. Capitalize on any phonetic similarities (e.g., *six* tens, *six*ty; *five* tens, *fif*ty). Repeat the activity with other numbers. Omit teens until later, when naming irregularities can again be pointed out.

2. **Start with tens.** Give the child 2 tens and 4 ones as in the preceding activity. "Let's write how many chips you have. Where do we start?" (Tens—2 tens.) "Write the '2' in green." "How many ones?" (4) "Write it in red (Figure 5.21a). What number did we write?" (Twenty-four.) "Finger trace the number as you say it . . . Now close your eyes and picture it while I say it . . . Open your eyes. Is this what you saw?" (refer again to Figure 5.21a). Prompt the child, as necessary, throughout this dialogue.

   - Show the child Figure 5.21b. "Which of these says 24?" (Last one.) "How do you know?" (It starts with 2 tens.) Have the child finger trace, as before.

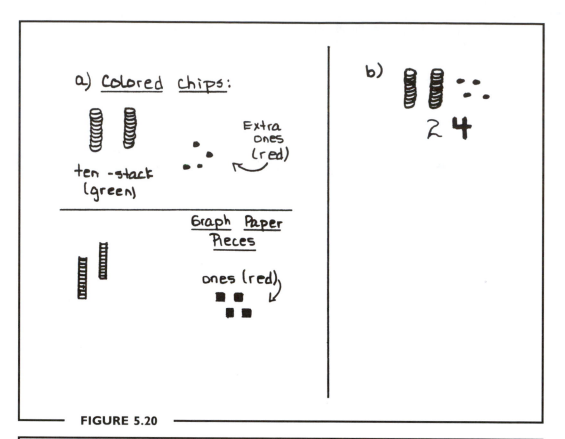

a) Colored chips:

ten-stack
(green)

Extra
ones
(red)

Graph Paper
Pieces

ones (red)

b)

2 4

FIGURE 5.20

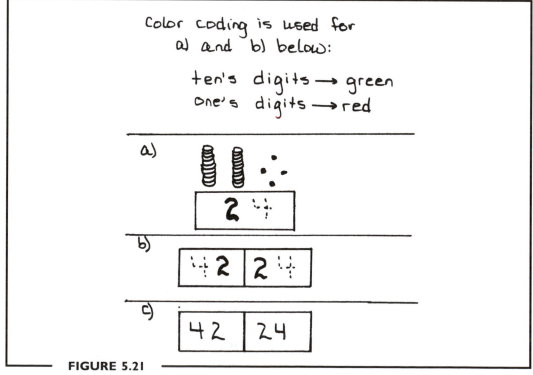

Color coding is used for
a) and b) below:

ten's digits → green
one's digits → red

a)

2 4

b)

4 2 | 2 4

c)

42 | 24

FIGURE 5.21

- Show the child Figure 5.21c. "This time there's no color. Can you remember which says twenty-four?" (Last one.) "How do you know?" (It starts with 2 tens.)

Repeat with other 2-digit numbers. A worksheet similar to that of Figure 5.22 can be used in conjunction with the activity. Boxes can be filled in during discussion with the child. Note that:

- It may be sufficient merely to underline the tens digit in green and the ones digit in red.

- The separation of tens-ones columns into individual boxes has been avoided. When this is done, some students, with closure problems, do not see "24." Instead, they see a 2 and a 4. In our experience, these same students accept and profit more from the color distinctions.

- *Follow-Up Worksheets:* Worksheets from commercial workbooks may be useful. Sometimes, particularly for children with sequential memory deficits, it might be necessary to color code these pages by underscoring the tens groups in green and the ones groups in red. Any response lines could be coded to match. It may be only necessary to color code the first problem on a page as an example for completing others. Alternately, it may be sufficient to make cards available showing the coding to which children can refer.

3. **Write and show.** Prerecorded cassette tapes are excellent for practice activities. Script suggestions include, "I'll say a number. You write it. Remem-

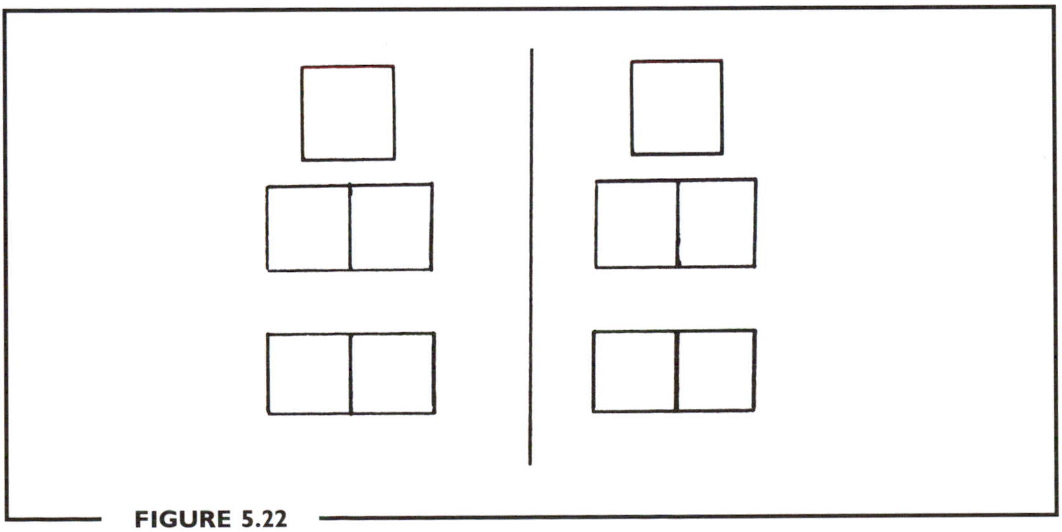

FIGURE 5.22

ber to start with tens. Here's the first number: twenty-four." (Tape off while the child writes.) "Now use tens and ones to show twenty-four." (Tape off while child selects the ten-stacks and ones needed.) "You should now have two tens and four ones, twenty-four. Check it out. Turn to page A of the answer book" (see Figure 5.23).

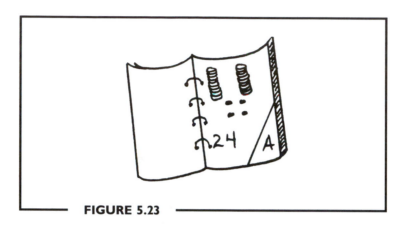

FIGURE 5.23

Providing paper with predrawn boxes for children's responses helps avoid random placement of numbers. Also, if a child is highly distractible, setting up a definite workspace is beneficial. Use a plain sheet of paper, a plastic mat, or a piece of smooth plastic tablecloth for this purpose. Use the workspace to focus the child's attention. For example, "Use tens and ones to show me twenty-four in your workspace. . . . Good! Now clear your workspace."

> • *Variation:* Provide a worksheet that is correlated to the cassette tape. Have the child circle the correct number: 24 or 42. For the first part of the tape, the tens digit could be color coded.

4. **Dot-to-dot.** Provide a prerecorded tape that dictates 2-digit numbers, with a pause between each. (If necessary, the tape can be turned off between each number.) Correlate a dot-to-dot pattern with the tape, so that a picture is formed if the child connects dots between each number dictated. The tape could begin with the reminder to "start with tens." If necessary, the tens place of each 2-digit numeral on the dot-to-dot sheet can be written or underlined in green.

5. **Secret message** (optional). Ask the child to number a paper 1 through 9. Now dictate a 2-digit number to be written beside each (see Figure 5.24a). Explain that the 2-digit numbers are page numbers in a book. Instruct the child to use the book to find the penciled letter written beside each page number. "Look up number 1 (page 32). Do you see an 'A'? Write 'A' in the number 1 box on your worksheet" (Figure 5.24b). "Do the same for the others. See if you can answer the riddle. Remember to start with tens when looking for pages."

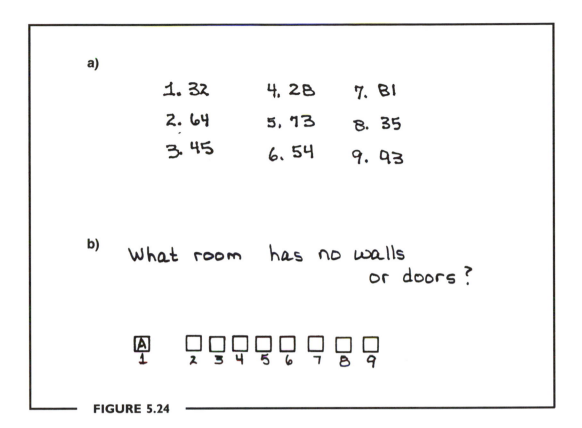

a)

1. 32   4. 28   7. 81

2. 64   5. 73   8. 35

3. 45   6. 54   9. 93

b)

What room has no walls or doors?

A
1   2 3 4 5 6 7 8 9

FIGURE 5.24

This has proven a very motivating activity for students with auditory-memory problems, and one that can be constructed quickly. Use a riddle book from a public library to help.

- Children with spatial or severe visual-perception difficulties may have trouble completing worksheets of this nature. The numbers 1 to 9 may "run together" with others written from dictation. It may be necessary to provide prenumbered sheets for the numbers 1 to 9 (numbers written in a distinctly different color than that to be used by the child during dictation). If lined paper is used, skip a line between numbers. Or provide centimeter grid paper (see Figure 5.25) and have the children write a dictated number in alternate squares. For severe cases, it may be necessary to omit worksheets of this type.

6. **Terrible teens!** The naming irregularities of the teens should be pointed out to students:

> 2 tens and 4: "twenty-four" (24);
>
> 4 tens and 6: "forty-six" (46); and
>
> *But→*   1 ten and 7: "seventeen" (17).

We still start with tens to write teens, but the verbal naming pattern does not hold. We must listen carefully to determine whether the ending is "teen" or "ty." (The numerals 11 and 12 are in categories all their own!) Worksheets like those of Figure 5.26 can help children focus on the ending.

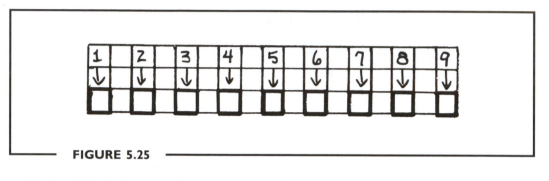

FIGURE 5.25

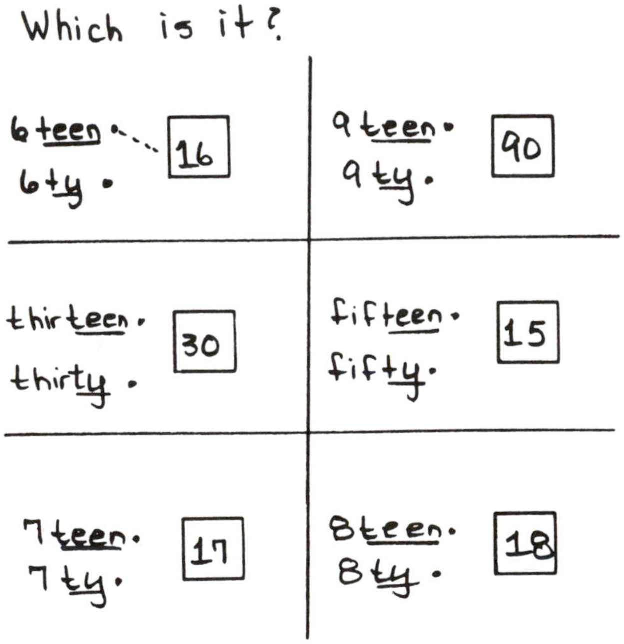

Which is it?

6 teen .... [16]   9 teen. [90]
6 ty .   9 ty .

thir teen. [30]   fifteen. [15]
thirty .   fifty.

7 teen. [17]   8 teen. [18]
7 ty.   8 ty .

FIGURE 5.26

NOTE: The "teen" and "ty" endings are written in red. The "6teen, 6ty" technique is effective even with nonreaders because the difference in configuration makes it easy to "read" the two forms.

EXTENDING COUNTING SKILLS: SKIP COUNTING BY 10S AND 5S

Problem Areas: Not understanding the patterning for continuing counting sequences (e.g., by 5s and 10s), even though basic place value concepts are well established.

Typical Disabilities Affecting Progress: Difficulties with abstract reasoning, auditory closure, visual or auditory association or discrimination, expressive language, and visual or sequential memory.

Background: Counting on by 5s or 10s is useful for mental addition and subtraction, for early multiplication, and for daily situations involving time or money. Some children, however, such as those with the disabilities listed here may be unable to continue even simple counting sequences involving these patterns. Suppose brownies should bake 25 minutes. These children may have difficulty counting on from the present time (by 5s) to determine when the brownies should be taken from the oven. Likewise, they may be unable to count by 5s or 10s to tell the value of given coins or to check change received. Applying these skills for mentally computing even simple sums may be difficult.

These children fail to make associations and recognize patterns that ordinarily make counting on by skip counting a reasonably simple task. Therefore, special instruction, such as that outlined in the following activities, is required. Rather than basing an activity immediately on numbers, the sequence first involves the child in *patterning*—the root of the processing problem. At first, the child is given simple shapes and visual/auditory cues to help in recognizing and extending a pattern. Then, when the child is successful with number sequences (easily distinguishable numerals), color-coded counting charts are introduced.

SUGGESTED SEQUENCE OF ACTIVITIES

1. **Finish the pattern.** Use wood or construction paper circles and squares (circles one color, squares another). Lay out a simple repeating pattern with the blocks. On two slips of paper, trace (same color as actual shapes) the dotted outlines of the next two blocks in the pattern (see Figure 5.27). Have

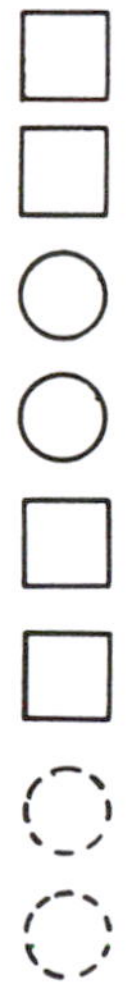

FIGURE 5.27

the child name the shapes, in order, so that the "square, square, circle, circle" auditory pattern is heard. Then ask the child to find the missing blocks and finish the pattern. When all blocks are in place, have the child "read" the pattern (name all the shapes displayed, in order). Finally, ask the child to use blocks to copy the completed pattern.

- *Follow-Up:* Repeat with other patterns, gradually omitting the dotted cue.

2. **Draw it in.** As in *Finish the Pattern,* but draw the repeating shape patterns on worksheets. At first, use two different colors and include the dotted outlines. Ask the child to "read" and complete each pattern. Then ask that the entire pattern again be read aloud. Provide space (and templates, if necessary), so that the child can copy the completed pattern. Gradually use more difficult patterns, fade the color cueing, and omit the dotted outlines. See if the child can add the next two or three shapes to the pattern without extra prompts. This is usually possible when pattern difficulty is gradually incremented along with gradual fading of prompts.

3. **What's next?** Follow the same "read, complete, read again, copy" format of the two preceding activities, but this time use numerals that can be readily distinguished (e.g., Figure 5.28). Similar cueing techniques can also be used if necessary.

4. **An easy one!** Show the child Figure 5.29. "This is an easy one. Tell me what's alike in the numbers." (All end in 0.) "Read the numbers." (To hear the auditory pattern.) "What comes next?" (70.) "How do you know?" (7 comes after 6.) Have the child finish the sequence and read it aloud. "Look at the numbers so you can picture them in your head. . . . Now close your

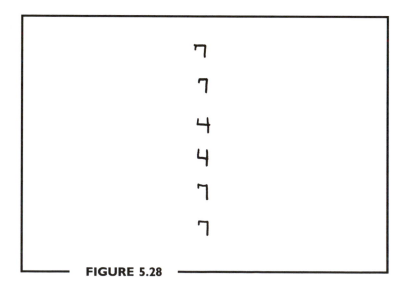

FIGURE 5.28

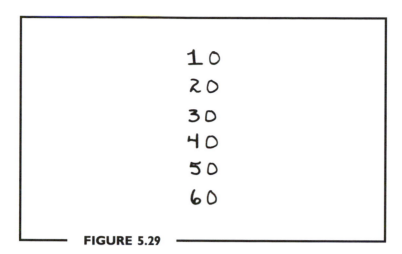

FIGURE 5.29

eyes and tell me the numbers." Prompt, as necessary, throughout the dialogue. Repeat parts of the dialogue, as necessary. If more patterning work is needed, adapt Activity 7 to provide practice.

5. **Count on.** Provide dimes the child can use for counting by 10s. If necessary, use a counting chart as in Figure 5.30, on which the child lays the dimes while counting. (If a child's money concepts are too weak for this activity, refer to the Chapter 4 suggestions.) Eventually, the child should be able to count by 10s independently of the chart.

   - *Extension* (to prepare for mental math, for counting money amounts and checking change received): Lay four dimes (40¢) on the counting chart and have the child *count on* by 10s from 40¢. Repeat, but vary the number of dimes initially laid on the chart.

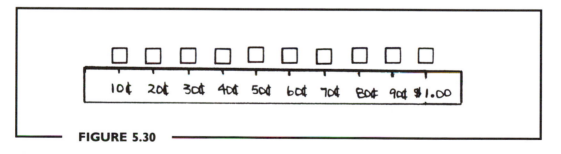

FIGURE 5.30

6. **To 100.** (Prerequisite: The child can count meaningfully to 10. It is also assumed that the numeration instruction summarized in the *Reversals* section on p. 169 has been carried out.) Show the color-coded counting chart of Figure 5.31 (tens digits green). This chart is sequenced vertically rather than horizontally as is commonly the case. Experience has shown that the vertical presentation makes it easier for children to see the patterning of the number sequence.

```
0    10   20   30   40   50   60   70   80   90   100
1    11   21   31   41   51   61   71   81   91
2    12   22   32   42   52   62   72   82
3    13   23   33   43   53   63
4    14   24   34   44
5    15   25   35
6    16
7    17
8    18
9    19
```

FIGURE 5.31

Have the child count by 10s *across* the columns. Now mask out all but the first column (0-9), and have the child read it aloud. Then slide the mask so the first two columns show. Discuss how the second column is like the first. (The ones column in both is the standard counting sequence. This can be related to the idea of "one more" as described earlier.) Have the child note the pattern that all numbers in the second column begin with 1. "This is the teen column." Count from 1 with the child, emphasizing the teen endings of the last numbers read. Slide the mask again to reveal the third column. "This is the 20s column." Have the child read the numbers in the column. "What numbers come next?" Write as the child orally continues the counting sequence to 29, prompting as necessary. For this, as for other columns on the chart, the child can be shown how the standard counting sequence of the ones digits will help.

Later retrace the tens digits with green, recounting aloud with the child to emphasize the "20" part of each number named. Have the child finger trace the first digits during an independent recount, if helpful. Let the child, eyes closed, count the 20s aloud. Then choose a number in a preceding column and count on from there—first using the chart, then looking away. Stress the 19–20 column shift. Repeat for other columns during this or any follow-up sessions. Make the chart available for reference. Use it as long as needed during review sessions in which the child either orally counts or writes the numbers in sequence.

- *Follow-Up Activity 1:* Reinforce the tens transition with repeated oral work. First the teacher says a few patterns emphasizing the switch. Then the student completes patterns started by the teacher.

Example:

A.   **Teacher**
"nineteen—twenty"
"thirty-nine—forty"
"eighty-nine—ninety"

B.   **Teacher   Student**
"twenty-nine"— "thirty"
"sixty-nine"—"seventy"

- *Follow-Up Activity 2:* When the auditory pattern for sequential counting is established, use objects (tens and ones) to dramatize and reinforce the meaning of the oral count.

  Example: Lay out 2 tens and one (to represent 21). "I will add sticks, one at a time. Count aloud so we can keep track of the number of sticks that are on the table each time" (see Figure 5.32). Repeat, varying the number of tens and ones initially placed on the table.

FIGURE 5.32

It may now also be necessary to redevelop concepts and skills for comparing and ordering two-digit numbers. Suggestions from the following section, *Comparing Numbers*, can be adapted to this purpose.

7. **By 5s.** Use a worksheet similar to that of Figure 5.33 to lay the groundwork for the patterning involved in skip counting by 5s. Following the sequence of patterns on the worksheet, first review the easier patterns with shapes, then turn to numbers used when counting by 5s.

    Next show Figure 5.34 (tens digits coded green). Ask the child to read the column, then to describe any patterns seen (numbers end in 5 or 0; in the tens place there are two 1s, then two 2s). In order for some children

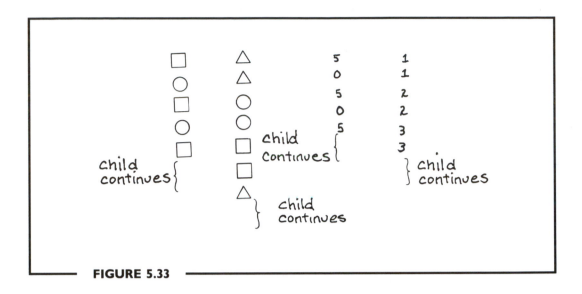

FIGURE 5.33

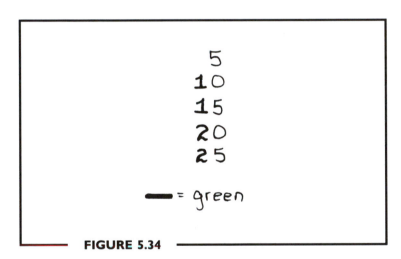

FIGURE 5.34

to see these patterns, they may need to cover first the ones column and then the tens column with a card.

"What two numbers would come next?" Write as the child says them: "30, 35." Prompt if necessary. Discuss why these two numbers were chosen. Then have the child say all the numbers aloud, continuing the count as far as possible (to 100). Write as the child gives the extended count. Underscore the tens digits green if this helps cue additional entries in the sequence. See if the child can repeat the counting pattern without looking at the chart. Make the chart available for future reference, and continue to use it, as needed, during review sessions.

8. **Nickel countdown.** Adapt *Count On* (Activity 5) to counting by 5s with nickels. The idea of counting by 5s and 10s can be extended to include (a) counting on from clock times or (b) using nickels and dimes first to count

by 5s, then switching to counting by 10s (and vice versa). The latter skill is often needed for counting money amounts or checking change received.

NOTE: *Follow-Up Activity 1 for* Turn Over *in Section 1 on page 165* (Counting in Early Number Work), *as well as dot-to-dot patterns, can be used to reinforce most of the activities of this section.*

COMPARING NUMBERS

Problem Area: Difficulty recognizing the greater of two numbers or correctly using greater than (>) and less than (<) symbols. (The use of these symbols is not recommended for all children and certainly not in lower grades.)

Typical Disabilities Affecting Progress: Difficulties with abstract reasoning, visual discrimination, visual association, spatial organization, and visual memory.

Background: When comparing numbers less than 10, a standard approach is to examine the linear sequence of digits and note that: "When you count, the numbers that mean *more* come after others in the count." The first set of activities that follow suggests ways of prefacing this instruction to build a better concept of *more* (or *less*) for numbers up to 10.

When comparing numbers greater than 10, children typically are asked to represent the numbers with grouping aids and to match one-to-one as in Figure 5.35. The focus is on starting big, with the tens (hundreds) to compare. Many children with the disabilities identified in this section can understand comparison when illustrated in this manner. Difficulties arise when materials are no longer used or when children are expected to use the "less than" and "greater than" symbols, without being able to associate any meaning with them. Some reverse the symbols when writing them, others forget "which means which."

More important than using the formal comparison symbols is the basic idea of "Which means more?" As a daily living skill, this concept is a critical one. It enters into comparison shopping—determining whether one has enough money to buy what is needed—and a myriad of other common situations. The important point of the second set of activities in the following sequence is to help students to compare larger numbers even when materials are no longer used. The use of symbols is secondary and in some individual cases would be omitted.

SUGGESTED SEQUENCE OF ACTIVITIES

Comparing Numbers to 10

Prerequisite Skill: Understanding the concepts "before" and "after" both orally and visually.

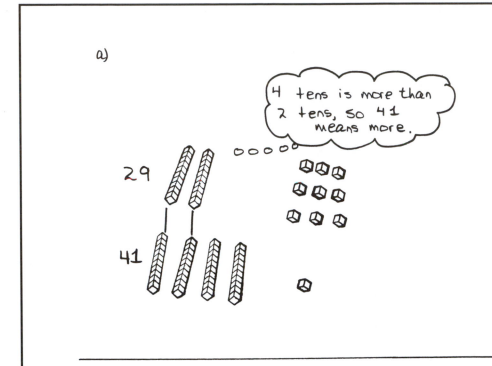

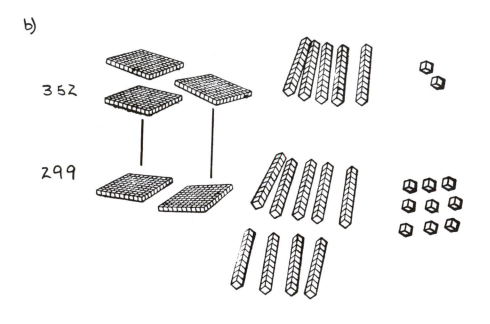

FIGURE 5.35

1. **Match up.** A first basic activity is to have children take two handfuls of objects or cubes (up to 10 in each hand) and lay them out or stack them so visual comparison is easy. Matching one to one, children can be led to observe: "The side or stack with extras has more" (Figure 5.36). Consistently and repeatedly, this verbal observation should be stated— both by the teacher and by the child: "The side with extras has more." The child can write or circle the greater number each time.

2. **"Comes after" in the count.** After repeatedly matching and writing to record the comparison of two numbers as before, the link to the counting sequence can be made. Simply ask children to write the numbers 1 to 10 at the top of a sheet of paper, or to use their ruler or a number line. Call out two 1-digit numbers and ask, " Which is greater?" If the child does not know, small counters can be used as in the Figure 5.36 "match up" to answer the question. If the child does respond correctly, it still is occasionally useful to "match up," as shown, to reinforce correct thinking. Commentary to be repeated in this activity is: "Yes, and did you notice that the greater number comes *after* the other in the count and on your number line?" Relate this idea to the pages in a book, as suggested in the Note to Activity 1, which follows, for larger numbers. When children can comfortably identify the greater of two numbers, then parallel activities focusing on "less/fewer than" can be presented.

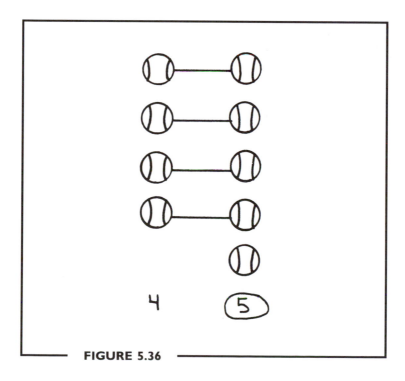

FIGURE 5.36

Comparing Multidigit Numbers

Prerequisite Skills:

a. Strong place-value understanding for the numbers involved, as suggested in the teacher *Background* of *Reversals* on page 169.

b. Prior work with grouping aids, as in Figure 5.35, for comparing 2- and 3-digit numbers.

c. Ability to use more/less to compare one-digit numbers.

d. Understanding of the concepts "before" and "after."

Basic Sequence

1. **See it.** Orally present 2- or 3-digit numbers with different first digits. Provide students with number line paper as in Figure 5.37. Have students write the numbers in the section using the correct section of the number line. They can then fill in the sentence (Figure 5.37a) or use symbols (Figure 5.37b), whichever is appropriate.

   NOTE: *This activity is a good starting point for students with spatial problems as it allows them to see that the greater number always comes after the other one in the count. When the numbers are "far apart" in the counting sequence, it is not practical to rely on counting alone to determine a comparison. Instead, the more general tactic of comparing the greater valued digits in the numbers (e.g., tens to tens, or hundreds to hundreds) is far more useful because: "The numbers compare the way the digits compare." Aligning numbers under each other, color cueing, or finger tracing lead digits in like positions is used throughout these activities to emphasize this approach. The link to the counting sequence is then made, often with the help of a library book or textbook.*

2. **More tens.** Present two 2- or 3-digit numbers with different first digits as in Figure 5.38. Have the children use materials (tens/ones) to represent each number (Figure 5.38b). Underscore the first digit of each number in green and discuss how you always "start big" to compare. Be sure children recognize that 32 has more tens than 24. "Yes, 3 tens is more than 2 tens, so 32 is more (greater) than 24. And, when you count, the number that is "more" always comes after the other." Repeat with other numbers.

3. **Feel it.** To reinforce the "more than" idea and to review the vocabulary "less than."

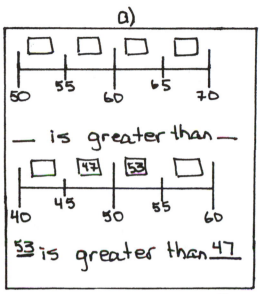

a)

— is greater than —

53 is greater than 47

"Which is greater?
47 or 53"

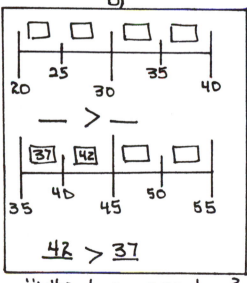

b)

— > —

42 > 37

"Which is greater?
42 or 37"

FIGURE 5.37

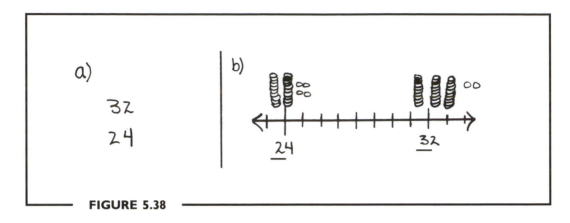

FIGURE 5.38

- Pose the situation where _____ and _____ (use names of people the children know) are reading the same book. Write two 2- or 3-digit numbers on the board and ask students to compare their location in a book (Figure 5.39). "Who has read more pages?" As in Activity 2 (*More Tens*), underscore the first digit of the numbers and have students note their location in the book. Place markers at each page, close the book, and have students feel that 215 pages is less. Repeat with other page numbers.

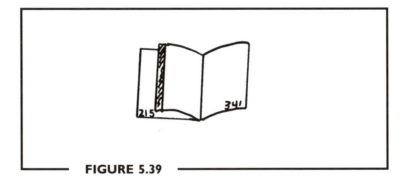

FIGURE 5.39

4. **Match and check.** Choose the approach from Activities 2 and 3 which seems to be the most effective. Use 2- or 3-digit numbers as in Activity 1.

   - Write two numbers. Have the children copy them onto a worksheet illustration where they "belong." For example, the child is given 118 and 231 and writes these numbers into a book to show which means more and which means less, as in Figure 5.40. Discuss how 231 means more pages.

   - Cut out the worksheet illustrations and glue them on cards (Figure 5.41). Write just the two numbers (in random order) on the front of the cards. Underscore the first digits if necessary. The children should then use the deck in the following manner: (a) study the numbers on the front; (b) close their eyes to imagine what the numbers

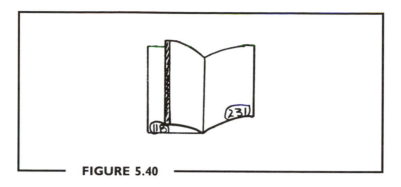

FIGURE 5.40

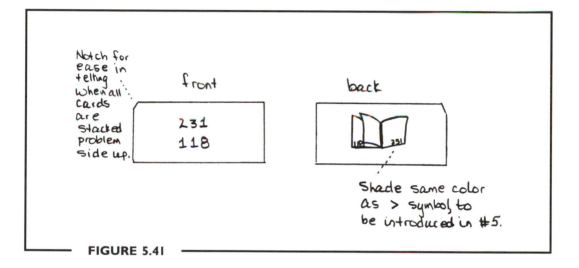

FIGURE 5.41

would look like if pictured; (c) write the number that means more and the number that means less; and (d) turn the card over to check their answer.

5. **Alligator Al.** Use auditory and tactile cues to help students attach meaning to the comparison symbols. For example, make an alligator hand puppet with its mouth clearly outlined. Use two different colors and textures, as illustrated in Figure 5.42a. Carry through the story line that Alligator Al is always hungry and always reaches for the greatest number. Make a poster or file card miniature of Al's two views for students. Provide sandpaper and felt symbols to be placed between numbers as you show students how to position and read the symbols (Figure 5.42b).

Use two 2- or 3-digit numbers with different first digits. Invite the children to finger trace the symbol while reading the comparison. For some number pairs, ask the children to retell Alligator Al's story (he always reaches for the greatest number). It is sometimes necessary to have children verbalize an association to ensure they grasp and retain it.

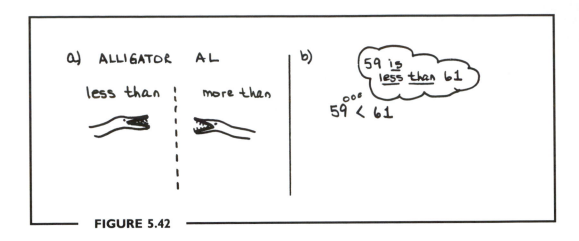

FIGURE 5.42

6. **More comparisons.**

- Dictate two numbers, a 2- and a 3-digit number, for children to write on the dotted lines (Figure 5.43). Discuss why the 2-digit number is placed on the last two lines (no hundreds). Write a dotted 0 in the hundreds place, if necessary, to help students with the comparison. Referring to Figure 5.43, you might note: "You always start big to compare. Here, 'big' means hundreds. One hundred is more than no hundreds, so 134 is more than 53." Repeat with other numbers. Use worksheet exercises to reinforce. At this point, the children could simply circle to indicate which number means more (less).

- Adapt the above activity to focus on two 2- or 3-digit numbers having first digits alike (e.g., 46, 49; 258, 262). "You always start big to compare. If the digits are alike, you compare the next two" (Figure 5.44).

- Provide mixed-review exercises that require students to use symbols for comparing all types of 2- and 3-digit numbers.

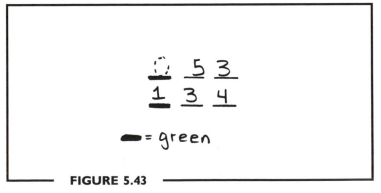

FIGURE 5.43

NOTE: Justifying digit placement by aligning digits one on top of the other, as in Figure 5.43, emphasizes the "greater than/less than" comparison.

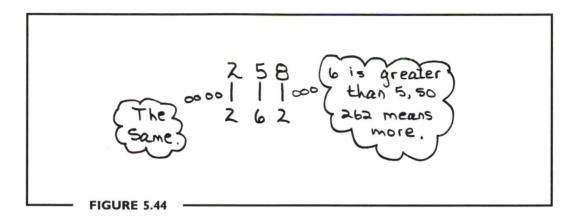

FIGURE 5.44

ROUNDING AND ESTIMATION

Problem Area: Difficulty rounding 2- and higher digit numbers to the nearest 10 or 100.

Typical Disabilities Affecting Progress: Difficulties with visual perception (figure-ground, visual discrimination), visual or sequential memory, abstract reasoning, or auditory processing.

Background: Most day-to-day work with numbers involves some sort of estimation which, in turn, generally involves rounding numbers to make a statement for decision. Clearly, the ability to round numbers is a functional skill, often underestimated in importance. Since it is a difficult skill to teach, it is frequently avoided, especially with students who already have trouble learning.

Mathematicians use one rounding "rule": look to the digit after. If it is 5 or more, round up; otherwise, round down. Social scientists sometimes use a different rule, one that is based on whether the number after is odd or even. In school, the mathematician guideline typically is adopted. Nonetheless, it is worthwhile discussing with students that the rule or procedure for rounding is man-made and, therefore, may differ across teachers.

SUGGESTED SEQUENCE OF ACTIVITIES

Round 2-Digit Numbers

1. **Feel the line.** Have students position the number to be rounded on the number line. At first, do not use a number ending in 5. As in Figure 5.45a, 53 would be placed on the line as shown. Have students visually inspect

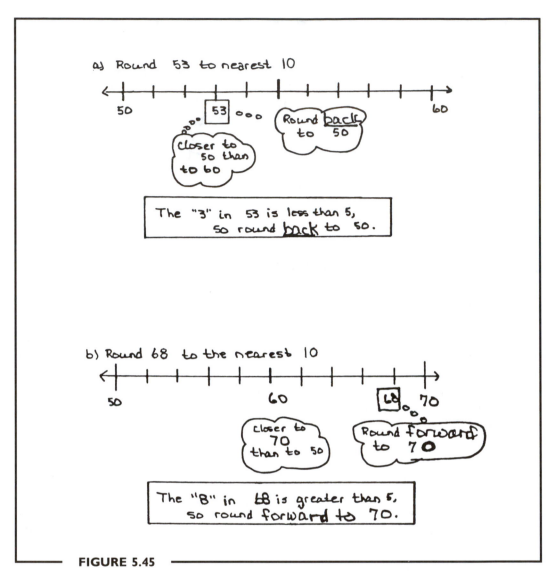

FIGURE 5.45

NOTE: Initially the use of *backward* and *forward* may help students more readily visualize the procedure. Later they can be taught the more commonly used synonyms.

the distance from the number to either end and then slide a finger along the line to each end.

NOTE: *If students are strong tactual learners, make the number line longer to involve more gross motor skill, or texturize the line. Also, have them close their eyes as they slide to either end of the line.*

As students inspect/feel the line, relate the idea of nearest endpoint to the concept and vocabulary of rounding numbers. "Sometimes exact numbers are not needed. A close estimate will do. So we often round numbers when we talk. If 28 people come to a party, we might say: 'About 30 people were there'."

Relate looking/sliding backwards on the number line to rounding *down*; and looking/sliding forward to rounding *up*. In the party example, we rounded *up*. Later extend to other number lines which involve more choices, as in Figure 5.45b.

Gradually include numbers ending in 5 and introduce the convention of rounding used in mathematics: "To round, examine the digit after. If less than 5, round down (backward); if 5 or greater, round up (forward)."

2. **A fast dime** (rounding to the nearest tenth. Small-group, teacher-led activity appropriate for students who cannot effectively use a number line). Provide two decks of cards: a "banker's deck" and a "fast dime" deck (see Figure 5.46). Place the banker's deck in a bank box along with extra dimes and pennies. This deck contains one card for each multiple of 10¢ (to 90¢). The fast dime deck contains cards that list amounts between 11¢ and 89¢ (no multiples of 10¢ included). Until the students understand the activity, remove all money amounts ending in 5 from the fast dime deck.

FIGURE 5.46

Shuffle the fast dime deck and place it face down between the players. Students take turns drawing the top card from the deck and placing it face up in the playing area. They then use dimes (as many as possible) and extra pennies to show the amount on the card.

The banker selects the two cards from the banker's deck that are closest in value to that displayed (see Figure 5.47). The child in this example must decide how a "fast dime" can be made. Is 34¢ closer to 30¢ or to 40¢? The child must either add extra pennies to the 34¢ pile or take some away to indicate the choice made. Thus, either six pennies are added (to make 40¢) or four pennies are taken away (leaving 30¢). The latter decision earns the child one point, since it involves the least number of coins. When the students are comfortable handling these tasks, return the money amounts ending in 5 to the deck. Introduce the "banker's rule" that for these cards the "fast dime" is always the greater 10¢ value.

- *Follow-Up 1:* Lay out cards from the fast dime deck, one at a time, and get the students to verbalize the fact that, for example, 34¢ is

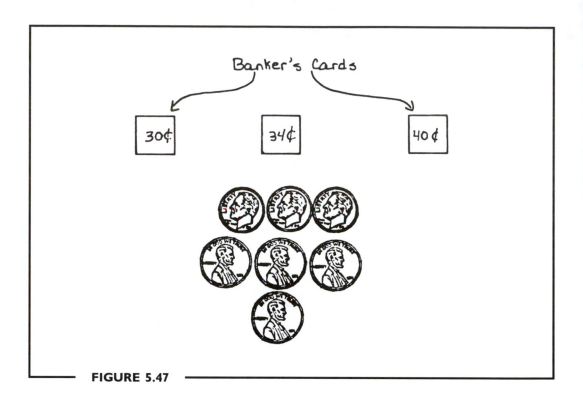

FIGURE 5.47

closer to 30¢ than to 40¢. Allow the students to use dimes and pennies to verify this if necessary.

- *Follow-Up 2:* As in Follow-Up 1, but use a new deck in which all cents signs have been eliminated. If the students hesitate, have them find the matching fast dime card. Seeing the card usually triggers the correct idea. If necessary, allow the students to use dimes and pennies to determine "closeness to." "Yes, 34 hundred is closer to 30 hundred than to 40 hundred."

- *Follow-Up 3:* Use worksheets like that of Figure 5.48. Allow students to use fast dime cards as well as dimes and pennies, if these help. When checking the worksheet, refer to the conventional rules for rounding. Post these rules or provide individual index card copies that can be kept in a file box at each student's desk. Be sure the students understand, procedurally, what rounding up (down) means. When rounding to the nearest ten, for example, all digits beyond 10 will be zeroes (and can be dropped). One uses the number *after* to determine whether the 10 digit itself is changed to a digit one higher (rounding up) or kept the same (rounding down).

3. **Color cue.** Help students focus attention on the "thinking digit" (the number after) by color highlighting, as in Figure 5.49, the "thinking digit" (4) in green and the "changing digit" (6) in red.

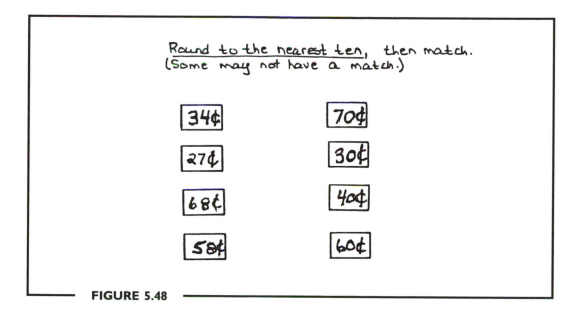

Round to the nearest ten, then match.
(Some may not have a match.)

34¢	70¢
27¢	30¢
68¢	40¢
58¢	60¢

FIGURE 5.48

Round to the nearest ten

4

■ = green   .... = red

FIGURE 5.49

4. **Numbered chips can help.** Use number lines the length of a standard sheet of paper (Figure 5.50a). Premade worksheets which can be filled in (Figure 5.50b) and numbered chips help students visualize the location of the nearest whole number as they place the chips on the number line and then fill in blanks.

5. **Focus here.** The preceding sequence may be adapted to rounding larger numbers and to rounding within numbers. The following idea may help students who understand the concept but have figure-ground difficulties. Using worksheets as in Figure 5.51 help children focus on the correct digit by highlighting the "thinking digit" (8) in green and the "changing digit" (5) *and the corresponding word* (ten) in red.

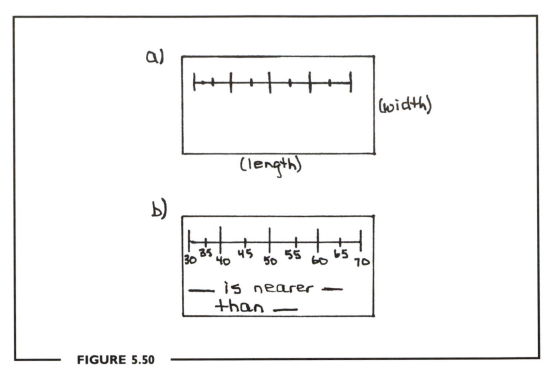

FIGURE 5.50

NOTE: Students with spatial problems especially seem to benefit from this method as the use of nearest, rather than rounding up, makes more sense to them. It is a more concrete, recognizable approach.

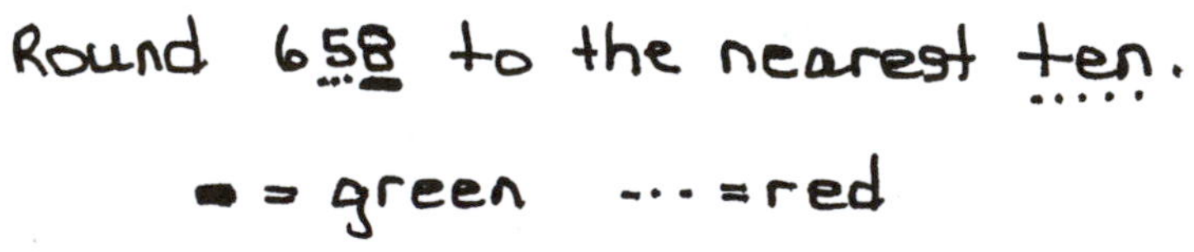

Round 658 to the nearest ten.

■ = green   ⋯ = red

FIGURE 5.51

READING AND INTERPRETING QUANTITATIVE DATA FROM THE PRINTED WORD

Problem Area: Interpreting visually and orally presented numerical information.

Typical Disabilities: Difficulty with abstract reasoning, auditory processing, the ability to generalize information, receptive and expressive language.

Background: At a very early age we help children begin to see the relationship between the spoken word and the written word. Often, however, we neglect to devote the same attention to helping them understand the relationship between numerical concepts and symbols, and oral and written language. Especially for students with visual memory or visual perceptual disabilities, nonverbal learning disabilities, and receptive or expressive language difficulties, confusion in this area can be problematic. Mathematics involves more than numbers; in fact, in today's technological world manipulating numbers can often be done much more rapidly and efficiently using calculators. Knowing when and how to use the available tools, however, involves language.

Many factors influence a child's success in reading and writing numbers. The ability to generalize is essential since, frequently, children hear familiar (mathematical) words. Even the individual numbers, 1 through 9, can have a variety of meanings depending on their use. Sometimes "4" means a quantity of items. At other times it identifies the place value in a larger number. Sometimes it is used as a preposition and it can also mean "pro," as in "I am for vacations!" Interpreting quantitative data used in charts and diagrams also involves a strong sense of language in order to visualize and understand the numerical representations. The following is just a brief list of ideas which have helped the authors improve students' ability to use language successfully. They are meant to be stepping stones to other ideas and an increased awareness on the teacher's part of the need to actively incorporate language into mathematics instruction.

SUGGESTED SEQUENCE OF ACTIVITIES

1. **Associate.** Provide students with ample opportunity to associate numerical symbols with what they hear and see. Instead of using word problems where the numbers are written in symbols, use ones where everything is in words and have students first "decode" the words by rewriting the problems using numerals.

   NOTE: *Students with fine motor problems might only cross out the word and write the number above the word. For others, however, just the copying (or typing) provides the needed reinforcement.*

2. **They're all around.** Encourage students to "listen for all the math around us." Break a hundreds chart into groups of ten. Each student would be assigned one of the groups with the goal of the day being to write down whatever is heard that is related to the number on the chart. The numbers should be written across a piece of lined paper which has been turned sideways, and whenever a child hears something related to that number he or she writes the word, draws a picture, or, if writing is difficult, uses a tape recorder and dictates what has been found.

3. **Explain it.** Using charts and tables from the newspaper, have children make up stories about the chart. They could do this in groups or individually, depending on their interests, abilities and disabilities, and confidence. At first, and especially for younger students, omit the explanations and have

students use their accurate narration skills to tell a story which goes along with the chart.

NOTE: *The goal of this assignment is to better understand the relationship between numbers and language. Some students may easily and willingly be able to write the stories. Others may prefer to dictate or draw a picture. Accept whatever presentation method is the child's strong area.*

WRITING MATHEMATICS

Problem Area: Difficulty writing multidigit numbers.

Typical Disabilities Affecting Progress: Difficulties with visual perception (figure-ground, visual discrimination), visual association, closure, abstract reasoning, and auditory processing.

Background: Coupled with the need for understanding the language components in math is the need to be able to accurately associate what is heard and/or seen with the ability to write a number. The opportunity to use materials such as those illustrated in Figure 5.52 to solve a wide variety of interesting problem

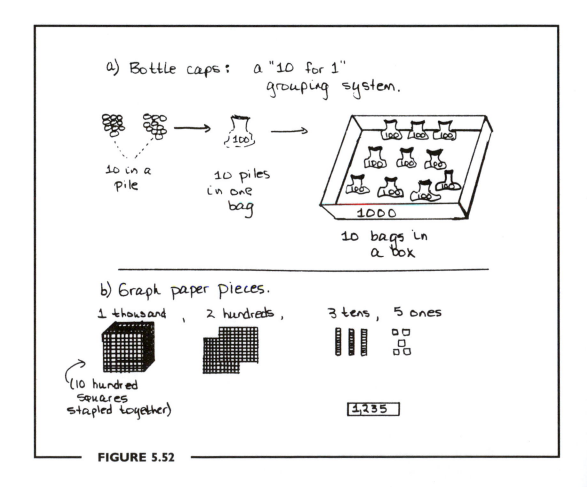

FIGURE 5.52

situations is beneficial for helping these students develop better intuitions for large numbers. Using such materials often precludes common difficulties, such as writing "20038" for "two hundred thirty-eight" or reading "415" as "forty-one, five"—or at least establishes a basis for treatment when these difficulties do emerge.

To remedy the first problem a teacher might, for example, ask a child to gather 2 hundreds, 3 tens, and 8 singles from a box of graph paper pieces. After recording the number of each kind of piece (Figure 5.53), the teacher might write the number in standard form and "model" the way it *should* be read. Teacher and child can then switch roles. After taking graph paper pieces and recording the number of each kind, the child could write the number in standard form and read it to the teacher. As follow-up, the teacher and student can take turns drawing a 3-digit number card, reading it, and asking the other to show it using graph paper pieces (Figure 5.54). Stamps for hundreds, tens, and ones, available from many school supply

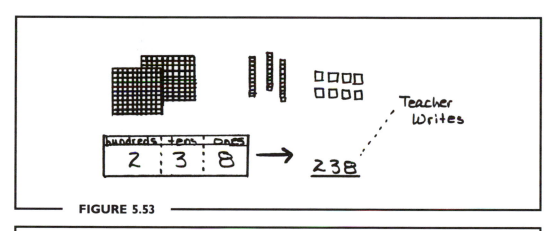

FIGURE 5.53

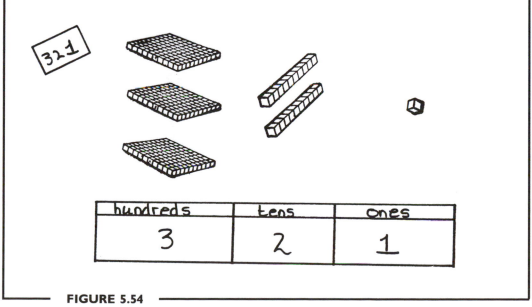

FIGURE 5.54

companies, can also be used. These should be among the teaching aids of every classroom in which mathematics is taught.

These activities provide an effective visual frame of reference that helps children read and write 3-digit numbers when concrete materials are no longer used. Teacher modeling—correctly writing and saying the number represented by the pieces—is a vital part of the sequence. Correct teacher modeling is also necessary to prevent children from reading "238" as "two hundred *and* thirty-eight." The "and" is properly reserved for the decimal point, as in $2.38 (two dollars and 38 cents) or 4.2 (four and two tenths). Only in special cases are children allowed to use "and." Some students may need to use the word as a pause for remembering how to group digits when reading a number. However, using "and" in this manner should be terminated when it is no longer needed. This situation parallels that of using "uh" or pausing to keep from stuttering.

For students who read "415" as "forty-one, five," underlining the hundreds digit sometimes helps.

- Examples:

$$\underline{4}15 \rightarrow \text{"4 hundred 15"}$$
$$\underline{2}23 \rightarrow \text{"2 hundred 23"}$$

Teachers might point out that the only new part is the first digit. Students already know how to read the rest. Provide a card for the child to move along, as in syllabicating, while reading the number. Further, illustrating each 3-digit number with graph paper pieces, as before, also helps.

Whenever possible, it is far better to embed number work and related problems in interesting or familiar contexts, rather than in isolation. Carefully selected applied or game settings tend to invite children's curiosity and interest, and hence better nurture their place value understanding and development of number sense. For example, as part of a unit on tropical rainforests, students might learn that, above the *forest floor,* the *understory* layer (smaller trees and bushes) might reach as high as 80 feet, the *canopy* (main tree) layer might reach another 50 feet above that and, finally, several giant trees in the *emergent* layer might be seen towering as high as 30 feet above everything else. Students might use materials (their choice) to determine the height of some of the tallest trees in the rainforest. Or, using the fact that it rains almost every day of the year in a rainforest—or up to 400 inches each year—students might use materials to help provide information for a graph of total rain that might fall in a rainforest over 2 years (800 inches), 3 years (1,200 inches), and 4 years (1,600 inches).

If the students have difficulties as they begin to work with larger numbers, or have difficulty interpreting quantitative data in printed material, more specialized techniques may be necessary. Several helpful techniques are outlined in the suggestions that follow.

SUGGESTED SEQUENCE OF ACTIVITIES

Reading and Writing 4- and 5-Digit Numbers

Prerequisite Skills:

a. Ability to read and write 3-digit numbers. This includes a firm grasp of place-value ideas for 3-digit numbers, including the understanding that "when you hear hundreds, the number has three digits. Sometimes a zero is needed to show no tens or ones, as in 403 and 620."

b. Prior work modeling 4-digit numbers with graph paper pieces (refer to Figure 5.52b).

Basic Sequence
---

1. **Look!** As a first step, present number pairs visually (Figure 5.55). The thousands digit is green; others are red. Explain that one comma in a number is read "thousand." The only new part comes before the comma. "You already know how to read the rest." Have children finger trace the part that is the same within the pair, then read both numbers.

   • Use no 0s in the hundreds place at this time.

   • Do not use colored digits with children having closure difficulties to avoid activating their tendency to treat multidigit numbers as a series of disjointed, unrelated digits.

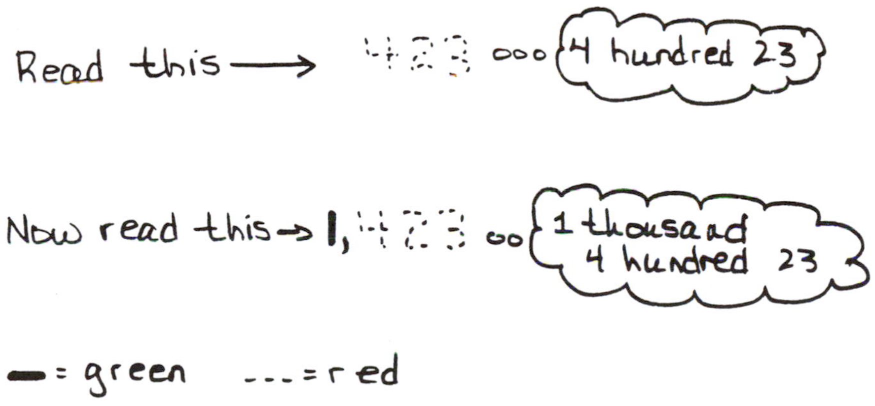

FIGURE 5.55

- *Alternative 1:* For children who need color coding but who have closure difficulties, underline the digits as in the example below. Generally, this approach can be used any time and, except in severe cases, works as effectively as color-coded digits.

  Example:

  "Read this: 4̲23"
  "Now read this: 1,4̲23"

- *Alternative 2:* Use no colors. Have the child use a card as when learning to syllabicate (Figure 5.56).

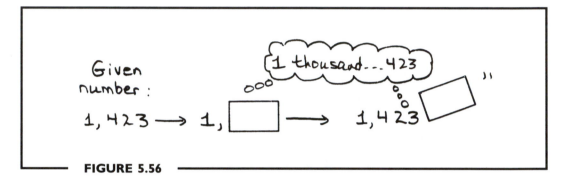

FIGURE 5.56

2. **Word match.** If the children can read number words, written practice exercises like those of Figure 5.57 can be given. The skill being reinforced is used in writing checks. In addition, the exercise prepares for the dictation in Activity 4 (*Hear and Find*). The number of thousands is written in green to match the green underlining of the thousands place. The 3-digit part, both underlining and words, is in red. The words *thousand* and the *comma* are the same color, so the children learn to associate the two. Later, when

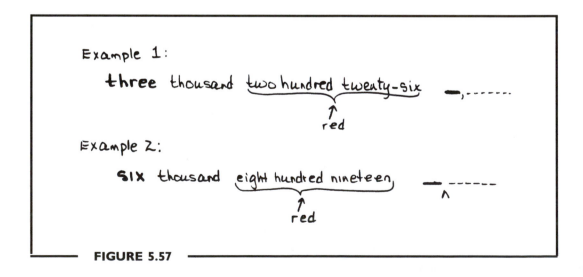

FIGURE 5.57

they need to learn to place the comma themselves, the format can be modified as in the second example of Figure 5.57.

3. **Find it.** Children match color-coded words (as in Figure 5.57) to non–color-coded numbers.

   • *Follow-Up:* Same type of match exercises, but without colors.

4. **Hear and find.** Dictate 4-digit numbers and have the children circle each from a group of numbers. Include 3-digit distractors. At first, use color coding as before.

5. **Zero holds the place.** Dictate "seventy-three" and ask children to write the number on the dotted lines (Figure 5.58a). Discuss why the digits are placed in the last two spots. (No hundreds.) Explain that in higher digit numbers, 0 is used to show no number in a given place. For example, 2,073 means "2 thousands, no hundreds, 7 tens, and 3 ones" (Figure 5.58b). Present color-coded number pairs for children to read (the thousands digit green; the hundreds group red). This time focus on 4-digit numbers having a 0 in the hundreds place.

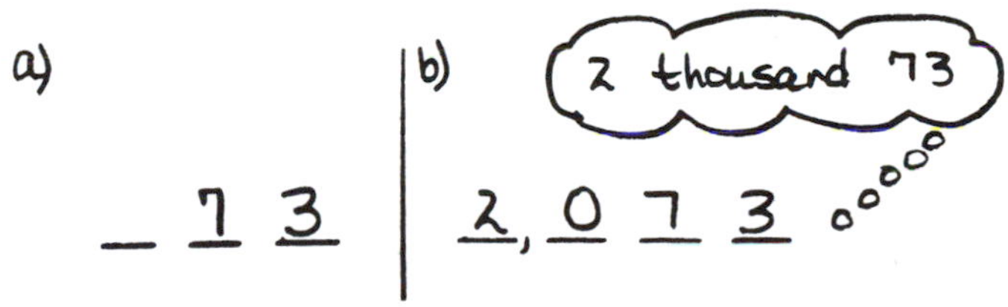

FIGURE 5.58

6. **More hear and find.** Adapt Activity 4 to focus on 4-digit numbers having a 0. Include numbers with 0 in the tens place and the hundreds place, as well as numbers without any zeroes. When the exercise is complete, have the children read aloud the 4-digit numbers they circled.

7. **Tape it to me.** Dictate 4-digit numbers and have the children write them. Alternatively, have the children play a prerecorded tape that dictates the numbers. Responses can be checked against an answer key.

> **Extending the Basic Sequence:**
> **Reading and Writing 5- and Higher Digit Numbers**

Ideas from the previous sequence can be adapted to help students read and write larger numbers. A card chart such as that illustrated in Figure 5.59 is also useful. Within each period, the child reads the familiar 1-, 2-, or 3-digit number and adds the "family" name (i.e., the name of the period). Except for students with

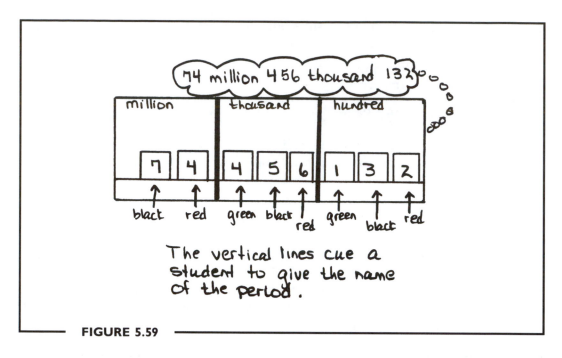

The vertical lines cue a student to give the name of the period.

FIGURE 5.59

closure difficulties, a green-black-red color coding of digits within each period can be used to emphasize the idea. The chart can later be extended and used for reading decimals.

A pleated modification of the chart is illustrated in Figure 5.60. Children enjoy "opening" a number at the comma to check that they are reading it correctly. Cover the writing surfaces with clear contact paper and use a wipe-off pen or pencil. This way the digits can easily be changed.

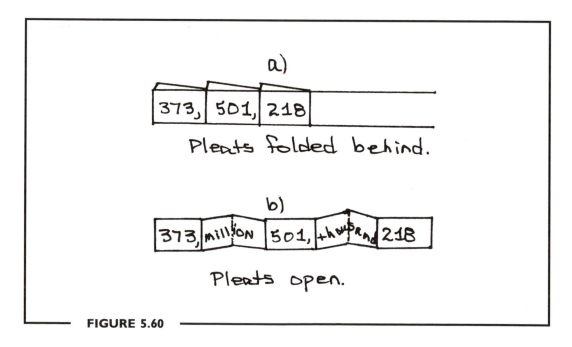

FIGURE 5.60

DEVELOPING "NUMBER SENSE"

A major goal of school mathematics is to help all children deal effectively in common, numerical situations like the following:

- Terry thought about the answer he had written for 26 + 48. "Can't be right. Both numbers are less than 50, so the total must be less than 100."

- Mary's mother had given her $10 for milk and bread. Mary knew that a gallon of milk was just under $2 and a loaf of bread was a little more than $1. At the store she put three gallons of milk and three loaves of bread in her cart. She was confident, as she stood in line at the checkout counter, that she would have enough money for the milk and bread, even with tax.

Experience has shown that when children feel comfortable with numbers, they develop a sense of control in numeric situations, in and out of school. They approach problems like these with a more positive attitude and get better results.

Some students reach this "comfort zone" naturally. Most children with learning disabilities do not, however. The key to success is the teacher in the daily mathematics lesson who:

- recognizes the importance of developing number sense in students;

- constructs situations which stimulate and develop number sense; and

- creates a positive climate where students can grow in their understanding and application of numbers.

The following facts are critical in an examination of how teachers can improve or further develop a positive climate for building number sense among students.

- Children are more willing to explore numeric situations that involve mathematical ideas with which they are familiar.

- Children approach numeric situations in different ways. Accepting and encouraging variety in pupil response results in more flexible thinking and nurtures a greater potential for student success in numeric situations.

- For students with learning disabilities who are mainstreamed, the use of cooperative learning groups, for example, provides opportunities to listen to each others' ideas about numbers. Therefore, children learn that more than one way of approaching a problem or a situation can lead to a successful outcome.

- Children will be more likely to take the risk and make decisions about numbers if they know it is all right not to be "right" or have the best estimate the first time. In a non-threatening atmosphere, and given many opportunities to practice, children have a greater potential to grow in their ability to make appropriate decisions about numbers.

- Social studies and science are among the content areas which come alive for students when they possess a sense of numbers. For example, while planning for a social studies field trip a teacher might ask, "Is one dollar per student enough spending money for the class field trip to the history museum? Why or why not?" When children see that number sense is useful throughout their day, they recognize a greater need for making better decisions involving numbers.

- Children are great imitators. Having a teacher who uses good number sense makes children want to be like the teacher and use good number sense, too.

Teachers who are committed to developing number sense in their students are dedicated to instruction that provides ongoing experiences such as:

- Flashing basic fact cards and having students indicate whether the answer is more or less than a given target number. (Then provide the exact answer or ask a child to do so.)

- Providing opportunities for children to think about and discover other relationships:

    > *For example:* "What's 5 + 5?" (10). "So is 5 + 9 more or less?" (More.) Have the child put five counters in each hand, while you or another child takes charge of the extra counters. "Do we have to give you more counters so you have 5 and 9?" (Yes.) Circle the second addend of each equation and note that 9 is more than 5.

- Having children take a few seconds before doing a row of problems to identify the one(s) that will have the greatest answer. (Discuss why.)

- Asking children to indicate those numbers that are "close to" another specified number (e.g., "Which fractions are 'closer to' 1 than to 0? Which are 'close to' $\frac{1}{2}$?" Or, "Which numbers are 'closer to' 50 than to 100?").

    NOTE: *If children have difficulty sensing "closeness," try a kinesthetic/ tactile approach. "What about 86?" Using a meter stick, the child can place a finger on 86 and close eyes while you run the finger from 86 to 100; from 86 to 50. Which "feels" closer?*

- Challenging children specifically to think about numbers in different ways.

For example: Frequently play "I'm thinking of a number." (To aid the thinking process, allow children to use number cards to 20. Have them laid out in two columns: 0–10 along the left edge of the desk; 11–20 along the right edge.)

— "It's between 9 and 14." (These cards are moved to the center of the desk.)

"It's a greater number than any you see on the classroom clock." (Child pushes back any cards that are not needed, i.e., 12 or less.)

"If I switch places with the digits, I will have 31. What's my number?" (13.)

— "I *don't* say it when I count by 2s." (Move odd number cards to center of the desk.)

"It's more than 8." (Child pushes back any cards not needed, those 8 or less.)

"It's less than 16." (Child pushes back any cards, 16 or more.)

"I *don't* say it when I count by 5s." (Child pushes back 10 and 15.)

"When it's two hours before 1:00 o'clock, the hour hands points to it. What's my number?" (11.)

This list samples number-related activities that are beginning to permeate the elementary-school mathematics curriculum in an effort to lead children to be friendly with and make better use of numbers. *The Arithmetic Teacher,* the official journal of the National Council of Teachers of Mathematics (NCTM), frequently carries practical articles related to the development of number sense. NCTM also has recently released *Number Sense and Operations, K–6* (1993) and *Developing Number Sense in the Middle Grades, 5–8* (1991).

There is a subtle difference between learning about numbers and learning enough about numbers to show good "number sense." The emphasis in working with students with learning disabilities is on structured, extended learning experiences which gradually will generate those number concepts, number relationships, and numeric skills which enable students eventually to demonstrate good number sense.

USING A HAND CALCULATOR

Exercises using a hand calculator can be designed to serve two purposes:

1. to reinforce basic number and place-value skills; and

2. to build visual and auditory memory skills.

Since some students with learning disabilities have difficulty merely locating the numbers on a calculator, teachers must check for the following prerequisites before requiring calculator use:

- *Prerequisite 1:* Students can discriminate among the numerals and locate the number on the calculator.

- *Prerequisite 2:* Students have sufficient eye-hand coordination to punch the correct key.

    When these prerequisites are established, exercises such as the following can be carried out.

> *Example 1 (visual memory):* Provide a list of numbers for the children to enter. For multidigit numbers, encourage them to look at, then punch, the *entire number* (or at least as many digits as they can) without looking back.

> *Example 2 (visual memory):* Provide a list of number pairs. The children enter the greatest (least) of each pair, then check against a key.

> *Example 3 (auditory memory):* Dictate a number (or use a prerecorded tape). Have the children punch in the number, then compare it with a key. In early phases of the activity children with severe problems may be allowed to write the number before entering it.

> *Example 4 (auditory memory):* Dictate a number (or use a prerecorded tape). Have the children enter the number that comes after the number given, then check with a key.

> *Example 5 (visual association):* Show students how to skip count, count on or back using a calculator. For example, to skip count by 10s on most calculators, the following sequence can be entered: 10 + = = = until the desired target number is reached. To *count on by 10s* from a given start number (e.g., 40), children can enter 40 + 10 = = = until the desired target or stop number is reached. To *count back by 1s* from a given start number (e.g., 12), children can enter 12 − 1 = = = until the desired stop number is reached.

REFERENCES

National Council of Teachers of Mathematics. (1991). *Developing number sense in the middle grades, 5–8.* Reston, VA: Author.

National Council of Teachers of Mathematics. (1993). *Number sense and operations, K–6.* Reston, VA: Author.

CHAPTER 6

The Four Operations: Basic Concepts, Basic Facts

IT IS ESSENTIAL FOR ALL STUDENTS, including those with learning disabilities, to understand what it means to add, subtract, multiply, and divide—and to develop a good sense of when to use each of these basic operations in day-to-day settings. Confidence in performing these tasks equips children with a certain power in mathematics. It provides them (a) with a strong conceptual base which enables them to reason in problem situations and (b) with a basis for developing successful computation skills involving mental and paper-and-pencil computation, estimation, or calculator use.

Much of children's success with these tasks depends on adequate mastery of the basic number facts. This chapter addresses the question of how to help students with learning disabilities develop a conceptual understanding of the basic operations and how to master the basic addition, subtraction, multiplication, and division facts. Specifically, the focus is on the following topics related to basic concepts or facts for each operation:

1. Building concepts for the four operations

2. Interpreting the printed word or sign for an operation

3. Comparison subtraction

4. Strategies for learning basic facts

5. Strategies for learning addition facts

6. Strategies for learning subtraction facts

7. Strategies for learning multiplication facts

8. Strategies for learning division facts

9. Using a hand calculator

Like their peers, students with learning disabilities typically need much oral and manipulative work to build a strong conceptual background for each mathematical operation. Suggestions for using and extending textbook treatments in this regard are discussed in Sections 1, 2, and 3. The other sections of the chapter focus primarily on ideas for helping students with learning disabilities memorize the basic facts. Section 4 presents suggestions that may be applied to facts for all four operations. Sections 5 through 8 look separately at facts for each operation. A final section outlines ideas for helping students with learning disabilities master basic concepts or facts for the four operations using a hand calculator.

Sometimes students get bogged down in higher level computation because they do not know the basic facts or because they do not recognize simple, known facts in multidigit problems. Specific ideas for how to handle these difficulties are outlined in the first sections of Chapter 7. It may be useful to consider those suggestions along with others which follow as background for planning a basic program of fact study for students with learning disabilities.

A general note regarding the importance of relating basic understandings and skills to common daily settings is in order at this point. Many students with learning disabilities need a structured program that emphasizes practical applications of the mathematics they are learning. Otherwise, they will not make the transfer and hence will fall short when it comes to using math where it counts—in day-to-day living. With respect to the four operations, activities like the following are helpful.

- *Activity 1:* Pose a situation, such as that involving money to purchase needed items, and ask the children to tell which of two given operations is appropriate.
  Example: "Buy a pencil for 5 cents and a small eraser for 8 cents. What is the cost?" Select situations very familiar to the children. If possible, involve them in dramatizing the situations.

- *Activity 2:* Have the children circle one problem on a practice sheet of number facts. Ask them to describe a situation outside the classroom that might involve that number fact.
  Example: $2 + 5 = \underline{\quad}$ is circled. The child might suggest: "Two red flowers, five yellow outside our front door; seven in all."

Other applications in the mathematics textbook might be highlighted and more carefully interwoven with the topics of this chapter. Selected story problems and measurement applications, such as finding perimeter and area, also fit this category.

BUILDING CONCEPTS FOR THE FOUR OPERATIONS

Problem Area: Inability to associate real meaning with written number sentences for addition, subtraction, multiplication, or division.

Typical Disabilities Affecting Progress: Difficulty with abstract reasoning, visual or auditory association, and receptive language.

Background: Diane looked at the problem "4×2" and quickly wrote 8. The teacher asked Diane to make a picture for "4×2." Diane did not hesitate at all.

She drew four dots beside the 4 and two dots beside the 2. It did not bother Diane that she had drawn six dots but had written 8 to indicate the total number. Conceptually, Diane is in trouble. Unless cued, she will not know when to multiply rather than add in a simple problem situation.

Diane's response is not atypical of other students with learning disabilities with reasoning or association problems. Children with expressive language difficulties may correctly select the one drawing from several that illustrates a basic fact, but, like Diane, they may be unable to represent it correctly. It is important that children have a good visual image of what it means to "add," "subtract," "multiply," or "divide." Then they will be more likely to use the appropriate operation to solve problems in day-to-day settings. In many situations, it also is necessary that they be able to assign meaning to the written sign for each operation.

"Big ideas" must be understood. Addition means "put together." Subtraction has several interpretations. The simplest, and that used in beginning instruction, is "take away," as in "8 cookies; 3 are eaten by the boys; how many then?" (Some children, for emotional reasons, have difficulty with subtraction because of the idea of take away. Being sensitive to this possibility is important.)

Children also can subtract instead of counting to compare two quantities. In Figure 6.1a, for example, "Dick has 7 balls and Jack has 4." To determine *how many more* balls Dick has then Jack (or, equivalently, *how many fewer* Jack has than Dick), children could match one-to-one and count the leftovers. By counting and comparing to the subtraction result, children may begin to realize that they can subtract to find the difference in situations like this—an understanding that is especially important as situations involve larger numbers. This under-

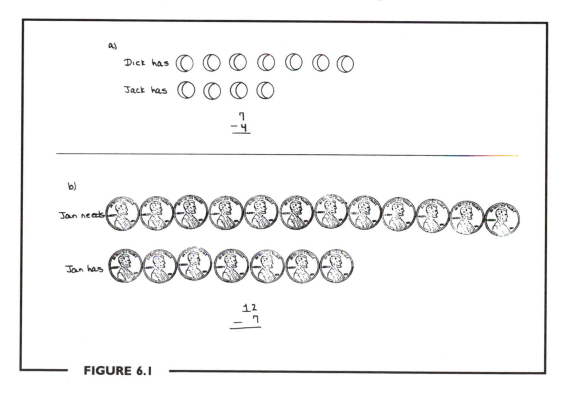

FIGURE 6.1

standing sometimes develops naturally, as children listen to solution approaches different children in a class or group present for problems like this, apart from direct instruction.

A second example of comparison subtraction, illustrated in Figure 6.1b, involves situations in which children are asked to compare what one has to what is wanted to determine *how much more* is needed. To develop a strong conceptual basis for addition and subtraction, children need systematic experiences with the full range of problem types.

Similar comments might be made about children's range of experiences with multiplication and division, which concern groups equal in number. To multiply we *join* or *put together* equal-sized groups, then tell how many in all. To divide we *share*. This is the simplest approach, now used with increasing frequency in beginning instruction. We start with a larger number of objects and give the same number to each of several persons. Children later learn both to tell the *number in each group* and the *number of groups* as the result of a division for particular situations (see Figure 6.2).

Most mathematics textbooks contain suggestions for developing these "big ideas." Too often, however, a very narrow view of problem solving is presented.

As a major focus for concept work, teachers today are encouraged to use action verbs in simple stories that informally involve children adding, subtracting, multiplying, or dividing to answer a question. These stories might be based on a literature theme or on some recent, shared experience.

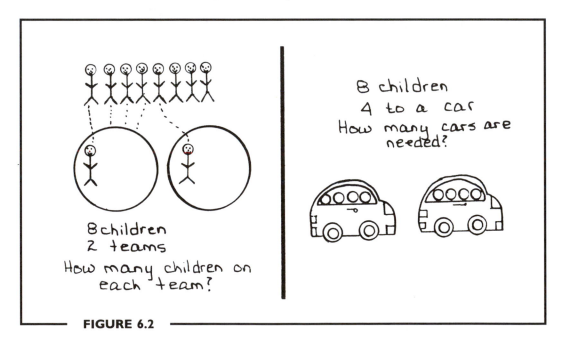

FIGURE 6.2

- *Addition Example (result unknown):* "The three bears picked berries. Baby Bear ate 2 berries. Mama Bear ate 3 berries. Papa Bear ate as many berries as Baby and Mama together. How many berries did Papa Bear eat?" (5, because 2 berries + 3 berries = **5** berries.)

Solving interesting problems should be the foundation of any effort to help children with learning disabilities understand an operation. Such problem solving should pervade the early school curriculum for all children and become part of the daily routine. During beginning phases one could expect, even encourage children to use objects to act out stories like that above in order to answer the question asked. *Children should always be expected to report on how they solved a problem and, eventually, to record their solution steps in some meaningful way.* As children become more comfortable with a type of problem, they will begin to use more efficient solutions and will be able to write appropriate number sentences to match their work. Gradually, for each operation, problems should be framed so the question shifts away from the result, as in the following example.

- *Addition Example (start unknown):* "Working together, the three bears picked several buckets of berries in the morning and 2 more buckets in the afternoon. By dinner time, they had picked 5 buckets of berries. How many buckets did they pick in the morning?"

Even very young primary children with learning disabilities have been observed to solve problems like this independently by using counters to mimic the action in the story. Following the storyline, these children do not initially know how many counters to put out for buckets picked in the morning, but they will place 2 counters on a workspace for the 2 buckets picked in the afternoon, then put out counters to make 5, the number of buckets picked by dinner time. Moving the 2 counters aside, most students will count and announce that "3 buckets were picked in the morning, because 3 and these 2 make the 5 they picked in all." (**2** buckets + 3 buckets = 5 buckets.) Note that children with poor auditory memory are helped by teachers who write numbers from the problem on the board as they are said and occasionally provide a visual sketch to correspond to the storyline.

It is possible to build three different types of addition problems around any simple number sentence having 3 numbers. We just leave out one of the numbers and fashion a story to find it. The first bear story above asked children to find the *result* (5); the second asked them to determine the number at the *start* (3). The second story could easily be modified to state the number of buckets picked by the bears in the morning and the total for the day, asking children how many were picked in the afternoon (2).

The thinking among leading mathematics educators today is that we have calculators readily available for computing. In today's technological age, children need to be better problem solvers, able to deal with many types of problems. The recommended curricular thrust, therefore, is to start problem solving earlier and to integrate this thrust throughout mathematics instruction. For each operation, it is necessary to increase the amount of time given to verbal problems—from early concept work on. Further, as in the three bears stories, there is the expectation to involve children with a broad variety of problem types. Teachers have the further responsibility to expect and encourage children to:

- *predict* problem solutions,

- use *different approaches* to solving any given problem, and

- be ready to *explain or justify* what was done to solve a problem.

As an attempt is made to provide this problem-solving integration in a child's mathematics program, it may be beneficial to consider specific suggestions, such as those outlined below, for supporting the efforts of students with learning disabilities who have reasoning or association difficulties.

SUGGESTED SEQUENCE OF ACTIVITIES

1. **Act it out.** Physically dramatize the "big idea" of an operation. Get children to show objects or act out what is meant (see Figure 6.3). This is the basis for what we say and later write with symbols in early addition, subtraction, multiplication, or division work.

    - *Example* (addition): "When we *add* we *put things together.* There are three pieces of chalk on the tray. Take these two pieces and add them to those on the chalk tray." (The child walks to the tray to do so.)

    - *Example* (division): "Eight cookies to share with two boys. *Divide.* Give *the same number* to each." (Physically act out this division.)

Emphasize oral-manipulative work to help children understand other vocabulary related to an operation.

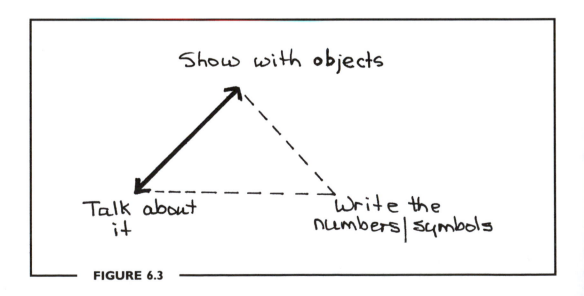

FIGURE 6.3

- *Example 1* (concrete multiplication): Introduce the idea of placing cookies on a cookie sheet. Then give the children a box of chips and ask them to lay out rows of four, as one might lay out cookies on a cookie sheet.

- *Example 2* (concrete abstract multiplication): Give the children a box of chips and have them lay out rows of four. Comment about the groupings made. "How many fours? (Figure 6.4). . . . One four, two fours, three fours—*three times* you laid out a row of four."

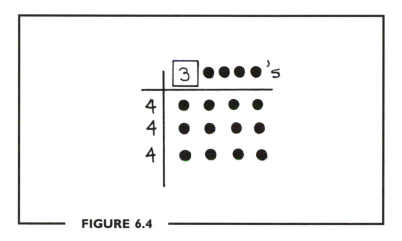

FIGURE 6.4

2. **Talk it out.** Encourage the children to use the new vocabulary for an operation. Hearing themselves often triggers the intended meaning or association.

3. **Tap it out.** If the children are strong auditorially, have them close their eyes and use sound or kinesthetic cues in association with new vocabulary.

- *Example 1* (subtraction): The children look at five felt hearts (Velcro stapled to the backs and attached to a Velcro strip as in Figure 6.5). They then close their eyes. "Feel the hearts now. How many? (5). Open your eyes so we can subtract. *Take away 2*. Now how many?"

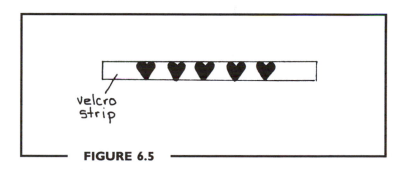

FIGURE 6.5

- *Example 2* (multiplication): The children close their eyes. Take one child's finger and tap it on the desk. "Let's tap out groups of four:

    (tap-tap-tap-tap) . . . . that's four—one four;
    (tap-tap-tap-tap) . . . . that's four again—two fours;
    (tap-tap-tap-tap) . . . . . . that's four again—three fours.

    Three *times* we tapped out a group of four." (Later we *will write 3 times 4,* or 3 × 4.)

    As follow-up, have the child independently identify the number of times a group of four (or three, or two . . .) is tapped.

4. **Small steps.** Building concepts with students with learning disabilities, particularly those having the difficulties identified at the beginning of this section, is often a slow process. Keep each instructional step size small, and use interesting or familiar contexts whenever possible. The following multiplication exercises illustrate these points.

    - *Activity 1:* Use colored loops and chips as in Figure 6.6, and use the context of placing cookies on a baking sheet. Reinforcing follow-up worksheets should use the same color coding. Key questions to ask are: "How many groups?" "How many chips in each group?" "How many chips in all?"

    - *Activity 2:* As before, with the modification suggested by Figure 6.7. (Note that the color coding is consistent with that used previously.) The children complete the example shown by filling in "3 5s = 15." Some children spontaneously draw five dots on the line instead of writing the digit 5. They say it makes more sense. (It does.)

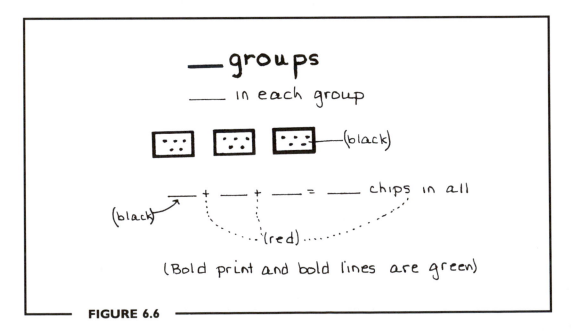

FIGURE 6.6

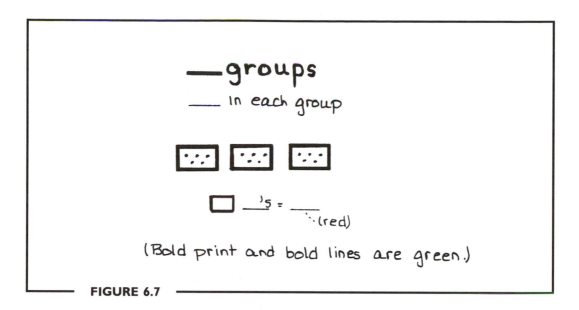

FIGURE 6.7

- *Activity 3:* Introduce the "times" sign (×). Use chips to form equal-sized groups as before. Have the children describe the grouping. In Figure 6.8 there are 4 threes. "Yes, four *times* we have a group of three. This '×' is the multiplication sign. When we see it, we *say* 'times' and *think* 4 threes. 4 × (times) 3, that's 12 in all." (The sign could be texturized or color coded. See *Symbol feel* and *Symbol look* activities on page 225.) Follow-up worksheets using the format of Figure 6.8 are then assigned with color coding as illustrated.

NOTE 1: *Discussion at this point should emphasize that multiplication deals with equal-sized groups. "When we have equal-sized*

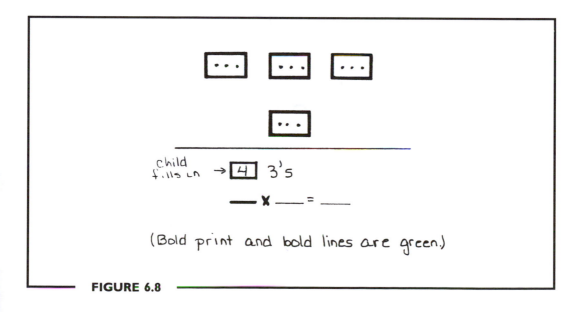

FIGURE 6.8

groups like this, and we need to know how many in all, we can multiply." Follow-up activities should present some situations in which equal-sized groups are not involved. This requires that students decide whether multiplication is indeed appropriate in a given situation. The ability to make this decision affects success with word problems.

NOTE 2: *New vocabulary must be carefully presented. The sequence of examples just illustrated how one might informally use the term* **times** *in a multiplication context both before and during presentation of the written multiplication sign. An activity sequence similar to that outlined, used remedially for Mark, led him to comment: "So that's what* **times** *is all about. I could get the multiply part, but I could never figure out that* **times."**

- *Activity 4:* Additional reinforcement is usually necessary. Use colored chips and frames as in Figure 6.8. Provide more chips than needed to force thinking. Have the children fill loops to picture 5 twos, 4 threes, or other groupings. For each, the corresponding multiplication sentence should be written. Next, follow-up worksheets using the format of Figure 6.9 are assigned, with color coding as illustrated.

- *Activity 5:* Have the children complete worksheets like that of Figure 6.10. Color code the sign to match the box as in previous activities. This helps establish the relationship between "Four 3s" and "4 × 3." For selected problems, the children may be asked to draw dots or use chips to show the number of *times* a group of a given size appears.

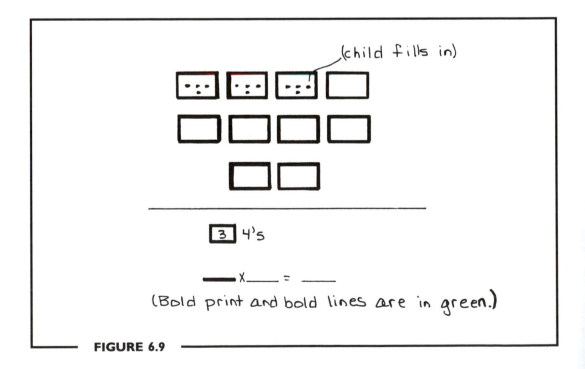

FIGURE 6.9

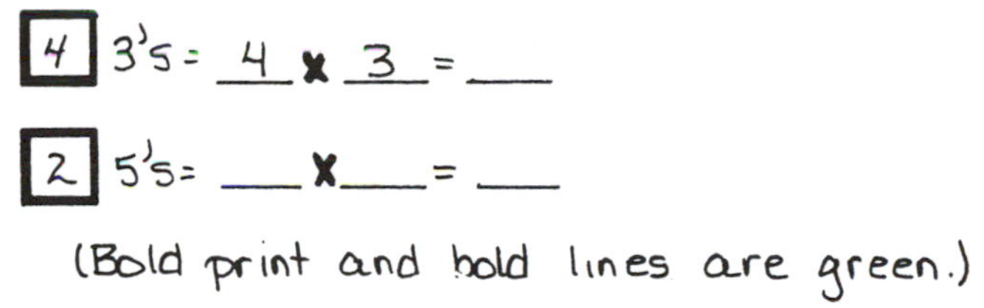

┌───┐

$\boxed{4}$ 3's = $\underline{\;4\;}$ **✗** $\underline{\;3\;}$ = $\underline{\qquad}$

$\boxed{2}$ 5's = $\underline{\qquad}$ **✗** $\underline{\qquad}$ = $\underline{\qquad}$

(Bold print and bold lines are green.)

FIGURE 6.10

└───┘

5. **Symbol feel.** Texturize the symbol for a new operation. Have children finger trace as they read an expression containing the symbol. Guide the hand, if necessary, so the writing movement is correct from the start. Next ask children to *close their eyes,* finger trace, and say the name for the symbol. As a follow-up, have children trace out the symbol on their desk or in midair.

6. **Symbol look.** Color code each operation a distinctly different color and place it on a wall chart for ready reference. In the chart of Figure 6.11, for example, all terms and symbols relating to subtraction are green. (Note that a diagram appears on the chart which illustrates the meaning of the symbol.) Use the color coding for the operation symbol during board work and on worksheets as long as it appears helpful.

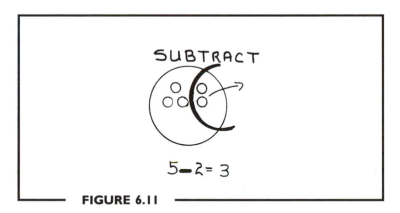

FIGURE 6.11

7. **Act it out.** Provide experiences where the children themselves use manipulatives to illustrate *written* work (Figure 6.12). For example, for a written fact like 3 + 2 = __, a child might count out three objects, then two more; then recount to find the number in all. Later, as they become more familiar with addition, encourage the children to *count on* from the number in a small sight group rather than count from one each time.

8. **Across and up and down.** Because it follows the left-right reading motion, many teachers introduce the horizontal before the vertical format for simple number combinations. Eventually, the vertical format must be introduced as a prelude to computation. To help the children associate the two forms,

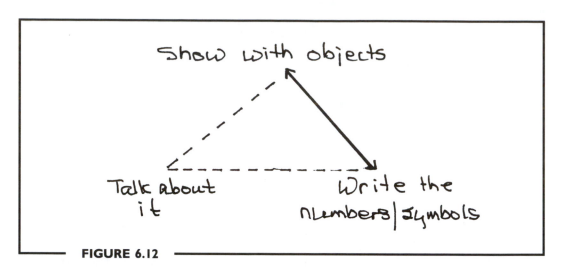

FIGURE 6.12

it may be helpful to use the technique of Figure 6.13 where the double bar simulates the equal sign.

9. **Turnarounds** (commutative property). Many children with learning disabilities need special help to recognize that $2 + 4$ and $4 + 2$ give the same answer, "When you know one you know the other, too." Glue chips to strips as in Figure 6.14.

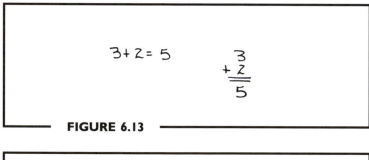

FIGURE 6.13

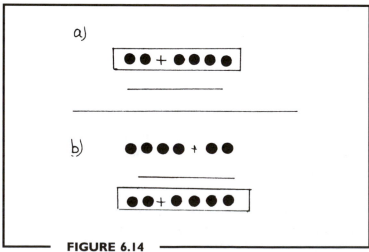

FIGURE 6.14

- Have the children write the expression illustrated by the strip (2 + 4).

- Use chips and a felt addition sign to lay out 4 + 2, as illustrated in Figure 6.14b. Have the children write the number sentence represented by this second configuration.

- "Are there as many chips in the first row as in the second?" Have children match the loose chips and the sign one-to-one with those on the strip. "Yes, there are just as many." Children should complete the number sentences to tell the number in all (4 + 2 and 2 + 4 = 6). Provide auditory reinforcement: "When you know one, you know the other, too."

- *Adaptation* (for multiplication): Use a similar approach. Provide cards such as that of Figure 6.15.

FIGURE 6.15

INTERPRETING THE PRINTED WORD OR SIGN FOR AN OPERATION

Problem Area: Failure to associate the correct process with the operation sign or with the written direction to add, subtract, multiply, or divide.

Typical Disabilities Affecting Progress: Difficulty with closure, expressive or receptive language, visual discrimination.

Background: This section deals with two related difficulties. The first, discussed in the introduction to this chapter, involves the printed symbol for each operation. For example, despite solid conceptual understandings, some students with learning disabilities either misperceive or misinterpret the written operation signs. A second difficulty involves not knowing what to do when presented with written directions to add, subtract, multiply, or divide. Without the sign as a guide, some children are at a loss as to how to proceed. Many mathematics textbooks present skill pages of the type shown in Figure 6.16. Within a structured program, this type of page is useful for building skills when there are not language deficits. Initially, however, children with receptive language difficulties may not be able to succeed independently with exercises of this type. A chart, such as that of Figure 1.19, can be especially helpful to these students.

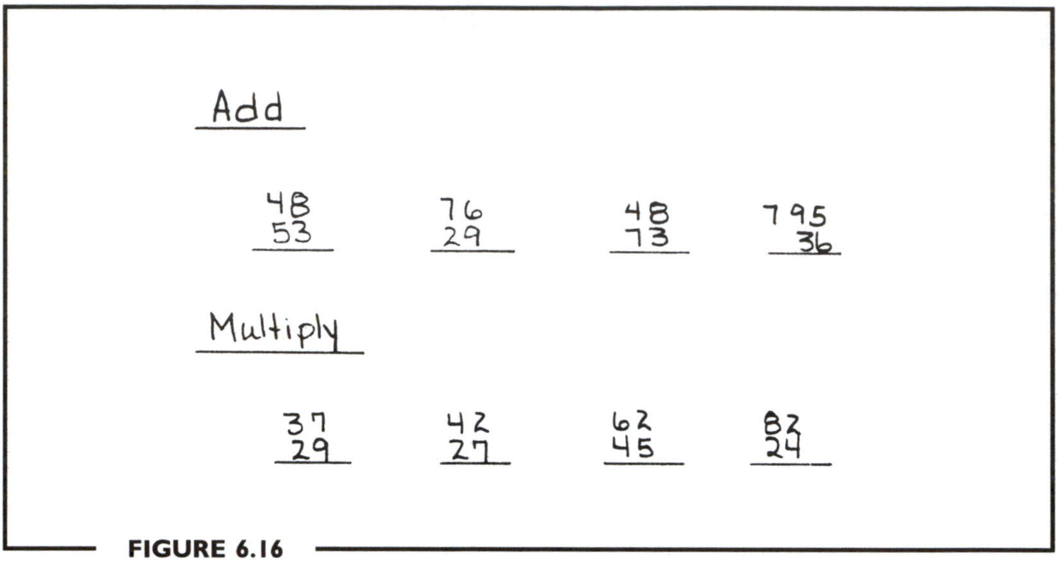

Add

| 48 | 76 | 48 | 795 |
| 53 | 29 | 73 | 36 |

Multiply

| 37 | 42 | 62 | 83 |
| 29 | 27 | 45 | 24 |

FIGURE 6.16

The following activities and exercises include techniques for dealing with each of the difficulties summarized in the preceding paragraph. The suggestions assume that students possess a well-established conceptual understanding of each operation. If this is not the case, before proceeding, return to work with physical materials, as outlined in the Building Concepts for the Four Operations section of this chapter.

SUGGESTED SEQUENCE OF ACTIVITIES

Interpreting the Operation Sign

1. **Circle.** Visual discrimination deficits may make it difficult to associate ideas properly. Use textbooks in which the operation signs have been circled, or ask the child to circle each sign on the page before solving the problem. In this way, attention is drawn more directly to the operation sign.

2. **What is the sign?** Use texture cues or color coding, or allow the students to finger trace before solving, as suggested in Activity 5 on page 225. Finger tracing a sign before solving is particularly useful on pages with mixed problem types (e.g., pages of addition and subtraction problems). Sometimes, a verbal reminder or visual cue to "Stop! Look at the sign" (see Figure 6.17) is helpful. In severe cases, require a student to circle all addition problems and work these before turning to the subtraction examples.

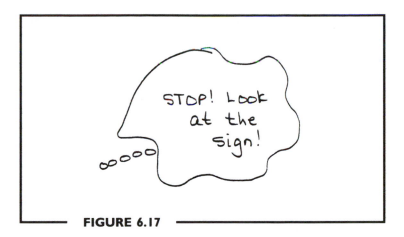

FIGURE 6.17

Interpreting the Sign or Word for Each Operation

1. **Chart it.**

   • Figure 6.18 shows one type of supplemental page that can be prepared at the beginning of the school year and kept on file for future use. Each symbol on the page should be the same color as the word that denotes the operation. If the chart shown in Figure 1.19 is present in the room, the colors on the exercise pages should match those of the chart. The teacher writes problems in the left column. The child recopies and solves them in the appropriate box as shown. For some, this might be a two-day assignment. On the first day, stu-

	Add	Subtract	Multiply	Divide
$\begin{array}{r} 48 \\ \times\ 6 \\ \hline \end{array}$			$\begin{array}{r} 48 \\ \times\ 6 \\ \hline \end{array}$	
$\begin{array}{r} 54 \\ -19 \\ \hline \end{array}$		$\begin{array}{r} 54 \\ -19 \\ \hline \end{array}$		
$\begin{array}{r} 36 \\ +\ 8 \\ \hline \end{array}$				

FIGURE 6.18

dents would merely copy each problem into the appropriate spaces. After the teacher has checked the paper, the student solves the problems.

- If a child has difficulty interpreting the operation sign, focus on internalizing its meaning. Eventually, these students learn to copy problems from their textbook into the proper space of the supplemental page.

- If a child has difficulty interpreting the written direction ("add," "subtract," "multiply," "divide"), focus on building vocabulary by association with numeric examples that use the operation sign. Similar sheets can be used to help children build associations for "sum," "difference," "product," or "quotient."

NOTE: *For many students, an operation sign is readily associated with the correct word and process when the numbers used are basic facts. However, when multidigit numbers are used in computation, these same children may experience difficulty with the association. For this reason, it is important that 2- or higher digit numbers be used in the problems of the left-hand column in Figure 6.18.*

2. **Page assignment sheets.** Many children perseverate and need continued help to associate the correct process with given words or symbols. Assign textbook pages or problems on a given page in random order as described in Chapter 1. Figure 6.19a shows an example of a page that can be kept on file and used as an assignment sheet for such children. The child first writes the symbol beside the word and then writes the appropriate problem number(s) in the right-hand column of the sheet (Figure 6.19b). If necessary, the operation word can be underlined to match the color used for the word on the wall chart.

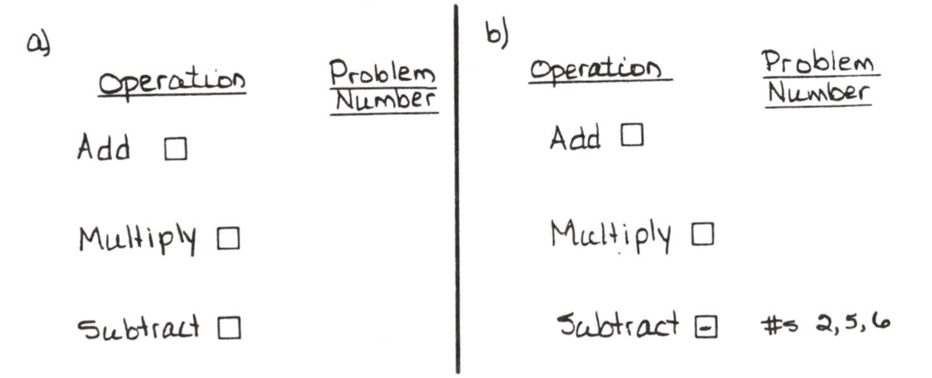

FIGURE 6.19

Interpreting Vocabulary for Each Operation

1. **Circle to match.** At the beginning of the school year, go through the text and find pages such as those illustrated in Figure 6.16. Circle direction words in the appropriate color to match the wall chart. Instruct the student to place the correct sign beside the word before solving the problems.

2. **Look to the chart.** When the words "sum," "product," "quotient," and "difference" are introduced, use a chart such as the one shown in Figure 6.20. Color the chart to match the coding scheme of Figure 1.19. A small copy of the chart can be pasted to the top of a child's worksheet. If the student needs more specific practice, use pages like that of Figure 6.21. The children can "X" (cross out) inappropriate problems, then work the correct ones. The color scheme adopted for the charts of Figures 1.19 and 6.20 should be carried through on pages of this type. In the example of Figure 6.21, if "sum" and "+" are green, then "−" could be black, "×" red, and ")‾‾" blue.

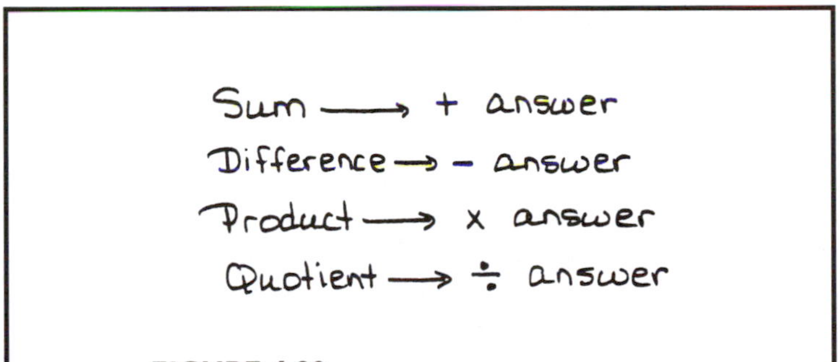

Sum ——→ + answer
Difference —→ − answer
Product ——→ × answer
Quotient ——→ ÷ answer

FIGURE 6.20

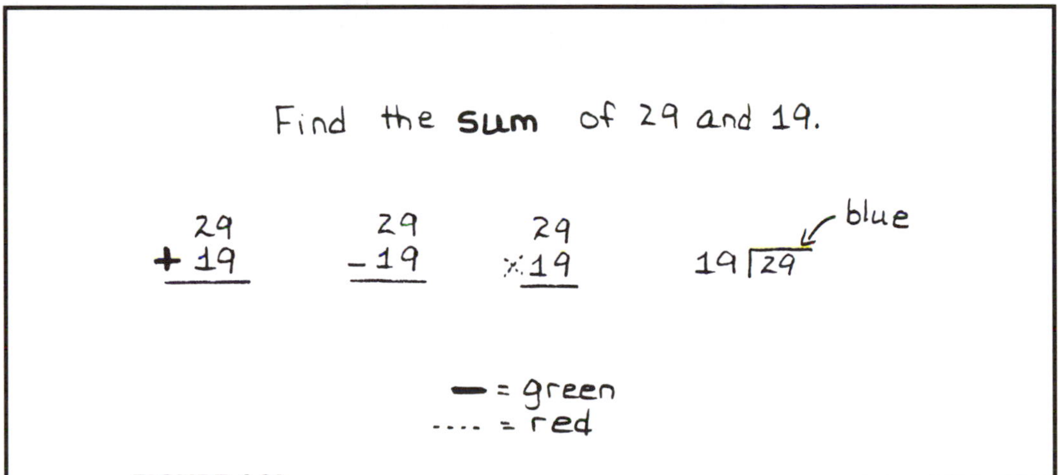

Find the **sum** of 29 and 19.

$$\begin{array}{r} 29 \\ + 19 \\ \hline \end{array} \qquad \begin{array}{r} 29 \\ - 19 \\ \hline \end{array} \qquad \begin{array}{r} 29 \\ \times 19 \\ \hline \end{array} \qquad 19\overline{)29} \quad \text{blue}$$

− = green
.... = red

FIGURE 6.21

COMPARISON SUBTRACTION

Problem Area: Adding instead of subtracting for word problems like: "Dick has 7 marbles. Jack has 4. How many more does Dick have than Jack?"

Typical Disabilities Affecting Progress: Difficulty with abstract reasoning, visual discrimination, and receptive or expressive language.

Background: Most young children, including those with learning disabilities, have difficulty with comparison word problems such as that represented by Figure 6.1. The situation of Dick and Jack represents one general type of comparison problem that can be solved by subtracting. It is a situation in which one determines *how much more one has than another.* A second type of comparison is that *which asks how much more is needed.* For example: "Jan has 7¢. An apple costs 12¢. How much more money is needed?" The comparison is between what Jan has and what she needs. Given a comparison situation, children are typically miscued by the word "more" and tend to add rather than subtract.

One root of the difficulty may be that a higher level of reasoning is required to handle problems like these successfully. A second reason is that teachers often do not give adequate attention to problems of this type. Most students need help setting up comparison situations as subtraction problems.

When children are confident with the basic subtraction idea modeled by "take away" situations and have learned at least a small number of subtraction facts, comparison subtraction problems should be introduced. Too often children are left, independently, to discover techniques for how to solve subtraction problems of this type. A worthy goal is to provide many informal opportunities for students to model comparison situations before these occur in word problems. Rather than simply assigning comparison word problems, specifically intervene using suggestions like the following to develop the idea of comparison subtraction. (Note that the step size of the instruction is kept very small.)

SUGGESTED SEQUENCE OF ACTIVITIES

1. **Picture it.** Orally pose a situation such as: "Dick has 7 marbles. Jack has 4." Or "Jan has 7¢. An apple she wants to buy costs 12¢." Tape a large sheet to the board and have the children help draw a picture to illustrate each situation. Repeat until the children are comfortable with this task. Save the sheets for use in Activities 2 and 3 below.

   • *Follow-Up:* Have children read situations from teacher-made cards. Help them picture each situation. For students with limited vocabulary, use pictograms as necessary (substitute pictures for words).

2. **Match.** Use the sheets from Activity 1. Review the sheets one at a time. For each, pose the problem to be solved: "How many more does one have

than the other?" or "How much more is needed?" Help children match one-to-one to compare the two groups pictured.

- When using the pages for the first time, allow the children to count the number remaining after the match.

- In subsequent sessions, help children recognize that they can simply subtract to find this number. Ask them to complete the subtraction sentence you have written on the sheet. They should then compare their answer with the number left over in the picture after the comparison.

- Eventually, the children themselves should write the subtraction sentences that solve situations pictured on the sheets. At this point, comment to the children that "It's good to know how to subtract. You can use it to solve so many different kinds of problems."

3. **Sort out.** Review the sheets from Activity 1 (p. 232). As a type of tracking exercise, have the children place in a special pile all the sheets that compare *how much more one has than another*. When the sorting is complete, have the children read (finger trace, if they are strong tactual learners) the subtraction fact that solves each situation. Orally emphasize the relationship between subtraction and this type of problem. "To find how much more one has than another, you subtract. Read the subtraction fact that solves this problem." Underline the question, "How much more does one have than another?" and the subtraction sign of the fact problem written to answer the question with the same color.

NOTE 1: *At another time, have the students sort out sheets for situations asking* how much more is needed.

NOTE 2: *Technically, the "How much more is needed?" type of question is a missing-addend problem. However, we do not emphasize it as such. Rather, we prefer to focus on the simple subtraction fact that will solve the problem.*

4. **Search.** As a follow-up tracking exercise, have the children search for comparison subtraction problems on worksheets or textbook pages that contain a mix of take-away and comparison types. For each comparison problem identified, ask them to draw a picture and write the subtraction sentence that solves the problem.

5. **Make up.** Help children make up their own word problems for the two types of comparison subtraction. If they demonstrate expressive language difficulties, provide a sheet of sentences they can draw from while creating their problems. Children could trade, picture, and solve each other's problems.

STRATEGY LEARNING FOR BASIC FACTS

Problem Area: Difficulty memorizing the basic facts.

Typical Disabilities Affecting Progress: Difficulties with visual, auditory, or long-term memory; visual or auditory discrimination; expressive language; sequencing.

Background: Children who have been involved in a rich, ongoing problem-solving program as suggested in the *Background* discussion for *Building Concepts for the Four Operations* in this chapter will learn many number facts just from the frequent exposure to them. It is important to realize, however, that basic facts are learned at a recall level over a much longer period of time than previously has been assumed, and that even for regular class students, school mathematics textbooks rarely include enough or the appropriate type of work to promote real mastery.

This problem is aggravated for children with learning disabilities. Memory, discrimination, or expressive language deficits may interfere to make learning facts very difficult. Many teachers find children can be successful when they specifically intervene to teach *recall strategies* such as those suggested in the remaining sections of this chapter. For students with learning disabilities, it will be necessary to carefully select numbers used in word problems to correspond to the small set of number facts currently being studied. A further critical part of this process is promoting the desired mastery by tracking as described and illustrated in the following sequence.

Tracking basically involves presenting only a few carefully chosen facts at a time. Much as a hunter would track a deer in the woods, children track or look for a small set of facts that are mixed in with others. Figure 6.22 shows a sample page with selected doubles at the top of the page. The technique (a) forces children to focus on given facts; (b) builds visual memory; and (c) assists with expressive language difficulties. The student follows the directions below the line. Short, frequent practice of this type helps students learn the facts faster and retain them longer.

Tracking is not a cure-all. Rather, it is a general approach that has proven especially useful in early fact work where the goal is to help children memorize the facts. Tracking can be applied to fact learning for all four operations as part of or as an alternative to a *strategy approach* for teaching basic facts (endorsed by the National Council of Teachers of Mathematics, 1989). Thornton (1989) suggested the following general 6-phase teaching framework:

1. *Look ahead* (to review or teach prerequisite concepts, counting and other skills which make it easier for children to learn helpful recall strategies).

2. *Teach* Retrieval *Strategies* (such as "Start with the greater number and count on"; or "Think of the picture to help with the double"; or "See × 5?"— "Think of the clock to help." These and other strategies are presented below and in the remaining sections of this chapter).

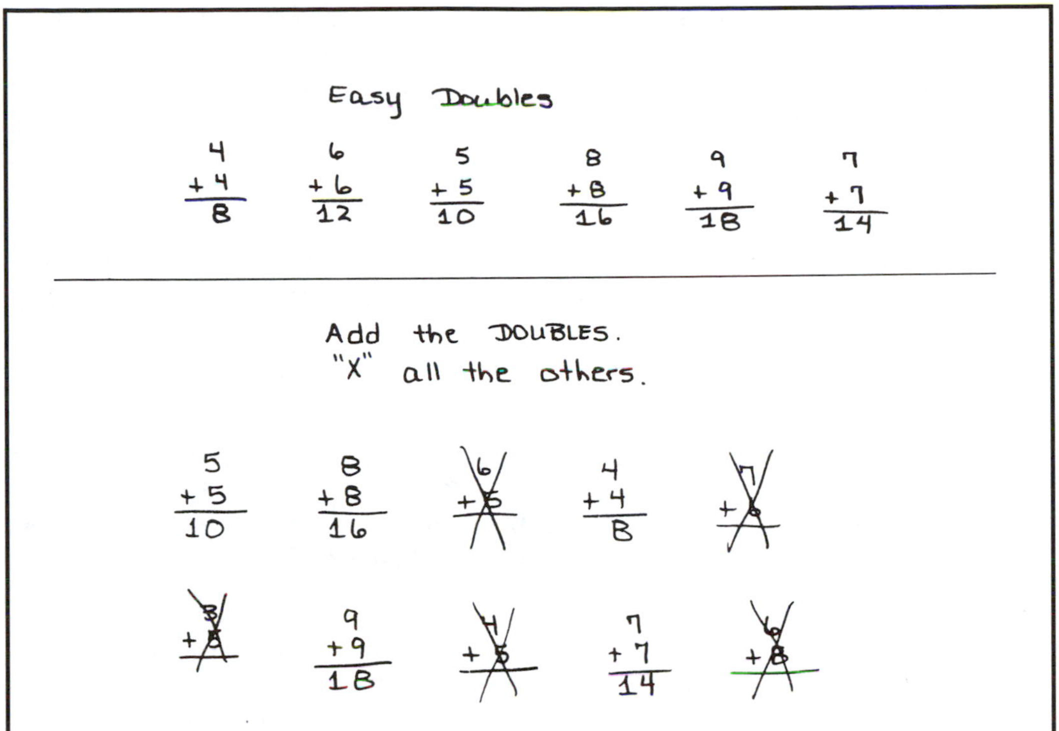

Easy Doubles

4 + 4 8	6 + 6 12	5 + 5 10	8 + 8 16	9 + 9 18	7 + 7 14

Add the DOUBLES.
"X" all the others.

5 + 5 10	8 + 8 16	6 + 6 (X'd)	4 + 4 8	7 + 6 (X'd)
3 + 4 (X'd)	9 + 9 18	4 + 5 (X'd)	7 + 7 14	6 + 8 (X'd)

FIGURE 6.22

3. Help children *use* the strategy (with emphasis on accuracy, not speed of response).

4. Help children *choose* when the strategy "fits." (This is an aspect of *tracking*.)

5. Provide practice to *speed up* response (so facts are answered *quickly* as well as *accurately*. Carry through to the point of overlearning, so *consistency* and *retention over time* also are promoted).

6. *Check up* (see Activities 10 and 11, p. 239).

Elements of this framework, highlighting the tracking technique, are emphasized in the following sequence. Since fact mastery implies giving accurate answers quickly, and being consistent in performance over time, follow-up exercises are necessary. Activities such as those described near the end of the following sequence are useful for this purpose.

SUGGESTED SEQUENCE OF ACTIVITIES

1. **Preassessment.** Determine each child's level of fact mastery. Timed written tests, of themselves, do not tell which specific facts are indeed mastered.

Individual assessment is best. Start by observing, over time, how individual children solve verbal problems—whether they rely on use of objects, whether they finger count or are able to count on or back for easier facts; whether they appear to "know" certain facts and whether they, in fact, can use easier facts to derive answers to other unknown facts. Some children, for example, may recognize that because $5 + 5 = 10$, then $5 + 6$ is "1 more" (11).

Create a checklist of those facts for which correct answers are given without hesitation. Follow through by using flash cards to individually interview the child to ascertain which facts have not been learned. Two piles can be formed: "mastered" and "not mastered."

2. **Cluster.** Group facts into clusters for easier learning. Count on facts, +2s and their turnarounds (commutatives), for example, might be grouped. That is: $2 + 1, 2 + 2, 2 + 3, 2 + 4, 2 + 5, 2 + 6, 2 + 7, 2 + 8, 2 + 9, 1 + 2, 3 + 2, 4 + 2, 5 + 2, 6 + 2, 7 + 2, 8 + 2,$ and $9 + 2$. Later, other easy facts such as 10 sums or doubles might be tracked. (Refer to the following sections for grouping facts, easy to hard.)

3. **Model it.** Continue the practice of carefully selecting numbers for oral problems. Supplement this focus by using special manipulatives to dramatize finding answers for facts within a cluster, as in the examples which follow.

   • *Example 1* (10 sums): Use chips (two colors) and a 10-frame made by stapling half-pint milk cartons together (Figure 6.23). Have the children: (a) Count the cartons in the frame (10). (b) Place a chip (all one color) in each of eight cartons. "How many chips are needed to *fill* the 10-frame?" (two). (c) Place two chips (second color) in the 10-frame to fill it up." (d) Pick out the flash card that describes this situation and tape it to the board or chart (Figure 6.24a). Picture the 10-frame as a visual cue with the chart. Repeat, using different combinations for 10.

   • *Example 2* (addition doubles): Use the suggestions of Activity 5 (p. 237). Picture the cues on a chart (Figure 6.24b).

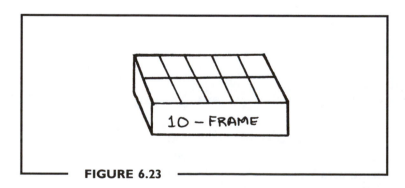

FIGURE 6.23

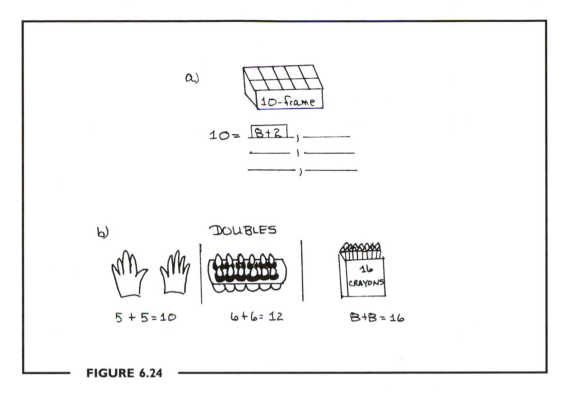

FIGURE 6.24

4. **Circle it.** Provide tracking pages on which the children find and circle, from among distractors, facts in a given cluster. Children can refer to the board or wall chart, or even use the model(s) if necessary.

5. **See and write.** Plan short sessions during which flash cards for selected facts in a cluster are presented one at a time. As the cards are flashed, the child says the problem, gives the answer, and writes it on the line of a worksheet such as that of Figure 6.25a or 6.25b. At first, present only a small

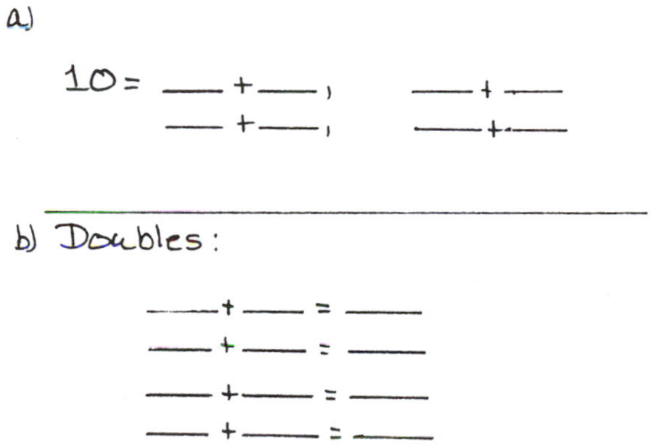

FIGURE 6.25

number of facts, those easiest or already known by the child. Then gradually, one at a time, introduce harder facts in the cluster.

6. **Match.** Provide worksheets such as those shown in Figure 6.26. As a form of visual training, the children study the top part of each page before completing the tracking exercise at the bottom.

7. **Find it.** Provide tracking pages like that illustrated in Figure 6.27. Have the children find and write answers *only to those facts in a given cluster.* Include about 20 problems from the cluster.

   - *Variation:* Have the children give answers orally to facts in the given cluster.

8. **Hear and write.** For each cluster, have the children read facts—problem and answer—into a tape recorder. Later they can listen to the playback for extra reinforcement.

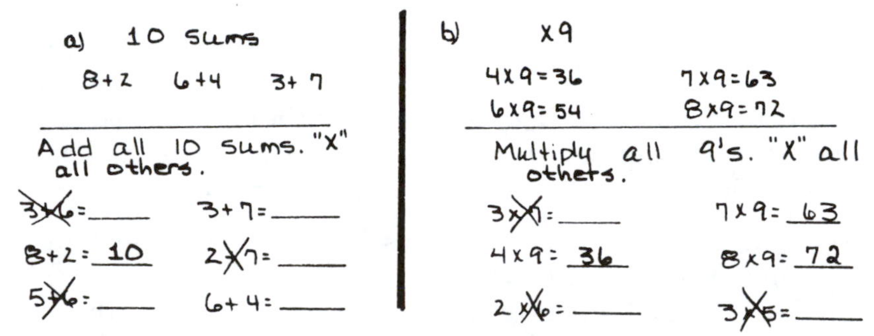

FIGURE 6.26

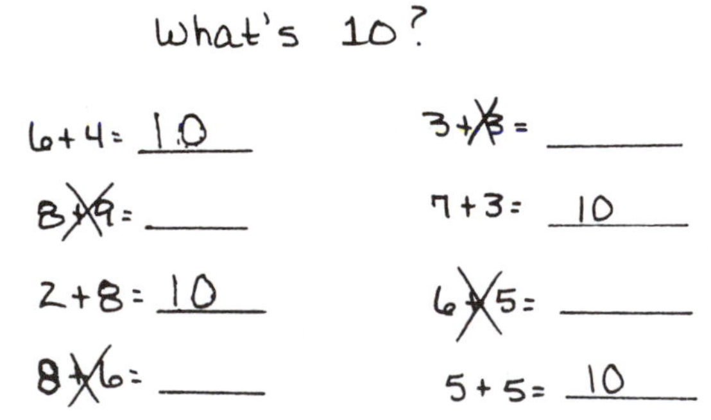

FIGURE 6.27

9. **Trace and write.** Use the answer side of flash cards. Have children finger trace facts within a cluster, problem and answer, as they read it aloud. Then have them close their eyes as they say the problem and answer quietly to themselves. Finally, ask the children to turn the flash card over, read the problem, and give the answer. If they forget, finger tracing the problem may trigger the response. Some teachers have found it helpful to trace over flash card answers with glue. When dry, the raised surface adds an extra stimulus to the finger tracing.

10. **Quiz.** Timed basic fact tests are very stressful for most children with learning disabilities and rarely provide information the teacher does not already know from daily observations of students. When an atmosphere that learning the facts is important, reasonable goals for mastery can be set and monitored through the use of checklists discussed later in this chapter.

11. **Review.** Systematically review facts from a cluster as other new facts are studied. Motivating games and activities are appropriate at this stage.

Strategies for Learning Addition Facts

Problem Area: Difficulty mastering the basic addition facts.

Typical Disabilities Affecting Progress: Difficulties with visual, auditory, or long-term memory; visual or auditory discrimination; expressive language.

Background: The activities of this section focus on strategies and models for learning the basic addition facts which can be nurtured and monitored as children solve problems which are part of their daily program. Children good at memorizing may not need to rely on such approaches. Children with learning disabilities, however, who have memory or other difficulties such as those previously identified, may profit from more specific and structured ideas like those outlined in the following activities. The basic approach is to help students master easy facts first. Models are used to help the children "picture" the facts in their minds. Then more difficult facts are mastered by relating them to the easier, known facts. This approach may involve deviating from approaches used in the school-adopted textbook. Be mindful that what helps one child may not prove effective with another. The teacher's role becomes one of suggesting relationships, models, or strategies while remaining open to children's ideas and being sensitive to individual learning styles.

One word of caution: Keep instruction for children with learning disabilities *very simple.* If presented too many "tricks" for remembering facts, some cannot sort out one from another. Others, however, can handle a variety of strategies during fact learning. Teachers may draw on the following suggestions, as needed, to plan a tracking sequence for individual or small groups of students. Ideas for adapting the basic sequence to meet remedial needs are included.

SUGGESTED SEQUENCE OF ACTIVITIES

Basic Sequence

Easy Facts First

1. **Count ons.** Review, if necessary, the extended counting activities of Chapter 4. For sums less than 10 and for other facts having 1, 2, or 3 as the addend, encourage the children to *count on* from the greater addend rather than starting from 1 each time.

   • *Example:* 6 + 3 = __. "That's 6—7, 8, 9." Experience shows that children with learning disabilities can perform this type of problem. Children do not need to count from 1 for addition facts.

   NOTE 1: *The relationship of a fact to its commutative should be stressed from the beginning. Use simple models like a card with dots or clothespins (Figure 6.28) to help children recognize that, for any given fact, its "turnaround" (commutative) has the same answer. "When you know one, you know the other, too."*

   NOTE 2: *Teachers may want to take time out at this point to help children note the "+ 0" pattern. 0 + 3 = 3; 7 + 0 = 7, and so on. Add 0, and the answer is what you started with.*

2. **10 sums.** Refer to Example 1 in *Model It*, page 236. Use chips and the 10-frame as a model or simply draw a 10-frame on cardboard or paper (Figure 6.29) to help the children learn sums of 10. Have the students themselves write the number sentences to describe each situation dramatized. Get children to the point where they track for 10 sums, using techniques discussed on page 234, then use the 10-frame to check.

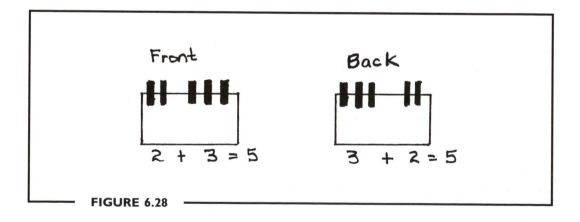

FIGURE 6.28

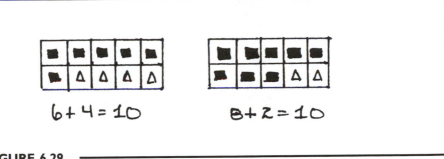

FIGURE 6.29

3. **Doubles.** Use models such as those of Figure 6.30 to help children memorize addition doubles. Among other activities, involve the children in:

- Writing number sentences to match cue cards;

- Reading cue and associated number sentences into a tape recorder and listening to the playback (e.g., "6 + 6 is the 'dozen eggs' fact; 6 + 6 = 12." Show students how, if you only want half of a dozen eggs, you would split as pictured);

- Finger tracing over the cue card and then writing the double that is illustrated;

- Tracking exercises, as in the section beginning on page 234;

- Practice activities where children match number sentences with associated cue cards. A variation on the card game Old Maid is good for this purpose (see Figure 6.31);

- Crossing off these and other facts as they are mastered. A chart such as that described in Activity 7, page 246, might be useful.

4. **Pattern 9s.** Use a 10-frame (see Activity 2 above) to illustrate that 9+ (any number) is just 1 less than 10+ (that number). This is a helpful *number pattern.* +9 facts are just "one step away" from easier +10 facts. Track +9 facts, as suggested in Section 4.

Other favorite patterns include:

- *Strategy 1:* "Make it a '10' problem." Use the "−1, +1" idea: "9 + 6 is the same as 10 + 5 (15)."

- *Strategy 2:* "Note the pattern." The ones digit of the answer is always 1 less than the digit added to 1 (see Figure 6.32).

| Now Harder Facts |

5. **One more than.** Help the students master harder facts by relating them to easier, known facts. The "one-more-than" strategy is a powerful help

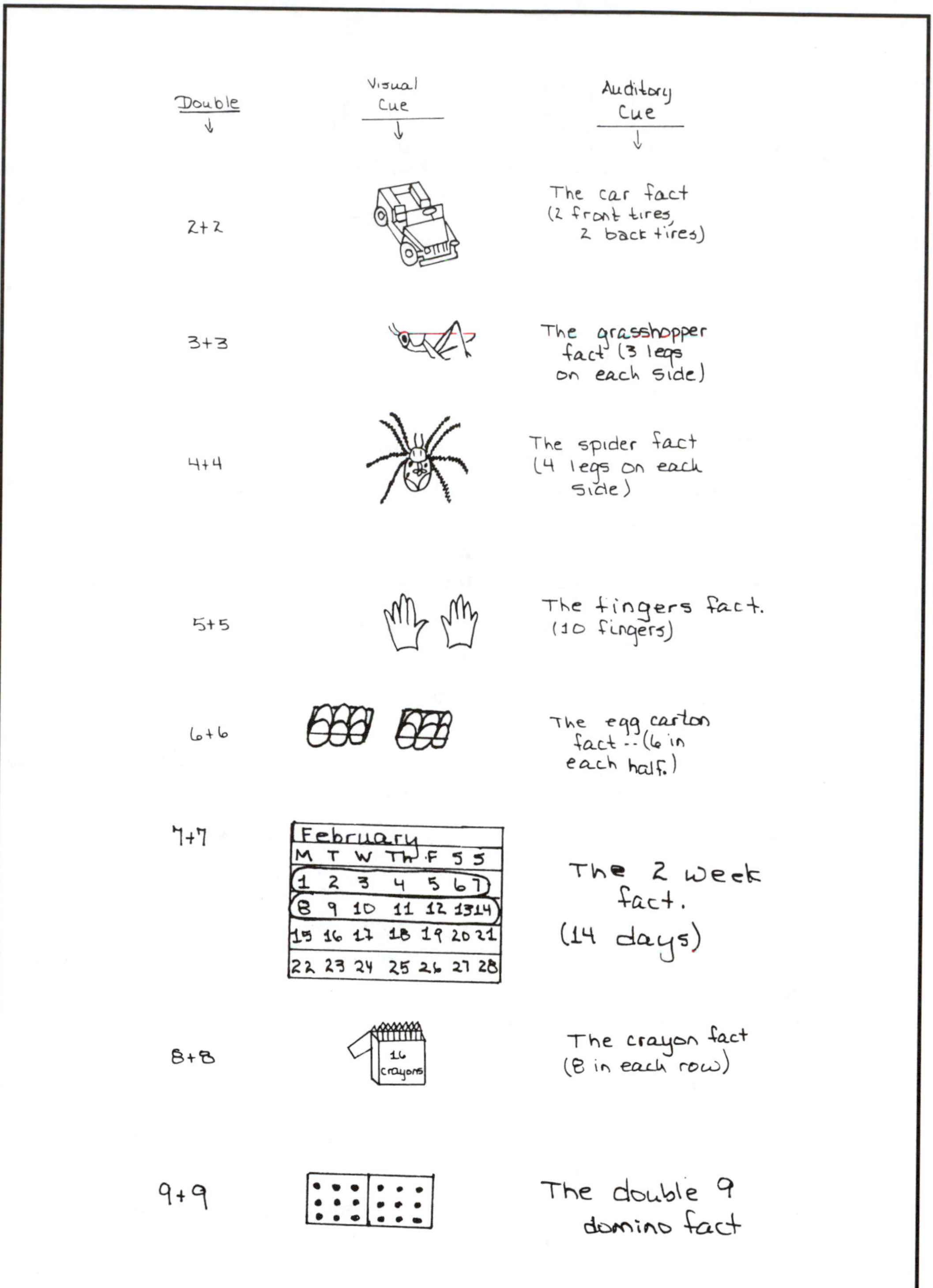
Double
Visual Cue
Auditory Cue
2+2
The car fact (2 front tires, 2 back tires)
3+3
The grasshopper fact (3 legs on each side)
4+4
The spider fact (4 legs on each side)
5+5
The fingers fact. (10 fingers)
6+6
The egg carton fact -- (6 in each half.)
7+7
February
M T W Th F S S
1 2 3 4 5 6 7
8 9 10 11 12 13 14
15 16 17 18 19 20 21
22 23 24 25 26 27 28
The 2 week fact. (14 days)
8+8
16 crayons
The crayon fact (8 in each row)
9+9
The double 9 domino fact

FIGURE 6.30

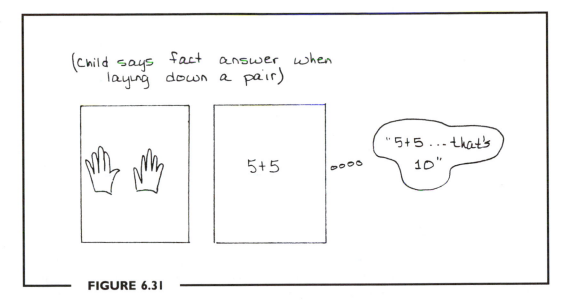

FIGURE 6.31

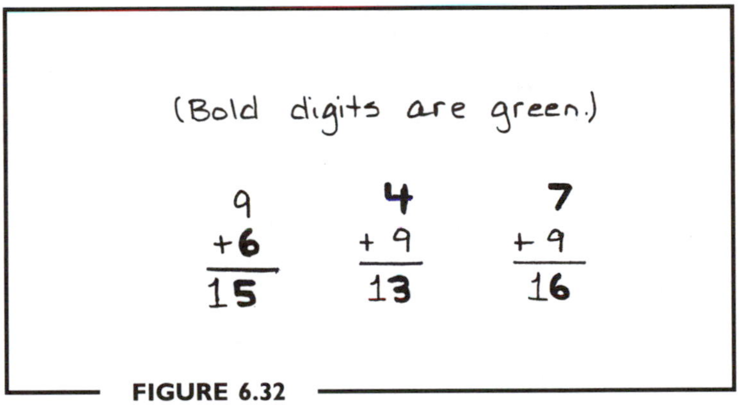

(Bold digits are green.)

$$9$$
$$+6$$
$$\overline{15}$$

$$4$$
$$+9$$
$$\overline{13}$$

$$7$$
$$+9$$
$$\overline{16}$$

FIGURE 6.32

NOTE: When *Pattern 9s* have been mastered, allow students to mark them off a master list, such as that described in Activity 7.

in this regard. Mastering a difficult fact is just "one step away." The strategy has a mushroom effect. As facts are mastered, they can be used to help learn others. Follow-up tracking (in the section on page 234) is usually necessary.

- *Example 1* (based on a double): $5 + 5 = 10$, so $5 + \underline{6}$ is 1 more (11). $5 + 6 = 11$, so $5 + \underline{7}$ is 1 more (12).

- *Example 2* (based on a 10-sum): $7 + 3 = 10$, so $7 + \underline{4}$ is 1 more (11). $7 + 4 = 11$, so $7 + \underline{5}$ is 1 more (12).

- *Assist 1:* When presenting examples like these, orally emphasize the underlined numerals.

- *Assist 2:* It sometimes helps to color code as in Figure 6.33 to emphasize the "one-more-than" relationship. The coding helps children focus

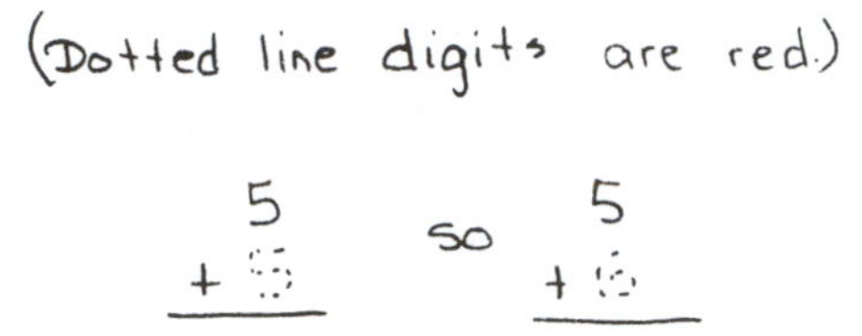

(Dotted line digits are red.)

$$5 \qquad 5$$
$$+\ :: \qquad so \qquad +\ ::$$

FIGURE 6.33

on the intended relationship. This approach is particularly helpful for children who are working independently or who, for auditory-discrimination reasons, may not hear the oral emphasis placed by the teacher when reading the pair of number sentences. Color coding may be necessary as well for students who are weak in making associations. These students may not relate the 5 and 6 without cueing.

- *Assist 3:* It is often necessary to dramatize a relationship for children. It is not enough simply to discuss it.

    For example: (a) Use rocks. Have the children make a picture of 5 + 5 and then write the number sentence to describe the picture (Figure 6.34a). (b) Give a child *one more* rock. "Place the rock with the others. It doesn't matter which side." Have the child write a second number sentence to describe the picture now. (c) Even as the child writes, emphasize the idea that you now have *1 more than 10* (11), as illustrated in Figure 6.34b.

- *Assist 4:* Many children, especially those with expressive language deficits, have trouble thinking of an easy, known fact to help them with a fact they do not know. These same children may be able to use a "helping fact" (the easier, known fact) once it is located. For these students, plan activities like the following with flash cards. (a) Present a fact the student has not yet memorized (4 + 7 in the

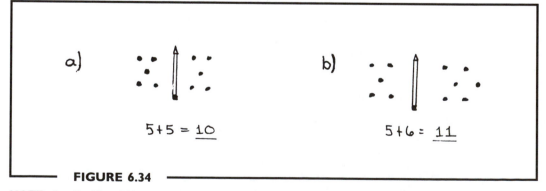

a) 5+5 = 10   b) 5+6 = 11

FIGURE 6.34

NOTE: For *Doubles*, children just add one more finger, egg, crayon, . . . to the picture.

example of Figure 6.35a). (b) Ask the students to select the easy "helping fact" from two other flash cards you place along the chalk tray. (c) Have the children turn over the card that does not help and give answers to the two related facts. ("3 + 7 = 10, so 4 + 7 is 11.") Follow-up worksheets, which direct children to select the helper from two given facts, may also be used. The fact that does not help should be crossed out, as in Figure 6.35b.

• *Assist 5:* Another alternative for helping children use an appropriate helping fact is illustrated in Figure 6.36. Although the exercise is related to missing addends, do not emphasize it as such. The focus should be on building new facts from easy, known facts (e.g., "3 + 7 = 10, so 4 + 7 is one more." [11]).

NOTE: *Although children typically find "one more" easier than the following strategies these are viable alternatives for some students:*

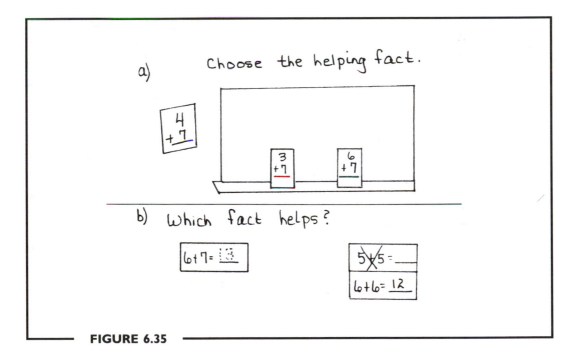

FIGURE 6.35

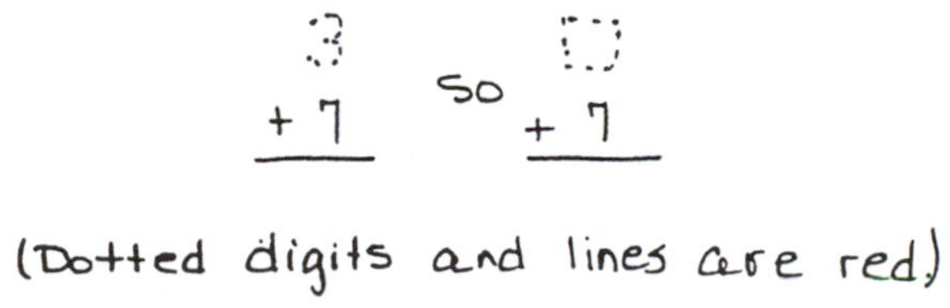

FIGURE 6.36

- *Strategy 1:* "Two more." 6 + 6 = 12, so 6 + 8 is 2 more (14).

- *Strategy 2:* "−1, +1." 6 + 8 is the same as 7 + 7 or 14.
  (Some children refer to this as the Robin Hood idea of sharing: Take 1 from the rich and give it to the poor.)

Allow students to use any strategy which seems helpful to them, as long as it shows correct thinking. Figure 6.37 illustrates two different approaches for figuring out 5 + 7. Since the addends are large, both illustrate a thinking process that is faster than counting on.

Although students with learning disabilities may not independently discover these strategies, many are able to use at least one of them if cued as previously suggested. Choose one strategy that you think will be easiest. Even if the child has difficulty, give it a good try (including tracking as in the section on page 234) before turning to a different approach. Too much change too fast is confusing.

6. **Other "1 less" facts.** Like the "1 more" relationship, the "1 less" idea is powerful. Many children use easier, known +9s to help with harder +8 facts like 8 + 4, 8 + 5, and 8 + 6. "I know 9 + 4 = 13, so 8 + 4 = 1 less." (12). Use a 10-frame to illustrate this. Reinforce with the tracking suggestions on page 234 as follow-up.

7. **Cross off known facts as these are learned.** Children who know the 45 "count ons," 19 zero facts, 10 sums, doubles, and 9s already have learned over 80 of the 100 basic addition facts. Consequently, these and other "one more than a double" and "10 sum" have been marked off the Figure 6.38 master list. Some children may also have mastered one or more of the remaining facts, perhaps by using strategies discussed in Activities 5 or 6.

As children progress, let them cross off facts they learn from a master list like that shown in Figure 6.38 or the one presented on page 273 in

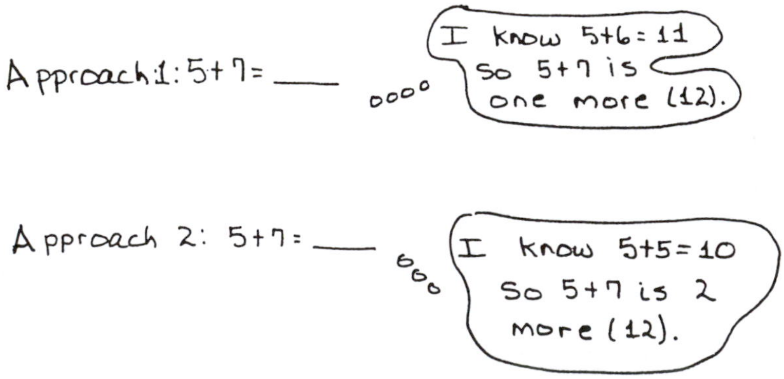

Approach 1: 5 + 7 = ____   ₀₀₀₀   I know 5+6 = 11
So 5+7 is one more (12).

Approach 2: 5 + 7 = ____   ₀₀₀   I know 5+5 = 10
So 5+7 is 2 more (12).

FIGURE 6.37

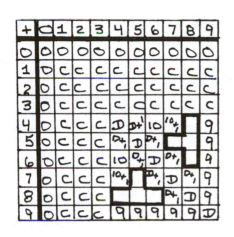

C: 45 Count Ons

O: 19 Zero Facts

D: 6 Other Doubles

10: 2 Other 10 Sums

9: 10 Pattern 9's

D+1: 8 Doubles Plus One Facts

10+1: 2 Facts 1 More

FIGURE 6.38

Chapter 7. Besides typically being very motivating by showing children how much they know, the list also provides a mind set for what should still be studied.

8. **Make 10, add extra.**

Prerequisite skills: Ability to add 10 to a 1-digit number.

- Visual color cueing, as in Figure 6.39, or auditory cueing through sound emphasis should be used if this seems helpful. The ones digit of the sum and of the digit added to 10 could also be texturized to allow for finger tracing.

- *Example:* (Use the answer side of a flash card [10 + 4 = 14], with both 4s texturized. Retrace each 4 with Elmer's glue. When the glue dries, it leaves a raised imprint of the digits.) "Read the number sentence." (The child reads 10 + 4 = 14.) "Now close your eyes and trace over the 4s as I read the number sentence . . . Now put your hands in your lap . . . Say the answer to this problem: 10 + 4 = __." Next ask the

(Bold digits are green.)

10	10	10
+ **3**	+ **6**	+ **4**
1**3**	1**6**	1**4**

FIGURE 6.39

child, with eyes open, to read the front side of the flash card problem and give the correct answer.

Use a 10-frame and chips to introduce the "make 10, add extra" strategy. The goal is to help children "see" that 8 + 5 is the same as 10 + 3 (13). The value of previous work with the 10-frame now pays off, because many children look at "8 + 5" and see that 8 and 2 more make 10, so it is a matter of adding in the extra 3. Continue until children can write the answer and use the 10-frame to check, then track on the new facts being learned, as suggested on page 234.

Remedial Sequence

Many older remedial children know most of the easier addition facts. Their greatest difficulty is often with more difficult teen sums. One approach is to start with *Doubles* and *Pattern 9s* (Activity 3 and 4 in the Basic Sequence). "Big" numbers like these seem sophisticated to students and tend to be more motivating for older learners than facts with smaller numbers. When these are mastered, review the *Count Ons* and *10 Sums* (Activities 1 and 2). Then treat the harder facts (Activities 5 through 8). Integrate tracking, as in the section beginning on page 234.

Strategies for Learning Subtraction Facts

Problem Area: Difficulty remembering subtraction facts, particularly those with teen minuends. Heavy reliance on counting.

Typical Disabilities Affecting Progress: Difficulty with visual, auditory, or long-term memory; visual or auditory discrimination; expressive language.

Background: Virtually without exception, subtraction facts are more difficult than addition for all children to master *and especially for those with learning disabilities.* In early work, very few children with learning disabilities can think of and use related addition facts to help. Most children will *count.* Unfortunately, many students continue to count even when larger numbers and longer counts are involved.

- *Example:* "13 − 6 = 7 because 7 + 6 = 13." A large number of students with learning disabilities do (among other things) the following:

  Count back: "13 − 6—that's 13—12, 11, 10, 9, 8, 7, 6."

  Count up: "13 − 6—that's 6—7, 8, 9, 10, 11, 12, 13." (The children finger count as they say the numbers.) "That's 7."

  Finger count everything: The children raise fingers to represent the minuend, they lower (take away) fingers to represent the subtrahend, and then count and tell the number left. These students face real trouble when having to work with teen minuends.

By observing children during problem solving and other computational work, it is possible to determine whether they are relying unduly on counters or becoming frustrated because subtraction facts are not mastered. The challenge, then, is to lead these students through a more structured program to use the most efficient strategy they are capable of learning to answer unknown facts. And, just as children grow from year to year, it is hoped that the kind of retrieval strategies they employ also might grow. For example, students may at first *always* count back or count up, as illustrated above, to answer unknown facts. Hopefully, if awareness of the addition-subtraction relationship is mastered, these same students later may use known addition facts or some other more efficient strategy instead of always counting to derive answers to facts they do not know.

The sequence below emphasizes counting only when *short counts* are involved. Visual cues are introduced to help students with subtraction doubles and 10-minuend facts. Throughout this work with easier facts, adding to check work is recommended. This approach nurtures an understanding of the addition-subtraction relationship and increases the possibility that children will *use* addition to help, especially when answering more difficult, teen-minuend facts.

Towards this end, we suggest that subtraction be delayed until students have mastered a modest group of addition facts. It also is better not to teach addition and related subtraction facts in back-to-back units of instruction. Students cannot use addition to check or to answer subtraction facts unless they first know related addition facts well. Delaying subtraction allows time for the necessary consolidation and the possibility that children will use addition as a retrieval strategy in subtraction number fact work. For students who continue to experience difficulty doing so, a method of using "10 as a bridge" is presented to help with more difficult, teen-minuend facts (see Note on p. 255).

SUGGESTED SEQUENCE OF ACTIVITIES

Prerequisite Skills:

- Ability to recognize when two or three numbers have been said;

- Ability to count on (from any number, 4 to 9);

- Ability to count back (from any number, 4 to 12);

- Mastery of related addition facts.

  NOTE: *Refer to* Counting in Early Number Work, *page 160 in Chapter 5, for help with the first three prerequisites.*

Instructional Overview

- 27 Count Backs: (10, 9, 8, 7, 6, 5, 4, 3, 2) −1; (11, 10, 9, 8, 7, 6, 5, 4, 3) −2; (12, 11, 10, 9, 8, 7, 6, 5, 4) −3.

- 19 Zeros: n − 0 and n − n (n = any number, 0 to 9).

- 6 New Doubles: $(8 - 4, 10 - 5, 12 - 6, 14 - 7, 16 - 8, 18 - 9)$.

- 7 Ten-Frame Facts: $10 - (9, 8, 7, 6, 4)$; also $9 - 5, 9 - 4$ (see Figure 6.40).

- 15 Count Ups: $(12, 11) - 9$; $(11, 9) - 8$; $(9, 8) - 7$; $(9, 8, 7) - 6$; $(8, 7, 6) - 5$; $(7, 6, 5) - 4$.

- 26 Harder Facts: $(17, 16, 15, 14, 13) - 9$; $(17, 15, 14, 13, 12) - 8$; $(16, 15, 13, 12, 11) - 7$; $(15, 14, 13, 11) - 6$; $(14, 13, 12, 11) - 5$; $(13, 12, 11) - 4$.

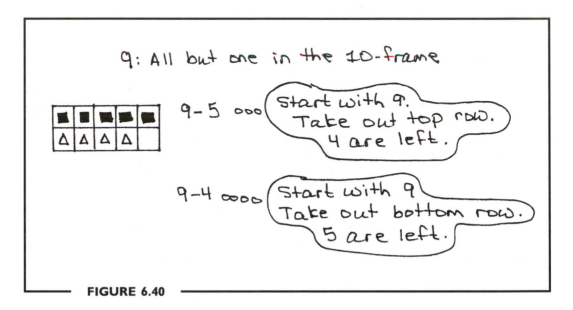

FIGURE 6.40

Basic Sequence

1. **Count back.** Let children use interlocking cubes. For each *Count Back* fact you select, students form a train with the cubes and count back as they break off cubes to model the subtraction. For example, students start with a train of 12 cubes and count back as, one by one, they break off three cubes. Initially, using cubes helps avoid counting pitfalls which leave a child one *off* in the backwards count. Get students to the point where they touch or look at the greater number (12 in $12 - 3$), count back mentally, and use the cube train to check. Follow with tracking exercises as in the section on page 234. *Language emphasis:* "See -1 (take away 1), -2, -3? Start big and count back."

2. **Add to check.** As soon as students can use a strategy accurately and efficiently to solve a group of unknown subtraction facts, provide *add to check* activities. These *should not be* introduced on the same day as a new strategy.

   - *Example 1:* **Break a stick.** For "$7 - 2$," children make a train of 7 cubes, break off 2, and write or tell (for teacher to write) the subtraction sentence that models what was done ($7 - 2 = 5$). They then put the parts back together: add to check. "7 − 2 = 5 *because* 2 + 5 = 7." Repeat for other facts.

- *Example 2:* **My favorites.** On a regular basis, invite students to circle two or three favorite problems on a worksheet and write the "add to check fact" beside each. Afterwards select one number fact pair on a page and ask the child to use counters to prove that what is written makes sense.

3. **Show with objects.** Introduce subtraction zero facts. Be sure students can use objects to illustrate number sentences involving zero.

4. **Use a picture to help.** Familiar pictures from addition can be used to help children with subtraction doubles (see Figure 6.30). For example: 10 fingers, remove 5: 10 − 5 = 5 are left. Or 12 eggs, remove 6: 6 are left. Integrate tracking suggestions from the section beginning on page 234, until children can *write* an answer, and then use the picture to check. Later emphasize "Add to check" activities, as in Activity 2, p. 250.

   NOTE: *As students master each new group of subtraction facts, cross them off a master list.*

5. **Use the 10-frame to help.** Provide counters and individual 10-frames. Starting with a full frame, students can take out some to model the subtraction (see Figure 6.41). Integrate tracking suggestions from Section 4 (see p. 234) until students can write an answer and then use the 10-frame to check. Later emphasize "Add to check," as in Activity 2.

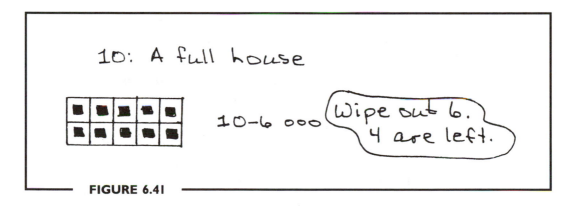

FIGURE 6.41

6. **Model the counting up.** When children do not know a fact and do not recognize it as a *Count Back* (a −1, −2, −3 fact), double, or 10-minuend fact, it often is easiest for them to count up. Start with counters, as suggested in Figure 6.42, use color coding to help students recognize, and start with the known part. When using the *Count Up* cards as in Figure 6.42b, alternate with the child as follows.

TEACHER: (showing the card): "Say the part you know."

CHILD: "7."

TEACHER (continues the count): "8,9. How many numbers did I say?"

CHILD: "Two."

TEACHER: "Yes, so the answer is *2*."

Repeat immediately for other *Count Ups*. At a later time, teacher and child can switch roles—the teacher can say the known part, the child can count on and say the answer. Alternating roles helps avoid counting pitfalls which leave students one off in the count. Integrate tracking suggestions starting

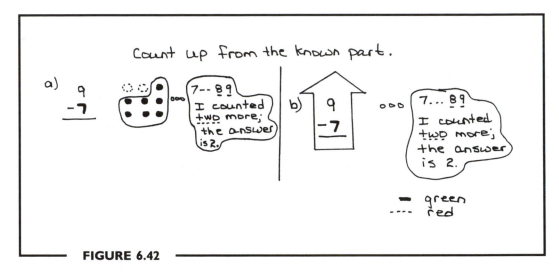

FIGURE 6.42

on page 234 until children can *write* an answer and use the *Count Up* card or counters only to check. Later emphasize "Add to check," as in Activity 2 (see p. 250).

NOTE: *If "Add to check" work has been carried out consistently in earlier work, some students may be able to use known addition instead of counting out answers.*

7. **Help with harder, teen-minuend facts.** Of the 100 basic subtraction facts, those with teen minuends are typically the most difficult to master. Some children with learning disabilities can learn to think of and use related addition facts as a help. For example: "13 − 6 = 7 *because* 6 + 7 = 13." Others find it easier to build on doubles or 10-minuend facts which they already know. For example: "12 − 6 = 6, so 13 − 6 is one more" (7); "12 − 6 = 6, so 11 − 6 is one less" (5); "10 − 7 = 3, so 11 − 7 is one more" (4); "10 − 7 = 3, so 9 − 7 is one less" (2). To subtract 9, some students notice and use one of the number patterns illustrated in Figure 6.43. In each case, follow-through tracking exercises, as suggested in the section starting on page 234, typically are useful.

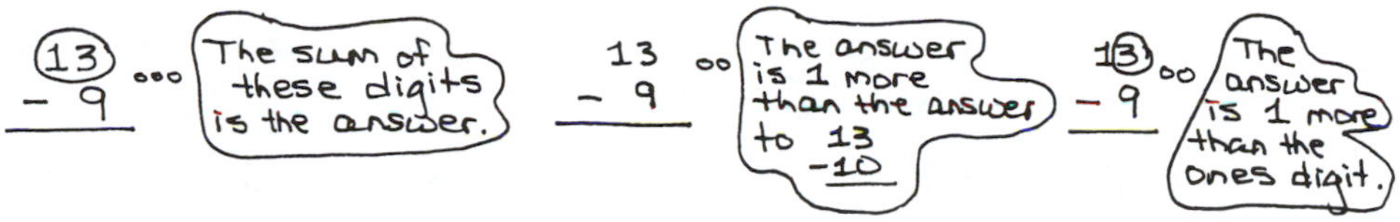

The sum of these digits is the answer.

The answer is 1 more than the answer to 13 −10

The answer is 1 more than the ones digit.

FIGURE 6.43

8. **Subtract through 10.** When none of the suggestions help students memorize harder, teen-minuend facts, teachers might:

- Help students recognize how fact pairs like those of Figure 6.44 differ. Color coding, as illustrated, may also help. Children should note that 13 is 3 more than 10. Model, if necessary, using a 10-frame: place *3* counters outside a full frame. Comment that the answer to 13 − 6, then, is just *three* more than that of 10 − 6. Repeat for other number pairs. For the moment, do not focus on answers at all. Continue until children are aware of the pattern. Then tell them that you will show them how to find answers to difficult problems like this (point to 13 − 6) by first thinking of the easy 10 problem (point to 10 − 6).

- Help students identify their "zero" finger. "You'll need a zero finger to help you think of the easy '10' fact." Have children examine the index fingers of their right hands. Help them to notice how the fingernail resembles a 0 (zero). Write a "0" on the nail or put a hole reinforcer on it. "This is your zero finger."

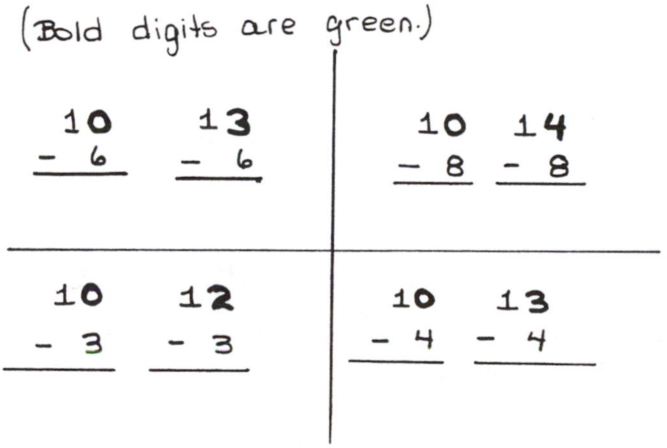

(Bold digits are green.)

| 10 | 13 | | 10 | 14 |
| − 6 | − 6 | | − 8 | − 8 |

| 10 | 12 | | 10 | 13 |
| − 3 | − 3 | | − 4 | − 4 |

FIGURE 6.44

- Show students how to use their zero finger. Refer to the sheet of Figure 6.44 again. Have the children use their zero finger to cover the ones digit of a problem like 13 − 6 (the second of a pair). "See how this problem now 'looks like' the easy '10' problem? With your finger in place it reads '10 − 6.'"

- Practice subtracting from 10 and adding the extras. (Refer to Figure 6.45.)

  — Write a teen-minuend problem like 13 − 6 on a sheet of paper.

  — Have children cover the ones digit of the minuend with their zero finger and give the answer to the easy 10 problem.

  — Children should then remove the zero finger and add in the extra ones.

  — Repeat for other teen-minuend facts. Incorporate tracking, as discussed starting on page 234, and follow through with an "Add to check" activity as in Activity 2 (see p. 250).

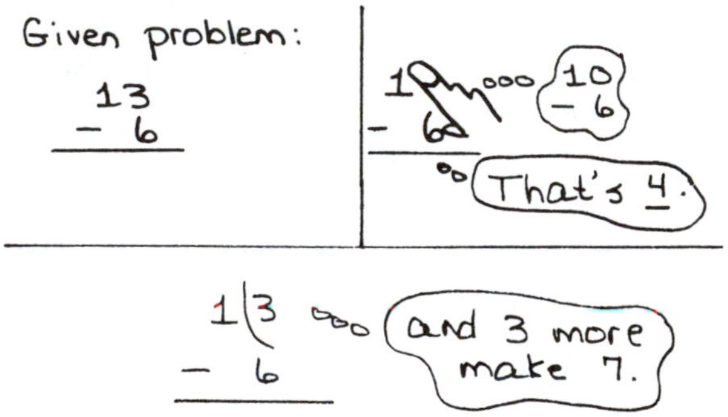

FIGURE 6.45

Strategies for Learning Multiplication Facts

Problem Area: Difficulty memorizing the basic multiplication facts. Use of wild guessing or inefficient counting techniques.

Typical Disabilities Affecting Progress: Difficulty with visual or auditory long-term memory; visual or auditory discrimination; expressive language.

Background: Two things for teachers to consider when planning a more structured program for helping students with learning disabilities are the following:

1. The techniques children use to figure out unknown facts. These can be assessed by observing and listening to children solve problems and explain their solutions.

2. The sequence in which unknown facts are clustered for study.

Children who have not yet mastered the multiplication facts often use wrong or inefficient techniques for arriving at answers to given facts. Sometimes, particularly when their concept of multiplication is weak, children tend to guess at answers and often miss. Or they may resort to some form of counting. Some, given a problem like 7 × 5, very tediously lay out counters or use tally marks to show seven groups of five, and then count by 5s to determine the total number. Some children do not rely on objects but skip count mentally to find simple products.

Skip counting by 2s and 5s is relatively easy and enables a child to figure out answers to multiplication fact answers. Otherwise, skip counting is difficult for children and, in general, slower than other techniques and models, such as those that follow. If the disability is so severe that children cannot learn to apply the more efficient approaches to memorizing the facts, serious thought should be given to using a hand calculator for multiplication and division.

The extent to which children succeed in fact mastery is tempered by the sequence in which facts are presented for study. Thus, traditional textbook sequences must often be replaced by a program of study that maximizes success and minimizes frustration in early sessions with facts. The following sequence has proven highly effective in this regard.

The basic plan in the suggested sequence is "easy facts first." Motivated by success at learning "so many facts so fast" (relatively speaking), students are encouraged to "study hard the few that remain." First 2s and 5s, then 9s—since, with the following approaches, these are the easiest to learn. (It is assumed that the commutatives of facts are studied at each step throughout the sequence.) Thus, if children also know 0s and 1s, there are only 15 other facts to be studied. Ideas for helping children master these last facts are included in the activities which follow.

NOTE: *Sometimes it is preferable that children begin memorizing their multiplication facts after they have learned the addition facts. Traditionally, however, addition and subtraction facts are presented first, then multiplication and, finally, division. For some students, especially those who require overlearning and are weak in abstract reasoning, a more reasonable sequence involves learning the multiplication facts before the subtraction facts. (The assumption is that the concept of multiplication is addressed first, even if only at a very concrete level.)*

SUGGESTED SEQUENCE OF ACTIVITIES

The following ideas are intended to be used in early sessions with each cluster of facts with tracking pages and reinforcing practice activities carried out systematically during later sessions.

1. **2s and addition doubles.** Children who know addition doubles usually have little difficulty with multiplication 2s. Use the models for doubles in Figure 6.31 to help with multiplication 2s.

   - *Example:* $2 \times 6 = 12$ (egg carton model). "Two rows of six, or 2 *times* 6—that's 12." After the $\times 2$ facts are established, children study the commutative facts. Model the commutative idea. For example, use the egg carton model or dots on cards to illustrate that 2 rows of six and 6 rows of two give the same total number: 12. Cueing exercises such as those suggested by Figure 6.46 can be used, if necessary. If additional auditory reinforcement is needed, have the children read matching pairs into a tape recorder and listen to the playback.

   - *Example:* The child reads into a tape recorder: "2×8. That's 16, the crayon fact." "2×6. That's 12, the egg carton fact . . . ." Matching pairs could also be colored or texturized alike on charts or cards for ready reference.

   NOTE: *Techniques similar to those just presented are used to reinforce the learning of other multiplication facts.*

2. **5s and clock times.** If children can tell time on the clock, use this skill to help them memorize multiplication 5s. (For special help in teaching clock times, refer to Chapter 4.) The half-hour time should cue the answer to 6×5 and 5×6 (30). For 9×5 and 5×9, the children should think of

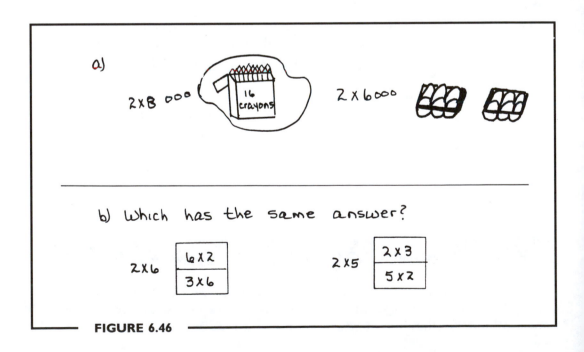

FIGURE 6.46

a time like 2:45 (big hand on the 9). For 7×5 and 5×7, children can think of the big hand on the 7 (2:35). If they cannot recall the minute time right away, cue them to think of the minute hand moving from the 6 to the 7: $5 \times 6 = 30$ (the half-hour fact), so 5×7 is 5 more (35). Similarly, if 3×5 and 9×5, facts associated with the quarter hour times, are learned first, then other more difficult facts can be related to them.

- *Example:* $3 \times 5 = 15$, so $4 \times 5 = 20$ (5 more). $9 \times 5 = 45$, so $5 \times 8 = 40$ (5 less). It usually helps to use a geared clock during instruction to illustrate answers to flash card problems. Visual, auditory, and kinesthetic cueing should also be used, as needed, to teach to the strengths of individual students. Ideas suggested in Activity 1 or in Figure 6.47 can be used for this purpose. Follow through with tracking, as suggested on page 234.

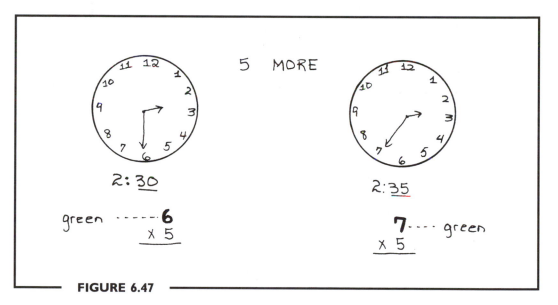

FIGURE 6.47

3. **9s patterns or finger cues.** Many patterns can be derived from the 9s tables (refer to Figure 6.48). For example, the sum of the answer digits is always 9; the first digit of the product is always one less than the factor being multiplied by 9. Some students with learning disabilities can learn to recognize and use these patterns as a help in fact recall. Most cannot, however—there are too many separate patterns to be integrated and remembered. But students can use their hands for multiplication 9s. To do so, they first "number" their fingers, left to right, from 1 to 10 as in Figure 6.49a. Then, to multiply 9×3 (or 3×9), students fold their 3rd finger down (Figure 6.49b) and read the product from their fingers: 2 fingers to the left and 7 to the right of the folded finger: 27. For 7×9 or 9×7, they fold their fingers: 6 fingers to the left and 3 to the right of the folded finger: 63. Whether 9s are approached through patterns or finger cues, reinforcement, as noted elsewhere in this chapter, should be provided, along with tracking pages (page 234).

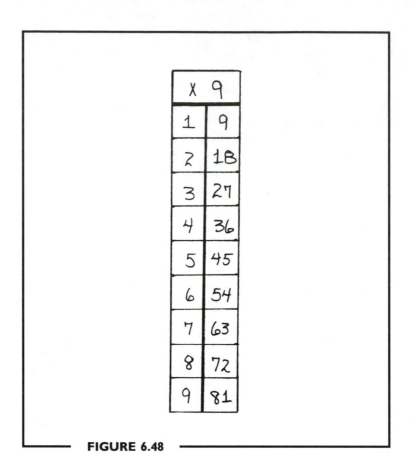

FIGURE 6.48

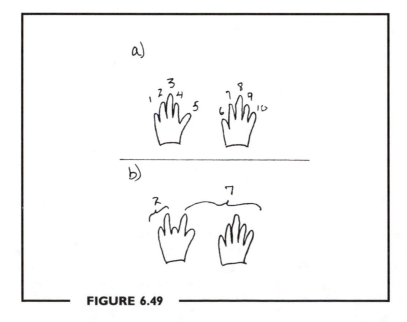

a)

b)

FIGURE 6.49

4. **About 0s and 1s.** If the students do not already know multiplication of 0s and 1s, they could be introduced now. It is common for students to be confused over fact answers to problems containing 0 (zero). Students with learning disabilities are no exception. Often the problem does not show itself right away in addition and subtraction. After students have been introduced to multiplication, however, the difficulty quickly emerges. When *multiplying,* the product for facts containing 0 as a factor is always 0. When *adding* 0 to any other addend, the non-zero digit is the sum. Children become confused about when to write 0 (zero) for a fact answer. The following ideas may help when these difficulties appear.

- *Act it out.* Introduce "0" facts dramatically. For example, have the students act out number facts containing 0.

  Example: "3 × 0." Use a bag filled with candy. Dramatize reaching into the bag *three times* and, each time, bringing out no candy. "How much candy did I pull out of the bag?" (None.)

- *Provide auditory cueing.* In the above activity and on other occasions when a "× 0" fact appears, use an auditory cue to reinforce (prompt) the correct answer.

  Example: "× 0 is a wipeout. You get nothing at all."

- *Have students "sort out" facts that have "0" as an answer from others.* Provide a mix of addition, subtraction, and multiplication cards with zeroes into two piles: "a zero answer" and "not-a-zero answer" pile.

5. **Take stock.** It is assumed that the commutatives of facts is studied throughout the sequence. So when students have mastered 0s, 1s, 2s, 5s, and 9s—the "easy" facts—there are only 15 facts (and their commutatives) left for study: 3 × (3, 4, 6, 7, 8); 4 × (4, 6, 7, 8); 6 × (6, 7, 8); 7 × (7, 8); and 8 × 8. Because the sequence to this point has emphasized the easy facts, it helps children learn many facts in a relatively short time. It is important now to determine along with the students what facts they have learned and what remains to be studied. Charts like those of Figures 6.50 or 6.51 can be used for this purpose.

NOTE: *While they are not technically "basic" facts, some students may enjoy studying 10s and 11s before turning to harder facts. Since they probably can already skip count by 10s, the multiplication pattern for 10s is easy to learn. Permit students to use a hand calculator to discover the patterning for 11s.*

6. **15 to go.** Some students with learning disabilities will need to rely solely on tracking pages and other practice activities to master the 15 remaining facts. Others can handle cues or strategies like the following in the early stages of learning the facts. Several of the following strategies, such as "twice

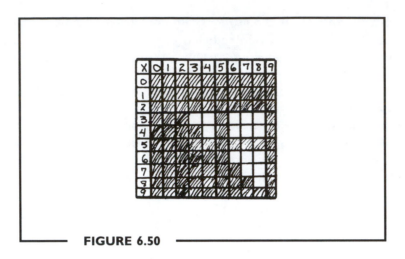

FIGURE 6.50

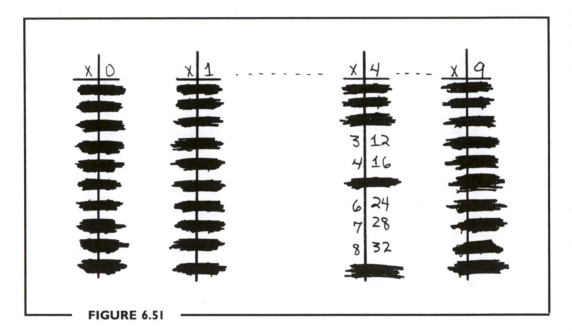

FIGURE 6.51

as much" and "add on," require a higher level of reasoning. If used, cueing techniques similar to those presented in Activity 1, are recommended.

- *Twice as much.* The distributive property can be applied to "slicing down" harder facts for easier study. The basic idea is to use two easier facts to figure out a harder one.

  Example: 7 × 8. The child can add as in Figure 6.52. Parentheses have purposely been avoided. Still, writing out everything is visually confusing to many children. Keep the presentation oral, perhaps writing just the "16 + 40 = 56." The easiest use of this idea is:

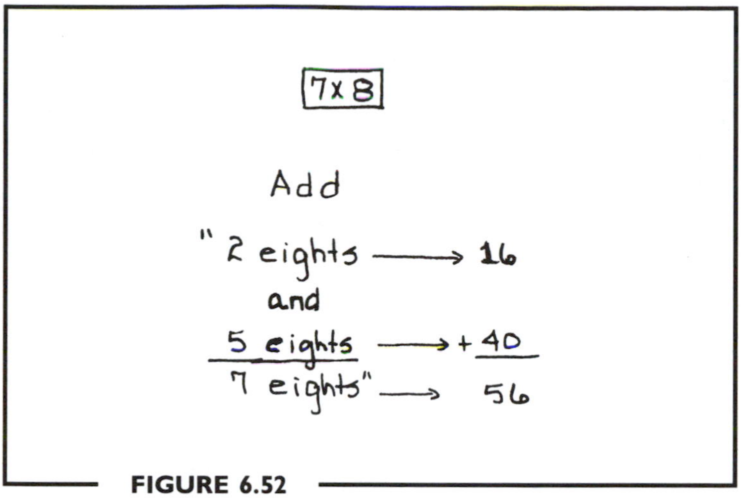

$$\boxed{7 \times 8}$$

Add

" 2 eights ⟶ 16
and
5 eights ⟶ + 40
7 eights" ⟶ 56

FIGURE 6.52

"Figure out half, then double it." Approximately half the remaining 15 facts can be learned using this approach.

Example: "4 × 6. Think of half: 2 × 6 = 12. Now double it: 4 × 6 = 24." "Twice as many cards," pictured in Figure 6.53, can be used to illustrate the point.

- *Add on.* An example of this familiar notion will serve to emphasize the idea: 5 × 8 = 40, so 6 × 8 = 48 (8 more). Children build from known facts. Encourage them to think: "5 eights. Now we have 6 eights. What do we add?" (8).

  Variation: Subtract from (a known fact): 5 × 4 = 20, so 4 × 4 = 16 (4 less). "5 fours. Now 4 fours. So 4 less."

- *It's a square.* Five of the remaining facts are perfect squares and can be shown as in Figure 6.54. Children with strong visual memories might be cued by thinking of the squares.

- *Other cues.* Children themselves have suggested the following cues. (a) 6s rhyme: 6 × 4, 24; 6 × 6, 36; 6 × 8, 48. (b) The "grade school"

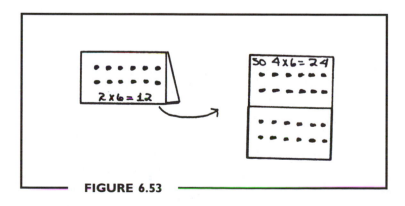

FIGURE 6.53

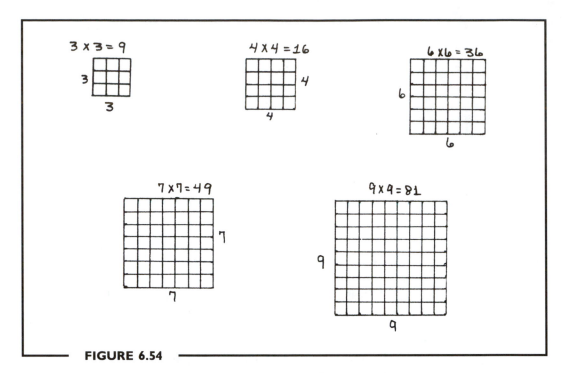

FIGURE 6.54

facts: In order, grades 1, 2, 3, and 4 (12 = 3 × 4); 5, 6, 7, and 8 (56 = 7 × 8). Sharing ideas like these sometimes helps children create their own.

Strategies for Learning Division Facts

Problem Area: Difficulty memorizing division facts.

Typical Disabilities Affecting Progress: Difficulty with visual, auditory, or long-term memory; visual or auditory discrimination; expressive language.

Background: Even with numerous problem-solving experiences, students with learning disabilities may find it difficult to master division facts for two major reasons: (1) they do not know related multiplication facts, thus using them to derive or check answers to related division facts is not possible, and (2) specific disabilities stand in the way. The suggestions which follow are based on the assumption that at least the first difficulty can largely be removed when division is delayed until a reasonable number of multiplication facts are mastered. The suggestions otherwise are based on structured cueing and tracking strategies which have helped many of our students.

SUGGESTED SEQUENCE OF ACTIVITIES

Easy Facts: ÷ 2s, ÷ 5s, ÷ 9s

1. **Teach a way to work out answers fast.** If students do not know ÷2s, ÷5s, or ÷9s, they can use retrieval strategies parallel to those for multiplication 2s, 5s, and 9s to help. *Language emphasis:*

> *"See ÷2? What's the picture?"* (For 14 ÷ 2, for example: 14 days, divided by 2 weeks—7 days in each week.)

> *"See ÷5? Think minutes after. Where's the minute hand?"* (For example: 35 ÷ 5: think 35 minutes after—minute hand is on the answer digit, 7.)

> *"See ÷9? What's the pattern?"* (Refer to the suggestions of Figure 6.55.)

In addition to the auditory language emphasis, visual cues including color coding, can be used to promote more rapid recall of unknown facts.

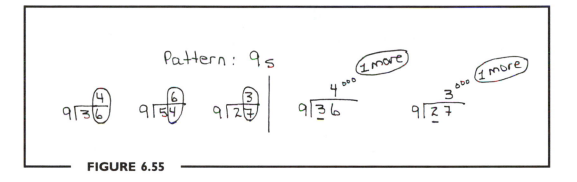

FIGURE 6.55

2. **Multiply to check.** No matter how the subtraction or division answer is obtained, follow through, when possible, with feedback like the following: "Yes, 15 ÷ 5 is 3 because 5 × 3= 15." Use materials to illustrate the relationship between a pair of facts: 15 objects shared among 3, each gets 5. And (return to the original position) 3 fives = 15.

   • *Variation:* Have the children write answers to a small set of division facts and listen to a tape recorder to check. The taped message should give not only the answer but the related fact each time.

3. **Find it.** Provide exercises like that of Figure 6.56 in which children cross out the wrong helping fact and answer the related helping fact along with the division fact given. Follow through with tracking as described starting on page 234. Include flash cards where children answer a given division fact, then flip over to the side with the related multiplication fact to check. Use color cueing as in Figure 6.57 if this seems helpful.

4. **Circle favorites.** On a regular basis, invite students to circle two or three favorite division problems on a worksheet and write the "multiply to check" fact beside each. Afterwards select one number fact pair on a page and ask the child to use counters to show that what is written makes sense.

$$35 \div 5 = \underline{}$$

$$5 \times 6 = \underline{}$$
$$5 \times 7 = \underline{}$$

FIGURE 6.56

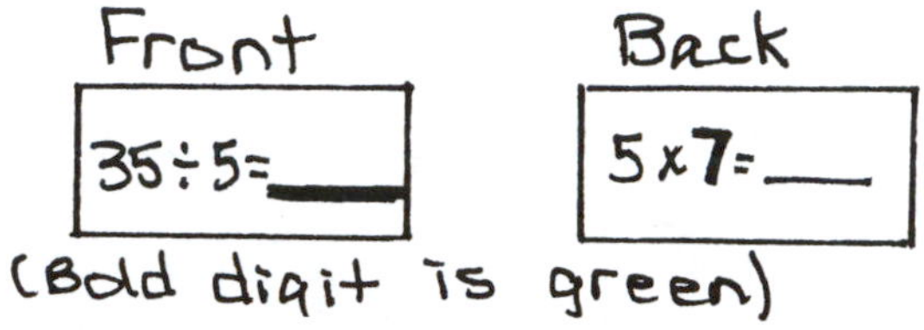

Front

$$35 \div 5 = \underline{}$$

Back

$$5 \times 7 = \underline{}$$

(Bold digit is green)

FIGURE 6.57

5. **Helpers.** Place multiplication facts that the children *know* at the top of a worksheet. Suggest that they use them to help answer the division fact problems on the page. Students may even write the helper fact beside the fact given.

6. **Throughout.** Encourage finger tracing (of textured number sentences) or use color coding throughout the preceding activities as necessary. Such cues are systematically withdrawn until the children can independently recall related multiplication facts to help with division problems.

7. **Teach related division facts.** For example, when students know $35 \div 5 = 7$, they can use this fact to learn $35 \div 7 = 5$. Or, if they know $36 \div 9 = 4$, they can use this fact to learn $36 \div 4 = 9$. Follow the previous suggestions including tracking, as described starting on page 234.

8. **Consolidate learning by finding fact "families."** Provide an opportunity for students to sort flash cards into families like $35 \div 5 = 7$, $7 \times 5 = 35$. Related facts could be color coded alike in early sessions. Alternatively, the backs of cards containing related facts could be keyed alike (e.g., all carry a red dot).

   - *Variation:* Provide puzzles of familiar objects with related facts written on the pieces of each puzzle (Figure 6.58). Encourage thinking by using the same color for pairs of puzzles the children are asked to piece together.

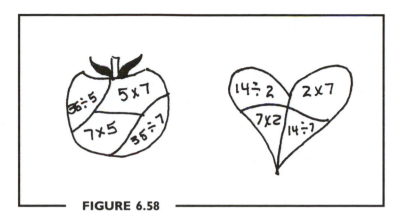

FIGURE 6.58

Special Facts

Use objects and story lines to help illustrate ideas. For example, $0 \div 5$ can be interpreted as having nothing to share—so each of the five gets 0 things. Carry out sorts in which students mark only those facts having an answer of 0 (or 1).

Harder Facts

If "multiply to check" work has been carried out systematically as suggested before, many students with learning disabilities will be able to use this technique to derive answers to the remaining, more difficult division facts. If not, use the tracking suggestions starting on page 234. As each new fact is mastered, help students learn related division facts. Consolidate learning by emphasizing fact families.

USING A HAND CALCULATOR

Several suggestions for using a calculator to build concepts or basic fact skills for the four operations follow.

- **Punch the sign.** Give the students sheets like the one presented in Figure 6.59. The children fill in the correct operation sign and punch out the problem on their calculators to see if they are correct.

- **Turnarounds.** To review or reinforce the idea of commutatives, give the children sheets like that of Figure 6.60. They can use the calculator to check if both facts of a pair have the same answer.

- **Beat the calculator.** Have students compare times for completing a practice sheet of facts—with and without a calculator. They should find that sometimes they can work faster without a calculator.

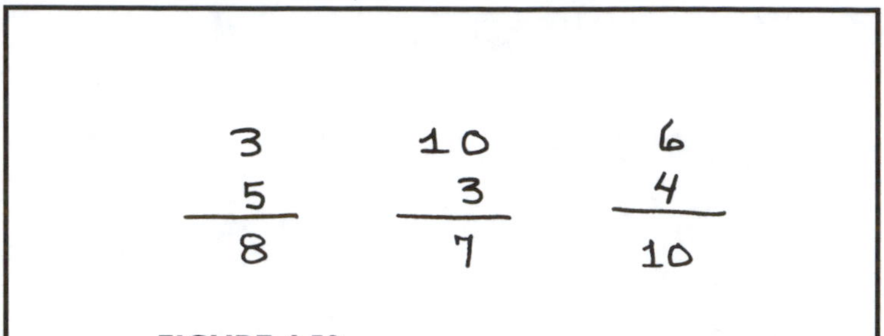

$$\begin{array}{r} 3 \\ \underline{5} \\ 8 \end{array} \qquad \begin{array}{r} 10 \\ \underline{3} \\ 7 \end{array} \qquad \begin{array}{r} 6 \\ \underline{4} \\ 10 \end{array}$$

FIGURE 6.59

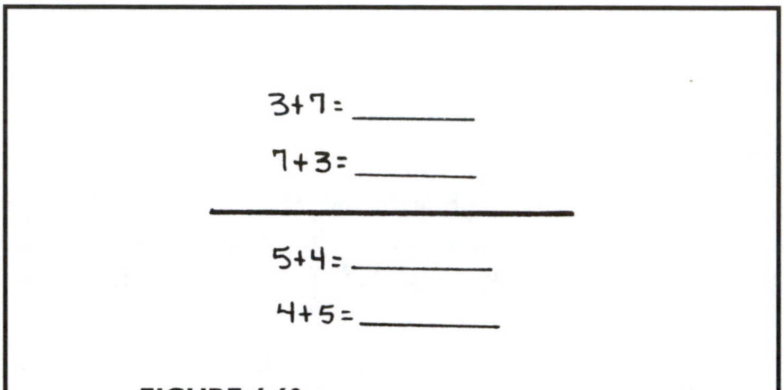

3+7 = _____

7+3 = _____

_____

5+4 = _____

4+5 = _____

FIGURE 6.60

- **Pick the helper.** (Subtraction or division facts.) Give the students a sheet like that in Figure 6.61. Have them circle the helper fact, then punch it into the calculator. If they get the green minuend (quotient) number as the answer, they know their response is correct.

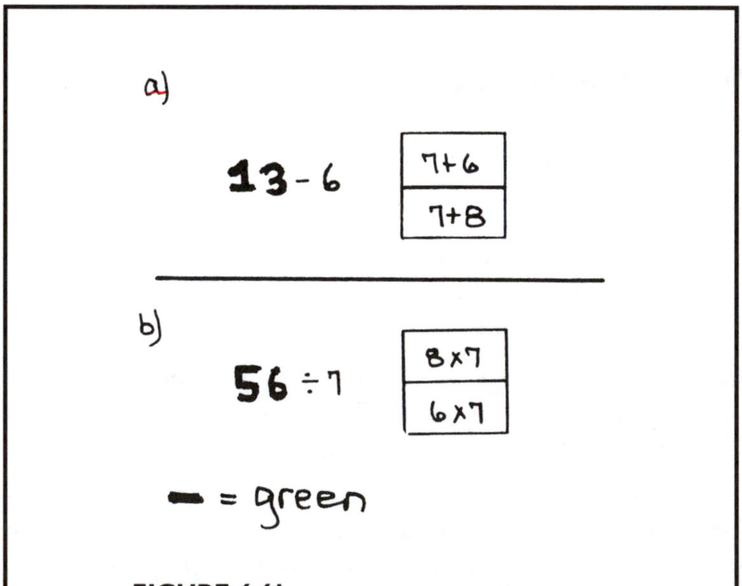

a)

$$13 - 6 \qquad \boxed{\begin{array}{c} 7+6 \\ \hline 7+8 \end{array}}$$

_____

b)

$$56 \div 7 \qquad \boxed{\begin{array}{c} 8 \times 7 \\ \hline 6 \times 7 \end{array}}$$

━ = green

FIGURE 6.61

CHAPTER 7

Whole Number Computation

IN THE PREVIOUS CHAPTER, whole number operations were discussed. Various methods were suggested as being effective ways to help students with learning disabilities understand and differentiate among the four operations. Ideas also were presented for helping students master the basic facts for each operation.

This chapter emphasizes being realistic about computation. One aspect of this effort toward practicality is embedding computation, whenever possible, in the context of motivational, interesting, or practical problems and applications—so students develop a sense of purpose about computation. A second aspect is to accept personally meaningful (but accurate) ways of recording in place of more "standard" computational procedures. A third aspect is to acknowledge the usefulness of the calculator as well as estimation and mental math, and to bring the focus on paper-and-pencil computation into perspective. There is very little use in today's technological society, for example, for 2-digit long division, so this should be reflected in the amount of time spent on this topic.

It is from this perspective that this chapter adopts three purposes: (1) to help students with learning disabilities select and use the appropriate computation method, particularly, estimation or mental calculation—in addition to calculator and paper-and-pencil approaches; (2) to help children extend and apply concepts and skills they know to computations with multidigit numbers; and (3) to provide remedial alternatives for how to cope with some of the difficulties students with learning disabilities encounter with basic paper-and-pencil computations at the abstract level.

Computation involves using symbols and operation signs to arrive at numerical answers. Some children, because of difficulty with abstract-reasoning, integrative processing, or auditory processing, lack important conceptual understandings necessary for success at the symbolic level. Other students with learning disabilities may, in fact, understand the concepts involved but still be unable to succeed with computation.

Children may lack the memory and association skills that normally allow one to incorporate previously learned skills and to arrive at correct answers. For example, associating the correct operation with a sign or symbol involves two skills:

1. the ability to differentiate among all the different symbols; and

2. the ability to associate the correct symbol with the correct process—addition, subtraction, multiplication, and division.

For many children, these steps are extremely difficult. These are the students who often say, "Tell me what to do; then I can solve the problem." That statement does not mean that they do not understand the isolated operations conceptually. They may be capable of showing what to do for each operation. However, at this stage they are not being asked to show what they know. Instead, they are being asked to determine the correct process based on a symbol. Once they identify that process, they are on their way.

Children with visual-perception problems may have trouble with this type of association because they incorrectly discriminate among the signs. Children with receptive language deficits, in turn, may be able to associate the sign with the correct word—add, subtract, multiply, or divide; but the word may carry no meaning for them! Another group of students, those with expressive language deficits, may not be able to elicit—either verbally or to themselves—the correct process without being cued visually or auditorially.

Once children have associated the correct symbol with the correct process, they must determine the sequence that applies. Since most estimation and computational procedures involve more than one step, confusion often arises. To further complicate the situation, many computations involve two or more operations, even though only one sign is used.

Consider the problem of Figure 7.1a. One common approach to the mental calculation is shown. Even though the operation sign is subtraction, the first step is addition: adding 1 to 19. Then, after the simple subtraction, $48 - 20$, is carried out, it is necessary to subtract 1 to adjust the result back to the original problem. To carry out the paper-and-pencil computation of Figure 7.1b in sequence it is necessary to subtract, add, subtract, and subtract; yet, the process is called subtraction.

Correct sequencing of steps is a difficult task for many students. Children with a memory-sequencing deficit, whether visual or auditory, find sequencing especially difficult.

Further, the child with a visual discrimination difficulty, who confuses the "+" and "×" signs, may perceive the operation differently each time it is seen. Figure 7.2 illustrates how this disability can affect paper-and-pencil computation. At first glance, it would appear that this student needs more work, conceptually, on the process of multiplying a 2-digit number by a 1-digit number. However, listening to the student verbalize the procedure revealed that after carrying the 7, the student misperceived the sign and completed the computation using addition.

Alignment poses another difficulty. Consider multiplication of two 2-digit factors. Even with a good understanding of place value, basic facts, and multiplication by ones and tens, the ability to align numbers accurately can be tedious for some children. Figure 7.3 shows a step-by-step breakdown of the mental process involved.

For the child with poor motor coordination or impaired spatial organization, the process of solving the problem becomes twice as long. Every time it is necessary to write a digit, this student must stop and look at the problem. The digits

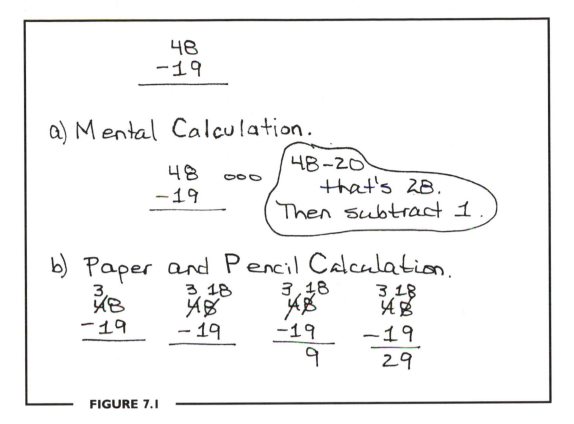

FIGURE 7.1

already present must be sorted out, and it is necessary to coordinate what is seen with what the hand does. Although this child may possess a solid understanding of place value and the steps involved, the sequence is interrupted, considerably and consistently, whenever it becomes necessary to write a number.

Visual figure-ground deficits and reversal tendencies also impede accuracy of paper-and-pencil computation. Consider Figure 7.4 in which a child is asked to perform a common subtraction problem. At first sight, it would appear that the difficulty might be inadequate mastery of facts (and, in many instances, it may well be). However, upon questioning the child, it became apparent that the difficulty lay in having to visually align the numbers in order to compute accurately. The first step was correct; the student thought "6 take away 5" and wrote 1. Next, the numbers were correctly regrouped. But then the student lost the place and saw "6 subtract 4." The last step, "8 subtract 2," is accurate.

$$
\begin{array}{r}
\overset{\diagup}{4}8 \\
\times\ 9 \\
\hline
112
\end{array}
$$

FIGURE 7.2

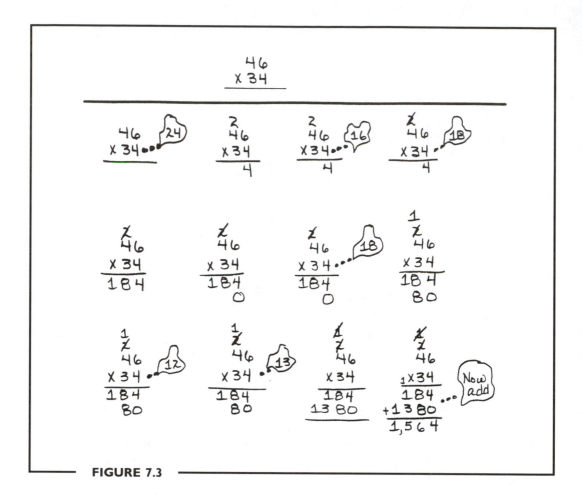

FIGURE 7.3

FIGURE 7.4

For students with reversal and visual memory deficits, regrouping causes special problems. So does long division. Figure 7.5a shows how a child who tends to reverse might solve a division problem. In the first example, the 6 was perceived as a 2, but otherwise the computation and the procedure are correct. Obviously, this student understands the steps for long division and knows the required facts for the problem.

Figure 7.5b shows the same division problem, but this time the way it would challenge somebody with reversal and discrimination difficulties. The student initially perceived the 6 as a "6" and wrote 1 in the quotient. However, at the multi-

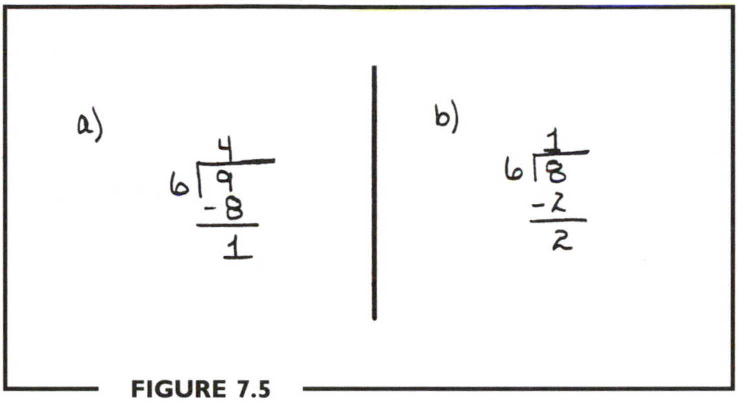

FIGURE 7.5

plication step, the divisor was seen as a 2, thus, the product 2. In the subtraction step, the 2 was perceived as a "6," resulting in a difference of 2.

At first glance, this student appears to be careless and unsure of the basic facts involved. However, in examples like this, questioning or looking at a computation in light of a child's previous work may reveal that the child does know the needed facts and is familiar with the correct process. Specific learning disabilities may be at the root of the problem.

Computational accuracy often involves estimating to check whether an answer is reasonable. This is difficult for most students and especially for many children with learning disabilities. Although an essential part of learning how to estimate involves concrete presentations, actual application of the skill is abstract and requires a considerable amount of reasoning and retention. Therefore, children who have any kind of processing deficit must learn to estimate through a highly structured approach. Many will not intuitively recognize when an answer is incorrect. Others may sense that something is wrong, but be unable to figure out or express exactly what it is.

In the following pages we recommend sequences and techniques for helping students who have difficulties like those previously described. Suggestions are clustered under five major headings. The first, general difficulties with whole number computation, examines special problems that children may experience with basic facts in computation or in associating operation sign and process. Thereafter, ideas are presented for how to handle computational difficulties for whole number addition, subtraction, multiplication, and division. Ideas for using the hand calculator to help students with learning disabilities master whole number computation are interwoven throughout the chapter.

GENERAL DIFFICULTIES

Controlling for Unknown Facts

Problem Area: Failure to succeed in estimation, mental or paper-and-pencil computation because of inadequate fact mastery.

Typical Disabilities Affecting Progress: Difficulty with visual, auditory, or long-term memory; visual or auditory discrimination; expressive language.

Background: Computing involves using the basic facts. Students with learning disabilities, like their peers, become frustrated and often fail on computation involving facts they have not yet mastered. Many students are ready, developmentally, to learn the more complicated computational procedures but have not yet committed the basic facts to memory. *To require them to learn the facts first may hold them back unnecessarily.* With these students, it is important to keep in mind, as noted in Chapter 1, the goal of a particular assignment. If the goal is to learn and use the various computational procedures, then memorizing the facts is a secondary and separate topic. The following are two approaches for dealing with this issue.

SUGGESTED SEQUENCE OF ACTIVITIES

1. **Controlled facts program.** One approach consists of controlling the entire math program around known facts. This very specialized approach involves considerable preparation and care. Specifically, it requires that one select or create problems and computational exercises so that only *known* facts are required for deriving answers. This approach is obviously not a practical one in mainstreamed or other instructional situations where teachers work with larger groups of students. However, it may be necessary in special cases.

   NOTE: *Most children know at least some of the easier facts, such as doubles in addition or twos and fives in multiplication. Easy facts like these can be used to present or review computational procedures. In this way, children with learning disabilities can still be a successful part of the class even though they may still be working on isolated facts.*

2. **Only known facts.** As in Figure 7.6, place two basic facts that are being worked in a prominent place. Review these facts at the beginning of the

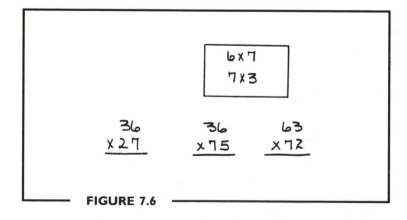

FIGURE 7.6

session, then select numbers for problems or exercises which involve only these facts and any other known facts, in this case twos and fives.

3. **Cross out.** Give each child a sheet of facts such as that shown in Figure 7.7. Help students cross out (blacken *completely*) all the facts they have already mastered. Then allow them to refer to the sheet whenever necessary. In the meantime, challenge them to learn several unknown facts each week. Choose the facts carefully, following the suggestions from Chapter 6.

> • *Example:* Select facts that are *one more than* some fact a child already knows. If a child knows $10 - 7 = 3$, select $9 - 7$ (1 less than $10 - 7$). Make sure the children are aware of any relationships between new and known facts; suggest that they use those relationships to figure out answers if they become confused. Each day, provide tracking pages on the three or four facts being studied. Then, at the end of the week, test the new facts in a mixed review quiz that also includes other known facts. These facts should be blackened as they are mastered.
>
> To check for consistency over time, some teachers circle or yellow highlight a fact the first time the student answers it correctly (and quickly) in an assessment setting. If the fact is also answered correctly (and quickly) in a second assessment setting, it is blackened *completely* as shown in Figure 7.7.

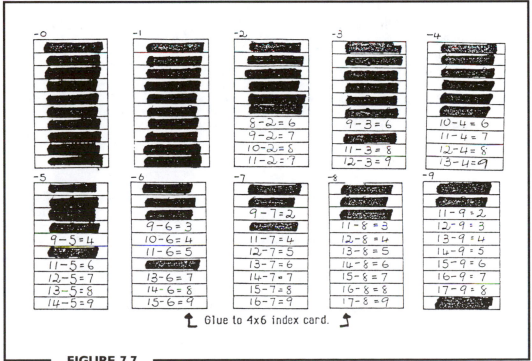

FIGURE 7.7

Basic Facts: Transfer to Larger Problems

Problem Area: Failure to answer correctly *known* facts embedded within larger computational problems.

Typical Disabilities Affecting Progress: Difficulty with visual discrimination or visual association; abstract reasoning; expressive language, memory.

Background: Many students with learning disabilities are unable, independently, to use basic facts within a computation until they have learned the procedure and feel comfortable with it. These are students who do reasonably well on fact tests. But they are unable to incorporate the facts into the computation until overlearning has occurred. It requires too much retention and sequencing for them to learn a new skill while trying to recall other isolated pieces of information. Hence they fail to transfer fact learning to computational situations. The suggestions that follow may help deal with this problem.

SUGGESTED SEQUENCE OF ACTIVITIES

---

1. **Write it out.** If children get stuck within a larger computation because they cannot recall a known fact, suggest that they write the problem fact to one side. Seeing the fact in isolation often triggers recognition and allows children to proceed.

2. **Finger trace.** If students are strong tactual learners, suggest that they finger trace over the problem fact, quietly saying it to themselves. If they are strong auditory learners, on the other hand, simply saying the fact to themselves may do.

3. **Circle.** Have students circle the problem fact within a problem or write over it as a means of better focusing on it.

4. **Side by side.** Help train for the desired transfer by providing practice sheets that place a basic fact beside a larger computational problem using this fact (Figure 7.8).

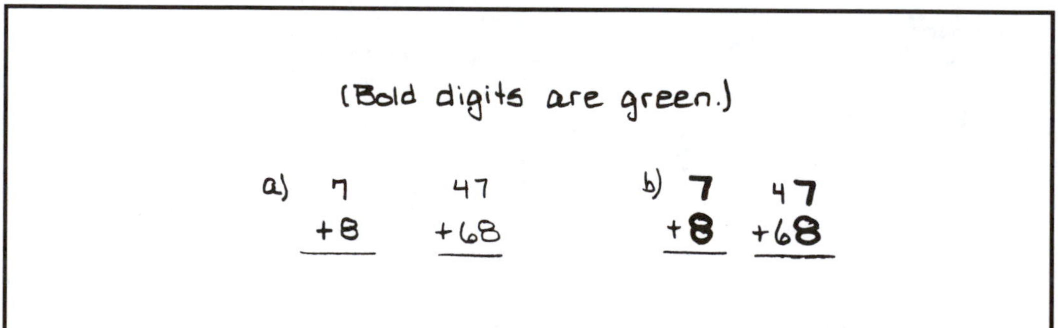

(Bold digits are green.)

a) 7   47   b) **7**   4**7**
   +8   +68   +**8** +**6**8

FIGURE 7.8

5. **Color code.** Provide extra visual reinforcement, if this is helpful, on the Activity 4 sheets, by color cueing as suggested by Figure 7.8b.

6. **Look to the chart.** Allow children to use a multiplication chart, their Cross Out sheet (modification of the Figure 7.7 chart, with all facts visible), or a fact box. Experience has shown that as children feel comfortable with the computational procedure, the need for these aids will disappear.

USING MENTAL COMPUTATION AND ESTIMATION

Problem Area: Lack of confidence or difficulty in mentally computing and estimating sums, differences, products, and quotients.

Typical Disabilities Affecting Progress: Difficulties with abstract reasoning, short-term and sequential memory, integrative processing; distractibility.

Background: The ability to be successful with mental calculation and estimation rests on several important prerequisites. To mentally add, for example, children must be able to visualize 2-digit numbers and either mentally count on or back by 10s and 1s or apply known facts. For any type of mental calculation or estimation, a firm understanding of place value and good number sense is required. Further, students must be able to retain information while simultaneously processing other information—a processing skill some students with learning disabilities lack. Using mental and estimation techniques for computation also involves risk-taking and a certain flexibility in one's abilities to think about and manipulate numbers. Typically, for any given problem, a variety of different, correct options might be pursued for calculating an answer mentally or making a computational estimation. Many students with learning disabilities, partially due to their learning deficit(s) but also partially because of their history of failure with computation, lack the confidence to function well in these situations which involve such flexibility and element of choice. Experience has shown that an early, consistent, structured emphasis on mental techniques, accompanied by expectations and opportunities to both explain one's solutions and listen to other different but correct approaches can help these students considerably.

In order to nurture personal confidence and a flexible mindset for employing a variety of useful computational approaches, the development of appropriate mental calculation and estimation strategies is a concern which should be met before paper-and-pencil computation is addressed within a school year. Otherwise, despite the fact these strategies could be learned to their advantage, students tend to show greater reluctance to abandon paper-and-pencil methods at times when mental approaches would be more appropriate and, often, much easier. The suggestions which follow are offered in the spirit of early and continuing intervention. As in all instruction, a positive, supportive environment and good role modeling, including "think aloud" techniques, are essential.

Making Mental Calculations

Learning to compute mentally, that is, to calculate exact numerical answers without the aid of calculators or paper-and-pencil algorithms, is a useful skill. Many everyday problems can be solved mentally. For example, "It is now 2:30. I should bake the brownies for 35 minutes. When do I take them out?" Or, "I want to buy a tape that costs $9.95. I have $7.15. If I make $2.50 cutting grass for the neighbor, will that be enough?"

Within the school curriculum, some of the standard computational textbook exercises which historically have caused many children great anxiety, such as 302 − 163, can, in fact, be computed mentally more readily than by using paper and pencil and regrouping over zeroes.

The premise pertinent to the focus of this section is that if students are eventually to select appropriately among computational alternatives, an effort must first be made to develop each individual's competence with each of these alternatives, thus making it possible for them to select appropriate alternatives. This section aims toward this goal by focusing on specific, systematic instruction to develop mental computation skills.

The ability to compute mentally requires integrative and simultaneous processing, short-term and visual memory, and reasoning skills, areas which some students find extremely difficult or lack entirely. In spite of their disabilities, other students can apply mental calculation procedures, as suggested below, when instruction is modified and approached in ways that accommodate their special learning needs.

One important aspect of teaching mental math is developing mental imagery to help students perform a computation "in their heads." Visual, auditory, kinesthetic/tactile approaches may be used. For example, students might use their fingers to "write" a problem in the air or on the desk. For some mental algorithms, using teaching aids such as hundreds charts, money, base-ten blocks, or number lines during initial instruction may provide a frame of reference for later recall. Perhaps the key with students with learning disabilities is to help them explore what they are able to do, place greater emphasis on the use of the hundreds chart in early instruction, and help them develop "modified mental algorithms." These are algorithms which also include writing some numbers as an aid to the mental thinking process. One approach which incorporates these aspects of instruction follows.

SUGGESTED SEQUENCE OF ACTIVITIES

1. **Develop basic prerequisite skills.** Specifically work to extend children's counting and basic fact work in areas which provide necessary prerequisites for mental computation. In particular, develop children's abilities to:

- Add multiples of 10 and 100 (3 + 4 = 7, so 30 + 40 = 70 and 300 + 400 = 700). If students experience difficulty with basic facts, use ideas from the first section of this chapter, General Difficulties, to help.

- Count on and back by 10s on the hundreds chart, using suggestions like the following.

2. **Look ahead to mental addition and subtraction.** Familiarize children with the hundreds chart and gradually build up appropriate counting skills. Provide individual hundreds charts and a 3 × 5 peep hole card with a center cut out the size of one square in the chart (see Figure 7.9). Teachers who prefer writing the numbers 0 through 9 in the first row, 10 through 19 in the second row, and so on; or who prefer the vertical format of Figure 5.31 can readily adapt the ideas of this activity and those that follow to other versions of the hundreds chart.

At first, children simply place the card over numbers you call out or write on the chalkboard. Later, the card can be used to count short sequences: by ones, by tens, forwards or backwards. The 39–40, 69–70, 89–90 decade shifts can be emphasized.

The next task consists of counting by tens. First start with 10 or some other number on the top row. A more sophisticated count is that which begins anywhere mid-sequence, and counts on or back by tens from that number. A final task is to count on or back by tens and then further by ones. *Bring children to the point where they count first without the chart, then afterwards recount using the peep hole card on the chart to identify numbers said.*

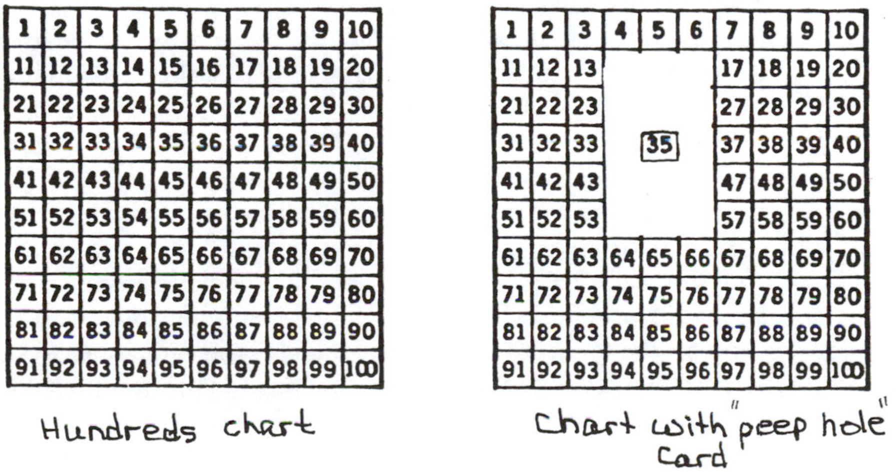

Hundreds chart   Chart with "peep hole" card

FIGURE 7.9

NOTE: *This approach provides visual support for counting on and back by 10s, an important prerequisite for mental math. This approach is especially appropriate for students with visual and kinesthetic-tactile strengths, as well as for those with short-term or sequential memory difficulties.*

3. **Start with, end with.** Write two 2-digit numbers (e.g., 29 and 54). Challenge students to find different ways to get from one number to the other on the hundreds chart. In this example, one could start with 29, count on by 10s to 59, then count back by 1s to 54 (29, 39, 49, 59—58, 57, 56, 55, 54). Or, one could start with 29, go forward 5 to 34, then count on by 10s to 54. Another strategy would be to move 1 space to 30, move down 2 rows (add 20) to 50, then count on 4 more to 54. One also might start with 54 and count backwards by 10s and 1s.

   Whenever possible, provide opportunity for different students to explain their strategy (based on 10s and 1s moves), and listen to different strategies others suggest. To foster the transition to mental addition and subtraction, summarize the counting moves in writing—and gradually let students take turns doing so. The first strategy above, for example, could be recorded as: 29 + 30 = 59; 59 − 5 = 54. Or, using arrows, an abbreviated version might be: 29 + 30 = 59 → −5 = 54.

4. **Apply to mental addition.**

   - Initially allow children to use a hundreds chart (Figure 7.9) to add mentally. Students should be provided individual hundreds charts for this purpose. Given a problem like 35 + 40, for example, children might place a peep hole card over the number for one addend and move the card down the column as they count on by tens: 35—45, 55, 65, 75. Because the connection to the written number sentence is critical, the teacher or a partner might write the sum after it is obtained (e.g., 35 + 40 = 75). Some teachers prefer writing these number sentences horizontally, to distinguish from the vertical, paper-and-pencil algorithm. *Whenever possible, provide opportunities for students to listen to strategies others might suggest and to share their own approaches.*

     Correct *alternate solution paths* should be respected and encouraged. For problems like 35 + 40, for example, some students may focus on the tens digits, use known facts, and immediately say "75." Activity 5, *Cue In,* (p. 280) suggests a way of supporting children who prefer this approach.

   - When children can comfortably add a 2-digit number to a multiple of 10, the idea of "Add to the nearest multiple of 10, then adjust," can be introduced for adding any two 2-digit numbers. Initially,

FIGURE 7.10

problems in which students add to adjust might be used (see Figure 7.10). Whenever possible, provide an interesting or practical context for the problems.

NOTE: *Children who are accustomed to the right-left, paper-and-pencil procedure of computing first with ones, then tens, may find it difficult to completely reverse their thinking and compute tens first, then ones. This latter approach generally is faster for mental calculation. Color coding may help students make this shift. To help these students learn to visualize and retain the relevant part of the addition problem, present flash cards with the important digits highlighted, as in Figure 7.11a. Ask the student to state and solve the highlighted part. Later, these cards can be used without highlighting as in Figure 7.11b.*

- Next consider 34 + 49 types. As in Figure 7.10, some students may find it easier to add 34 + 50, then subtract 1 to compensate. Others may prefer to add 34 to 40, and count on 9! While the second approach clearly is less efficient, it may be more straightforward for some and could be allowed. On the other hand, some students might initially prefer the second approach only because they do not understand any

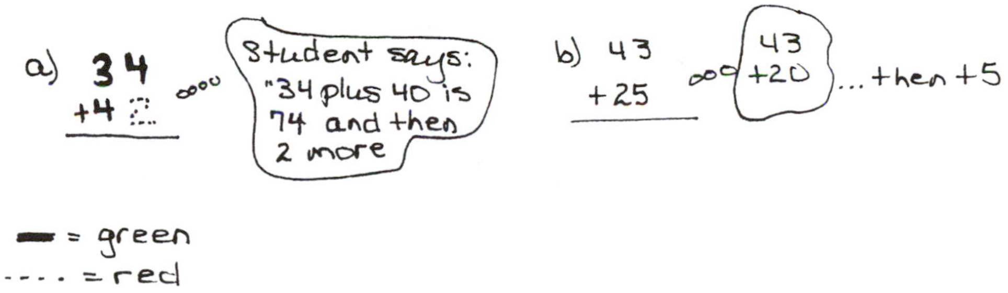

FIGURE 7.11

other. Most teachers at least introduce the first (more efficient) method to see whether it is within a student's range of thinking.

NOTE: *If children have used the vertical hundreds chart of Figure 5.31, the ideas can be easily adapted for use on the horizontal chart.*

5. **Cue in.** (A more sophisticated approach for students who have good mastery of basic facts.)

First present problems in which a 2-digit number is added to a multiple of 10 (Figure 7.12a). *Whenever possible, do so in the context of a problem situation to which the children can relate.* To help students solve the problem mentally, color code green the tens digits of the numbers. "Cue in on the tens digits of each number first—'35 + 40: that's 3 tens and 4 tens, which is 7 tens. Now add in the 5 ones. The answer is 75.'" (It helps to verbalize the pattern for students.)

At a later time, problems requiring no regrouping can be paired as shown in Figure 7.12b. Children first complete the problem in the cue bubble. Point out that this is similar to what they have been practicing previously (Figure 7.12a). Then problems like those shown in Figure 7.12c can be

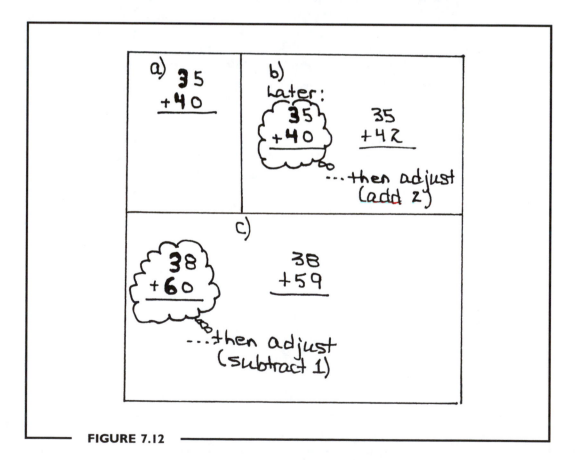

FIGURE 7.12

presented. As above, we add to the nearest multiple of 10 (in this case, 38 + 60, or 98); then adjust. In this case we go back one, to 97.

NOTE: *It may be necessary to practice extensively with mental calculation and counting on before introducing counting back.*

Students with short-term memory or sequential-memory deficits can use this approach to mental calculation, but may need to write down what they are thinking as they proceed, especially when regrouping is involved.

- *Example:*

    "38 + 45 is 3 tens and 4 tens."
    (student writes 70)

    "8 ones and 5 ones is 13."
    (student writes 13)

    "38 + 45 is 83."

6. **Apply to mental subtraction.** Similar procedures can be used to help students subtract 2-digit numbers mentally. As with addition, respect students' choice of strategy and their need to write down their thought processes—a technique some students may have to use throughout life.

    - As in addition, initially allow children to use a hundreds chart (Figure 7.9) to subtract mentally. Given a problem like 65 − 40, for example, children might place a peep hole card over 65 and count backwards by 10s (move back four rows) to 25. Other students may prefer to start with 40 and count on (40—50, 60—and 5 more is 25). Still others may focus on the tens digits, use known facts, and immediately say "25."

    - Next introduce mentally subtracting problems like 65 − 42, as in Figure 7.13, and emphasize subtracting the nearest multiple of ten, then adjusting. Placing problems in a story context rather than as

FIGURE 7.13

isolated numbers helps students develop intuitions about the direction of the adjustment. 65 − 42 might suggest, for example, that "On Monday only 42 fish could be taken from a lake stocked with 65 fish. If only 40 are caught, then fishing could continue until another 2 are taken from the lake (i.e., adjust by subtracting 2)."

- Finally introduce 65 − 49 types. As in Figure 7.14, some students may find it easier to subtract 65 − 50, then add 1 because they subtracted 1 too many. Again, the story context may help students' intuitions about the direction of the adjustment: "On Tuesday the lake was restocked so it started the day with 65 fish, and 49 could be taken. If a fisherman catches 50 fish, 1 too many are taken, so 1 fish must be put back into the lake (i.e., adjust by adding 1)." As before, different correct solution approaches should be expected, respected, and supported.

7. **Look ahead to mental multiplication and division.** Specifically work to extend children's counting and basic fact work in areas which provide necessary prerequisites for mental computation. In particular, develop children's abilities to:

- Skip count by 10s, 20s, 30s . . .;

- Skip count by 25s, 50s . . .; and

- Multiply multiples of 10 and 100 ($3 \times 2 = 6$, so 3×20 and $30 \times 2 = 60$; $30 \times 20 = 600$; 3×200 and $300 \times 2 = 600$).

8. **Apply to mental multiplication and division.** The major use of the basic skills involves multiplying multiples of 10 or 100 to check whether a given product or quotient is reasonable, as in Figure 7.15. Some students can learn to carry out simple 1-digit multiplications like 12×3, 31×4, or $\$2.50 \times 2$ mentally. Unless the student is interested in doing so, further mental calculation of products may not be useful. The value of mentally computing simple quotients beyond division basic facts is limited.

FIGURE 7.14

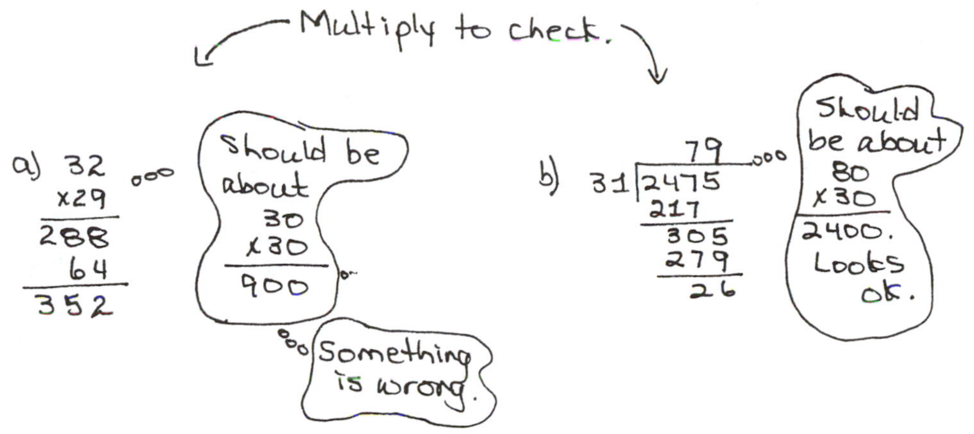

FIGURE 7.15

Using Computational Estimation

Estimation applied to computation involves giving an answer that is "close to" the actual one. As such, it involves the ability to carry out some calculations mentally and assumes skills related to place value, rounding, and basic facts. Everyone estimates every day in one form or another. "I think I can eat that much bread." "I think I have enough time to get to school." "I think this is enough to pay for what I'm taking to the checkout counter." Every day, newspaper headlines are full of estimates, and referring to them is a good way to acquaint students with the fact that in most everyday situations involving number, an estimate is "good enough."

Instructional emphasis focusing on the following steps is useful:

- Developing an awareness of what estimation is about (an approximate rather than an exact answer, as one is used to giving in math).

- Developing an awareness of how frequently an estimate is used in everyday numeric situations.

- Developing an awareness of when an estimate is "good enough" and when one is not "good enough."

- Developing a range of estimation strategies.

- Using estimation strategies in practical and other problem-solving situations.

- Using estimation to judge whether results obtained are reasonable ones.

At times, exact answers are needed. If your neighbor agreed to pay you $2.10 an hour for a job, and you worked 2 hours, then "about $4 is *not* good enough." If there are 23 people at a party and the host thought "about 20" when she brought out the party treats, that is *not* good enough.

On the other hand, there are times when an estimate might actually be the better choice. Consider the following. You are going to meet some friends at 8:00. It usually takes about two and one half hours to drive to the meeting place. You may want to allow a little more time than that just in case something happens. An estimate is certainly "good enough" and probably better than relying on the exact time it took on previous trips.

When one estimates, a certain amount of mental calculation is involved. Exact answers, however, are not a goal. In fact, one typically computes with numbers that have been rounded off or otherwise simplified rather than with the actual numbers in the problem. The activities presented below first focus on helping students with learning disabilities learn and use the more important estimation strategies that are now a standard part of school mathematics curriculum. As in their work with mental calculation, these students may need to write out intermediate numbers as the basis for a final estimation.

SUGGESTED SEQUENCE OF ACTIVITIES

1. **Focus on front end addition.** Figure 7.16a suggests one way of helping students understand estimating by focusing on the "lead" digits of a problem. This approach is actually easier than rounding for many children. Instead of boxing lead digits, they could be color coded green during initial phases of instruction.

2. **Adjust the estimate.** In some situations, the rough estimate may be formed by calculating with lead digits. In other cases, a closer estimate may be more desirable. When children have made an initial estimate by focusing on front end digits, then they might consider whether this estimate is good enough, or whether they can "get closer."

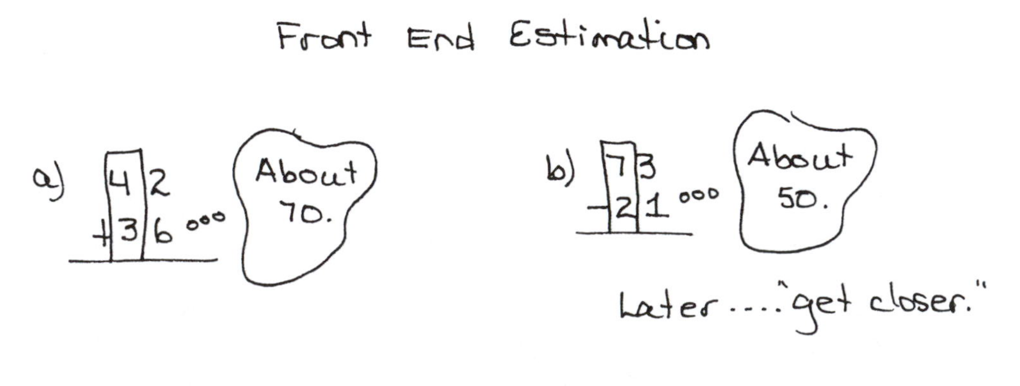

FIGURE 7.16

For the example of Figure 7.16a, since there are 8 ones, that means that 70 is an underestimate. If the decision is to get a closer estimate, students need to note that "there is almost enough to make another 10. A closer estimate is 80." Students might work a series of problem like that given in Figure 7.16a in steps. As a first step, they might make just the rough "lead digit" estimate. As a second step, perhaps taking turns with the teacher or a partner, they might decide whether they are close to making another 10.

3. **Front end subtraction.** Figure 7.16b suggests how similar work might be structured for subtraction. At first, only a rough "lead digit" estimate is made. Later, they might be helped to determine at least whether the actual difference is "more" or "less."

   In Figure 7.16b, for example, because 3 (in the one's place) is *more* than 1, then the actual difference is a little *more* than 50 (for there would be extra ones after subtracting). In a problem like 73 − 29, where the 3 (in the one's place) is less than the 9, then the actual difference is a little *less* than 50 (for one would "take away" one of the tens when regrouping).

4. **Rounding.** Some students may prefer using rounding techniques. In Figure 7.16a, one might think: "About 40 + 40, or 80." This is the estimation method typically emphasized in school textbooks. It involves applying rounding skills (developed in *Rounding and Estimation* section of Chapter 5), the ability to retain each rounded digit, and then mentally computing with these digits. As with other attempts at mental math, some students will need to write the digits they have rounded as an intermediate step and reference for completing the estimation.

5. **Use "nice numbers."** Introduce the idea of looking for "nice numbers." In Figure 7.17a, there clearly is enough to pay for one tape, but not enough for two. In Figure 7.17b, if only one can is needed, it is easier to overestimate as shown.

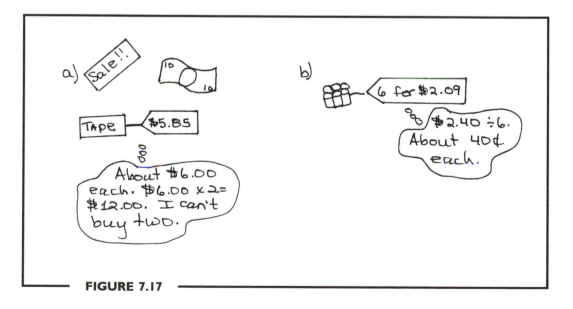

FIGURE 7.17

6. **Use averaging.** Introduce the idea of averaging in order to get an estimate. When all numbers are "about the same"—as they may be in rainfall patterns in some areas; or in the individual meal costs of people sitting together in a restaurant—use the number that seems to be central. This number is sometimes called a "cluster point" or "average"—though an average is not actually calculated.

7. **Use estimation to enhance number sense and concept for the operation.** See the section on *Division of Whole Numbers, Two-digit divisors* (page 344). If students can respond well, apply these ideas to other operations.

Determining Whether Results Are "Reasonable"

An important aspect of number sense is detecting whether a given estimate or other computational result is reasonable. This is a very difficult skill for many students with learning disabilities. Some of these students may be able to detect unreasonable answers only when results examined are "way off," but not otherwise. We consider this last achievement to be major and worth working toward. The suggestions that follow emphasize determining whether a stated result "makes sense." In implementing these suggestions care should be taken to make directions explicitly clear. Otherwise students will tend to redo the computation rather than simply estimating, which is desired.

SUGGESTED SEQUENCE OF ACTIVITIES

1. **Select the most reasonable.** Students need opportunities to react to what is reasonable in a variety of contexts and situations. Noncomputational examples like those of Figure 7.18 may be used.

   NOTE: *In order to estimate, some students (not just small children) will need visual reminders. It may be helpful to provide real objects, have students weigh them, and then decide. Alternatively, use pictures of*

1) The telephone weighs about _____ pounds.

3   30   300

2) The number of books Tom carried in his bag to school was about _____.

4   40   400

FIGURE 7.18

common objects accompanied by approximate weights. In this way, especially students with expressive-language or memory problems will have something upon which to draw to help them estimate.

2. **Predict the number of answer digits.** Having students identify the number of answer digits for specific computational examples helps them focus on the size of the answer. Later they can examine the "size" of an answer to judge, rather quickly, whether it is unreasonable. One would expect the Figure 7.19 problem, for instance, to contain three digits. So "something" is wrong.

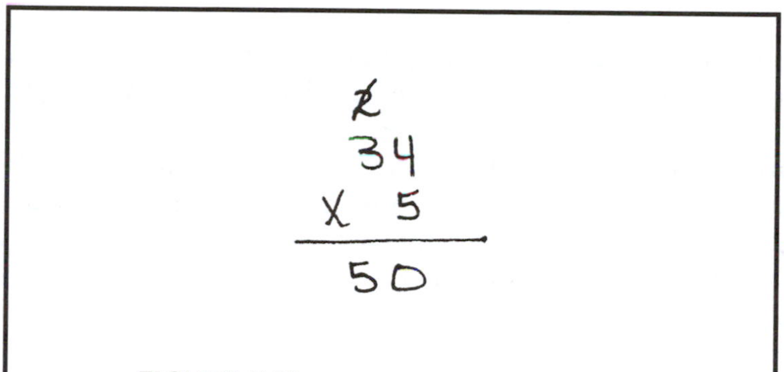

FIGURE 7.19

3. **One right on, one way off.** To start, it is easier for students to detect unreasonable answers when the *same problem* is presented twice: once with a correct answer; once with an answer which is "way off" as in Figure 7.20. Many students find it easier to detect wrong answers when they are paired with correct ones or when they know that one of the pair is wrong. Each time, talk through the estimate(s) used to make the decision. This type of activity prepares for the recommendation in Activity 4.

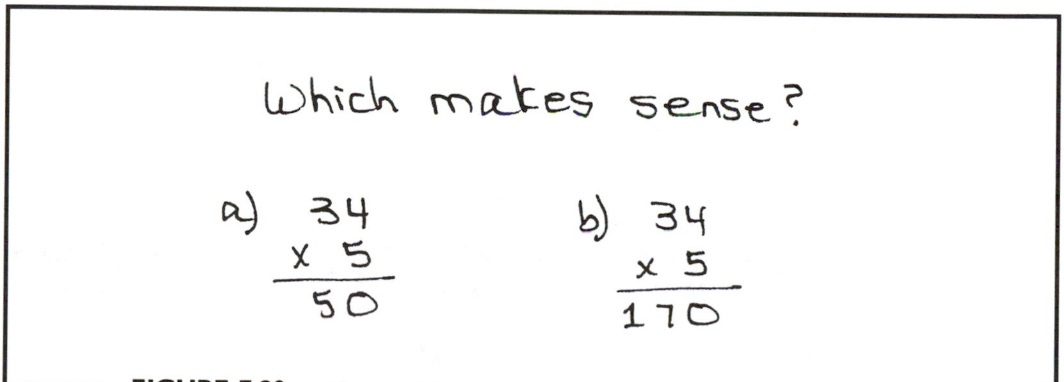

FIGURE 7.20

4. **Does my answer "make sense"?** Give students calculations as in Activity 3, but mix the problems in with others. Gradually present random problems of the same general type:

   - some which have correct answers; and

   - others with answers that are "way off target."

Ask students to identify those that "make no sense." Talk through the estimate(s) used to make the decision.

SELECTING THE COMPUTATION METHOD

Problem Area: Difficulty recognizing that a computation can be carried out best by estimating or making a quick mental calculation, rather than computing by hand.

Typical Disabilities Affecting Progress: Difficulty with abstract reasoning; short-term and sequential memory; integrative processing.

Background: Because of changes in technology, it is no longer necessary or useful for students to spend large amounts of time learning to perform routine computations by hand. This was recently emphasized by the National Council of Teachers of Mathematics in its *Curriculum and Evaluation Standards for School Mathematics* (1989), and already is having impact on school mathematics textbooks. Perhaps the greatest implication for the teaching of computation involves:

- restricting paper-and-pencil computations to simpler numbers, and

- fostering an emphasis on selecting and using the most appropriate method for performing a given computation.

In a given situation it might be both easier and more appropriate to use a calculator, to make a quick estimation, or to calculate mentally rather than to complete a paper-and-pencil computation. On the other hand, particularly if a calculator is not readily available, one might compute by hand the total cost of an order being placed by mail, figure out the amount of cloth needed for a costume, or even balance a checkbook! Different sections which follow in this chapter examine instructional techniques for helping students with learning disabilities become more confident and competent with the many aspects of computation. The suggestions below emphasize ways to help these students decide when one of these computational methods is more appropriate than others in a given situation.

SUGGESTED SEQUENCE OF ACTIVITIES

1. **Look for very big numbers.** As computation for each operation is treated, provide exercises which present a mix of problems, including smaller and

larger numbers of digits. Have students just look for problems with larger digits and use a calculator to solve them.

NOTE: *To assess students' progress in estimation skills, consider a two-part assignment. Provide an assignment of mixed problems in a multiple-choice format. In the first part of the assignment the student merely decides which method of calculation is most appropriate and circles the choice. After the answers are checked, the student proceeds to solve the problems using the different methods.*

2. **Look for quick ones.** Similarly, provide a mix of problems which include some that can be computed very quickly using mental calculation techniques students have mastered. Students who mentally can add problems like 34 + 40, but not 34 + 42 (see Figure 7.11) might be given just the first type of problem along with others which they would normally hand compute. More capable students might be given both types mixed with others. Directions for this exercise would be to "Look for and write down quickly the answer to just those problems you can work out in your head." When this step is checked, the remaining problems can be computed using the standard paper-and-pencil algorithm.

3. **Just do those with answers more than 40 (or any other target number).** Students must first develop estimation skills as previously suggested. Then ask them to apply that skill in an interesting way. For example, ask them to estimate and then hand compute just those problems for which they think the answers are above the target number.

    It may be necessary to ask some students first to estimate and circle problems with answers over the target number. When this step is checked, students could be directed to hand solve the circled problems. Students working out of hardback books could place an acetate sheet over a page before circling. After this part of the assignment is checked, they could solve the circled problems on paper.

    Each of the above activities required students to decide between hand computation and some other calculation method. It also would be useful to systematically ask students to decide between estimation and mental calculation, estimation and using a calculator, and mental calculation and using a calculator. These types of activities involve viable alternatives and provide students with a background for deciding which computation method is "best" in a given situation in light of their abilities.

Comments on Assessment

Alternative ways of assessing progress with mental calculation and estimation must be devised, as controlling time on each individual problem is critical. This can be accomplished by displaying each problem on an overhead transparency for only a brief time (10 seconds, or 15 seconds, or . . .) and then removing it. Each time, students would try to solve the problem mentally and record only the answer in the time allotted.

WRITTEN COMPUTATION

Recent reform recommendations in school mathematics emphasize the need to place written computation in perspective. Thoughtful teachers today, rethinking teaching and learning in relation to computation, recognize the need to balance the time spent on teaching calculation techniques with the time spent on developing children's intuitive and informal knowledge to nurture their ability to be good mathematical thinkers and problem solvers.

For these reasons, whenever possible, computation should be presented in the context of interesting and relevant problems or situations, not as isolated numbers to be added, subtracted, multiplied, or divided. As children work to solve problems, they should be encouraged to record their solution steps in personally meaningful ways, and be expected to explain or justify their thinking. As they listen to each other, greater flexibility of thinking about and processing numeric information should be learned as different solution approaches are shared.

Indeed, while a certain level of competence with written computation is expected, formal time for developing standard computational algorithms should occupy less instructional time and may, for some students, be abandoned in favor of (accurate) algorithms invented by the children themselves. Throughout, every effort should be made to integrate and systematically include significant emphasis on mental calculation and estimation strategies and appropriate calculator use. Ideally, students should always be free to select the computation method that seems most appropriate for any given situation. From the perspective of this general philosophy, the following suggestions are offered to provide insight into ways of helping students handle paper-and-pencil computation when specific difficulties are recognized.

ADDITION OF WHOLE NUMBERS

Multiples of Ten

Problem Area: Difficulty adding 10 or a multiple of 10 to other 1- or 2-digit numbers.

Typical Disabilities Affecting Progress: Difficulty with auditory association, auditory memory, auditory figure-ground, and visual figure-ground.

Background: The ability to add multiples of 10 to other numbers is especially helpful for regrouping in subtraction or performing other mental calculations. Many children who have difficulty recognizing relationships or patterns have difficulty with these additions. For example, they may not recognize—visually or auditorially— the relationship between "30 + 40" and "3 + 4." Some students even have difficulty with the simpler additions, such as adding 10 to a single-digit number. For these students, it is essential to work on the underlying pattern of "adding 10" before introducing regrouping. Once regrouping has been introduced, frequent review may still be necessary to ensure that the students incorporate the skill.

The suggestions that follow have proven helpful in our work with students with learning disabilities who have difficulty "adding tens." The ideas assume that the children have already worked extensively with materials—tens and ones—as the basis for understanding the computational procedure required to add 2-digit numbers: Add like units; if there are 10 or more singles, trade for 1 ten. As the children turn to work at the symbolic level, activities and exercises such as those that follow frequently are necessary.

SUGGESTED SEQUENCE OF ACTIVITIES

> **Adding 10 to a Single-Digit Number**
> **(Helpful for regrouping in subtraction)**

1. **A bundle plus.** Provide numeral cards (one each for 1, 2, 3, ... 9), a bundle of 10 popsicle sticks, and 9 extra single sticks. Lay out the 10-bundle, making sure the children realize that there are 10 sticks banded together in the bundle. Mix the cards and place them face down in a pile. The children, in turn, draw a number card and place the corresponding number of single sticks beside the 10-bundle (Figure 7.21a). They then tell the number of sticks in all (16 in this example). If a child does not know, ask for a guess

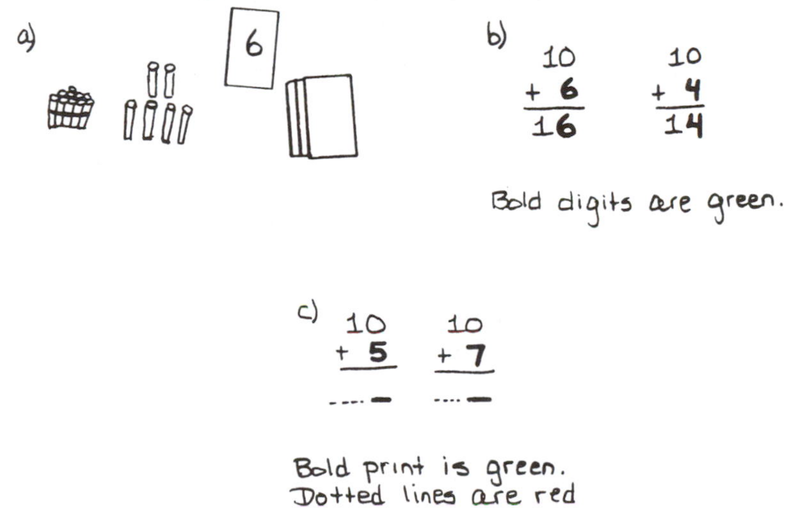

FIGURE 7.21

before a count is made to check. Encourage the students to count on from 10 rather than count from 1 each time. Make a chart showing the result of each draw (Figure 7.21b). Color-emphasize the like digits.

- *Follow-up 1:* Assign exercises like that of Figure 7.21c. Allow the students to use a 10-bundle and extra sticks if needed.

- *Follow-up 2:* To encourage mental calculation, use a mask like that of Figure 7.22 on the chart of Figure 7.21b. Ask the children to give answers orally. Allow them to use a 10-bundle and extra sticks if they get stuck.

2. **Slide and see.** Use a ruler and a "+10" card like that shown in Figure 7.23a. (A laminated worksheet of Figure 7.23b should also be provided.) The teacher writes a single-digit number on a green line of the worksheet to indicate where the student should place the green circle on the ruler (in this example, on the "6"). The child slides a finger along the arrow to get the "feel" of "adding 10." Then the ruler number sentence is read aloud: "6 + 10 is 16." The child writes the result of the addition on the red worksheet line. A 10-bundle and extra sticks could be used to verify the result. Repeat with the other numbers, until four or five examples are written on

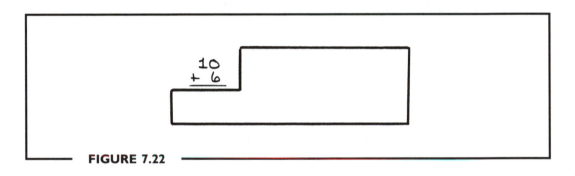

FIGURE 7.22

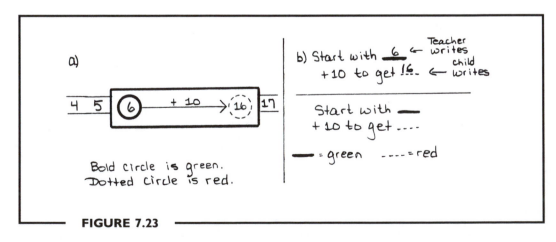

FIGURE 7.23

the sheet. Help the children analyze their written work. Model the auditory emphasis of the two like digits in each example: "*Six* plus ten is *sixteen*." If the children benefit from kinesthetic involvement, have them finger trace the like digits in each example they read.

3. **Slide and check.** Tape a flap over the red hole of the "+10" card (Figure 7.24). Repeat Activity 2, but this time have the child tell the sum, then lift the flap to check the answer.

4. **On their backs.** Copy incomplete "+10" problems like those of Figure 7.25 on the board, and provide the numeral card deck of Activity 1. Mix the cards and place them face down in a pile. In turn, the children draw a card, look at it, show it to the teacher, and place it upside down on the table or desk. After the teacher traces the numeral on each child's back, the child walks to the chalkboard and completes one of the "+10" problems. (The walk provides a medium for forcing the child to think about the numeral that recurs twice in the completed problem.) When the "+10" problem is complete, ask the student to read it aloud. Encourage auditory emphasis of the repeated digit. Then hold up the card the child left behind. Check that the numeral on the card does appear twice in the completed problem. If necessary, the child can use the "+10" card and ruler of Activity 1 to correct any error.

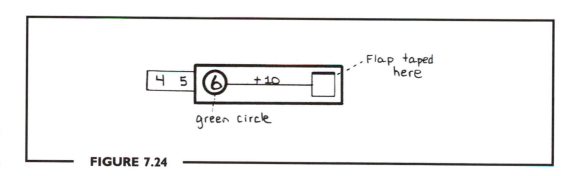

FIGURE 7.24

FIGURE 7.25

Adding 10 to 2-Digit Numbers

1. **Calculator help.** If children possess the necessary skills, allow them to use a hand calculator to complete exercises such as that shown in Figure 7.26a. When a page is complete, have the student read across each row as follows: "26 plus 10 is 36; 48 plus 10 is 58." It often helps to give the child a card to uncover the numerals while reading (Figure 7.26b). Toward the end of the page, cover up the answer and have the child say the sentences, giving answers without the visual reinforcement.

2. **Highlight the pattern.** In exercises of this type some children are helped when a vertical format and colors are used, as in Figure 7.27. Highlighting the digits helps emphasize the pattern of change in the tens digits. The children could be instructed to complete the first part of a page with problems like those shown, leaving the last six or seven problems unsolved. When they have completed the first part, have the children analyze their work. Help them notice the pattern by pointing (a) first to the green tens digit in the problem and (b) then to the tens digit in the sum. While pointing, say each numeral: "two . . . three," "four . . . five," "six . . . seven." Continue this verbal patterning as the children fill in the green blanks of the unsolved problems. A similar procedure is used with the ones digits. When the page is complete, have them read the problems as in Activity 1. Model the auditory emphasis of the tens digit pattern. For example, "*Twenty*-six plus ten is *thirty*-six."

   - *Follow-Up:* To encourage mental calculation, follow up with similar worksheets in which children give answers orally (or dictate them into a tape recorder) before writing.

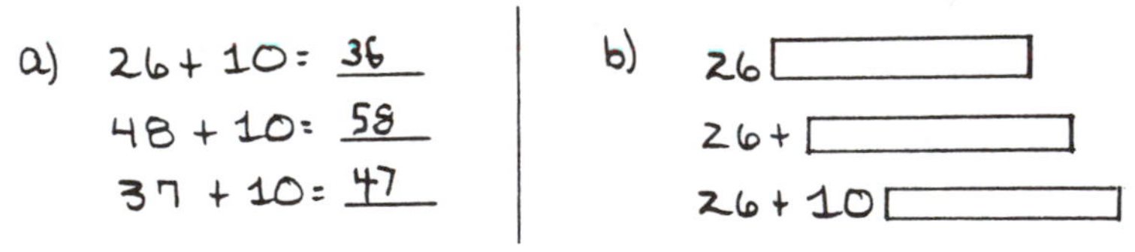

a) 26 + 10 = 36
    48 + 10 = 58
    37 + 10 = 47

b) 26 [   ]
    26 + [   ]
    26 + 10 [   ]

FIGURE 7.26

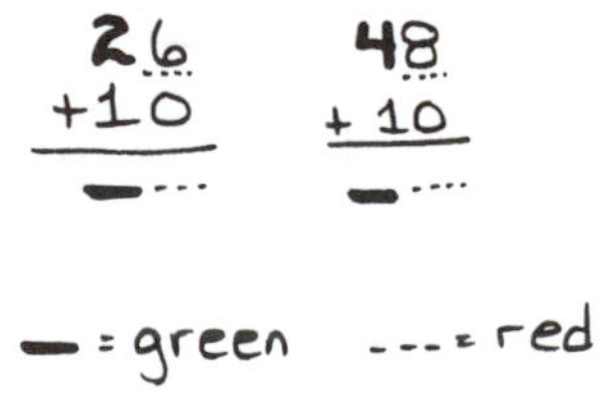

26   48
+10   + 10
─ ···   ─ ····

─ = green   ---- = red

FIGURE 7.27

3. **Practice.** To build up automatic addition of tens, present pages with color-coded horizontal problems, as in Figure 7.28. The colors are used for focusing and visual association with the vertical problems previously completed. The students read the problems as in Activity 1 and fill in the blanks.

4. **Toss up** (a practice activity for two players). Prepare a gameboard as in Figure 7.29 and laminate the center strip. Using a grease pencil, write fifteen 2-digit numbers in the center strip. Provide about 10 markers for each player and two dice:

> Die 1: Marked 4, 5, 6, 7, 8, 9.
> Die 2: Marked 1, 2, 3, 4, 5, 6.

In turn, the players roll the dice and place them in the squares to the left of the center strip to form a 2-digit numeral. This number is added to 10. If the sum is on the board, a marker is placed beside it as shown. If players give an incorrect answer, they must remove one marker from their side of the board. If the sum is correctly stated but not on the board, the dice go to the next player. The winner is the first player to place five markers in a row.

- *Variation:* To encourage mental calculation, give each player markers of two different colors (e.g., orange, worth 2 points; blue,

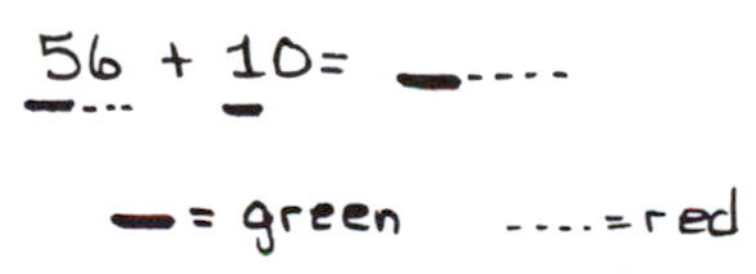

$$56 + 10 = \underline{\quad} \cdots$$

— = green   .... = red

FIGURE 7.28

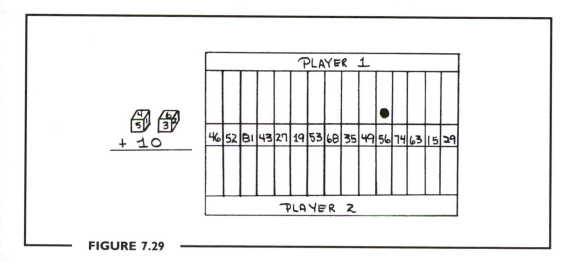

FIGURE 7.29

worth 1 point). The game proceeds as in Activity 4, but use an orange marker if answers are given after mental calculation; blue otherwise. The winner is the first to accumulate 6 points.

| **Adding Other Multiples of 10 to a 2-Digit Number** |

---

1. **Calculator help.** As in Activity 1, page 294 (*Calculator Help*), but introduce multiples of 10 (20, 30, . . . 90) as the second addend.

2. **Relate to the basic fact.** To help develop the visual/auditory pattern and relate the addition to basic facts, exercises such as that shown in Figure 7.30 are helpful. Colors or bold print and underline could be used to focus attention on the related basic facts. In Figure 7.30a, the child begins on the left and reads across the line, filling in the answer on the line. Encourage auditory emphasis to highlight the relationship: "*Six* plus *two* is eight, so *sixty* plus *twenty* is *eighty*." Examples of this type may later be extended to include adding a multiple of 10 to any 2-digit number, as in Figure 7.30b. The vertical format of the second set of problems is more effective for some students. Whatever the format, finger tracing like parts of related problems might be encouraged for a student who requires a high degree of kinesthetic involvement.

   - *Follow-Up:* Encourage mental calculation. Use the exercises described above, but ask the students to give the answers orally before writing. Provide answer keys so that students who work independently can check their own work.

3. **Pick up** (for two or three players). This game reviews adding 10 or other multiples of 10 to a 2-digit number. Provide a laminated gameboard such as that illustrated in Figure 7.31, 25 chips, and two dice:

   Die 1: green numerals, 1–6.
   Die 2: red numerals, 1–6.

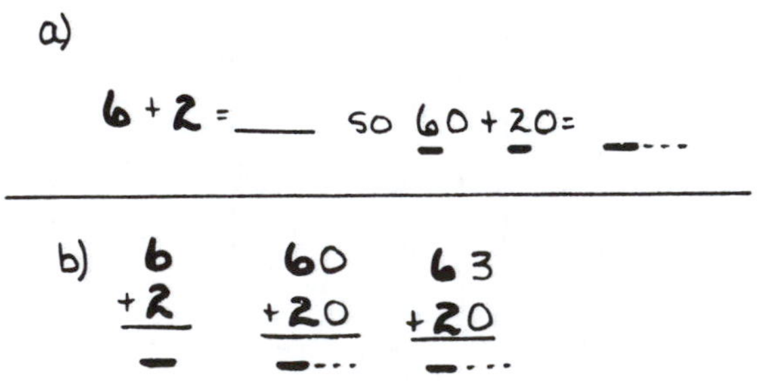

a)

6 + 2 = ___ so 60 + 20 = ___

b)
| 6 | 60 | 63 |
| +2 | +20 | +20 |

FIGURE 7.30

The numerals in the left column of the gameboard are green; those in the top row are red. To begin, the students cover the entire board with chips. In turn, they roll the dice to see which numbers should be added. In the example of Figure 7.31, the green "3" refers to the 3rd green number (left column); the red "4" refers to the 4th red number (top row). These two numbers, 36 and 10, are to be added. The student locates the numbers and says, "36 plus 10 is 46." To check, the player removes the chip corresponding to the addends. If the answer is correct, the child keeps the chip. Otherwise it is replaced. The player who has the most chips when the board is uncovered (or at the end of a given number of rounds) wins.

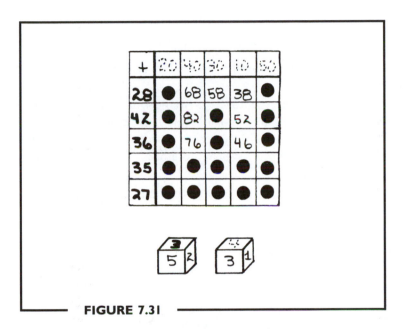

FIGURE 7.31

One- and Two-Digit Addends

Problem Area: Difficulty adding a single-digit and a 2-digit number.

Typical Disabilities Affecting Progress: Difficulty with visual memory, visual discrimination, auditory figure-ground or sequencing, abstract reasoning, and closure.

Background: Study the problems of Figure 7.32. In early developmental work, as background to paper-and-pencil computations like these, children typically use

$$\begin{array}{r} 17 \\ +\ 6 \\ \hline \end{array} \qquad \begin{array}{r} 32 \\ +\ 5 \\ \hline \end{array}$$

FIGURE 7.32

10-stacks and 1s or other physical materials to dramatize the combination of two 2-digits or a 1- and a 2-digit addend. At this stage, children learn to combine like units—all the ones, all the tens—and to trade 10 singles for 1 "ten" whenever possible (Figure 7.33a).

The result of combining ones and tens is written (Figure 7.33b), so the children have a record of what they did. Gradually, because the children "see" what the computational procedure is all about, the materials are dropped, and they learn to compute independently of manipulative aids. They now enter a practice phase that emphasizes obtaining the correct answers more rapidly.

At this skill level, addition involving a 1- and a 2-digit addend can be approached in two ways:

1. as a paper-and-pencil computation, with or without regrouping; or

2. as a mental computation—an extension of the basic facts.

By the time a child is doing fourth- or fifth-grade work, problems such as those of Figure 7.32 can be treated as an extension of the basic facts. Since the problems can be computed mentally, it is unnecessary to use regrouping marks.

There are payoffs to handling problems of this type mentally.

• The mental calculation approach may help children "add by endings" in column addition (Figure 7.34a).

• The mental calculation approach prepares children for multiplication with regrouping (Figure 7.34b).

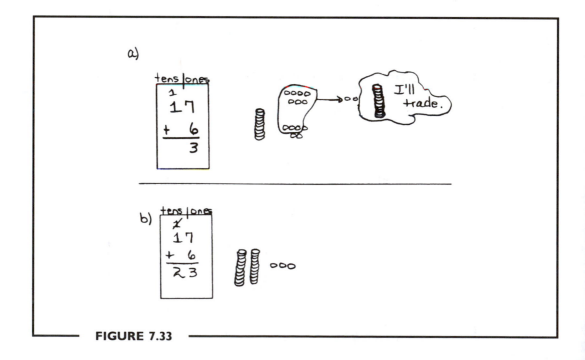

FIGURE 7.33

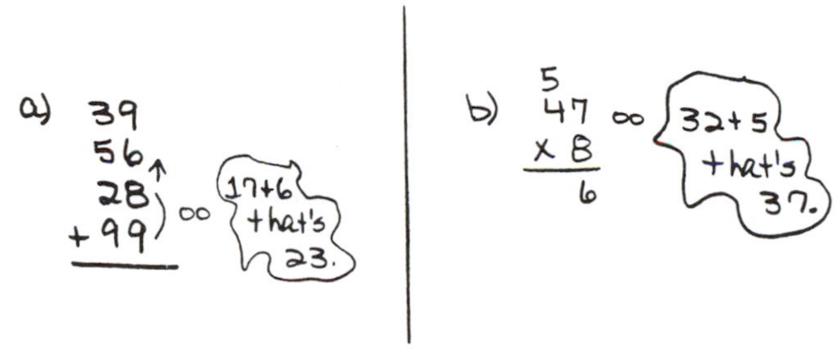

FIGURE 7.34

Many children who *do* know their basic facts are unable to recognize them in the context of a bigger problem (e.g., 32 + 5, not just 2 + 5). The single-digit addend causes confusion that may be linked to a visual-perception or memory difficulty, or to an inability to reason abstractly. Alternately, it may be that, auditorially, the children do not hear the basic fact within the problem. Although they say the problem to themselves (silently or aloud), they may not recognize the particular fact. This latter difficulty may be due to auditory figure-ground or closure deficits. (See Chapter 1 for definitions of terms.) If the problem is presented visually, the empty space in the tens place can be confusing, even for students who demonstrate solid place value comprehension. For many, adding a "concrete" symbol to an empty space is more difficult than adding two 2-digit numerals.

The following exercises are intended to build or reinforce skill in adding a 1- and a 2-digit number. The emphasis is on developing confidence with mental calculation. A suggestion for paper-and-pencil computation of these problem types is included at the end of the section. It is assumed that extensive work with materials, such as those previously outlined, has already been carried out. This is a necessary prerequisite to ensure that the children possess an intuitive basis for work at the symbolic level like that described.

SUGGESTED SEQUENCE OF ACTIVITIES

1. **How does it end?** Figure 7.35 shows an exercise that has proven helpful for relating problems involving a 1- and a 2-digit addend to basic facts. At first, only problems that require no regrouping are presented. Blank file pages, using the format of Figure 7.35b, can be kept on hand and filled in as needed by the teacher. The colors will:

   • Focus attention on the basic fact;

   • Develop reasoning and language skills;

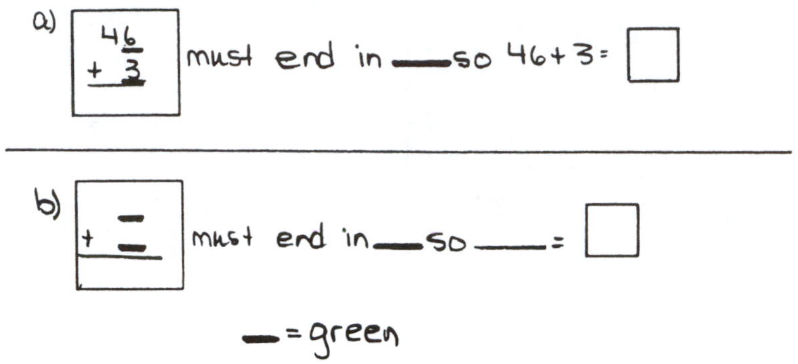

a) 46 / + 3   must end in ____ so 46+3 = ☐

b) ▬ / + ▬   must end in ____ so ____ = ☐

▬ = green

FIGURE 7.35

- Give visual reinforcement to students with auditory deficits; and
- Give auditory reinforcement to children with poor visual memory.

As previously pointed out, it is necessary to check for intact color vision. In serious cases of color blindness, bold print and underscoring can be substituted to highlight and cue responses. In the example of Figure 7.35a, the student begins on the left, reading silently or aloud, depending on preferred learning style. The horizontal part of the exercise follows the left-right reading sequence and reflects what a child should *think* while computing a problem of this type. The blanks are filled in as the student approaches them verbally. Figure 7.36 suggests a sequence that may be used to help build the

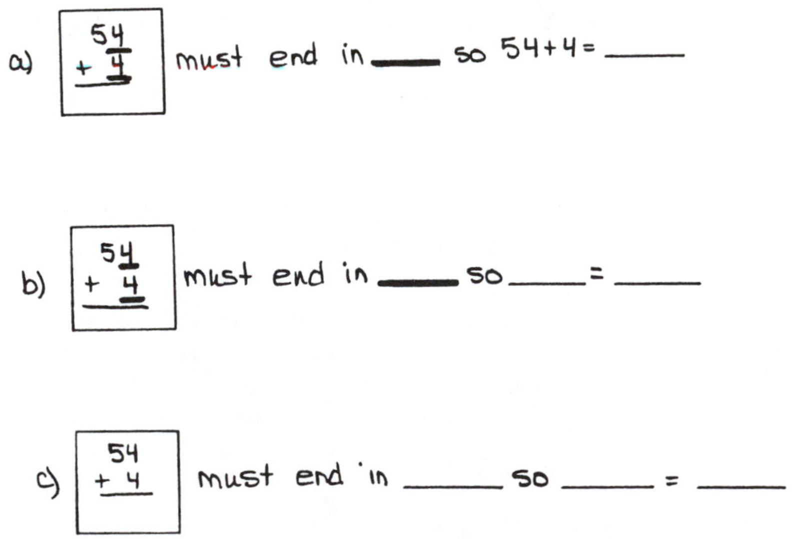

a) 54 / + 4   must end in ____ so 54+4 = ____

b) 54 / + 4   must end in ____ so ____ = ____

c) 54 / + 4   must end in ____ so ____ = ____

FIGURE 7.36

needed skill. By the time a child is working exercises like that in Figure 7.36c, colors may no longer be needed. If they are still necessary, however, the student could underline with a green pen before solving.

2. **Help for book problems.** These same pages can be used, if necessary, for textbook problems. Have the student copy out the problem, place it in the left-hand box, and then compute.

3. **Listen and read.** For students who need the verbalization illustrated in Figures 7.35 and 7.36 but cannot read or express themselves well, prepare cassette tapes that match pages you keep on file. Have the child read along with the tape, problem by problem, until the process is internalized and the student feels comfortable. Experience has shown that use of the tape or other external verbalization can be eliminated within a relatively short time.

4. **Flash! How does it end?** Once the student has internalized the thought process, flash a color-coded card like that of Figure 7.37. With the card as a cue, the child states the problem and completes the sentence, as in the exercises of Figures 7.35 and 7.36.

5. **Side by side.** For children who have either internalized the preceding pattern or who can readily recognize visual patterns, present practice pages containing exercises like that of Figure 7.38. (Though similar to many now presented in texts, the exercise uses a discontinuous pattern.) The child is forced to focus on the pattern in each problem, thus eliminating the tendency to perseverate. By encouraging children to recognize and use a pattern, the approach fosters reasoning skills.

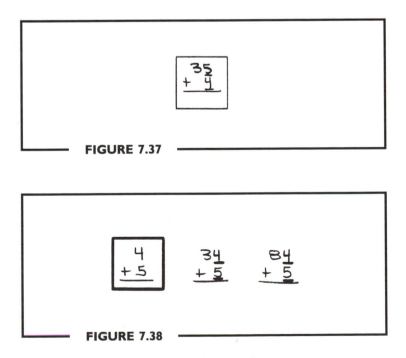

FIGURE 7.37

FIGURE 7.38

NOTE: *If color coding is necessary, the original basic fact—in this case 4 + 5—should be written or outlined in green. In the remaining problems, the fact is underlined in green by the teacher or the student before the problem is solved. Figure 7.39 shows a sample format for sheets that can be prepared in advance and kept on file. These pages can also be used with the controlled fact program described in Activity 1 of the section on General Difficulties earlier in this chapter. The specific facts being worked on are immediately incorporated into actual problem situations.*

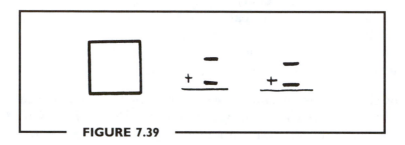

FIGURE 7.39

6. **Three by three.** Keep blank gameboards like that shown in Figure 7.40 on hand. Put the boards in plastic holders and give one to each child. Use a grease pencil to fill the boxes along the left side and top with numbers appropriate to the child's level. (Figure 7.40 uses numbers that require regrouping only sometimes.) Use a standard deck of cards, with picture cards and 10s removed. Each child is given a set of chips. The child draws two cards (e.g., 5 and 3) and tells the sum.

   If possible, the fact is related to the numbers on the gameboard, and the child finishes by saying, "So 85 + 3 must be 88." If the answer is correct, the child places a chip in the appropriate square. Answers can be checked on a calculator or against an answer sheet. The first person to cover a 3 × 3 square wins.

7. **Paper-and-pencil work.** When paper-and-pencil computation is to be carried out, allow the children who need the help to place a zero in the empty 10s space before computing.

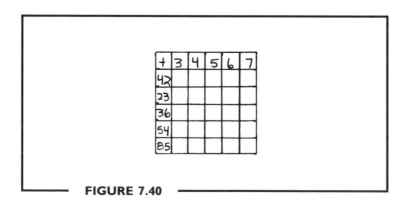

FIGURE 7.40

NOTE: *Do not place the zero in the space for the child. Force the child to deal with the problem. Most children place the zero in the space when it is time to add the 10s digits.*

Regrouping for Addition

Problem Area: Difficulty regrouping when adding 2-digit numbers.

Typical Disabilities Affecting Progress: Difficulty with abstract reasoning, perseveration, figure-ground, and reversals.

Background: Many students are unable to retain a lot of information at one time. The many discrete steps involved in adding 2-digit numbers are difficult enough for them, and they may not readily recognize when or know how to regroup. Automatic recognition becomes even more difficult as regrouping is extended to the 100s place. The student must continually make decisions while trying to recall correctly the sequence for carrying out the computation. In many cases, regrouping difficulty is a result of poor conceptual understanding of place value. For the child with learning disabilities, however, all too often it is simply due to an inability to think without obvious, visual cues.

The following suggestions are helpful for children who have difficulty knowing when or how to regroup when adding two 2-digit numbers. The suggestions assume that the children

- Possess adequate numeration understanding for 2- and 3-digit numbers (see Chapter 5); and

- Understand, at least informally, that when adding two 2-digit numbers you add like units and trade 10 ones for 1 ten whenever you have 10 or more ones.

The latter prerequisite assumes that the students have used grouping aids such as popsicle sticks (10-bundles and extra sticks), chips (10-stacks and extra chips), or graph paper (10s and 1s) to dramatize these ideas. Once this foundation is established and the child is ready to begin regrouping with symbols only, perceptual or other deficits may make it necessary to use activities like those that follow to aid in the transition. These same activities can, of course, be used in remedial situations as well.

SUGGESTED SEQUENCE OF ACTIVITIES

Chips, 10-stacks, and ones are used. In implementing the sequence, use any grouping aid with which the children are familiar.

1. **Picture it: 10 ones for 1 ten.** Review the idea of exchanging 10 ones for 1 ten, using color-coded tens-ones frames as in Figure 7.41a. The child fills in the spaces to describe the picture on the left and is then reminded that

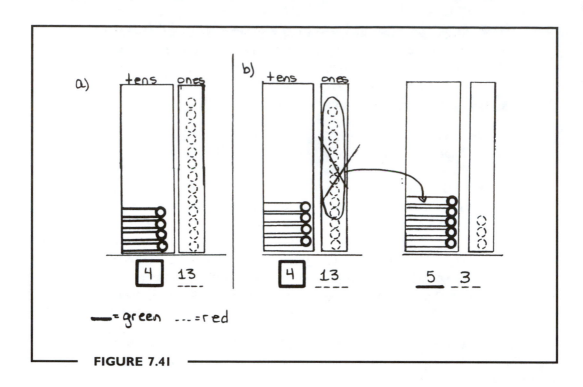

FIGURE 7.41

"Something is not right. There are two digits in one of the spaces." The student crosses out 10 red chips and replaces them with a green 10-stack on the right-hand frame, again filling in the blanks (Figure 7.41b). Auditorially reinforce what is being done: "Yes, if there are 10 or more ones, trade 10 ones for a 10-stack."

NOTE: *For students needing concrete aids to review, use 10-stacks and extra single chips together with laminated tens-ones frames as illustrated in Figure 7.42. Design the frame so that no more than nine chips can be placed in the ones column. (The inside of a file folder can be used to draw the frames. Simply use a felt-tipped pen to outline the slots in which you wish children to place their 10-stacks and single chips.) Problems may be set up as in Activity 1, but students can trade 10 single chips for one 10-stack. Using grease pencils or wipe-off markers, they can fill the spaces to describe the pictures both before and after the trade. The limited frame-space idea can also be carried out in follow-up paper-and-pencil work.*

2. **Picture the picture.** Once a student masters the work presented in Activity 1, introduce exercises like that illustrated in Figure 7.43. Fill in the left-hand boxes with numbers previously used with the tens-ones frames. The basic teaching sequence is illustrated in the following narration:

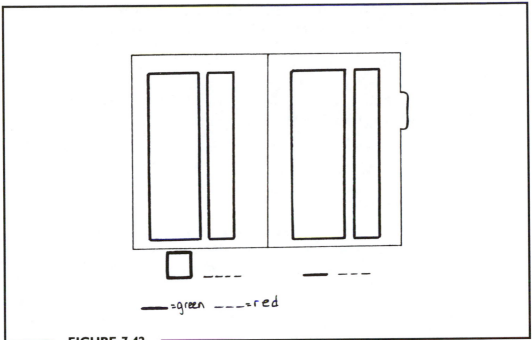

FIGURE 7.42

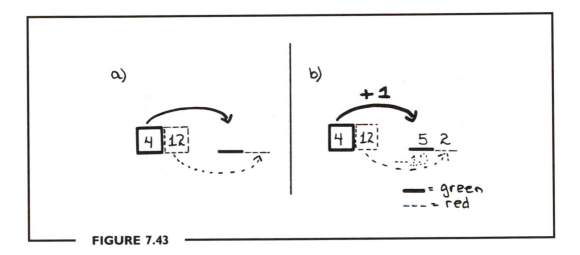

FIGURE 7.43

TEACHER: (pointing to the left-hand box of Figure 7.43a): "Something is not right. There are two digits in one of the spaces. What did we do with the chips whenever there were 10 or more ones?"

STUDENT: "Traded 10 loose chips for a 10-stack."

TEACHER: "Yes, and what did we do every time we put another 10-stack in the frame?"

STUDENT: "We wrote a different number on the green line, because now there's one more." (At this point, the teacher writes + 1 on the green arrow and instructs the students to do the same on their sheets.)

TEACHER: "That's right, and 4 + 1 is 5" (writing "5" on the right-hand green line). "Whenever we put another 10-stack in the frame, what did we do with the red chips?"

STUDENT: "Took off 10." (At this point, the teacher writes "−10" on the red arrow, instructing the children to do the same.)

TEACHER: "That's right, and 12 − 10 is 2" (writing "2" on the right-hand red line).

NOTE: *For the first few examples, particularly for students with visual-memory or sequencing deficits, it may be necessary to use 10-stacks and single chips with the tens-ones frames to dramatize each step.*

3. **Need to trade?** An important question should now be asked in conjunction with exercises like those illustrated in Figure 7.44: "Are there two digits in one space?" Children may be asked to examine the right-hand boxes to answer this question for each example. They may then be instructed to circle those boxes that "are not right"—those in which the ones place is overloaded.

4. **If yes, then trade.** Children who have mastered the previous step have an edge in recognizing *when* to regroup. The issue now is knowing *how* to regroup at the symbolic level. The answer to the question in Activity 3 is now given direct attention (Figure 7.45). A procedure similar to that out-

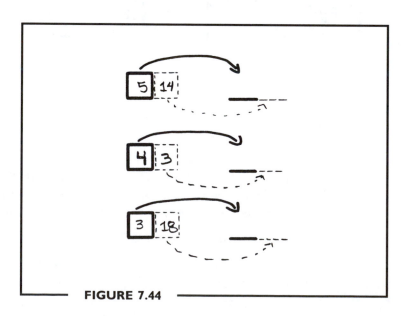

FIGURE 7.44

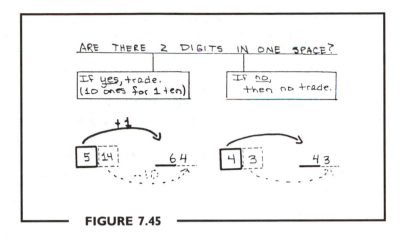

FIGURE 7.45

lined in Activity 2 (*Picture the Picture*) is carried out. At this stage, however, most students do not need to relate vocally each step of a problem to the movement of chips. They already have internalized the concept and need to practice to build skill in regrouping whenever there are two digits in the ones column. Previous work is extended as the children fill in the right-hand box in exercises (see Figure 7.46). To encourage the child to consider when regrouping is necessary, some of the problems do not require regrouping (Figure 7.46b). A wall chart similar to Figure 7.45 or a mini-pasteup on the child's page is helpful during early stages of independent work with exercises of this type.

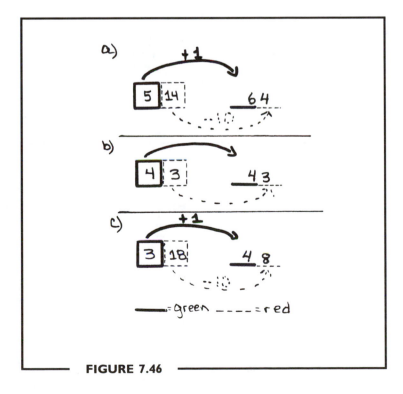

FIGURE 7.46

5. **Now add.** The previous exercises required that students, working with numerals alone, recognize when the ones place was overloaded. When this skill is mastered, apply it to 2-digit addition problems. Figure 7.47 shows one type of page that can be used. *Part of the page is visually similar to previous work. This may take some pressure off the student.* Each problem is first solved without regrouping. The answer is then examined, and the student decides whether or not to regroup. If it is necessary to point out the similarity to previous work, provide the child with a card to cover up the actual problem. The extra step of seeing two digits in the ones place often provides the necessary reinforcement to remember to think about regrouping.

   NOTE: *The discrete steps of the preceding sequence are essential for many students with learning disabilities, particularly for overlearners or those with sequencing or abstract-reasoning difficulties. Using colors (or other visual highlighting techniques) and repeated drills helps the child more readily learn* when *and* how *to regroup.*

6. **A box cue.** Color-coded reminder boxes, such as that pictured in Figure 7.48a, serve two needs by providing:

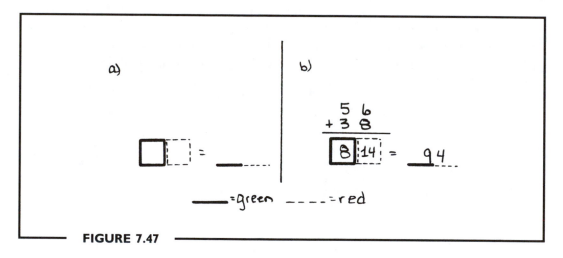

FIGURE 7.47

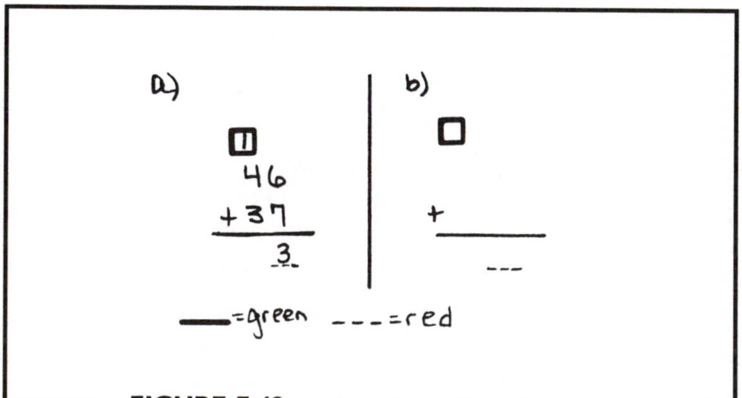

FIGURE 7.48

- help in the transition to the standard computational format for addition with regrouping; and

- help for students with reversal tendencies.

In the example of Figure 7.48a, the children first add to obtain 13 ones. The normal pattern for writing 13 is "1" then "3"; so urge the children to follow this sequence when recording their answer. The color scheme of Figure 7.48 encourages this: 1 first (in the *green* box), then *3* on the *red* "stop" line. Figure 7.48b suggests how to format pages in advance. Pages can be filed and pulled later as needed. When preparing the pages, include the boxes on all problems, even when regrouping is not needed. This forces the students to determine whether regrouping is needed.

7. **Doctor the text.** When using a text or workbook page, allow the students to draw dashes under each problem to match the columns (e.g., two columns, two dashes). This often serves as a reminder that only one digit is allowed per space. (If the textbook problems are too small for the students to mark, ask adult volunteers to help prepare texts in advance.)

Column Addition

Problem Area: Inability to complete the sequence in column addition.

Typical Disabilities Affecting Progress: Difficulty with short-term or sequential memory and visual figure-ground.

Background: Although a student may, conceptually, understand column addition, perceptually, this can be extremely difficult, especially when "ragged columns" or regrouping are involved as in Figure 7.49. Children with figure-ground difficulties find it especially hard to "keep the place" while copying or computing problems of this type. To complicate matters, the three-addend problem is really a four-addend problem because of the regrouping. The child who worked the example of Figure 7.49 handled the ones column addition correctly, even the regrouping, but forgot the "1" while adding the tens column.

For some students, using a hand calculator for column addition is a viable alternative to paper-and-pencil computation. Indeed, sometimes calculator use or estimation should take precedence over hand calculations. Yet, most students with

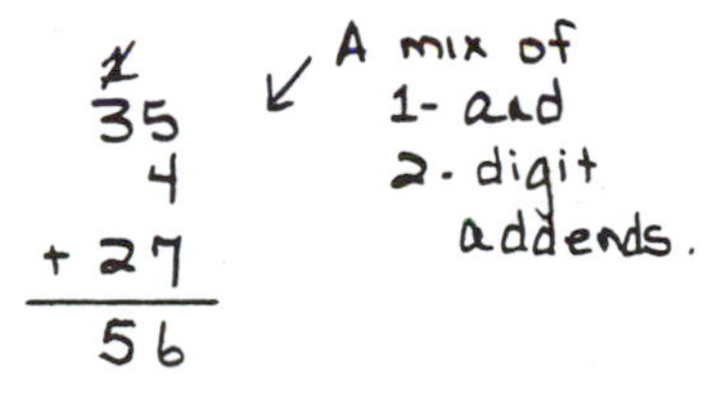

$$
\begin{array}{r}
\overset{1}{3}5 \\
4 \\
+\ 27 \\
\hline
56
\end{array}
$$

A mix of 1- and 2-digit addends.

FIGURE 7.49

learning disabilities can learn to add a sequence of three or four numbers. Compensatory techniques such as the following have proven effective in helping students acquire this skill.

SUGGESTED SEQUENCE OF ACTIVITIES

1. **One step at a time.** Approach column addition one step at a time. Prepare practice pages containing problems like that shown in Figure 7.50a. Use green for the first two addends and the answer line, red for the arrow and the last addend. Before writing the final sum, the student fills in the blank line with the sum of the first two addends.

   NOTE: *Pages using the problem format of Figure 7.50b can be kept on file and used as needed. The teacher fills in specific numbers if a controlled-fact program is used. Students can also copy problems from the text onto these pages. Alternatively, if textbook space is not too confining, the students can color code text problems before solving. If difficulty with column addition is anticipated, textbooks could be coded in advance (perhaps at the beginning of the school year) by adult volunteers.*

2. **Cross out means 10.** For children with good visual but poor sequential memory, the approach of Figure 7.51 has proven helpful. The child adds down the column until a 2-digit answer (8 + 9 = 17) is reached. The last digit added, in this case 9, is crossed out to represent the 10 in the sum. The student retains the 7 mentally and combines it with the 6. The 6 is crossed out to indicate the one 10 in 13, and the child writes down the 3. The number carried is the same as the number of digits crossed out, in this case 2. The same approach is used for remaining columns.

3. **Write the ones.** If visual memory or reversal deficits require that a child write subsums, the procedure suggested in Figure 7.52 can be used. The student adds the first two addends. Since the sum (16) is a 2-digit number,

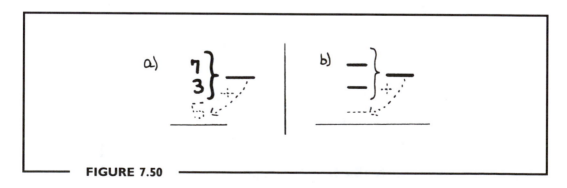

FIGURE 7.50

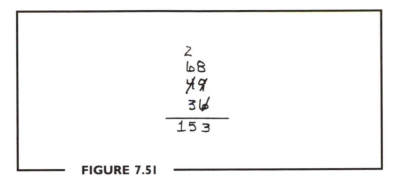

FIGURE 7.51

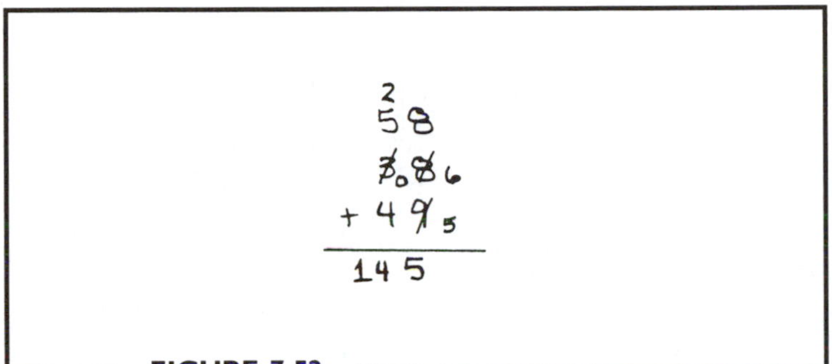

FIGURE 7.52

the second 8 is crossed out and the 6 is written down, in that order. 6 + 9 is 15, so the 9 is crossed out and the 5 is written below the line. As before, the number of crossed digits represents what should be carried.

4. **Visual helps.** For students having visual figure-ground or other perceptual deficits, any of the following techniques may be used.

- Teach the children to color highlight a column before adding it (Figure 7.53a).

- Provide square centimeter paper and instruct the students to write one digit per square (Figure 7.53b).

- Provide vertically lined paper and instruct the students to write every digit on a line (Figure 7.53c).

- Provide a tachistoscopic card for covering columns not being added. The card should only cover the problem, with room to write the carried number at the top and the answer in the proper place. As the student works, the card is moved along so that only the numbers being added show through the slot. Figure 7.53d shows a step-by-step approach for using the card to solve an addition problem with three 3-digit addends.

  NOTE: *The entire card may be covered with acetate and children be allowed to use a grease pencil to write the ones digit of sub-sums directly on it (see Activity 3). The acetate is wiped clean before another column is added.*

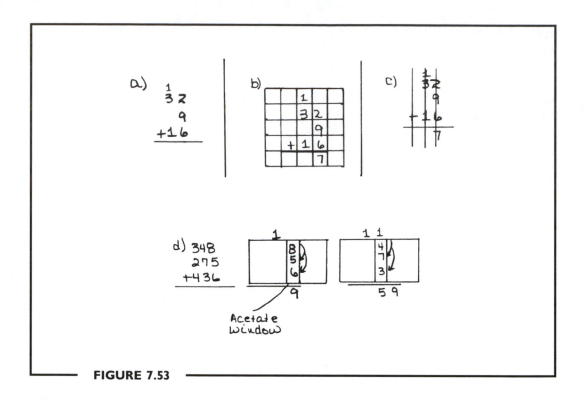

FIGURE 7.53

SUBTRACTION OF WHOLE NUMBERS

When children turn to subtraction, they meet difficulties similar to those encountered in whole number addition. It is not uncommon for students to have problems subtracting a single-digit from a 2-digit number; some find it hard to subtract multiples of 10. Knowing *when* and *how* to regroup is a major challenge in subtraction, as in addition, especially for children with learning difficulties. Many of the activities described in the previous sections can be adjusted and used to aid in handling parallel difficulties in subtraction. Since some problems with regrouping require slightly different techniques than those previously discussed, the following two sections will present additional suggestions for this topic.

As with addition, be accepting of invented algorithms which may be more meaningful for individual children than "standard" approaches. Continue to embed subtraction computation in interesting, relevant problem settings.

Two- and Three-Digit Subtraction with Regrouping

Problem Area: Difficulty knowing when and how to regroup in subtraction of 2- and 3-digit numbers.

Typical Disabilities Affecting Progress: Difficulty with abstract reasoning, perseveration, visual figure-ground, reversals, and sequencing.

Background: As with addition, knowing when to regroup in subtraction is difficult for many students. Many tend to subtract the smaller from the larger number,
regardless of position within the problem. Figure 7.54 illustrates this error, typical
also of children who do not exhibit specific disabilities. Often this error stems from poor
conceptual understanding of the process of subtracting with regrouping. Some children
with learning disabilities have strong concepts, but visually reverse the numbers.

Other factors contribute to the widespread difficulty in this area. Figure 7.1
illustrated, step by step, how subtraction with regrouping is really a combination
of subtraction and addition. The process requires a tremendous amount of mental
computation and constant switching from one operation to the next and then back
again. Thus, children are continually having to make decisions—they must not only
know when to regroup, but also how. That involves realizing what operation to use
and then applying it at each discrete step.

Several approaches may be used to develop the proper procedure for 2-digit and
3-digit subtraction with regrouping. Generally, it is most helpful to use the simplest
model, that of "take away," as the basis for subtraction computation. In the problem
68 − 49, for example, students can be cued to think: "8 take away 9. Since there
are not enough ones, a trade must be made (1 ten for 10 ones)." The "take away"
approach aptly dramatizes the "big ideas" underlying subtraction computation:
subtract like units; if there are not enough, make a trade. This approach consti-
tutes the basis for the suggestions that follow.

$$\begin{array}{r} 64 \\ -35 \\ \hline 31 \end{array}$$

FIGURE 7.54

SUGGESTED SEQUENCE OF ACTIVITIES

1. **Fair trade** (to prepare for a natural, meaningful transition to 2-digit subtraction with regrouping). Provide a deck of laminated cards like that pictured in Figure 7.55a and a "band" of 10-stacks and loose chips. In turn,
   the children draw a card and use the chips to picture the problem on the
   card. The teacher leads the following discussion:

   > "The bank needs another 10-stack. Will you trade
   > one of yours for loose chips? How many loose
   > chips would make a fair trade? (10 loose chips
   > for the 10-stack.) Write what you have now" (see
   > Figure 7.55b).

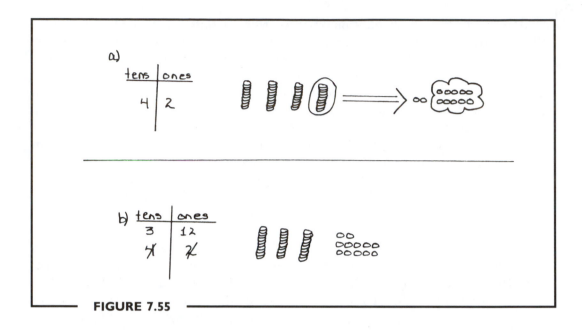

FIGURE 7.55

Repeat with other cards, making a record of the trade each time.

2. **Take away.** Relate the trade idea of Activity 1 to 2-digit subtraction with regrouping. In the example of Figure 7.56a, the children use 10-stacks and loose chips to show what you start with (42). Now subtract: "2 take away 8." There are not enough loose chips to take 8, so trade a 10-stack for 10 chips and write to tell the number of remaining 10s and 1s (Figure 7.56b). Now the children can "take away" 8 loose chips and one 10-stack, leaving two 10-stacks and four loose chips (Figure 7.56c).

3. **Are there enough?** Some children—particularly the careless, the impulsive, and those who perseverate—may fall into the pattern: regroup, subtract, regroup, subtract. This pattern is continued whether regrouping is required or not. Force children to decide about regrouping. One suggestion is to present mixed problem types like those of Figure 7.57. Note that the ones digit of the minuend has been visually highlighted to focus attention on it. The children start with this digit each time and decide whether there are enough, so they can "take away" the number represented by the digit directly beneath it. (Use chips as in Activity 2, if necessary, to dramatize the first few problems.) Ask the children to circle the problem if there are not enough. Do not require that they complete the problems at this time.

4. **Help them decide.** Some students need more structured assistance before they can succeed with the task presented in Activity 3. Figure 7.58 shows one type of exercise that can be used. The underlining helps the children focus on the correct starting point in each problem. To force them to think more clearly about the relationship between the numbers, ask them to read

a)

tens	ones
4	2
− 1	8

b)

tens	ones
3	12
4̸	2̸
− 1	8

c)

tens	ones
3	12
4̸	2̸
− 1	8
2	4

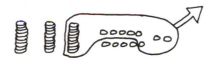

FIGURE 7.56

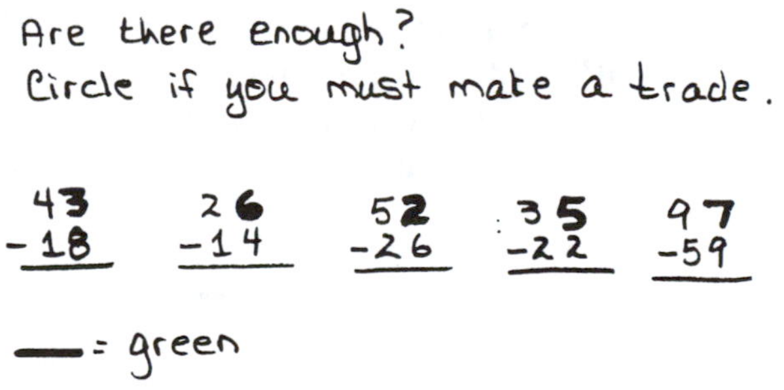

Are there enough?
Circle if you must make a trade.

43	26	52	35	97
− 18	− 14	− 26	− 22	− 59

_____ = green

FIGURE 7.57

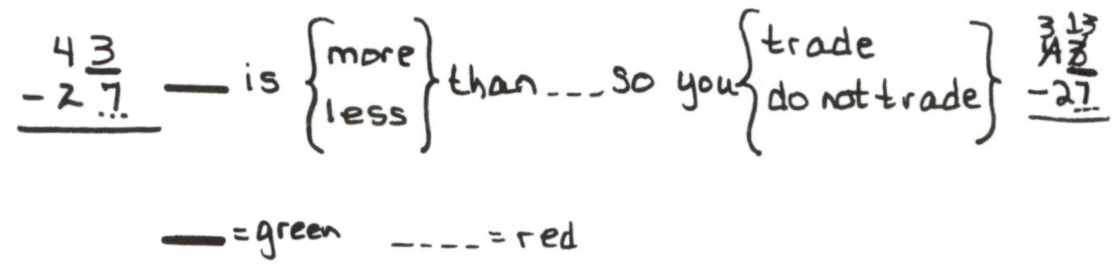

FIGURE 7.58

across the line and fill in while doing so. Eventually, they internalize the sentence. As they do other problems, they are more likely to think about the way the exercise has prompted them.

NOTE: *The phrase "make a trade," used during work with 10-stacks and loose chips in previous activities, is used throughout the rest of this sequence. Some teachers may prefer to use the term "regroup." Whatever the students understand best should be adopted.*

5. **Cue box.** For children who have trouble sequencing or who do not automatically associate written words with numbers, the cueing technique in Figure 7.59 has proven helpful. Problems of this type can be used to reinforce the last step of the sequence discussed in Activity 4. Even with the cueing, the students must decide whether it is necessary to make a trade. If so, the teacher can help by discussing the number available and the number to be "taken away;" 10-stacks and chips could then be used to verify thinking. If a trade must be made, then there is "1 less ten, 10 more ones."

6. **Block out.** As regrouping is extended to the tens and hundreds places, it is often necessary to remind students to continue thinking in the correct way. The "block out" card shown in Figure 7.60 is helpful in this regard. Used by the child as a marker while solving subtraction problems, the card serves to block out extraneous numbers, thereby allowing the child to focus on the pertinent numbers.

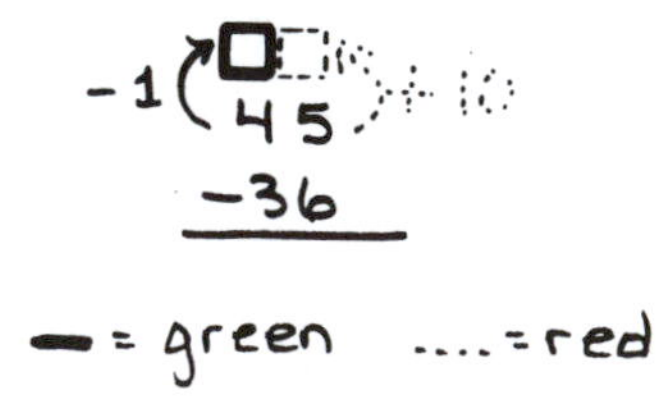

FIGURE 7.59

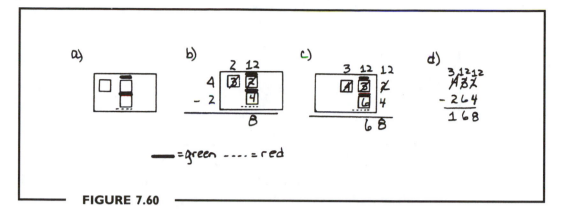

FIGURE 7.60

7. **Different strokes.** Subtract like units . . . if there are not enough, make a trade. These are the "big ideas" behind subtraction. Some students apply these ideas, step by step, when computing: first ones, then tens, and so on. Others benefit by first going through an entire problem, noting all places where regrouping is necessary. Once this is done, they can backtrack and perform the computation. Children who benefit most from this latter method are those who have trouble sequencing or making switches in their thought process, and those who have difficulty with number alignment. Rather than forcing one procedural pattern on all students, note which method is easiest for an individual.

8. **Do it backwards!** Children with severe reversal problems often benefit from working problems left to right (see *Note* to Figure 7.61). In the example shown in Figure 7.61 the child begins with 9 − 2 = 7. Next, the student thinks, "5 take away 9." Recognizing the need to make a trade, the child crosses out the 7 and writes 6 beneath it. The 5 is crossed out and 15 is written above. The explanation is that, after the first subtraction, we still have 7 hundreds left, enough to trade, when necessary, for the 5. A similar procedure is used to complete the problem. (The approach is similar to the equal-additions methods illustrated in Figure 7.62, but it is easier for chil-

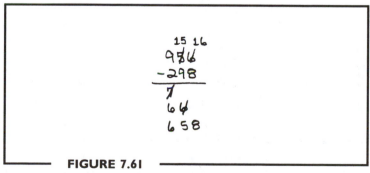

FIGURE 7.61

NOTE: This method looks longer and more cumbersome to many of us, yet for the child with learning disabilities with visual-perceptual problems, it eliminates one obstacle to learning—the tendency to reverse.

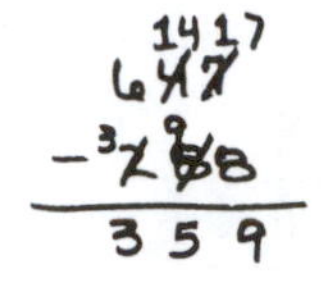

$$
\begin{array}{r}
\overset{\overset{14}{1}\overset{1}{4}\overset{1}{7}}{6\,\not4\,\not7} \\
-\,\overset{3}{\not3}\,\overset{9}{\not8}\,\not8 \\
\hline
3\ \ 5\ \ 9
\end{array}
$$

FIGURE 7.62

dren with reversal tendencies to understand and follow.) For those who need help with number alignment, use graph paper or pages containing examples like that of Figure 7.63.

9. **Into the maze** (for two or three players). To reinforce the correct sequence, the need to regroup, and the skill of adding 10 to a number, prepare a game-board as in Figure 7.64a. Also provide a grease pencil and wipe-off rag, a deck of laminated cards with subtraction problems like those of Figure 7.64b,

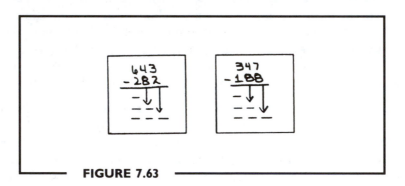

FIGURE 7.63

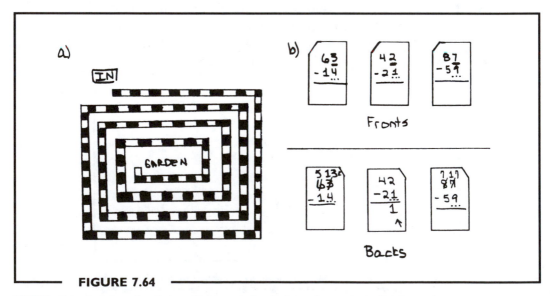

FIGURE 7.64

NOTE: If the deck is used up before the winner is found, the cards are wiped off and reused.

an envelope for the cards, and a game marker for each player. To begin, cards are mixed and placed in the envelope. In turn, the players draw a card, state the problem, and decide whether or not a trade is necessary. If so, a grease pencil is used to show the trade. After the players add 10 to the green number, they move that many spaces. If no trade is needed, the players simply subtract the two numbers. The result is the number of spaces they may move. Answers can be checked by flipping to the back sides of cards. The first student to reach the garden in the rear of the maze wins.

Zero in Subtraction

Problem Area: Difficulty regrouping when zero appears in the minuend.

Typical Disabilities Affecting Progress: Difficulty with sequencing, spatial organization, memory, and reversals.

Background: Zero difficulties are more prominent in subtraction than in addition. In subtraction of 2-digit numbers with zero minuend digits, for example, the tendency to reverse is more dominant than when only nonzero digits appear (see Figure 7.65). Some children simply ignore the zero (Figure 7.66). Because of these and other erratic errors children often make, it is generally more beneficial to teach the concept and process of subtraction with regrouping before introducing zero in the problem. The specific lessons, incorporating ideas such as those that follow, could be carried out to help the children deal with zero in subtraction computations.

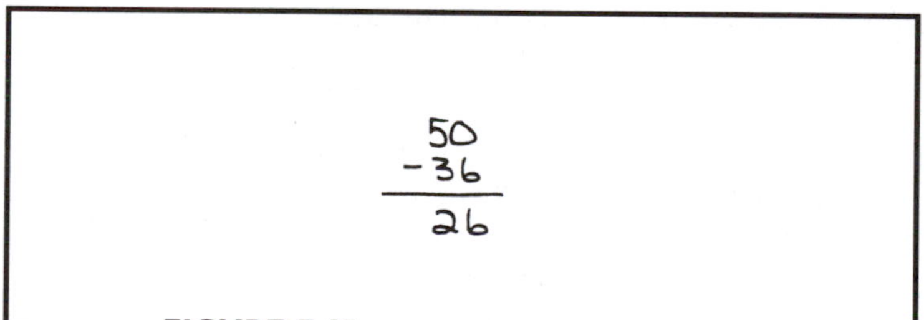

$$\begin{array}{r} 50 \\ -36 \\ \hline 26 \end{array}$$

FIGURE 7.65

$$\begin{array}{r} 415 \\ \cancel{5}0\cancel{5} \\ -196 \\ \hline 39 \end{array}$$

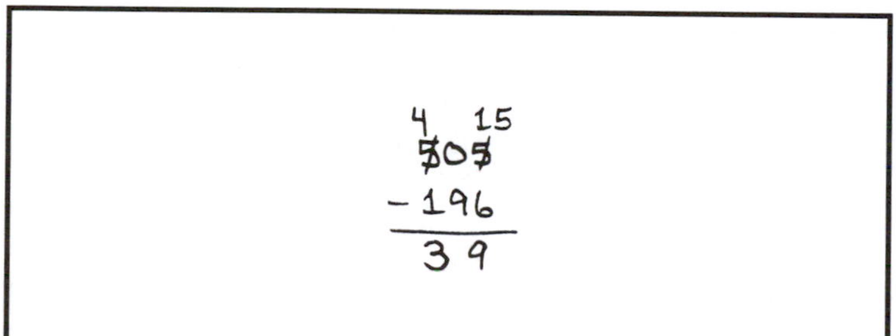

FIGURE 7.66

SUGGESTED SEQUENCE OF ACTIVITIES

1. **Act it out.** Use the *Fair Trade* and *Take Away* activities of the previous section to provide a physical frame of reference for 2-digit subtraction with 0 in the minuend. Use multiples of 10 (20, 30, . . . 90) for the "fair trade" activity and include these same numbers in the minuend for the "take away" activity. (A sample problem for this latter activity is 60 − 13.)

2. **Think about it.** Prepare pages using the format of Figure 7.58, placing zero on the green line. If the child does not respond to the verbal association, adapt the *Cue Box* activity of the previous section to work with zero.

3. **Circle.** Follow up with pages that mix zero and nonzero digits in the minuend for 2-digit subtractions. Include both regrouping and nonregrouping. At first, just ask students to circle problems where a trade must be made. At a later time, they can complete the subtractions.

4. **One step.** Show the children how to make a trade (regroup) in one step, as in Figure 7.67. Initially, underline the 60 to focus attention. "We can think of this as 6 one-hundreds and no tens. We can also think of it as 60 tens. That's easier. When we borrow 1 ten we have 59 tens left. Now we give that 1 ten to the 2."

5. **Hidden zero.** The method of Activity 4 can also be used with a hidden 0, as shown in Figure 7.68. The student still views 71 as 71 tens, thus eliminating one regrouping step.

6. **Do it backwards.** An alternative to the "one step" is the method of subtraction explained in Activity 8 of the previous section (*Do It Backwards!*).

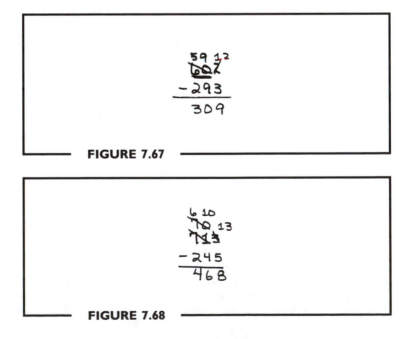

FIGURE 7.67

FIGURE 7.68

This approach (as in Figure 7.69) has proven helpful to some students when a zero is in the tens place. Often children become confused when they reach the step shown in Figure 7.70. Continuity has been broken, and many, particularly those with short-term memory deficits, forget why they were doing what they did. The "backwards" left-right approach may help eliminate this problem.

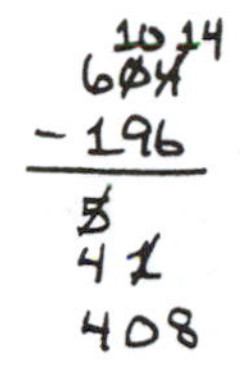

FIGURE 7.69

FIGURE 7.70

MULTIPLICATION OF WHOLE NUMBERS

This section troubleshoots to give targeted special needs children experience with whole number multiplication. These problems may emerge as students work cooperatively or individually to solve problems in which multiplication is needed. Some teachers may choose to implement suggestions presented as a way of anticipating students' needs and thereby alleviating difficulties which might otherwise arise.

Though both 1-digit and 2-digit factors are treated, the need to be sensitive to individual needs and abilities is paramount. Written computation that is longer and more complex for any individual student might well be bypassed by employing a stronger program of calculator use, so that more important "thinking" aspects of the mathematics curriculum can be addressed. For all students, systematic review and integration of mental calculation and estimation strategies is important, as well as the expectation to continue to select the most appropriate computation method in any given problem situation.

SUGGESTED SEQUENCE OF ACTIVITIES

1. **Side by side.** Present multiplication problems like those shown in Figure 7.71. Children solve the first problem in each pair. Then, using a calculator, they arrive at the product for the second problem of the pair. (If there are not enough calculators for each student to have one, the children take turns.) When the product is read to the class, it can be written on the board or an overhead. Use the colors as indicated to help the students notice the pattern. Gradually, extend the process to higher multiples of 10 and color code in the same manner.

2. **Relate.** A problem sequence like that of Figure 7.72 can be used effectively with students who, perceptually, cannot work the calculator. Remind the students of the relationship between multiplication and addition by initially setting up the problems as in Figure 7.72a. Most children who know their facts and are strong conceptually will use multiplication to solve the problem, even in this form. Students who do not know the facts, but understand the relationship between addition and multiplication can use a multiplication chart to solve the problems and cue them to the general pattern. The following narration, based on the problem of Figure 7.72a, suggests the type of discussion that might take place.

> TEACHER: "Did you add the zeros each time?"
>
> STUDENT: "No, they sort of tagged along each time."
>
> TEACHER: "Right. What about the 4s? Did you add them?"
>
> STUDENT: "No. 6 × 4 is 24, and that's easier."

By the time the students are working problems like those of Figure 7.72d, they generally note how "It's like multiplying by 2; since 90 ends in 0, so does the answer." A similar rationale can be used to support the multiplication of Figure 7.71. For 48 × 20, you write a 0 in the product

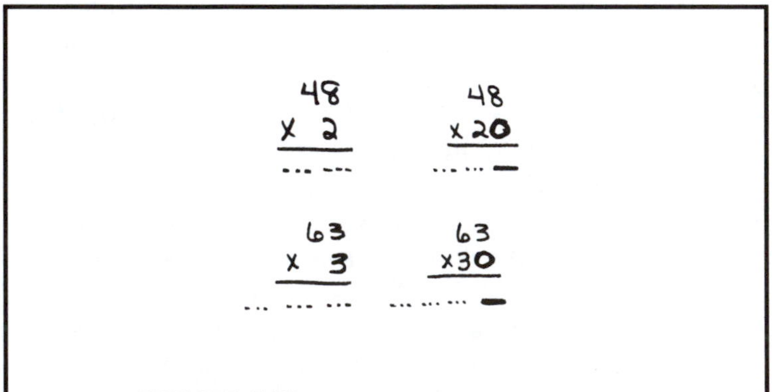

FIGURE 7.71

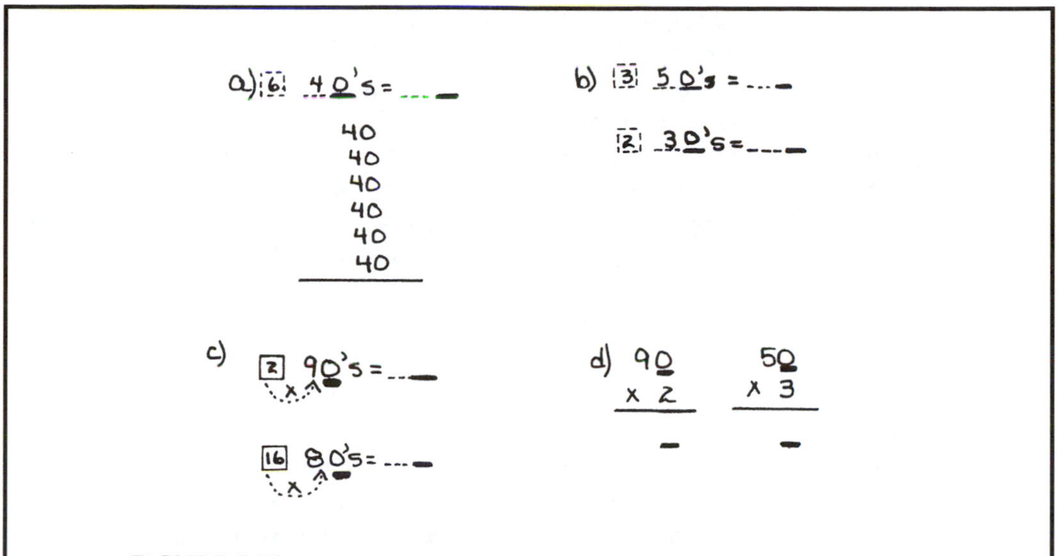

a) 6 40's = _ _ _ _

40
40
40
40
40
40
_____

b) 3 50's = _ _ _

2 30's = _ _ _ _

c) 2 90's = _ _ _
x

16 80's = _ _ _
x

d) 90
x 2
—

50
x 3
—

FIGURE 7.72

to show you are multiplying by a multiple of ten. Otherwise, it is just like multiplying 2. Placing related pairs side by side on worksheets, as shown, reinforces this idea.

3. **Call it** (a practice activity for two players). Prepare a laminated gameboard like that of Figure 7.73. Write the numerals 1 to 6 (in green) along the bottom row and 1 to 6 (in red) up the left-hand column. All other gameboard spaces should show a product, with one factor being a multiple of 10. For students who are just beginning, it is best to make one of the factors 10. As the students gain experience in the game and confidence in themselves this can be changed. Provide an answer sheet of possible factors for each product and two dice:

Die 1 (green): Marked 1, 2, 3, 4, 5, 6;
Die 2 (red): Marked 1, 2, 3, 4, 5, 6.

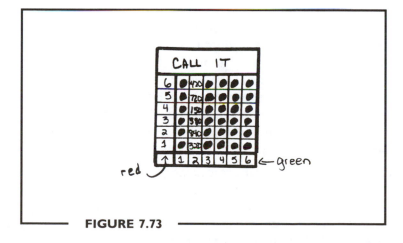

FIGURE 7.73

Also provide three sets of markers, each a different color: one set for each player, and one set to cover the entire board at the beginning of play. In turn, the players throw the dice and read them as points on a graph. For example, a green 2 and a red 5 correspond to (2, 5) or 720 on the gameboard of Figure 7.73. If the player can correctly name two factors forming the product (one must be a multiple of 10), the black chip is replaced with the child's colored one. If necessary, the student can consult the answer sheet to check. The winning pattern should be determined before the start of the game.

Beyond One-Digit Multipliers

Problem Area: Difficulty multiplying two multidigit numbers.

Typical Disabilities Affecting Progress: Difficulty with spatial organization, integrative processing, sequencing, abstract reasoning, visual memory, and reversal.

Background: Many children have trouble multiplying two numbers when both factors contain two or more digits. The sequence is long and continually broken up by addition; a considerable amount of spatial organization is required, not only to place the numbers on the correct line, but also to align the digits properly; and visual memory is needed to retrieve the basic fact and to regroup the correct number.

For many students, it is necessary to provide visual or auditory cues in early work involving 2- or higher digit multipliers although they have a strong place value comprehension and understand the use of the distributive idea for multiplication computation. The following activities suggest ways in which this can be done once the children are ready to begin this work at the symbolic level. It is assumed that the students can multiply 2-digit numbers by 1-digit factors and by multiples of 100.

SUGGESTED SEQUENCE OF ACTIVITIES

1. **Color cue.** Color-coded grid boxes, as in Figure 1.16, have been most effective in helping students organize the multiplication process, both spatially and sequentially. Figure 7.74 shows a sample problem completed by a child using the grid boxes. The student first multiplied by the green number (3). The digit to be carried was recorded in the green circle, and the units digit was placed in the appropriate green box. Next, the child multiplied 3×4, and added the 2 in the green circle. After crossing out the 2, the answer (4) was recorded in the two green boxes. The student proceeded similarly with the multiplication by 20, this time using the red carrying circle and red boxes.

   NOTE: *Students must be taught to write the carried digit first at all times and thereby avoid any tendency to reverse. Crossing out the carried digit should be a carryover of work with 1-digit multipliers. When the colored circles are no longer used, the crossing-out technique will eliminate confusion over which digit to add whenever two or more carry digits appear.*

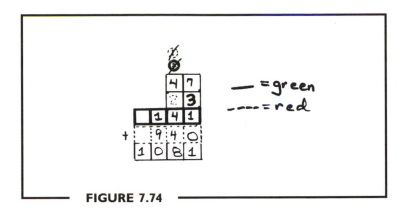

FIGURE 7.74

2. **Fade out.** As the students begin to feel comfortable with the process, the colors can gradually be eliminated, depending on the student's progress. Two suggestions follow.

- Children whose major difficulty appears to be spatial organization may be able to do without all the colors almost immediately. They will continue to need grid paper for a while, however, until they have overlearned the kinesthetic feeling and sequence. Gradually, the grid paper sheets can be replaced with pages using the format illustrated in Figure 7.75.

- Students having primarily sequencing difficulties may need to retain the color cue for the factor digits and carrying circles for quite some time.

3. **A special case.** Using the same color-coded grids as described previously, the presentation can be varied for children with more severe reversal difficulties. For these students, the 10s digit of the multiplier is green and the 1s digit is red. The child "goes on green" (Figure 7.76) and multiplies 2(0) × 7. As the product is said, the student writes 1 in the green circle and 40 in the appropriate green boxes. The procedure continues in a similar manner for the remaining digits.

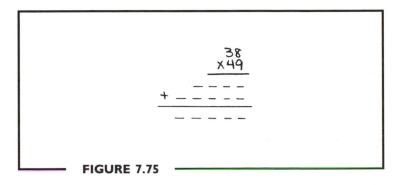

FIGURE 7.75

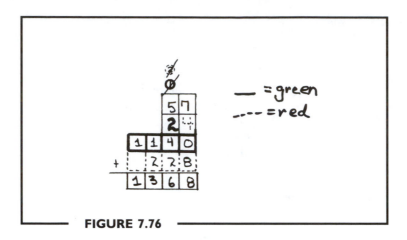

FIGURE 7.76

4. **A zero card.** Children with figure-ground or abstract-reasoning deficits often benefit from being allowed to use a zero card or factor slide. Figure 7.77 shows, step by step, how a child uses a zero card. The student first uses the blank side of a card and covers the 6 (to block out extraneous numbers). After completing this multiplication, the card is flipped over and the 0 is placed over the 4. The idea being reinforced is that, to multiply by 64, you multiply first by 4 then by 60. Finally, you add the result. Figure 7.78 shows how a factor slide can be used in a similar way.

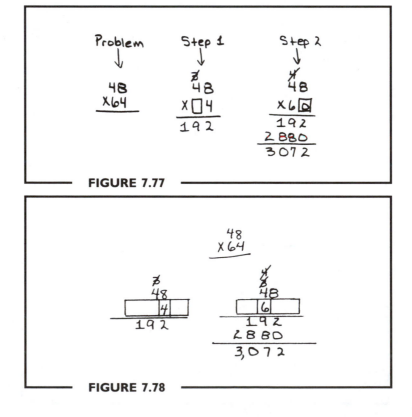

FIGURE 7.77

FIGURE 7.78

Regrouping in Multiplication

Problem Area: Difficulty adding the carried digit.

Typical Disabilities Affecting Progress: Problems related to short-term memory, visual memory, reversals, sequential memory, and figure ground.

Background: Many students have trouble adding the carried digit because they cannot perform the required mental computation. They may know the basic facts, but, if they cannot retrieve an accurate image of the 2-digit number, they are bound to have trouble computing with it. Consider Figure 7.79. This student had no trouble with multiplication. Numbers were carried properly and aligned properly, and the operations were sequenced correctly. What happened then? Notice the 85 in the product. After correctly recording first the 10s and then the 1s digit of 48, the student mentally reversed the digits for 18 (6 × 3). The child thought "81," and for that number the sum 85 (81 + 4) is correct. The digits of the product 48 were probably not reversed because they were recorded as said. There was no need to sort out a confused visual image.

We have noted how, as computational skills are expanded, the number of steps increases and accurate sequencing becomes essential. Unless children have a clear conceptual understanding of the process and have overlearned each discrete procedure involved, it is often difficult for them to maintain the correct sequence and compute successfully at the symbolic level.

The activities that follow address one small step of the computational process for multiplication: adding the carried digit. The suggested exercises have proven effective in dealing with the problem highlighted in the example of Figure 7.79 as well as other related difficulties.

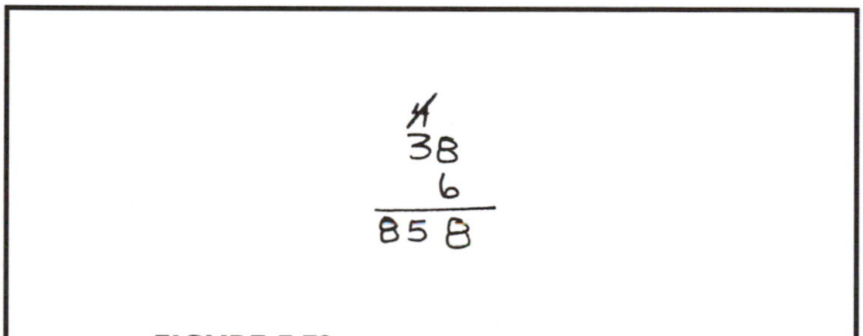

FIGURE 7.79

SUGGESTED SEQUENCE OF ACTIVITIES

1. **Relate.** If students have difficulty regrouping in multiplication, exercises like those of Figure 7.80 often prove helpful. These are an extension of the

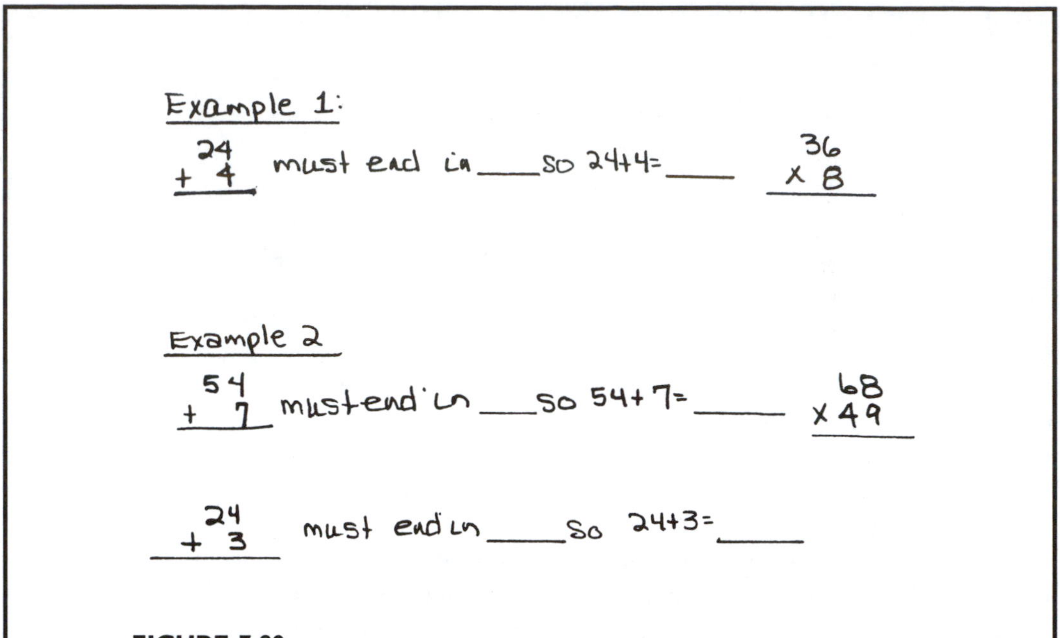

Example 1:

$$\begin{array}{r} 24 \\ + \ 4 \end{array}$$ must end in ____ so 24+4= ____ $$\begin{array}{r} 36 \\ \times \ 8 \end{array}$$

Example 2

$$\begin{array}{r} 54 \\ + \ 7 \end{array}$$ must end in ____ so 54+7= ____ $$\begin{array}{r} 68 \\ \times 49 \end{array}$$

$$\begin{array}{r} 24 \\ + \ 3 \end{array}$$ must end in ____ so 24+3= ____

FIGURE 7.80

work begun in Section 2 of the addition part of this chapter, illustrated in Figures 7.35 and 7.36. Now an effort is made to relate the addition to its role in multiplication computation. In Figure 7.80 the student first solves an embedded addition problem and then a related multiplication problem. In example 1, students first find the sum of 24 and 4, filling in the spaces as they approach them verbally. The related multiplication is then carried out. When they reach the addition part of the problem, the children can look back at the answer. This eliminates the need to retain a reversed digit mentally.

In the second example, the students complete the first addition and multiply 68 by 9. Then they do the second addition before finishing the multiplication. The speed with which the children can independently incorporate the addition procedure into multiplication will depend on how comfortable they are with the entire multiplication process. Allow them to use pages of this type so they can multiply with a minimum of interference from their learning deficits.

2. **Color cue.** Figure 7.81 shows how to use color coding to help students who have trouble sequencing even though visual discrimination presents little difficulty. The children are reminded to use the colors as a stoplight—multiplying first and then adding.

3. **Different strokes.** The previous example can be adjusted as in Figure 7.82 for students who have trouble revisualizing the product in order to be able to combine it with the carried number. After multiplying the 10s digit, the product (45) is written on the green line and added to the number carried.

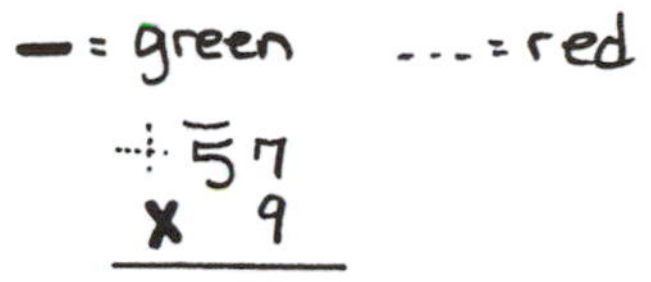

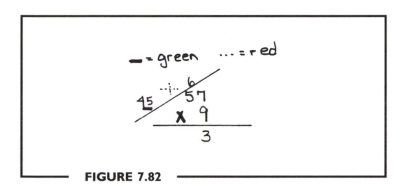

FIGURE 7.81

FIGURE 7.82

4. **Another alternative.** Students whose major difficulty is digit reversal when having to retain a number mentally should be encouraged to write the number down. Providing a box to the side of the problem, as in Figure 7.83, often is sufficient to avoid digit reversal. For left-handed students, place the box to the left of the problem.

5. **In and out.** A board game that provides practice in adding the carried number is shown in Figure 7.84. Each child needs a marker and, if necessary, an answer key. Provide a maze board and a set of cards containing partially completed multiplication problems. Each child, in turn, draws a card and states the remaining partial product. In this case, 44. If correct, the child advances a marker as many steps into the maze as indicated by the carry number. In case of a wrong answer, the marker is moved back an equivalent number of spaces. The winner is the first to get out of the maze.

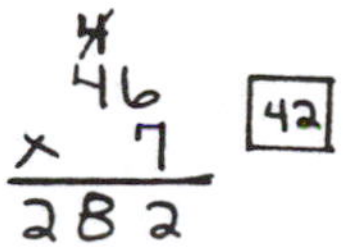

FIGURE 7.83

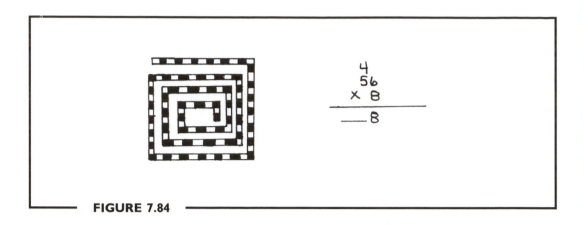

FIGURE 7.84

DIVISION OF WHOLE NUMBERS

The increased availability and lower cost of hand calculators, together with the infrequent need to use long division in day-to-day situations, has caused mathematics educators to question whether we should continue to teach the long-division algorithm. In a real sense, the long division algorithm is as archaic as the square root algorithm. It clearly does not make much sense to spend 5 weeks on the long division! In favor of emphasizing richer aspects of mathematics, this section will focus only on finding exact answers for division involving 1-digit divisors as a way of reinforcing numeration understandings.

Instead of dealing with 2-digit divisors for obtaining exact answers, this topic is *treated*, but from the perspective of nurturing number sense and estimation. The activity suggestions throughout this section are offered to provide ideas for working with individual students to meet targeted needs. While they do not refer to problem settings, it is assumed that this emphasis is a consistent one during instruction. As with other operations, the integration of other computation methods should be integrated and encouraged, when appropriate. Further, the students themselves should be allowed, even encouraged, to use personally meaningful methods of recording their solutions to division situations.

If the standard algorithm is used, it is important to be sensitive to the fact that, aside from being sequentially difficult, it also requires good visual perception. Even with strong place-value comprehension, many students have difficulty aligning the digits in the quotient. Others, like the child who worked the problem in Figure 7.85a, are miscued perceptually by the problem itself. In this case, the child understood the long division process. He or she knew the remainder was too large but was confused because there appeared to be nothing more to bring down! When questioned regarding digit placement in the quotient, the child could only correct the error when a card was placed over the 26 (Figure 7.85b) to make the placement more obvious. This technique and others described below make it possible for students with learning disabilities to succeed with the standard algorithm for 1-digit divisors, should this algorithm be used.

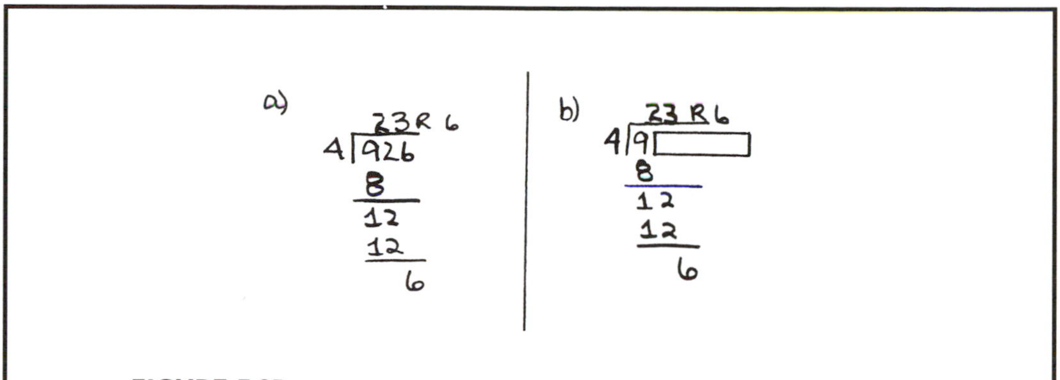

FIGURE 7.85

Beginning Long Division

Problem Area: Difficulty transferring from the concrete to the symbolic level for long division; inability to interpret meaningfully written long division problems.

Typical Disabilities Affecting Progress: Difficulty with visual memory, sequencing, abstract reasoning, retrieval, and figure ground.

Background: For many children, the concept of division—using blocks, chips, money, and other concrete aids—is relatively easy to grasp. Thus, they soon learn to divide (separate) things into groups with the same number in each group. The difficulty arises when only symbols are used in the written problem. The functional division sign (⟌) tends to confuse students with reversal tendencies, whether visual or auditory. Yet, the other division sign (÷) is not particularly useful, at this point. Generally, rather than confronting children with both symbols simultaneously, it is better to teach them to use the more functional one first, relating it as much as possible to concrete aids.

Because of the inherent reversal tendencies and involved sequencing in division, the process lends itself well to color coding. The colors provide the student with a starting point as well as a way of determining and maintaining the sequence. Suggestions along this line follow.

SUGGESTED SEQUENCE OF ACTIVITIES

1. **Say it with chips.** As children make the transition to symbolic work for long division, it is often helpful to relate the work with materials directly to the written computational problems. Make puzzles available like those shown in Figure 7.86. Have the children cut the puzzles apart before beginning, then place the two pieces of each together, upside down, at the side of the desk. Using an overhead projector or felt board, the teacher places

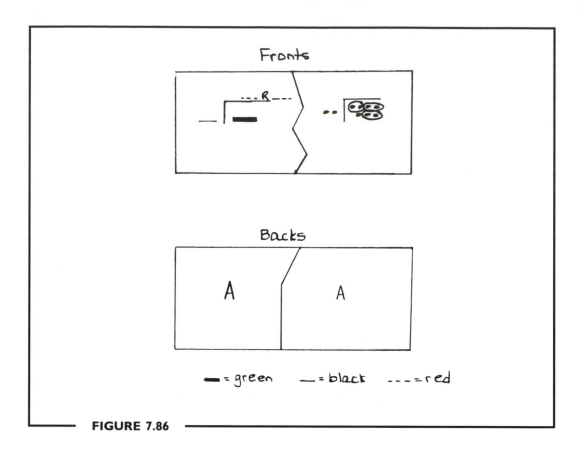

FIGURE 7.86

chips under the division sign ($\overline{)}$) and goes through the sequence described below. The chips should be colored green, black, and red to match the colors on the puzzles. For each puzzle, the presentation is similar to that indicated below. The children work with real chips and the *left* side of each puzzle.

> TEACHER: "Start with seven green chips." (After the seven green chips are taken, the teacher tells the students to find the left piece of the puzzle A.) "Write 7 on the green line to stand for the seven chips."

> TEACHER: "Use your chips again. Let's put two chips in each group." (In conjunction with this activity, the children write a 2 on the black line of the puzzle piece.)

> TEACHER: (Using the chips under the $\overline{)}$ forms groups of two.) "How many groups did I make? Right. I made three and had one chip left over." (The children are instructed to put numbers in the appropriate places of their puzzle pieces to indicate this.)

This procedure continues until all left-hand puzzle pieces have been filled in. The children then put the puzzles back together to check their work.

2. **Puzzles alone.** Once students understand the previous work at the concrete level, show them the picture part of the puzzles and ask them to rewrite each problem on their own paper, using *numbers* rather than dots. To check, the children again match the puzzle pieces.

    NOTE: *This method of presentation and reinforcement is effective even with upper-primary grade children. First it offers the concrete aspect so essential to comprehension. In addition, the direct teaching of the transition and the overlearning help build a strong base. Visual memory, sequencing, auditory memory, and abstract reasoning are all reinforced.*

3. **Follow-up.** After work with chips and puzzles, exercises like those of Figure 7.87 can be used by students with adequate reading skills. These pages are especially good for children who need to verbalize while learning, but have trouble retrieving the words. Before solving the problem using numbers, the left-hand section is completed. The teacher fills in divisor dots at the presentation. Then the children fill in the numbers at the right and solve the problems.

4. **Transition.** Figures 7.88 and 7.89 show transitional pages that can be used as the children develop better conceptual understandings and become able to sequence using symbols only. In Figures 7.88b and 7.88c the student can fill in numbers from textbook problems or the teacher can fill in numbers

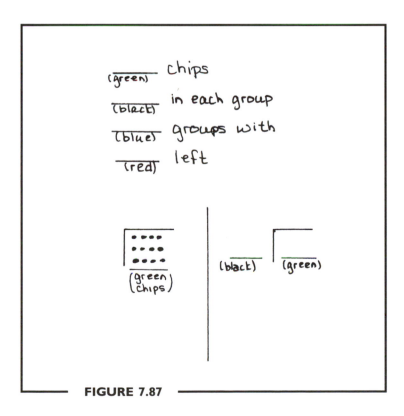

FIGURE 7.87

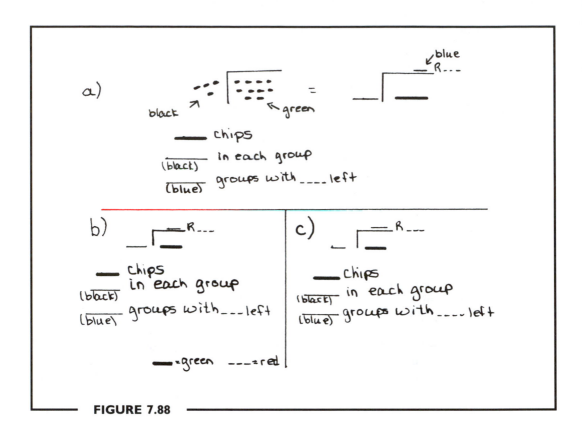

FIGURE 7.88

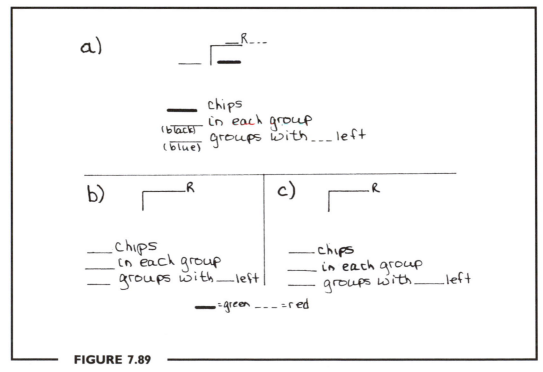

FIGURE 7.89

which are appropriate to the student's level. Figure 7.89a acts as an example which the teacher can fill in before the student begins copying textbook problems in the rest of the page.

Beginning Long Division: Special Help

Problem Area: Using only symbols to solve division problems.

Typical Disabilities Affecting Progress: Difficulty with auditory processing, perseveration, sequencing, visual memory, and closure.

Background: Even when the concept of division is established and the students can interpret the written long division problem, many children are still unable to proceed independently. For many, it is due to an inability to retrieve the needed facts. For others, the required sequencing and constant operation switch make it difficult to complete a problem accurately. Memory deficits may have prevented them from learning the basic facts and perseveration makes skip counting or the use of charts too difficult.

The following activities contain suggestions for how to help children deal with these problems. The assumption is that students' concept base is strong and that the division problem difficulty is primarily due to individual learning difficulties.

SUGGESTED SEQUENCE OF ACTIVITIES

1. **In the squares.** Many children need to see and feel what they are saying. Figure 7.90a illustrates a format idea for pages that can be kept in the file

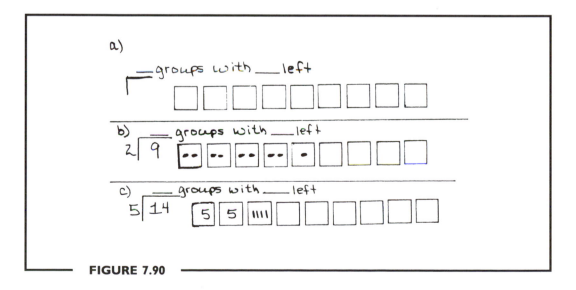

FIGURE 7.90

and used, as needed, to provide such reinforcement. The children place dots, lines, or chips (if necessary) in each square as they skip count (Figure 7.90b). For those who need assistance with stopping, provide a stoplight above the last box needed or outline this box in red. Encourage the students to keep one finger on the dividend number and to compare it with the number of chips placed.

NOTE: *As overlearning occurs, the children independently place numbers rather than pictures or objects in the squares to show the skip count (Figure 7.90c).*

2. **Transition.** As a transition to the long division procedure, Figure 7.91 illustrates a format for pages that can be filed and used. The teacher fills in dividend and divisor numbers at the time of presentation (Figure 7.92a). The student fills in the squares and determines the number of groups that have been made. Then a count is made to see how many things have been "used up" (15 in this example). The child now subtracts to find the number left over.

NOTE: *For right-handed children the boxes should be to the right of the computation. For left-handed children they should be on the left.*

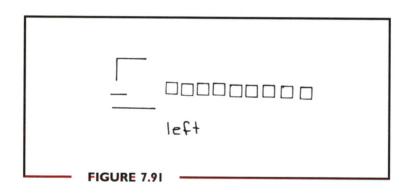

FIGURE 7.91

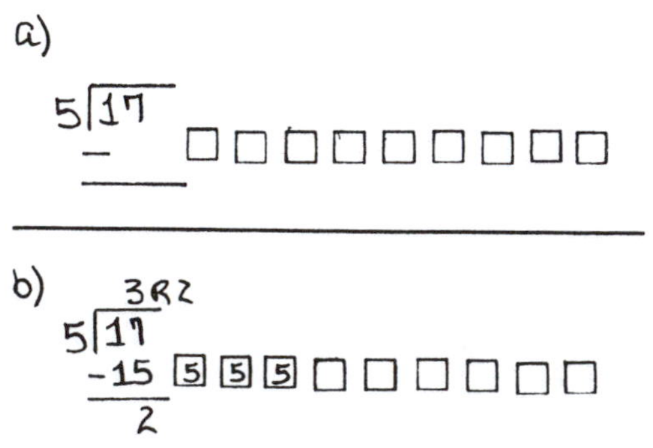

FIGURE 7.92

3. **Help for sequencing.** As students need the squares less, but still require visual cues for sequencing, use pages containing problems like that of Figure 7.93. After filling in the quotient, the student is reminded to multiply by the box at the left. Figure 7.94 shows an alternative format designed to help with sequencing. Pages of this type are especially useful for students who have receptive language deficits. The pages can be color coded if necessary. Assuming there is no perceptual or spatial organizational difficulty to bar copying, the student can fill in the blanks with problems from the text. Ideally, the problems should be copied as one assignment and solved as a second.

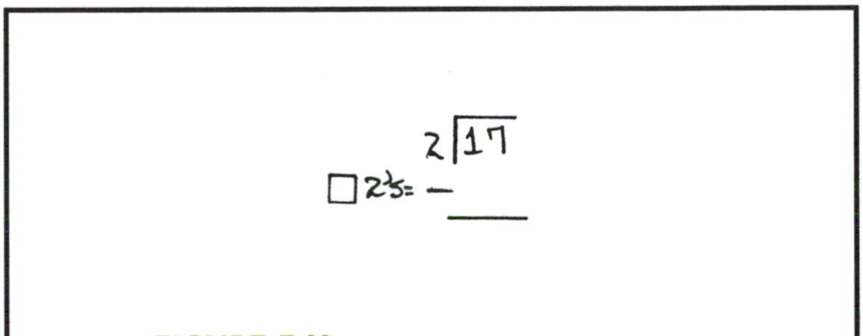

FIGURE 7.93

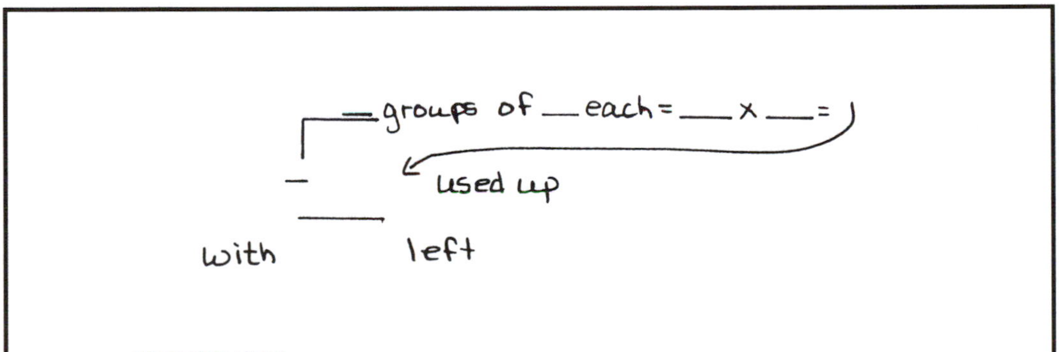

FIGURE 7.94

4. **Relate.** The sequence suggested by Figure 7.95 can be used to help students more readily determine the correct quotient digit. An effort is made to relate division with remainders directly to basic facts. In the first set of problems, the basic fact answer is given. The child is cued to use this to help solve the given division with remainder. In Figure 7.95b, the students must answer the basic fact problem themselves before computing the long division example. The last problem set (c) requires that students write in the dividend closest to, but less than that of the given long division problem. The idea of a left-hand basic fact problem can also be used in conjunction with the exercises suggested by Figures 7.93 and 7.94.

NOTE: *Throughout these explanations, the divisor has been used to describe the number of objects in each group. This interpretation has proven successful, given our approach, with LD students with whom we have worked. Obviously, the divisor can also mean the number of needed groups, with the quotient describing the number of objects in each group. This latter interpretation describes situations in which the children divide or share a given number of objects (see Figure 7.96). Because of research documenting the ease with which regular class children relate to the idea of sharing, the concept is becoming increasingly popular in mathematics textbooks that present long division. Whatever the approach, it is important to be consistent until the process is learned. Once understanding and retention have been achieved, it is essential to introduce also the other interpretation. A suggestion for how to introduce the "sharing" idea is outlined in the story line that follows.*

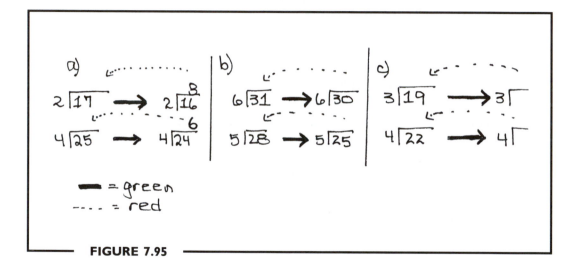

FIGURE 7.95

FIGURE 7.96

5. **Story line for sharing money.** A money story line can be used to provide auditory reinforcement for and give meaning to the procedure for long division. The problem of Figure 7.97a can be related to four students who find a bag of money containing 2 one-hundred dollar bills, 3 ten-dollar bills, and 5 one-dollar bills. They cannot locate the owner. After turning the bag in to the police, the boys are allowed to keep the money and split it among themselves. How do they go about sharing the money? They are most excited about splitting the one-hundred dollar bills first. (This fact reinforces the left-to-right procedure for computing long division problems.) With only 2 one-hundred dollar bills and four people, what should they do? Tear the bills? No! They trade the 2 one-hundred dollar bills in for 20 ten-dollar bills. Now with 23 ten-dollar bills, what's the *greatest number* of ten-dollar bills each can receive? (Refer to Figure 7.97b.)

The story continues along these lines as the children divide what is left, thereby computing the long division problem. With 1-digit divisors, play money can be used to dramatize the story. Eventually, the students should be asked to analyze the sequence suggested by the story line, noting that there are *five basic steps* (Figure 7.98). Further ideas for focusing on the five basic steps of the long division process are contained in the following section.

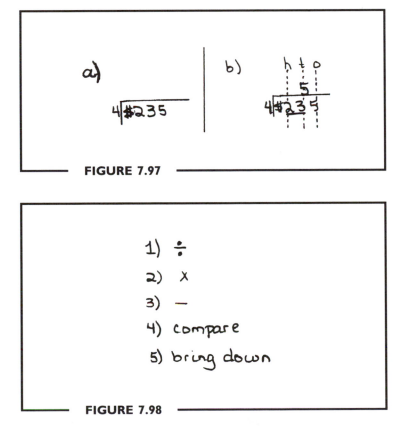

FIGURE 7.97

FIGURE 7.98

Five Basic Steps

Problem Area: Difficulty retaining and sequencing steps in long division.

Typical Disabilities Affecting Progress: Difficulty with memory, sequencing, figure-ground, integrative processing, and spatial organization.

Background: The long division process is cumbersome and often unnecessary, particularly for children with the learning deficits just noted. Although their conceptual understanding is adequate, these children may not be able to sequence the steps and place the numbers correctly to arrive at an answer. Sometimes the use of a calculator for long sequences is a viable and preferable alternative. However, if students are not able to use the calculator at this level (i.e., for division which involves remainders) or if their visual perceptual difficulties make the calculator more complicated than paper-and-pencil exercises, then repeated drill, with the goal of overlearning the sequence, is recommended.

SUGGESTED SEQUENCE OF ACTIVITIES

1. **Fill in.** Figure 7.99 shows a way of helping students organize their thoughts and build up a mental image of the sequence for long division. Before computing, the student fills in the blanks of the rectangle as a reminder of what the numbers represent. The student then continues, reading the words as they are approached to help with the sequencing and to give meaning to the numbers. If necessary, chips may be used to dramatize problems. Eventually, the procedure should be related to the basic steps of Figure 7.98. It is often helpful to display these steps on a wall chart or write them on cards the children can keep at their desks for ready reference.

   NOTE: *If color coding is necessary during early work with exercises of this type, colors would match those of Figure 7.87.*

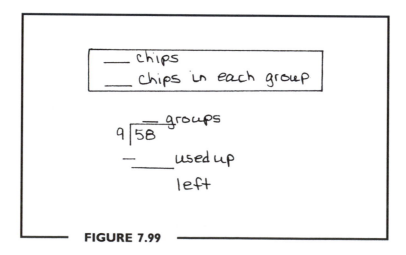

FIGURE 7.99

2. **Longer problems.** As problems become longer and more involved, students typically encounter even greater difficulty in correctly placing digits. Figure 7.100 suggests one way of handling this situation. The words in the center column aid sequencing and eventually lead to overlearning. Encourage students to memorize them. The color coding within the problem helps students organize the sequence and properly place the numbers while computing. When dividing by the green 3, for example, the student writes the quotient on the green line. When multiplying by the green numbers, the product is recorded on the green line.

NOTE: *Examples of pages similar to that of Figure 7.100 are shown in Figures 1.14 and 1.15. These can be prepared in advance, filed, and used as needed. Problems from the text can be copied directly into the boxes by students. If students need help with spatial organization, draw lines on some of the pages. This also helps those who have difficulty copying.*

3. **Card slide.** For children who tend to reverse or for those with figure-ground deficits, provide a sliding card as in Figure 7.101. Instruct the children to cover up the digits not being used, as in the sequence shown.

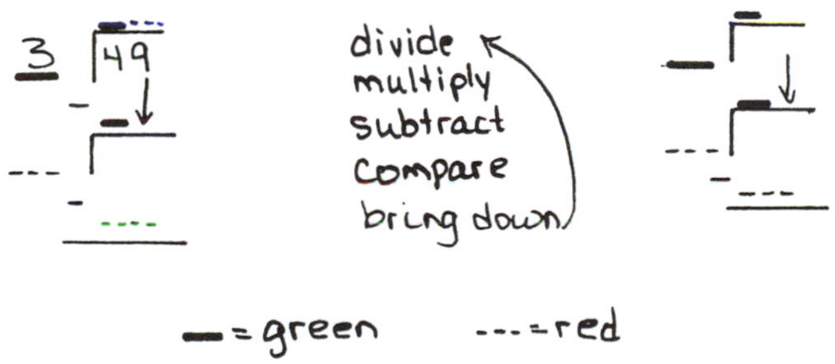

FIGURE 7.100

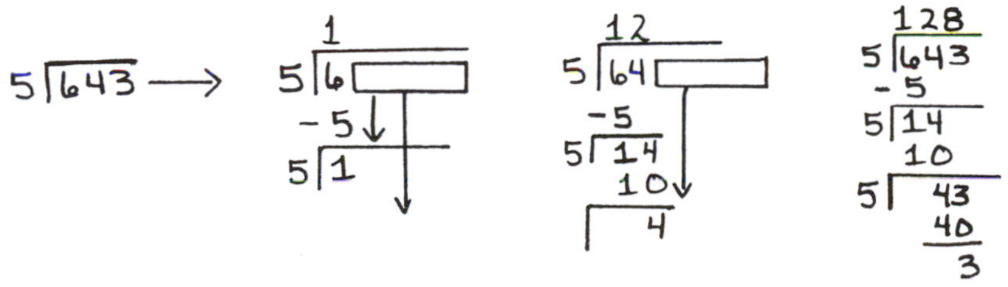

FIGURE 7.101

4. **Problems within problems.**

- *Middle zero in the quotient.* In early work, avoid giving the students problem types for which you anticipate a high percentage of errors. For example, give students the chance to feel comfortable with the computational process for long division before introducing more difficult problems such as those with a middle zero in the quotient.

- *Think ahead.* The formatted pages of Figures 1.14, 1.15, and 7.100 can be prepared in advance, filed, and used to help students, as needed, with digit placement in long division.

- *Show where.* Many children find it necessary to determine the number of digits in the quotient before solving. To help, they can use a finger or a card and uncover the digits in the dividend one at a time, as in Figure 7.102. As the student determines where quotient digits should be placed, short lines are drawn to indicate the placement over the appropriate dividend figures.

- *Placing quotient digits.* Some children have trouble reasoning and, therefore, do not automatically notice if an answer does not make sense. (They will only notice if there is not enough room or if there is too much room for the digits.) For them it often helps merely to practice determining where quotient digits should be placed. Have the students place lines above the dividend numbers to show the correct placement, as in Figure 7.102. Do not require that they complete problems at this time. Gradually, through discussion and repetition, the student should begin to notice that when the divisor is larger than the first digit of the dividend that space must be empty.

- *Graph paper.* As with multiplication, graph paper is helpful for aligning digits in long division. Keep some pages set up as in Figure 7.103. Many children, especially those with severe figure-ground problems, cannot copy numbers on to the graph paper unless it is spatially organized as shown. However, once the initial organization is provided, the graph paper boxes help with alignment. Gradually, as the child feels comfortable determining the number of digits in a quotient, it also becomes easier to set up and compute the problem independently.

FIGURE 7.102

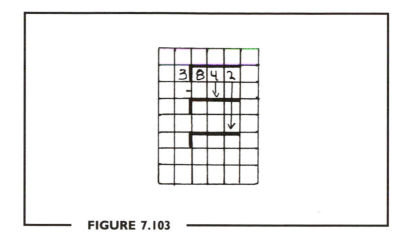

FIGURE 7.103

- *Block out.* Keep tachistoscopes, as in Figure 7.104, that can be used to block all but the relevant part of a long division problem.

- *Transition.* As a transition to working the problems independently, have the child use the tachistoscope before solving. Figure 7.105a shows the original problem. The student decides where the first digit of the quotient will be, in this case over 6, and places a line to mark that position. The tachistoscope is then placed as shown, and the student traces around the rectangle before removing the stencil (Figure 7.105b). The problem of Figure 7.105c is now "ready" for the child to compute.

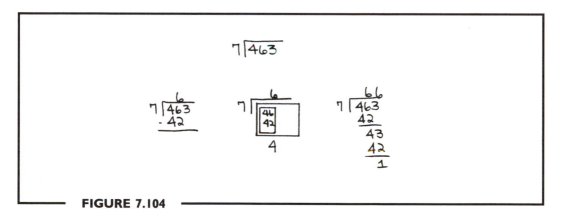

FIGURE 7.104

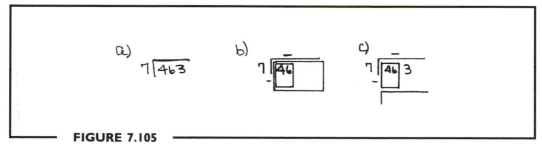

FIGURE 7.105

- *Outline the sign.* Sometimes it is helpful to outline the division sign in a bright color. This helps the student distinguish the isolated parts of the problem.

- *Circle.* Provide practice pages of *completed* problems, as in Figure 7.106. Have the student circle each subtraction (or just the first) within the division. This could be part of a 2-day assignment. On the first day, the student circles the subtraction problems. The next day, after the page is checked, the student receives a second sheet containing the same problems (*not* worked) to solve independently.

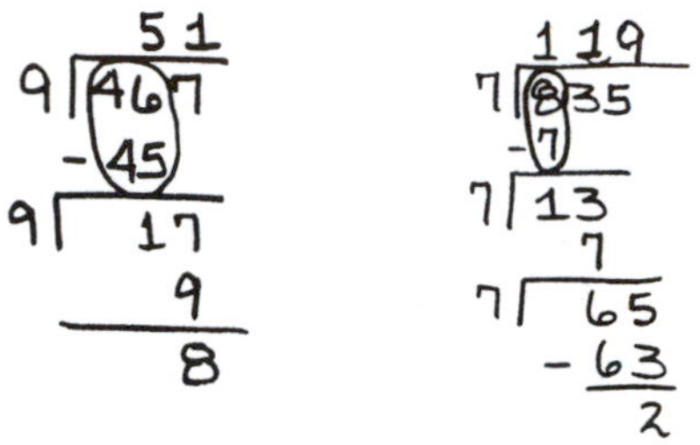

FIGURE 7.106

5. **2-digit divisors.** The *Background* introduction to this section highlighted our philosophy on the need to replace the time traditionally spent on paper-and-pencil computation of 2-digit divisors with more significant mathematics. Instead of assigning children to actually hand compute textbook exercises for 2-digit divisors, use these exercises in a different way to nurture number sense. Four major types of activity thrusts are valuable:

- *Roughly identify the range of the quotient.* Ask students just to tell whether the quotient (division answer) will be a 3-digit or a 2-digit number. Rather than dealing with isolated numbers, placing the problem in a money story line helps students gain intuitions about the range of the quotient and, therefore, places them in a position to be successful. The problem of Figure 7.107, for example, might be viewed as sharing $2,176 with 31 people. Using the card slide of Figure 7.101, we can help children realize that there are not enough thousand-dollar or one-hundred-dollar bills to share among too many people. However, bank trades would give us enough ten-dollar bills:

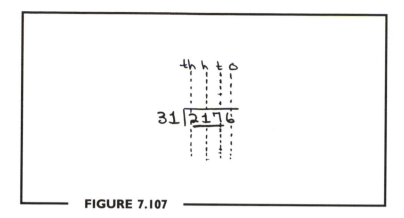

FIGURE 7.107

a total of 217. Hence, we can share out ten-dollar and one-dollar bills, which means that the number of dollars each of the 31 people will get in the sharing is some 2-digit number.

- *Get closer.* Relying on multiplying multiples of 10, as in Figure 7.108, students can get a little closer to the actual answer. Note the continued use of the storyline, at least initially, to place the numbers in a context which will nurture better intuitions.

- *Arrange low to high.* Make clear to students that there is no need to work any of the problems in a given row. Just *"Roughly identify the range of the quotient"* and then *"Get closer"* so you can rank order the problems low to high, based on their quotients. Allow students to explain their thinking and (later) do a calculator check.

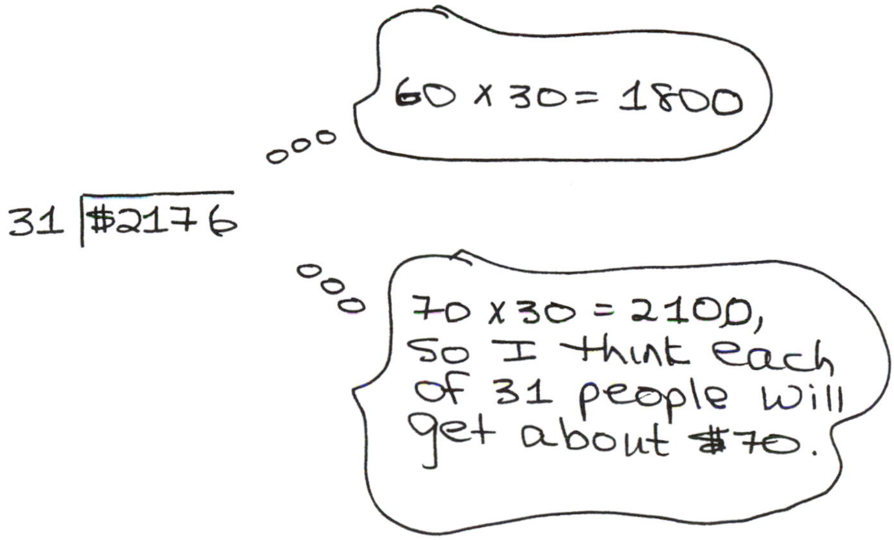

FIGURE 7.108

- *Create a problem.* Challenge students to copy the first problem in a row, then to:

  — create a verbal problem that might use those numbers in its solution;

  — create a second problem whose answer is more than the first.

Alternately, students might be challenged to create a second problem whose answer is less than the first; about twice as much as the first; about half the first; and so on.

NOTE: *Students can use a calculator to check whether the problems they create come close to meeting the requirements set.*

USING CALCULATORS

Most students with learning disabilities will readily turn to calculators as an alternative to paper-and-pencil computation because they can be used to get answers quickly. And, when calculators are in good working condition and properly used, they are accurate. Ideas for integrating calculator use in instruction on the paper-and-pencil algorithms have been embedded in several sections of this chapter. This section offers several practical suggestions for selecting among and using calculators.

Since there are many different models from which to select, students typically can find one that works well for them. For example, calculators which have a print out are helpful for students with motor or memory difficulties. The tape can be used for reference when input cannot be remembered. The tape also can be used to check whether digits were entered accurately.

Calculators with larger numbers on the print out, or ones which print out in different colors accommodate students with visual deficits. Talking calculators, if the auditory output is very clear and consistent with what is displayed, are useful or even necessary for others.

Some calculators display outputs in the thousands or greater with commas at the top of the number (e.g., 3'765). This type of display can not only be confusing, but also requires that students must learn and then ignore (unlearn) a procedure, and it is not the best purchase.

In general, a calculator should be selected that carries out simple arithmetic functions like $3 + 4 = $ _____ in the typical linear sequence:

- Enter first addend;

- Enter "+";

- Enter second addend;

- Enter "=."

Some calculators would have the user enter the two addends, then push the operation symbol, "+." This style, of course, is more difficult. Some calculators display the entire input, such as $6 + 4 = 10$. Although difficult to find, the latter models are not expensive and for students with memory and sequencing problems might be the best choice.

Some children, for example, work with calculators inefficiently because they do not know how to use the memory key. This is a particular skill that should be specifically addressed. Whatever the model, instructional emphasis in mathematics should include helping children to use calculators accurately and effectively as a viable option to other forms of computation, with all the power they possess.

REFERENCE

National Council of Teachers of Mathematics. (1989). *Curriculum and evaluation standards for school mathematics (draft)*. Reston, VA: NCTM, 1906 Association Drive, 22091.

CHAPTER 8

Rational Numbers: Early Concept Work with Fractions and Decimals

CHILDREN'S EARLY IDEAS about number pertain primarily to whole numbers. When they extend these whole number ideas, their first intuitions stem from day-to-day settings: half a glass of milk, part of a cracker. As children turn symbolically to fractions and then to decimals, their mathematical power grows, enabling them to represent and solve a new variety of problems involving measurement, geometry, probability, graphing, and other topics. They learn ideas that later can be applied to proportion, algebra, and other advanced topics.

Acquiring a good sense for fractions and decimals involves, first, developing a solid understanding of and good intuitions about the relative size of given numbers. It also requires the ability to relate fractions and decimals in accurate, meaningful ways. Number sense for fractions and decimals improves students' abilities to use and apply these numbers in appropriate day-to-day settings. Furthermore, a strong "number sense" leads to a more solid "operation sense," which enables students to judge whether the results of their computation are reasonable.

In the typical school curriculum, early work with fractions precedes work with decimal numbers. Generally, however, beyond that introduction, the emerging trend is to address decimal topics before parallel fraction topics. The rationale for this change is that:

- computation with decimals generally is easier and more closely related to whole number computation than is computation with fractions, and

- calculators and microcomputers use decimal notation.

As pointed out in the following pages, however, for some students with learning disabilities and in some topics, the use of fractions in basic developmental work is more effective than other techniques. The rationale for this sequence is to first build strong concepts with fractions and then proceed to use the more concrete path of fractions to develop related concepts in early work with decimals. Finally, with a strong base of each type of number, students can more easily begin to apply their knowledge to daily activities such as measurement and problem solving. Instruction can then focus on helping children (a) select the correct operation; (b) decide on the most efficient method of arriving at a workable answer (e.g., mental calculation, calculator, paper and pencil); and (c) use a calculator efficiently and accurately. Additionally, students can more easily develop the ability to estimate so they can check whether answers are reasonable.

This chapter presents an instructional sequence for students with learning disabilities that integrates early work with fractions and decimals. The focus is on developing a basic understanding of rational number and on nurturing students' abilities to *read, write,* and *interpret* fractions and decimals in meaningful ways. The overriding goal is to enable students to demonstrate a good sense for these numbers in a variety of settings. To prepare for this, early fraction experiences should include some work with tenths, along with fractions having denominators of 2, 3, 4, 5, 6, 8, and 16 (for inch rulers).[1] Five major sections provide a framework for discussion:

1. Rational numbers: general areas of difficulty

2. Number sense for rational numbers

3. The language of rational numbers

4. Equivalent numbers

5. Selected real-life applications

Rational Numbers: General Areas of Difficulty

Perceptual Skills

Perceptually, both fractions and decimals can be difficult. The mere act of correctly writing a fraction requires spatial organization that many children with learning disabilities lack. It is not unusual to see children writing fractions or mixed numbers as in Figure 8.1. This type of copying tends to appear careless when, in fact, children may be perceiving the positions exactly as written.

Figure-ground deficits also can make it difficult for some students to sort out the relevant parts of a picture or to locate the decimal point in a decimal number. Textbook illustrations, like that shown in Figure 8.2, can be visually confusing, making it impossible for students to use them effectively. These same children may have trouble computing because all the isolated digits of the fraction or the decimal "run together."

---

1. The National Council of Teachers of Mathematics (1989) recommends that only these more familiar fractions be emphasized and, when possible, in applied settings.

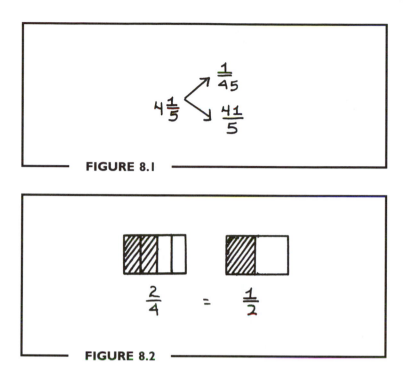

FIGURE 8.1

FIGURE 8.2

Abstract Reasoning

Students with abstract-reasoning deficits often encounter difficulty with rational numbers regardless of how concrete the approach is. Using objects and pictures, we can actually show students that $\frac{1}{10}$ means 1 out of 10 equal parts. There are words and manipulatives to match each symbol in $\frac{1}{10}$. When faced with .1, however, even manipulatives do not always help; there are not words and manipulatives to match each symbol.

Similarly, consider Figure 8.3, in which both pictures represent the fraction or $\frac{2}{5}$. Children who have trouble with multiple meanings find this idea extremely complex. While the concept of "two out of five equal parts" may be clear, the difficulty arises because the equal parts of the two shapes are different sizes. The unit, the "one whole," in each case is different.

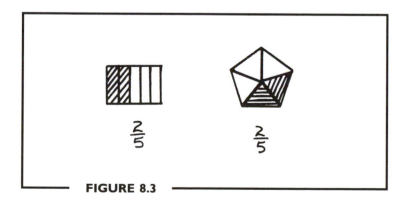

FIGURE 8.3

Language and Vocabulary

Expressive and receptive language problems also commonly interfere with the ability to understand and use rational numbers. The language of fractions involves many familiar words used in a new context. Most children have heard the words *third, fourth, fifth,* and so on. By about second grade, it generally is expected that they can readily relate numeric symbols to them. However, they also must begin to apply new meanings to these words and make immediate decisions about how they are being used. Students are accustomed to "hearing horizontally" and may have trouble associating the vertical fraction with the words. For example, suppose a teacher writes $\frac{3}{4}$ on the board and (a) instructs the student to shade three fourths of a rectangle or (b) asks how many people are in three fourths of the class. The child hears the fraction and may even be able to relate the words to the correct written form. However, when asked to apply the fraction in this new context, which is no longer horizontal (linear) in nature, the student becomes confused. ("What does 'three fourths of the class' mean? There are 20 people in here. I can't divide a person into fourths.")

These same children frequently experience difficulty when other vocabulary is introduced: *equivalent, common, simplest, reduced, improper.* The words may be used over and over again—not necessarily in the same contexts—and many students find it difficult to retrieve and associate the proper meanings at the proper time. For example, each of the numbers in Figure 8.4 can be referred to using a different word, yet they are all equivalent numbers.

$$\frac{8}{6} = 1\frac{2}{6} = 1\frac{1}{3}$$

FIGURE 8.4

Auditory Discrimination

Students with auditory discrimination difficulties may have trouble orally interpreting, reading, and understanding decimals. Distinguishing *tenths* and *hundredths* from *tens* and *hundreds* can be quite disconcerting and slow down the ability to process and apply their knowledge.

NUMBER SENSE FOR RATIONAL NUMBERS

Problem Area: Poor intuition regarding the relative size of and relationship between fractions and decimals; difficulty making an appropriate estimate using fractions or decimals in practical settings.

Typical Disabilities Affecting Progress: Difficulty with abstract reasoning, receptive and expressive language, short-term and sequential memory, and visual perception.

Background: Number sense develops slowly, even with the best role modeling and structured, ongoing experiences. Consistent efforts along the lines suggested in the following activities and exercises are critical. If we are to nurture a student's potential to develop good number sense for fractions and decimals, structured activities related to this goal belong as an ongoing, important thrust of both the fraction and the decimal programs.

SUGGESTED SEQUENCE OF ACTIVITIES

1. **Sort Fractions.** Use fraction cubes, fraction bars, and numerical representations to conclude that a fraction is close to:

   - 0 when the numerator is very small in comparison to the denominator;
   - $\frac{1}{2}$ when the numerator is about half the size of the denominator; and
   - 1 when the numerator is very close in size to the denominator.

   Ask students to sort fractions, as suggested by Figure 8.5.

2. **Sort decimals.** Similar activities can be carried out with decimals to determine whether a given decimal is closer to 0, .5, or 1. (See Figure 8.6.)

Approximating Fractions and Decimals

Problem Area: Difficulty noting relationships between fractions; difficulty noting relationships between decimals; good number sense.

Typical Disabilities Affecting Progress: Difficulty with abstract reasoning, sequential memory, expressive language.

Background: Number sense for fractions and decimals involves the ability to (a) demonstrate good conceptual understanding, (b) use relationships between numbers, and (c) think about and use rational numbers in meaningful ways. Mental activity, a degree of critical thinking, and the ability to use common sense and evaluative thinking are all important components for success in this area.

A classroom atmosphere in which the emphasis is on thinking rather than on exact answers helps students become comfortable in any of these areas. Written

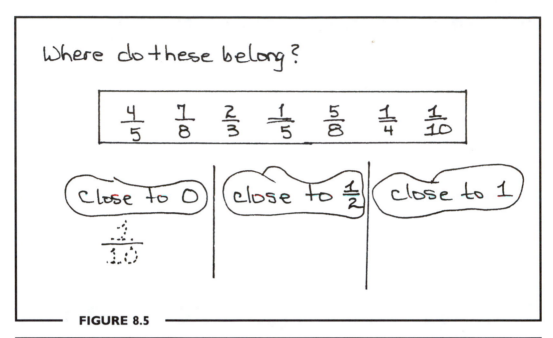

FIGURE 8.5

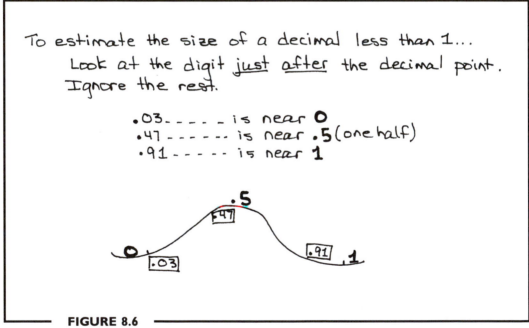

FIGURE 8.6

NOTE: Providing a number line and allowing students to finger trace the distance from a given fraction/decimal to each of the target numbers (0, half, 1) may help them make the correct decision.

work is an essential component but need not, in fact should not, be the primary means of solving problems. Rather, written work should be a tool to assist the child with retention, sequencing, expressive language, and so on.

If common-sense thinking about fractions is an important goal, suggestions like the following may be in order.

SUGGESTED SEQUENCE OF ACTIVITIES

1. **"Close to."** Ask students to study a list of fractions or answers to problems they have completed. Ask them to identify fractions/decimals that are "close to" 0, $\frac{1}{2}$/.5, 1/1.00, 2/2.00, $2\frac{1}{2}$/2.5, or some other related target number.

   NOTE: *Some students, such as those with short-term memory problems, may need to have a number line in front of them to use as a reference point.*

   - *Variation:* Students can apply knowledge developed in this activity to estimating answers to computation problems. For example, given 1.75 × 2.3, a student might estimate the product as "close to 2 × 2, or about 4."

2. **Adjusting estimates.** In many cases, estimates may be adjusted. In Figure 8.7, for example, each addend is less than the number used in the estimate, so the estimate given is an overestimate. Students should consider whether estimates they have given are *over* or *under* the actual figure. In many practical situations, as when buying material to make a dress or build a fence, it is better to be over than under.

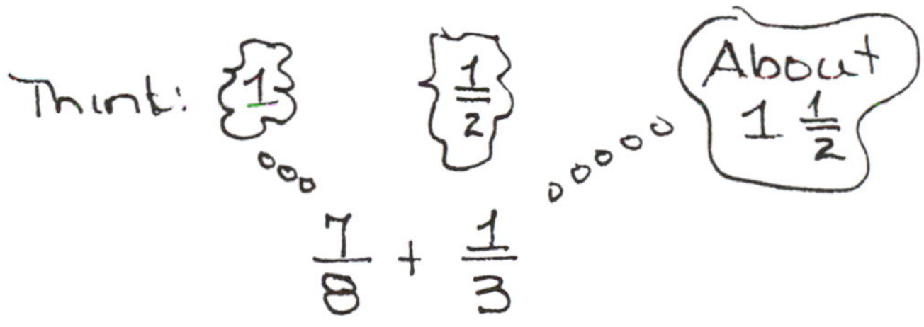

FIGURE 8.7

3. **Accept a range of estimates.** Knowing that any number of alternate responses can be correct is helpful to timid students. Particularly in early stages, when the goal is to encourage students to take a risk and make an estimate, an accepting, supportive environment is critical. For the problem in Figure 8.7, for example, any of the following responses might be accepted:

   - about $1\frac{1}{2}$ or 1.5
   - a little more than 1

- about 1
- $1\frac{1}{2}$ – (the "–" indicates that the estimate is a little less than $1\frac{1}{2}$)
- less than 2

In early stages, accept a broader range of estimates and help students explain their thinking rather than concentrating on very close estimates.

4. **Listen.** Encourage students to explain how they thought out given estimates. ("What did you think of to help you work that out?")

5. **Does my answer make sense?** Prior to introducing or reviewing a paper-and-pencil computational procedure, give students completed calculations, some with correct answers and others with answers that are way off target.

Ask students to identify those answers that make no sense. Talk through the estimate(s) used to make the decision. Given this background of experiences, students typically have a more positive attitude toward rational numbers and often are more likely to catch errors when they turn to a variety of forms of computation.

THE LANGUAGE OF RATIONAL NUMBERS

"As the complexity of mathematical symbolism increases, students become more dependent on their prior learning and their language to lend meaning to more technical mathematics language. Accordingly, we need to give students many opportunities to form connections to the language of mathematics" (Capps & Pickreign, 1993, p. 9). Students with learning disabilities, especially those with nonverbal learning disabilities and those who have trouble with receptive language and/or spatial organization, may need some additional assistance understanding and applying the language of rational numbers in written form. Although it often is preferable simply to use a calculator and read the answer, or do the work mentally and state the answer, many of these students need the additional visual cue or motor involvement. Writing something down on paper helps them recall, focus, understand, and apply what they are learning.

Reading and Writing Fractions

Problem Area: Accurately writing fractions and mixed numbers.

Typical Disabilities Affecting Progress: Difficulty with spatial organization, eye–hand coordination, and receptive language.

Background: Once fraction concepts have been established using physical materials, it generally is assumed that children will have little difficulty reading and writing the numbers. This is not always the case, however. Sequentially, students may know the order in which fraction digits should be read or written, but, spatially, they may be unable to place the digits properly (see Figure 8.8). Similarly, they may hear the correct sounds and associate them with the symbols, but retrieving and writing them properly may be an entirely different matter.

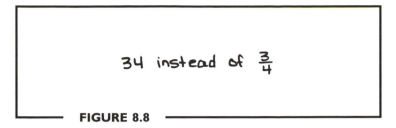

FIGURE 8.8

For younger students or for those who have learning difficulties, it often is necessary to provide specific practice in writing and reading fractions, much like what is done with handwriting. As students make the transition from concrete or pictorial representations to symbolic representations, it may be especially necessary for the teacher to review the goal of individual lessons. Is the goal to associate the correct fraction with its concrete or pictorial representation? Is it to write the correct fraction for a given model? Is it to write a fraction that is heard? Is it to read a fraction that has been written?

Too often we think of these steps as one and the same, but for many children with learning disabilities they are not. Often, these students must internalize, for example, what it *feels like* to write the digits of a fraction in the proper spaces. Even older students often benefit from the gross motor involvement of writing fractions on the blackboard. Until they begin to feel more comfortable with the spatial orientation needed to write fractions, most of their energy will be expended on number placement rather than on understanding.

The following activities suggest ways to help children write fractions correctly. The major assumption is that difficulties are not due to conceptual misunderstanding.

SUGGESTED SEQUENCE OF ACTIVITIES

1. **Trace.** Felt numbers, rainbow writing on the chalkboard, or a sand or salt tray often are helpful for students who need kinesthetic involvement and gross motor activity while learning to write fractions. Children trace over a given fraction and then immediately write it, perhaps starting on large art-sized paper or on the blackboard and then moving progressively to smaller surfaces.

2. **Color cue.** When students are ready for paper-and-pencil work, start by using exercises like those in Figure 8.9. The goal is to develop the spatial organization, visually and kinesthetically, required to write fractions correctly. Colors are used to help with sequencing and number placement: "When you write, green goes first—on top." Coat the green shading and box outline of several examples with glue. When the glue is dry, the children can finger trace over the raised surfaces. Eventually, they will write the number independently (at the end of the line following the equals sign).

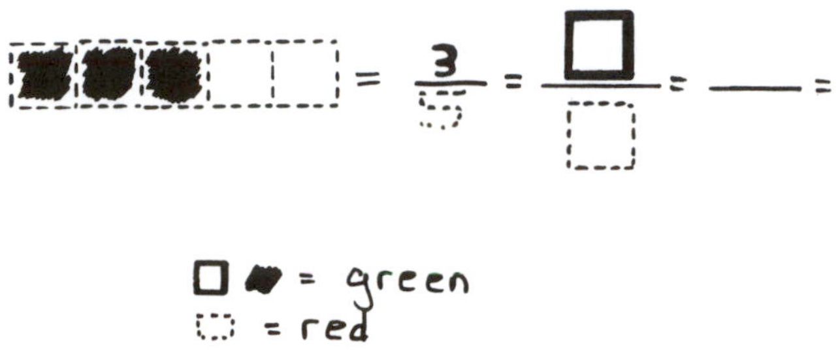

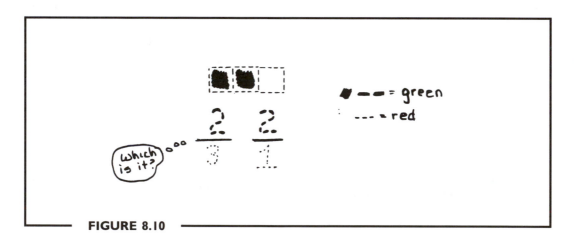

FIGURE 8.9

3. **Choose.** If the goal of the assignment is to write fractions to describe a shaded region, the example in Figure 8.10 shows how to avoid difficulties due to spatial deficits. The children cross out the wrong answer and write over the correct one. The fraction then is written independently, immediately after tracing.

FIGURE 8.10

4. **Mixed numbers.** Writing mixed numbers presents even greater problems for children with spatial difficulties. Now a sense of midpoint is added, in addition to up and down movements. Figure 8.11 shows one type of exercise that can be prepared in advance and kept on file. The colors are used to help students:

- develop the correct sequence for writing numbers;
- locate the correct position for each digit; and
- associate the parts of the number with the related parts of the picture.

The goal of the assignment is to help students spatially organize their writing of mixed numbers.

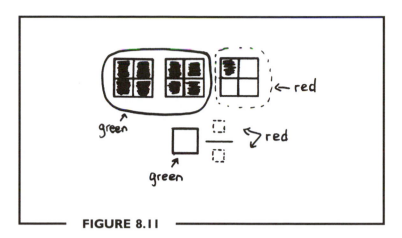

FIGURE 8.11

5. **Stencil first.** For students with more severe deficits, keep stencils on hand (see Figure 8.12a). Instruct students first to use a stencil to write a fraction, and then to write it again without the stencil. The two fractions—the stencil and the nonstencil copy—should be written side by side. In this way, the first serves as a pattern for writing the second.

6. **Tape it.** The stencils shown in Figure 8.12a can be used for students who have trouble writing fractions without a visual cue. Provide boxed paper as described in Chapter 1. Have students listen to a tape recorder and write the dictated fractions. If color coding is needed, put tape around the sides of the stencil as in Figure 8.12b. Students "go" on green and write the first digit of each proper fraction dictated on top (in the numerator) and the second digit dictated on the bottom (in the denominator).

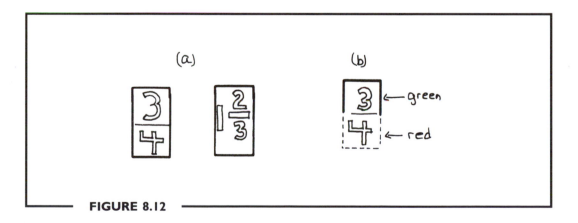

FIGURE 8.12

7. **Words to numerals.** Many students have trouble associating number words with the correct position of the digits in a fraction. Color-coded exercises, as in Figure 8.13, often help with both spatial organization and language association. Note that the students rewrite the fraction independently as a last step of the exercise.

$$\frac{\text{three}}{\text{fifths}} = \frac{3}{5} = \qquad \blacksquare = \text{green}$$
$$\cdots = \text{red}$$

FIGURE 8.13

- *Extension:* To develop the idea further, the colors can be used as in Figure 8.14. In the first two examples, children read the words, fill in the blanks, then write the fraction independently. The variation in the last example requires that students describe the picture verbally before proceeding.

  NOTE: *Throughout these exercises, bold, dotted, or regular line drawings can be used instead of color cuing for students who are color blind.*

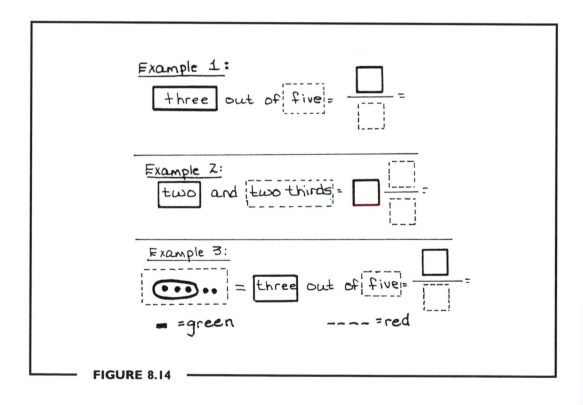

FIGURE 8.14

8. **Fringo.** A variation of bingo can be used to reinforce basic fraction concepts and provide practice writing fractions. Make a set of calling cards representing fractions, as in Figure 8.15a. Also make a set of game boards with fractions in each square (see Figure 8.15b). Instead of chips, provide the students with plastic overlays and grease pencils. Players take turns pulling a card and stating the fraction name. If the symbol is on the game board, the student writes over it with a pencil. The winning pattern should be determined before the game.

Writing Improper Fractions and Mixed Numbers

Problem Area: Difficulty writing a quotient as a mixed number; difficulty changing an improper fraction to a mixed number.

Typical Disabilities Affecting Progress: Difficulty with spatial organization, visual figure-ground, abstract reasoning, sequencing, and auditory processing.

Background: Even with the increased use of calculators and the decreased emphasis on long division, students still must understand the relationship among the decimal answer on the calculator, the quotient in a division problem that has been done using paper and pencil, and the solution to a problem situation. There are times when it is most expedient to use either mental calculation or paper and pencil, especially for problems involving small numbers. At these times, in order for the work to have meaning students must be able to express the answer as a mixed number. However, spatially, writing and aligning the numbers can be demanding. Additionally, at the symbolic level, even when the division is simple, because there are many numbers to sort out, children may forget what the numbers mean. As a consequence, they lose track of the correct sequence for writing the digits. Certain techniques may be used to deal with these types of problems. The exercises that follow have proven effective in our own work with students with learning disabilities.

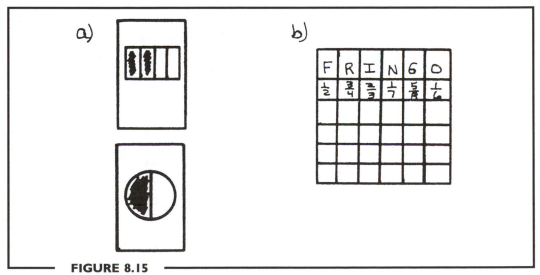

FIGURE 8.15

NOTE: For students with auditory sequencing or memory problems, the calling cards can be color coded, if necessary. Use the suggestions from the exercises in this section for the coloring scheme.

SUGGESTED SEQUENCE OF ACTIVITIES

1. **Color code.** Color-coded pages for simple division problems with remainders, as in Figure 8.16, constitute the initial practice needed to help students spatially organize their work. First, they follow the color cuing and merely copy the numbers in the correct boxes. (The completed division example is given at this stage.) Then, the mixed number is rewritten, independently, to provide extra reinforcement. The goal is to help students learn the correct placement of the digits. The color scheme controls for extraneous interferences by drawing students' attention only to relevant digits and their placement.

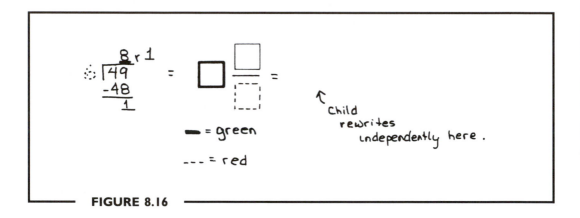

FIGURE 8.16

2. **Divide, too.** Once students feel more comfortable about transferring the quotient to a mixed number, have them do the division as well. Generally, it is a good idea to encourage students first to write the final answer in the form ____R____. This method tends to prevent them from losing the remainder in the mass of the other numbers; it also emphasizes the meaning of what they are doing.

   • *Variation:* For students with language difficulties, use the form ____ Remainder ____.

3. **Sample problems.** Pages with color-coded examples at the top can be used to help students make the transition from colors to no colors. Colors are not used for the other problems on the page. If children become stuck, they can refer to the coded examples at the top of the sheet.

4. **Relate.** Figure 8.17a shows a way to help students discover the relationship between a fraction and the division process. This exercise also paves the way for changing improper fractions to mixed numbers (see Activity 5). Students solve the division problems and fill in the blanks. Have them read aloud and, for selected examples, partition the objects into groups to dramatize what is said. As a follow-up, present exercises like those of Figure 8.17b.

   The children could copy mixed numbers from previously worked division problems into the boxes and rewrite each in the form ____R____ (see Figure 8.17b). Ask them to verbalize how the quotient and the mixed-number expressions mean the same thing. Tie this in with the work of Figure 8.17a by allowing students to place small objects in groups to prove the equivalence. Sample file pages are shown in Figure 8.17c.

5. **Improper fractions to mixed numbers.** Figure 8.18a suggests a preformatted page that can be kept on file and used with teacher-made problems or with problems students copy from the text. As suggested by the example, colors often are essential at this point. Specifically, they reduce difficulties due to deficits in visual perception and spatial organization; they emphasize associations that help students understand the process of changing from an improper fraction to a mixed number. As before, the objects can be divided into groups to dramatize what is said. A completed example is presented in Figure 8.18b.

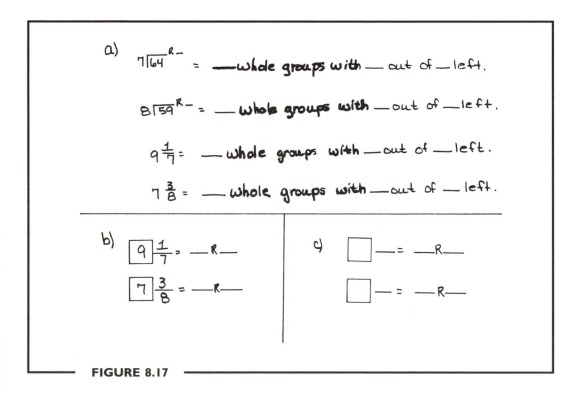

FIGURE 8.17

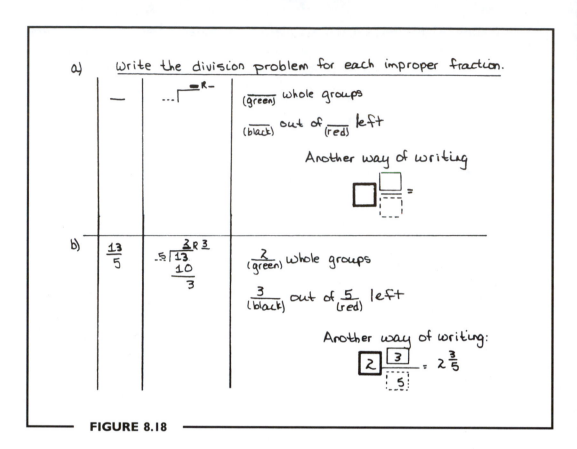

FIGURE 8.18

6. **Tic–tac–toe.** Make a set of cards with division problems, like those shown in Figure 8.19a. Until the children are more advanced, do not include problems whose quotients require reducing when written as a mixed number. Have the children fill in tic–tac–toe boards with the mixed number for each quotient (see Figure 8.19b). After checking the boards, laminate them or cover with clear contact paper. For practice, the students play tic–tac–toe, alone or with a partner, by drawing a card and circling the correct mixed number if it is represented on the board. The first person to circle three in a row wins.

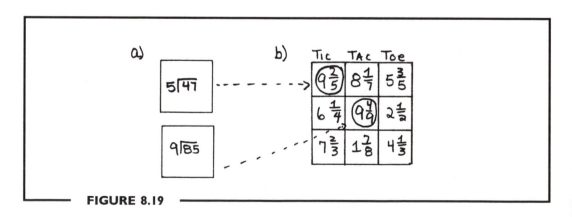

FIGURE 8.19

Reading and Writing Decimals

Problem Areas: Difficulty interpreting written decimals in a meaningful way; difficulty appropriately attaching *tenth, hundredth,* and other decimal names to decimals.

Typical Disabilities Affecting Progress: Difficulty with abstract reasoning, auditory or visual memory, auditory discrimination, and expressive language.

Background: Decimals typically are introduced using models like that of Figure 8.20a. As long as the models are present, students may be able to write and read the decimals associated with them, as in Figure 8.20b. However, the same

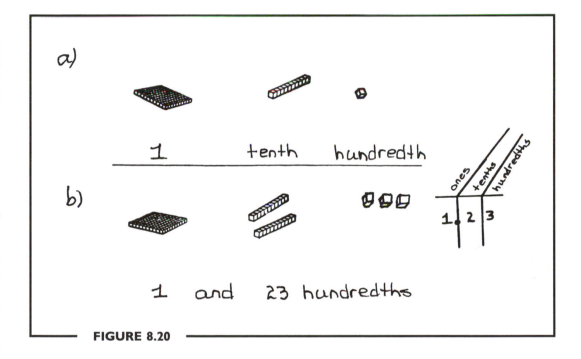

FIGURE 8.20

students, particularly those with the deficits identified above, may be unable to read written decimals without visual aids. A meaningful and effective way to help students become functionally independent with written decimals is to relate them to the familiar fractional notation. Even in the symbolic form, fractions are more concrete than decimals. The 10 in the denominator of $\frac{1}{10}$, for example, cues one to say "one tenth." No similar cue for saying "tenth" is given by ".1." Thus, students must simply remember what to say, and this can be difficult.

The following sequence outlines steps for helping students with learning disabilities read and write decimals by relating them to fractions. It is assumed that the students have a firm understanding of the fraction concept as equal parts of a whole. It also is necessary that they have worked with the blocks (or graph-paper substitutes) to illustrate decimal numbers.

SUGGESTED SEQUENCE OF ACTIVITIES

1. **Review.** Present the three blocks shown in Figure 8.21 and help students write the fraction for each. Discuss the name of each, orally emphasizing the *th.*

   NOTE: *Sometimes it is necessary to color-emphasize the th in words for students with auditory discrimination deficits. Doing so focuses attention on the endings and on how they differ from whole numbers.*

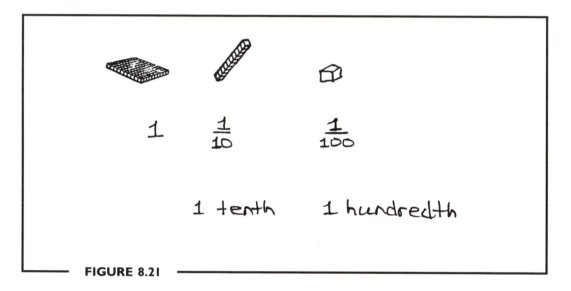

FIGURE 8.21

2. **Tell it to me.** Present pages like that in Figure 8.22. At first, cover the bottom of the page and have the children match real blocks to those appearing in the top row. Discuss the fraction written beneath each. Have the students read the fraction and note the color cuing: "One tenth has one zero, .1 (point one) has one decimal place," and so on.

3. **Write it out.** Help students complete the bottom part of the page in Figure 8.22. Here an effort is made to relate the visual model (the blocks) and the familiar fraction notation to the decimal form. Cue students to look at the number of zeros in the fraction, which tells the number of decimal places needed. "One zero (one decimal place) for tenths; two for hundredths."

   NOTE: *Omit decimal examples like .03, which require a zero in the tenths place, until children are more at ease writing other numbers with two decimal places.*

4. **Reinforce with money.** Once the concepts of decimal place value and writing decimals are established to the hundredths place, decimals can be related to money, as in Figure 8.23. Review how to write money (Figure 8.23a), but focus on the decimal part. Eventually, eliminate the dollars and just

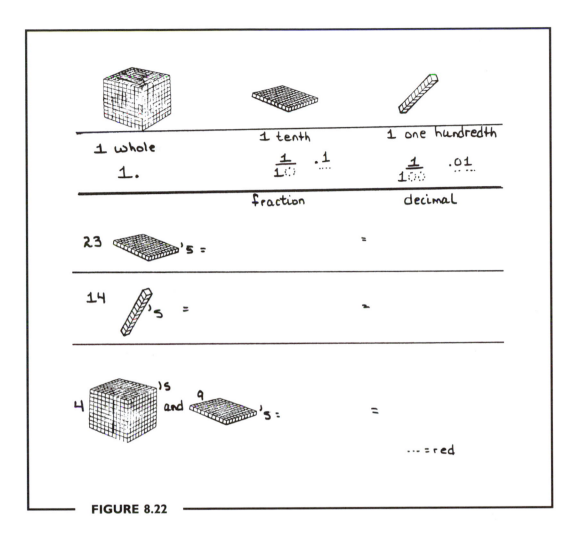

FIGURE 8.22

use pennies (Figure 8.23b). Now is a good time to introduce zeros in the tenths place: "$.06—That's 6 out of 100 possible pennies." Continue color coding, if needed.

NOTE: *When money concepts and skills are strong, students with expressive language or visual memory deficits may benefit from using money as a base for the introduction of decimals.*

5. **Relate.** To make use of students' strong visual association skills, pages like that of Figure 8.24 can be provided as follow-up to the work in Activity 4. Pages with mixed-fraction and decimal problems also can be presented.

6. **Phase out.** Eliminate picture cues except at the top of the page, and require students to complete exercises like those shown in Figure 8.25.

7. **Decimal number words.** If students have auditory weaknesses but can read, have them complete exercises like that of Figure 8.26. Initially, they

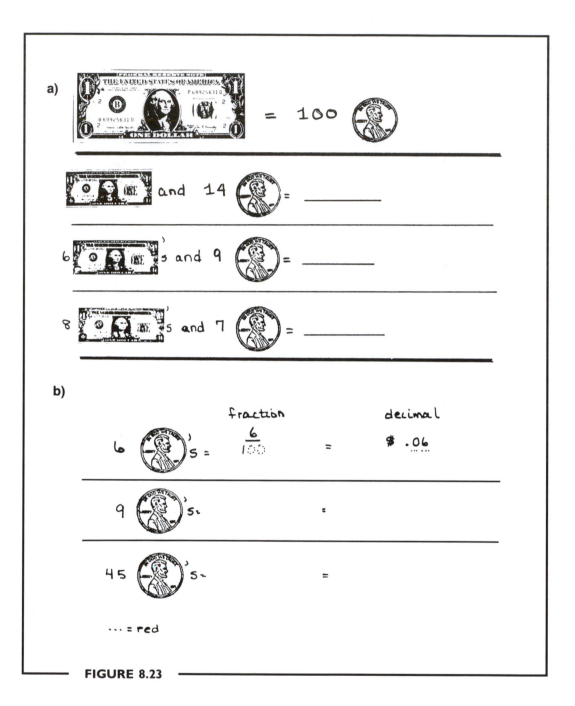

FIGURE 8.23

write the fraction form first, then the decimal. This sequence helps internalize the association between the decimal number names and the numerals themselves. Throughout decimal work, if the students become confused when reading or writing a decimal, encourage them to think of or write the related fraction. The denominator of the fraction should help cue them to say "tenths" or "hundredths" and also indicate the appropriate number of decimal digits.

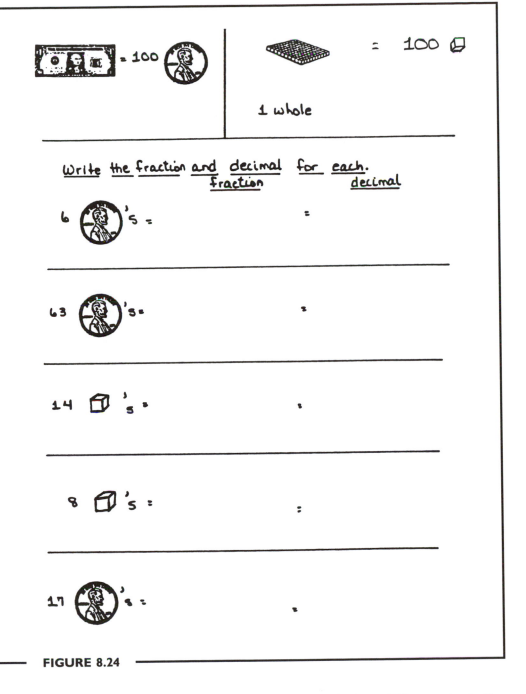

FIGURE 8.24

8. **Punch it in** (a practice activity for two players). As a follow-up to Activity 7, provide a hand calculator for each student and a deck of cards, such as those in Figure 8.27. The children mix the cards and spread them face up. Then, in turn, each draws a card. After both players punch the numbers into their calculators, they compare the visual displays. Then they turn the cards over to check. Players earn one tally point for each correct entry.

1 whole = 1. $\frac{1}{10}$ = .1 $\frac{1}{100}$ = .01

Write the decimal form for each fraction.

$\frac{4}{10}$: ____ $\frac{7}{100}$: ____

$\frac{32}{100}$: ____ $\frac{3}{10}$: ____

Write the fraction form for each decimal.

.9 =   .47 =

.06 =   .2 =

FIGURE 8.25

$\frac{6}{100}$ = six one hundredths = .06

$\frac{9}{10}$ = nine tenths = .9

Write the fraction and decimal for each.

	fraction	decimal
four tenths =		=
eighteen one hundredths =		=
seven one hundredths =		=

Write the decimal for each.

		decimal
nine one hundredths	=	
sixteen one hundredths	=	
five tenths	=	

··· = red

FIGURE 8.26

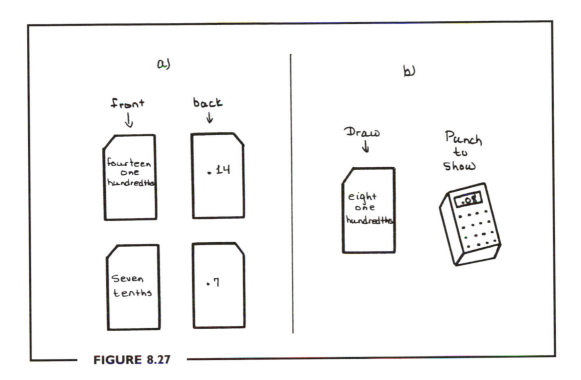

FIGURE 8.27

- *Variation* (to build auditory memory and association skills): Ahead of time, read (or have the child read) the numbers on the cards into a cassette tape recorder. The child listens to the tape, punches the number heard, and uses the card deck to check the answer. If the tape does not allow sufficient pause between entries, instruct the child to push the "stop" button after each number has been heard.

EQUIVALENT NUMBERS

Problem Area: Difficulty identifying equivalent numbers.

Typical Disabilities Affecting Progress: Difficulty with closure, visual memory, integrative processing, abstract reasoning, retrieval, and visual figure-ground.

Background: Understanding the conceptual base for rational numbers involves a clear understanding of the meaning of the word *equivalent*. Students use this idea daily, often without even realizing it, in activities such as sharing items by ensuring that "my friend has something of the same value that I do" even if they look different. Teachers use the idea by scheduling the day so that equivalent time is spent on activities of equal or similar importance. Often, however, relating this idea to the concept of numerical equivalence is more complicated. Although the concept itself is readily illustrated with physical models, the application of the concept requires several discrete subskills, including:

- knowing when it is appropriate to find an equivalent number;
- knowing what type of equivalent number is needed; and
- knowing how to find the equivalent number.

The following are some ideas that have been used successfully to teach students the underlying concept of equivalence and to enable them to apply their knowledge in a variety of situations. The section begins with ideas to help foster understanding of equivalent fractions, then equivalent decimals, and then equivalence of all kinds. This is not necessarily the only sequence to follow but one that is often preferable since overlearning in one area helps students apply their knowledge more confidently in other areas.

Finding Equivalent Fractions

During early developmental work with equivalent fractions, when the emphasis is on understanding the concept, physical and pictorial models must be used to dramatize the concept of equivalence. Typically, students are asked to compare shaded parts of regions, as in Figure 8.28. Children with abstract-reasoning, figure-ground, or spatial deficits may not readily recognize that an equal amount of space is colored in both drawings. The added lines in Figure 8.28b can be very confusing and prevent children from making the comparison visually.

Though specialized techniques like those that follow can help establish a conceptual basis for equivalence, other difficulties related to finding equivalent fractions also must be resolved. Some children can write a "family" of equivalent fractions by multiplying a given fraction first by $\frac{2}{2}$, then by $\frac{3}{3}$, $\frac{4}{4}$, and so on. These same children, especially those with memory, sequencing, or closure difficulties, may have difficulty finding the numerator for a given denominator, as in Figure 8.29. Consider what is involved in locating a fraction equivalent to $\frac{3}{4}$ with a denominator of 24. The student must:

- find the missing factor for the equation $4 \times \underline{\hphantom{XXX}} = 24$;
- switch the thought process to a more standard form of an equation;

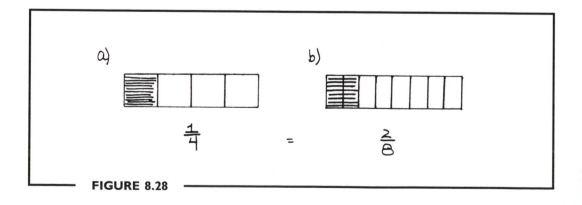

FIGURE 8.28

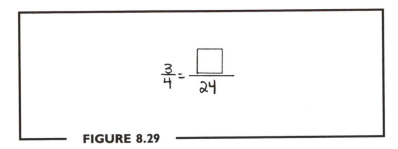

FIGURE 8.29

- find the product of 3×6; and

- determine the numerator.

Students *can* learn to deal with these problems. To this end, they must be actively involved in a learning program that is carefully tailored to meet their special learning needs. Suggestions for how to plan such a program for early work with equivalence are outlined below. The emphasis is on developing strong visual images with language and kinesthetic reinforcement, keeping the step size small, and, equally important, making provisions for overlearning.

SUGGESTED SEQUENCE OF ACTIVITIES

1. **Match ups.** Give students a construction-paper rectangle like that in Figure 8.30a. Have them state the name of the fractional part that is colored. If the children are strong tactual learners, texturize the shaded part. Glue pieces of felt, or spread glue and sprinkle salt or sand over the region; then glue string or straws over the lines that partition the shape. Have the students close their eyes, feel, and then name the fraction represented by the texturized area.

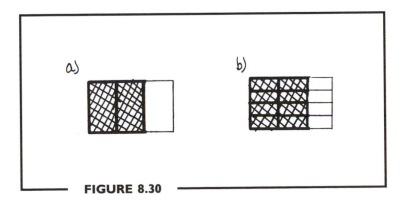

FIGURE 8.30

Repeat the procedure with the rectangle in Figure 8.30b. Encourage students to use their eyes and their hands to see and feel that the second rectangle is the same shape and size as the first. For an additional check, they can place the two shapes on top of each other.

2. **Pictures now.** Because many children cannot readily recognize equivalence when comparing two pictures they cannot move (see Figure 8.28), it often is helpful for them to use only one picture. In Figure 8.31, the students are presented first with the rectangle divided into thirds. Have them tell you, then write, that two thirds of it is colored. Next, direct them to connect the hatch marks with a ruler and write the fraction that describes the colored part. Several problems of this sort, in which the student actually uses the same space, help build up the equivalence idea without relying totally on visual perception.

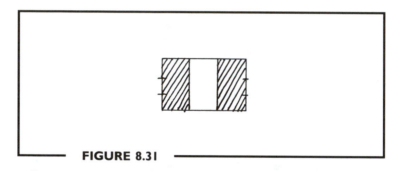

FIGURE 8.31

3. **Plastic overlays.** Using a permanent marker and clear plastic overlays, draw rectangular shapes as shown in Figure 8.32a. Provide predrawn worksheets (see Figure 8.32b) that contain shapes congruent to those on the overlays, as shown. In the first part of the assignment, the children color in a designated fractional part of each shape on the worksheet (see Figure 8.32c). To determine equivalence, they then match the plastic overlays with the rectangles they colored. When they think they have a matching shape, they can use a grease pencil to outline the shaded area as a means of checking for accuracy. The fractions represented by the colored regions of the two rectangles are written below the worksheet shape, as in Figure 8.32d.

4. **Dot it.** Figure 8.33 illustrates another technique that helps eliminate visual confusion and focuses attention correctly. Matching shapes are aligned one above the other on worksheets, and a dotted line is used to help students recognize the equivalence being demonstrated. It also helps to have the children draw around the colored (uncolored) area of both figures to get a better feel for the congruence in size.

5. **Talk about it.** Set aside time to analyze the equivalence demonstrated by picture pairs. The following dialogue, based on the example in Figure 8.34, suggests how a discussion might proceed.

> TEACHER: "You said that $\frac{2}{5}$ of this figure is colored. Into how many equal parts is the rectangle divided?"

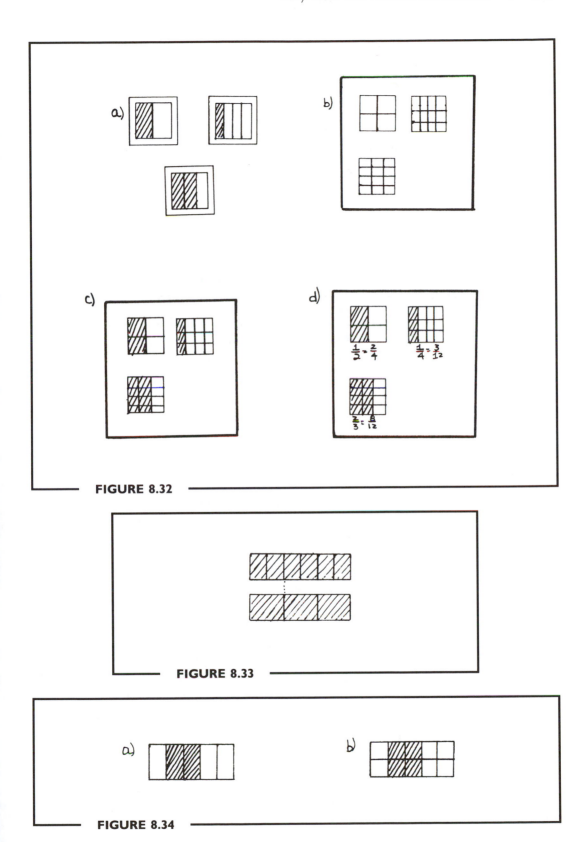

FIGURE 8.32

FIGURE 8.33

FIGURE 8.34

STUDENT: "Five."

TEACHER: "Correct. In this second rectangle, the same amount of space is colored, but we divided it up differently. How many total parts are there in the second rectangle?"

STUDENT: "Ten."

TEACHER: "Yes, we could also say the second rectangle has *two times as many total parts* as the first. Compared to the first, how many times as many colored pieces are in the second rectangle?"

STUDENT: "Two times as many."

TEACHER: "That's right, we colored in four parts of that rectangle, which is *two times as many* as were colored in the first one."

NOTE 1: *Make sure students understand the expression "two times as many as." Sometimes it is necessary to review this idea even though students understand the concept of multiplication. They may not automatically relate the phrase to the concept of equivalence.*

NOTE 2: *Tenths were used for this activity and should be used along with halves, thirds, fourths, and other commonly used fractions during early developmental work. The way then will be paved for an earlier introduction and use of decimals.*

NOTE 3: *Encourage students to understand that a similar comparison can be made using the expression "half as many." Be sure they understand that using the word "half" means the same as "dividing by 2." Much work in this area will help children develop a broader understanding of the concept of equivalence.*

6. **The general idea: multiply and divide.** When children are comfortable with discussions like that in Activity 5, introduce the idea of forming equivalent "families" by multiplying and dividing. Have children use fraction strips for $\frac{1}{3}$ and $\frac{2}{6}$. If necessary, lay them on paper and draw in a dotted line. Students should verbalize the different ways of comparing. Compared to the strips for $\frac{1}{3}$, $\frac{2}{6}$ has two times as many colored parts and two times as many total parts. ("We can also say that the strips for $\frac{1}{3}$ have half as many colored parts and half as many total parts.") Using numbers, help students see that $\frac{2}{2} \times \frac{1}{3} = \frac{2}{6}$ and $\frac{2}{6} \div \frac{2}{2} = \frac{1}{3}$. Lead children to see how a whole family of equivalent fractions can be formed by multiplying or dividing both numerator and denominator by 2, or by 3, and so on. In early work, children should use fraction strips to verify the multiplication and division. Three or four strips can be placed under each other (on paper, using dotted lines to picture families that have been formed).

7. **Talented "1."** Gradually, strips or pictures are eliminated, and the children use the multiplication and division technique to find fractions equivalent to a given fraction. One final point should be made before pictures are laid aside entirely. Use the technique in Figure 8.35 to color-emphasize that you really multiply or divide by $\frac{2}{2}$, $\frac{3}{3}$, $\frac{4}{4}$, and so forth when finding equiva-

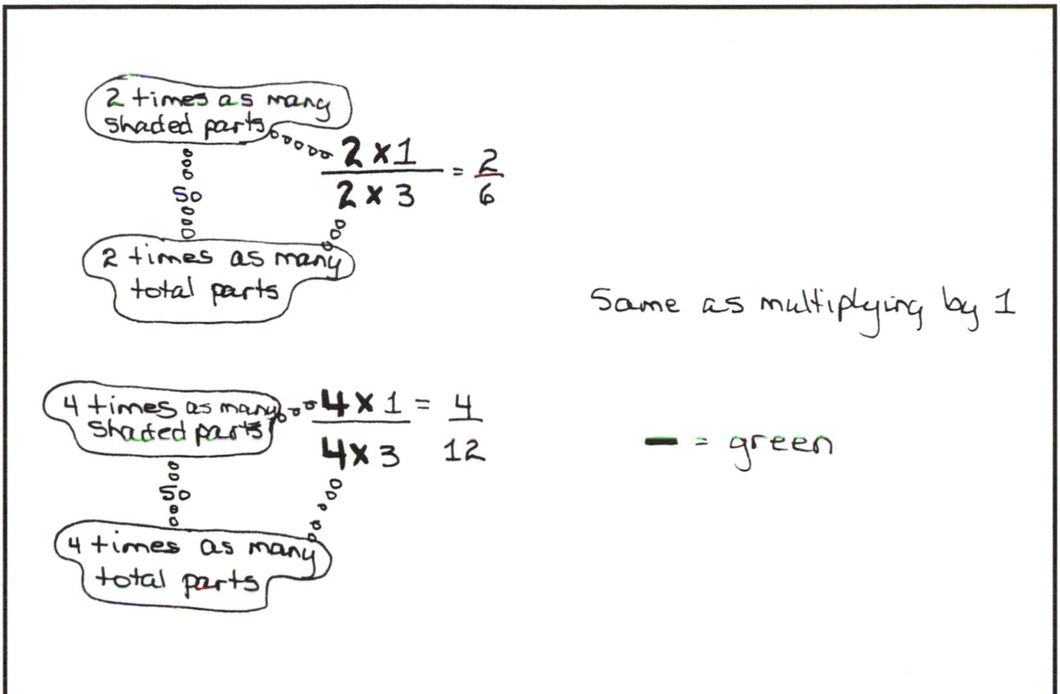

2 times as many
shaded parts

$$\frac{2 \times 1}{2 \times 3} = \frac{2}{6}$$

So

2 times as many
total parts

Same as multiplying by 1

4 times as many
shaded parts

$$\frac{4 \times 1}{4 \times 3} = \frac{4}{12}$$

So

4 times as many
total parts

━ = green

FIGURE 8.35

lent fractions. That is the same as multiplying or dividing by 1, so the area you end with is the same as the area with which you start. All you actually change are the size and number of pieces on the strip. The colored space stays the same size.

8. **Find the numerator.** Difficulty finding a new numerator for a given denominator is often the result of an inability to retrieve the missing factor. Many students need specific training before they can retrieve the factor as well as a controlled fact program like that described in Chapter 7. Initially, the equivalent fractions used on work pages would involve only basic facts the children have worked on, as in the examples in Figure 8.36. The examples represent three different formats, each gradually eliminating cues related to finding equivalent fractions but still retaining the "help box" at the top for the facts. By the time Example 3 is used, students extend the fraction line themselves and write in the multiplication facts. This way, students who are having trouble memorizing their facts can still progress conceptually.

NOTE: *It generally is preferable not to encourage dividing the new denominator by the old one in order to determine the missing factor. This practice adds an extra step to the already complicated thought process. Although the correct missing factor may be obtained using this technique, the division step often interferes with what should be done in the numerator. The visual cuing of Figure 8.36 prompts children to "think multiplication" instead.*

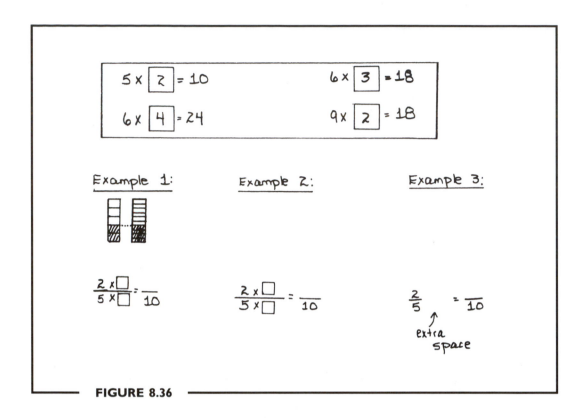

FIGURE 8.36

9. **Turn over** (a practice activity for two players). Make a game board and an answer sheet for missing numerators as shown in Figure 8.37. Also make two sets of 50 circles, each set a different color. Write the numbers 1 through 20 on the circles and give each child a set of circles. To begin, all circles are placed upside down. Children take turns flipping one of their circles to expose a number and placing the circle on the board so that an equivalent pair of fractions is formed. A player can be challenged if it is thought an error has been made. If the person challenged cannot prove, by correctly stating what to multiply the numerator and denominator by, the circle must be removed. The answer sheet, or a calculator, can be used to resolve differences. The winner is the first to form five pairs of equivalent fractions.

Finding Equivalent Decimals

As noted in previous sections, an understanding of fractions is often a prerequisite to an understanding of decimals. Students should be encouraged to write the fraction equivalent for the decimal and convert that to equivalent fractions. The final step would be converting back to a decimal. Many of the activities in the previous section can be adapted to help students understand and apply the equivalence of decimals.

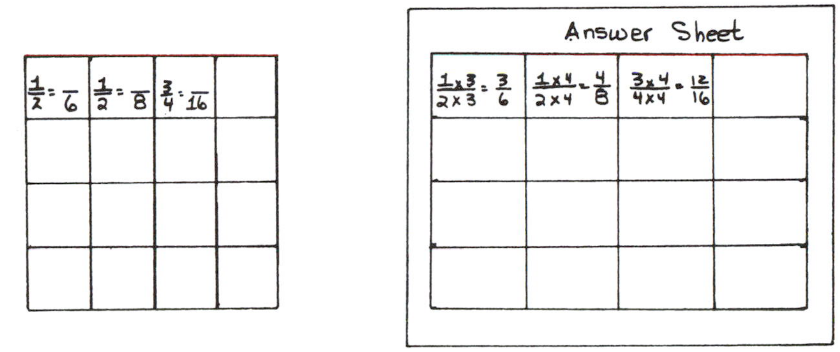

$$\frac{1}{2} = \frac{}{6} \quad \frac{1}{2} = \frac{}{8} \quad \frac{3}{4} = \frac{}{16}$$

Answer Sheet

$$\frac{1 \times 3}{2 \times 3} = \frac{3}{6} \quad \frac{1 \times 4}{2 \times 4} = \frac{4}{8} \quad \frac{3 \times 4}{4 \times 4} = \frac{12}{16}$$

FIGURE 8.37

SUGGESTED SEQUENCE OF ACTIVITIES

1. **Decimal equivalents.** Finding decimal equivalents for given fractions is an important skill. It generally is necessary to convert fractions to decimals in order to compute with a calculator. Some fractions, like those in Figure 8.38, are equivalent to fractions that have 10 or 100 in the denominator. When the exercises in this section are extended to help students deal with these fractions, the changeover to decimals is relatively simple for those who can read and write decimals (e.g., $\frac{5}{10} = .5$; $\frac{75}{100} = .75$).

2. **Divide to find.** Sometimes children find it easier to divide, as in Figure 8.39, in order to find the decimal equivalent of a fraction. The "divide

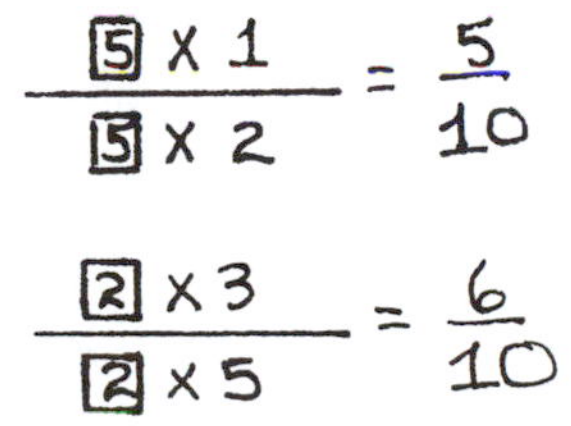

$$\frac{\boxed{5} \times 1}{\boxed{5} \times 2} = \frac{5}{10}$$

$$\frac{\boxed{2} \times 3}{\boxed{2} \times 5} = \frac{6}{10}$$

FIGURE 8.38

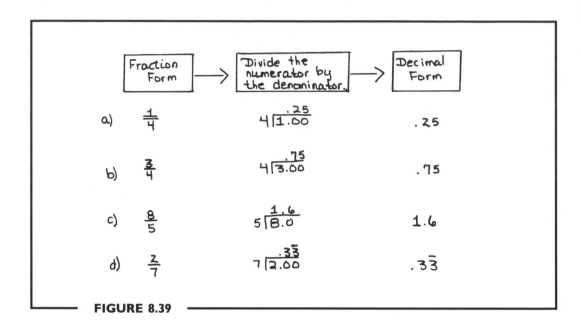

FIGURE 8.39

numerator by denominator" rule is simple enough, and a calculator can be used to carry out the division. Some children can understand why the division works. The focus, of course, is on the denominator, which tells the number of parts into which the whole is divided. For the fraction in Figure 8.39a, the whole is divided into fourths (.25) and we have one of those parts—.25 of the whole. In Figure 8.39b the whole also is divided into fourths, but we have 3 of them, or .75 of the whole. Instead of dividing into fourths and then multiplying by 3, we combine steps when we divide 3 by 4— numerator by denominator.

Finding Equivalent Numbers

Once students fully understand the idea of equivalence within an area, help them see the relationship between a variety of types of numbers. Work in this area can begin even with very young students. Coloring activities can help them see the relationship between a whole, or 1, square being colored and two out of two parts of the square or three out of three parts of the square being colored in. Similarly, "Look. We connected *all* the dots and made *one* whole picture. That's like saying we connected *12 out of 12* dots and made *one whole* picture."

NOTE: *Verbally and visually emphasize the italicized words at this level so that, at an early age, students become familiar with hearing those words in similar contexts.*

SELECTED REAL-LIFE APPLICATIONS

Using an Inch Ruler

Problem Area: Difficulty reading fractional parts of an inch ruler.

Typical Disabilities Affecting Progress: Difficulty with abstract reasoning, visual perception, and visual motor coordination.

Background: To date, the United States still has not made giant strides toward "going metric." As a result, students must continue to use inch rulers even as they learn to use centimeter rulers (see page 384 for further discussion of centimeter rulers). Visually the inch ruler causes more problems than the centimeter ruler. Rather than just being able to associate a specific number with a specific line, the student must be able to:

- differentiate visually among four different lengths;

- associate the length of the line segment with the preceding ideas; and

- read or write a symbol that is visually, spatially, and auditorially difficult to sequence.

When using an inch ruler to draw a line, students must know where to place the ruler in relation to the object to be measured. Visual motor coordination problems often interfere. This section will not deal with this problem except to say that, if the goal is accurate measuring, the instructor should give students guide lines to follow, as in Figure 8.40, or allow them to use lined paper. For children with figure-ground deficits, however, the latter alternative can be more difficult than using guide lines.

The basic approach to teaching students how to use a ruler involves measuring many objects. In addition, some children may require more specialized instruction, such as that outlined below.

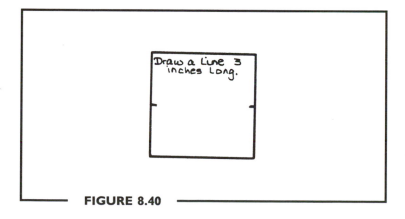

FIGURE 8.40

SUGGESTED SEQUENCE OF ACTIVITIES

1. **Simplified rulers.** Younger children and children with learning disabilities usually start out with simplified rulers, ones that show only quarter, half, and whole inches. Even then, they may have trouble perceiving size differences for the various parts of an inch. Colors are often helpful. Properly used, colors can focus student attention and make size differences more obvious. Figure 8.41a shows an example of a homemade ruler that can be run on ditto paper and kept on file. As children become ready, the paper can be cut, glued to cardboard, and marked, as in Figure 8.41b. Covering rulers with clear contact paper makes them more durable.

   NOTE: *For students who are color blind, use bold, dotted, and regular line markings.*

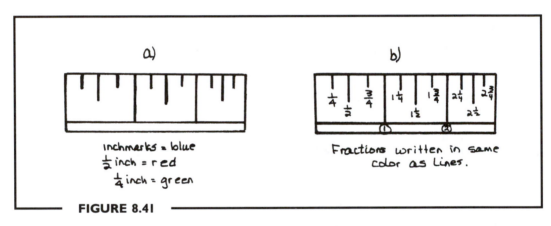

FIGURE 8.41

2. **Measure.** To help children use the ruler in Activity 1, provide opportunities for them to measure many objects. Structure these experiences as follows. Attach masking tape strips to several items, as shown in Figure 8.42a. At first, make sure the measurement is an exact number of inches. Later, the tape mark can be slightly longer or slightly shorter so children can learn how to measure to the nearest inch.

   Gradually introduce half- and quarter-inch lengths. If the measurement is to be made to the nearest inch, the colored line segment on the tape should be blue to match the inch marks on the ruler Similarly, the tape markers should be red (green) when half-inch (quarter-inch) measurements are to be made.

   This color-cuing technique draws the child's attention to the appropriate ruler mark needed for a given measurement. Having the numbers on the ruler is especially important for students who require overlearning or have difficulty with retrieval. After an object is measured, the measurement is recorded on the worksheets that picture the object. (See Figure 8.42b.)

   • *Extension:* As a follow-up to work with objects, have the children find and record the measurements of line segments drawn on paper.

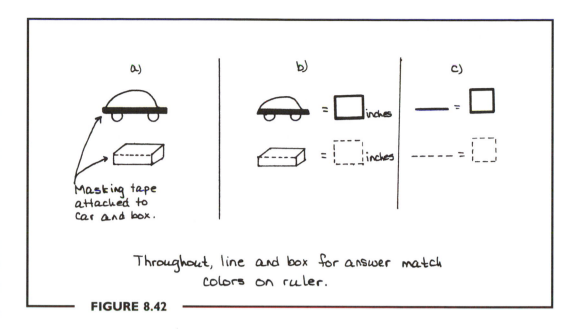

FIGURE 8.42

Figure 8.42c shows a sample exercise. Figure 8.43 shows another type of page which is helpful for students who have spatial deficits that make it difficult to write proper fractions and mixed numbers, or for children who have retrieval or expressive language deficits and, therefore, need visual cues. The color-coding scheme, introduced earlier, is used as long as it seems helpful.

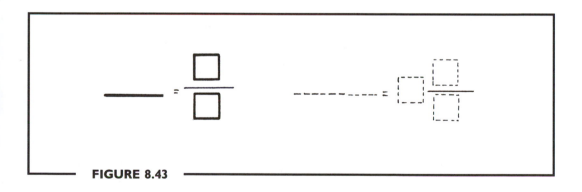

FIGURE 8.43

3. **Draw a line.** The color coding of Activity 2 also can be used to help students draw a line of a specific length. A sample exercise is presented in Figure 8.44a. Children use their rulers to draw over a given line then draw another line of the same length under it. Gradually, still using color to specify the length (see Figure 8.44b), instruct students to draw the segment indicated. This latter exercise still provides some guidance because the color used for the written direction draws attention to the appropriate marks on

the ruler. Even nonreaders quickly pick up the color cuing and learn to perform the measurements accurately.

NOTE: *Some students may require the additional guidance of start and stop marks (see Figure 8.44c) as a transition between exercises like those shown in Figure 8.44a and 8.44b.*

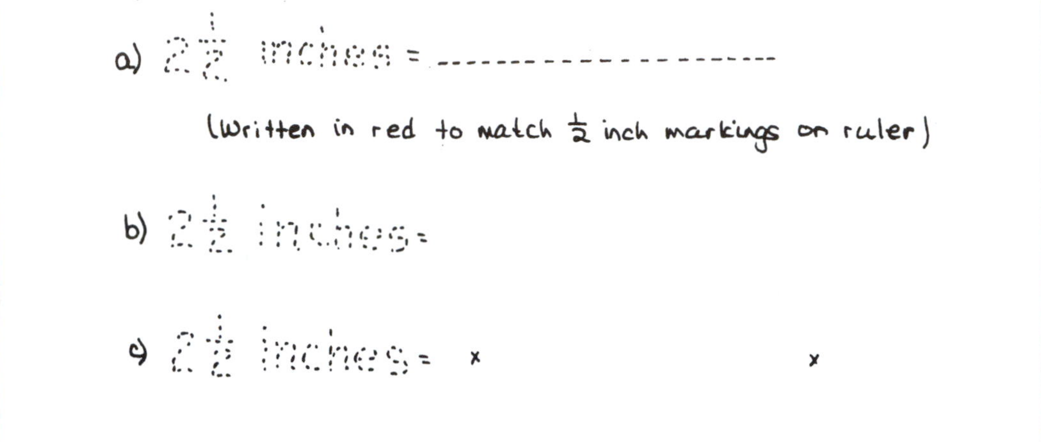

---

a) $2\frac{1}{2}$ inches = ----------------------------

(written in red to match $\frac{1}{2}$ inch markings on ruler)

b) $2\frac{1}{2}$ inches =

c) $2\frac{1}{2}$ inches = ✗   ✗

FIGURE 8.44

Using a Centimeter Ruler

Problem Area: Difficulty interpreting or writing centimeter measures.

Typical Disabilities Affecting Progress: Difficulty with abstract reasoning, visual perception, and visual motor coordination.

Background: Centimeter rulers are considerably easier for children to use than inch rulers, which are based on fractions. Visually, centimeter rulers are less confusing. Each line on the ruler can be associated more readily with a verbal expression. Even if students have trouble retrieving the correct decimal number name, there is still the readily available "one point three centimeters"—an important idea for these children in terms of being able to interact with their peers.

SUGGESTED SEQUENCE OF ACTIVITIES

1. **Simplified ruler.** Younger children with learning disabilities should use centimeter rulers with a midline between each centimeter. As with inch rulers, different colors can be used for the centimeter versus the midline.

2. **Overhead rulers.** Enlarge a ruler and create a transparency (see Figure 8.45) so students can more easily examine the subdivisions. Project the picture onto a wall and let children run a finger from the left ("start") edge to the first midline.

A fraction bar, as in Figure 8.45, can be used to illustrate that the distance from the end covers 5 out of 10, or $\frac{5}{10}$ (.5) of the total distance to the centimeter mark. Continue to read other measures as the children, each time, run a finger from the left edge of the ruler: 1 cm, 1.5 cm, and so on. Later have students write what is read. Accept responses that use fraction answers, such as "one and a half," even though technically it may not be appropriate to use the fraction instead of the decimal notation.

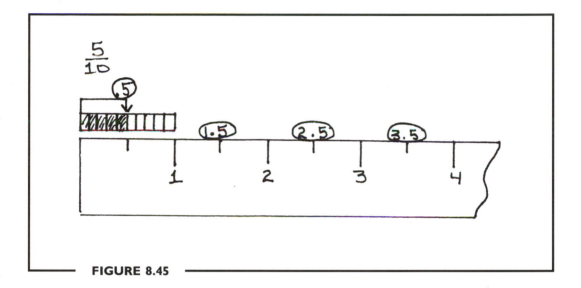

FIGURE 8.45

Estimating

Problem Areas: Difficulty remembering the sequence of steps; difficulty retaining information mentally.

Typical Disabilities Affecting Progress: Difficulty with abstract reasoning, closure, memory sequencing, nonverbal learning disabilities.

Background: Estimation is an essential component of a strong mathematics program and is often a more important area than the actual ability to use computation. Increasingly, as technology becomes more exact and less expensive, calculators and computers make more sense than using paper and pencil for longer calculations. Students with learning disabilities, however, often have difficulty in this area and need additional practice in related areas, such as rounding fractions and decimals, which others may be able to determine and apply intuitively.

The following activities are suggestions for helping students develop and improve their ability to use estimation. Rather than being taught as an isolated skill, as it has been in the past, rounding should be thought of as a tool to help students process and use language as they apply estimation.

SUGGESTED SEQUENCE OF ACTIVITIES

1. **Review.** Most students fairly readily understand that 38 is about the same as 40. Many even rather easily, but intuitively, understand that $3\frac{1}{3}$ is closer to 3 than to 4. Applying this concept to decimals is a little more difficult since there are often fewer visual and auditory cues. Practicing with a number line, as in Figure 8.46, helps these students develop a mental image that makes it easier for them to develop some automaticity.

   NOTE 1: *Initially, the use of backward and forward may help students more readily visualize the procedure. Later, they can be taught the more commonly used synonyms.*

   NOTE 2: *If students are strong tactual learners, texturize the number line or make it longer to encourage more gross motor involvement. Have students close their eyes as they slide their fingers to either end of the line. Later extend to other number lines that involve more choices, as in Figure 8.47b.*

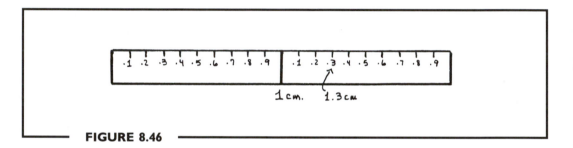

   FIGURE 8.46

2. **A fast dime.** Provide two decks of cards: a "banker's deck" and a "fast dime" deck (see Figure 8.48). Place the banker's deck in a bank box along with extra dimes and pennies. This deck contains one card for each multiple of $ .10 (to $ .90), whereas the fast dime deck contains cards that list amounts between $ .11 and $ .89 (no multiples of $ .10 included). Until students understand the activity, remove all money amounts ending in 5 from the fast dime deck.

   Shuffle the fast dime deck and place the cards face down between the players. Students take turns drawing the top card from the deck and placing it face up in the playing area. They then use dimes (as many as possible) and extra pennies to show the amount on the card.

   The banker selects the two cards from the banker's deck that are closest in value to that displayed (see Figure 8.49). The child in this example must decide how a "fast dime" can be made. Is $ .34 closer to $ .30 or to $ .40? The child must either add extra pennies to the $ .34 pile or take some away to indicate the choice made. Thus, either six pennies are added (to make $ .40) or four pennies are taken away (leaving $ .30). The latter decision earns the child one point, since it involves the least number of coin moves. When students are comfortable with this activity, return the money amounts

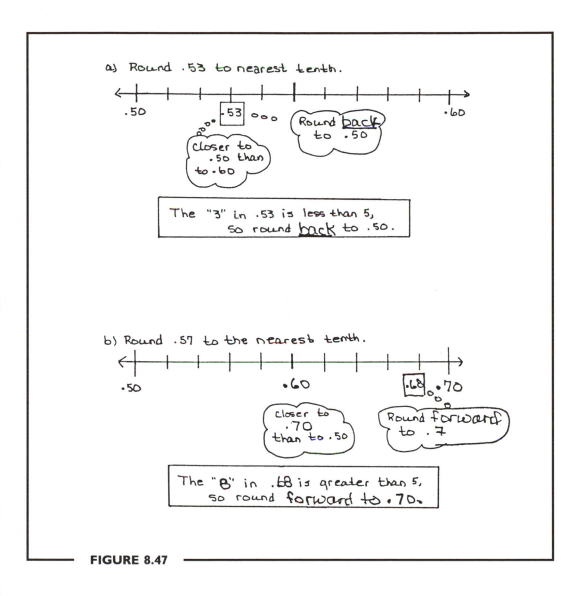

FIGURE 8.47

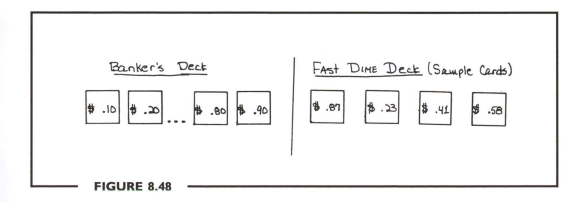

FIGURE 8.48

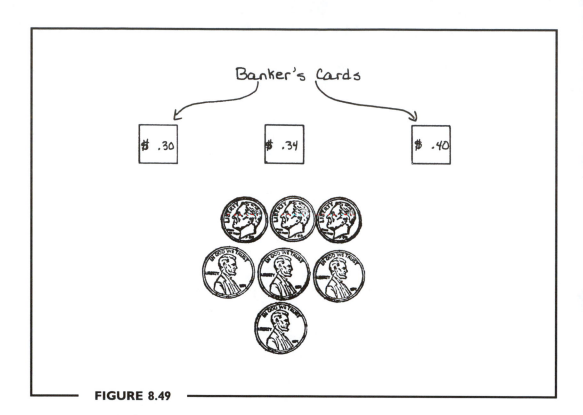

FIGURE 8.49

ending in 5 to the deck. Introduce the "banker's rule" that for these cards the fast dime is always the greater $ .10 value.

- *Variation:* Play the same game but now use a deck in which all dollar signs have been eliminated. If the students hesitate, ask them to find a matching fast dime card. Seeing the card usually triggers the correct idea. If necessary, allow the students to use dimes and pennies to determine "closeness to." ("Yes, 34 hundredths is closer to 30 hundredths than to 40 hundredths.")

3. **Color cue.** Help students focus attention on the "thinking" digit (the number after) by color highlighting that digit, as in Figure 8.50.

- *Extension 1:* For students who are strong in money concepts and skills, Figure 8.50b suggests one way to use money to build or reinforce rounding skills for decimals. In the example illustrated, green represents the thinking number, while red indicates the number of digits in the final answer.

- *Extension 2:* A natural progression from the example in Figure 8.50b consists of introducing students to rounding off, using a calculator. Provide a calculator and worksheets or index cards as in Figure 8.51.

a)

Round to the nearest
whole number.

_ _ 6.4̲5

■ = green
- - - = red

b)

Round to the nearest dime.
$ 1̲.4̲5̲

Round to the nearest penny.
$3.94̲7̲

■ = green   · · · = red

FIGURE 8.50

Round to the nearest tenth

→ _ _ . _ □ → _____

CHILD COMPLETES
INDEPENDENTLY

Interpret as money and
round to the nearest cent.

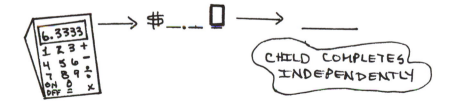

→ $ _ . _ □ → _____

CHILD COMPLETES
INDEPENDENTLY

FIGURE 8.51

Highlight as needed. (Prerequisites: (a) determine the child's visual perceptual skills and (b) provide appropriate practice with a calculator.)

- *Follow-Up Practice Game: Rounding War* (for two players): The students mix and deal out all cards of a two-digit decimal deck. Each player turns over the top card and rounds it to the nearest tenth. The player with the greatest tenth captures both cards. Ties are resolved in the traditional "war" fashion. The winner is the first to capture all cards.

REFERENCES

Capps, L. R., & Pickreign, J. (1993). Language connections in mathematics: A critical part of mathematics instruction. *Arithmetic Teacher, 41*(1), 8–12.

National Council of Teachers of Mathematics. (1989). *Curriculum and evaluation standards for school mathematics*. Reston, VA: Author.

CHAPTER 9

Extending Understanding and Application of Fractions and Decimals

IN THE TYPICAL SCHOOL CURRICULUM, early work with fractions precedes and, as has been suggested in the previous chapter, can be integrated with decimal topics to help children with learning disabilities develop understanding and skills for successfully using rational numbers. Generally, however, beyond that introduction, different patterns emerge. Because computation with decimals is generally easier and closely related to whole number computation, it often is treated *before* fraction computation. On the other hand, because tedious paper-and-pencil computations for rational numbers are being abandoned in favor of estimation or calculator approaches in which fractions, decimals, or even percents may be used interchangeably, these topics may need to be *integrated* during instruction.

Rather than hand computing a tricky fraction computation, for example, the student might translate it to decimal form before computing it by hand or on a calculator. In other instances (e.g., when multiplying decimals), some students might gain better intuitions about a general procedure when decimals are translated to fractions as part of the initial development. Because of their interface in practical use and instruction, both fraction and decimal computation are discussed in this chapter.

Whenever possible, as with whole numbers, it is suggested that the computational work be embedded in applied settings or in interesting or relevant problem contexts. The National Council of Teachers of Mathematics (NCTM) highlighted this very point: "The ability to correctly compute 0.17×45 is not so interesting for its own sake as it is, perhaps, for estimating the number of times a certain result will occur on a spinner in a game or in determining a discount when buying a new tennis racquet" (1989, p. 95).

In other words, computation should arise from students' need to do or know, not merely as an end in itself. As a consequence, nurturing good understanding of and proficiency with simple paper-and-pencil fraction and decimal computations is an appropriate instructional goal, but the need for involved computations and work with any but the more commonly used fractions or decimals is obsolete.

The National Council of Teachers of Mathematics is quite explicit on this point:

> The mastery of a small number of basic facts with common fractions (e.g., $\frac{1}{4} + \frac{1}{4} = \frac{1}{2}$; $\frac{3}{4} + \frac{1}{2} = 1\frac{1}{4}$; and $\frac{1}{2} \times \frac{1}{2} = \frac{1}{4}$) and with decimals (e.g., $0.1 + 0.1 = 0.2$ and $0.1 \times 0.1 = 0.01$) contributes to students' readiness to learn estimation and for concept development and problem solving. This proficiency in the addition, subtraction, and multiplication of fractions and mixed numbers should be limited to those with simple denominators that can be visualized concretely or pictorially and are apt to occur in real-world settings; such computation promotes conceptual understanding of the operations. This is not to suggest, however, that valuable instruction time should be devoted to exercises like $\frac{17}{24} + \frac{5}{18}$ or $5\frac{3}{4} \times 4\frac{1}{4}$, which are much harder to visualize and unlikely to occur in real-life situations. Division of fractions should be approached conceptually. An understanding of what happens when one divides by a fractional number (less than or greater than 1) is essential.
>
> Similarly, students should learn to compute decimal products like 0.3×0.6, especially as a means of locating the decimal point. Although such problems train students to estimate more difficult computations, valuable instructional time should not be devoted to calculating products such as 0.31×0.588 with paper and pencil. (1989, p. 96)

The general perspective taken in the following sections is that, throughout work involving fraction and decimal computation, number sense and the practical usefulness of rational numbers should be nurtured. On a consistent basis, instruction should focus on helping children (1) select the correct operation for solving a problem; (2) decide on the most efficient method of arriving at a workable answer (i.e., mental calculation or estimation, calculator, paper and pencil); (3) explore or respect different correct solution paths; and (4) explain and justify their solution approaches.

Perspectives on Students with Learning Disabilities

Even with a strong conceptual understanding of fractions and decimals, many students with learning disabilities still have trouble, especially as they begin to compute. Techniques for handling problem areas of fraction and decimal computation that typically are troublesome for students with learning disabilities are discussed in the five sections of this chapter:

1. General areas of difficulty

2. Comparing rational numbers

3. Simplifying fractions

4. Developing computation sense for fractions and decimals

5. Written computation for fractions and decimals

Calculator work is integrated throughout the suggestions of this chapter. It is assumed that prerequisite understandings of rational numbers, addressed in the previous chapter, are intact as the basis for the computation program selected for an individual child.

GENERAL AREAS OF DIFFICULTY

Because of their level of involvement, individuals with learning disabilities may have great difficulties extending or applying even stable understandings to computation. General areas of difficulty related to disabilities may be due to any of the three aspects of computation in which students may be involved when working with fractions and decimals, including:

- the use of a hand calculator to compute,

- estimation and mental calculation, and

- paper-and-pencil computation.

These difficulties tend to be idiosyncratic to each student, depending on the nature and severity of the disability, as well as on the kind of compensatory techniques that the student had adopted. This section addresses each of these three areas of difficulty.

General Difficulties with Calculator Use

In addition to special sections devoted to using a hand calculator in previous chapters of this book, suggestions for using the calculator to both accommodate and compensate for specific disabilities have been provided. Many of these suggestions specifically apply or can be readily adapted to students' work with fractions and decimals. Some of the more important of these suggestions include:

- the use of a printing model for students with motor or memory difficulties, so they can refer to the printed tape to check what has been keyed;

- the use of headphones and a calculator model with a voice synthesizer for students who need or benefit from auditory input; and

- the use of a larger, desk-size calculator model for students with motor or visual perception deficits, so they can more easily see the keys and read the visual display.

Several calculator models are available commercially that allow fractions to be keyed, processed, and displayed. Because these models use a modified version of the standard fraction form, some students may find it too frustrating to use them. Other students may in fact be motivated by their use.

The use of concrete aids is essential during early developmental work with fractions. Manipulative experiences help give meaning to the written work. Eventually, however, the use of physical objects becomes cumbersome and it is necessary to rely on pictures. For most children the use of pictures is not a problem; they make the transition from objects to pictures easily. However, some children with learning disabilities have real trouble with textbook illustrations.

General Difficulties with Estimation and Mental Calculation

Even when students have strong concepts for fractions and decimals, estimation and mental computation may be very difficult. The major difficulty inhibiting the success of many students with learning disabilities in these areas is parallel to that highlighted in their work with whole numbers: their inability to retain information while simultaneously processing other information. This difficulty often is accompanied by related problems. For example, the student may reverse digits while attempting to retain information and then proceed to process the wrong data. Or, a student may know but, for language reasons, be unable to express an estimation or mental calculation.

As has been suggested in Chapter 7, in the Using Mental Computation and Estimation section, many of these students should be encouraged to use a modified mental procedure in which intermediate data is written for later reference. This has proved to be an effective approach, one which some students will need to use throughout life. Students with expressive language difficulties may need to write the resulting estimate or mental calculation to trigger their own speech or to convey their result to others.

General Difficulties with Written Computation

Figure-ground

As pointed out earlier, children may be unable, visually, to interpret shaded fraction or decimal pictures as intended. Suppose the task requires adding fractions with unlike denominators, such as $\frac{3}{4} + \frac{1}{3}$. The children may understand and enjoy representing each fraction with its fraction strip, then trading the $\frac{3}{4}$ for a $\frac{9}{12}$ strip, the $\frac{1}{3}$ for a $\frac{4}{12}$ strip, and adding the twelfths. However, these same children may have difficulty sorting out the necessary steps from textbook pictures that accompany the explanation of how to find common denominators. They may even have difficulty interpreting pictures for simpler problems, such as the addition in Figure 9.1a.

For textbook illustrations like this, it is sometimes necessary to provide children with unshaded pictures, but ones that are otherwise similar to those of the textbook, as in Figure 9.1b. Placing a card over all but the first addend in the equation, as in Figure 9.1c, the student colors $\frac{1}{6}$ of the figure. By moving the card, the

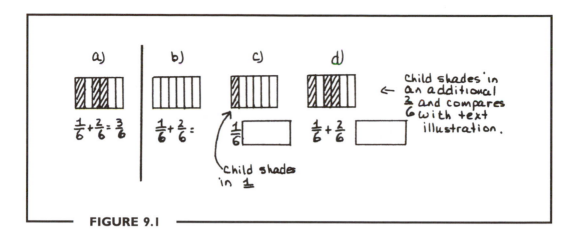

FIGURE 9.1

student exposes the next addend (see Figure 9.1d) and proceeds to color in an additional $\frac{2}{6}$ of the rectangle. The card is then removed and the answer written down. Finally, a comparison is made between the worksheet and the textbook page.

Patterning

Patterning requires that students be able to draw conclusions, a skill specifically taught in reading but not always in mathematics. Making the transition from concrete aids to symbolic understanding requires a strong ability to recognize number patterns. Generally, specific work on recognizing patterns is limited to kindergarten and first grade. At about fourth or fifth grade a high degree of abstraction is required as explanations begin to deal more with numbers than with either concrete aids or pictures. As the children begin to use symbols, their ability to recognize patterns, both obvious and implied, is important.

The fractions in Figure 9.2a, for example, illustrate an often unnoticed need for pattern recognition. The primary goal in changing mixed numbers to improper numbers is to understand, conceptually, what is happening. Ultimately, however, students remember what to do because they know they must "multiply the 4 and 3 and then add 2." In order to determine and retain the pattern, it helps students to see what the numbers do.

To help students see and "hear" what the numbers do as they conceptualize what is actually happening (see Figure 9.2b), "think bubbles," tape recordings to match problems, and teacher verbalization are effective.

Spatial organization

Generally, we write letters or numbers in one direction, horizontally and left to right. With fractions, however, that organization is different. Students now are required to switch between horizontal and vertical alignment. Many students, especially younger ones, cannot clearly discriminate these differences. It is not unusual to see children writing fractions or mixed numbers as in Figure 9.3. As children mature they usually develop an ability to handle these distinctions unless specific learning disabilities interfere.

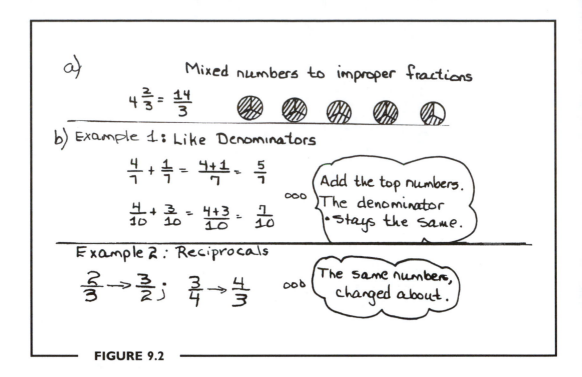

FIGURE 9.2

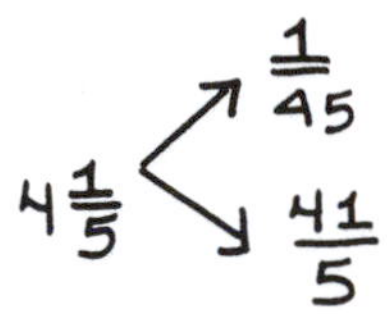

FIGURE 9.3

Figure 9.4 presents ideas for types of preformatted pages that can be kept on file and used to help students with fractions. Example 1 in the figure is useful when teaching children to add or subtract mixed numbers. With the boxes already there, students need not be as concerned with number placement. Instead, they can focus on the major goal: deciding whether to find a common denominator. The page is set up in two columns to help children in the decision-making process. The child writes in the first column when it is necessary to find a common denominator, and in the second when this is not necessary. Example 2 illustrates a similar idea for multiplication of fractions, while Example 3 suggests a format that can be adapted to either addition or subtraction of fractions.

In relation to decimals, many students, particularly those with abstract-reasoning, motor, or visual perception deficits, have difficulty aligning digits for computing. For example, when problems like $6 - 2.4$ or $.8 + 2.34$ are presented

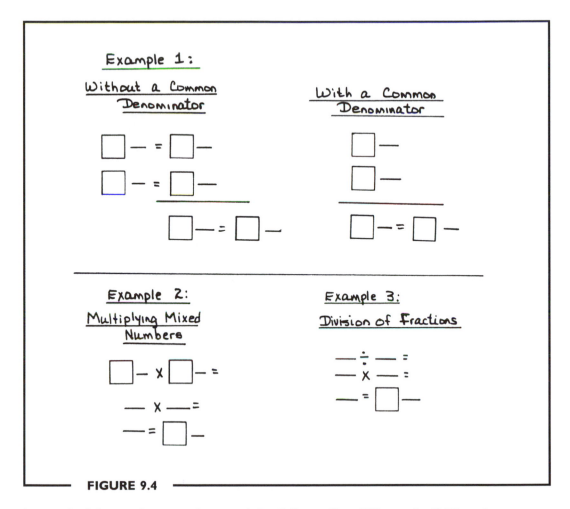

FIGURE 9.4

in vertical form, these students might fail to align "like units." Visual cues can be used to guide correct writing or placement of the decimals and fractions as the students learn the various computational processes.

The items in Figure 9.4 reinforce reasoning as well, since the maximum number of spaces is presented. The student must decide whether it is necessary to use all the spaces. Figure 9.5, for example, shows a sample problem that does *not* require use of all the spaces provided.

$$\frac{2}{3} = \frac{16}{24}$$
$$+ \frac{1}{8} = \frac{3}{24}$$
$$\frac{19}{24}$$

FIGURE 9.5

Another simple yet important practice that helps students spatially organize the writing of fractions deals with the fraction bar separating numerator and denominator. Encourage children to draw this line *horizontally* ($\frac{3}{5}$) not diagonally (3/5). With the horizontal bar, there is less tendency to read a fraction as a whole number (35 or 315 for 3/5) or to misread mixed numbers (15/8 for $1\frac{5}{8}$).

A final suggestion, helpful to children who must copy fraction problems from a textbook, is to provide a stencil as in Figure 9.6. The stencil should be made of clear plastic so that the entire problem can be viewed. The framing helps the students focus on just one fraction at a time. As a result, the children tend to make fewer errors in copying.

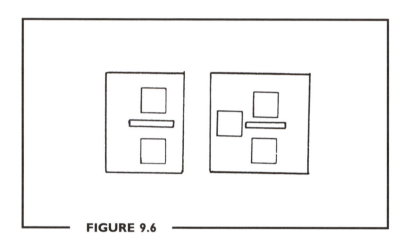

FIGURE 9.6

Sequencing

Aside from spatial organization, sequencing is probably the next greatest problem and particularly influences a student's success with the more complex and less familiar fraction algorithms. As computational processes become more involved, what appears to be a single step actually may be two or three. Consider the problem in Figure 9.5, in which the student is required to add two proper fractions with unlike denominators. What generally is considered the first step, that of finding the common denominator, is actually three steps:

1. deciding whether or not a common denominator is required;

2. deciding what the common denominator should be; and

3. deciding what each numerator should be.

Children who have trouble retaining the isolated steps of a sequence often benefit from doing one step at a time until they can perform the sequence automatically. For example, if students fail to check whether a common denominator is needed, have them focus on this one step before introducing additional steps. (The practice page ideas presented in Figure 9.7a may help.) Instruct the students to

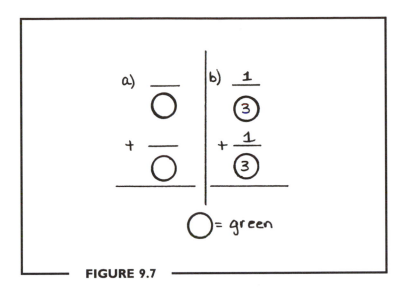

FIGURE 9.7

copy the problems from the book onto the pages, as in Figure 9.7b. The green circles in the denominators will help draw attention to what the first step should be: check for common denominators. For children who have difficulty copying problems from a text, use workbooks or textbooks in which the denominators have already been circled in green. This preparatory work could be done in advance, even at the beginning of the school year.

After children have mastered individual steps and must put them all together, pages with the format shown in Figure 9.8 are helpful. This example is set up to show the maximum number of steps needed to add or subtract fractions. Encourage decision making. Remind the students that *not all problems require all steps.* If necessary, a sample problem can be placed at the top of the page or on a 5″ × 8″ index card.

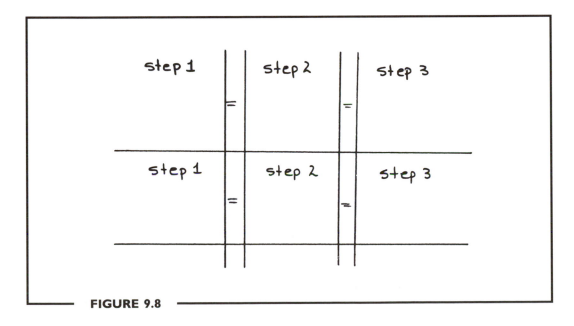

FIGURE 9.8

COMPARING RATIONAL NUMBERS

Problem Area: Tendency to focus on numerals rather than on the value represented. For example, when comparing .48 and .6, calling .48 greater or, when comparing $\frac{1}{2}$ and $\frac{3}{8}$, calling $\frac{3}{8}$ greater.

Typical Disabilities Affecting Progress: Difficulty with abstract reasoning, spatial organization, and auditory memory.

Background: Even students with no disabilities tend to have trouble comparing rational numbers. For those students with abstract-reasoning deficits, the difficulty is compounded. It often is necessary to teach these students a procedure for comparing, then, when they feel comfortable with that procedure, to use visuals to demonstrate that it is a reasonable one. For students with spatial organization difficulties, the standard sequence of using objects/pictures first in developmental work is appropriate, given that care is taken to avoid number lines or other aids that rely on accurate size perception.

We propose that comparison skills be grounded in ongoing problems that have meaning for students. The storyline of these problems might be presented orally while pertinent numbers and simple illustrations to help retain the storyline are provided on a transparency, card, or classroom chalkboard. Alternately, while students work individually or in small groups, the full text of the problem might be provided and read or given to them as an aid to solving. By carefully selecting the problem types and the numbers used in these problems, students can gradually be involved in making more difficult comparisons. By varying the theme or numbers used for each problem type, students also can be led to making important generalizations about comparing the numbers. Several examples for fractions follow. Similar approaches can be used for developing and extending comparisons for decimals.

- "At [name of a child in the class]'s birthday party, 6 children were at one table and 4 children were sitting at another. Both tables had the same size chocolate chip cookie cake. At each table the cakes were shared equally among all the children so that each one of them got the same size piece at each table. Who got more chocolate chip cookies—those at the table with 6 children or those at the table with 4 children?"

- "[Name of child in the class] had an overnight and invited many friends. Two tables were set up for lunch. Each table was given two pizzas [each the same size] to be shared equally among the children at the table. If all children took what was served to them, who got more pizza—the children at the table with 4 children or those at the table with 3 children?"

- "At [name of the child in the class]'s birthday party, the children also were seated at two tables for ice cream and cake. Mom had prepared many small cakes, each the same size. At one table 6 children shared 3 cakes. At another table 6 children shared 4 cakes. Who got more cake?"

As children work, some flexibility in personal choice of materials for assisting or demonstrating ideas might be allowed, depending on individual needs and learning style. Always, students should be expected to explain their thinking. If more than one student is involved in the instructional group, listening to others' solutions and seeing how different students record their solution steps often broadens individual perspectives.

To meet individual needs, special techniques may need to be used in conjunction with problem-solving work for both decimals and fractions. The first section that follows, on comparing decimals, provides a sequence that has been used effectively with students who have spatial organization deficits. Beginning with Activity 4 (saving the "prove" step until later), the same sequence has been successfully modified for students who have abstract-reasoning deficits. Other children with learning disabilities, including those with visual perception and visual or auditory memory difficulties, also have been helped by the suggestions, generally retaining the sequence presented. Ideas for helping students compare fractions are then presented in a separate sequence of activities and may be modified in a similar manner to meet special learning needs of individual students.

SUGGESTED SEQUENCE OF ACTIVITIES

Comparing Decimals

1. **Shade in.** Assigning them a pair of decimals, have the students shade hundredths squares as in Figure 9.9 to see which is greater.

2. **Use money** (if money concepts and skills are strong). Figure 9.10 suggests how dimes and pennies can be used to compare decimals to hundredths.

3. **On the line.** Many school textbooks suggest that students position decimals on a number line as an aid to comparing and ordering decimals (Figure 9.11). (This approach is inappropriate for students with spatial organization deficits.) "Walk-on" number line segments where students walk from the lesser to the greater number helps children who benefit from kinesthetic/motor involvement.

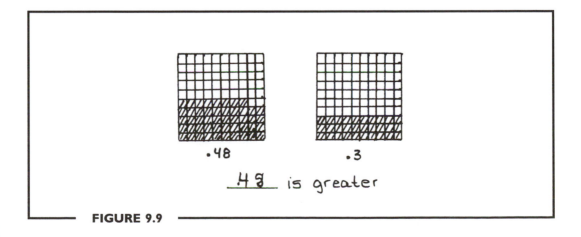

.48   .3

___48___ is greater

FIGURE 9.9

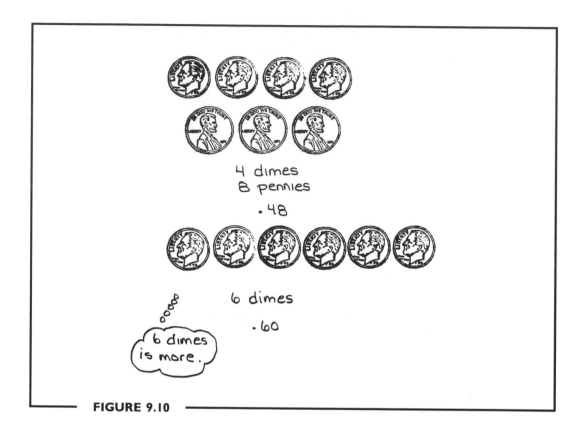

4 dimes
8 pennies
.48

6 dimes
.60

6 dimes
is more.

FIGURE 9.10

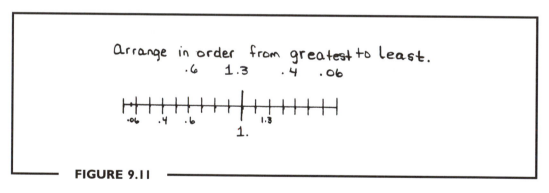

arrange in order from greatest to least.
.6   1.3   .4   .06

.06   .4   .6   1.3
1.

FIGURE 9.11

4. **Line them up.** Typically, it is effective to have students align decimal points to compare decimals, as in Figure 9.12. Then, digit by digit, they can "read" left to right to compare the numbers. (This procedure is similar to placing words in alphabetical order.) As soon as the child finds a difference in a column, the number with the greater digit has the greater value. If students require kinesthetic involvement, have them finger trace digit pairs, stopping when they find a difference. Using ideas from Activities 1, 2, or 3, help students "prove" that this procedure always works.

5. **Color cue.** Figure 9.13 illustrates how color coding can be used to draw attention to critical digits in the comparison. This technique is especially helpful during early developmental work for students with figure-ground

FIGURE 9.12

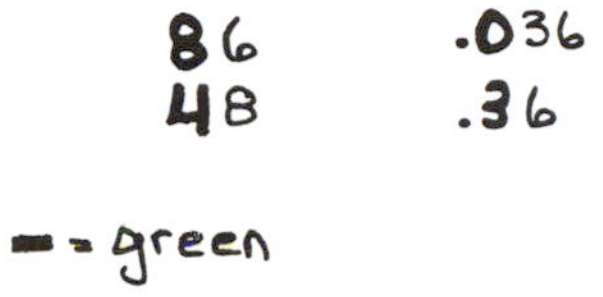

86
48

.036
.36

■ = green

FIGURE 9.13

or other perceptual deficits. Eventually, students themselves can learn to color highlight critical digits as a way of internalizing the comparison.

6. **Add zeros.** Whenever the number of decimal places in two given numbers differs, many students find it easier to compare when extra zeros are added, as in Figure 9.14a. Evening out the number of decimal digits as shown makes the comparison more obvious, particularly when decimal points are aligned as previously suggested. In this case, 360 thousandths, which is greater than 36 thousandths, is illustrated: "We have 360 of the thousand it takes to make one whole, which is much more than having just 36 of the thousand needed."

NOTE: *Adding zeros frequently is helpful when interpreting calculator displays as money, as in Figure 9.14b. Shading as in Figure 9.9 can be used to illustrate that the two decimals, .7 and .70, are equivalent.*

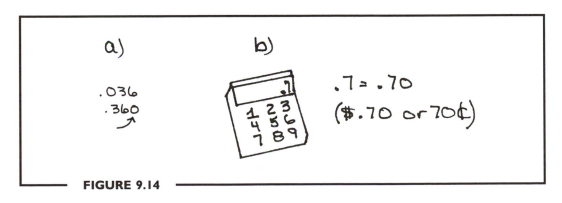

FIGURE 9.14

SUGGESTED SEQUENCE OF ACTIVITIES

Comparing Fractions

---

1. **Show and write.** Students with learning disabilities generally have little difficulty at the concrete level in using physical models to compare fractions. When a storyline provides a context for using the models, as suggested in the *Background* introduction to this section, so much the better. Some students who need more structured assistance can be encouraged to use fraction pieces on workmats like those in Figure 9.15a. Loose pieces laid on the workmat can be compared visually or tactually to the unit as well as to each other.

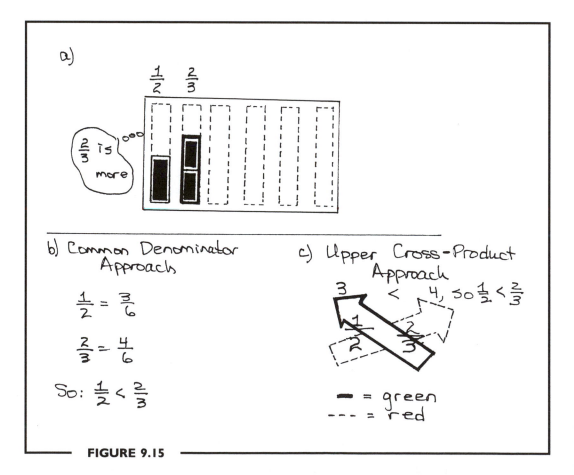

FIGURE 9.15

It is better if the students themselves can discuss the fraction pieces then fold and cut the pieces on premarked division lines. The strips and pieces can be used on the workmat during early work to illustrate certain specific fractions and to help students see, for example, that $\frac{4}{4}$, as well as $\frac{2}{2}$ or $\frac{3}{3}$, equals one whole unit. To compare fractions, students can again use the workmat as a base and, for example, lay a $\frac{1}{2}$ piece on top of two $\frac{1}{3}$ pieces to see that $\frac{2}{3}$ is more. Alternately, using preshaded bars, they might compare shaded parts of fraction strips, as in Figure 9.15a. Getting students themselves to write the fraction represented by each set of fraction pieces and to verbalize the result of the comparison is necessary to enable them to form important connections.

NOTE: *Problem storylines can be created to provide progressively more difficult comparisons. The following list suggests one such sequence, in which the last two examples are particularly difficult: $1\frac{1}{2}$ cakes and $1\frac{1}{3}$ cakes; $\frac{1}{3}$ of a cake and $\frac{5}{12}$ of a cake; $\frac{3}{4}$ of a cake and $\frac{9}{12}$ of a cake; $\frac{3}{4}$ of a cake and $\frac{8}{12}$ of a cake; $\frac{6}{8}$ of a cake and $\frac{9}{12}$ of a cake; $\frac{2}{3}$ of a cake and $\frac{3}{5}$ of a cake.*

2. **Special cases.** Students with perceptual deficits might experience some difficulty when asked to compare preshaded fraction bars or pictures of shaded regions on worksheets or textbook pages. (Ideas from the "Plastic overlay" and "Dot it" activities on page 374 help these students.)

NOTE: *The real difficulty arises when students are asked to compare fractions using either the common denominator or the cross-products method illustrated in Figures 9.15b and 9.15c. Of these two approaches, the more popular one for early work involves changing each fraction to an equivalent fraction with a common denominator.*

3. **Cross products.** Teachers interested in developing the cross-products approach in Figure 9.16 with students can use fraction strips as shown to validate results. The upper cross products are really the numerators of fractions equivalent to the original. The common denominator is the product of the denominators in the original fraction (6 in Figure 9.16c).

4. **Color cue.** Students can cross multiply and chart several examples of each type of comparison shown to develop or verify the general pattern: the fractions compare the way their upper cross products compare. The color cuing illustrated in this Figure 9.16 is helpful to many students: green first, then red when finding upper cross products.

SIMPLIFYING FRACTIONS

Problem Area: Difficulty writing fractions in simple form.
Typical Disabilities Affecting Progress: Difficulty with visual memory, sequencing, abstract reasoning, and expressive language.

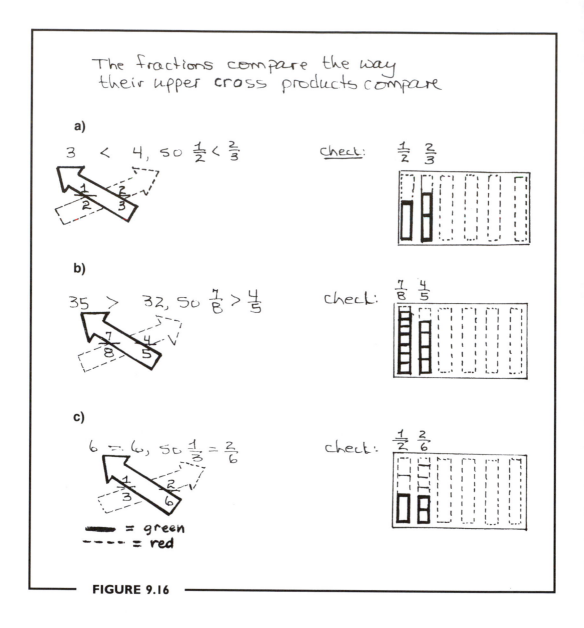

The fractions compare the way their upper cross products compare

a)

$3 < 4$, so $\frac{1}{2} < \frac{2}{3}$ Check: $\frac{1}{2}$ $\frac{2}{3}$

b)

$35 > 32$, so $\frac{7}{8} > \frac{4}{5}$ Check: $\frac{7}{8}$ $\frac{4}{5}$

c)

$6 = 6$, so $\frac{1}{3} = \frac{2}{6}$ Check: $\frac{1}{2}$ $\frac{2}{6}$

━━━ = green
---- = red

FIGURE 9.16

Background: When children compute, we generally ask that they express all answers in the simplest form. The ability to simplify fractions, however, involves more than understanding what to do. Actually, the easiest part is dividing the numerator and the denominator by the same number. The difficulty arises because children either:

- do not know which divisor to use for numerator and denominator in order to simplify a fraction; or

- fail to recognize the need to simplify further.

Initially, to help students concentrate on each step of the sequence, do not require the final step of simplifying an answer when teaching to add or subtract fractions. This way students are not forced to learn to do two new things simultaneously:

- add/subtract in the new context of fractions; and

- simplify in the new context of computation.

In early work with equivalent fractions, it also is important to examine equivalences like fractions $\frac{4}{6} = \frac{2}{3}$ or $\frac{6}{8} = \frac{3}{4}$. This will provide the children with a background for *dividing* numerator and denominator by the same number. All too often this emphasis is slighted, since most examples are those in which one *multiplies* to find an equivalent fraction.

Deal directly with the problems children encounter when reducing fractions to simple form. The following ideas have proven helpful with students who have learning disabilities. The focus is on:

- recognizing the correct divisor for numerator and denominator, and

- knowing when to reduce.

SUGGESTED SEQUENCE OF ACTIVITIES

1. **Number strip.** Prepare a strip listing the numbers 2 through 9, as in Figure 9.17. Tape the strip along the chalkboard or have students glue strips to individual index cards they can keep for personal reference. As the children begin reducing, they can use the strip to assist thinking as they answer the following questions:

   - *What's the greatest number or "factor" that will divide both numerator and denominator?* If the given fraction is $\frac{6}{8}$, then the greatest factor is 2 (see Figure 9.18a). For $\frac{12}{18}$ (see Figure 9.18b), one could

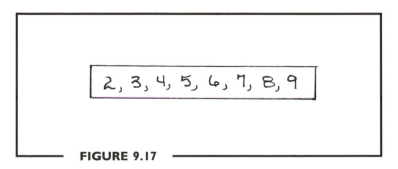

2, 3, 4, 5, 6, 7, 8, 9

FIGURE 9.17

divide by 2 and then by 3; but the greatest factor, 6, makes it necessary to divide by just one number rather than by two.

- This done, look once more. *Can I divide both numerator and denominator by any other number?* Because fraction computation is more limited in focus, size of number used, and quantity of problems listed in exercises, the typical answer to this question will be *no.* Using this process, occasionally, as in Figure 9.19, fractions may require two divisions.

a)
2, 3, 4, 5, 6, 7, 8, 9
6 ÷ 2 / 8 ÷ 2 = 3/4
b)
2, 3, 4, 5, 6, 7, 8, 9
12 ÷ 6 / 18 6 = 2/3

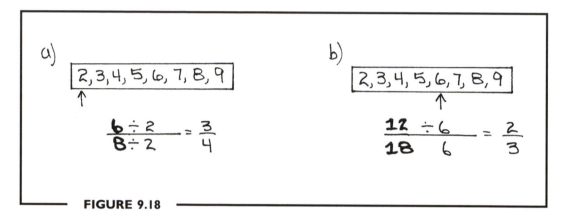

FIGURE 9.18

Divide once:
2, 3, 4, 5, 6, 7, 8, 9
24 ÷ 6 / 36 ÷ 6 = 3/6
Divide again:
2, 3, 4, 5, 6, 7, 8, 9
3 ÷ 3 / 6 ÷ 3 = 1/2

FIGURE 9.19

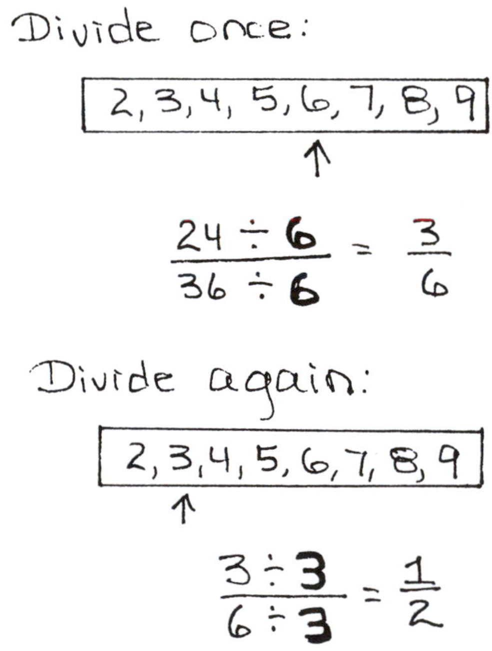

DEVELOPING COMPUTATION SENSE FOR FRACTIONS AND DECIMALS

Problem Areas: Difficulty recognizing and using number relationships for decimals and fractions, making mental estimations or calculations, meaningfully interpreting written equations and algorithms, selecting and using appropriate computation procedures.

Typical Disabilities Affecting Progress: Difficulty with abstract reasoning, sequential memory, visual perception, expressive language.

Background: Computation sense for fractions and decimals is demonstrated by students' abilities (a) to interpret written number sentences as well as mental and written computational procedures in meaningful ways; (b) to choose appropriate calculation methods for given situations; and (c) to be able to judge whether computational results are reasonable. These abilities imply strong conceptual understandings for the numbers and operations involved and the ability to reason critically.

Besides the demands on decoding and processing skills, being skilled in any one of these areas requires time and frequent opportunities to carry out activities related to these areas. To nurture better *thinking,* less computation of exact answers is sometimes preferable. At other times, written work can be reused in different ways, as suggested in several of the activities in this section.

Just as important, however, is a positive, supportive environment and good role modeling that emphasizes common-sense estimation with fractions and decimals. Hearing teachers and other students think aloud as they compute to solve problems, to summarize or defend the procedure(s) used, often provides a new perspective for individual students.

If common-sense thinking about fractions and decimals is an important goal, suggestions like the following may be in order. Emphasis on appropriate use of physical models and invented, personally meaningful algorithms, as well as on mental techniques and calculator experiences, should occur before formal paper-and-pencil procedures are introduced or reviewed within a school year.

Interpreting Written Equations and Computational Procedures

Computation needs to be taught and learned meaningfully. Many students, sadly, have no intuitions about what $\frac{3}{4} \div \frac{1}{2}$ or $4.2 \times .51$ means. For the first example they may be unable to tell whether the result is more or less than 1 (more, for there are more than just one $\frac{1}{2}$ sized piece in $\frac{3}{4}$). For the second example they may be unable to recognize that the result is very close to $\frac{1}{2}$ of 4 (because .51 is very close to .5, or $\frac{1}{2}$, of 4.2) and conclude that the answer is very close to 2.

Good beginnings toward nurturing this kind of thinking requires careful attention to underlying concepts and number relationships. A problem-centered, conceptual approach to computation is suggested, which precludes many of the difficulties children otherwise typically experience in learning to compute and which also reduces the amount of instructional time that must be devoted to it.

Consistent with this suggestion, a successful approach for developing good intuitions about written number sentences and computational algorithms includes:

- basing computation instruction for fractions and decimals on problem situations that have meaning for students;

- allowing students to select personally meaningful ways to solve these problems, including their choice of any manipulative or teaching aid that may be helpful in working out a solution;

- alllowing, even encouraging students to record their solution steps in personally meaningful ways, including any intermediate recordings that may be needed by the students to assist in decoding or processing information;

- expecting and encouraging different solution approaches; and

- expecting students to justify their thinking and explain their recording methods (if any).

As part of this approach, students eventually are expected to use their own language to interpret or describe number sentences and computational procedures. They also should be expected to collaborate with others or independently write their own story problems that provide realistic contexts for the numbers being used.

For example, one child wrote the following story for $1\frac{1}{2} + 2\frac{1}{2} =$ _____.

> Mom made cookies. She put $1\frac{1}{2}$ cups of flour into the bowl then added another $2\frac{1}{2}$ cups. How much flour did she use for the cookies?

The child then used paper strips for the cups of flour (halves and whole strips) and illustrated how it was decided that 4 cups were used. Being able to translate freely from:

- the problem in numbers (the equation or computational exercise),

- the problem in words, and

- the problem illustrated with some physical model

is a powerful indicator of good number sense and can be nurtured through varied and rich problem-solving experiences. As students report on their solution strategies, different models and mental solution strategies typically emerge. The overall result of this approach, nurtured by a risk-free classroom environment and supported by frequent "think aloud" exchanges between the teacher and the student(s), is greater flexibility in thinking about rational numbers and more accurate intuitions for interpreting written aspects of computation.

Choosing the Calculation Method

As mentioned previously, technology has changed drastically the methods by which we compute. We have inexpensive, readily available calculators that perform routine computations with fractions or decimals. This fact broadens our concept of *meaningful approaches to computation,* which includes being able to easily compute previously complicated problems. The suggestion of the National Council of Teachers of Mathematics (1989) is that students should be encouraged to choose and use the method that is most appropriate in a given situation. This should be especially true when working with rational numbers. Sometimes it is far preferable to use a calculator for part or all of a problem.

- *Mental calculation first,* then try paper and pencil or a calculator. For example: 30.15 + 26.14 is about the same as 30 + 26, or about 56. Similarly, $25\frac{5}{8}$ + $15\frac{1}{3}$ is about the same as 26 + 15 or close to 41.

- *Let's estimate.* Figure 9.20 suggests how, when working with fractions, students might think about individual addends to estimate sums. It is also useful for students to think about whether estimates they have made are over or under the actual answer. In Figure 9.20, for example, each addend is less than the number used in the estimate, so the estimate given is an overestimate. In Figure 9.21, the estimate calculated is an underestimate. Students

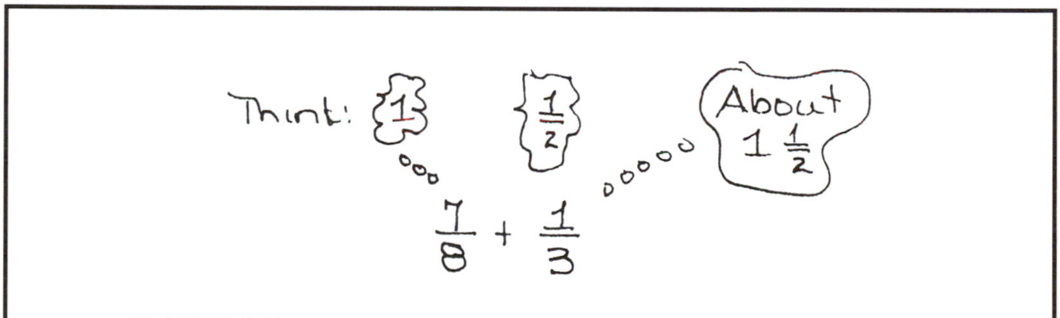

FIGURE 9.20

FIGURE 9.21

need to realize that, in many practical situations such as buying material needed to make a dress or deciding how much money to have with you, it is better to be over than under.

Allow for alternate responses to encourage those students who are timid or insecure. For example, in Figure 9.21, some students might round $19 up to $21 and decide that a reasonable answer is "about $7 off." In early stages, it makes more sense to accept a broader range of estimates and to help students explain their thinking than to concentrate on close estimates. Help them understand what kinds of estimates are best in what types of situations.

When considering the computation $3\frac{7}{8} \div 1\frac{1}{4} = $ _____ for the problem "How many costumes requiring $1\frac{1}{4}$ yard of fabric can be cut from $3\frac{5}{8}$ yards of material?" some students think of the problem as $3 \div 1$ and estimate 3. Others may mentally add: $1\frac{1}{4} + 1\frac{1}{4}$—that's $2\frac{1}{2}$. So another $1\frac{1}{4}$ makes $3\frac{3}{4}$. There is enough material for 3 costumes." For similar problems, responses like the following can be accepted.

- More than 1 ($3\frac{1}{4} \div 2\frac{1}{2}$)
- About 2 ($5\frac{1}{4} \div 2\frac{1}{8}$)

WRITTEN COMPUTATION FOR FRACTIONS AND DECIMALS

Problem Area: Difficulty carrying out written computations with fractions or decimal numbers.

Typical Disabilities Affecting Progress: Difficulty with closure, visual figure-ground, spatial organization, sequential and long-term memory, visual perception, and visual memory.

Background: An earlier section of this chapter, *Developing Computation Sense for Fractions and Decimals,* highlighted students' needs to:

- initially learn and consistently apply computation in problem-solving settings;

- be allowed to use solution approaches that make sense to them, record their solution steps, and explain their thinking in personally meaningful ways; and

- develop appropriate mental calculation, estimation, and calculator techniques before or at least at the same time as formal work with written computation is addressed.

As the result of a rich, problem-centered introduction to computation like that suggested above, some students may develop personally meaningful computational approaches, which preclude the need to teach more standard algorithms. Other students will require direct intervention because approaches attempted have been inaccurate or grossly inefficient. Many students will require special intervention to overcome difficulties arising from a specific disability.

As we observe, listen to, and monitor what students do and say, decisions about intervention emerge. Clearly, because of calculators, there is no need to focus on learning tedious or complex written computations, or on requiring students to spend an inordinate amount of time learning a written algorithm when an estimate is just as appropriate. Further, if the level of students' disabilities is profound and the student is able to use a calculator effectively, it is better to spend precious instructional time exploiting the full use of the calculator, with an emphasis on developing the student's abilities to think mathematically in problem-solving situations. Following the suggestions of Chapter 8, this may include translating fractions to decimals before computing, or using a calculator that accommodates numbers in fractional form. This approach should free instructional time for pursuing other rich areas of mathematics like data analysis and probability or computer explorations in geometry and algebra.

The reader is referred to the *Developing Computation Sense for Fractions and Decimals* section on page 409 for suggestions for treating difficulties with mental techniques or calculator use. The following ideas provide a reference for accommodating special areas of difficulty related to *written* computation. Although not specifically addressed, an area that often interferes with successfully using fraction and decimal skills is the increased vocabulary and the need to apply new meanings to old words. Teachers need to be aware of this situation and consider previewing vocabulary wherever and whenever needed.

Fraction Computation

Adding or Subtracting Fractions

Given the current de-emphasis on fraction computation and the rare need to add or subtract fractions in daily living, many teachers seek to balance out the amount of time students spend on involved paper-and-pencil computations in relation to other more important areas of mathematics. As suggested in the previous section, sometimes an estimate is sufficient.

Given that some paper-and-pencil calculation with familiar fractions is needed if (a) this type of calculation is still part of the curriculum, or (b) a calculator is not available, it typically is helpful to emphasize two "big ideas" which apply to fractions as well as to whole number and decimal computation:

For addition:

1. Add like units.

2. If there are enough of a kind to trade up (regroup), do so.

For subtraction:

1. Subtract like units.

2. If there are not enough to take what is needed, trade down.

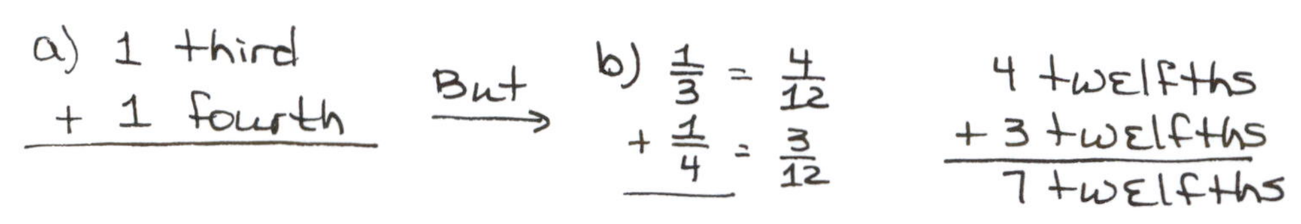

a) 1 third
+ 1 fourth   But →   b) $\frac{1}{3} = \frac{4}{12}$ 4 twelfths
                              $+ \frac{1}{4} = \frac{3}{12}$ + 3 twelfths
                                                               7 twelfths

FIGURE 9.22

The first big idea—adding or subtracting like units—is directly related to finding a like denominator when a computation involves fractions with different denominators. Good number sense for fractions includes the recognition that, when the sum or difference of two *unlike* fractions is needed, as for $\frac{1}{3} + \frac{1}{4}$, a common label for both fractions must first be found. Otherwise, how should the sum be labeled? (See Figure 9.22a.) If fractions equivalent to each of those in the original problem are found, as in Figure 9.22b, completing the computation makes sense.

Beyond recognizing *why* and *when* like (common) denominators are needed, perhaps the most difficult aspect of hand calculating the sum or difference of unlike fractions involves finding like denominators.

Locating equivalent fractions when the new denominator is already given and determining the common denominator for two given fractions are two completely different skills. The former requires far less abstract thinking because much of the final answer is already in sight. The latter skill, on the other hand, requires a great deal of visual association, overlearning, and quick retrieval. Students must master this latter skill in order to be successful with addition and subtraction of unlike fractions.

Finding the lowest common denominator

In line with the desire to balance out the amount of time spent on fraction computation in relation to other more important mathematical topics, many teachers have adopted the following approach to finding a common denominator:

1. Check: *Is one denominator a multiple of the other? If so, that number is the lowest common multiple.*

   Let students use multiple strips (see Figures 9.23 and 9.24) to help determine the answer to the question. In the $\frac{1}{2} + \frac{3}{4}$ example of Figure 9.23a, 4 is on both strips so 4 is the lowest common multiple of both numbers. Used as the new denominator for the two fractions, it is called the lowest (least) common denominator.

2. *If one denominator is not a multiple of the other, multiply the two denominator numbers to find a common denominator.*

   This step does not always provide the *lowest* common denominator. On the other hand, it very quickly provides a denominator that works and allows students to move on to more important mathematics topics.

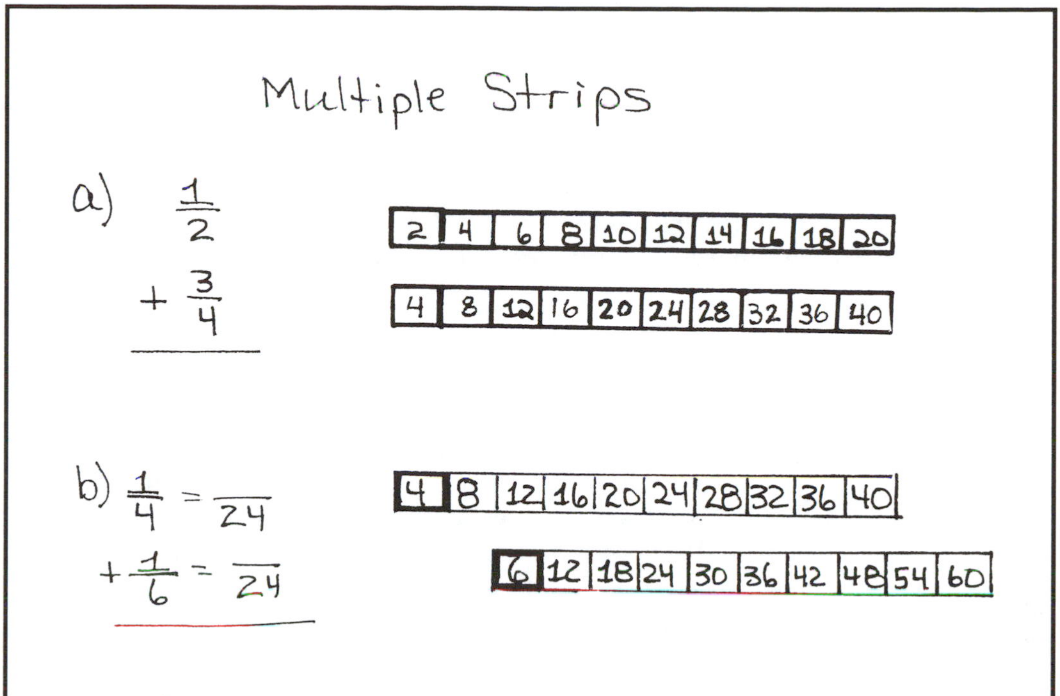

Multiple Strips

a) $\dfrac{1}{2}$

| 2 | 4 | 6 | 8 | 10 | 12 | 14 | 16 | 18 | 20 |

$+\ \dfrac{3}{4}$

| 4 | 8 | 12 | 16 | 20 | 24 | 28 | 32 | 36 | 40 |

_____

b) $\dfrac{1}{4} = \dfrac{\ }{24}$

| 4 | 8 | 12 | 16 | 20 | 24 | 28 | 32 | 36 | 40 |

$+\ \dfrac{1}{6} = \dfrac{\ }{24}$

| 6 | 12 | 18 | 24 | 30 | 36 | 42 | 48 | 54 | 60 |

_____

FIGURE 9.23

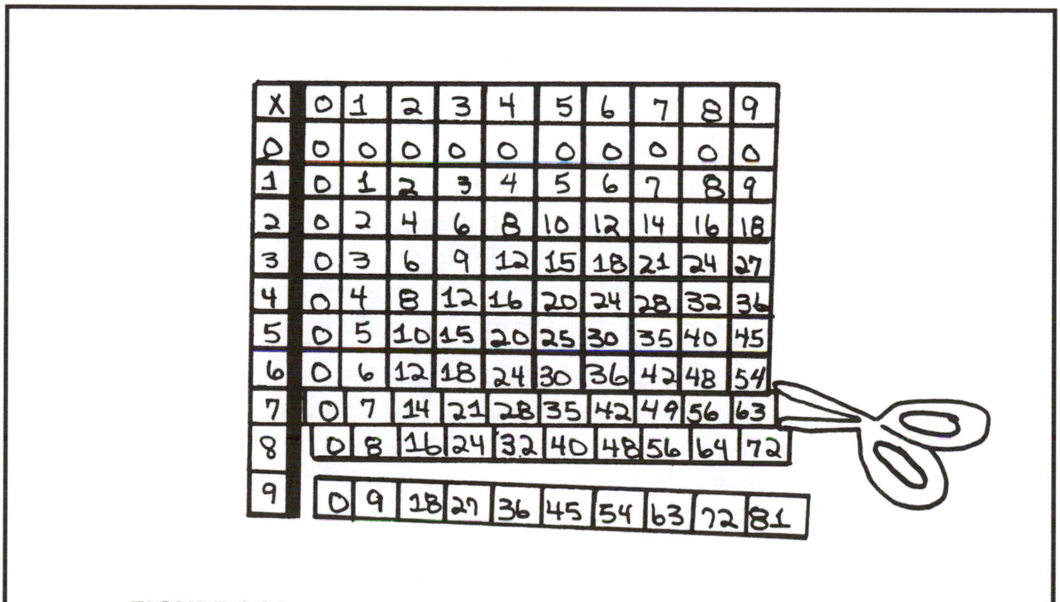

X	0	1	2	3	4	5	6	7	8	9
0	0	0	0	0	0	0	0	0	0	0
1	0	1	2	3	4	5	6	7	8	9
2	0	2	4	6	8	10	12	14	16	18
3	0	3	6	9	12	15	18	21	24	27
4	0	4	8	12	16	20	24	28	32	36
5	0	5	10	15	20	25	30	35	40	45
6	0	6	12	18	24	30	36	42	48	54
7	0	7	14	21	28	35	42	49	56	63
8	0	8	16	24	32	40	48	56	64	72
9	0	9	18	27	36	45	54	63	72	81

FIGURE 9.24

Teachers who consider it desirable for students always to find the lowest common denominator when comparing, adding, or subtracting fractions can select from two alternate approaches:

1. Use individual multiple strips (Figure 9.23b) to locate the least common multiple as the new denominator. (This is the approach typically presented first in school mathematics textbooks.) Help students slide one strip under the other stationary one until the least common multiple is found.

2. Find the prime factors of each denominator and multiply, being careful to use as factors only the minimum number of primes needed to make the product a multiple of each denominator number.

Both of these methods can be cumbersome and difficult. In our experience, the first approach has proven easier, given that the goal is always to find the *lowest* common denominator. Listing the multiples also reinforces the basic multiplication facts for children who still need practice. If necessary, provide individual *cross out* sheets for unknown facts, as suggested in Chapter 7.

When dealing with more frequently used denominators, it is desirable that students automatically recognize the lowest common multiple. Though some children may find it difficult at first, it generally comes with practice for more common pairings. In the interim, ideas for helping students become familiar with the "listing multiples" procedure for determining the lowest common denominator of two fractions follow.

SUGGESTED SEQUENCE OF ACTIVITIES

Teachers interested in students always using the lowest common denominator may use the following activities.

1. **Multiple strips.** Use heavy tagboard to make a personal set of multiple strips for each student (see Figure 9.23a). If the children are familiar with multiplication charts, have them cut apart the rows, as in Figure 9.24, and glue them onto tagboard. If possible, laminate the strips or cover them with contact paper. Check that students understand that the meaning of *multiples* is "answers you get when you multiply."

2. **Find it** (developmental activity for individuals or small groups). Provide two decks of cards. The first deck should contain a card for each of the commonly used denominator numbers: 2, 3, 4, 5, 6, 8, and 10. Make the second card deck a different color, and have two cards for each number between 2 and 50. Arrange the cards *sequentially* to make it easier to locate specific cards.

Also make a pocket chart like that in Figure 9.25a, or use masking tape on the floor or desk to partition a space into three columns. The chart should be labeled as shown. The children take turns drawing two cards from the first deck. In the example in Figure 9.25a, the cards 6 and 8 were drawn. After the cards are placed in the chart, the children work together, using multiple strips if needed, to take multiples of 6 and 8 from the second deck. These cards are placed in the appropriate multiple column of the chart. The children then examine the chart and remove any numbers that appear in both multiple columns. One card for each of these numbers is moved to the "common multiple" section of the chart (see Figure 9.25b). Finally, the lowest or smallest multiple (24) is moved to the "lowest common multiple" section. Replace the cards in the decks and draw again to continue.

3. **Just the denominator.** Give the students a work page of about 10 addition or subtraction problems with unlike denominators. Allow them to use

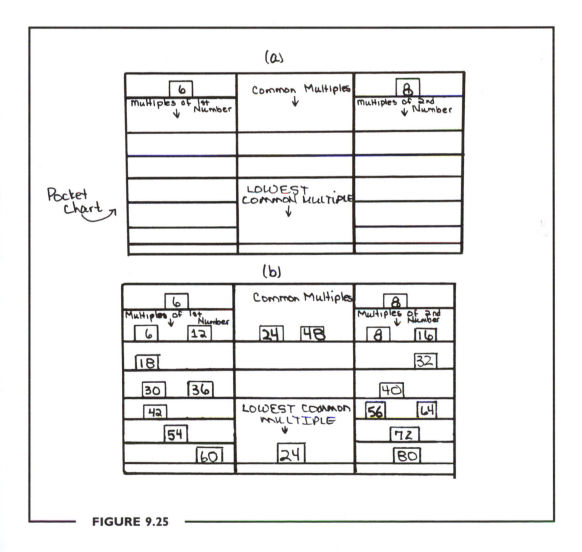

FIGURE 9.25

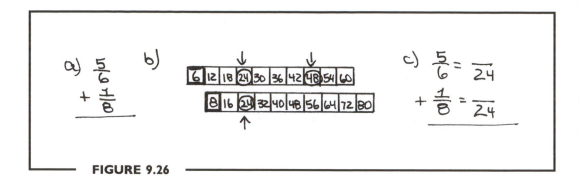

FIGURE 9.26

their multiple strips (to build visual memory) and find just the *lowest common denominator* of the two fractions. Given the problem of Figure 9.26a, for example, the students may find it helpful to circle common multiples on the laminated strips, match up the strips as in Figure 9.26b, and then write the smallest of the common multiples (24) as the new denominator for the problem (see Figure 9.26c).

Do not require the children to finish the problems at this time. The sheets can be collected, checked, and redistributed at a later date so that the problems can be completed.

NOTE: *If the multiple strips are not laminated, show the students how to place them under a clear plastic sheet so they can circle common multiples (see Figure 9.27a). Alternatively, for children with severe motor, figure-ground, or discrimination problems, glue the multiple strips to longer pieces of paper for use in a homemade tachistoscope. Children pull the strips through the tachistoscope and stop when one number appears on both strips—this is the lowest common multiple (Figure 9.27b).*

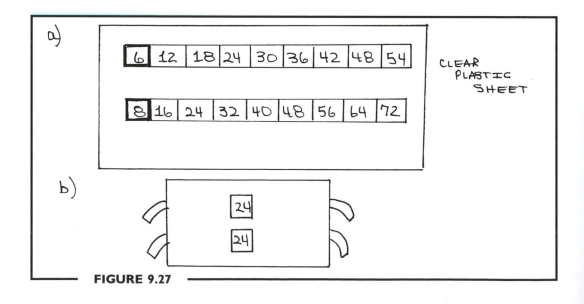

FIGURE 9.27

4. **Color cue.** Some students need to write out the multiples of each denominator to be able to identify the least common multiple. To help students organize their work space when listing the multiples, set up pages as shown in Figure 9.28. Highlighting the space where the common multiple will fall helps children with perseveration or figure-ground deficits know when to stop.

5. **Say aloud.** Some students benefit from hearing themselves count the multiples in order to memorize them. Oral skip counting practice is necessary.

6. **Transition.** As the students become more proficient at finding multiples, a simpler cuing system, as suggested by Figure 9.29, can be used. Instead of listing all the multiples, the child skip counts until the circle is reached and then writes the number in that circle. This method has proven particularly effective with students who need help organizing their work for computation.

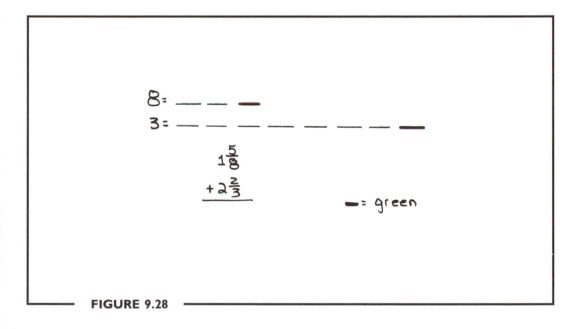

FIGURE 9.28

7. **Concentration** (a practice activity for two players). Students enjoy *Concentration*, a game that helps build retrieval and visual memory. The game requires two sets of cards. The cards of one set each show two numbers from the commonly used denominator numbers: 2, 3, 4, 5, 6, 8, and 10. The cards of the second set should show the least common multiple for each pair in the first deck. Shuffle the decks and lay them out in two separate groups, face down. Players take turns turning over one card from the first deck and trying to select its match from the other set of cards. *Concentration* game rules are followed. The winner is the one with the most pairs of cards at the end.

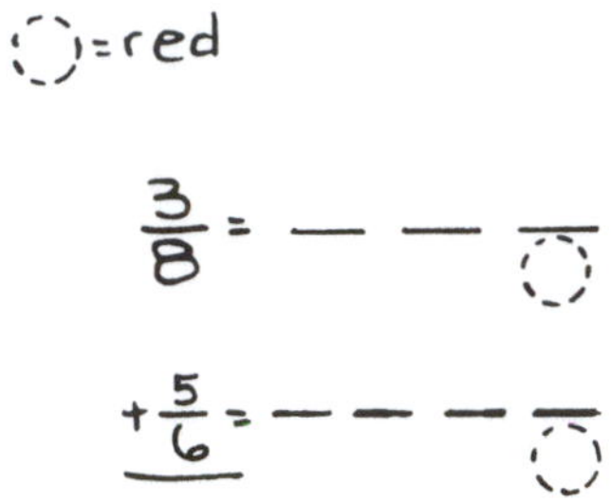

FIGURE 9.29

- *Variation:* As an independent activity, have the students time how long it takes them to pair cards from the two sets. Encourage them to keep a log of their time and gradually try to improve their records.

Regrouping in subtraction

Students may realize *when* they must regroup and even *why* they need to do so. However, these same students may not know *how* to regroup. The error in the problem in Figure 9.30 is typical. The student confused the regrouping with the familiar whole number procedure: 1 less ten, 10 more ones. Having completed the subtraction, the child reduced to lowest terms, unaware that anything was wrong.

Anticipating difficulties like this during early developmental work, many teachers dramatize the regrouping. Thus, trading activities often are used. In the example of Figure 9.31a, the children use materials to model $3\frac{1}{8}$. They trade 1 whole for 8 eighths and record the total number of eighths (9 eighths). Repeated experiences with fair-trade activities of this type for different fractions help most children see what is happening. This enables them to correctly apply the regrouping procedure to subtraction problems like that of Figure 9.31b. The similarity between the record-keeping format of Figure 9.31a and the regrouping shown in Figure 9.31b helps children transfer the regrouping skill to computation with fractions.

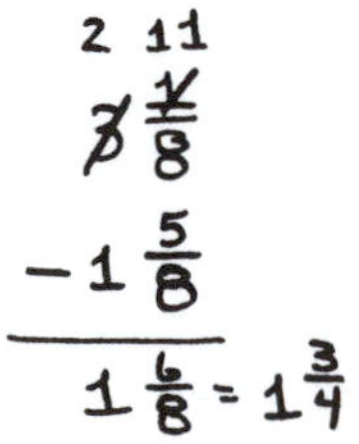

FIGURE 9.30

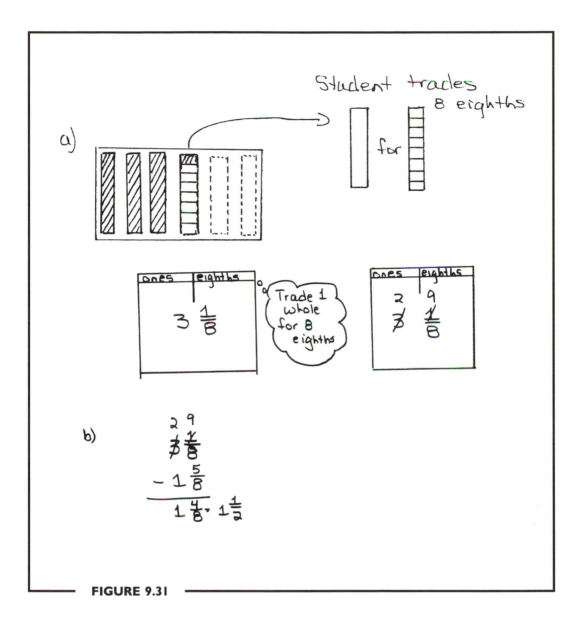

FIGURE 9.31

Some students do not make the transfer, however. Despite any care taken in early developmental work, specific learning disabilities cause them to fail at the symbolic level. For example, abstract-reasoning difficulties may inhibit the meaningful transition of the procedure to paper-and-pencil computation, or memory sequencing deficiencies may make it difficult to remember all the isolated steps of the regrouping process.

Given subtraction problems requiring regrouping, these children may refuse even to attempt the work, or they may revert to the more familiar procedure of always adding 10 when regrouping is necessary. For these students, more specialized cuing techniques, such as those illustrated in the following sequence, are necessary.

SUGGESTED SEQUENCE OF ACTIVITIES

1. **Regroup.** Before turning to regrouping within subtraction, focus on just renaming numbers that might appear in the minuend of subtraction problems. Figure 9.32a presents the format for a color-coded page that can be kept on file and used as needed. This type of page has proven helpful with children who have visual, sequential, or abstract-reasoning difficulties. Figure 9.32b presents a completed example of the problem. If the children recognize the need for regrouping, the colors remind them what to do by ordering the steps and increasing reasoning. Experience has shown that, because the students notice the different colors, they tend to recall more readily the reason why the steps are carried out.

2. **Talk about a shorter way.** After practicing the preceding isolated step, most students begin to notice the regrouping pattern. Some, however, will need extra help to eliminate the longer procedure. Make a chart of problems that have been solved previously through the longer procedure (Activity 1), but this time write only the original number and the regrouped one, as in Figure 9.33. If the students have figure-ground deficits and cannot readily sort out the numbers, use the colors as shown. The denominator of the second fraction is green to indicate a starting point. Most students quickly will notice that the denominators in both pairs are the same. The discussion can then focus on the pairs of black numbers and finally on the red ones.

   The basis of discussion for the sample problem in Figure 9.33 is the idea that 1 whole, or 3 thirds, is taken from the 8 and added to the $\frac{1}{3}$, resulting in 7 wholes and 4 thirds. Similar discussions would take place for other number pairs. If helpful, materials could be used to show that the regrouping is correct. After analyzing the chart numbers in this manner, the students should be given other problems for which they independently carry out the regrouping.

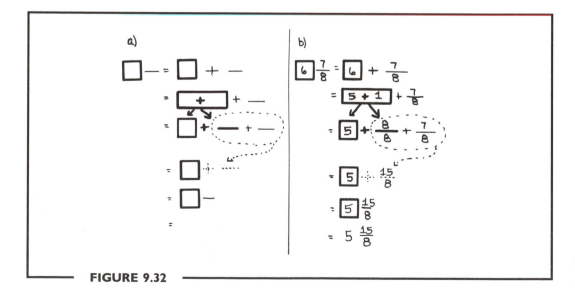

FIGURE 9.32

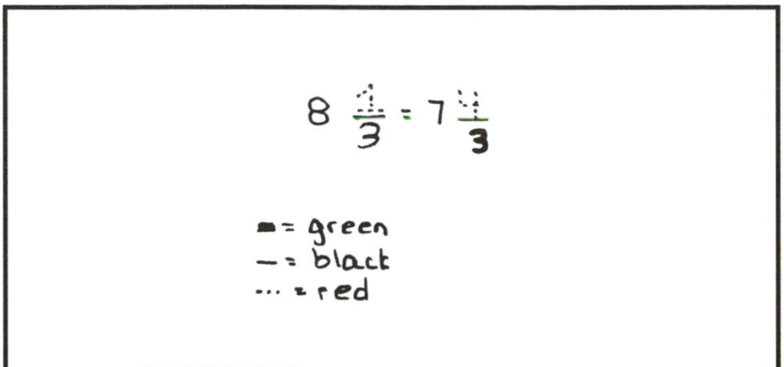

$$8 \frac{1}{3} = 7 \frac{4}{3}$$

■ = green
— = black
··· = red

FIGURE 9.33

3. **A middle step.** To help children retain the sequence while going to the standard format for regrouping, the intermediate step shown in Figure 9.34 is often useful.

4. **Now subtract.** Next, present subtraction problems like that in Figure 9.35. Once the children recognize the need to regroup, allow them to use a card, if necessary, to block out all but the minuend number until the regrouping is complete.

   NOTE: *If the students have difficulty recognizing whether regrouping is needed, adapt suggestions from Chapter 5 on whole number subtraction to work with fractions; then proceed with the ideas just outlined.*

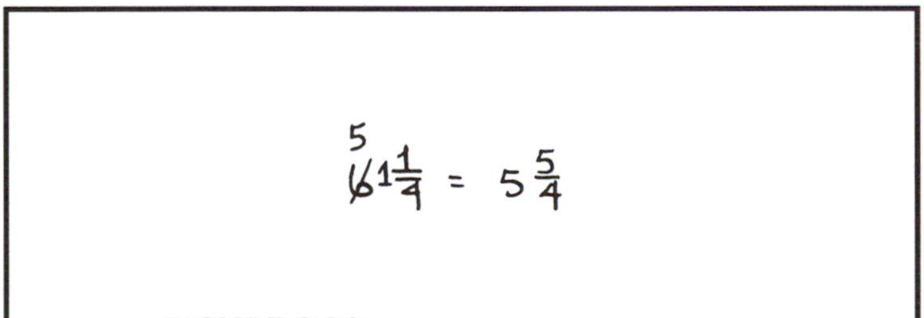

$$\overset{5}{\cancel{6}}1\tfrac{1}{4} = 5 \frac{5}{4}$$

FIGURE 9.34

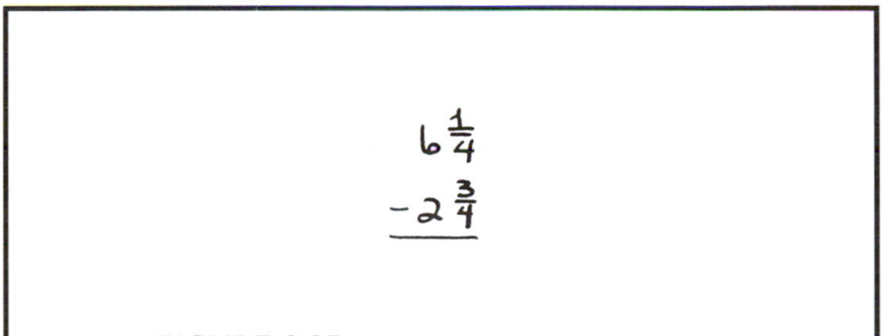

$$\begin{array}{r} 6\frac{1}{4} \\ -2\frac{3}{4} \\ \hline \end{array}$$

FIGURE 9.35

Multiplying fractions

In daily situations, we rarely need to carry out paper-and-pencil calculations involving multiplication of fractions. Yet, sometimes the skill is useful for converting recipes, buying material, or deciding how much carpet is needed to cover a room. If necessary, however, one can convert fractions to decimals and use a hand calculator to derive these answers.

On the other hand, the skill must be taught to those who can learn it because multiplication of fractions (a) is still part of the modern mathematics curriculum and (b) is sometimes easier if no calculator is available or if a student has trouble retaining the conversions. Finally, it is a prerequisite for students who plan to take algebra in high school, since the procedures for handling rational algebraic expressions have their basis in the simpler computations with fractions.

Multiplication of fractions is relatively easy to teach. Some teachers, particularly those planning upper-grade review sessions, prefer to present multiplication as the first area of computation with fractions. Because there are no common denominators to be found, most students have greater success with multiplication than with addition or subtraction. Therefore, the goal is to build in many success experiences by dealing with multiplication early in the computational sequence.

The suggestions that follow have been used successfully with students who have learning disabilities. The format includes a basic sequence as well as alternative techniques that have been helpful in meeting special needs. Regardless of whether the multiplication topic is approached first or introduced after addition and subtraction, the ideas should prove useful.

SUGGESTED SEQUENCE OF ACTIVITIES

1. **Shaded discs.** Using discs or construction-paper circles, shade $\frac{1}{2}$ of 2, $\frac{1}{3}$ of 6, $\frac{2}{5}$ of 10, $\frac{2}{3}$ of 9, and so on. Help the students write equations to describe the shaded parts. Example: $\frac{1}{2}$ of 2 = 1; $\frac{1}{3}$ of 6 = 2.

2. **Picture it on paper.** Provide worksheets that contain geometric regions like that of Figure 9.36. Have the students use pencil or crayons to color

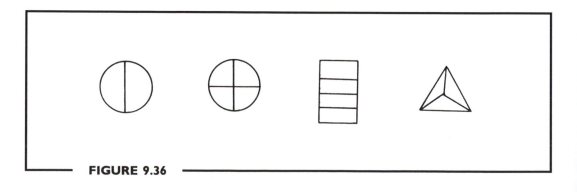

FIGURE 9.36

$\frac{1}{2}$ of 2, $\frac{2}{3}$ of 6, $\frac{2}{3}$ of 9, and so on. As in Activity 1, have the students write equations to describe the shaded parts.

3. **Look for patterns.** Have the students note that answers could be found simply by multiplying numerators and multiplying denominators (or, alternately, multiplying numerators then dividing by the denominators). To reinforce the idea that *of* means *times* or *multiply*, rewrite each equation to use the multiplication symbol ($\times$) instead of the word *of.* Examples: $\frac{3}{4}$ of 8 = $\frac{3}{4} \times 8 = \frac{24}{4} = 6$.

4. **Different strokes.** Some students may suggest the pattern of dividing first, then multiplying. Example: $\frac{2}{3}$ of 63. First, divide 63 into 3 equal groups (21 in each group). Then take 2 of the groups, or 42 things.

- This approach may be the best one for students who have trouble sequencing. Figure 9.37 illustrates how color coding can be used to support this thinking. Because the vocabulary is simple, reading generally causes no difficulty.

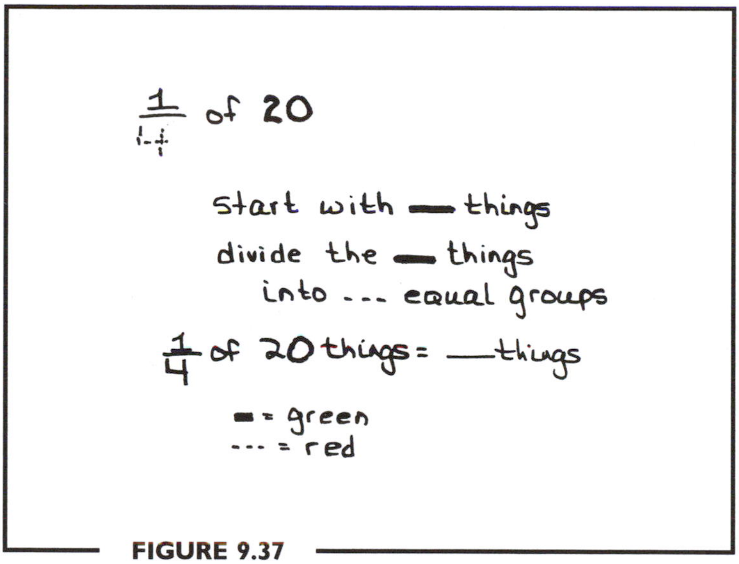

FIGURE 9.37

- Figure 9.38a presents a variation of color cuing for factors other than unit fractions. In this example, a child's attention is focused first on the number of equal groups into which 16 is divided (8), and then on the number of groups to be used (5). To help students picture this multiplication, give them a sheet like that of Figure 9.38b and a set of geometric shapes. After the shapes are drawn, the children place chips in the shape to illustrate the problem (see Figure 9.38c).

For this example, the children take 16 chips and place them, one by one, into the shapes until all 16 are distributed. They then note that 10 of the 16, or $\frac{5}{8}$, are inside the red frame. When they are ready to eliminate visual/manipulative aids like this, color coding

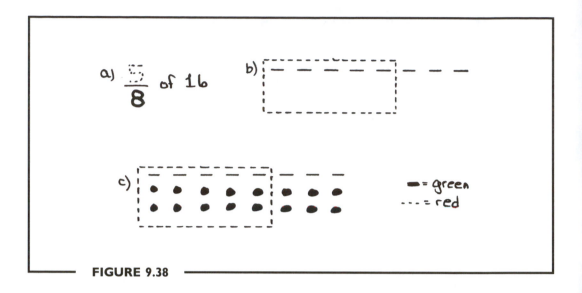

FIGURE 9.38

digits as in Figure 9.38a can serve to remind them of what was done previously with shapes and chips. As before, help the students see that there is a pattern in what the numbers do.

NOTE: *Placing chips in the shapes requires one-to-one matching. Some students may need specific help with or review of this skill.*

5. **Whole number × fraction.** Use construction-paper fraction strips (all the same size.) Subdivide some into halves, thirds, fourths, and so on. Have the students label the pieces and cut them apart on the subdivision lines. (Strips and pieces are illustrated in Figure 9.39). Ask the students to place the pieces into the workmat (see Figure 9.39): 2 of the $\frac{1}{2}$ pieces, or 6 of the $\frac{1}{3}$ pieces, or 10 of the $\frac{2}{5}$ pieces, and so on. They should write equations to describe the finished picture each time. Example: $2 \times \frac{1}{2} = 1$; $6 \times \frac{1}{3} = \frac{6}{3}$, or 2; $10 \times \frac{2}{5} = \frac{20}{5}$, or 4.

6. **Both factors a fraction.** Repeat Activities 1 to 3, asking students to show $\frac{1}{2}$ of $\frac{1}{8}$, $\frac{1}{4}$ of $\frac{1}{3}$, $\frac{1}{3}$ of $\frac{1}{2}$, and so on. Have them verbalize the pattern for multiplying fractions: multiply numerators, multiply denominators. Ask students to check each equation to see if it follows the pattern.

7. **Alternative approach.** Some students have difficulty changing a mixed number to an improper fraction in order to carry out the computation. Given a problem like $4 \times 2\frac{3}{5}$, they may multiply the whole number 4 by both the numerator *and* the denominator of $\frac{3}{5}$. To eliminate confusion while allowing this alternate procedure, it is helpful at times to teach students to multiply a whole number by a mixed number using the distributive property. (Figure 9.40 presents an example using this approach.)

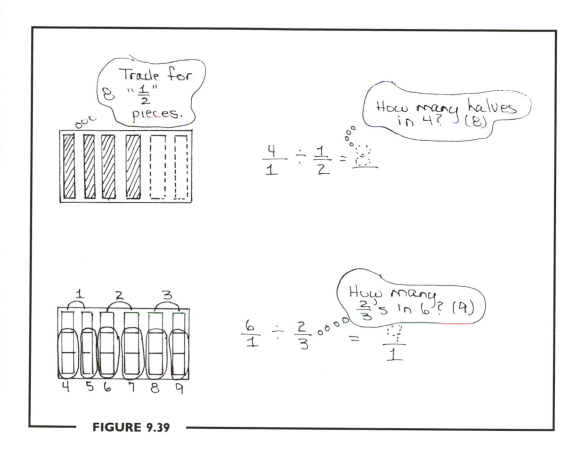

FIGURE 9.39

$$4 \times 2\tfrac{3}{5} = 4 \times \left(2 + \tfrac{3}{5}\right)$$
$$= \left(4 \times 2\right) + \left(4 \times \tfrac{3}{5}\right)$$
$$= 8 + \tfrac{12}{5}$$
$$= 8 + 2\tfrac{2}{5}$$
$$= 10\tfrac{2}{5}$$

FIGURE 9.40

Dividing fractions

Many students, not just those with learning disabilities, lack good intuition for division of fractions. For that reason they are unaware that their answers are "unreasonable" when they make common mistakes like inverting the dividend rather than the divisor before computing. The activities of the following sequence have proved helpful in addressing these problems.

SUGGESTED SEQUENCE OF ACTIVITIES

1. **Use fraction strips and pieces.** Present problems like those of Figure 9.41 (whole numbers divided by a unit fraction).

   - Students fold and cut unit strips (or trade fraction pieces for unit strips) to find the number of divisor-size pieces that can be had.

   - Show students that the same result can be found by multiplying by the reciprocal of the divisor: "invert and multiply." (Confine numbers to those that can be checked using strips and pieces.)

   NOTE: *NCTM (1989) does not recommend a heavy emphasis on division of fractions beyond what can be modeled. Should district policy or student interest proceed beyond this point, the following suggestions may be helpful.*

2. **Color highlight.** To divide fractions, invert the divisor and multiply. When students understand this notion, color underscore the divisor in each of several problems to emphasize which fraction should be inverted.

3. **Box it.** As a follow-up, provide a sheet with several fraction division problems. Instruct the students to box or finger trace the divisor (the number to be inverted) for each problem on the sheet.

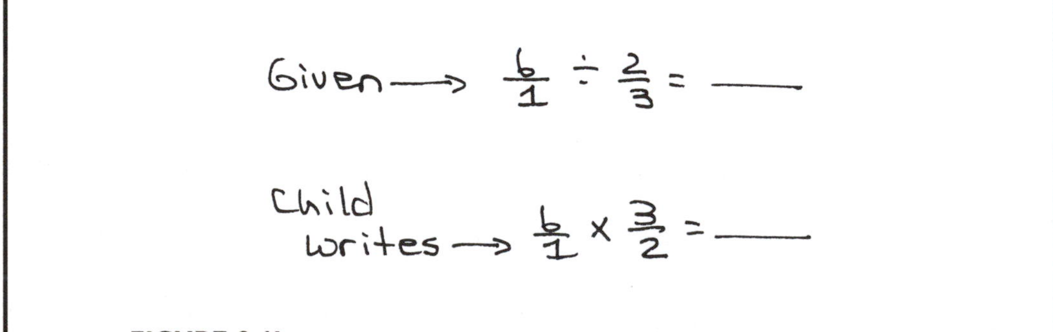

Given $\longrightarrow \dfrac{6}{1} \div \dfrac{2}{3} =$ _____

Child writes $\longrightarrow \dfrac{6}{1} \times \dfrac{3}{2} =$ _____

FIGURE 9.41

4. **Do just one step.** Have the students perform just the one step of writing the first equation toward solving each problem on the sheet (see Figure 9.41).

Decimal Computation

Adding or subtracting decimals

It is common for students with learning disabilities to make mistakes like those illustrated in Figure 9.42a. In Joey's work, digits rather than decimal points were aligned. Ann mistakenly added the 4 to the 5 as the first step of her computation. In the last step, she skipped columns and added the whole number 8 to 2 before completing the addition.

In Figure 9.42b the child started by bringing down the 3, then continued the subtraction. In Figure 9.42c, the decimal part, then the whole number part was added. Both subsums were recorded independently. Although mistakes like these are sometimes careless ones, they can stem from specific disabilities, particularly those identified at the beginning of this chapter. Children forget what to do, find it difficult to relate meaningfully to numbers (and then make all kinds of errors), or have problems sorting out all the numbers within the computation. Ideas for how to deal with problems such as these, in relation to decimal addition and subtraction, are outlined on the following pages.

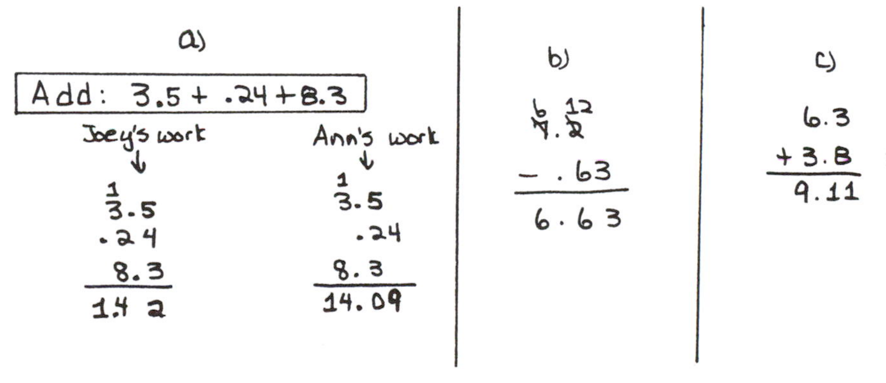

FIGURE 9.42

SUGGESTED SEQUENCE OF ACTIVITIES

1. **Use base-10 blocks** (or graph-paper pieces) to help children understand when decimals need to be aligned. Have students use blocks to picture written problems, then physically move the materials to carry out the indicated operation. At each step, the student or teacher should record what is being done

in the problem itself. This step is often essential for students with learning disabilities who do not readily transfer concepts based on concrete aids to the written task. Doing this now will make it easier, at a later stage, for students to check their work with or without blocks.

2. **Use auditory cuing.** Encourage the students themselves to verbalize what they are doing. If necessary, review the first "big idea" of addition (subtraction) of decimals: add (subtract) like units (see Figure 9.43). Help the students recognize that doing so helps align decimal points.

   NOTE: *If the students have abstract-reasoning difficulties, use the idea of auditory cuing first until they feel comfortable with a procedure they can follow. Then help them recognize that the procedure makes sense by using the idea in Activity 1.*

3. **Line them up.** If the students have visual perception difficulties, encourage them to do the following:

   • Add extra zeros to right-justified problems like that of Figure 9.42a (Ann's) and Figure 9.42b. Use shading as in Figure 9.9 to illustrate, for example, that 3.5 = 3.50 (i.e., adding the 0 does not change the value of the decimal).

   • Use a highlighter, pen, or pencil to mark vertically all digits in a column before adding or subtracting.

   • Use square centimeter paper and write one digit per space. Show the students how to place decimal points on a line.

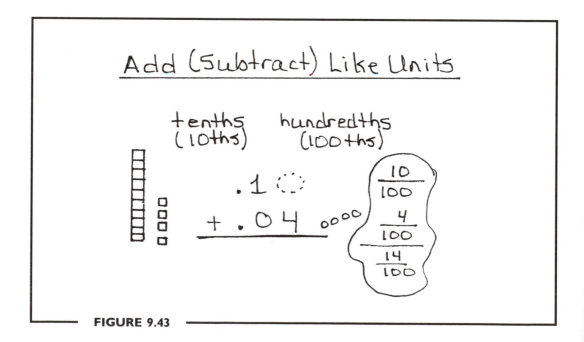

FIGURE 9.43

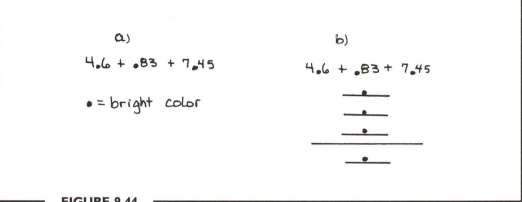

FIGURE 9.44

- Turn lined paper 90° and use the lines as a vertical guide to column alignment.

- Make the decimal point a bright color, as in Figure 9.44a. This helps the students notice it when they recopy the problems to compute. For special cases, color highlight the decimal point for the students and, during early work, also align the points in vertical form as shown in Figure 9.44b. Children with spatial or figure-ground deficits may require such additional assistance until they have learned to deal with the decimal point.

NOTE: *If children are strong tactual learners, it helps if they are allowed to finger trace all numbers in a column (all like units) before adding or subtracting.*

Multiplying decimals

Students who have mastered written whole number multiplication have a good start toward learning to multiply with decimals. The focus now is on learning to place the decimal point in the product. For many students with learning disabilities this can be difficult. One of the most common errors made by students, including those with specific disabilities, is illustrated in Figure 9.45. Although the problem may stem from confusion over the familiar procedure for addition and subtraction, other reasons, including those linked to the preceding disabilities, also may contribute to mistakes in this area. Assuming that skills for multiplying

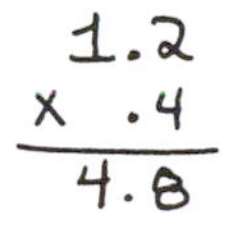

$$
\begin{array}{r}
1.2 \\
\times\ .4 \\
\hline
4.8
\end{array}
$$

FIGURE 9.45

whole numbers are strong, the following suggestions have proven effective for helping students avoid decimal multiplication errors. They also have been useful for correcting erroneous practices.

SUGGESTED SEQUENCE OF ACTIVITIES

Prerequisite Skills: The most critical prerequisite for decimal multiplication is the student's ability to handle whole number multiplication. Another prerequisite—one that is often overlooked—is the ability to locate and count the digits of a given number. Students may have trouble interpreting and following instructions because of difficulty related to understanding and applying the meaning of *number* and *digit.* Keep pages like that in Figure 9.46 on hand and fill in the first blank before giving it to students. The color cuing and verbal patterning help focus students properly so they can differentiate between the meaning of *number* and *digit.*

Later, when the students recognize the distinction, they can independently copy given numbers into the circles before rewriting the digits. In exercises patterned after Figure 9.46b, numbers are given for which students indicate the number of digits involved before writing them in the spaces provided.

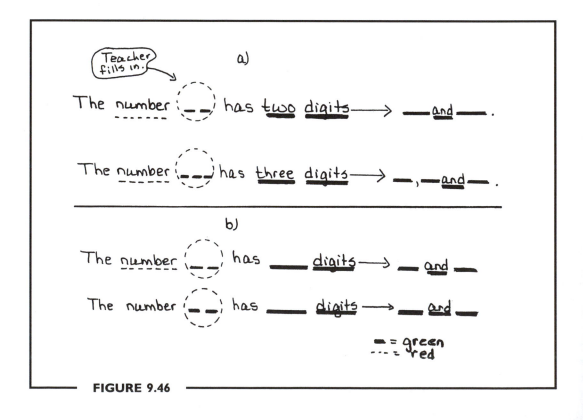

FIGURE 9.46

1. **Find and chart.** Students with sequencing or memory problems and/or abstract-reasoning deficits may benefit from the approaches that follow. Make a chart of all completed problems. (See Activity 2, *Study the chart.*)

   - *Use fractions.* If students can multiply fractions well and have no difficulty changing from decimal to fraction form (and vice versa), have them solve decimal multiplications as illustrated in Figure 9.47. Choose problems that can be readily calculated mentally (though the student is required to change to fractions, compute, and rewrite as directed).

     NOTE: *Encourage students to think ahead about the answer. ("Where will the decimal point go?") Some children may be helped if asked to write down their "think ahead" answer.*

   - *Use area.* If students have studied area, this topic can be used to help with decimal products. Figure 9.48 illustrates, for example, how .1 × .1 = .01 (1 of the 100 squares) and .6 × .2 = .12 (12 of the 100 squares).

   - *Estimate.* (Prerequisite: Understanding the language involved: ".5 times [a number]" means the same thing as "$\frac{1}{2}$ of [a number].") Present problems like those of Figure 9.49a, where .5 (one-half) and .9 (almost 1) are used as factors. (Notice that the product is complete except for placing the decimal point.) Help students estimate placing the point correctly in the product. Suggestions for how to do so are illustrated in Figure 9.49b.

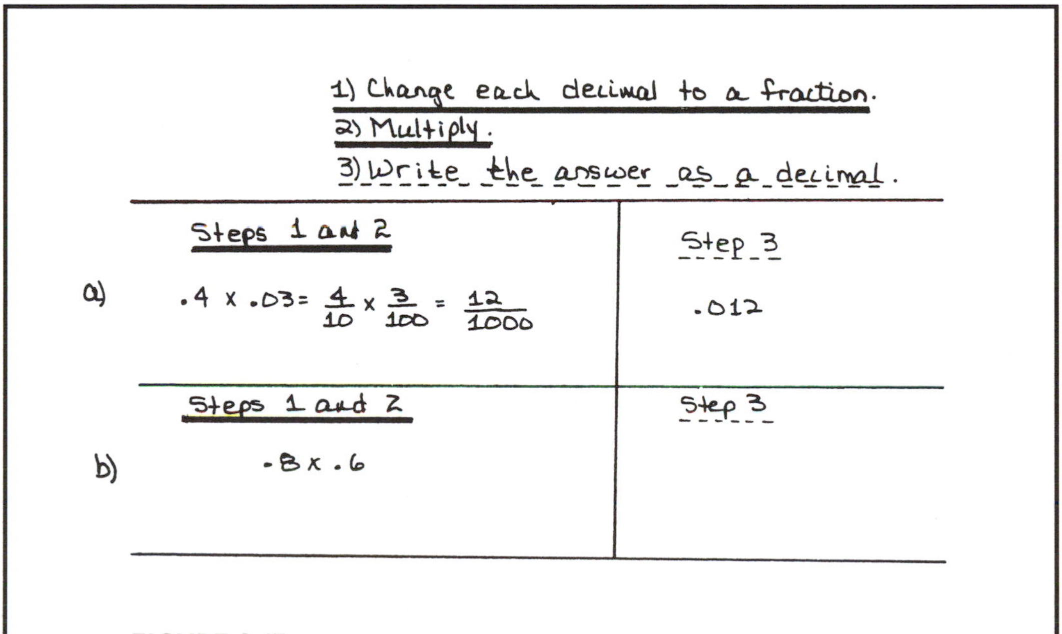

1) Change each decimal to a fraction.
2) Multiply.
3) Write the answer as a decimal.

Steps 1 and 2	Step 3
a) $.4 \times .03 = \frac{4}{10} \times \frac{3}{100} = \frac{12}{1000}$	.012
Steps 1 and 2	Step 3
b) $.8 \times .6$	

FIGURE 9.47

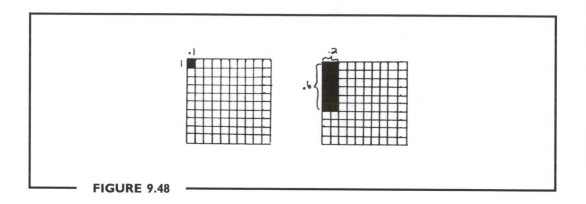

FIGURE 9.48

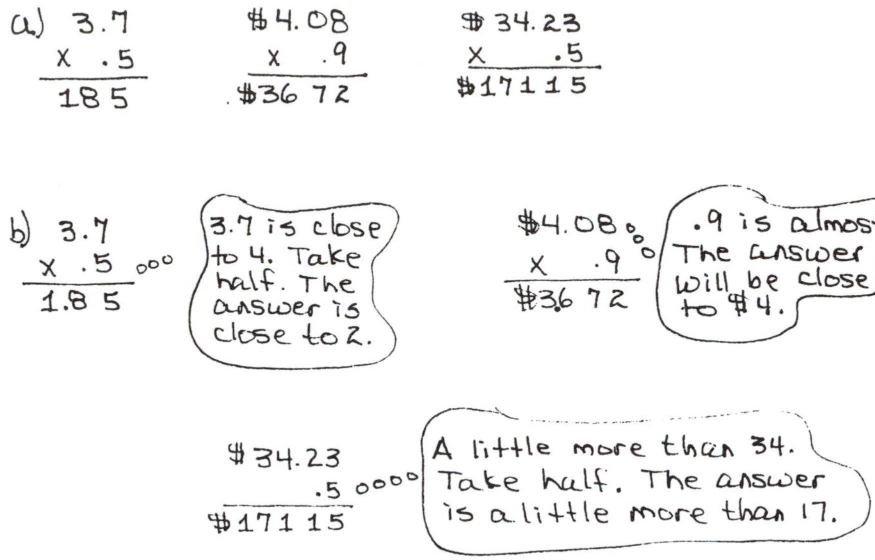

a) 3.7 $4.08 $ 34.23
   X .5   X .9   X   .5
  ────   ──────   ────────
  18 5   .$36 72 $171 15

b) 3.7   3.7 is close
   X .5 ₀₀₀   to 4. Take
  ──────   half. The
   1.8 5   answer is
                         close to 2.

                          $4.08 ₀₀   .9 is almost 1.
                             X .9 ₀   The answer
                          ──────────   will be close
                          $36 72   to $4.

              $ 34.23   A little more than 34.
                  .5 0000   Take half. The answer
              ──────────   is a little more than 17.
              $171 15

FIGURE 9.49

- *Use a calculator.* A final alternative for students who can read a calculator accurately is to allow them to use a calculator to obtain decimal products for given problems.

2. **Study the chart.** (Prerequisite: Ability to readily associate numbers [number parts] with the words *problem, digit,* and *product.*) When decimal products are determined and charted using one of the approaches outlined in Activity 1, help students study the chart and note the recurring pattern (see Figure 9.50a). Color coding as in Figure 9.50b (same colors as in Activity 1a) helps the students with self-discovery, a skill that frequently is difficult to develop. Leading questions also help: "Two decimal digits in the problem (circle the problem part). How many are in the product?"

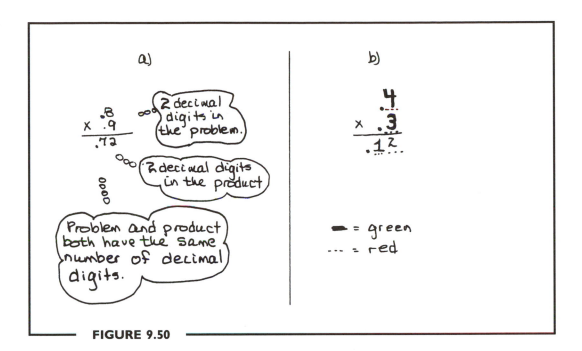

FIGURE 9.50

3. **Carry through.** Assign problems like that of Figure 9.51, using either a horizontal or a vertical format. The color scheme, the same as that used earlier, outlines the sequence to be followed. The green box and digits cue the first step: "Multiply given digits." Red indicates the last step: "Count digits and place the decimal point."

4. **The one-step.** To reinforce the pattern for decimal point placement in products, gradually eliminate colors and present problems like those of Figure 9.52. The students complete just the one last step of each problem: that of placing the decimal point in the product.

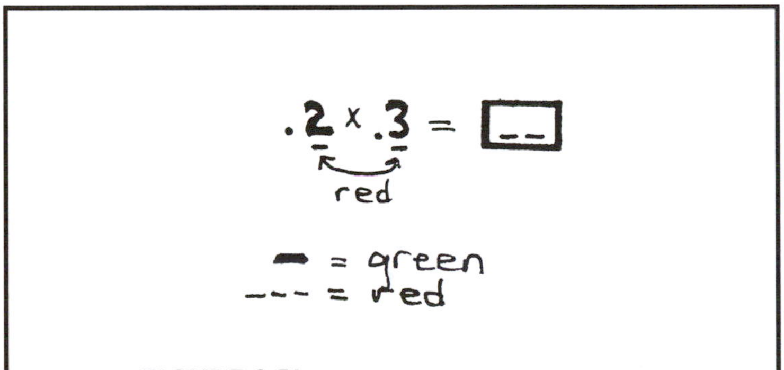

$$.2 \times .3 = \boxed{\,\_\_\,}$$

red

━ = green
--- = red

FIGURE 9.51

NOTE 1: The red digits are purposely placed in the center of the green box to force thinking when placing extra zeros.

NOTE 2: Keep the products simple so they can be computed mentally.

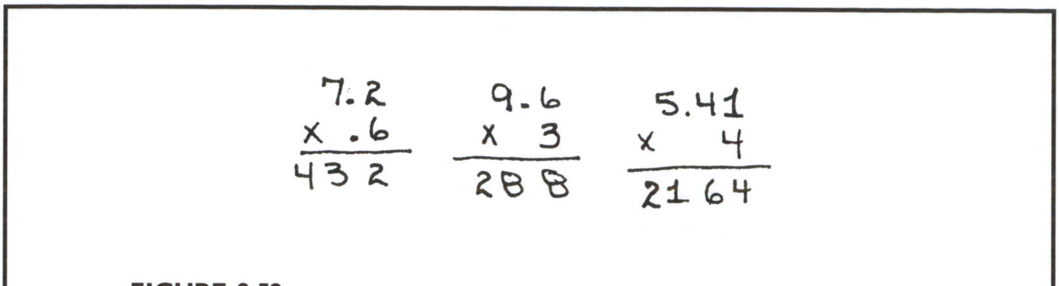

$$
\begin{array}{r}
7.2 \\
\times .6 \\
\hline
432
\end{array}
\qquad
\begin{array}{r}
9.6 \\
\times 3 \\
\hline
288
\end{array}
\qquad
\begin{array}{r}
5.41 \\
\times 4 \\
\hline
2164
\end{array}
$$

FIGURE 9.52

5. **Different from +, −:** To reinforce the decimal multiplication procedure, present exercises like those of Figure 9.53. Pages like that shown can be prepared in advance and kept on file. The teacher (and later the students themselves) fills in addition, subtraction, and multiplication problems

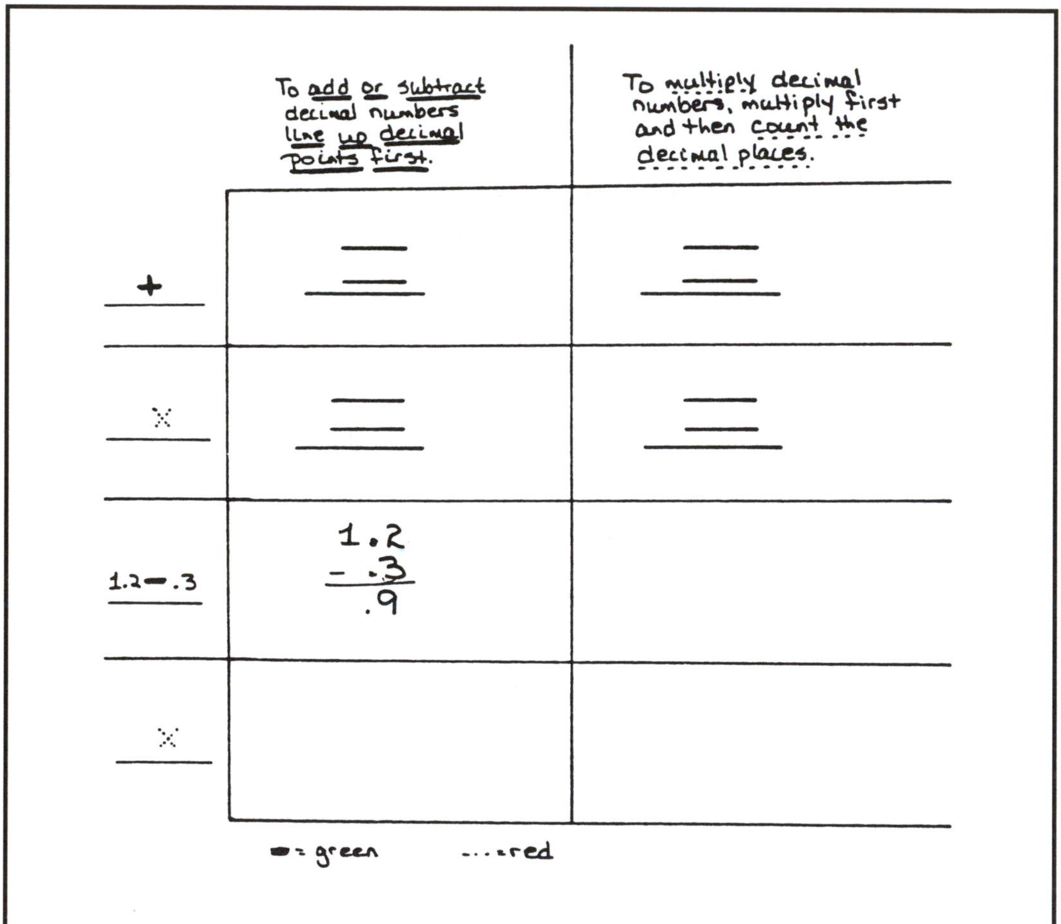

	To add or subtract decimal numbers line up decimal points first.	To multiply decimal numbers, multiply first and then count the decimal places.
+		
×		
1.2 − .3	$\begin{array}{r} 1.2 \\ - .3 \\ \hline .9 \end{array}$	
×		

●= green   ...red

FIGURE 9.53

NOTE: Problems along the left edge of the paper are purposely written in horizontal form. This forces the students, when recopying into vertical form, to think whether it is necessary to align decimal points to carry out the computation. For students who have visual motor or other perceptual deficits that make the transfer from horizontal to vertical form difficult, provide lines as in the first two problems to help with alignment.

involving decimals down the left edge of the sheet. The children recopy in the appropriate column. The two-column arrangement highlights, procedurally, the basic distinction between addition/subtraction and multiplication. The column headings serve as backup in case the students forget or confuse the sequence for adding, subtracting, and multiplying. When the work is checked, get the students themselves to read or verbalize independently the procedures summarized in the column headings.

Dividing decimals

Even students with learning disabilities who are confident with the long-division process may have special problems with division involving decimals. Figure 9.54 illustrates a typical error. This student automatically placed the decimal point in the quotient above that in the dividend, just as he or she would do when dividing money amounts by whole number divisors. If written computation for decimal division is included as a mathematics learning goal for a child with learning disabilities, the suggestions that follow may be helpful. Note that, as with whole numbers, work has been confined to single-digit divisors, with the expectation that calculators would be used for more complex work beyond this.

$$\begin{array}{r} 5.3 \\ .3\overline{)15.9} \end{array} \qquad \begin{array}{r} 1.21 \\ .04\overline{)4.84} \end{array}$$

FIGURE 9.54

SUGGESTED SEQUENCE OF ACTIVITIES

1. **Color highlight.** School textbooks typically begin decimal division with easy problems first: those with counting numbers as divisors. Since the need to divide money amounts is a common occurrence in daily life, problems like that illustrated in Figure 9.55 often are posed. Some textbooks may include problems like that of Figure 9.56. In either case, cuing can be used as illustrated in Figure 9.57 to help students focus on the decimal placement in the quotient of an "easy" problem: right above that of the dividend.

2. **"Hard" problems: decimal divisors.** Rather than including these types of problems in a child's instructional program, allow students to estimate or to use a calculator. If paper-and-pencil calculation with decimal divisors is included as a learning objective, the child's interests and learning

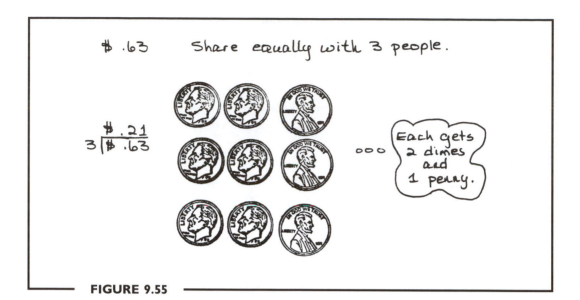

FIGURE 9.55

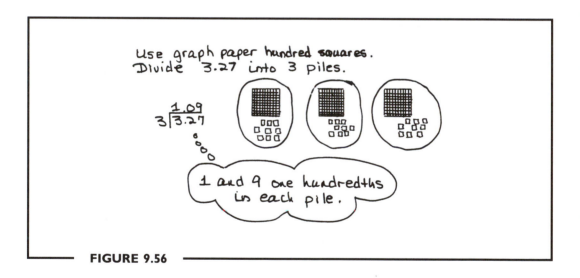

FIGURE 9.56

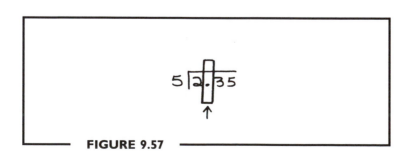

FIGURE 9.57

strengths will dictate which of the following approaches might be used to introduce problems with decimal divisors.

- *Use fractions.* If the students are skillful with fractions, they can find answers to given decimal division problems by (a) rewriting as a fraction and dividing; (b) writing the answer as a mixed number; and (c) rewriting, finally, as a decimal. Figure 9.58 illustrates the format of a color-coded worksheet that can be used to help students with memory, sequencing, and perceptual or spatial organization deficits.

- *Use a calculator.* (Prerequisites: The students can carry out decimal divisions for problems having whole number divisors, and they can use a calculator accurately.) Allow students to use a calculator to find answers to problem sets like that of Figure 9.59. They will find that each pair of problems has the same answer. "To divide hard problems with decimal divisors, change them to easy problems like those shown."

- *Follow-Up 1: Should I move it?* To change a hard problem into an easy one, the student must move the decimal point in the divisor to make it a counting number. Of course, the decimal point in the dividend must be shifted similarly, as illustrated in Figure 9.60a.

    What shifting the decimal point really means is illustrated in Figure 9.60b. Review whole number operations to help students understand that multiplying both divisor and dividend by the same number does not change the answer. Similarly, a quick calculator check may be a simpler way of verifying that multiplying both divisor

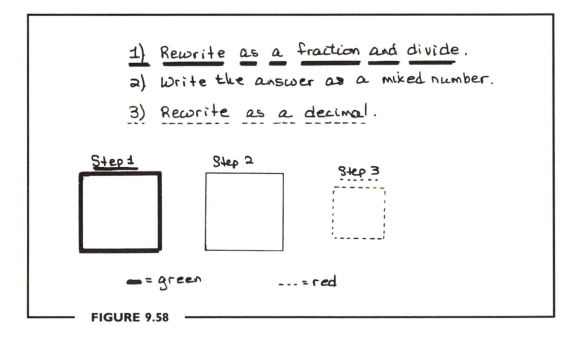

FIGURE 9.58

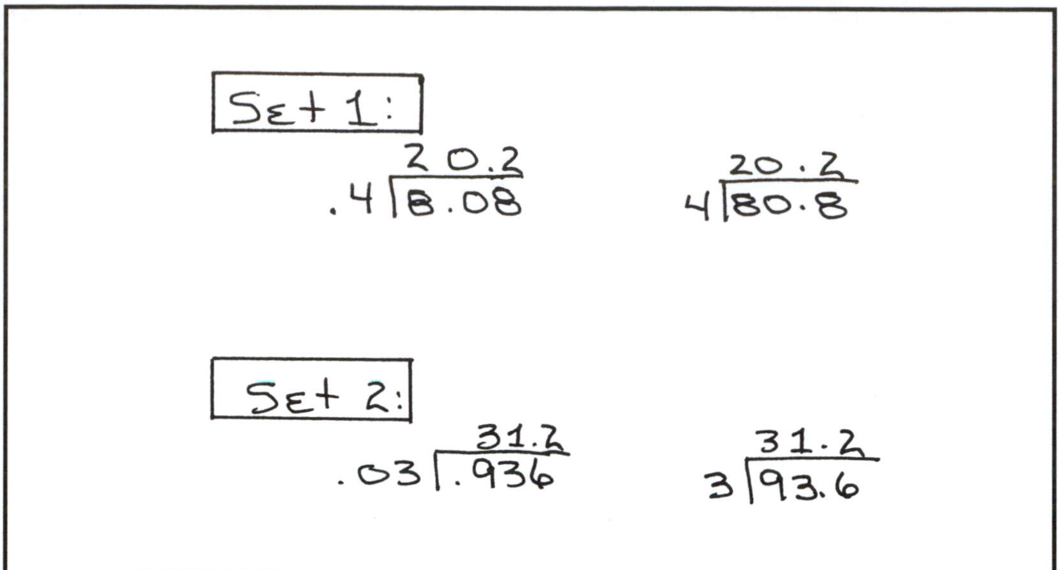

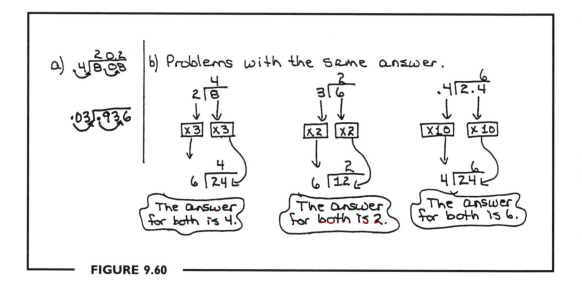

FIGURE 9.59

FIGURE 9.60

and dividend by the same decimal number yields a problem with the same answer.

An important first step when dividing with decimals is to recognize whether a decimal shift is needed. To focus on this, present a mixture of problems—some with decimal divisors, others with counting numbers as divisors. Have students circle any problem for which the decimal point should be moved to turn it into an easy problem. Save student papers for use in the following activity, to be carried out during a subsequent session.

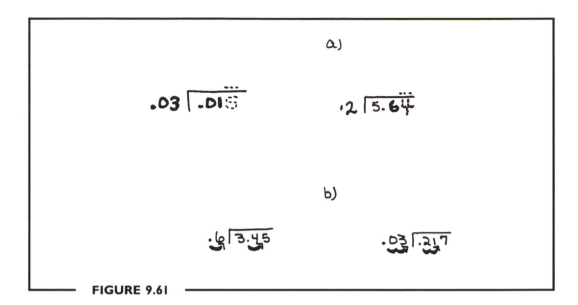

FIGURE 9.61

- *Follow-Up 2: Then do it.* (Use papers from the preceding activity.) Re-examine the above problem set. Many students can be helped using ideas from Figure 9.60 to realize that, in moving the decimal point to get a counting number as divisor, one really multiplies *both* divisor and dividend by 10 or by 100 (or by some power of 10). Procedurally, one must orally emphasize: "What you do to the divisor, you do to the dividend, too."

Color-coded exercises using the format of Figure 9.61a or 9.61b emphasize the movement of the decimal point within given problems. In Figure 9.61a, color highlighting is used to help the student focus on the number of digits involved in the decimal point shift. In Figure 9.61b, the green coding emphasizes the need to move the decimal point first. Last of all, students divide.

NOTE: *Omit decimal division problems like 24 ÷ .3, where extra zeros must be added in the dividend, until students are comfortable carrying out other decimal divisions.*

REFERENCES

National Council of Teachers of Mathematics. (1989). *Curriculum and evaluation standards for school mathematics.* Reston, VA: Author.

National Council of Teachers of Mathematics. (1991). *Developing number sense: Addenda series, grades 5–8.* Reston, VA: Author.

National Council of Teachers of Mathematics. (1993). *Number sense and operations: Addenda series, grades K–6.* Reston, VA: Author.

CHAPTER 10

Hard-to-Learn, Upper-Grade Topics

THIS CHAPTER DEALS WITH some of the topics generally developed in the upper-elementary and junior high grades. The following areas are emphasized.

- Ratio

- Proportions

- Percents

- Integers

- Exponents

Each of these topics involves the transfer of lower-level concepts to new contexts. For students with learning disabilities this transition is not easily made. Many students can, for example, master simpler concepts or computations related to ratio, proportion, and percent; they may be able to solve a proportion problem by filling in a missing numerator or denominator but be unable to set up the correct proportion in a given situation. Students may be able to describe the shaded part of a 10×10 grid using percents yet be unable to determine the percent for a base other than 100. They may even be able to carry out some or all of these rubrics yet have little sense of what they are doing or how to apply that learning in practical situations.

In some instances, students may not have mastered prerequisite concepts and procedures, hence they cannot make important associations. At other times, nonverbal learning disabilities or difficulties with sequencing, abstract reasoning, or visual or auditory memory may interfere with retrieval and application of previously learned material.

As integers, exponents, and rules governing the order of operations are introduced, other difficulties emerge. Visual perception problems, for example, are at the root of many errors in this area. The exponent is easily misperceived; some students even interpret a number written in exponential form as a whole number (see Figure 10.1). Many students with abstract-reasoning or receptive and/or expressive language deficits have difficulty with the new "language" they encoun-

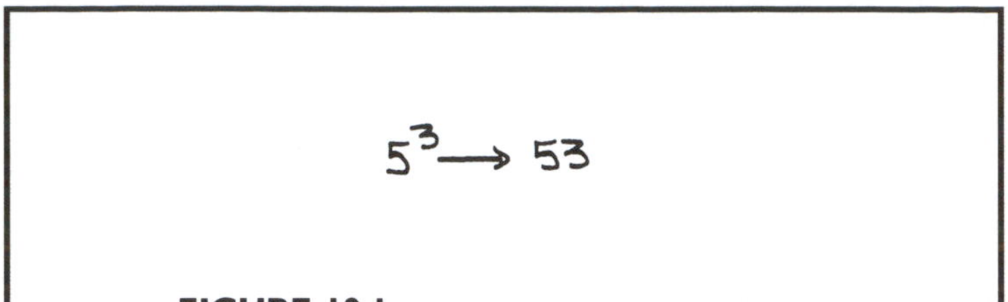

$$5^3 \longrightarrow 53$$

FIGURE 10.1

ter (see Figure 10.2). Success with integers requires good visual memory and discrimination as well as memory sequencing skills. A strong language base also helps. Difficulties like those identified in the preceding paragraph, as well as the fact that the context is new, leave many students with learning disabilities unsuccessful with mental or paper-and-pencil computations.

An effort has been made to deal with several of the hard-to-learn, upper-grade topics from the point of view of how learning disabilities affect understanding, retention, and application. In some instances, the suggested sequence differs from that commonly used. Generally, however, the emphasis is on directly relating new material, visually and aurally, to previously learned concepts and skills. The approaches outlined are among those that have proven effective in our own work with students with learning disabilities.

$$5^3 \longrightarrow \text{Five to the third power}$$

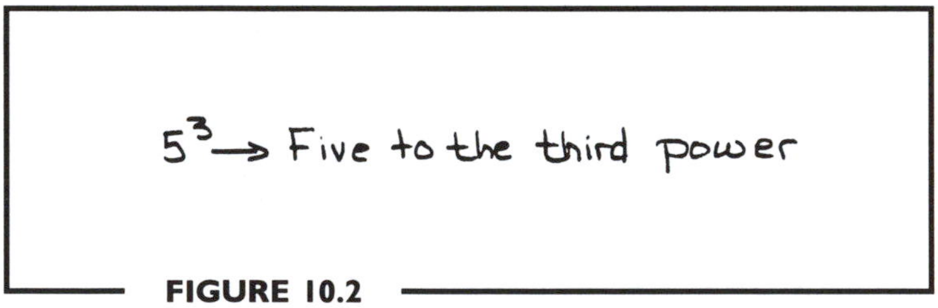

FIGURE 10.2

RATIO

Problem Area: Difficulty with the language and symbolism of ratio.

Typical Disabilities Affecting Progress: Difficulty with receptive and expressive language, abstract reasoning, closure, and visual perception.

Background: Ratio involves comparing the number of one group to that of another. Typically, the comparison is between dissimilar units: balls to bats, or cups to spoons, as in Figure 10.3a. However, ratio situations also can involve similar units, like that in Figure 10.3b (balls to balls).

Although a ratio is not a fraction, the fraction form often is used to represent a ratio (see Figure 10.4). Conceptually, this can be very confusing to students who are used to thinking of $\frac{7}{4}$ in the manner illustrated in Figure 10.5. When introduced to ratios, students, therefore, must learn to relate a familiar symbol in a new con-

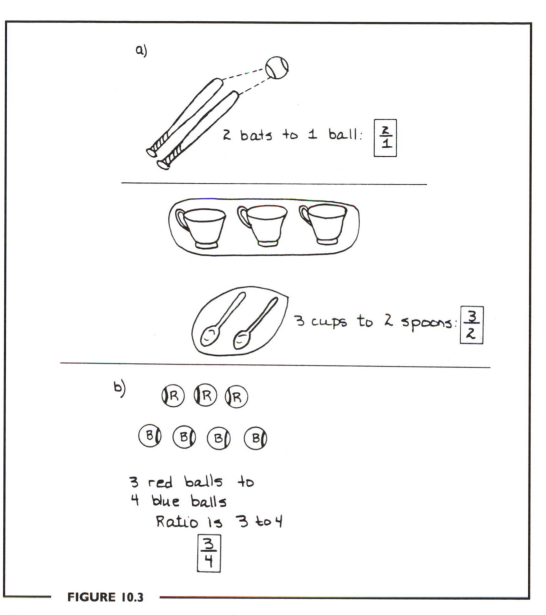

FIGURE 10.3

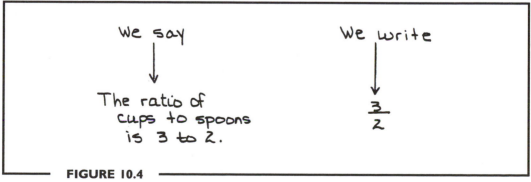

FIGURE 10.4

7/4 means
seven fourths
one and three fourths
seven divided by four

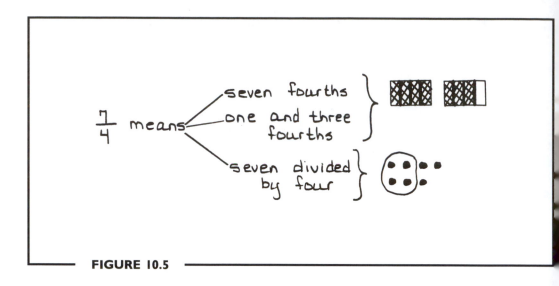

FIGURE 10.5

text and then give that symbol a different interpretation. What used to be thought of as a fraction is now visually the same but means something different. The language of ratio is abstract, and that adds to the difficulty. The ratio $\frac{7}{4}$ is often read "7 to 4." This statement itself is confusing. A much more meaningful, but longer statement would be: "Think: for every 7 (cups of flour) we need 4 (cups of milk)." The second type of expression makes the necessary language association far easier.

Setting up a ratio from a simple one-step problem like that of Figure 10.6 generally is easy for students. The word *ratio* triggers the general idea, and the problem presents the number in the correct order for writing the ratio. The difficulty arises when the numbers are not presented in the correct order and when the word *ratio* is not used. Students also have trouble finding equal ratios. (This problem will be discussed in the section on Proportion.) The suggestions that follow focus on the needs of students with learning disabilities and on ways to supplement standard approaches for introducing ratio to meet those needs.

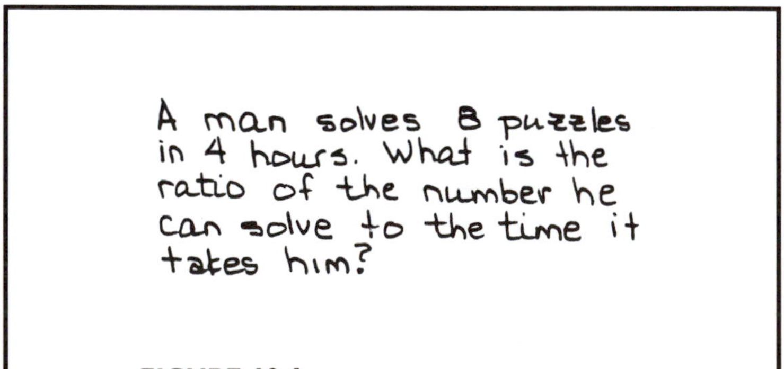

A man solves 8 puzzles in 4 hours. What is the ratio of the number he can solve to the time it takes him?

FIGURE 10.6

SUGGESTED SEQUENCE OF ACTIVITIES

1. **Focus.** Figure 10.6 presents a typical introductory ratio problem. When asked to find the ratio, students commonly say "2." To help children focus on the notion of comparing one thing to another, have them underline related parts of the problem using the same color. For example, underline in green everything associated with the first number, and underline everything dealing with the second number in red. Figure 10.7 illustrates this technique.

   NOTE: *Initially, it might be best for the teacher to underline the related parts ahead of time. A follow-up discussion should help students understand the thought process.*

2. **Match.** It often is necessary to practice determining the proper ratios for given situations. Even if students understand that a ratio is written in the form of a fraction, deciding where to place the numbers may be difficult. A combination card game and puzzle is fun and helpful at this point. Use large index cards (8″ × 12″) and make puzzle shapes as in Figure 10.8. On the left side of each puzzle piece write a problem, on the right fill in the ratio. Cut the puzzle pieces apart on the dotted lines. The problem side of

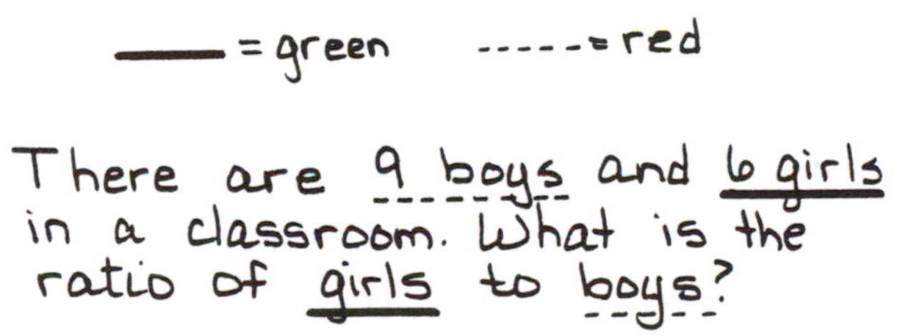

FIGURE 10.7

FIGURE 10.8

the card is placed in a central draw pile, and each player is dealt five ratio cards. The remaining ratio cards are placed face down in a second pile.

The first player turns over a problem card. If the player already has the correct ratio on a card, a match is made and placed on the board. If not, the player calls for the ratio card. If another player has the requested card, he or she gives it to the caller. Otherwise, the caller draws one ratio card from the pile. When a match is made, the caller puts the pair of cards down on the board. Should an incorrect ratio be requested (the puzzles act as a check), the caller keeps that ratio card and draws another from the pile. The winner is the first person to run out of cards.

3. **Write it out.** Encourage children to write the words as well as the numbers when setting up a ratio. Seeing and saying the words help give the numbers more meaning (see Figure 10.9).

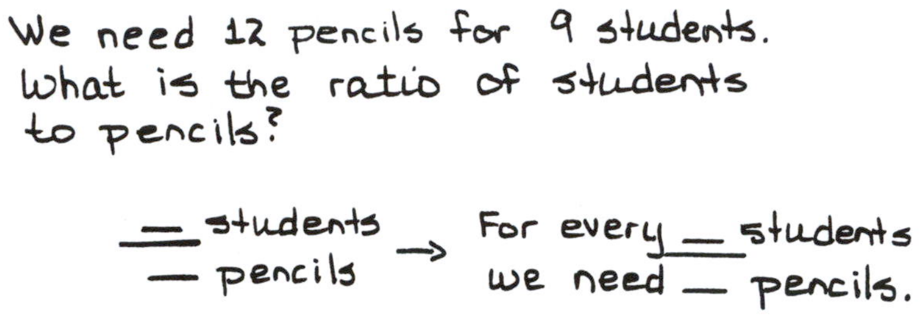

We need 12 pencils for 9 students. What is the ratio of students to pencils?

$$\frac{\underline{} \text{ students}}{\underline{} \text{ pencils}} \rightarrow \text{For every } \underline{} \text{ students we need } \underline{} \text{ pencils.}$$

FIGURE 10.9

NOTE: *At this point, it is unnecessary to simplify (reduce) the ratio. The primary goal is to understand and set up a ratio.*

4. **Three ways.** To help students recognize and use the three ways of writing a ratio, post a chart like that shown in Figure 10.10 for students to

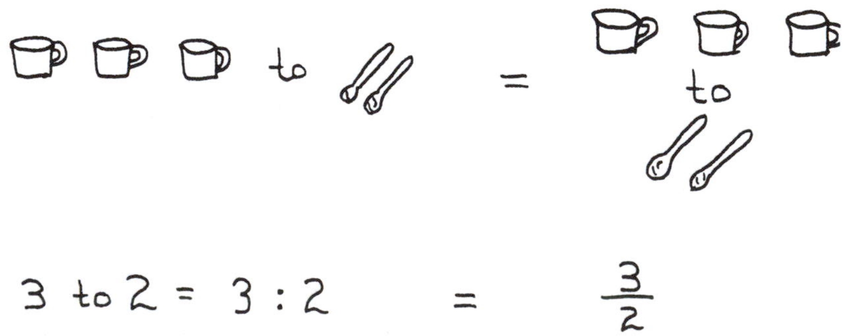

$$3 \text{ to } 2 = 3 : 2 \quad = \quad \frac{3}{2}$$

FIGURE 10.10

refer to. The chart is especially helpful to children with language or visual memory difficulties.

5. **Practice.** Using manipulatives and real-life materials, encourage children to develop their own ratios based on their experience. For example, young children enjoy building; help them see the relationship between the concept of ratio (even if the word is not used) and the materials they are using to build. When they are older, the word *ratio* can be introduced and related back to their enjoyment of building.

6. **Color code.** Similarity involves ratio; thus, it is often helpful to use colors to focus attention. Keep a set of pages, as in Figure 10.11, with color coding as shown. To aid the transition to non–color-coded presentations, have students color code the figures to match statements. In written work, it may help at first to color code statements to match the figures. For children who have trouble processing what they read, this approach helps break the steps down to a manageable size. The focus here, of course, is on recognizing ratios in an applied setting rather than on setting up or solving proportions.

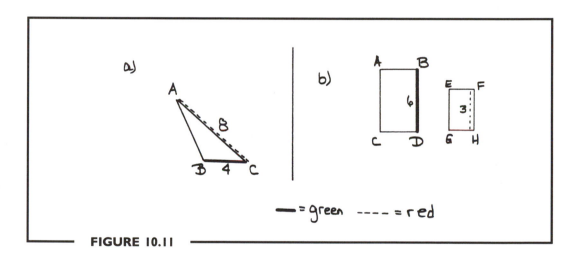

FIGURE 10.11

PROPORTIONS

Problem Area: Difficulty setting up proportions for given situations.

Typical Disabilities Affecting Progress: Difficulty with receptive language, sequencing, abstract reasoning, and closure.

Background: Once they have learned about equivalent fractions and solving equations, most students with learning disabilities have little difficulty solving proportions that already have been set up. (Figure 10.12 illustrates typical approaches students might use.)

Problems arise, however, when students must independently determine the proportion that applies to a given situation. Consider the example in Figure 10.13. The wording in this problem does not allow the use of key words to set it up. Stu-

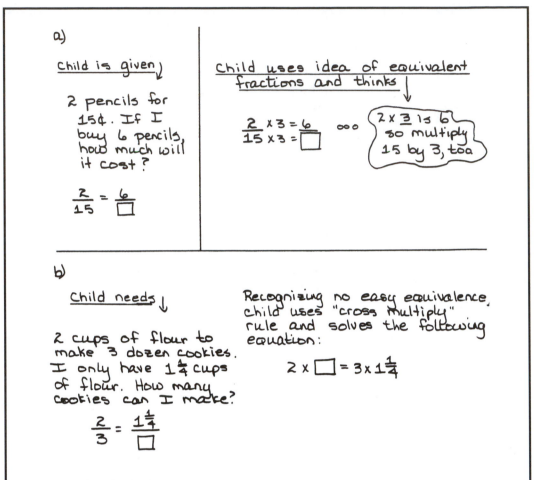

a)

Child is given

2 pencils for 15¢. If I buy 6 pencils, how much will it cost?

$$\frac{2}{15} = \frac{6}{\Box}$$

Child uses idea of equivalent fractions and thinks

$$\frac{2 \times 3 = 6}{15 \times 3 = \Box}$$ ∘∘∘

2 × 3 is 6 so multiply 15 by 3, too

b)

Child needs

2 cups of flour to make 3 dozen cookies. I only have 1¼ cups of flour. How many cookies can I make?

$$\frac{2}{3} = \frac{1\frac{1}{4}}{\Box}$$

Recognizing no easy equivalence, child uses "cross multiply" rule and solves the following equation:

$$2 \times \Box = 3 \times 1\frac{1}{4}$$

FIGURE 10.12

A recipe for 3 dozen cookies uses 2 cups of flour. How many cookies can you make if you only have 1¼ cups of flour?

FIGURE 10.13

dents must fully understand the concepts of ratio and proportion. Many, including those with the above-described learning disabilities, *are* able to set up simple ratios and solve proportions. They just need help getting started so that they:

- recognize the need for a proportion in a given situation and
- can set up the correct proportion.

Many of these same students need help in developing a better sense of proportions so that they can judge whether results are reasonable. The suggestions that follow may prove helpful in this regard.

SUGGESTED SEQUENCE OF ACTIVITIES

Help Students with Computation

1. **Construct a chart.** Drawing a chart, like that in Figure 10.14, can help students organize their thinking so that they set up the proportion properly. The sample chart is based on the following problem: "On the map 1 cm equals 80 km. If the distance from Santa Barbara to Los Angeles is about 144 km, how far away are the two cities on the map?" The chart helps students recognize and compare like terms of the written problem.

2. **Map out an alternative.** It often is effective to present alternate methods to help students solve problems. For example, although proportions can be used to compare prices at a grocery store, it is easier for many students to use unit pricing, as in Figure 10.15. Many stores display unit pricing labels on the shelves, so children need to learn what the labels mean and how to use them to buy wisely.

Help Students Develop Number Sense

1. **Establish benchmarks.** As a first step, help children sort ratios as "close to 0", "close to $\frac{1}{2}$," and "close to 1." For example, in $\frac{80}{144}$ (see Figure 10.14) the numerator is about half the denominator, so this ratio is close to $\frac{1}{2}$. If a numerator is very small in comparison, as in $\frac{2}{40}$, the ratio is close to 0. Numerators that are comparatively large in relation to the denominator, as in $\frac{87}{90}$, characterize a ratio that is close to 1.

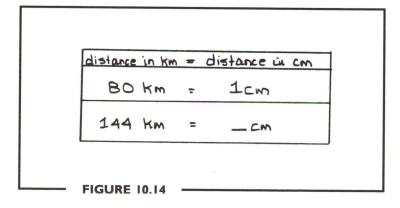

FIGURE 10.14

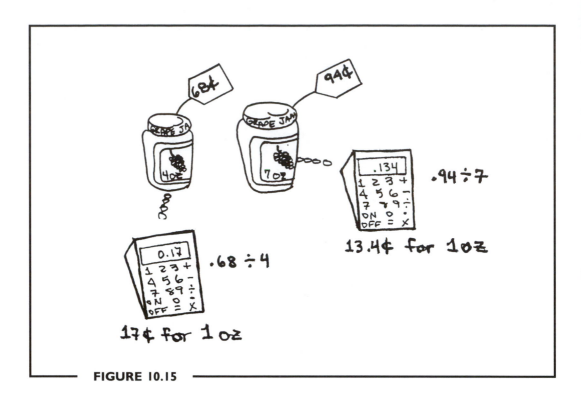

FIGURE 10.15

2. **Does my answer make sense?** Encourage students to plug computed elements of a proportion back into the original problem to check whether the result makes sense. To develop this skill, present computed elements—some correct and some way off. Students plug the number back into the problem and, using ideas from Activity 1, examine whether both ratios in the proportion are similar. $\frac{88}{144} \sim \frac{1}{20}$, for example, makes no sense. The first ratio is a little more than $\frac{1}{2}$. The second is closer to 0.

PERCENTS

Number Sense for Percents

Problem Area: Difficulty estimating in practical situations that involve percents.

Typical Disabilities Affecting Progress: Difficulty with abstract reasoning, receptive and expressive language, short-term and sequential memory, and visual perception.

Background: An instructional focus on estimation and mental computation in relation to percent situations is receiving renewed interest in school mathematics. In most day-to-day situations, people make quick estimates. When exact answers are required they typically work out simple percent problems in their heads and use a calculator for more difficult ones. They rarely make paper-and-pencil calculations.

Needed insights, experiences, and skills take time to develop. Given this time, sound teacher modeling and systematic instruction based on ideas like those that follow will enable many students with learning disabilities to develop adequate estimation skills to handle percents successfully. Actually, many of these students prefer estimation as an alternative to difficult, cumbersome, and easily forgotten rules associated with paper-and-pencil procedures.

SUGGESTED SEQUENCE OF ACTIVITIES

1. **"Closer to."** In early work with percents, help students develop intuitions about the relative size of percents. For example, 3%, 12%, and 21% are each closer to 0% than to 50% or 100%. If necessary, have students close their eyes as they run a finger on a meter stick from 12 (for example) to the 0 end, and then from 12 to 100, to develop the notion of *close to*.

2. **Benchmark estimation**. When converting between fractions, decimals, and percents, certain "nice" numbers are good benchmarks or points of reference. For example, 1%, 50%, and 100% are good benchmarks, as is the fact that $\frac{1}{2}$ = 50%. Seven out of 15 is pretty close to 7 out of 14, which is about $\frac{1}{2}$ or 50%. Similarly, a fraction with a very small numerator as compared to the denominator, such as $\frac{2}{87}$, is about 1%, and a fraction with a numerator that is very close to the denominator, such as $\frac{49}{53}$, is very close to 100%.

   Parallel observations can be made in terms of decimals and percents. It is important to verbalize observations like these often in order to model appropriate thinking and a good attitude toward percent.

3. **What is likely?** Students with learning disabilities need opportunities to explore and discuss questions such as the following. (A hand calculator can be used in some instances, *after* the student has offered an opinion, to work out an exact answer in comparison to the initial response.)

   - Can we have 100% attendance at school today? 200%?
   - Can a price increase 40%? 100%? 300%?
   - Can a price decrease 50%? 200%?
   - What does it mean to have 10% unemployment? 10.5%?

4. **What is meant?** Discuss common occurrences of percents like: orange juice—100% pure; paper towels—20% more absorbent; mixed nuts—less than 50% peanuts; hamburger—at least 70% lean.

5. **Mentally take 1%, 10%, and 100% of a number.**

100% of \$3,518 = \$3,518	100% of \$423 = \$423.00
10% of \$3,518 = \$351.80	10% of \$423 = \$42.30
1% of \$3,518 = \$35.18	1% of \$423 = \$4.23

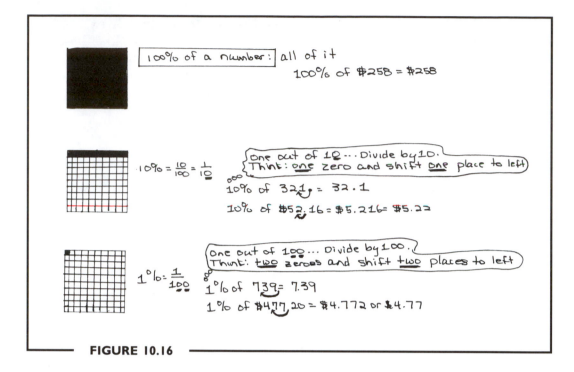

FIGURE 10.16

Using both place value cubes, as shown in Figure 10.16, and a calculator helps students notice the general pattern of shifting the decimal point one or two places to the left.

6. **Estimate using 1%, 10%, and 100% of a number**. Three examples of estimating using these "nice" percents are shown in Figure 10.17. Another nice number is 50%.

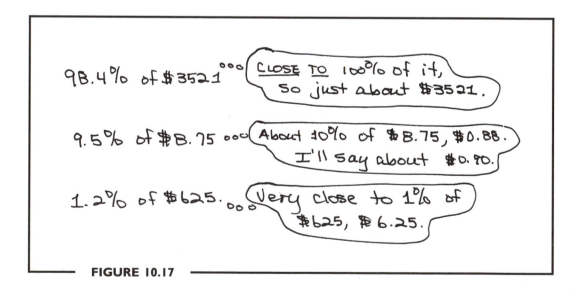

FIGURE 10.17

7. **Lots of ways.** Flexibility is important to estimation. No one way is right. Students enjoy hearing how their peers solved a problem differently and got different answers even though everyone got the "right answer."

- *Example:* 61% of 847 can be estimated by:

  a) breaking 61% apart:

  $$50\% \text{ of } 847 = \text{about } 425$$
  $$10\% \text{ of } 847 = \text{about } 85$$
  $$\underline{1\% \text{ of } 847 = \text{about } 9}$$
  $$61\% \text{ of } 847 \text{ is about } 500+$$

  b) approximating 61% as 60% and rounding 847:

  60% of 850 = 6(10% of 850) = 6(85), or 510

  c) rounding 61% and 847 to the closest nice percent:

  50% of 850 is about 425.

This type of situation also allows students to understand when using nice numbers works and when it does not work. As their estimation abilities improve, children should routinely be asked to decide whether the results of their estimates make sense with regard to either the computation or the situation. For example, 61% of 625 is not 200 (61% is close to 50%, so a more sensible estimate would be at least 300). Similarly, even though Step c in the problem above is accurate in terms of computation, using the result to buy food for a graduation party where 61% of the class will be attending might cause some problems.

Percent Equivalents

Problem Area: Changing percents to decimals or fractions.

Typical Disabilities Affecting Progress: Difficulty with sequencing and visual discrimination.

Background: Generally, when students are introduced to percents, they are shown a hundreds square with part of it shaded. Often the explanation is given that percent means "per one hundred" or "out of one hundred." These examples and explanations are understood rather easily by most students. Quite often, in fact, the basic concept of percent is less difficult for students with learning disabilities than some of the topics presented up to this point. The difficulty arises when students need to develop good number sense in relation to percent and then apply it to everyday situations. Students who have good number sense may be able to estimate to solve a problem, making cumbersome computations unnecessary. They also are more likely to judge whether statements or computations involving percent are reasonable. When using paper and pencil to solve problems involving percent, students usually need to express a percent either as a fraction or as a decimal. Changing whole-number percents to fractions typically is not very difficult for students. Most children readily recognize what to do and remember to put the number itself over 100. Similarly, two-digit whole-number percents are fairly easy to convert to decimals. However, single-digit percents are sometimes more difficult, and it is not uncommon for teachers to see the following: $6\% = .6$. Even harder is the conversion of percents to decimals or fractions, like that in Figure 10.18. When learning this latter skill, children must think through each step to the point of overlearning. The ideas that follow should help with this and other aspects of instruction related to finding percent equivalents.

SUGGESTED SEQUENCE OF ACTIVITIES

1. **Fractions first.** As noted in other parts of this book, decimals are often more meaningfully introduced when related to the familiar, less abstract fraction notation. When converting percents to decimals, it is often preferable first to change the percent to a fraction with the denominator 100. Seeing the two zeros in the denominator often instantly reminds students where to place the decimal point. This approach is particularly effective for helping students avoid the $6\% = .6$ error cited above. The underscoring technique shown in Figure 10.19 can be used to emphasize the fact that the correct decimal equivalent of a single-digit percent has two decimal places.

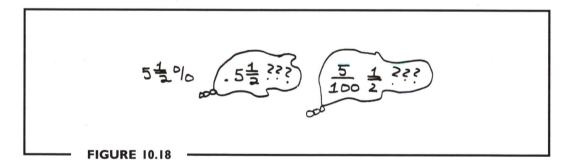

FIGURE 10.18

$$6\% = \frac{6}{100} = .06$$

FIGURE 10.19

$$5\tfrac{1}{2}\% = 5.5\% = \frac{5.5}{100} = \frac{55}{1000} = .055$$

FIGURE 10.20

2. **Make it easier.** Given a percent like $5\tfrac{1}{2}\%$, students can be instructed to change the $\tfrac{1}{2}$ to .5 right away. This step makes it easier to change the percent to a fraction. In Figure 10.20, 5.5% first is expressed as a fraction with a denominator of 100, then is changed, as necessary, to eliminate the decimal.

3. **Chart it.** Using charts, as in Figure 10.21, helps students who have trouble with memory sequencing. Such a chart provides structure. For many students who enter the fifth or sixth grade with an intuitive understanding of the relationship of percents to fractions and decimals, this structure is especially important as it helps them begin to realize how the conversions are derived.

4. **Make a book** (a practice activity for two or three players). Provide a deck of 51 cards—17 showing percents, the remainder giving the fraction or decimal equivalent of each percent. After each player has been dealt five cards, the rest of the deck is placed face down between the players. The object of the game is to make books of three cards: the percent and its fraction and decimal equivalent. If, at a player's turn, there is not a book in hand, the player takes top card from the discard pile or from the draw pile. The player discards one card and the next person has a turn. During a player's turn, all exposed books can be played. The winner is the one with the most books when one of the players runs out of cards.

Percent	=	Fraction (Denominator of 100)	=	Decimal	=	Reduced Fraction
50%	=	$\frac{50}{100}$	=	.50	=	$\frac{1}{2}$
8%	=	$\frac{8}{100}$	=	.08	=	$\frac{2}{25}$
$5\tfrac{1}{2}\% = 5.5\% =$		$\frac{5.5}{100} = \frac{55}{1000}$	=	.055	=	$\frac{11}{200}$

FIGURE 10.21

Percent Form of a Fraction

Problem Area: Difficulty changing fractions to percents.

Typical Disabilities Affecting Progress: Difficulty with memory, abstract reasoning, and closure.

Background: It is relatively easy to convert fractions to percents when the denominator is 100. The difficulty arises when the denominator is not 100. The general technique for handling situations like this is illustrated in Figure 10.22: cross-multiply and solve the equation for *x*. Most textbooks include problems of this type in the section on proportion. For students with good memory and abstract-reasoning skills, this approach is fine. In fact, for students who have closure difficulties it is sometimes simpler than alternate methods. However, for some students with learning disabilities the following sequence has proven more effective. The sequence (a) involves very small learning increments, (b) relates to the familiar process of finding equivalent fractions, and (c) makes adequate provision for overlearning.

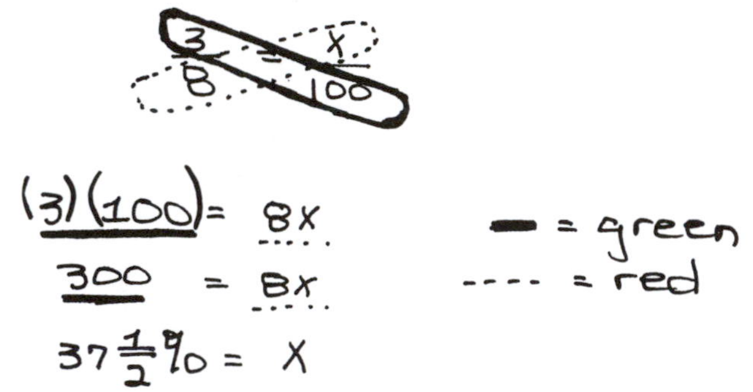

$$\frac{3}{8} = \frac{x}{100}$$

$$(3)(100) = 8x$$

$$300 = 8x$$

$$37\tfrac{1}{2}\% = x$$

—— = green

---- = red

FIGURE 10.22

SUGGESTED SEQUENCE OF ACTIVITIES

1. **Build prerequisites.** Be sure that the children can name and write fractions and their equivalents successfully. Then introduce the concept of percent in the usual manner.

2. **Easy things first.** Now help students write percents as fractions, in unreduced (unsimplified) form, and fractions with a denominator of 100 as percents.

3. **Review.** Be sure children can apply the idea of equivalent fractions to reducing given fractions to lowest terms.

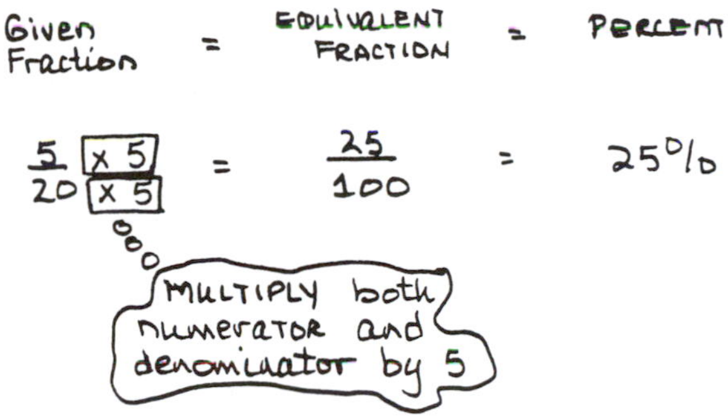

FIGURE 10.23

4. **Now reduce.** Students should now be able to write percents as fractions in reduced form.

5. **Use what you know.** Next, turn to writing fractions, with the denominator a factor of 100, as percents. Help students use the idea of equivalent fractions, as in Figure 10.23. First they locate an equivalent fraction having a denominator of 100, then they rewrite it as a percent.

6. **One last step.** Finally, have students write, as percents, fractions whose denominators are not factors of 100. As before, students first rewrite the fraction with a denominator of 100. To find this fraction, they must divide (see Figure 10.24a) to determine the factor for multiplying numerator and denominator (see Figure 10.24b). Then they can rewrite the fraction as a percent.

NOTE: *Students who have difficulty with both the proportion and the equivalent fraction approaches to writing fractions as percents should be allowed to use a calculator. (This alternative is viable only if the students have adequate visual perception skills or a large calculator is used.)*

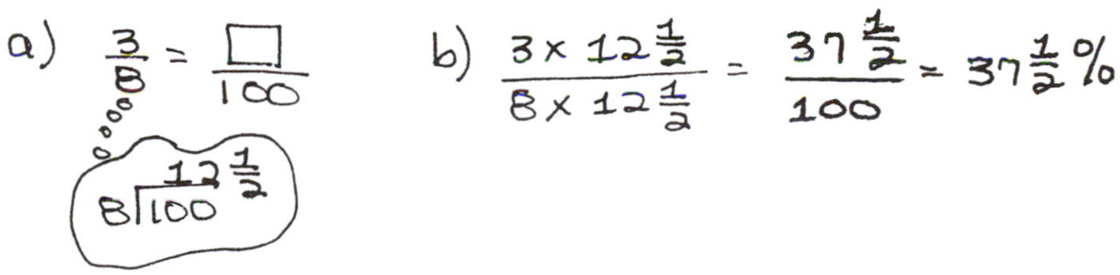

FIGURE 10.24

Initially, assign fractions that have exact two-digit decimal equivalents. Review the idea of converting a fraction to a decimal, and allow students to use a calculator to divide the numerator by the denominator. The students then can move the decimal point two places to the right (to show division by 100) and add the percent sign in forming the percent equivalent. (See Figure 10.25.)

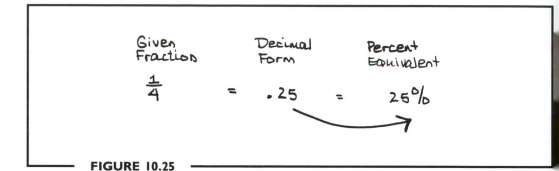

FIGURE 10.25

Percent in Everyday Situations

Problem Area: Difficulty using percent to solve problems.

Typical Disabilities Affecting Progress: Difficulty with abstract reasoning, sequencing, visual perception, and short-term memory.

Background: Many students with learning disabilities intuitively are able to solve problems using common percents such as 50%, 10%, and, sometimes, 25% and 75%. They are able to estimate, and some students can calculate mentally with easy percents. However, as they begin to deal with other percents, things become more difficult.

- "What method should be used to solve the problem?"

- "Should a fraction or a decimal equivalent be used?"

- "Now that I've found the answer, does it need to be rounded off?"

Decisions like these must be made, and longer, more complex sequences must be employed. In addition, applying meaning to the final answer is usually difficult. Too often, a student ends up knowing only that $x = 20$ without being able to relate the number to the original problem. The following are ideas for helping students handle difficulties.

SUGGESTED SEQUENCE OF ACTIVITIES

1. **From problem to equation.** Determining the appropriate equation for a given word problem can be the most difficult part. It often is helpful to teach children the vocabulary related to the work and then use the color coding techniques of Figure 10.26 to help them set up the equation. Dur

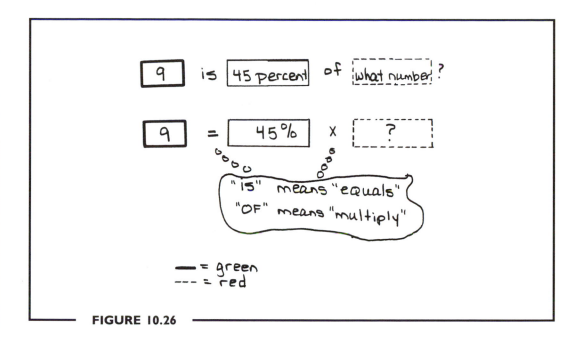

FIGURE 10.26

ing early work, structuring problems into "one-lines," so that the equation can be written directly beneath the problem, helps students translate the verbal statement into an equation. Children learn, for example, to associate the word *of* with the "×" sign and *is* with the "=" sign.

2. **Three easy pieces.** Provide preformatted pages using the idea in Figure 10.27. Help students analyze sample problems to recognize that percent situations typically involve three pieces of information (refer to the three boxes in the figure): the part, the whole or the base, and the percent figure. A percent problem-solving exercise provides two of these pieces of information and requires that the student find the third. The format shown in Figure 10.27 can be used to solve any of the three types of percent problems:

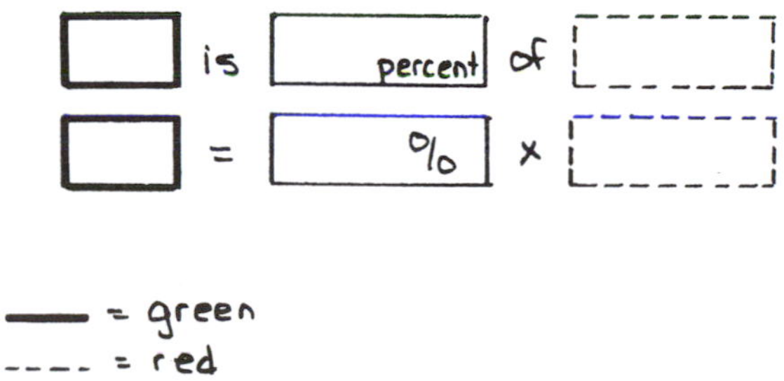

FIGURE 10.27

1. percent figure missing;
2. the "part" missing; or
3. the "whole" or base missing.

Using this approach, it becomes a matter of placing information from the verbal statement into the appropriate boxes and then solving to determine the unknown piece of information. Gradually, the students themselves learn to format their own papers, when necessary, to solve percent problems. When an answer is found, encourage students to write it above the appropriate box in the problem statement. This step is necessary for some students so they relate the answer to the original problem.

3. **Using proportion.** Students with good sequencing, abstract-reasoning, and spatial organization skills may prefer the proportion method to solve percent problems. The color-coding technique in Figure 10.28a, similar to that discussed earlier, can be used. Figure 10.28b illustrates how a page can be preformatted for this purpose and kept on file. If the proportion method is used, encourage students, as suggested in Activity 2, to relate the answer back to the original problem statement.

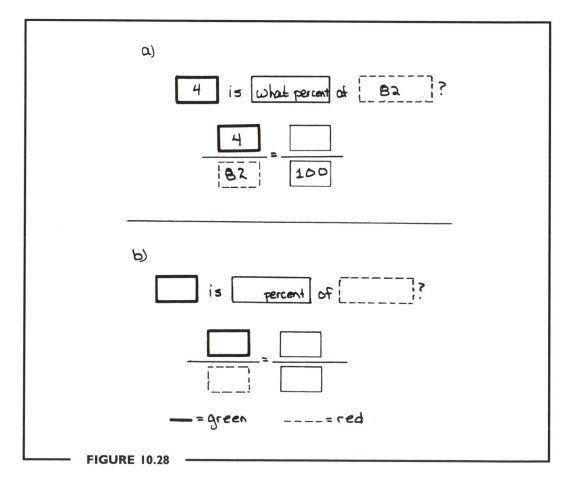

FIGURE 10.28

INTEGERS

New Symbolism

Problem Area: Difficulty associating meaning with abstract representations.

Typical Disabilities Affecting Progress: Difficulty with visual or auditory association, integrative processing, visual perception, and receptive or expressive language.

Background: We use the idea of integers regularly in our everyday lives. We borrow money from a friend then we pay it back. Do we still owe money? The temperature drops 8° but then climbs 9° the next morning. A salary increase means we earn more money, but then we might take a cut in salary of $10 when we switch jobs. All of these ideas are familiar to children. Even students with learning disabilities have little difficulty comprehending the meaning in context. However, when the same ideas are expressed symbolically using positive or negative integers, many children become confused. Most can readily tell you how much a friend owes them if $4 was borrowed, and they may even use the expression "I'm $4 in the hole." However, the mathematical representation is not as easily explained, although it may have the same meaning.

Poor visual or auditory association skills, coupled with poor integrative processing abilities make it difficult for students to deal meaningfully with the written integer form. Students are asked to relate an old idea to old signs (+ and −) in a new way using new language. That is, they have to decide what the familiar sign now means: *add* or *positive*; *subtract* or *negative*. To complicate matters, new skills and new language often are presented simultaneously. Those with expressive or receptive language deficits may understand the similarity in meaning between words such as *add* and *positive* or *subtract* and *negative* but find it hard to elicit or associate the word with the correct meaning in context. These students require considerable overlearning, consistent verbal and pictorial association, and small learning increments in early work with integers.

The following are suggestions for how to deal with these difficulties during early concept development with integers. The ideas presented can be used to supplement textbook treatments that typically focus on the application of integers in real-life situations.

SUGGESTED SEQUENCE OF ACTIVITIES

1. **Color code.** Children with language deficits often benefit from color-coded pages like that in Figure 10.29. The assumption at this point is that the student understands the vocabulary used. The colors help reinforce understanding by allowing the student to focus directly on the ideas of *more* and *less*. Related symbolism is highlighted and associated with the corresponding terminology.

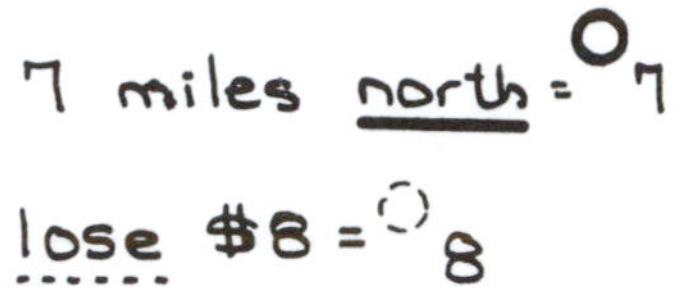

7 miles <u>north</u> = ⁰7

<u>lose</u> $8 = ○8

FIGURE 10.29

2. **Time out.** To help students develop an automatic association of integers with their use in real-life situations, take time to build up vocabulary. Exercises like those in Figure 10.30 make it easier for students to focus on the necessary language. A sense of usefulness develops, and children begin to use the numbers more successfully. The exercise also serves as a transition to eventually eliminating colors.

3. **Number line: Develop good number sense.** As children begin to use the number line, have them select examples from everyday situations to verbally describe several points on the line. Figure 10.31 presents a sample exercise.

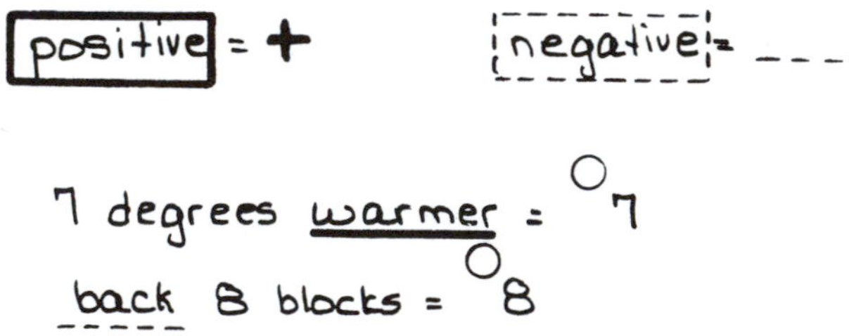

positive = **+**   negative = ---

7 degrees <u>warmer</u> = ○7

<u>back</u> 8 blocks = ○8

FIGURE 10.30

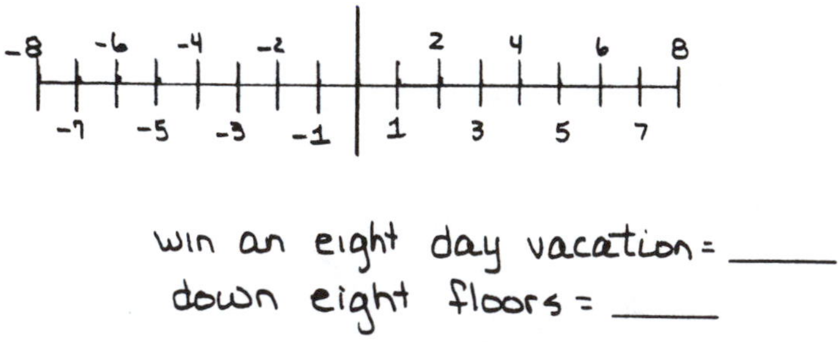

win an eight day vacation = ____
down eight floors = ____

FIGURE 10.31

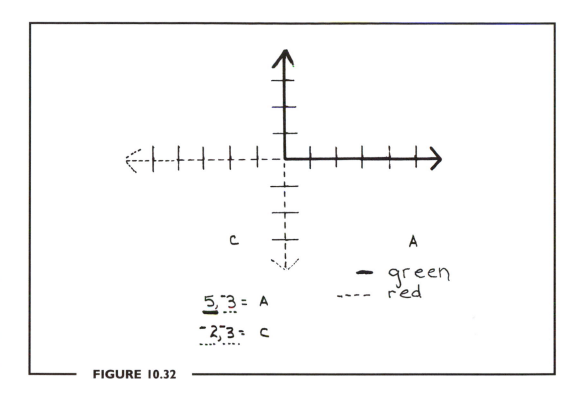

FIGURE 10.32

4. **Picture it.** As a class activity, present pictures with related phrases that describe "positive" or "negative" situations. (Figures 10.29 and 10.30 show sample ideas for such situations.) If possible, put the pictures and matching phrases on a ditto with the guide words *positive* and *negative* at the top in two different colors. Discuss the meaning of the two terms and have students underline the key words or phrases to match the color of the guide words.

5. **Point plotting.** As students begin to plot points in all four quadrants, a color-coded grid, like that in Figure 10.32, often helps with directionality. Order pairs are coded according to the quadrant, as shown.

Positive and Negative Signs

Problem Area: Difficulty interpreting signs used with integers.

Typical Disabilities Affecting Progress: Difficulty with visual perception, spatial organization, and closure.

Background: For many students, the greatest difficulty in dealing with integers is misreading or misplacing the sign. For this reason, it is essential that the teacher be consistent in the placement of these signs. When signs are to be interpreted as negative or positive, they should be placed in a raised position, as in Figure 10.33. When used to denote an operation, the sign should be centered between the two numbers that are involved. Figure 10.34 shows a typical problem that can be very confusing. Does the sign in front of the 8 mean "subtract" or "negative"? The

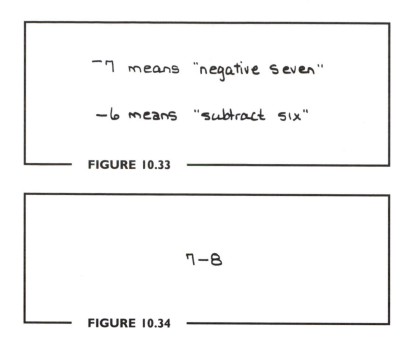

⁻7 means "negative seven"

−6 means "subtract six"

FIGURE 10.33

7−8

FIGURE 10.34

following ideas have proven useful in dealing with problems related to sign interpretation. In our experience, they have helped make computation with integers easier for students.

SUGGESTED SEQUENCE OF ACTIVITIES

1. **Circle to focus.** Preview the text used and circle the raised signs on the first several pages of the chapter on integers. Adult volunteers can be called upon to help.

2. **Label all numerals.** Some students, especially those with memory difficulties, forget that numbers without signs are assumed to be positive. Therefore, it is not unusual for them to misread the 9 in Figure 10.35 and treat it as a negative integer. For these students, it helps to label all numerals until they become more comfortable with integers.

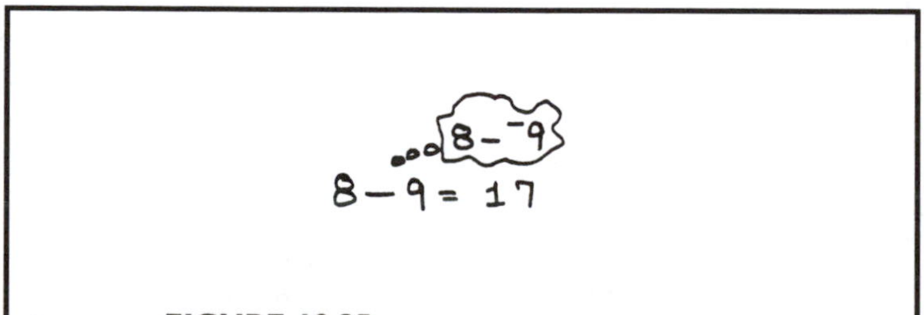

8−⁻9
8−9 = 17

FIGURE 10.35

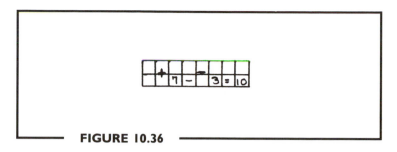

FIGURE 10.36

3. **Do it first.** Until students become familiar with the raised positive and negative signs, teach them to circle the signs in the text or on a worksheet prior to carrying out the computation. This will help them remember later, when actually computing, that "this sign means something different."

4. **Use graph paper.** If students need help spatially organizing their writing of signed numbers, allow them to use graph paper. Show them how to place the signs and numbers on the lines, as in Figure 10.36. Students with severe visual perception deficits will find this activity difficult. For others, the graph paper technique simplifies the task of writing integers and computing.

   NOTE: *Graph paper with six squares to the inch works well.*

   - *Variation:* For students needing additional assistance to organize their writing spatially, use the format in Figure 10.37a to prepare sheets in advance. The students fill in the problem as shown in Figure 10.37b. The adaptation for vertical alignment of numbers is shown in Figure 10.38.

5. **Use parentheses.** Often, just inserting parentheses within a problem, as in Figure 10.39, is sufficient to make signs easier to interpret. Parentheses, instead of circles, could be used to mark raised signs on textbook pages, as suggested in Activity 1.

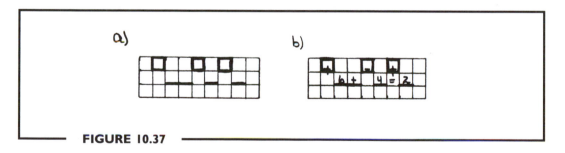

FIGURE 10.37

Computation with Integers

Problem Area: Difficulty computing with integers.

Typical Disabilities Affecting Progress: Difficulty with visual perception, sequencing, abstract reasoning, and memory.

Background: Assuming that visual perception or spatial deficits do not interfere or that such deficits have been controlled, computing with integers still requires

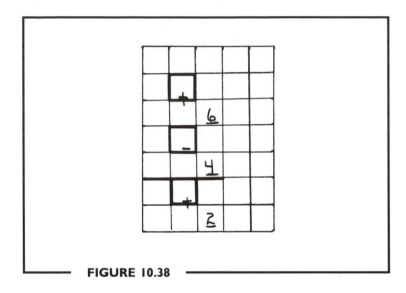

FIGURE 10.38

$$9 - (^-3) + (^+4) = 9 + 3 + 4 = 16$$

FIGURE 10.39

more sequencing and mental regrouping than previous computation involving positive integers. As with all calculation, easy problems can be completed more quickly if done mentally. For others, it may be more appropriate to hand compute or use a calculator. A major instructional goal is to help children develop expertise with all three methods and be able to choose between them.

When teaching any of the computation skills, encourage students with learning disabilities to proceed step by step through *all* steps, even when they think they can do the work mentally. It also may be necessary for these students to spend more time practicing than others in order to assure overlearning. Suggestions for how to supplement or reinforce textbook treatment of integer computation for the four operations follow.

SUGGESTED SEQUENCE OF ACTIVITIES

Addition

1. **Informal beginnings.** Most textbooks suggest activities involving chips, cards, charged particles, or walk-on number lines to introduce, informally,

addition of integers. It is especially important to carry out rather than omit these activities for students with learning disabilities because they help develop the mental imagery necessary to deal successfully with addition of integers. Figure 10.40a suggests a number line activity. Alternately, the charged particle model might be used, as in Figure 10.40b.

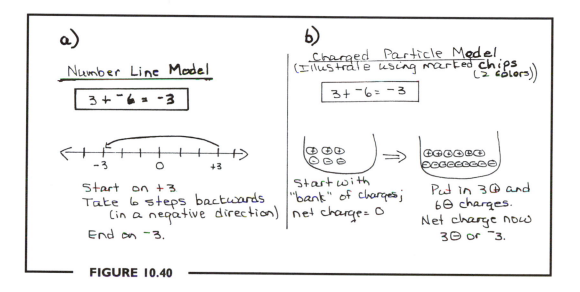

FIGURE 10.40

2. **Different strokes.** Textbook treatments typically present number lines or other models in an effort to lead students to verbalize the patterns or rules for adding integers. A chart, similar to that in Figure 10.41, often helps in this area too. For students with abstract-reasoning difficulties it generally is helpful to:

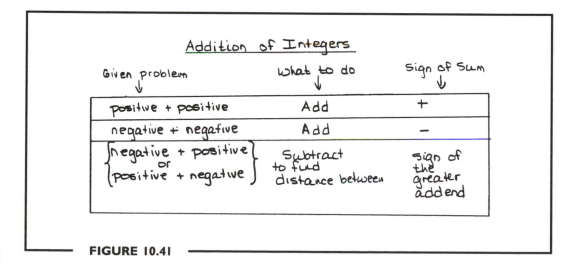

FIGURE 10.41

- present the chart and discuss it in conjunction with several examples so that, procedurally, the students can use the chart to solve integer addition problems;

- have students copy the chart onto a file card for ready reference;

- have students use the rules to work out a number of problems until they become familiar with the general procedures for adding integers; and

- use a walk-on number line to verify that the sums derived in this manner actually make sense before attempting to memorize the procedural rules.

This last step usually is first in the standard sequence, but the authors' experience has been that it is more important as a tie-in to earlier informal work.

3. **For other folks.** For other students, such as those with memory or perceptual difficulties, the standard sequence is followed with additional reinforcing measures like: (a) color coding signs to emphasize them whenever they appear in integer addition problems; (b) using the graph-paper technique in Figures 10.37 and 10.38 when helpful; and (c) providing kinesthetic/motor involvement in analyzing or certifying the procedural rules for adding integers.

- Allow students to dramatize simple additions, as in Activity 2, on a walk-on number line.

- Have students think of their bodies as number lines. When both arms are spread out, the left arm can represent the negative integers, the right arm the positive ones. The body is zero. To add a negative 5 to a positive 4, for example, students must pass through 0 and on to negative 1. Doing this for several sample problems helps children internalize the action of crossing the midline when needed, as is often the case in integer addition.

- *Variation:* An alternative to arm stretching involves taping a smaller number line from shoulder to shoulder across a child's back. The body midline is zero. As the teacher dramatizes a simple addition problem by finger movement on the child's back, the student can either (a) close eyes and reverbalize the problem as it is enacted or (b) with eyes open, mimic the teacher's movements by finger walking the addition on a personal number line placed on the desk in front of the child.

Subtraction

NOTE: *Suggestions for successful integer addition have obvious implications for integer subtraction. Informal introductory work is important. Variation of the standard subtraction sequence for students with abstract-reasoning difficulty is similar to that outlined for integer addition. Likewise, the compensatory techniques outlined in Activity 3 of the addition sequence can be reviewed and adapted to work with integer subtraction. The following ideas, based on the number line model, also deserve special emphasis. Similar activities can be carried out using the charged particle model.*

1. **Act it out.** There generally is great value in having students use a walk-on or "body" number line (as in Activity 3 in the previous section). This enables the student to:

   - solve simple integer subtraction problems that often involve the pattern summarized in Figure 10.42; and

   - verify that given answers, or those obtained using a calculator, also can be derived by following this rule.

To subtract two integers:
add the 1st integer to
the opposite of the 2nd.

FIGURE 10.42

2. **Use the number line.** A problem like that in Figure 10.43a might be posed and the students cued to think of the related addition problem: "What must be added to ⁺4 to get ⁻7?" Starting at ⁺4 on the number line, the children find that they must take 11 steps in a negative direction to arrive at ⁻7.

a)

sum   addend   addend

$$^-7 - {}^+4 = \square$$
$$\square + {}^+4 = {}^-7$$
$$\square = {}^-11$$

b)

$$^-7 - {}^+4 = {}^-11$$
$$^-7 + {}^-4 = {}^-11$$

FIGURE 10.43

The result should be charted along with others obtained in this manner. Using previously solved problems, help students notice the pattern by grouping like problems, as in Figure 10.43b. Have them verbalize that the pairs $^-7 - {}^+4$ and $^-7 + {}^-4$ have the same answer. Repeat with other similar examples to help students arrive at the conclusion: "To subtract two integers, the first can be added to the *opposite* of the second." Use the number line to verify the equivalence.

- *Extension 1:* Design worksheets or card-sort activities in which students solve and then match an integer subtraction problem to an equivalent addition problem. For example:

  Solve:

  $^-7 - {}^+4 = $ _____ $^-8 + {}^+5 = $ _____

  $^+3 - {}^-2 = $ _____ $^-7 + {}^+4 = $ _____

  $^-8 - {}^-5 = $ _____ $^+3 + {}^+2 = $ _____

  Pair them:

  a. $^-7 - {}^+4 = $ _____ and $^-7 + {}^+4 = $ _____

  b. _____ = _____ and _____ = _____

  c. _____ = _____ and _____ = _____

  When all matches are made, the students must use a number line to verify the equivalence of each match.

- *Extension 2:* Next, give students integer subtraction problems and instruct them to carry out just the first step of each. As in Figure 10.44a, have students merely rewrite the problem without solving. After the papers are checked, the problems can be completed.

  NOTE: *Most texts present integer computation horizontally; for many students with learning disabilities, however, the vertical format is easier. As shown in Figure 10.44b, it may be necessary to help the students rewrite the horizontal format.*

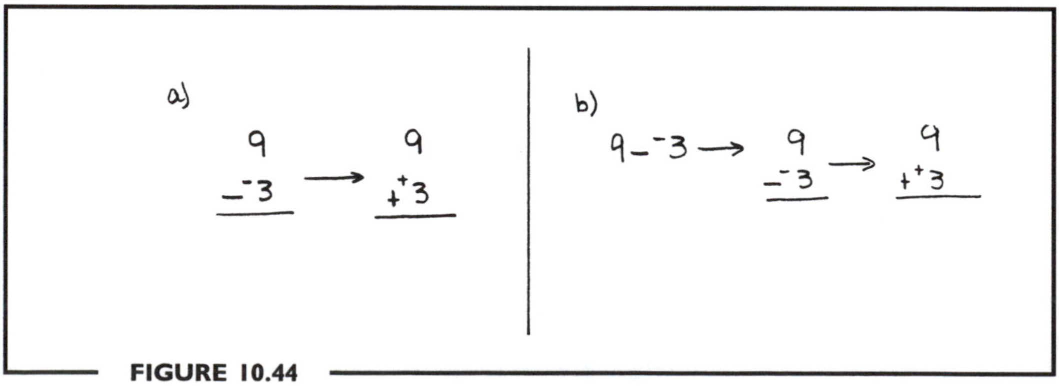

FIGURE 10.44

3. **Different strokes.** The sequence outlined in Activity 2 starts intuitively with number line moves, notes an equivalent method for finding answers (adding the opposites), then provides practice to understand and retain the process. Some students may have difficulty with this more sophisticated, standard method of using the additive inverse to solve integer subtraction problems. The following are suggestions for instructing these students.

- *Use number line moves* as before to introduce integer subtraction intuitively. As before, cue students to think of the related addition problem. Using the example in Figure 10.45a, ask students, "What must be added to a positive 4 to get a negative 7?" The students rewrite the problems, as in the second line of Figure 10.45b, to match the question. Starting at $^+4$, children move back to 0 and on to $^-7$, for a total of 11 spaces in the negative direction. This result ($^-11$) is now recorded, as in Figure 10.45c.

NOTE: *Either the walk-on or the body number line discussed earlier can be used in this activity.*

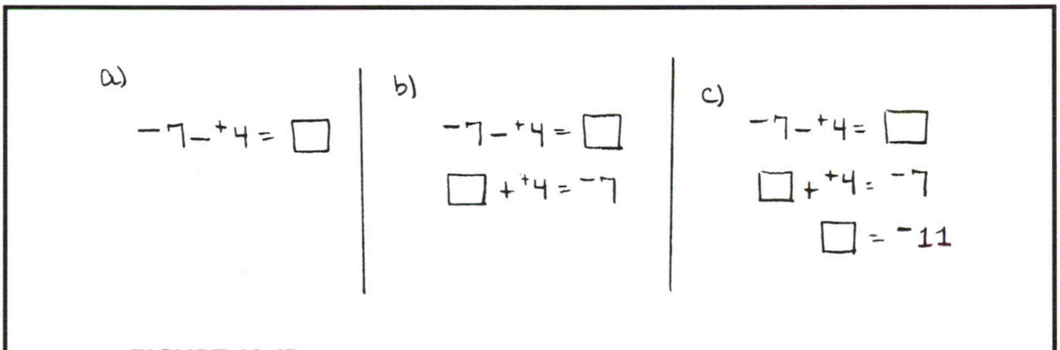

a)

$$^-7 - {}^+4 = \square$$

b)

$$^-7 - {}^+4 = \square$$
$$\square + {}^+4 = {}^-7$$

c)

$$^-7 - {}^+4 = \square$$
$$\square + {}^+4 = {}^-7$$
$$\square = {}^-11$$

FIGURE 10.45

- *Write it out.* To reinforce the subtraction–addition relation and to help students internalize the procedure for subtracting, use the technique in Figure 10.46. (The subtraction sign in the problem is

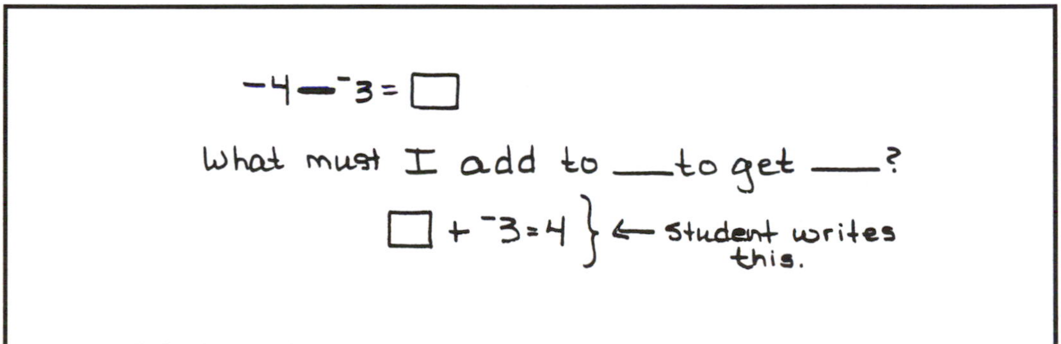

$$^-4 - {}^-3 = \square$$

What must I add to ___ to get ___?

$$\square + {}^-3 = 4 \;\}\; \leftarrow \text{student writes this.}$$

FIGURE 10.46

written in a bright color.) Write out the procedure for subtracting as shown. The students solve the problem by filling in the blanks. Later, just put an example at the top of the page as a reminder, but continue to highlight the subtraction signs for all problems.

- *The whole thing.* As children begin to solve integer subtraction problems independently, encourage them to picture the number line.

  Example:

  $$8 - {}^-3 = \underline{\hspace{2cm}}$$

  Child writes: $\underline{\hspace{2cm}} + {}^-3 = 8$

  Child thinks: "Start at ⁻3, move forward to 0, then on to 8.

  That's a move of ⁺11. $8 - {}^-3 = {}^+11$."

NOTE: *This method does not utilize the traditional rule for subtracting integers—that of adding the opposite (additive inverse). It is based on the addition–subtraction relationship, and it allows those children who respond best to concrete approaches to use this strength in their thinking. Children are encouraged to picture (or actually make) number line moves, first to zero, then on to a target number. This two-step process also can be used with larger two- and three-digit numbers.*

Multiplication and Division

- *Prerequisite Abilities:* An understanding of the concepts of multiplication as repeated addition and multiplication as commutative.

For those students who understand these concepts at the initial stages, the following activities have proved helpful in applying their comprehension to higher-level topics such as integers.

1. **Products and unlike signs.** Given mastery of the prerequisites, the sign for the product of a positive and a negative can readily be identified.

   - *Example:* $7 \times {}^-6$. "That's seven negative sixes." One could repeatedly add, if necessary, to obtain the ⁻42. Since multiplication is commutative $7 \times {}^-6 = {}^-6 \times 7 = {}^-42$.

2. **Products and like signs.** Many students can recognize and continue the pattern to the answers in Figure 10.47a. Each product is 5 less than the one directly above it. Similarly, in Figure 10.47b, each product is 4 less than that directly above it. Further, when the answers are filled in, the

a)

$$5 \times {}^-5 = {}^-25$$
$$4 \times {}^-5 = {}^-20$$
$$3 \times {}^-5 = {}^-15$$
$$2 \times {}^-5 = {}^-10$$
$$1 \times {}^-5 = \underline{\quad}$$
$$0 \times {}^-5 = \underline{\quad}$$
$${}^-1 \times {}^-5 = \underline{\quad}$$
$${}^-2 \times {}^-5 = \underline{\quad}$$
$${}^-3 \times {}^-5 = \underline{\quad}$$
$${}^-4 \times {}^-5 = \underline{\quad}$$

b)

$$5 \times {}^-4 = {}^-20$$
$$4 \times {}^-4 = {}^-16$$
$$3 \times {}^-4 = {}^-12$$
$$2 \times {}^-4 = {}^-8$$
$$1 \times {}^-4 = \underline{\quad}$$
$$0 \times {}^-4 = \underline{\quad}$$
$${}^-1 \times {}^-4 = \underline{\quad}$$
$${}^-2 \times {}^-4 = \underline{\quad}$$
$${}^-3 \times {}^-4 = \underline{\quad}$$
$${}^-4 \times {}^-4 = \underline{\quad}$$

FIGURE 10.47

students can see how, each time, the product of two negative numbers is positive. Some students, particularly those with abstract-reasoning difficulties, may not follow the logic of this exercise but will merely remember that, as long as the signs are the same, the product is positive.

3. **Mail time.** A table like that in Figure 10.48 also can be used as a story line to dramatize the sign patterns for products. Since most students like to get mail, that is positive. No one likes to receive bills; that is negative.

4. **Same as multiplication.** Most students have little difficulty remembering how to handle the signs in division once they are comfortable with multiplication of integers. They are used to relating multiplication and division, so it is easy to remember (and verify) that sign rules for quotient figures are analogous to those for products:

Divisor and Dividend	Quotient
Like signs	Positive
Unlike signs	Negative

If letters (+) are brought (+) that's positive (+).
If bills (−) are brought (+) that's negative (−).
If letters (+) are taken away (−) that's negative (−).
If bills (−) are taken away (−) that's positive (+).

FIGURE 10.48

- *Example 1:* $^-45 \div 5 = {}^-9$ ("Yes, because $^-9 \times 5 = {}^-45$.")
- *Example 2:* $^-63 \div {}^-7 = 9$ ("Yes, because $9 \times {}^-7 = {}^-63$.")

EXPONENTS

Basic Concept

Problem Area: Difficulty understanding, reading, and writing exponents.

Typical Disabilities Affecting Progress: Difficulty with short-term memory, visual perception, expressive language, and abstract reasoning.

Background: Students are introduced to the concept and symbolism of exponents as early as the fifth or sixth grade. At that point, the idea is dealt with basically in conjunction with factoring and primes. As students advance in mathematics, computation involving exponents becomes more commonplace. Mathematical problem-solving applications in a number of fields, including medicine, science, and computer science, regularly use exponents to express both very large and very small numbers. Students with interest in these fields benefit from a firm foundation in exponents.

At the pre-algebra level, development of adequate understanding of and ability with exponents is both important and necessary for students planning to continue mathematics in high school. The topic itself is not particularly difficult, except that it introduces new terminology and new notation that can be visually confusing. The following activities suggest ways of making exponents more understandable and usable, especially for those with language deficits. Previewing language and/or providing vocabulary cards may be needed by some students.

SUGGESTED SEQUENCE OF ACTIVITIES

1. **Helpful models.** At an intuitive level, prior to the textbook introduction of exponents, squares and cubes of various dimensions can be used, as in Figure 10.49, to acquaint students with exponential notation and language.

2. **Factors first.** Color coding can be used in the previous activity to help students remember how to read and write exponents. Since an exponent indicates the amount of times a number is used as a factor, generally it is best to have students first write the exponential form from a list of factors (see Figure 10.50). This sequence especially seems to help students with expressive language deficits as it reinforces the meaning of the numbers used. Figure 10.50 contains an exercise that can be kept on file and used prior to the textbook introduction of exponents. The color coding, of course, can extend beyond the second and third powers of the base.

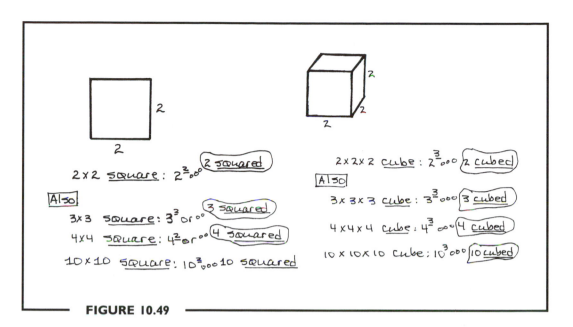

FIGURE 10.49

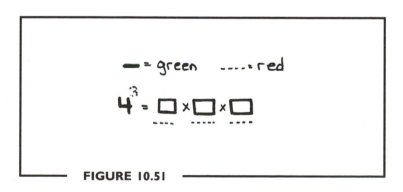

FIGURE 10.50

3. **Reverse what's given.** Once students can write the exponential form of the factored form, provide practice translating the exponential form. Color coding again can be used, as in Figure 10.51.

4. **I call.** Make a deck of 52 cards. Twenty-six should show a number in exponential form, and 26 should show factored form, as in Figure 10.52.

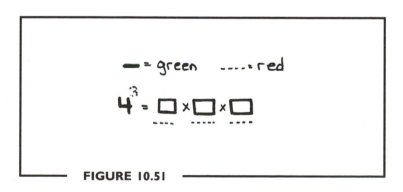

FIGURE 10.51

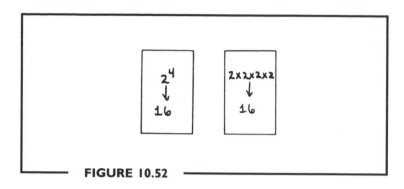

FIGURE 10.52

After each child has been dealt five cards, the rest of the deck is placed face down between the players. The game is played by making pairs of one exponential card and one with matching factors. In turn, players request one card from the player on the left. If that player has the requested card, it is given to the caller, who can then lay a pair down. A turn continues until no more pairs can be drawn from the pile, and play continues. The first player to run out of cards wins.

5. **New terminology.** For many students, the language involved in exponents is the most difficult part of the subject. These students have trouble meaningfully associating the words, such as "six to the third power," with any visual image. To help build up the necessary language, provide language practice that is separate from computational practice. Pages such as those shown in Figure 10.53a are useful as they present the new symbolism together with the associated language. Figure 10.53b suggests an alternate exercise that visually reinforces the fact that the exponent is raised.

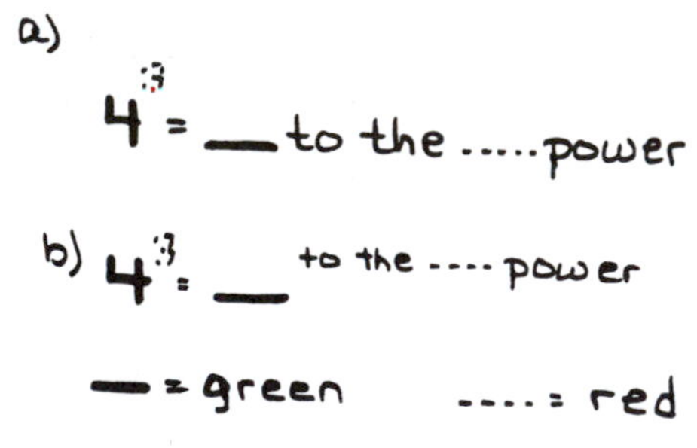

a)

$$4^{:3} = \underline{\quad} \text{to the} \dots\text{power}$$

b) $$4^{:3} = \underline{\quad} \text{to the} \dots\text{power}$$

$$\underline{\quad} = \text{green} \qquad \dots = \text{red}$$

FIGURE 10.53

Scientific Notation

Problem Area: Using exponents in scientific notation.

Typical Disabilities Affecting Progress: Visual perception, figure-ground, sequencing, and closure problems.

Background: Scientific notation is used in many fields to express both very large and very small numbers. The successful conversion of numbers to (or from) scientific notation requires several major prerequisites, including:

- strong numeration concepts and skills;
- ability to multiply and divide powers of 10;
- basic understanding of and skill with exponents; and
- ability to read decimals.

Application of all these isolated understandings and skills when writing numbers in scientific notation requires good reasoning, recall, and sequencing. These are typically weak areas for students with learning disabilities. In addition, closure or visual perception deficits can lead to confusion when reading the numbers. Too often, these deficits make it seem as if the student does not understand what to do when, in fact, it really may be a matter of the student losing the place or not being able to recall information. The following suggestions offer ideas for how to handle some of the common problems children face as they deal with scientific notation.

SUGGESTED SEQUENCE OF ACTIVITIES

1. **Color highlight.** During early work, for students with figure-ground deficits, it sometimes helps to highlight the digits to be used. Figure 10.54 illustrates two alternatives for color coding digits. Highlighting in this manner helps minimize the chance that students will lose their place or misperceive the numbers read.

2. **Use a mask.** Some students need to use a card, as in Figure 10.55, to block out part of the number field while counting digits. Students write the answer, digit by digit, while moving the card.

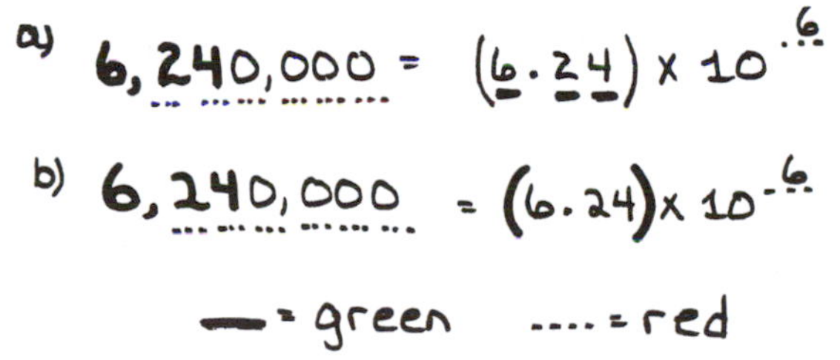

a) $6,240,000 = (6.24) \times 10^{.6}$

b) $6,240,000 = (6.24) \times 10^{-6}$

— = green   .... = red

FIGURE 10.54

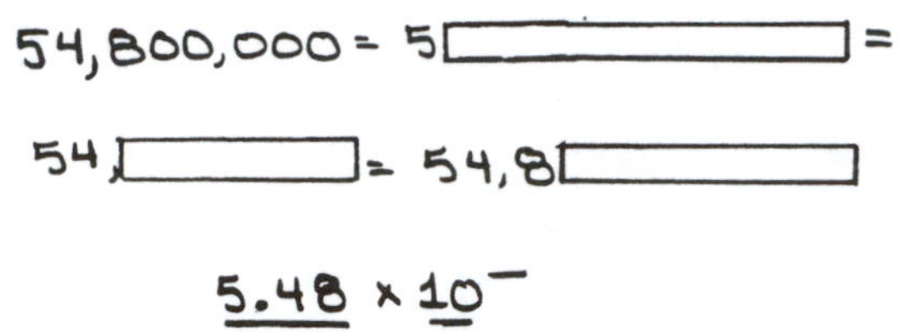

FIGURE 10.55

3. **Help for computation.** When multiplying with scientific notation, color highlight, as in Figure 10.56, to help students apply the distributive law. Otherwise, the visual field can be confusing. Texts can be highlighted as in Figure 10.56a. Pages, formatted as in Figure 10.56c, can be kept on hand for students to use.

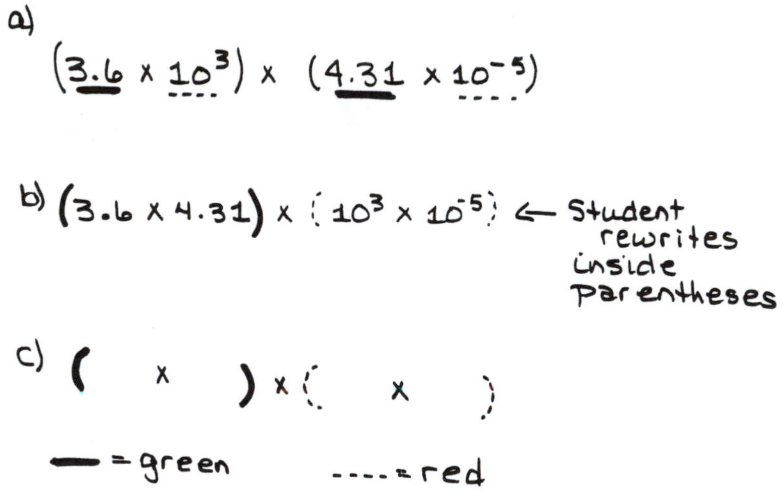

FIGURE 10.56

Index